THE FRESH WATERS
OF SCOTLAND

Proceedings of the 50th Meeting
of the Scottish Freshwater Group

FRONTISPIECE   Falls of Acharn, Tayside Region. Photograph: Lorne Gill, Scottish Natural Heritage

THE FRESH WATERS OF SCOTLAND

A National Resource of International Significance

Edited by

P. S. MAITLAND
Fish Conservation Centre,
Stirling, UK

P. J. BOON
Scottish Natural Heritage, Edinburgh, UK

D. S. McLUSKY
University of Stirling, UK

JOHN WILEY & SONS
Chichester · New York · Brisbane · Toronto · Singapore

Other Wiley Editorial Offices

John Wiley & Sons, Inc., 605 Third Avenue,
New York, NY 10158–0012, USA

Jacaranda Wiley Ltd, 33 Park Road, Milton,
Queensland 4064, Australia

John Wiley & Sons (Canada) Ltd, 22 Worcester Road,
Rexdale, Ontario M9W 1L1, Canada

John Wiley & Sons (SEA) Pte Ltd, 37 Jalan Pemimpin   05–04,
Block B, Union Industrial Building, Singapore 205

Library of Congress Cataloging-in-Publication Data

A catalog record for this book is available from the Library of Congress

British Library Cataloguing in Publication Data

A catalogue record for this book is available from the British Library

ISBN 0-471-94462-9

Typeset in 10/12 pt Times by Acorn Bookwork, Salisbury, Wiltshire
Printed and bound in Great Britain by Bookcraft (Bath) Ltd

Contents

Contents

List of Contributors

R. Allcock   Tay River Purification Board, 1 South Street, Perth, PH2 8NJ, UK

T. E. H. Allott   Environmental Change Research Centre, University College London, 26 Bedford Way, London, WC1H 0AP, UK

A. E. Bailey-Watts   Institute of Freshwater Ecology, Bush Estate, Penicuik, EH26 0QB, UK

R. W. Battarbee   Environmental Change Research Centre, University College London, 26 Bedford Way, London, WC1H 0AP, UK

S. L. Bell   Cobham Resource Consultants, 7 Mentone Gardens, Edinburgh, EH9 2DJ, UK

G. A. Best   Clyde River Purification Board, Murray Road, East Kilbride, G75 0LA, UK

M. C. M. Beveridge   Institute of Aquaculture, University of Stirling, Stirling, FK9 4LA, UK

P. J. Boon   Scottish Natural Heritage, 2 Anderson Place, Edinburgh, EH6 5NP, UK

V. Brazier   Scottish Natural Heritage, 2 Anderson Place, Edinburgh, EH6 5NP, UK

A. J. Brook   Dept of Life Sciences, University of Buckingham, Buckingham, MK18 1EG, UK

D. Buchanan   Highland River Purification Board, Strathpeffer Road, Dingwall, IV15 9QY, UK

R. N. Campbell   Tigh-Ur, Bonskeid, Pitlochry, PH16 5NP, UK

R. N. B. Campbell   The Tweed Foundation, Drygrange, Melrose, TD6 9DJ, UK

B. E. Clelland   Tay River Purification Board, 1 South Street, Perth, PH2 8NJ, UK

C. P. Cummins   Institute of Terrestrial Ecology, Abbots Ripton, Huntingdon, PE17 2LS, UK

T. N. Dixon	Scottish Trust for Underwater Archaeology, Dept of Archaeology, University of Edinburgh, Edinburgh, EH8 9JZ, UK
C. R. Doughty	Clyde River Purification Board, Murray Road, East Kilbride, G75 0LA, UK
I. R. Fozzard	Forth River Purification Board, Avenue North, Riccarton, EH14 4AP, UK
C. A. Galbraith	Joint Nature Conservation Committee, Monkstone House, City Road, Peterborough, PE1 1UA, UK
D. J. Gilvear	Dept of Environmental Science, University of Stirling, Stirling, FK9 4LA, UK
J. E. Gordon	Scottish Natural Heritage, 2 Anderson Place, Edinburgh, EH6 5NP, UK
J. Green	Vincent Wildlife Trust, Barjarg, Barrhill, Girvan, KA26 0RB, UK
R. Green	Vincent Wildlife Trust, Barjarg, Barrhill, Girvan, KA26 0RB, UK
J. D. Hamilton	65 Main Road, Elderslie, Johnstone, PA5 9AZ, UK
D. Hammerton	Clyde River Purification Board, Murray Road, East Kilbride, G75 0LA, UK
R. Harriman	Freshwater Fisheries Laboratory, Faskally, Pitlochry, PH16 5LB, UK
N. T. H. Holmes	Alconbury Environmental Consultants, The Almonds, 57 Ramsey Road, Warboys, PE17 2RW, UK
D. L. Howell	Scottish Natural Heritage, 2 Anderson Place, Edinburgh, EH6 5NP, UK
A. D. Jamieson	Dept of Planning, Lothian Regional Council, Edinburgh, EH1 1PT, UK
F. G. Johnson	Mott MacDonald, 15 Cadogan Street, Glasgow, G2 6NW, UK
A. A. Lyle	Institute of Freshwater Ecology, Bush Estate, Penicuik, EH26 0QB, UK
T. D. Macdonald	Scottish Office Environment Dept, 27 Perth Street, Edinburgh, EH3 5RB, UK
D. W. Mackay	North East River Purification Board, Greyhope Road, Aberdeen, AB1 3RD, UK
D. S. McLusky	Dept of Biological and Molecular Sciences, University of Stirling, Stirling, FK9 4LA, UK
J. McManus	School of Geography and Geology, University of St Andrews, St Andrews, KY16 9ST, UK

P. S. Maitland Fish Conservation Centre, Easter Cringate, Stirling, FK7 9QX, UK

D. W. Minns RSPB, 17 Regent Terrace, Edinburgh, EH7 5BN, UK

B. R. S. Morrison Freshwater Fisheries Laboratory, Faskally, Pitlochry, PH16 5LB, UK

R. S. Oldham Dept of Applied Biology and Biotechnology, De Montfort University, Leicester, LE7 9SU, UK

M. A. Palmer Joint Nature Conservation Committee, Monkstone House, City Road, Peterborough, PE1 1UA, UK

K. B. Pugh North East River Purification Board, Greyhope Road, Aberdeen, AB1 3RD, UK

J. C. Sheldon Dept of Planning, Lothian Regional Council, Edinburgh, EH1 1PT, UK

I. R. Smith 18 Torphin Road, Colinton, Edinburgh, EH13 0HW, UK

R. W. Summers RSPB, Etive House, Beechwood Park, Inverness, IV2 3BW, UK

M. J. S. Swan Amphibian Habitat Advisory Services, 19 St Judith's Lane, Sawtry, Huntingdon, Cambridgeshire, PE17 5XE, UK

S. E. Walker Centre for Leisure Research, Heriot-Watt University, Cramond Road North, Edinburgh, EH4 6JD, UK

A. Werritty School of Geography and Geology, University of St Andrews, St Andrews, KY16 9ST, UK

R. B. Williamson Scottish Office Agriculture and Fisheries Dept, Pentland House, 47 Robbs Loan, Edinburgh, EH14 1TW, UK

Preface

This volume was conceived to mark the first 25 years of the Scottish Freshwater Group. It is intended as a contemporary account of the fresh waters of Scotland – the extent of the freshwater resource, its value and uses, threats to Scotland's rivers and lochs and possible remedial measures. Most of the chapters were presented as papers at the 50th meeting of the Scottish Freshwater Group held at the University of Stirling on 2 and 3 February 1993. Manuscripts were revised following discussion at this meeting and comments from expert reviewers, and then edited to form an integrated account of this important national and international resource.

Authors were asked to cover their topic within a fairly precise framework but inevitably there is some duplication among a few chapters. This is as it should be – the intention being that each chapter is a reasonably self-contained account of its subject. The term "national" refers to Scotland unless otherwise indicated (e.g. GB).

Scotland is fortunate in being very richly endowed with numerous rivers and lochs. These constitute on the one hand an attractive feature of the landscape and on the other a major resource for industry and recreation. It was not until the 19th century that limnology developed properly as a science. At that time several classical studies were innovated in both Europe and North America. The bathymetrical survey of the freshwater lochs of Scotland, initiated by Sir John Murray in 1897, is recognized as the start of organized limnology in the British Isles. Since then, freshwater science in Scotland has developed substantially and an extensive literature is now available.

The Scottish Freshwater Group was first formed in the autumn of 1968 as an open forum to facilitate contact and discussion among the many people in Scotland concerned with fresh water. One-day meetings have been held every spring and autumn since then at the University of Stirling and have taken the form of several informal talks and demonstrations on each occasion. From time to time, individual meetings have dealt with single topical issues (e.g. acid precipitation). The knowledge of current work gained from these meetings has proved of real value and allowed much closer liaison throughout Scotland among the individuals and groups concerned over the past quarter of a century. During that time the Group has grown from some 50 members in 1968 to over 300 in 1993.

The Scottish Freshwater Group is indebted to the University of Stirling for the excellent facilities provided at the university over this long period. It was particularly appropriate that the opening address at the 50th Meeting of the Group was given by

Professor Sir F. G. T. Holliday, formerly Professor of Biology at the University of Stirling, and instrumental in providing facilities there after the formation of the Group. The 50th meeting of the Group happily coincided with the Silver Jubilee celebrations of the University of Stirling and a major address on "Science and technology 2000, and beyond" was given jointly to the University and the Group by Professor W. D. P. Stewart (Cabinet Office, Office of Science and Technology). Again, appropriately, Professor Stewart, then Professor of Biology at the University of Dundee, was an early member and strong supporter of the Scottish Freshwater Group.

The Editors are grateful to a number of people who assisted at the 50th Meeting of the Scottish Freshwater Group and with the production of this volume. The meeting was sponsored by the Scottish Freshwater Group, Scottish Natural Heritage and the University of Stirling. Mrs Sue Dyer helped with the organization and secretarial work. Chairmen of the various sessions at the Meeting were: Mr W. Halcrow, Mr J. D. Hamilton, Professor A. D. Hawkins, Mr S. Pepper, Professor R. J. Roberts, Professor J. R. Sargent and Professor M. B. Usher. Reviewing of the chapters was greatly facilitated by comments from: Dr C. E. Adams, Dr J. Berry, Dr M. C. M. Beveridge, Professor D. M. Bryant, Mr J. C. Currie, Dr D. J. Gilvear, Professor D. Hammerton, Dr D. M. Harper, Mr R. Harriman, Ms A. Henderson, Mr A. V. Holden, Mr D. L. Howell, Mr T. Huxley, Dr R. C. Johnson, Dr H. Kruuk, Dr O. L. Lassière, Professor D. W. Mackay, Mr W. G. McGregor, Dr C. Martin, Dr D. H. Mills, Dr K. J. Murphy, Mr T. Poodle, Dr F. E. Round, Dr D. B. C. Scott, Dr R. G. J. Shelton, Dr A. B. Stephen, Mr G. Struthers, Professor M. F. Thomas, Dr A. Werritty, Mr C. Wishart and Dr J. F. Wright.

Peter S. Maitland
Philip J. Boon
Donald S. McLusky

SECTION I

DEFINING, CLASSIFYING AND EVALUATING THE RESOURCE

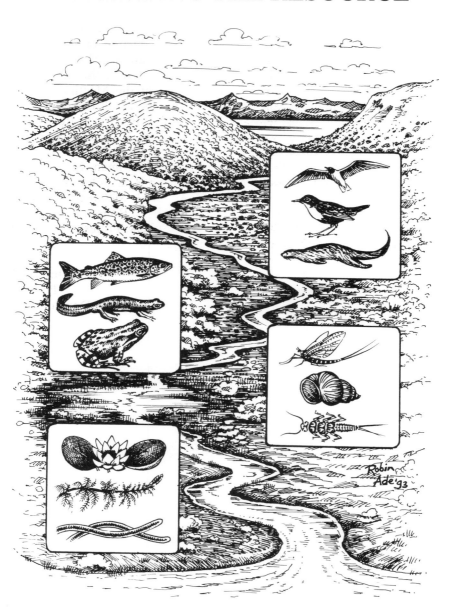

1

History of Freshwater Science

P. S. MAITLAND

Fish Conservation Centre, Easter Cringate, Stirling, FK7 9QX, UK

and

J. D. HAMILTON

65 Main Road, Elderslie, Johnstone, PA5 9AZ, UK

INTRODUCTION

The history and development of freshwater science in Scotland follows a pattern similar to that of other branches of modern science which had their beginnings in the early part of the 19th century. A few perceptive individuals, scattered in space and time, recorded their observations and experiments, thus providing stimulation for others. They remained, however, largely independent of one another. As the other sciences advanced – especially chemistry, physics, geology and cartography – investigations in freshwater science also increased in number and variety, reaching a peak around the turn of the century. There followed something of a slackening off with only slow growth during the early part of the 20th century until the quickening demonstrated by all sciences from the late 1940s onwards (Maitland, 1983).

Over these two centuries the kinds of investigations and the manner in which they have been carried out have varied enormously making it difficult to give a continuous history of any one branch of limnology. The compromise chosen in this review is first to describe the early Scottish contributions to freshwater science, highlighting those of special significance and culminating in the important work of Murray and Pullar (1910). For the period since then it is more appropriate to look at the research carried out by organizations and at special projects which often involved several institutions.

The present short review deals only with the major aspects of limnological work carried out to date in Scotland and only a few of the many hundreds of references available are quoted. More detail and further references on many of the studies carried out before 1980 can be found in Maitland (1983). Other authors in this volume also make reference to historical aspects of their subject.

The Fresh Waters of Scotland: A National Resource of International Significance
Edited by P. S. Maitland, P. J. Boon and D. S. McLusky. © 1994 John Wiley & Sons Ltd

EARLY STUDIES

Most published information relating to freshwater science in Scotland appeared during the 19th and 20th centuries. However, some publications of relevance did appear before this, many of them casual and anecdotal and most related to applied topics such as water supply or fisheries (Franck, 1658; Figure 1.1). *The Statistical Account of Scotland* (Sinclair, 1791) was one of the first attempts at a comprehensive review of the natural resources of Scotland. Its many volumes of accounts by ministers of all the Scottish parishes included information and observations on numerous lochs and rivers and their wildlife (including fish and fisheries). Though the geographic coverage of Scotland was comprehensive, the accounts varied in quality.

In the field of physical limnology, the early studies were for the most part occasional and unsystematic. The remarkable waves observed in Loch Lomond and other lochs during the great Lisbon earthquake of 1755 excited considerable interest at the time but gave rise to more theories than observations. Thus, although a number of early physical studies were available (e.g. Fleming, 1788) it was not until the 19th century that freshwater studies began to develop properly as a science, and in the second half of the 19th century a number of important papers were published. Among the first of these were the studies of Buchan (1871) on the deep-water temperatures of Lochs

FIGURE 1.1. One of the earliest "limnological" descriptions is of the River Endrick (seen here near Wester Cringate), described by Franck in 1658 as "The memorable Anderwick, a rapid river of strong and stiff streams; whose fords, if well examined, are arguments sufficient to convince the angler of trout, as are her deeps, when consulted, the noble race and treasure of salmon". Photograph: Peter S. Maitland

Lomond, Katrine and Tay, and of Buchanan (1879) on other lochs. The interest in Loch Katrine was partly due to the creation of the scheme there to supply water to Glasgow (see Chapter 16), and Napier (1875) published observations on the effect of Katrine water on various metals.

In the field of hydrology, the innovative work on river flows by McClean (1933) was well ahead of its time and, ironically, though it was not supported by the government of the day it now forms the basis of present river flow gauging in Scotland supported almost entirely by public funds.

In the field of biology a considerable amount of work was done by eminent naturalists of the day. Prominent among these were McLachlan (1881), Morton (1883) and King (1890) who were especially interested in dragonflies, caddisflies and stone-flies and made notable contributions to knowledge of their distribution and biology in Scotland. During the early 20th century, some workers, as well as describing individual groups, ventured into broader accounts of the entire animal communities of whole systems. Notable among these was W. Evans who published a whole series of papers on different invertebrate communities – for example on the fauna of Upper Elf Loch (Evans, 1906).

However, it was the bathymetric survey initiated by Sir John Murray in 1897 and discussed below which must be regarded as the start of organized limnology, not only in Scotland but also in the British Isles.

THE BATHYMETRIC SURVEY

While carrying out research on the sea lochs of Scotland, Sir John Murray made several excursions into the freshwater lochs of the Caledonian Canal – Lochs Lochy, Oich and Ness. Following these studies he concluded that a systematic survey of the freshwater lochs of Scotland would result in many new additions to scientific know-ledge, and would be especially important for comparisons with data in other fields of science. Many geologists were anxious for bathymetric data on these lochs, and fishermen and water supply engineers were also interested in the subject. Murray's proposal was brought before the Councils of the Royal Societies of both Edinburgh and London and both Councils made strong representations to the Government urging that such a survey should be carried out at once in the interests of scientific progress. There was no practical outcome from these representations.

In 1897, Murray, with the assistance of Fred Pullar, started a private systematic survey of Scottish freshwater lochs. "We were led to take up this self-imposed task because ... there was no hope of the work being undertaken by any government department" (Murray and Pullar, 1910). After overcoming various technical and logistic difficulties a number of lochs were surveyed and the first paper – on the lochs of the Trossachs and Callander district – was published in 1900. Murray went abroad that winter and when he returned he found that Pullar had lost his life while trying to rescue people during an ice accident at Airthrey Loch (Figure 1.2). The survey was brought to a standstill and it was Murray's intention to abandon it altogether. However, as a memorial to his son, Laurence Pullar offered to help as much as possible and gave £10 000 to finance the project. The work was renewed in 1902 and proceeded steadily; by 1904, 562 lochs had been surveyed. These included most of the larger lochs in Scotland and bathymetric maps of each one were published.

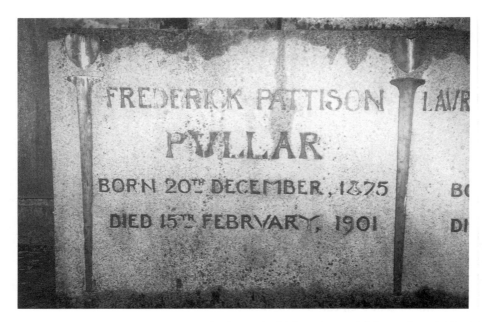

FIGURE 1.2. The memorial to F. P. Pullar in Logie Kirkyard near Stirling. Though his death interrupted the Bathymetric Survey, the money subsequently provided by his father ensured the Survey's eventual success as a major international contribution to limnology. Photograph: Peter S. Maitland

As well as the sounding work for bathymetry, biological studies were carried out by James Murray, and Wedderburn (1910) and others carried out numerous physical observations. Altogether, nearly 50 people took part in the work of the loch survey for shorter or longer periods. Special attention was paid to Loch Ness in order to obtain continuous physical and biological observations from one loch, and for this purpose several staff were stationed for a time at Fort Augustus. The results of all these studies were published in a series of papers, many of them in the *Geographical Journal*, but the project culminated in a definitive six-volume multi-author work published by the Challenger Office (Murray and Pullar, 1910).

In addition to the bathymetric maps and related data, an enormous amount of new data were collected and published, some of major importance – for example the early studies of seiches, and particularly the discovery of internal seiches. More than 700 different animal species were identified during the survey, about 50 of them new to the British Isles and at least 29 described as new to science. In the field of aquatic macrophytes, the extensive survey carried out by West (1910) as part of the bathymetric survey was a major contribution and for many years after this only occasional papers on macrophytes appeared.

There can be no doubt that the Bathymetric Survey was of seminal importance to the development of freshwater science in Scotland and most of the organizations referred to below have made use, at some time, of the information and maps published by Murray and Pullar. The survey was also recognized internationally for its comprehensive coverage of Scotland's lochs and its high standard of accuracy which has been confirmed many times in subsequent investigations.

ORGANIZATIONS

Fishery Board of Scotland

The earliest formal organizations concerned with Scottish fresh waters and their biota were the Commissioners of the Scotch Salmon Fisheries (established 1862) and their successor the Fishery Board of Scotland (established 1882) whose Inspectors of Salmon Fisheries published reports from 1883 onwards. Although they were principally concerned with regulating fishing for Salmon and Sea Trout, valuable contributions to our knowledge of the biology of these fish were made by members of the Inspectorate, notably on hatching and migration (Calderwood, 1931; 1945), and on migration and stock improvement (Menzies, 1939; 1949). T. Scott, whose main concern was with marine fish, collected and described plankton from lochs and rivers, producing a notable series of papers on the invertebrate fauna of Scotland's inland waters (e.g. Scott, 1890; 1895) which are of considerable interest today. For example, the paper on Loch Leven (Scott, 1895) provided a benchmark against which the present fauna of that loch can be compared.

After 1945, supervision of basic Salmon research was transferred to the Director of Fisheries Research (at first under the Scottish Home Department, then in 1960 under the Department of Agriculture and Fisheries for Scotland (DAFS) which became the Scottish Office Agriculture and Fisheries Department (SOAFD) in 1991) and was continued at the Freshwater Fisheries Laboratory (FFL) (see below). In recent years the Salmon Inspectorate has been much involved in monitoring, and advising on, the development of Salmon farming.

The District Salmon Fishery Boards (DSFBs) also originated in 1862 with a remit to regulate local matters. Over the years they have assessed stocks of fish, carried out hatchery work and co-operated in tagging programmes and other research projects.

Hydro-Electric Board

Hydro-power is an important segment of electricity production in Scotland (see Chapter 17). The Caledonian Power Bill 1936 was thrown out largely because of the potential impact on fisheries (John Berry, personal communication) and was replaced eventually by the Hydro Act 1943. From the mid-1940s the North of Scotland Hydro-Electric Board (NSHEB) (now Scottish Hydro-Electric plc) was thus concerned with the conservation of migratory salmonid stocks and joint work with the Salmon Inspectorate, the FFL and some DSFBs led to improved design of fish passes (Aitken *et al.*, 1966) and large-scale hatchery provision. The attention given by NSHEB to fish conservation has had an important effect internationally (John Berry, personal communication) and many other countries have copied Scottish standards in designing their schemes.

More recently, the Board commissioned research into the effects of pumped storage schemes (Maitland, 1981). Thus, although the development of power generation from water has altered considerably the hydrological map of Scotland, especially in the central Highlands, the Board has maintained a sensitive and co-operative attitude to the environmental consequences of its activities (NSHEB, 1978; Chapter 17).

An important aspect of this has been the appointment of fisheries advisers, notable among whom have been W. L. Calderwood, W. J. M. Menzies, Dr John Berry and Dr Derek Mills.

Freshwater Fisheries Laboratory

In 1948, an initiative by the NSHEB led to the setting up of the first laboratory in Scotland dedicated to research into freshwater fish. This was subsequently supported by the Scottish Home Department. Although the Brown Trout Research Laboratory at Pitlochry concentrated its efforts on the eponymous species over the first 10 years of its existence (Pyefinch, 1960), it gave increasing attention to Salmon and Sea Trout and was renamed the Freshwater Fisheries Laboratory in 1957.

The early work of the Laboratory looked at development, growth, spawning and behaviour of Brown Trout and also examined the chemistry, especially the phosphorus content, of Highland waters (Holden, 1966). The components of the Trout's food web were also studied, and fishery management techniques such as nutrient enrichment and population control were examined. Research activity then turned to Salmon and the DAFS Fisheries of Scotland Reports of the 1960s show that FFL staff published over 70 papers on Salmon, 30 or so on water chemistry (including pesticides and pollutants) and more than 20 on fish parasites and diseases. In the 1970s the FFL Triennial Research Reviews show that of more than 100 published papers about one third were on Salmon and another third concerned with pesticides and heavy metal pollutants. Several major contributions to Salmon biology were made during this period (e.g. Thorpe, 1977). In the 1980s, well over 100 of the 230 papers listed in the FFL Annual Reviews were on Salmon research (many on physiology and behaviour), almost 50 on "acid rain" topics and 25 on methods developed at the Laboratory.

A recent review of work at the Laboratory (SOAFD, 1992) includes items on Arctic Charr, Grayling, Rainbow Trout and sawbill ducks in addition to the main studies on Atlantic Salmon and Trout; topics covered range from genetics, development, nutrition, behaviour and migration to catches, fish farming, environmental conditions and management of freshwater fish resources.

Throughout its 45 years of existence the Laboratory has also provided an information and advisory service to the public which has contributed much to the general appreciation of Scotland's salmonid fauna.

University Field Station

Following the introduction of courses in freshwater ecology at Loch Lomond in 1938 by Dr Harry Slack, the University of Glasgow established a Field Station at Rossdhu in 1946. This was the first, and for many years the only, such facility of a British university. In 1964 the original hutted laboratory was replaced by a purpose-built field station across the loch at Rowardennan and this was extended in 1976 in collaboration with the University of Stirling, who now share the teaching and research premises. Other universities also bring their students to Rowardennan for field courses. Apart from the many undergraduate and graduate students trained there, a very wide range of freshwater research has been conducted over the years. Much of the early work on the characterization of Loch Lomond is reviewed by Slack (1957) and since then research on a wide range of topics has been published: for example on the phytoplankton (Maulood and Boney, 1980), zooplankton (Chapman, 1972), profundal fauna (Slack, 1965), fish (Maitland, 1972; Scott, 1975; Adams, 1991 and others). Work has also been carried out on important adjacent waters: for example the River Fruin (Hamilton, 1961) and River Endrick (Maitland, 1966).

From 1987 onwards research publications have been listed in the Field Station's Annual Report and a recent review can be found in the symposium volume edited by Tippett *et al.* (in preparation).

Natural Environment Research Council

The concept of a Freshwater Biological Association (FBA) was first discussed at a meeting of the British Association in Glasgow in 1928. It was founded in London in 1929 by a group of biologists who wished to further the study of fresh waters by establishing a permanent laboratory provided with full-time staff and the necessary equipment. The Freshwater Biological Association was established in 1931, supported initially by the Development Commission and since 1965 by the Natural Environment Research Council (NERC). Most of the FBA's work has been in England but occasional studies have been undertaken in Scotland (e.g. Mortimer, 1955; Gorham, 1957; Pennington *et al.*, 1972).

In the early 1960s, the Nature Conservancy (then part of NERC) obtained official approval to initiate work on freshwater biology in Scotland and in 1964 it was proposed that a programme of research on Loch Leven would be developed as part of the International Biological Programme (IBP). The combined research work was initiated in 1966 by staff of the Wetlands Research Group of the Nature Conservancy, the Freshwater Fisheries Laboratory and the Wildfowl Trust. The project ran for several years, culminating in a successful symposium at the University of Stirling in 1973 (Anonymous, 1974).

In 1974, the Nature Conservancy Wetlands Research Group became part of the Institute of Terrestrial Ecology, and more recently (1989) has been taken into the Institute of Freshwater Ecology. The post-IBP work of the Group has been very productive with over 120 papers on Scottish freshwater research published between 1974 and 1986. Over 20 of these were synoptic studies on regional groups of waters such as Shetland, Hebrides and Tayside and most notably Scotland's five largest lochs (Maitland, 1981).

The Institute of Hydrology (IH) was formed from the NERC Hydrological Research Unit in 1968. The IH headquarters is still in Wallingford where a wide range of research is carried out, from forest evaporation processes to water quality modelling. Two out-stations, Plynlimon and Stirling, carry out more field-oriented research programmes. The IH base in Scotland was established in 1981 when the Balquhidder catchment water balance and water quality experiment was initiated (Johnson, 1990). Research in Scotland currently covers a diverse range of issues including flood modelling, hydrology of wetlands, snow melt and long-term acidification, as well as continuing with the forest research in the Balquhidder catchments (Johnson and

Whitehead, 1993). Much of this work is carried out in association with other research bodies in Scotland.

Scottish Natural Heritage

In 1974, the executive arm of the Nature Conservancy was moved out of NERC and became directly responsible to the Department of the Environment as the Nature Conservancy Council. More recently, this has been split into three country agencies, the Scottish arm becoming the Nature Conservancy Council for Scotland (1991) and a year later merging with the Countryside Commission for Scotland to form Scottish Natural Heritage.

A relatively small portion of the work of these conservation bodies in Scotland has been basic freshwater research. However, there have been a number of useful monitoring studies, substantial survey and classification work (e.g. Ratcliffe, 1977) and many commissioned projects (e.g. Tivy, 1980; Maitland and Lyle, 1992; see also Chapter 29).

Academic research

The universities, colleges and other academic establishments in Scotland have played a major role in research in freshwater science. The strength of the research and its emphasis has relied very much on individuals and so the relative importance of freshwater studies has varied enormously from decade to decade. Much of the research has been short-term and often produced in the form of student theses (many of which have never been published).

At the University of Aberdeen, early innovative work on rivers and benthos sampling (Neill, 1938) was followed some years later by a number of studies on invertebrates by Young and Williams (1983) and on fish by Treasurer (1981), Laird and Needham (1986), Lucas *et al.* (1991) and others.

The new University of Dundee developed a very strong freshwater group specializing in algal physiology and led by Stewart (Stewart and Pearson, 1970) and later Codd (Codd and Stewart, 1973). Geological studies on the sediments of estuaries and lochs using sidescan sonar were carried out from the Tay Estuary Research Centre (Duck and McManus, 1985; McManus and Alizai, 1987).

In the Zoology Department at the University of Edinburgh the early work on Arctic Charr in Scotland was initiated by Friend (1959). This emphasis on salmonids was continued by Mills (1964; 1969) and his students in the Department of Forestry and Natural Resources.

As well as the many studies on Loch Lomond carried out from the University Field Station (discussed above), workers at the University of Glasgow have studied freshwater molluscs (Hunter, 1953), triclads (Calow, 1977) and algae (Boney, 1975).

At the University of St Andrews, the extensive work by Spence (1982) and his colleagues has considerably extended the knowledge of aquatic plant communities in Scotland. Scott (1975) and his students have studied the biology of Powan in Loch Lomond for three decades.

Research at the University of Stirling has included a strong aquatic component with studies by Holliday *et al.* (1974), McLusky and McFarlane (1974) and others. In addition, the development of the Institute of Aquaculture there by Roberts *et al.* (1970) and his staff (e.g. Stephen, 1984) has created an internationally renowned centre of research.

At the former Colleges of Technology (Glasgow, Napier, Paisley and Robert Gordon's) – all of them recently made universities – there has been a strong tradition of teaching in aquatic biology and many former students are now working in this field.

Other institutions have also had a strong involvement in freshwater science in Scotland; for example, the Royal Museum of Scotland in Edinburgh (Waterston *et al.*, 1979) and the Kelvingrove Museum in Glasgow.

Water Boards

The earliest example of a water supply reservoir in Britain appears to have been one at Whinhill, constructed in 1796 to supply water to Greenock (Henderson-Sellars, 1979). The history of the development of such systems is typified by that of the City of Glasgow whose engineers pioneered the use of large lochs (notably Loch Katrine) for water supply (Hunter, 1933). After the opening of the Loch Katrine scheme in 1859, numerous smaller local schemes were developed all over Scotland. Various changes took place in the organization of the authorities responsible for the provision of water, and eventually in 1972 water supply became the responsibility of the nine regional and three islands councils together with the Central Scotland Water Development Board which had been set up in 1968.

These Water Boards, in addition to carrying out their statutory function in providing water to domestic and industrial users, have also carried out substantial research and monitoring in relation to water resources and drinking water quality (Benton, 1983). In addition, many of the Boards have looked ahead to problems within their catchments and to methods of solving these or counteracting them by controls on land management (e.g. the restriction of afforestation in some areas).

Water Research Centre

The Water Research Centre (now WRc plc) was established in 1974, combining the Water Research Association, the Water Pollution Research Laboratory and the research section of the Water Resources Board. From 1979, an office in Stirling has provided a technical and advisory service on water quality, waste water and environmental management in Scotland.

Various research topics have also been tackled since then, including the effects of land use on water quality (Water Research Centre, 1992). This has included the effects of afforestation (Water Research Centre, 1990a) – for example, the quantification of run-off of phosphate fertilizer and a desk study of the effects of fertilizer applications (Water Research Centre, 1990b). Other studies have investigated the effects of sewage sludge application in forests on run-off water quality, the effects of oil spills on groundwater and the effects of sheep dipping practices. Since 1989, WRc has carried out numerous research projects on behalf of SNIFFER (the Scotland and Northern Ireland Forum for Environmental Research). These include the development of a Eutrophication Risk Assessment procedure for fresh and coastal waters and a river water quality classification scheme.

River Purification Boards

The first attempt to obtain a picture of the pollution of rivers in Scotland was the report of a Royal Commission (appointed in 1868) in 1872. The Report noted "examples of river pollution of nearly every kind to be met with in Great Britain, and of every degree of intensity between the slightest departure from the purity of the original rain water and a filthiness offensive to nearly every sense and destructive of nearly every use to which water can be put". The Commissioners recommended the enactment of general standards of purity for liquid discharges to watercourses but this never reached the statute book and it was not until the River Pollution Act 1876 that their report had any practical outcome.

This Act was ineffectual in keeping rivers clean and in 1928 the Scottish Advisory Committee on Rivers Pollution Prevention was appointed. This published seven reports prior to the outbreak of the Second World War but it was not until after the report of the Rivers Pollution Prevention Sub-Committee in 1950 that the Rivers (Prevention of Pollution) (Scotland) Act 1951 was passed. This Act gave statutory powers to local river purification authorities, which have since been amalgamated in various ways to form the present seven River Purification Boards (RPBs) and three Islands Authorities. These Boards have made a notable contribution, not only in pollution prevention in Scotland, but also in research terms.

Unlike the all-embracing Regional Water Authorities of England and Wales, the Scottish RPBs were established as single-purpose authorities (Hammerton, 1983) and so far have argued successfully for this to remain so. Much of what they have attained can be attributed to this degree of independence and also their conviction that success in pollution control and prevention comes from obtaining accurate and long-term hydrological, chemical and biological records (Best, 1974; Sargent, 1981; Poodle, 1987). On the research side, Chandler (1970), Mackay *et al.* (1973) and others have helped to develop and test methods of assessing river pollution.

Scottish Development Department

Part of the remit of the Scottish Development Department (SDD), which was formed in 1962 and became the Scottish Office Environment Department (SOEnD) in 1991, is to administer government policy on public water supplies, sewerage and the prevention of air and water pollution. In doing this it has encouraged best practices and has played an important role in promoting and co-ordinating Scotland-wide surveys of river and estuarine pollution (Scottish Development Department, 1972; 1976; 1980).

Scottish Freshwater Group

The Scottish Freshwater Group was first formed in 1968 to facilitate contact and discussion among the many people in Scotland concerned with fresh water. Meetings have been held every spring and autumn since then at the University of Stirling and take the form of several informal talks and demonstrations. The knowledge of current work gained from these meetings has proved of real value and allowed much closer liaison throughout Scotland among the individuals and groups concerned.

The meetings are always open to all those interested as is the membership of the Group itself. All members receive regular notices of meetings and occasional revised lists of members and their interests. By the 50th meeting of the Group, some 250 talks and 300 poster demonstrations had been heard and seen by members of the Group.

COLLABORATIVE PROJECTS

In recent years, the increasing expertise and effort required to research complex issues in the field has resulted in a number of valuable collaborative projects. These have included the International Biological Programme Study on Loch Leven (Anonymous, 1974), the Balquhidder Project (Johnson and Whitehead, 1993), the Loch Dee Study (Burns *et al.*, 1984), the Loch Fleet Project (Howells and Brown, 1986) and others.

CONCLUSIONS

A good proportion of those who made important contributions to the early knowledge of freshwater science in Scotland have been included in this account. However, the burgeoning of limnological research over the past 50 years, as demonstrated by the number of organizations cited here, has restricted reference to only a few examples of publications by individuals from each organization. As it is estimated that the number of published papers in freshwater science has doubled in each decade since the 1940s, clearly much research and many research workers have been left out. While the selection of what has been included is the authors' responsibility, more details can be obtained from the annual reports and publication lists of the various organizations. Perhaps also this paper will encourage more workers to produce historical accounts of their own institutions or research area.

ACKNOWLEDGEMENTS

We are grateful to Dr Philip Boon and Dr John Berry for useful comments on an early draft of this review. Ruth Wolstenholme and R. C. Johnson were kind enough to supply details of the work of WRc and IH respectively in Scotland, and Eileen Moran and Sheila Adair helped to supply some of the references.

REFERENCES

Adams, C. E. (1991). "Shift in Pike, *Esox lucius* L., predation pressure following the introduction of Ruffe, *Gymnocephalus cernuus* (L.) to Loch Lomond", *Journal of Fish Biology*, **38**, 663–667.

Aitken, P. L., Dickerson, L. N. and Menzies, W. J. M. (1966). "Fish passes and screens at water power works", *Proceedings of the Institution of Civil Engineers*, 1963, 34–42.

Anonymous (1974). "The Loch Leven IBP Research Project", *Proceedings of the Royal Society of Edinburgh*, **74**, 45–416.

Benton, C. (1983). "Seagull pollution of reservoirs", *Journal of the Institution of Water Engineers and Scientists*, **37**, 347–363.

Best, G. A. (1974). "Continuous monitoring of water quality", *Proceedings of the Society for Analytical Chemistry*, **11**, 268–269.

Boney, A. D. (1975). *Phytoplankton*, Arnold, London.

Buchan, A. (1871). "Remarks on the deep-water temperature of Lochs Lomond, Katrine and Tay", *Proceedings of the Royal Society of Edinburgh*, **7**, 791–795.

Buchanan, J. Y. (1879). "Note on the distribution of temperature under ice in Linlithgow Loch", *Proceedings of the Royal Society of Edinburgh*, **10**, 56–58.

Burns, J. C., Coy, J. S., Tervet, D. J., Harriman, R., Morrison, B. R. S. and Quine, C. P. (1984). "The Loch Dee Project: a study of the ecological effects of acid precipitation and forest management on an upland catchment in south-west Scotland", *Fisheries Management*, **15**, 145–167.

Calderwood, W. L. (1931). *Salmon Hatching and Salmon Migrations*, Arnold, London.

Calderwood, W. L. (1945). "Passage of smolts through turbines", *Salmon and Trout Magazine*, **115**, 214–221.

Calow, P. (1977). "The joint effect of temperature and starvation on the metabolism of triclads", *Oikos*, **29**, 87–98.

Chandler, J. R. (1970). "A biological approach to water quality management", *Journal of Water Pollution Control*, **69**, 415–422.

Chapman, M. A. (1972). "The annual cycles of the limnetic cyclopoid Copepoda of Loch Lomond, Scotland", *Internationale Revue der gesamten Hydrobiologie und Hydrographie*, **57**, 895–911.

Codd, G. A. and Stewart, W. D. P. (1973). "Pathways of glycollate metabolism in the blue-green alga *Anabaena cylindrica*", *Archiv für Mikrobiologie*, **94**, 11–28.

Duck, R. W. and McManus, J. (1985). "Bathymetric charts of ten Scottish lochs", *Tay Estuary Research Centre Reports*, **9**, 1–31.

Evans, W. (1906). "Fauna of the Upper Elf Loch", *Annals of Scottish Natural History*, 1906, 57.

Fleming, T. (1788). "Account of a remarkable agitation of the waters of Loch Tay", *Transactions of the Royal Society of Edinburgh*, **1**, 200.

Franck, R. (1658). *Northern Memoirs, Calculated for the Meridian of Scotland*, Mortlock, London.

Friend, G. F. (1959). "Subspeciation in British charrs", *Systematics Association Publication*, **3**, 121–129.

Gorham, E. (1957). "The chemical composition of some natural waters in the Cairn Gorm – Strath Spey district of Scotland", *Limnology and Oceanography*, **2**, 153–154.

Hamilton, J. D. (1961). "The effect of sand pit washings on a stream fauna", *Verhandlungen der Internationalen Vereinigung für theoretische und angewandte Limnologie*, **14**, 435–439.

Hammerton, D. (1983). "The history of water quality management in Scotland", *Journal of the Institution of Water Engineers and Scientists*, **37**, 336–346.

Henderson-Sellars, B. (1979). *Reservoirs*, Macmillan, London.

Holden, A. V. (1966). "A chemical study of rain and stream water in the Scottish highlands", *Freshwater Salmon Fisheries Research Scotland*, **37**, 1–17.

Holliday, F. G. T., Tytler, P. and Young, A. H. (1974). "Activity levels of Trout (*Salmo trutta*) in Airthrey Loch, Stirling, and Loch Leven, Kinross", *Proceedings of the Royal Society of Edinburgh*, **74B**, 315–331.

Howells, G. D. and Brown, D. J. A. (1986). "Loch Fleet: techniques for acidity mitigation", *Water, Air and Soil Pollution*, **30**, 593–599.

Hunter, R. (1933). *The Water Supply of Glasgow*, Menzies, Glasgow.

Hunter, W. D. R. (1953). "On migrations of *Lymnaea peregra* (Muller) on the shores of Loch Lomond", *Proceedings of the Royal Society of Edinburgh*, **65**, 84–105.

Johnson, R. C. (1990). "The interception, throughfall and stemflow in a forest in highland Scotland and the comparison with other upland forests in the UK", *Journal of Hydrology*, **118**, 281–287.

Johnson, R. C. and Whitehead, P. G. (1993). "An introduction to the research in the Balquhidder experimental catchments", *Journal of Hydrology*, **145**, 231–238.

King, J. J. F. X. (1890). "Neuroptera from the island of Unst", *Entomologist's Monthly Magazine*, **26**, 176–180.

Laird, L. M. and Needham, E. A. (1986). "Salmon farming and the future of the Atlantic Salmon", *Institute of Terrestrial Ecology Symposium*, **15**, 66–72.

Lucas, M. C., Priede, I. G., Armstrong, J. D., Gindy, A. N. Z. and De Vera, L. (1991). "Direct measurements of metabolism, activity and feeding behaviour of Pike, *Esox lucius* L., in the wild, by the use of heart rate telemetry", *Journal of Fish Biology*, **39**, 325–345.

McClean, W. N. (1933). "Practical river flow measurement and its place in inland water survey as exemplified on the Ness (Scotland) basin", *Transactions of the Institute of Water Engineers*, **38**, 233–267.

Mackay, D. W., Soulsby, P. G. and Poodle, T. (1973). "The biological assessment of pollution in streams", *Association of River Authorities Year Book*, 1973, 189–197.

McLachlan, R. (1881). "Description of a new species of Trichoptera (*Polycentropus kingi*) from Scotland", *Entomologist's Monthly Magazine*, **17**, 254–255.

McLusky, D. S. and McFarlane, A. (1974). "The energy requirements of certain larval chironomid populations in Loch Leven, Kinross", *Proceedings of the Royal Society of Edinburgh*, **74B**, 259–264.

McManus, J. and Alizai, S. A. K. (1987). "Variations in marsh surface levels in the upper Tay Estuary", *Proceedings of the Royal Society of Edinburgh*, **92B**, 345–358.

Maitland, P. S. (1966). *The Fauna of the River Endrick*, Blackie, Glasgow.

Maitland, P. S. (1972). "Loch Lomond: Man's effects on the salmonid community", *Journal of the Fisheries Research Board of Canada*, **29**, 849–860.

Maitland, P. S. (Ed.) (1981). *The Ecology of Scotland's Largest Lochs: Lomond, Awe, Ness, Morar and Shiel*, Junk, The Hague.

Maitland, P. S. (1983). "Two hundred years of the biological sciences in Scotland: freshwater science", *Proceedings of the Royal Society of Edinburgh*, **84**, 171–210.

Maitland, P. S. and Lyle, A. A. (1992). "Conservation of freshwater fish in the British Isles: proposals for management", *Aquatic Conservation: Marine and Freshwater Ecosystems*, **2**, 165–183.

Maulood, B. K. and Boney, A. D. (1980). "A seasonal and ecological study of the phytoplankton of Loch Lomond", *Hydrobiologia*, **71**, 239–259.

Menzies, W. J. M. (1939). "Some preliminary observations on the migrations of the European salmon", *American Association for the Advancement of Science*, **8**, 13–25.

Menzies, W. J. M. (1949). *The Stock of Salmon. Its Migrations, Preservation and Improvement*, Arnold, London.

Mills, D. H. (1964). "The ecology of the young stages of the Atlantic Salmon in the River Bran, Ross-shire", *Freshwater Salmon Fisheries Research Scotland*, **32**, 1–58.

Mills, D. H. (1969). "The growth and population densities of Roach in some Scottish waters", *Proceedings of the British Coarse Fish Conference*, **4**, 50–57.

Mortimer, C. H. (1955). "Some effects of the earth's rotation on water movements in stratified lakes", *Verhandlungen der Internationalen Vereinigung für theoretische und angewandte Limnologie*, **12**, 187–192.

Morton, K. J. (1883). "Notes on the Trichoptera of upper Clydesdale", *Entomologist's Monthly Magazine*, **19**, 194–196.

Murray, J. and Pullar, L. (1910). *Bathymetrical Survey of the Fresh Water Lochs of Scotland*, Challenger Office, Edinburgh.

Napier, J. R. (1875). "On the action between the Loch Katrine water supplied to Glasgow and various metals", *Proceedings of the Glasgow Philosophical Society*, **9**, 202.

Neill, R. M. (1938). "The food and feeding of the Brown Trout (*Salmo trutta* L.) in relation to the organic environment", *Transactions of the Royal Society of Edinburgh*, **59**, 481–520.

NSHEB (1978). *Power from the Glens*, North of Scotland Hydro-Electric Board, Edinburgh.

Pennington, W., Haworth, E. Y., Bonny, A. P. and Lishman, J. P. (1972). "Lake sediments in northern Scotland", *Philosophical Transactions of the Royal Society*, **264B**, 191–294.

Poodle, T. (1987). "Factors affecting the future of the Scottish hydrometric network", *Transactions of the Royal Society of Edinburgh*, **78**, 269–274.

Pyefinch, K. A. (1960). *Trout in Scotland*, HMSO, Edinburgh.

Ratcliffe, D. A. (1977). *A Nature Conservation Review*, Cambridge University Press, Cambridge.

Roberts, R. J., Shearer, W. M., Elson, K. G. R. and Munro, A. L. S. (1970). "Studies on ulcerative dermal necrosis of salmonids. I. The skin of the normal Salmon head", *Journal of Fish Biology*, **2**, 223–229.

Sargent, R. J. (1981). "A river coding system for water quality archives", *Water Pollution Control*, **80**, 682–686.

Scott, D. B. C. (1975). "A hermaphrodite specimen of *Coregonus lavaretus* (L.) (Salmoniformes, Salmonidae) from Loch Lomond, Scotland", *Journal of Fish Biology*, **7**, 709.

Scott, T. (1890). "Notes on a small collection of Ostracoda from the Edinburgh district", *Proceedings of the Royal Physical Society of Edinburgh*, **10**, 313.

Scott, T. (1895). "Notes on freshwater Entomostraca, with special reference to Loch Leven", *Annals of Scottish Natural History*, 1895, 163–173.

Scottish Development Department (1972). *Towards Cleaner Water*, Edinburgh.

Scottish Development Department (1976). *Towards Cleaner Water 1975*, Edinburgh.

Scottish Development Department (1980). *Water in Scotland: A Review*, Edinburgh.

Sinclair, J. (1791). *The Statistical Account of Scotland*, Creech, Edinburgh.

Slack, H. D. (1957). *Studies on Loch Lomond. I*, Blackie, Glasgow.

Slack, H. D. (1965). "The profundal fauna of Loch Lomond, Scotland", *Proceedings of the Royal Society of Edinburgh*, **69B**, 272–297.

SOAFD (1992). *Freshwater Fisheries Laboratory, Pitlochry, Annual Review 1990–91*, Edinburgh.

Spence, D. H. N. (1982). "The zonation of plants in freshwater lakes", *Advances in Ecological Research*, **12**, 37–125.

Stephen, A. B. (1984). "Electrophoretic evidence for population variation in Brown Trout (*Salmo trutta* L.) and the implications for management", *Institute of Fisheries Management Annual Study Course*, **15**, 119–127.

Stewart, W. D. P. and Pearson, H. W. (1970). "Effects of aerobic and anaerobic conditions on growth and metabolism of blue-green algae", *Proceedings of the Royal Society of London*, **175B**, 293–311.

Thorpe, J. E. (1977). "Bimodal distribution of length of juvenile Atlantic salmon (*Salmo salar* L.) under artificial rearing conditions", *Journal of Fish Biology*, **11**, 175–184.

Tivy, J. (1980). *The Effect of Recreation on Freshwater Lochs and Reservoirs in Scotland*, Countryside Commission for Scotland, Perth.

Treasurer, J. W. (1981). "Some aspects of the reproductive biology of Perch, *Perca fluviatilis* L. Fecundity, maturation and spawning behaviour", *Journal of Fish Biology*, **18**, 729–740.

Water Research Centre (1990a). "A review of the effects of afforestation and forestry activities on upland water quality", *WRc Report No. PRS 2422-M*, Medmenham.

Water Research Centre (1990b). "Nutrient enrichment of Scottish lochs and reservoirs with particular reference to the impact of forest fertilisation", *WRc Report No. PRS 2457-M*, Medmenham.

Water Research Centre (1992). "Measures for protecting upland water quality", *WRc Report No. SR 3052*, Medmenham.

Waterston, R., Holden, A. V., Campbell, R. N. and Maitland, P. S. (1979). "The inland waters of the Outer Hebrides", *Proceedings of the Royal Society of Edinburgh*, **77B**, 329–351.

Wedderburn, E. M. (1910). "Current observations in Loch Garry", *Proceedings of the Royal Society of Edinburgh*, **29**, 312–323.

West, G. (1910). "A further contribution to a comparative study of the dominant phanerogamic and higher cryptogamic flora of aquatic habit in Scottish lakes", *Proceedings of the Royal Society of Edinburgh*, **30**, 65–181.

Young, M. R. and Williams, J. C. (1983). "The status and conservation of the freshwater pearl mussel (*Margaritifera margaritifera* Linn.) in Great Britain", *Biological Conservation*, **25**, 35–52.

2

Running Waters

I. R. SMITH

18 Torphin Road, Colinton, Edinburgh, EH13 0HW, UK

and

A. A. LYLE

Institute of Freshwater Ecology, Bush Estate, Penicuik, EH26 0QB, UK

INTRODUCTION

This chapter outlines the properties of river networks which form the basis for assessing the extent of running water resources. Estimates of the numbers and distribution of river systems and associated streams are presented. A brief account of the physical characteristics of running waters and how these compare, nationally and internationally, is included.

CATCHMENT STRUCTURE

Scotland is traditionally divided, in terms of topography, into Highlands, Midland Valley and Southern Uplands (Figure 2.1) but, when dealing with water resources, drainage patterns and catchment areas are more significant. For administrative and statistical purposes, the whole of the United Kingdom is divided into Hydrometric Areas. These are not always single catchments; the basins of small streams draining directly into the sea are often combined. There are 47 such areas in Scotland but, to simplify the presentation of results here, they have been grouped into seven Hydrological Regions (Figure 2.2 and Table 2.1). Hydrological Regions contain basins having broadly similar characteristics but there are anomalies. For example, Hydrometric Area 85, the Loch Lomond catchment, is taken to be part of the South West Scotland Region. This is appropriate for the River Endrick flowing into the South Basin of the loch, but other parts of the catchment are more likely to have the characteristics of the West Highlands Region. The most obvious feature of Figure 2.2 is the closeness of the east–west watershed to the west coast in central and northern Scotland. This has a pronounced influence on the characteristics of running waters (see Chapter 5).

The Fresh Waters of Scotland: A National Resource of International Significance
Edited by P. S. Maitland, P. J. Boon and D. S. McLusky. © 1994 John Wiley & Sons Ltd

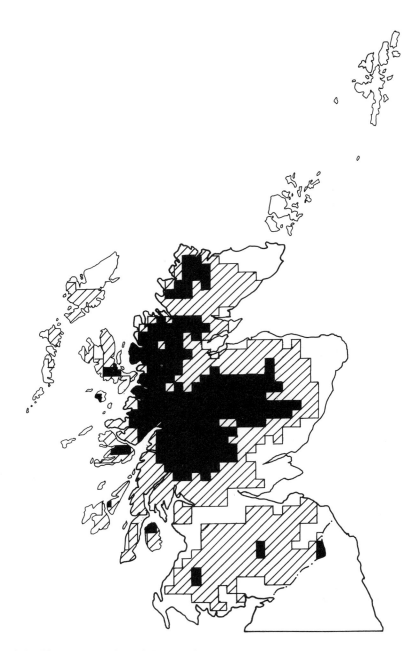

FIGURE 2.1. The topography of Scotland. The black areas indicate 10 km grid squares containing some land over 760 m (2500 feet) and the hatched areas some land over 300 m (1000 feet). The map is based on overlays published by the Institute of Terrestrial Ecology (1978)

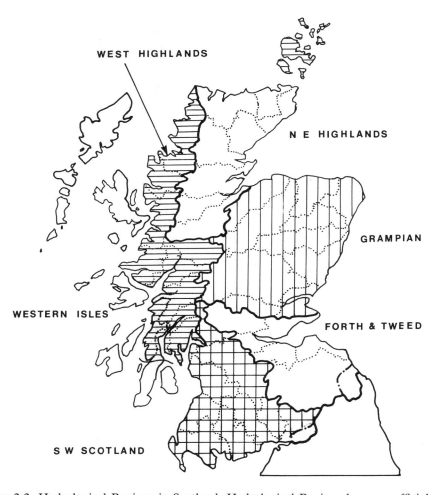

FIGURE 2.2. Hydrological Regions in Scotland. Hydrological Regions have no official status and are delineated solely to indicate broad regional patterns. The dotted lines define Hydrometric Areas and the chain dotted line indicates the national boundary where it does not coincide with watersheds

CLIMATE AND HYDROLOGICAL CHARACTERISTICS

Climate

In a world context, the whole of Scotland has a temperate, maritime climate characterized by the absence of extremes in temperature and rainfall throughout the year. A detailed account of climate is given, for example, in Gregory and Chandler (1976). Within this broad class, two more detailed features are worth emphasizing. The first concerns the degree of wetness. Green (1964) compared the annual cycles of rainfall and evaporation for the whole of Great Britain. From his maps, three water balance zones can be identified (Figure 2.3):

- the waterlogged zone where the rainfall normally exceeds evaporation in every month of the year – the region of climatic bog formation
- the dry zone where the reverse occurs in summer so that evaporation is frequently restricted by lack of water in the soil, the area being very small in Scotland
- an intermediate zone where reduction in evaporation due to water shortage may occur in some years

The other feature is the mountain climate which prevails in many areas of the Highlands and some of the Southern Uplands, and also the partially Alpine climate of the Cairngorm Massif. This relatively small area, at the eastern edge of the Highlands, is sufficiently far from the sea for its moderating influence to be reduced. Snowfall may form an appreciable part of winter precipitation and winters can be markedly colder.

Seasonal run-off patterns

The annual pattern of river flow associated with a temperate, maritime climate is a simple cycle with maximum flows in winter, the volume of run-off in summer being reduced by evaporation (Pardé, 1949). The timing of maximum and minimum monthly flows can be affected by the degree of wetness. In the waterlogged zone, flow extremes virtually coincide with rainfall extremes while, in the dry zone, peak flows occur when the soil is saturated and field drains flowing. For the River Ewe (West Highlands Region), for example, the highest monthly average rainfall occurs in November and the highest monthly average flow in December. For the River Tyne (Forth and Tweed Region), the corresponding months are August and January. There is less difference in the timing of the corresponding summer monthly minimum values. In some years, the Alpine character of flows from the Cairngorms can be seen. High spring flows due to snowmelt, accompanied by marked diurnal variations in flow, can occur during fine weather, and some of the lowest recorded flows occur in winter because of sub-zero temperatures.

Other flow characteristics

There are about 200 stations in Scotland where river flow is measured continuously although there appear to be none in the two island Regions. Summaries for all stations

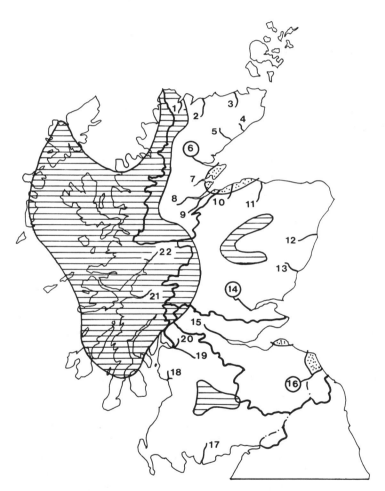

FIGURE 2.3. Soil moisture zones and principal rivers in Scotland. The horizontally hatched areas indicate the waterlogged zones and the dot shaded areas the dry zones. The numbers indicate the seaward end of fourth and fifth order river systems in the original count, the fifth order rivers being circled. 1, Strathmore; 2, Naver; 3, Thurso; 4, Berriedale; 5, Helmsdale; 6, Shin; 7, Conon; 8, Beauly; 9, Ness; 10, Findhorn; 11, Spey; 12, Dee; 13, North Esk; 14, Tay; 15, Teith; 16, Tweed; 17, Dee; 18, Garnock–Irvine; 19, Clyde; 20, Leven; 21, Awe; 22, Lochy

are published by the Institute of Hydrology and the British Geological Survey (annually) and various computer print-out options are also available. It is worth emphasizing that the frequency distribution of daily flows is not symmetrical and that, as a rough rule, flows are below average for about two thirds of the time.

Table 2.1 shows the average total annual run-off from each Hydrological Region. The average total run-off from Scotland in a year, i.e., 80.6 km^3, is equivalent to a little over one metre depth over the entire area of Scotland. Within individual Hydrometric Areas, the depths of run-off vary from 250 mm in the dry area of the Forth and Tweed Region to 2300 mm in the wettest parts of the West Highlands Region.

TABLE 2.1. Hydrological Regions and total run-off in Scotland

Hydrological Region	Hydrometric Areas	Total area (km^2)	Depth (mm)	Specific flow (L s^{-1} km^{-2})	Total volume (m^3 × 10^6)
				Mean annual run-off	
Orkney and Shetland	107, 108	1 976.4	950	30.1	1 877.6
North East Highlands	96, 97, 1–6	12 212.5	1090	34.5	13 311.6
Grampian	7–16	20 428.4	742	23.5	15 157.9
Forth and Tweed	17–21	10 015.8	593	18.8	5 934.4
				Totals discharged to North Sea	36 286.5
South West Scotland	77–85	13 457.6	979	31.0	13 175.0
West Highlands	86–95	12 373.2	1950	61.8	24 127.7
Western Isles	104–106	7 404.5	950	30.1	7 034.3
	Total	77 063.4	Totals discharged to Atlantic		44 337.0
			Totals discharged from Scotland		80 623.5

Run-off values are unpublished data made available by the Institute of Hydrology

These volumes of water are made up of flood or quick flow water discharged after only a few hours contact with the ground, and base flow which is discharged after weeks or even longer stored in soil and rock. The duration of contact has obvious implications for the chemical composition of stream water. Data published by the Institute of Hydrology and the British Geological Survey (1988) show that there is some tendency for the Base Flow Index – the fraction of the total run-off that is composed of base flow – to increase with catchment area, although not consistently. It appears that the mean value of the Index throughout Scotland for catchments greater than 500 km^2 is almost exactly 0.5. Lower values are found in smaller catchments in the North East Highlands, South West Scotland and West Highlands Regions, the extreme value being 0.10 in the headwaters of the River Nith, South West Scotland Region. A high proportion of the run-off in Scotland is, in these terms, flood water. The quantity in tonnes of solid and dissolved matter discharged to the sea per 1 mg L^{-1} concentration is numerically equal to the run-off volume in m^3 × 10^6.

NUMBERS AND DISTRIBUTION OF RUNNING WATERS

River network properties

The pattern of converging tributaries that form a river network contains more ordered structure than is first apparent from a casual look at a map. Network properties, therefore, provide a useful means of assessing the numbers and distribution of river and stream systems. They do not, however, provide a consistent means of describing the physical characteristics and habitats within a river. This is discussed below.

Stream order, as defined by Strahler's (1957) modification of Horton's (1945) original scheme, classifies a stream without tributaries as first order, a stream below the confluence of two first orders as second order and so on (Figure 2.4a); the order of the outfall stream can be dependent on the inclusion or omission of a single first order tributary. The omission of stream A on the figure would reduce the outfall order number from 4 to 3. The basis of pattern in river networks is the existence of a linear relation between order number and the logarithm of the number of streams in that order – effectively the ratio of the number of streams in a given order to that in the next higher order is constant. This is termed the 'bifurcation ratio'. A number of more complex procedures have been devised to analyze river networks (see, for example, Smart, 1978). Although these procedures are geomorphologically more precise, their additional complexity is not necessarily justified for resource assessment and ecological classification.

The stream order of a channel entering the sea clearly depends on the scale of the map used. Since this forms the basis of the river survey described below, the effect of map scale is important. Figure 2.4b shows the change in stream order on a sample of 28 river systems examined at map scales of 1:625 000 and 1:63 360. 68% of the sample increased by an order number of 2.

Other properties of river networks, besides the number of streams, are related to order number. Correlations between catchment area and stream length are commonly reported by geomorphologists (Knighton, 1984). A survey of the River Tay at 1:50 000 scale (Smith, 1992), showed that network laws also apply to average stream width (W) and depth (h) (in metres) such that, for a stream of order, u,

$$W = 0.51e^{0.72u} \quad r = 0.992$$
$$h = 0.097e^{0.32u} \quad r = 0.961$$

(These correlations are based on data collected during a survey in April when the flow was below average.) The ratios of change in width and depth values between adjacent orders are 2.05 and 1.39 respectively. It is thus possible to estimate the lengths, water surface areas and volumes associated with each order number (Figures 2.4d, e, f). The total stream length for the Tay system (5827 km) is more than 40 times the length of the main river stem (137 km) which is virtually identical to the sum of the mean lengths of each order. It is not known how typical the Tay results are for Scotland as a whole. At 1:250 000 scale the total length of rivers in Scotland has been measured at 50 737 km (Scottish Office Environment Department, 1992).

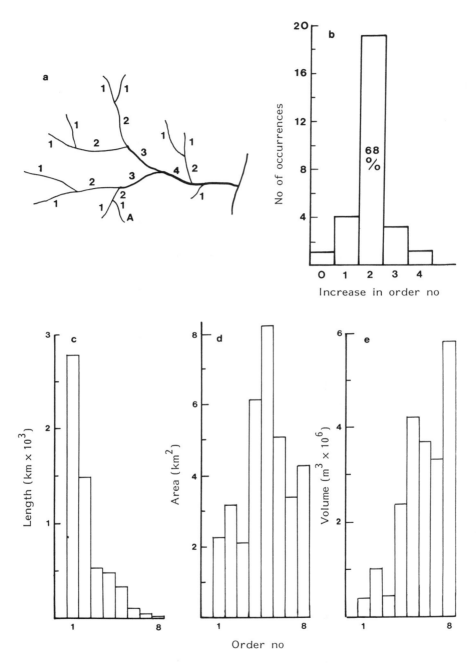

FIGURE 2.4. The properties of river networks. Figure (a) illustrates the definition of stream order. Figure (b) shows the increase in stream order when comparing maps at scales of 1:625 000 and 1:63 360. Figures (c), (d) and (e) show the total stream lengths, water surface areas and volumes respectively for the River Tay Basin network, by stream order

TABLE 2.2. Results of the original river count at 1:625 000 map scale (Smith and Lyle, 1979)

Hydrological Region	Systems						Mean system area[a]	Streams					
	1	2	3	4	5	Total		1	2	3	4	5	Total
Orkney and Shetland	112	46	4	–	–	162	12.2	252	55	4	–	–	311
N E Highlands	42	23	13	8	1	87	140.4	635	154	37	10	1	837
Grampian	27	9	6	4	1	47	434.6	426	96	23	6	1	552
Forth and Tweed	14	5	4	1	1	25	400.6	160	46	15	4	1	226
S W Scotland	20	15	13	4	–	52	258.8	350	92	22	4	–	468
W Highland	135	92	22	2	–	251	49.3	686	169	26	2	–	883
Western Isles	213	106	7	–	–	326	22.7	552	121	7	–	–	680
Totals	**563**	**296**	**69**	**19**	**3**	**950**		**3061**	**733**	**134**	**26**	**3**	**3957**

[a] Total area of Region divided by the total number of systems

River systems and streams

A count of the running waters shown on the 1:625 000 scale Ordnance Survey Physical Map is given by Smith and Lyle (1979). A Strahler-type network analysis was done for every river system entering the sea. The total number of river systems, the order number of the channel entering the sea, and the total number of streams of different orders associated with these systems can be computed immediately (Table 2.2). The regional variation in river characteristics is highlighted by the mean system area values.

Thirteen sample lengths of coastline were examined at a map scale of 1:63 360 in order to estimate the number of systems and their order number that were omitted in the original count. Because the primary concern is the effect of map scale, the original results, including those from England and Wales, have been retained. If X is the number of systems in the original count and Y the corresponding number of

TABLE 2.3. Estimates of the numbers of systems and streams on 1:63 360 maps

(a) Distribution, by stream order, of systems omitted in the original count

Order number	1	2	3	4
Percentage of total	67.5	25.5	6.9	0.1

(b) Estimated total number of river systems in Scotland

| | Order number | | | | | | | |
	1	2	3	4	5	6	7	Total
Transformed from original count	–	–	563	296	69	19	3	950
Estimated total number of uncounted systems	3848	1448	392	6	–	–	–	5694
Total	3848	1448	955	302	69	19	3	6644

(c) Estimated total number of streams associated with these systems

Order number	1	2	3	4	5	6	7	Total
1	3848							3848
2	5589	1448						7037
3	14229	3686	955					18870
4	17369	4500	1166	302				23337
5	15318	3968	1028	266	69			20649
6	16281	4218	1093	283	73	19		21967
7	9923	2571	666	173	45	12	3	13393
Totals	82557	20391	4908	1024	187	31	3	109101

systems on 1:63 360 maps, then,

$$Y = 5.98X - 2.95 \ (n = 13, r = 0.83)$$

The order numbers (on 1:63 360 maps) of omitted streams are shown on Table 2.3a. The majority, as might be expected from the earlier discussion on the effects of map scale, correspond to a shift of two order numbers, but not consistently. It is thus possible to estimate the approximate total number of river systems in Scotland (Table 2.3b) and, by using the mean bifurcation ratio of 3.86, the total number of associated streams (Table 2.3c). These totals include some streams in England. Parts of Hydrometric Areas 21 and 77 are in England and no logical separation seems possible when the national boundary is the centre of the river.

The seaward ends of major rivers, i.e., fourth and fifth order systems in the original count, are shown on Figure 2.3. The results may not be what might have been expected. The River Clyde, for example, appears to be no more significant than the Garnock–Irvine system. These anomalies are partly cultural – some rivers are famous for other reasons – but they also emphasize the difficulties with stream order. River networks and the branching structure of trees have features in common so that the Clyde can be considered *coniferous*, having a main stem and a number of small branches, while the Garnock–Irvine is *deciduous* – two relatively small systems merge just before entering the sea. There is also an apparent discrepancy with the River Tay. The original count identified a fifth order river, equivalent to a seventh order system on 1:63 360 maps, while Figure 2.4 indicates that the Tay is an eighth order river. Figure 2.4 is based on a separate survey using 2nd Edition 1:50 000 maps. One additional stream on the most recent map raises a main tributary, the River Isla, to seventh order and thus the lower reaches of the Tay are eighth order.

PHYSICAL CHARACTERISTICS OF RIVERS AND STREAMS

The pattern in stream networks is useful in determining the total extent of running water resources, but a first order stream may be a mountain headwater or a coastal drainage channel. How do the physical characteristics of rivers and streams determine the habitat of plants and animals and how do they vary across the country?

Commonly quoted indicators of physical conditions are channel dimensions, slope, and bed particle size. Current speed is not a good basis for comparison between sites. Ledger (1981) showed that, in the River Tweed, the variation in velocity with discharge at a point is much greater than any variation along the whole length of the river at discharges with the same frequency of occurrence. The ratio of the water depth (h) to bed particle size (d) determines the nature of the flow within a river, i.e.,

(1) If h/d is large, then the turbulent flow is characterized by a logarithmic velocity profile away from both bed and banks. This results in the maximum velocities being found near or at the surface in the centre of the channel. Standard equations relating flow resistance to velocity will then obtain.
(2) If $h/d<1$ (i.e., boulders protrude through the flow) none of the above obtains and the pattern of flow and the attendant velocities are highly variable.

Channel dimensions

Relationships between channel width and depth in terms of stream order have already been indicated. However, since a river channel is itself created by the flowing water, a more logical approach is to seek relations between channel dimensions and flow. This is a major topic and the subject of continuing controversy. All that is attempted here is a gross simplification in order to indicate order of magnitude.

Most relationships refer to "bankfull" conditions, i.e., a moderate flood flow where water is about to break out of the confined channel (Figure 2.5a). One that is well established is that the bankfull width (W_b) is proportional to the square root of the bankfull discharge (Q_b). An appropriate equation for Scottish conditions is that given by Charlton *et al.* (1978), i.e., on average,

$$W_b = 3.72Q_b^{0.44}$$

The width varies with the erosion resistance of the banks, particularly the presence or absence of trees. There remains the problem of estimating the bankfull discharge.

(a)

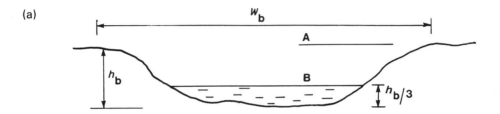

(b)

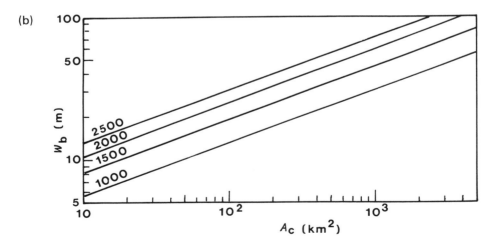

FIGURE 2.5. Bankfull conditions in a river channel. (a) Definition sketch. Line A corresponds to bankfull conditions. The ratio of width to depth increases as a river becomes wider. As a rough guide, water depth at average flow is about one third the bankfull depth, i.e., line B. (b) Approximate relationship between bankfull width, W_b, and catchment area, A_c, for different values of the average rainfall (in mm) over the catchment

Assuming that Q_b has an average recurrence interval of 1.5 years, it is possible to produce Figure 2.5b using information in the Flood Studies Report (Institute of Hydrology, 1975) and the above equation shows that, given the high rainfall that occurs, particularly in the West Highland Region, quite wide rivers can occur on small catchments.

Slope

The range of longitudinal profiles found in Scottish rivers is illustrated in Figure 2.6; these were derived from 1:50 000 scale maps. Greater insight into the nature of river beds is obtained from a slope frequency analysis although the definitive accuracy of these particular intervals (below) is uncertain (Figure 2.7) The units of slope are m k^{-1}.

> 25   mountainous, the bed being a sequence of chutes and pools with very large boulders and bedrock exposed
> 10–25   uneven distribution of boulders on the bed
> 2–10   pool and riffle sequence very obvious
> 1–2   pool and riffle sequence less obvious because water depth is large compared to the bed particle size
Up to 1   lowland river where water depth is large compared to the bed particle size

Figures 2.6 and 2.7 are essentially illustrative but, despite the small sample size, certain features are fairly clear. The difference between east- and west-flowing rivers

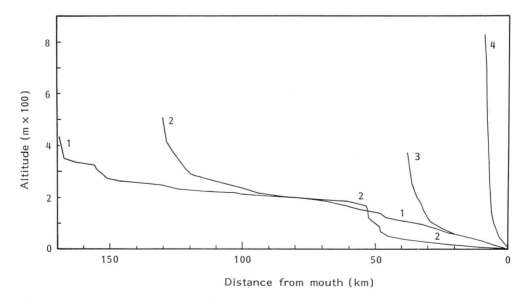

FIGURE 2.6. Longitudinal profiles for selected Scottish rivers. 1, River Spey (Grampian) – the longest river in Scotland; 2, River Clyde (S W Scotland); 3, River Tyne (Forth and Tweed); 4, River Finnan (West Highland)

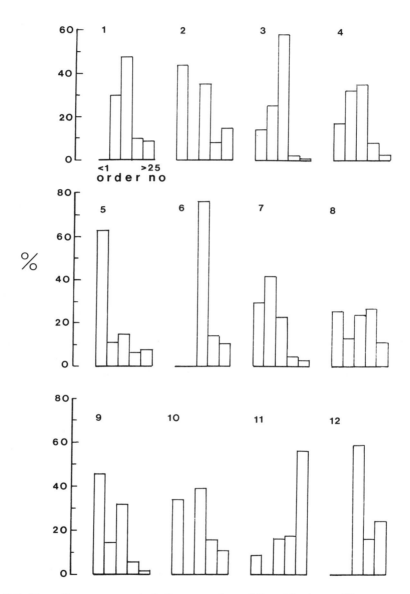

FIGURE 2.7. Slope frequency analysis for a number of Scottish rivers. Histograms show the percentage of the river length in different slope classes. The classes from left to right are: up to 1, > 1–2, > 2–10, > 10–25 and more than 25 m km^{-1}. Lengths of standing water are excluded. 1, Thurso River; 2, River Moriston; 3, River Spey; 4, River Tay; 5, River Forth; 6, River Tyne; 7, River Tweed; 8, River Dee; 9, River Clyde; 10, River Endrick; 11, River Finnan; 12, River Carron

in central and northern Scotland is obvious and follows directly from the catchment structure. Slopes corresponding to the occurrence of pool and riffle sequences are common and the larger east-flowing rivers do not have extensive, flat, lowland reaches. Where flat reaches do occur, they may not be at the seaward end. Rivers that do have marked lowland sections, such as the Endrick and Forth, are the exception in Scotland.

Bed particle size

Smith (1992) shows that the ratios of the median bed particle size (d_{50}) to channel slope (S), for catchments up to 1000 km^2, are defined by power functions of catchment area. For larger catchments, the d_{50}/S ratio tends to be constant and independent of catchment area. Given the slopes occurring in Scottish rivers, this indicates that particle sizes less than 2 mm (coarse sand) are rare. Most Scottish rivers have coarse bed material, the bulk of the sediment movement is in contact with the bed, and rough turbulent flow where some boulders are greater than the water depth is a common feature, especially at lower flows.

RIVER WATER TEMPERATURES

The volumes of water in rivers are small so that relatively little heat exchange is required to change river water temperatures. The temperature of river water, unlike that of large standing waters, is not markedly out of phase with air temperature. A number of observers, for example Smith (1981) and Crisp and Howson (1982), have shown that mean river water temperature for periods of more than five days can be adequately predicted from air temperature, provided that the air temperature is above zero. Air–water temperature relationships are of less value for estimating extremes. A comparison of the temperature of the Water of Leith in Edinburgh with air temperature showed that the mean monthly maximum air temperature was, on average, 2.3°C higher than the corresponding water temperature. The reverse occurs with mean monthly minima, water being, on average, 3.0°C warmer (Smith, 1981).

Air-water temperature relations compensate, partly, for the lack of systematic published temperature data as are available for stream flow and meteorology. The only published data are based on observations as part of the sampling associated with the Harmonised Water Quality Monitoring Programme operated by the Department of the Environment, and not on continuous observations. The obvious feature is the limited regional variation at this level of detail. Over the whole country, the mean annual temperature ranges from 8.5 to 10.3°C, the ranges for the 5 and 95 percentile values being 1.5 to 2.5°C and 15.2 to 20.0°C respectively. The recorded lowest summer mean temperatures are in the West Highland Region.

NATIONAL AND INTERNATIONAL COMPARISONS

The nature of rivers is ultimately determined by climate and topography. The high rainfall, low evaporation and lack of temperature extremes in Scotland leads to rivers that are large for their catchment area, dense river networks and a small range in water temperature. The topography creates steeply sloping rivers formed of coarse

FIGURE 2.8. The upper end of the River Cononish, near the source of the River Tay. Small streams such as this are not included in the original count. The pool and chute structure associated with steep slopes is clearly visible. Photograph: Kenneth H. Morris

FIGURE 2.9. The River Tay at Perth. The Tay is Britain's largest river in terms of discharge and one of the three fifth order river systems recorded in the original count. Photograph: Kenneth H. Morris

bed material – few rivers are navigable above their estuary. There is relatively little interference with the rivers themselves as a result of land drainage and flood control works. The most obvious artificial influence on flows is that below controlled reservoirs (Chapter 25).

The 950 river systems in Scotland from the original count at 1:625 000 scale represent two thirds of the Great Britain total but, because of the large number of small systems (Figure 2.8) in the West Highland and Island Regions, the number of the streams associated with these systems are only half the Great Britain total. There is greater diversity of river types in England and Wales in terms of both dryness and slope as well as more interference with river structure for drainage and navigation. As all British rivers have an island location, nowhere is far from the sea and full development never occurs. The lower reaches of the Tay (Figure 2.9) and of the Humber on the east coast of England are eighth order rivers. On the same map scale, the Mississippi in North America above its delta is an eleventh order river (Leopold *et al.*, 1964). Even a look back over 10 000 years shows that the river created by the joining of the Tay, the Humber and the Rhine from Europe would still not rank among the world's large rivers.

ACKNOWLEDGEMENTS

We would like to thank the Institute of Hydrology, particularly Dr Terry Marsh, for making available area and run-off data for Hydrometric Areas in Scotland. We also thank Mrs Marjorie Ferguson who typed the manuscript.

REFERENCES

Charlton, F. C., Brown, P. M. and Benson, R. W. (1978). "The hydraulic geometry of some gravel rivers in Britain", *Hydraulics Research Station Report*, **IT80**.

Crisp, D. T. and Howson, G. (1982). "Effect of air temperature upon mean water temperature in the North Pennines and the Lake District", *Freshwater Biology*, **12**, 359–367.

Green, F. H. W. (1964). "A map of potential water deficit in the British Isles", *Journal of Applied Ecology*, **1**, 151–158.

Gregory, S. and Chandler, T. J. (1976). *The Climate of the British Isles*, Longman, London.

Horton, R. E. (1945). "Erosional development of streams and their drainage basins", *Bulletin of the Geological Society of America*, **56**, 275–370.

Institute of Hydrology (1975). *Flood Studies Report*, Vol. 1, Hydrological Studies, Natural Environment Research Council, Wallingford.

Institute of Hydrology and British Geological Survey (Annually). *Hydrological Data: UK*, Natural Environment Research Council, Wallingford.

Institute of Hydrology and British Geological Survey (1988). *Hydrometric Register and Statistics: 1981–5*, Natural Environment Research Council, Wallingford.

Institute of Terrestrial Ecology (1978). *Overlays of Environmental and Other Factors for Use with Biological Records Centre Distribution Maps*, Natural Environment Research Council, Cambridge.

Knighton, D. (1984). *Fluvial Forms and Processes*, Edward Arnold, London.

Ledger, D. C. (1981). "The velocity of the River Tweed and its tributaries", *Freshwater Biology*, **11**, 1–10.

Leopold, L. B., Wolman, M. G. and Miller, J. P. (1964). *Fluvial Processes in Geomorphology*, W. H. Freeman, San Francisco.

Pardé, M. (1949). *Fleuvers et Rivieres*, Armand Collin, Paris.

Scottish Office Environment Department (1992). *Water Quality Survey of Scotland 1990*, Scottish Office, Edinburgh.

Smart, J. S. (1978). "The analysis of drainage network composition", *Earth Surface Processes*, **3**, 129–170.

Smith, I. R. (1992). *Hydroclimate: The Influence of Water Movement in Freshwater Ecology*, Elsevier Applied Science, London.

Smith, I. R. and Lyle, A. A. (1979). *Distribution of Fresh Waters in Great Britain*, Institute of Terrestrial Ecology, Cambridge.

Smith, K. (1981). "The prediction of river water temperature", *Hydrological Sciences Bulletin*, **26**, 19–32.

Strahler, A. M. (1957). "Quantitative analysis of watershed geomorphology", *Transactions of the American Geophysical Union*, **38**, 913–920.

3

Standing Waters

A. A. LYLE

Institute of Freshwater Ecology, Bush Estate, Penicuik, EH26 0QB, UK

and

I. R. SMITH

18 Torphin Road, Colinton, Edinburgh, EH13 0HW, UK

INTRODUCTION

This chapter describes the extent and distribution of standing waters – lochs and lochans – in Scotland and gives simplified accounts of loch morphometry, dynamics and their interrelationships. Relevant aspects of climate and topography are given in Chapter 2.

The account of resources is based mainly on the survey of fresh waters in Great Britain by Smith and Lyle (1979). However, the chapter relies heavily on the work of others, in particular the *Bathymetrical Survey of the Fresh Water Lochs of Scotland* by Murray and Pullar (1910) and associated studies both within that work (Chrystal, 1910; Peach and Horne, 1910; Wedderburn, 1910) and thereafter (Gorham, 1958).

The range of types of standing waters in Scotland extends from small peat pools and mountain corrie lochs to expansive waters in shallow basins and large, deep valley lochs. The geomorphological processes involved in the creation of these lochs, or more correctly their basins, are described elsewhere (see Chapter 5) and are many and varied. Peach and Horne (1910) define 15 methods of loch formation in Scotland in seven main categories ranging from basins caused by chemical dissolution to those formed by geological disruption.

EXTENT AND DISTRIBUTION

Resources

The actual number of lochs and lochans in Scotland is not known – they have not yet been fully counted. The distribution of standing waters in Great Britain was surveyed

The Fresh Waters of Scotland: A National Resource of International Significance
Edited by P. S. Maitland, P. J. Boon and D. S. McLusky. © 1994 John Wiley & Sons Ltd

TABLE 3.1. The numbers, areas and volumes of Scottish lochs shown on 1:250 000 maps. (Partly from Smith and Lyle, 1979). (Note: For lochs <2 km^2, areas and volumes are estimates, for those $\geq$2 km^2 actual values are used.) The number of water bodies classified as Large Raised Reservoirs (see text for explanation) are also listed

Area class (km^2)	Number	Estimated accumulated area (km^2)	Estimated accumulated volume (m$^3 \times 10^6$)	Large Raised Reservoirs
<0.25	2973	296.9	744.0	436
0.25–0.49	417	147.6	1 901.1	96
0.50–0.99	209	147.8	1 252.5	54
1–1.99	83	117.4	677.5	43
2–3.99	54	147.0	1 943.1	19
4–7.99	27	148.6	2 598.9	16
8–15.99	12	124.4	3 025.1	11
16–31.99	9	199.4	10 730.4	6
32–63.99	3	127.7	9 374.9	3
64–127.99	1	71.1	2 627.9	1
Totals	3788	1527.9	34 875.4	685

by Smith and Lyle (1979) for those depicted on the 1:250 000 scale Ordnance Survey maps. At this scale the lower limit of inclusion for waters is about 4 ha (0.04 km^2) and the total number counted in Scotland was 3788 (Table 3.1). However, many more waters appear on larger scale maps and from sample counts at 1:63 360 scale Smith and Lyle (1979) estimated there to be an *additional* 27 672 lochs (see also Table 3.2). More information on the number of these smaller lochs may become available from a digitized map survey of Scotland at 1:25 000 scale currently being carried out by the Macaulay Land Use Research Institute. Any final number must depend on what is considered to be the minimum size for a loch or lochan, but this is not defined and remains subjective. The Ordnance Survey does not measure the area of any "parcel" less than 0.04 ha (Harley, 1975), and this could be considered a convenient minimum

TABLE 3.2. Comparison of the numbers of lochs counted by Smith and Lyle (1979) at 1:250 000 scale with the results of other counts at larger map scales

Location	1:250 000 scale Smith and Lyle (1979)	+ 1:63 360 scale * 1:50 000 scale
Tayside Region (part)	103	*733 Maitland *et al.* (1981)
Tweed Basin	38	*324 unpublished
Isle of Arran	4	*65 unpublished
Outer Hebrides	1094	+6038 Waterston *et al.* (1979)
Inner Hebrides	249	+1542 Maitland and Holden (1983)
Shetland	195	+1596 Lyle and Britton (1985)

since it ties in with statistics of inland water areas (e.g. Scottish Office, 1992), but there may be problems of permanency at this size.

Smith and Lyle (1979) grouped the lochs larger than 25 ha into nine logarithmic area classes (Table 3.1) and there is a clear relationship here between the numbers of lochs (N_L) and the geometric mean areas ($\overline{A}g$) of the classes, given by the expression:

$$N_L = 146.6\ \overline{A}g^{-1.029} \text{ correlation coefficient, } r = 0.994$$

This implies a natural order in the frequency of occurrence of lochs in Scotland based on surface area – within the range examined. Without similarly categorized data for the numbers of smaller lochs the validity of this relationship down to a chosen "minimum" size cannot be confirmed and extrapolated speculation towards a "final" total would be unsafe. What is certain, however, is that there are over 30 000 lochs in Scotland and the vast majority are small waters less than a few hectares in area (e.g. Figure 3.1).

The accumulated areas of the lochs in each of the classes do not demonstrate any strong trend in relation to size (Table 3.1). There is reasonable constancy between them, their mean accumulated area being 136.8 km^2 (standard deviation = 34.1 km^2). It is unlikely that this holds throughout the range of smaller, uncounted lochs – say, down to the limit of Ordnance Survey measurement (0.04 ha), since this would add

FIGURE 3.1. Peat lochans in the north of Scotland. There are many thousands of small waters such as these in Scotland but most will not be included in the count by Smith and Lyle (1979). Despite their vast number, collectively they contribute little to the volume of fresh water in Scotland. Photograph: Scottish Natural Heritage

a further nine size classes and effectively double the area in Table 3.1. This area already accounts for 90% of the measured area of inland water in Scotland, including rivers, which currently stands at 1703 km² (Scottish Office, 1992) taken from 1:2500 scale maps, except for mountain areas where 1:10 000 scale is used (Harley, 1975; Ordnance Survey, personal communication). The proportions of standing and running water in that figure are not separately identifiable but, for example, in Tayside Region a survey at 1:50 000 scale showed that lochs accounted for 80% of inland water (Maitland *et al.*, 1981).

The distribution of accumulated volume by area class is more complex than for numbers or accumulated areas. There appears to be a bi-modal distribution in Table 3.1 which peaks in the 0.25–0.49 and 16–31.99 km² classes. The central trough occurs in the 1–1.99 km² class which also falls below the relationship for numbers (Figure 3.2) and has a low accumulated area. However, the mean loch volume per class ($\bar{V}$) is more readily related to class geometric mean areas ($\bar{A}g$) and is given by the expression,

$$\bar{V} = 10.6\,\bar{A}g^{1.35} \qquad r = 0.98$$

An obvious feature in Table 3.1 is the pronounced increase in the volumes of lochs larger than 16 km² and this shows that the bulk of standing water in Scotland is held in a few very large lochs. The 13 lochs in the top three area classes account for 66% of the Scottish total. Conversely, the 2973 lochs less than 25 ha are estimated to contain only 2%. This can be further exemplified by considering Scotland's four largest lochs by area – Lomond, Ness, Awe and Shin – which cover almost 200 km² and contain some 12 km³ of water (one third of the national total). Two hundred lochs of 1 km² at a typical mean depth of 6 m (see Smith and Lyle, 1979) would hold only one thousandth of that volume.

The relationships between class geometric mean areas and the numbers, areas, and volumes of lochs are collectively illustrated in Figure 3.2 which demonstrates that from the data presently available there appear to be natural patterns in the occurrence, extent and quantity of standing waters throughout Scotland.

Artificial alterations to the resource

It is difficult to determine whether there has been a net gain or loss in the number of standing waters with time. The natural process is to lose waters by siltation. Man's influence is both to create and destroy water bodies for his own purposes. The most significant constructions have been for water supply and hydro-electric power, but many small waters are built for amenity, recreational or industrial uses. Losses are only sustained in the smaller sizes, usually by deliberate infilling or drainage. There is no comprehensive record of such changes and national information sources are limited by the criteria of their purpose. For example, information on water dams in Scotland is available from a worldwide register, but only for structures greater than 15 m in height (British National Committee on Large Dams, 1983). Some 137 water bodies are included and range in size from a few hectares up to Loch Shin (32.5 km²). Also, Regional Councils compile lists of Large Raised Reservoirs – a title which is misleading since it contains any structure retaining over 25 000 m³ of water. This is

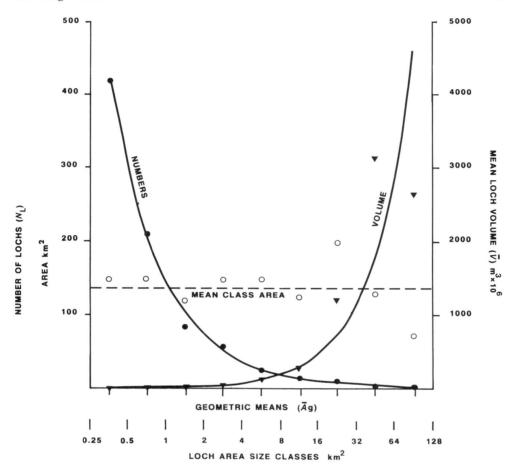

FIGURE 3.2. The relationships between the geometric means ($\bar{A}g$) of the loch area classes and: the numbers of lochs (N_L) in each class (●), and the mean loch volume ($\bar{V}$) in each class (▼). Also shown are the class accumulated areas (○) and the mean class area

a relatively small amount, equivalent to only a 1 cm level change in St Mary's Loch (2.5 km²) which is included because of outflow control (as are many others) but could not be considered an artificial water. Almost 700 sites are listed (including the 137 above) (Table 3.1) the majority (>60%) of which are less than 25 ha. Neither source gives details of changes from original lochs (if any); such information must be derived independently (e.g. from Murray and Pullar, 1910). There is no national account of water bodies in Scotland such as flooded quarries, gravel pits and ponds.

Of the 28 largest dammed reservoirs (all > 2 km² in area) eight are completely new and artificial, the remaining 20 being a range of enlargements of one or more natural lochs. The process of creating the latter engulfed 30 smaller lochs, giving a net loss overall of two.

It seems in little doubt that there has been a net gain in water area caused by recent artificial alterations. For example, the creation of the above 28 reservoirs alone has added 115 km^2 to the national total – equivalent to twice the surface area of Loch Ness.

The most detailed survey of change carried out in Scotland is that of Lassière (1993) who, as part of a survey of the conservation value of lochs, examined the standing waters depicted on 1:63 360 and 1:50 000 scale maps for Central Region (see Figure 3.3d for location) from 1896 to 1990. This showed a net increase in numbers from 207 to 355, a 71% gain, and in total area from *ca.* 140 to 150 km^2. The increases were predominantly in very small waters less than 1 ha (quarries and gravel pits). While it is certain that an overall gain has occurred, improved mapping standards must contribute to its apparent scale.

Distribution

For simplification and clarity the distribution of standing waters is considered in seven regionalized groupings of Hydrometric Areas, characterized by similarities in their topography and climate (see also Chapter 2). The relative regional distribution of numbers of lochs, accumulated areas, volumes and percentage land cover for the 3788 lochs counted by Smith and Lyle (1979) are described below and illustrated in Figure 3.3.

The Western Isles clearly dominate in terms of numbers (Figure 3.3a) which, in the main, is due to the abundance of small lochans in the Outer Hebrides where 30% of all Scotland's lochs smaller than 25 ha are found. At larger map scales than that of the original survey (i.e. 1:250 000) this proportion would be expected to increase substantially (see also Table 3.2). There is a clear decline in numbers towards the eastern side of the country which seems relatively impoverished. Indeed, the combined number of lochs in the four regions in the lowest category is less than that for the Outer Hebrides alone.

In terms of overall water area, the highest regions are West Highlands and North East Highlands (Figure 3.3b) which together account for 50% of the total (notably the Western Isles now falls into the lowest category). The position of these two regions as the principal locations for fresh water in Scotland is confirmed when volume is considered (Figure 3.3c). Together they hold 66% of the Scottish total and this is due mainly to the presence of nine of the 13 very large lochs referred to above.

Standing waters cover about 2% of the land area of Scotland, and the regions most densely covered are the North East Highlands and the island groups (Figure 3.3d). Again the tendency is for higher values in the north and west than in the south and east of the country. The Forth and Tweed Region has consistently been the most poorly represented in all aspects of standing water distribution. Clearly the north-west of mainland Scotland is the most important in terms of resources but, as a consequence of their relative sparsity, lochs in the southern and eastern sectors may have greater individual value.

Examination of the distribution of lochs by area class in the altitude bands on the 1:250 000 scale maps used in the original survey (i.e. nine bands: 0–61, –122, –183, –244, –305, –427, –610, –914, > 914 metres) shows a general decrease in numbers with altitude, although there are a few minor reversals of this trend in all but the two smallest size classes. Only in the 0–61 m band, which has 36% of the total number, are all the size classes present, and most lochs (55%) are to be found below 122 m.

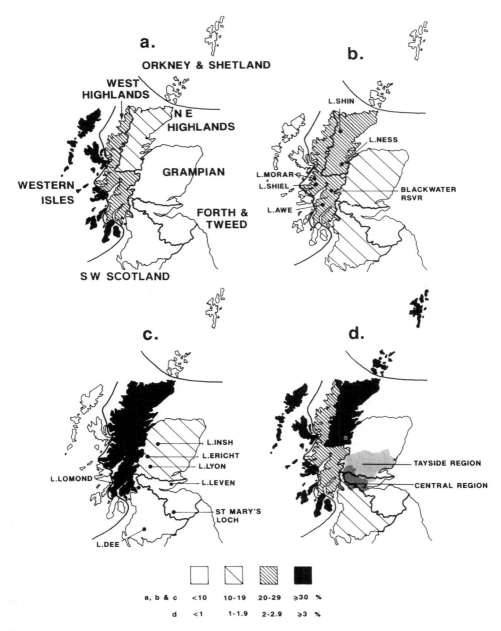

FIGURE 3.3. The relative distribution of standing waters in Scotland, by seven regional divisions. Shading refers to the percentage share of the total resource for, a – numbers, b – accumulated area, and c – accumulated volume. Part (d) shows the percentage of land area covered by standing waters. Also shown are the locations of lochs (in b and c) and the two administrative regions (in d) mentioned in the text

However, over 500 lochs (14%) do appear at high altitude (i.e. > 305 m (1000 ft)) and, as would be expected, are predominantly the smaller waters less than 25 ha, five of which are over 914 m (3000 ft). The three largest waters above 305 m are dammed reservoirs. Two – Blackwater Reservoir (10.4 km^2) and Loch Lyon (5.0 km^2) – were created from much smaller lochs, but the original Loch Ericht was artificially increased in area from 18.7 to 23.3 km^2 in 1931 and was the only natural, large, high altitude loch in Scotland, "*one of the wildest and most magnificent lochs in Scotland, presenting all along its shore scenes of lonely grandeur and sublimity*" (Murray and Pullar, 1910).

MORPHOMETRY AND DYNAMICS

This section gives a simplified account of the structural characteristics of Scottish lochs and the principal physical processes which take place within them. (The locations of lochs mentioned in the text are shown in Figure 3.3 and their physical dimensions in Table 3.3.)

Morphometry

The first requirement of an analysis of loch form and structure is a survey of depths and the construction of bathymetric maps from which physical parameters can be derived. In this it is fortunate that 562 Scottish lochs were surveyed by Murray and Pullar (1910) and that for 399 of them interrelationships between the principal morphometric parameters were examined by Gorham (1958); these are outlined below. As a preliminary step he separated the lochs into two groups based on their geological origin, i.e. those which sit in rock basins (262) and those which lie in, or are created by, drift deposits (137). These are broad classifications based on the more detailed descriptions given by Peach and Horne (1910).

The parameters considered here are loch length, mean width, maximum and mean depth, and surface area. There are, of course, many other morphometric parameters relevant to limnological studies which are not mentioned here – see, for example, Hakanson (1981).

The ratio of loch length to mean width is a useful indication of shape. Some smaller lochs of both basin types may be almost circular (1:1) but with increasing size rock basins become relatively more linear than those in drift. The largest (and longest) lochs lie in narrow rock valleys and are distinctly elongated with high length/mean width ratios of up to 44:1 (Loch Awe). Large "broad" lochs (e.g. Loch Leven 2.6:1) lie in drift basins. Regression analysis shows reasonable correlation coefficients (r) of 0.75 (rock) and 0.69 (drift), the relationship being steeper for the latter. This feature is particularly relevant to hydrodynamic performance in terms of the scale and extent of wind-induced mixing, but these also depend on the orientation of the main axis.

The regression relationships between maximum and mean depth for both basin types are very close ($r = 0.95$ rock, 0.92 drift) with similar slopes. However, their ratios of maximum to mean show opposite trends. In rock basins, as mean depth increases it becomes closer to the maximum (i.e. the ratio decreases) indicating a shift from V-shaped to U-shaped basins – again a feature of the large, glacially eroded, valley lochs.

TABLE 3.3. Physical parameters of lochs and lakes mentioned in the text

Name	Altitude (m)	Area (Km²)	Maximum depth (m)	Mean depth (m)	Volume (m³ × 10⁶)	Length (Km)	Mean width (Km)
Shin	93	32.5	61	20.3	660	28.3	1.15
St Mary's	247	2.5	47	22.2	56	4.9	0.51
Ness	16	56.4	230	132.0	7452	39.0	1.45
Blackwater Reservoir	325	10.4	27	9.9	103	12.9	0.81
Lyon	343	5.0	54	16.7	83	8.9	0.56
Ericht	359	23.3	164	53.4	1243	26.4	0.88
Leven	107	13.3	25	4.0	52	5.9	2.25
Awe	36	38.5	94	32.0	1230	41.0	0.94
Lomond	7.9	71.1	190	37.0	2628	36.4	1.95
Shiel	4.5	19.6	128	40.5	793	28.0	0.70
Morar	10	26.7	310	86.6	2307	18.8	1.42
Insh	220	1.1	30	11.4	13	1.7	0.65
Dee	225	1.0	14	4.5	4.5	1.9	0.53
Windermere	39	14.8	64	23.8	316	17.0	0.87
Neagh	15	396.0	31	12.2	4831	27.4	14.45
Baikal	456	31 500	1741	680.0	22 995 000	635	49.60

In drift basins a similar shift in shape occurs, but in this case with decreasing mean depth, illustrating the "shallow pan" nature of the smaller lochs of this type. The importance of basin shape in terms of bed slope can be illustrated if we consider the effect of a 1 m water level drop in two basins of contrasting form. In Loch Ness (deep, rock) such a change would reduce the surface area by 0.25 km² (0.45%), whereas in Loch Leven (shallow, drift) 2.82 km² (21.2%) would be lost (Smith, 1992). The average maximum and mean depths for rock basins are 18.4 m and 6.8 m respectively with corresponding standard deviations equivalent to 4% and 11%. For drift basins the figures are 5.9 m and 2.4 m, but standard deviations are higher at 12% and 26%, reflecting not only the basins' shallower nature but also greater variability in form (and origin).

A mean depth to loch area relationship is potentially valuable in limnological studies as mean depth is an important hydrobiological parameter and area is readily obtainable. Unfortunately the relationships are not close, particularly for drift basins ($r = 0.68$ rock, 0.24 drift). The general trend is that in small lochs of both basin types mean depths are about the same (*ca.* 2 m), but as area increases rock and drift basins diverge such that mean depths in the former become about four times greater. The large valley, rock basin, lochs have the greatest mean depths, the extreme being 132 m in Loch Ness, and in respect to their relationship with area they are similar to Alpine lakes.

Thermal properties

The thermal regime of standing waters is intrinsically important to their hydraulic structure and biological functioning.

The Scottish lochs fall into two distinct temperature classes as defined by Hutchinson (1957): namely, warm monomictic and dimictic. The former never fall below the temperature of maximum density (4°C) and are typified by the large deep lochs, particularly those in the milder western climes. Dimictic waters pass through 4°C twice each year, as is usual for most Scottish lochs. They may experience thermal stratification in summer and can freeze over in winter.

Wedderburn (1910) identified radiation and conduction at the air/water interface as the two major factors in heat gain or loss, but also gave importance to the influence of rivers (and rain), internal convection and mixing by wind. Clearly, altitude is also important (the standard air temperature lapse rate is 0.6 °C per 100 m rise). Principally, therefore, heat exchange occurs at the loch surface and, due to vertical dispersion, the rate of temperature change is strongly dependent on depth. Based on data from 370 lochs, Gorham (1958) showed that in summer, deeper lochs were cooler and exhibited a greater separation between top and bottom temperatures. Maximum temperatures attainable in the largest lochs will be around 15°C (Smith *et al.*, 1981); shallow, low altitude lochs may peak in excess of 20°C (A. Kirika, personal communication). The former respond more slowly to temperature change, lagging behind the latter by up to three months in reaching their summer maxima, with a lower amplitude of variation. In winter, because of their smaller heat storage per unit area, shallow lochs cool more rapidly and may freeze. Again, because of their inertia in this respect, large waters are relatively "warm" during early and mid-winter and indeed may influence local climate. The amounts of energy involved are enormous. For example, Wedderburn (1910) estimated that, over winter, Loch Ness emitted the equivalent of burning 2.4 million tons of coal; Smith *et al.* (1981) calculated that the energy required to raise Loch Awe by a single degree Celsius was the equivalent of the 400 MW Cruachan power station there running continuously for over eight days.

In summer, thermal stratification may take place. This is one of the more important physical features affecting the ecological characteristics of a loch (e.g. Golterman, 1975) and occurs when heating and wind mixing of the surface waters effectively creates a warm, buoyant, top layer – the epilimnion – which progressively deepens throughout the summer. The metalimnion – the layer where temperature changes rapidly with depth (and including the thermocline which is the plane of maximum temperature discontinuity) – separates the epilimnion from the cooler, less turbulent bottom waters – the hypolimnion.

Susceptibility to wind mixing is important in determining the depth of stratification which can be mathematically predicted from morphometric parameters. From an evaluation of 17 predictive models (Hanna, 1990), the maximum effective length (the maximum length of water uninterrupted by land) is the best single predictor. For convenience many empirical models use the square root of area (A) as a measure of length. For lakes in New Zealand (which has similarities in climate and topography to Scotland) thermocline depth (D_T) in late summer can be estimated from:

$$D_T = 9.52 \ (A^{0.5})^{0.425} \qquad r = 0.98 \ \text{(Davis-Colley, 1988)}$$

Gorham and Boyce (1989) calculated that if the ratio of D_T to maximum depth (D_{max}) is greater than *ca* 0.6, then consistent stratification is unlikely because of the influence of friction stress from the loch bed. If $D_T/D_{max} < 0.6$ then the loch could experience extensive and prolonged stratification which will affect its hydrological, hydrodynamic and ecological functioning. In general, because of their greater depth, lochs in rock basins are more prone to stratification than those in drift basins. Due to maritime influences, frequent cloud cover and strong winds are a feature of the Scottish climate. Surface warming by solar radiation is therefore reduced and disruptive mixing increased. Consequently, stratification is deeper but less pronounced, stable or reliable here than in, say, a continental climate at similar latitudes.

In winter, inverse stratification is possible (i.e. when the buoyant surface layer is < 4°C) but density differences, and therefore stability, are low at these temperatures. In practice, wind mixing usually causes uniform cooling of the full water depth, often taking temperatures well below 4°C. Under such conditions, with calm weather and sub-zero air temperatures, ice can form at the surface. Again depth is significant, shallow areas being more susceptible to freezing. A good account of the processes involved is given by Hutchinson (1957) amongst others. There are few sites monitored for ice in Scotland and a study of 10 years of records for Loch Leven (Figure 3.4) by

FIGURE 3.4. Loch Leven, a shallow drift basin loch, shown here partially covered by ice.
Photograph: John Dewar Studios

Lyle (1981) showed a high correlation ($r = 0.98$) between extensive ice cover (i.e > 50%) and sub-zero mean air temperatures. However, at this site the influence of wind disturbance in maintaining ice-free areas was greater than that of depth. In Loch Leven, and many other lochs, the occurrence or extent of freezing is not annually consistent, but shallow mountain lochans may freeze for much of their depth each winter, while the largest, deepest lochs have never been recorded to freeze over.

Hydrology

The rate at which water passes through a loch is an extremely important factor in determining its hydrological, chemical and biological character. A long-term average value of water replacement time (or alternatively flushing rate) may be estimated simply from rainfall and evaporation statistics for the catchment (i.e. run-off) divided by loch volume. This is particularly useful for site classification in limnological studies; for example, small lochs situated on large rivers may have a mean replacement time of only a few days (e.g. Loch Insh – 17 days (Bailey-Watts *et al.*, 1992)) whereas in large rock basins this may take years (e.g. Loch Morar – 6.9 years (Smith *et al.*, 1981)). Such information is valuable in understanding loch responses to nutrient budgets (e.g. Bailey-Watts *et al.*, 1992) or pollutants (e.g. Lyle, 1987). However, there are limitations to the application of such estimates since in reality the situation is much more complex and variable, especially for periods less than one year.

For increased accuracy, account must be taken of annual and seasonal variations in run-off, plus several other factors. River flows are at average levels or higher for only a minority of the time so the bulk of loch inflows are received in short surges. This is very relevant at small sites such as Loch Dee (1 km^2) which has a measured mean replacement time of *ca* 40 days but a ten-fold range from 12 to 120 days (Werritty *et al.*, 1993). In very small sites complete flushing may occasionally occur within a few hours (Lyle, 1987). Seasonal differences are important from a biological aspect: for example, algal blooms may not have time to develop in a rapidly flushed system. In Scotland, run-off is generally higher in winter when flushing may be several times more rapid than in summer, although in high catchments snow storage and freezing may cause lowest flows to occur in winter. If thermal stratification occurs, then the effective volume being replaced is only that of the epilimnion, thus reducing inflow residence time during that period but greatly increasing that of water trapped below in the hypolimnion. In addition, changes in loch level alter the volume which is to be replaced. Basin shape and orientation determine the extent of wind-driven circulation and mixing, and the relative locations of major inflows to the outflow can be important. All these factors have a bearing on the real rate of water exchange in lochs.

Hydrodynamics

The analysis of hydrodynamics is extremely complex and only a broad outline of the principal features can be given here (see, for example, Smith, 1992). The main forces which induce water movement in lochs are the momentum forces of inflows, thermal density gradients and wind stress at the air/water interface. Of these, wind-driven effects are by far the most powerful and are given preference below.

Wind stress at the surface creates waves and currents, the strength and direction of which are governed by wind speed, the deflecting force of the Earth's rotation (Coriolis) and the influences of shoreline shape and the loch bed. Subsequent reductions in wind speed will set up oscillations of the surface (seiches).

Wave dimensions (length, height and period) can be predicted if wind speed and effective fetch are known (US Army, 1962), the validity of which has been tested at Loch Leven by Smith and Sinclair (1972). Effective fetch is not a simple linear measure but incorporates a component of width, and since Scotland's largest lochs are narrow their wave sizes are not great. The largest freshwater fetch in Scotland is found at the north-east end of Loch Ness (Figure 3.5) where a wind of 10 m s^{-1} will generate waves 11 m long and 0.5 m high (Smith *et al.*, 1981).

FIGURE 3.5. Loch Ness, a massive body of water in British terms. The volume of Loch Ness, about 7.5 km^3, constitutes almost one fifth of the Great Britain total and is nearly twice that found in the standing waters of England and Wales combined. This scene shows the largest freshwater fetch in Great Britain. Photograph: Aerofilms Ltd

The idealized isothermal circulation in a long, narrow loch of uniform depth assumes that approximately the upper third moves in the direction of the wind, and that this transport is balanced by a slower moving current in the opposite direction over the lower two thirds of depth – a "conveyor belt" system (Smith, 1979). In round shallow lochs, downwind central axis currents are balanced by semi-circular return currents around the shores. In reality, actual circulation is complicated at any site by the relative influences of the governing factors mentioned above. At Loch Leven, which is broad and shallow, Smith (1974) found complex circulation patterns including some surface currents in direct opposition to the wind. Simplified models can be used to estimate the net wind-driven transport and for a moderate wind of 10 m s^{-1} at Lochs Lomond, Awe, Ness, Morar and Shiel this was found to be an order of magnitude greater than throughflow (Smith *et al.*, 1981) which, at these sites, demonstrates wind to be the overriding force of motion. In small lochs with very short replacement times throughflow will be influential and may be the dominant force in determining circulation. In a stratified loch, circulation in the epilimnion is similar to that described above, the thermocline acting as the loch bed.

Early studies of seiches were carried out on Scottish lochs by Chrystal (1910) and more recently on Loch Ness by Thorpe (1971) (see also Hutchinson, 1957). Wind stress applied across the surface of a loch will cause it to tilt (set-up). A cessation, reduction, or even change of direction in wind force will cause the surface to oscillate around a nodal line (or lines) determined by basin shape. The period of the primary surface seiche is also solely dependent on basin geometry and can be calculated with reasonable accuracy (Hutchinson, 1957). The largest period for a Scottish loch would appear to be about one hour, at Loch Awe, but is only about half of that at Loch Ness (Smith *et al.*, 1981). If the loch is stratified then a reverse seiche will also be set up in the thermocline inducing gradient currents in the hypolimnion. In general, the magnitude of such oscillations in Scottish lochs is small and does not have a major influence on water levels – even in gales (20 m s^{-1}) the set-up in Loch Awe is only about 10 cm (Smith *et al.*, 1981). However, an earth tremor in 1755 set up an oscillation in Loch Lomond with a reported amplitude of 0.76 m (Chrystal, 1910).

NATIONAL AND INTERNATIONAL COMPARISONS

From the survey of the extent and distribution of fresh waters in Great Britain (Smith and Lyle, 1979), Scotland clearly possesses the major share of standing water resources. It contains 69% of the standing waters, 79% of the total surface area and 91% of the included volume. The 25 largest lochs in Scotland cover an area similar to that of the 1717 lakes counted in England and Wales. Loch Ness alone holds almost double their volume. The largest lake in England and Wales – Windermere, at 14.8 km^2 – would rank only 14th in Scotland, but the largest water body in the United Kingdom is Lough Neagh in Northern Ireland. Its waters cover 396 km^2 (equivalent to one quarter of the Scottish total), although it is relatively shallow and holds only two thirds of the volume of Loch Ness. However, from the above survey it is estimated that the uncounted number of very small (< 4 ha) waters in England and Wales approaches 50 000 – almost double the estimated number at that size in Scotland.

The percentage area of Scotland covered by fresh water (2%) is about four times that in the remainder of the United Kingdom, but its human population density is only about one fifth. Due to these facttors and the remote locations of many Scottish lochs, a greater propoortion are perhaps under less environmental pressure than elsewhere.

In a global context, Scotland's lochs are not significant in terms of size. Indeed, if the entire Scottish resource were contained in a single basin its area would rank no higher than 93rd in order of the world's largest lakes (see Herdendorf, 1982). Only in terms of depth do Scottish lochs appear on a world scale (although many of the world's large lakes are uncharted). Only 10 are known to have a greater mean depth than Loch Ness (132 m), and Loch Morar, with a maximum depth of 310 m, is ranked 39th in that respect.

Fresh water is a valuable commodity and Scotland is fortunate in having an abundance of high quality water for domestic, industrial, recreational and environmental requirements. Management is of prime importance if this is to be safeguarded. Lake Baikal in Russia, the world's largest freshwater lake by volume, contains over 600 times the water in Scotland, but it is noticeably damaged by indiscriminate pollution.

ACKNOWLEDGEMENTS

We wish to acknowledge the assistance given by the following who provided information on resources: Regional Council Water Departments, Dr Olivia Lassière and Dr Terry Marsh. We also thank Mrs Marjorie Ferguson who typed the manuscript.

REFERENCES

Bailey-Watts, A. E., May, L., Kirika, A. and Lyle, A. A. (1992). *Eutrophication Case Studies: Phase II, An Assessment Based on Desk Analysis of Catchments and Summer Limnological Reconnaissances*, report to the Nature Conservancy Council for Scotland, Edinburgh.

British National Committee on Large Dams (1983). *Dams in the UK 1963–1983*, Institution of Civil Engineers, London.

Chrystal, G. (1910). "Seiches and other oscillations of lake-surfaces, observed by the Scottish lake survey", in *Bathymetrical Survey of the Fresh Water Lochs of Scotland* (Eds. J. Murray and L. Pullar), 1, pp. 29–90, Challenger Office, Edinburgh.

Davis-Colley, R. J. (1988). "Mixing depths in New Zealand lakes", *New Zealand Journal of Marine and Freshwater Research*, **22**, 517–527.

Golterman, H. L. (1975). *Physical Limnology*, Elsevier, Amsterdam.

Gorham, E. (1958). "The physical limnology of northern Britain: an epitome of the bathymetrical survey of the Scottish freshwater lochs 1897–1909", *Limnology and Oceanography*, **3**, 40–50.

Gorham, E. and Boyce, F. M. (1989). "Influence of lake surface area and depth upon thermal stratification and the depth of the summer thermocline", *Journal of Great Lakes Research*, **15**, 233–245.

Hakanson, L. (1981). *A Manual of Lake Morphometry*, Springer, New York.

Hanna, M. (1990). "Evaluation of models predicting mixing depth", *Canadian Journal of Fisheries and Aquatic Sciences*, **47**, 940–947.

Harley, J. B. (1975). *Ordnance Survey Maps, A Descriptive Manual*, Ordnance Survey, Southampton.

Herdendorf, C. E. (1982). "Large lakes of the world", *Journal of Great Lakes Research*, **8**, 379–412.

Hutchinson, G. E. (1957). *A Treatise on Limnology*, John Wiley, New York.

Lassière, O. L. (1993). Central Region lochs and ponds, *Unpublished Report, University of Stirling*.

Lyle, A. A. (1981). "Ten years of ice records for Loch Leven, Kinross", *Weather*, **36**, 116–125.

Lyle, A. A. (1987). "The bathymetry and hydrology of some lochs vulnerable to acid deposition in Scotland", in *Acidification and Fish in Scottish Lochs* (Eds P. S. Maitland, A. A. Lyle and R. N. B. Campbell), pp. 22–34, Institute of Terrestrial Ecology, Cambridge.

Lyle, A. A. and Britton, R. H. (1985). "The fresh waters of Shetland: II Resources and distribution", *Scottish Geographical Magazine*, **101**, 157–164.

Maitland, P. S. and Holden, A. V. (1983). "Inland waters of the Inner Hebrides", *Proceedings of the Royal Society of Edinburgh*, **83B**, 229–244.

Maitland, P. S., Smith, I. R., Jones, D. H., East, K., Morris, K. H. and Lyle, A. A. (1981). *The Fresh Waters of Tayside*, Report to the Nature Conservancy Council, Edinburgh.

Murray, J. and Pullar, L. (1910). *Bathymetrical Survey of the Fresh Water Lochs of Scotland*, Challenger Office, Edinburgh.

Peach, B. N. and Horne, J. (1910). "The Scottish lakes in relation to the geological features of the country", in *Bathymetrical Survey of the Fresh Water Lochs of Scotland* (Eds J. Murray and L. Pullar), **1**, pp. 439–513, Challenger Office, Edinburgh.

Scottish Office (1992). *The Scottish Environment – Statistics No. 3 1991*, Edinburgh.

Smith, I. R. (1974). "The structure and physical environment of Loch Leven, Scotland", *Proceedings of the Royal Society of Edinburgh*, **74B**, 81–100.

Smith, I. R. (1979). "Hydraulic conditions in isothermal lakes", *Freshwater Biology*, **9**, 119–145.

Smith, I. R. (1992). *Hydroclimate: The Influence of Water Movement on Freshwater Ecology*, Elsevier Applied Science, London.

Smith, I. R. and Lyle, A. A. (1979). *Distribution of Freshwaters in Great Britain*, Institute of Terrestrial Ecology, Cambridge.

Smith, I. R. and Sinclair, I. J. (1972). "Deep water waves in lakes", *Freshwater Biology*, **2**, 387–399.

Smith, I. R., Lyle, A. A. and Rosie, A. J. (1981), "Comparative physical limnology", in *The Ecology of Scotland's Largest Lochs: Lomond, Awe, Ness, Morar and Shiel* (Ed. P. S. Maitland), pp. 29–65, Junk, The Hague.

Thorpe, S. A. (1971). "Asymmetry of the internal seiche in Loch Ness", *Nature*, **231**, 306–308.

US Army (1962). *Waves on Inland Reservoirs*, Technical Memorandum No 132, Beach Erosion Board, Corps of Engineers, Washington, D.C.

Waterson, A. R., Holden, A. V., Campbell, R. N. and Maitland, P. S. (1979). "The inland waters of the Outer Hebrides", *Proceedings of the Royal Society of Edinburgh*, **77B**, 329–351.

Wedderburn, E. M. (1910). "Temperature of the Scottish lakes", in *Bathymetrical Survey of the Fresh Water Lochs of Scotland* (Eds J. Murray and L. Pullar), **1**, pp. 91–144, Challenger Office, Edinburgh.

Werritty, A., Harper, F. and Burns, J. (1993) "Rainfall and runoff responses in the Loch Dee sub-catchments", *Proceedings of the Loch Dee Symposium*". Foundation for Water Research, pp. 13–21.

4

Tidal Fresh Waters

D. S. MCLUSKY

Department of Biological and Molecular Sciences, University of Stirling, Stirling, FK9 4LA, UK

INTRODUCTION

The upper reaches of coastal estuaries are known by various names, including tidal fresh waters, upper, or inner reaches of an estuary and the oligohaline region. They have been little studied perhaps for several reasons. Freshwater scientists have traditionally ceased their activities once the river became tidal, and marine (or estuarine) scientists have, like many animals, migrated into estuaries from the nearshore marine waters and once the number of animal species reached a minimum level, at about 5‰ salinity, have often ceased their activities.

This chapter examines the problems facing animals and plants in these tidal freshwater areas in Scotland. Tidal freshwater environments experience a great deal of natural stress, associated with the chemical and physical processes which characterize these regions, as shown by Meire and Vincx (1993) and McLusky (1993). The dominant processes are those concerned with sediment transport and turbidity, coupled with chemical changes, particularly marked by the appearance of saline waters, and including reduced dissolved oxygen and fluctuating salinity.

The animal and plant communities of rivers are living in conditions dominated by a uniform downstream flow of oxygenated fresh water. Within the tidal freshwater sections of an estuary they need to cope with the increasing turbidity of the water, a lower oxygen content, and a change in bottom sediment from coarse sand or gravel into very fine muds. In many estuaries of the world, including some of those in Scotland, these natural stresses are exacerbated by the effects of human activities, as wastes from the cities and towns adjacent to the upper estuarine reaches are discharged into the estuary in the belief that tides will convey the waste away. A dip in oxygen content, known as an oxygen sag, is typical and associated with natural decay and decomposition processes at the zone of maximum turbidity (Griffiths, 1987). The introduction of organic waste into such a region only serves to enhance the oxygen sag already there, and has led in some cases to severe oxygen depletion.

Few species are able to make these adjustments and, as Remane (1934) first noted, the number of species in these reaches is invariably lower than that of the parent river.

The Fresh Waters of Scotland: A National Resource of International Significance
Edited by P. S. Maitland, P. J. Boon and D. S. McLusky. © 1994 John Wiley & Sons Ltd

TABLE 4.1. Classification scheme for estuaries proposed by
McLusky (1993)

Division	Tidal	Salinity (‰)	Venice system
River	Non-tidal	<0.5	Limnetic
Head	The highest point to which tides reach		
Tidal fresh	Tidal	<0.5	Limnetic
Upper	Tidal	0.5–5	Oligohaline
Inner	Tidal	5–18	Mesohaline
Middle	Tidal	18–25	Polyhaline
Lower	Tidal	25–30	Polyhaline
Mouth	Tidal	>30	Euhaline

Similarly, few or no marine species which enter the estuary from the seaward end are able to penetrate below a salinity of 5‰. The tidal freshwater reaches are thus characterized by a declining number of species of freshwater origin, supplemented by a few species which live in estuaries but may be absent from both rivers and the sea.

In order to clarify the terminology associated with these regions, McLusky (1993) proposed a consistent classification for estuaries (Table 4.1). The present paper is only concerned with the "Head – Tidal fresh – Upper" estuary regions. It should be emphasized that the limits in the first two columns are geographical terms (in particular, the Head is marked on UK Ordnance Survey maps as the tidal limit, indicated by a change in colour of the river bank from black to blue), whereas the limits of the latter two columns may oscillate with the tides.

Within these low salinity waters, Morris *et al.* (1978) and Mantoura (1987) have identified that most of the biogeochemical processes involved in the meeting of fresh water and sea water occur at salinities below 1‰, at what is known as the "fresh-water–seawater interface" (FSI). At the FSI, which is located generally at the border between the tidal fresh waters and the upper reaches of an estuary, major biological changes occur, especially the release of soluble and particulate organic material, as well as major changes in the composition and speciation of the chemical ions within the water. The organic material released by these changes is carried down the estuary, and in the adjacent upper reaches (0.5–5‰) supports bacteria and ciliates, which are often fed upon by abundant populations of the copepod *Eurytemora affinis*.

Many authors (see Deaton and Greenberg, 1986) report a minimum number of species at approximately 5‰. Whilst there has been some debate about the cause of this ecophysiological minimum, it should be emphasized that this point (also some-times known as "Remane's minimum", or "the horohalinicum") is not the same as the FSI, and usually occurs downstream from the tidal freshwater regions.

The term "turbidity maximum" describes a zone with maximum suspended sedi-ment (McCave, 1979). The position of the turbidity maximum varies from estuary to estuary, and within an individual estuary can change depending on the spring/neap tidal cycle and river flow fluctuations. The term should not therefore be used as a general descriptor of the upper or tidal freshwater reaches of an estuary.

Biological and chemical changes are thus well characterized by salinity, with the FSI at <1‰ and the horohalinicum at approximately 5‰; however, the physical changes, in particular the position of the turbidity maxima, can vary from estuary to estuary or within an estuary and can occur in a variety of salinities.

CASE STUDIES

Tay

The River Tay, with a mean discharge of 167 m³ s⁻¹, has the greatest river flow in Britain, to which is added 31 m³ s⁻¹ from the River Earn. The Tay estuary is tidal up to Perth, but salt water normally only reaches to Newburgh, and then only during conditions of low river flow (Williams and West, 1975). The tidal freshwater area is thus approximately 16 km in length (Perth to Newburgh) (Table 4.2).

The Tay estuary was the site of one of the earliest investigations into estuarine science in Britain by Alexander *et al.* (1935). Their main task was to investigate pollution in the Tees estuary, and in order to distinguish man-induced changes from the natural changes which occur in any estuary, they surveyed the Tay estuary in considerable detail, as an "unpolluted" control area. Their findings (Figure 4.1) revealed a clear pattern of freshwater animals and plants entering the estuary from the Rivers Tay and Earn, extending as far as Newburgh. They showed that the number of freshwater species declined over this distance with, for example, 20 species at Bridge of Earn dropping down to 0 below Newburgh. This classical study occurred in parallel with Remane's (1934) work in Baltic waters, and to a large extent marked the beginning of an appreciation of the need to examine the life of estuaries with care, and to distinguish natural change from that caused by man.

Khayralla and Jones (1975) resurveyed the Tay 38 years later, confirming that it remained virtually unpolluted, except for some localized effects near the city of Dundee. Unfortunately for the present review, they omitted the upper three (freshwater) sampling sections of Alexander *et al.* (1935). They found that few significant changes had occurred over the intervening years. The main freshwater species, reaching into the estuary to below Newburgh, were *Tubifex tubifex, Potamopyrgus jenkinsi, Gammarus zaddachi* and chironomids. The estuarine/marine species which reached furthest into the estuary (to Newburgh) were *Enteromorpha* sp., *Corophium*

TABLE 4.2. Physical characteristics of the tidal freshwater reaches of the three major Scottish estuaries. Data from Williams and West (1975), Poodle (1986), Leatherland (1987) and Henderson (personal communication)

	Tay	Forth	Clyde
Mean river discharge (m³ s⁻¹)	167 (+ 31 from Earn)	44.5 (Teith, Forth, Allan)	41
Tidal freshwater length (km)	16	9–21	2
Head	Perth	Craigforth	Tidal Weir
Downstream limit	Newburgh	Cambuskenneth–Fallin	Broomielaw

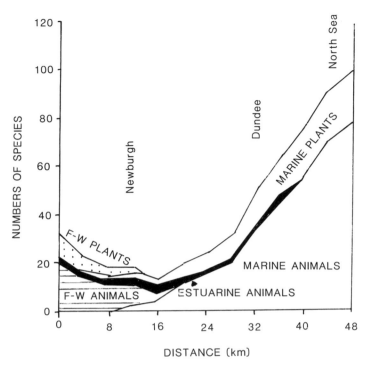

FIGURE 4.1. Composition of the fauna and flora along the Tay estuary, Scotland. The numbers of species, for each grouping, is shown against distance from the tidal limit. The tidal freshwater area is upstream of Newburgh, (After Alexander *et al.* 1935)

volutator, Bathyporeia pilosa, Nereis diversicolor, Nerine cirratulus and *Neomysis integer*. In the upper estuary they particularly reported large numbers of oligochaete worms (up to $14\,000 \text{ m}^{-2}$). They were able to record interstitial salinities near Newburgh with a maximum of 0.26‰ representing the lowest recorded salinities at which *Corophium* and several other estuarine species have been reported.

Maitland and Smith (1987) surveyed the River Tay from its source downstream into tidal fresh waters, a distance of 160 km. Their results showed the changeable nature of the substrate in the tidal freshwater areas, with a mixture of silt, gravel and stones, as well as maximal levels of suspended solids. Their faunal records confirm the general position established by Alexander *et al.* (1935), with taxonomic improvements iden-tifying more accurately the insects which reach furthest into the freshwater tidal areas as: Ephemoptera: *Baetis rhodani, Baetis muticus, Rhithrogena semicolorata, Ephe-merella notata*; Coleoptera: *Latelmis volckmari, Oulimnius tuberculatus*.

From these findings it can be seen that the number of species declines within the tidal freshwater region even when there are no pollution effects. This decline may be due to changes in the sediment or else to occasional episodes of salt penetration. The latter is unlikely since Williams and West (1975) report Newburgh as the limit of salt intrusion during low river flows. During high river flows the limit of salt intrusion will be even further downstream. The detailed sedimentary maps of Buller and McManus

(1975) for the Tay estuary show that the subtidal sediments of the tidal freshwater region are composed of poorly sorted fine sands or pebble and boulder patches, flanked by narrow intertidal areas of mud and reed. These substrates may be relatively hostile to animals entering the area from more stable substrates of either the river or the main estuary.

Forth

The River Forth, together with flow from the Rivers Teith and Allan, has a mean discharge of 44.5 m^3 s^{-1} (Leatherland, 1987) (Table 4.2). The upper part of the estuary, from the tidal limit (6 km above Stirling, at Craigforth) down to Alloa (21 km below Stirling) follows a series of meanders, known locally as the "Windings", which experience salinities of up to 20‰ at Alloa, and a tidal amplitude decreasing to 2.8 m at Stirling (MHWS–MLWS) (Webb and Metcalfe, 1987). The turbidity maximum migrates between 3 and 15 km downstream of Stirling. The tidal freshwater area is thus between the tidal limit and a distance of 9–21 km below it (Craigforth to between Cambuskenneth and Fallin, see Figures 4.2 and 4.3).

Throughout its length the upper parts of the Forth estuary are flanked by short (5–10 m) steep intertidal areas. There is a clear gradient in sedimentary conditions over the length of the tidal freshwater area, with coarse sand (phi −0.87, median size

FIGURE 4.2. Tidal freshwater stretch of the Forth estuary at Stirling (Stirling Castle on the skyline), 4 km below the tidal limit. Photograph: D. S. McLusky

1.8 mm) at the tidal limit, changing to fine-grained silt (phi > +4, median size <60 μm) at 8 km (McLusky *et al.*, 1993). The organic content of the intertidal sediments increases from 1 to 7% over the same distance.

There is a pronounced oxygen sag between Stirling and Alloa which Webb and Metcalfe (1987) attribute to the suspended solids for 50–90% of the biochemical oxygen demand. The main dissolved oxygen minimum occurs in the vicinity of Alloa, well below the tidal freshwater area, with the worst deficit occurring when low river flows coincide with spring tides. This marked oxygen sag is attributed to organic waste discharges, mainly from Alloa, but also in the past to discharges from Stirling and Cambus, superimposed on a region of natural stress (Griffiths, 1987). Changes in discharges of recent years have caused a clear improvement in water quality and although there remains a dip in oxygen, it is not as severe as in the past.

The fauna of the intertidal areas in the tidal freshwater zone in 1988/89 consisted of 10 species at the tidal limit, decreasing to two at 8 km, thereafter remaining at two or three until 20 km, and then increasing to six at 32 km (Table 4.3). Within the tidal freshwater area the fauna at first consists of a typical variety of freshwater species, but as these decline Chironomidae larvae, among the insects, persist furthest. The oligochaetes *Limnodrilus hoffmeisteri* and *Tubifex tubifex* are the only species to persist throughout the zone.

Subtidal sampling has not occurred quite as far up the estuary as the intertidal sampling; however, it has taken place up to 4 km below the tidal limit (McLusky *et*

FIGURE 4.3. Tidal freshwater stretch of the Forth estuary at Upper Taylorton (the Wallace Monument on the skyline), 12 km below the tidal limit. Photograph: D. S. McLusky

TABLE 4.3. The fauna of the tidal freshwater region of the Forth estuary. NS means not sampled, + indicates presence, blank indicates absence. (Source: McLusky *et al.*, 1993)

Distance from tidal limit (km)	0	2	4.5	7	8	10
Interstitial salinity (‰)	0	0	0	0	0	<1
Intertidal						
Median particle diameter (phi)	−0.87	+2.8	+4.2	+4.4	+3.7	+3.9
% carbon (sediment)	1.3	1.6	4.7	7.2	6.6	4.6
Number of Taxa	10	8	5	3	2	2
Lymnaea sp.	+	+				
Potamopyrgus jenkinsi	+	+				
Pisidium sp.	+	+				
Notonecta sp.	+	+	+			
Arachnida (unidentified)	+	+	+			
Trichoptera	+					
Tipulidae	+					
Chironomidae	+	+	+	+		
Limnodrilus hoffmeisteri	+	+	+	+	+	+
Tubifex tubifex	+	+	+	+	+	+
Total oligochaetes m^{-2}	8533	40 319	60 450	15 1300	20 693	12 066
Subtidal						
Limnodrilus hoffmeisteri	NS	NS	+	+	NS	+
Tubifex tubifex	NS	NS	+	+	NS	+
Total oligochaetes m^{-2}	NS	NS	49 214	1739–97 141	NS	8228–10 607

al., 1993). Throughout the tidal freshwater region the subtidal fauna is dominated by the same two oligochaete species found intertidally (*Limnodrilus hoffmeisteri, Tubifex tubifex*). Occasional specimens of typical freshwater animals, such as *Potamopyrgus* and Chironomidae, are also found. The subtidal sediments also show considerable short-term variations, as a consequence of seasonal erosion and depositional cycles.

Over the past decade, the abundance of oligochaetes in the tidal freshwater region of the Forth estuary has declined and there is some evidence of increased downstream penetration of non-oligochaete species. These trends are mainly attributed to the reduction in organic waste discharged to the area from the town of Stirling.

Zooplankton in tidal fresh waters face a particular problem of being carried down the estuary by the ebbing tide. Roddie *et al.* (1984) studied the zooplankton in the tidal freshwater and upper reaches of the Forth. They showed that the freshwater Crustacea (*Bosmina, Daphnia, Diaptomus*) were carried well down the estuary, but their abundance of 10^2 m^{-3} at the beginning of the tidal freshwater reach declined markedly as they reached > 1‰ salinity waters in the upper estuary (Figure 4.4). *Eurytemora affinis* was also present in the tidal freshwater reaches, but did not reach its maximal abundance (max. mean 50 119 m^{-3}) until the upper reaches. Experimental studies of *Eurytemora* showed that its survival decreased steeply at salinities below 3‰. This study revealed freshwater zooplankton species as being typical of the tidal freshwater area, and *Eurytemora* as being more typical of upper estuarine areas.

Throughout its recent history the Forth has remained of sufficient quality to permit the passage of migratory fish such as salmonids, although hitherto this was prevented

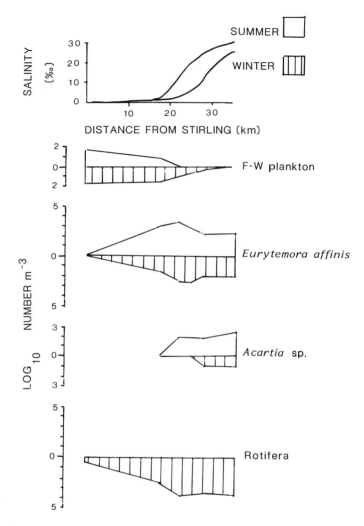

FIGURE 4.4. Distribution of salinity and the main groups of zooplankton in the Forth estuary, Scotland, in summer 1980 and winter 1982, shown against distance from Stirling. The tidal freshwater area is approximately the first 10 km, (After Roddie *et al.*, 1984)

during summer months by the low oxygen conditions. The recent improvements in water quality in the upper estuary now permit the passage of salmonids throughout the year, except for perhaps a few days in summer. In 1989 the tidal freshwater section witnessed the return of the Sparling (*Osmerus eperlanus*), and a survey in 1992 has established that it is now breeding in the tidal freshwater reach of the Forth.

Clyde

The River Clyde has a mean discharge of 41 m^3 s^{-1} (Poodle, 1986) (Table 4.2). The penetration of tidal or saline waters into the uppermost reaches of the Clyde is

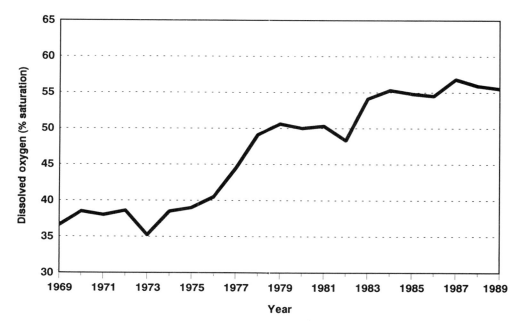

FIGURE 4.5. Dissolved oxygen in the Clyde estuary at King George V Dock, expressed as a five-year moving mean of depth averaged data. (From Clyde River Purification Board)

prevented by the Tidal Weir, situated upstream of the Albert Bridge. Below the weir salinity fluctuations can be extreme, with 0‰ salinity recorded in bottom waters as far downstream as Erskine (16 km). Equally, saline waters (> 15‰) can penetrate to King George V Bridge/Broomielaw. The 2-km-long area between Broomielaw and the Tidal Weir can be reliably regarded as the tidal freshwater section of the Clyde estuary.

The tidal freshwater and upper reaches of the Clyde estuary have suffered historically from severe pollution. Fish populations were probably eliminated from the upper estuary by 1845–1850 due to industrialization and urbanization (Henderson and Hamilton, 1986). From that date until 1972 the poor oxygen conditions prevented any fish at all living there. Since 1972, clearly improving trends in dissolved oxygen (Figure 4.5) have been detected, although an oxygen sag still occurs during summer dry weather flow. Concomitant with this improving trend the number of fish in the upper estuary has steadily increased, to 18 in 1978, 34 in 1984 and 40 in 1992, including the first run of Atlantic Salmon (*Salmo salar*) through the estuary in autumn 1983 (Mackay and Doughty, 1986; Henderson, personal communication).

The condition of the Clyde used to be so bad that, when the benthos was first systematically surveyed in 1967, there was a complete absence of macrofauna, and only very few oligochaetes over the 19.2 km distance of the upper estuary from Milton to King George V Bridge (Mackay *et al.*, 1978). Indeed the first oligochaete was recorded at Broomielaw only in 1972, and the area at the mouth of the River Kelvin was devoid of all macrobenthos until 1976. Over the 16 km from King George V Bridge to Erskine Bridge, the benthic fauna then became characterized by abundant

60

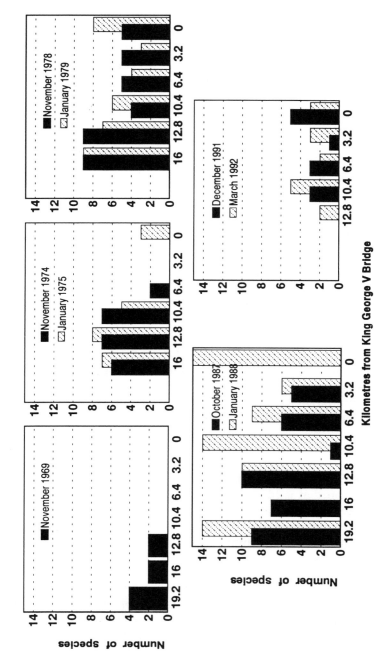

FIGURE 4.6. Variation in winter benthic faunal colonization of the upper Clyde estuary over the period 1969–1992. (From Clyde River Purification Board)

oligochaetes. From 1989/90 onwards, the regular appearance of various polychaete species as well as some Crustacea and Mollusca from the Cart confluence downstream indicates frequent saline intrusions, as well as the biological recovery of the Clyde (Figure 4.6) (Henderson, personal communication)

In the tidal fresh water, which is the 2-km-long section from the Tidal Weir to Broomielaw, the fauna now includes leeches and the isopod *Asellus aquaticus* as well as many oligochaetes, especially *Tubifex tubifex, Limnodrilus hoffmeisteri, Nais elinguis, Paranais littoralis and Lumbricillus lineatus*, and Chironomidae, with 15 species in January 1988 (Figure 4.6) (Henderson, 1984, and personal communication).

The Clyde is unique in Scotland in having the physical barrier of the Tidal Weir to prevent saline intrusion, which makes comparisons with the Tay and Forth rather difficult. Nevertheless it can be seen from the faunal records that the short stretch of the Clyde above Broomielaw is comparable to the other tidal freshwater reaches.

Other estuaries

It is apparent that other large Scottish estuaries, such as the Solway Firth, and the estuaries which lead into the Moray Firth, have a tidal freshwater region, but either it has not been studied or no records have been published. For the smaller estuaries, such as those at the head of the west coast sea lochs, the tidal freshwater reach may be effectively non-existent, as in many cases the strongly flowing rivers debouch directly into saline waters with little gradation.

DISCUSSION

A general pattern can be seen in all the tidal fresh waters studied in Scotland, of a declining diversity of species compared to the adjacent rivers. At the heads of the estuary a variety of typical freshwater species can be found, including several types of insects and molluscs. Within the tidal freshwater area the Chironomidae are the insects which persist furthest, but in all estuaries it can be seen that the oligochaete worms *Tubifex tubifex* and *Limnodrilus hoffmeisteri* dominate and persist. Below the oligochaete-dominated area, other species such as *Corophium volutator* or *Nereis diversicolor* appear as soon as some trace of salinity is reached, and as the salinity increases so the diversity of marine and/or estuarine species increases.

These patterns occur in both clean and polluted estuaries. In a non-polluted estuary such as the Tay, the non-oligochaete species may penetrate furthest (e.g. *Corophium* at Newburgh). As the Forth has become cleaner there has been some evidence of an increased penetration of various species. In moderately polluted conditions the abundance and biomass of oligochaetes increases, but not necessarily their diversity. In grossly polluted situations, such as the Clyde before 1972, no macrobenthos lives.

The faunal sequence of oligochaete species, with *Tubifex tubifex* and *Limnodrilus hoffmeisteri* in the tidal fresh waters, and *Limnodrilus* penetrating furthest down into the estuary, before being replaced by *Tubifex costatus* in low salinity areas, and then replacement by other species such as *Tubificoides benedeni*, has been found in many estuaries, including the Forth (Bagheri and McLusky, 1982), the Clyde (Mackay *et al.*, 1978; Henderson, 1984), the Weser (Schuchardt *et al.*, 1993), the Somme

(McLusky *et al.*, 1994), the Thames (Birtwell and Arthur, 1980) and the Elbe (Pfannkuche, 1981).

The tidal freshwater area of the Weser estuary (Germany), which is 40–70 km long, has been defined by Schuchardt *et al.* (1993) as being a different biotope from adjacent areas and having its own community structure. Mainly due to physical processes, such as tidal movements and prolonged residence time, the tidal freshwater area is different from river habitats, and due to a lack of salinity and lower concentrations of particulate suspended matter it is different from the upper reaches of the estuary, where the turbidity maximum occurs.

From the various case studies within Scotland, as well as the limited general literature available, it is clear that whilst salinity may be the dominant factor in the estuary below the tidal freshwater area, it cannot be the controlling factor in tidal fresh waters, since saline waters do not reach them, and the tides are solely due to fresh water being temporarily dammed back by the seawater flood tide further down the estuary. We must therefore look to other ecological factors, such as the sediment, which result from physical or hydrographical changes.

In the Tay, for example, Oligochaeta became dominant and there was a marked species decline within an area which never experienced any salt penetration. This suggests either substrate changes and/or tidal conditions as being responsible. The tidal freshwater area is different from the river because it is tidal and experiences currents which flow in either direction with velocities ranging from nil to strong. There is therefore a longer residence time of water, resulting both in sedimentation during slack currents as well as re-suspension of sediments during tidal flow and ebb. A river, by contrast, has a permanent uni-directional flow. The tidal freshwater area will thus have markedly increased silt deposition compared to a river. This fine sedimentary silt would certainly clog the respiratory structures of many typical freshwater species.

In conclusion, it must be stressed that it is the change in sedimentary conditions from the adjacent rivers which imposes the greatest limit on the faunal composition. These sediments may also vary seasonally, imposing a further stress on the fauna in these regions. The fauna is a complex mixture, some of which is transient and arrives through drift in times of high river flow, and otherwise is composed of a few oligochaete species. The oligochaete worms, as "opportunistic" species, are thus exploiting a biotope which other species shun. The species composition varies seasonally in response to river flow, and the whole situation may be further complicated by seasonal dissolved oxygen sags.

The evidence from the three large Scottish estuaries, the Tay, Forth and Clyde, is that despite their varied histories the tidal freshwater areas can be considered as a distinct biotope, with a fauna of freshwater origin adapted to fluctuating tidal currents and their associated sedimentary regime.

ACKNOWLEDGEMENTS

Anne Henderson of the Clyde River Purification Board kindly supplied up-to-date data on the fauna and conditions of the Clyde estuary, as well as valuable discussion of the manuscript.

REFERENCES

Alexander, W. B., Southgate, B. A. and Bassindale, R. (1935). "Survey of the River Tees. Part II. The estuary–chemical and biological", *DSIR Water Pollution Research Technical Paper*, **5**, 1–171.

Bagheri, E. A. and McLusky, D. S. (1982). "Population dynamics of oligochaetes and small polychaetes in the polluted Forth estuary", *Netherlands Journal of Sea Research*, **16**, 55–66.

Birtwell, I. and Arthur, D. R. (1980). "The ecology of tubificids in the Thames estuary, with particular reference to *Tubifex costatus*", in *Aquatic Oligochaeta Biology* (eds R. O. Brinkhurst and D. G. Cook), pp. 331–381, Plenum, New York.

Buller, A. T. and McManus, J. (1975). "Sediments of the Tay estuary. I. Bottom sediments of the upper and upper middle reaches", *Proceedings of the Royal Society of Edinburgh*, **75B**, 41–64.

Deaton, L. E. and Greenberg, M. J. (1986). "There is no horohalinicum", *Estuaries*, **9**, 20–30.

Griffiths, A. H. (1987). "Water quality of the estuary and Firth of Forth", *Proceedings of the Royal Society of Edinburgh*, **93B**, 303–314.

Henderson, A. R. (1984). "Long term monitoring of the macrobenthos of the upper Clyde estuary", *Water Science and Technology*, **16**, 359–373.

Henderson, A. R. and Hamilton, J. D. (1986). "The status of fish populations in the Clyde estuary", *Proceedings of the Royal Society of Edinburgh*, **90B**, 157–170.

Khayrallah, N. and Jones, A. M. (1975). "A survey of the benthos of the Tay estuary", *Proceedings of the Royal Society of Edinburgh*, **75B**, 113–135.

Leatherland, T. M. (1987). "The estuary and Firth of Forth, Scotland: uses and aims", *Proceedings of the Royal Society of Edinburgh*, **93B**, 285–297.

McCave, I. N. (1979). "Suspended sediment", in *Estuarine Hydrography and Sedimentation* (Ed. K. R. Dyer), pp. 131–185, Cambridge University Press, Cambridge.

Mackay, D. W. and Doughty, C. R. (1986). "Migratory salmonids of the estuary and Firth of Clyde", *Proceedings of the Royal Society of Edinburgh*, **90B**, 479–490.

Mackay, D. W., Taylor, W. K. and Henderson, A. R. (1978). "The recovery of the polluted Clyde estuary", *Proceedings of the Royal Society of Edinburgh*, **76B**, 135–152.

McLusky, D. S. (1993). "Marine and estuarine gradients – an overview", *Netherlands Journal of Aquatic Ecology*, **27**, 489–493.

McLusky, D. S., Desprez, M., Elkaim, B. and Duhamel, S. (1994). "The Inner Estuary of the Baie de Somme", *Estuarine, Coastal and Shelf Science*, **38**, 313–318.

McLusky, D. S., Hull, S. C. and Elliott, M. (1993). "Variations in the intertidal and subtidal macrofauna and sediments along a salinity gradient in the upper Forth estuary", *Netherlands Journal of Aquatic Ecology*, **27**, 101–109.

Maitland, P. S. and Smith, I. R. (1987). "The River Tay: ecological changes from source to estuary", *Proceedings of the Royal Society of Edinburgh*, **92B**, 373–392.

Meire, P. and Vincx, M. (Eds) (1993). "Marine and estuarine gradients", *Netherlands Journal of Aquatic Ecology*, **27**, 71–496.

Mantoura, R. F. C. (1987). "Organic films at the halocline", *Nature*, **328**, 579–580.

Morris, A. W., Mantoura, R. F. C., Bale, A. J. and Howland, R. J. M. (1978). "Very low salinity regions of estuaries: important sites for chemical and biological reactions", *Nature*, **225**, 472–474.

Pfannkuche, O. (1981). "Distribution, abundance and life cycles of aquatic Oligochaeta in a freshwater tidal flat of the Elbe estuary", *Archiv für Hydrobiologie*, **43**, 506–524.

Poodle, T. (1986). "Fresh water inflows to the Firth of Clyde", *Proceedings of the Royal Society of Edinburgh*, **90B**, 55–66.

Remane, A. (1934). "Die Brackwasserfauna", *Verhandlungen Deutsche Zoologische Gesellschaft*, **36**, 34–74.

Roddie, B. D., Leakey, R. J. G. and Berry, A. J. (1984). "Salinity–temperature tolerance and osmoregulation in *Eurytemora affinis* in relation to its distribution in the zooplankton of the upper reaches of the Forth estuary", *Journal of Experimental Marine Biology and Ecology*, **79**, 191–211.

Schuchardt, B., Haesloop, U. and Schirmer, M. (1993). "The tidal freshwater reach of the Weser estuary: riverine or estuarine region?", *Netherlands Journal of Aquatic Ecology*, **27**, 215–226.

Webb, A. J. and Metcalfe, A. P. (1987). "Physical aspects, water movements and modelling studies of the Forth estuary, Scotland", *Proceedings of the Royal Society of Edinburgh*, **93B**, 259–272.

Williams, D. J. A. and West, J. R. (1975). "Salinity distribution in the Tay estuary", *Proceedings of the Royal Society of Edinburgh*, **75B**, 29–39.

5

Geomorphology

A. WERRITTY

School of Geography and Geology, University of St Andrews, St Andrews, KY16 9ST, UK

V. BRAZIER and J. E. GORDON

Scottish Natural Heritage, 2 Anderson Place, Edinburgh, EH6 5NP, UK

and

J. MCMANUS

School of Geography and Geology, University of St Andrews, St Andrews, KY16 9ST, UK

INTRODUCTION

The geomorphological freshwater resources in Scotland afford a richer diversity of processes, forms and patterns than in any other part of the UK. This arises because of the highly resistant underlying bedrock, deeply dissected relief (particularly in the Highlands), the juxtaposition of highland and lowland environments in the piedmont zone, and the marked climatic gradients (especially in terms of precipitation) from west to east across the country. The aim of this review is to demonstrate the geomorphological diversity found in stream, river, loch and estuary, and to explain their origins and significance for conservation and management. The review concludes with a discussion of some of the key issues to be addressed by conservation agencies as they seek to sustain this valuable geomorphological resource for future generations.

The manner in which geological history has influenced the freshwater resources of Scotland is addressed in detail in the next section. Here it is appropriate to indicate that this control has been exercised over a very large timespan (stretching back over 60 million years) and has included a range of spatial scales extending from the evolution of the largest drainage basin – the Tay – to the development of "badland" gullies within sites occupying only tens of hectares. This account thus encompasses a

The Fresh Waters of Scotland: A National Resource of International Significance
Edited by P. S. Maitland, P. J. Boon and D. S. McLusky. © 1994 John Wiley & Sons Ltd

great variety of scales both in terms of formative time periods and the areas within which the streams, rivers, lochs and estuaries are to be found.

By way of more specific introduction it might be helpful to the non-specialist reader to be offered an imaginary journey through mountain, piedmont, lowland and estuarine zones along a major Scottish river system (echoing a similar exercise undertaken by Geikie (1865)). This journey begins in the "mountain zone" (Newson, 1981) alongside a boulder-bed torrent often interrupted by bedrock reaches. Such channels are steep, generally very stable and subject to major adjustment only during rare extreme floods (e.g. the Allt Mor, Glenmore; McEwen and Werritty, 1988). The presence of bedrock reaches, including gorges, at this stage in the journey is highly significant and points to the efficacy of erosion by meltwaters during and immediately after the repeated glacial stages of the Pleistocene. In addition to these "meltwater gorges" (often locally referred to as "linns") our traveller is likely also to encounter "alluvial basins" (glaciated valley floors infilled with alluvium) often occurring like beads on a string where they are separated from each other by further bedrock reaches. Downstream of this initial channel type, a concurrent reduction in channel slope and size of the bed material combined with a widening of the valley floor typically results in a low sinuosity wandering gravel river which, depending on local controls, may exhibit both divided and undivided channels of variable sinuosity (e.g. the Rivers Tulla and Feshie (Bluck, 1976; Werritty and Ferguson, 1980)). In terms of sediment transport such reaches are "bedload channels", but their activity and ability to migrate across and thus rework the valley floor is determined by the number of times per year the bed becomes mobile. This, in turn, will depend upon the size of the bed material to be transported and the velocity of the flows delivered to that reach. The mobility of the channel can also depend upon the amount and size of the material supplied from tributary valleys and undercut terraces adjacent to the valley floor. If the sediment is coarse, the main channel may become stabilized in position since it is unable to transport very coarse bed material (e.g. reaches on the Rivers Findhorn and Feshie). In such "piedmont zone" reaches (Newson, 1981) the channel is overwhelmingly alluvial (incised within sediments the river itself deposited at an earlier stage) and only rarely confined by bedrock reaches and gorge-like sections. The channel may also be temporarily interrupted as it flows into a loch (which acts as a major regulator of flow, as a sediment trap and as a geomorphic unit in its own right; McManus and Duck, 1988). However, at the outflow the channel gradient downstream combined with a renewed sediment supply from banks and tributary streams usually ensures that the river continues to display many of the characteristics noted above.

Truly lowland reaches are likely to be short-lived as the lowland areas of Scotland are generally restricted to a narrow coastal fringe around the Highlands and Southern Uplands and become extensive only within Central Scotland. The Spey is thus still a gravel-bed river when it reaches the Moray Firth. More typically, rivers in the lowlands are sand-bedded rather than gravel-bedded, although the point at which this transition is made can be quite close to their final outlet to a loch or the sea (e.g. the River Endrick; Bluck, 1971). Low channel gradients together with river training (to control the position of the river within the valley floor) mean that these channels are generally highly stable, and it is only rarely that active meandering and major reworking of the floodplain occur (e.g. the River Clyde meanders at Carstairs; Brazier *et al.* (1993)). Even in the lowland zone, bedrock controls can still provide dramatic changes in channel types, and gorge-like reaches are locally significant (e.g. the River Clyde at the Falls of Clyde and the River Devon at Rumbling Bridge). Finally, as the tidal limit is reached the fresh water becomes brackish, and the river gives way to a firth or estuary.

THE EVOLUTION OF SCOTLAND'S RIVERS, LOCHS AND ESTUARIES

Geological framework of the Scottish fluvial system

The structure provided by the rock formations of Scotland and their varied resistance to erosion constitutes the starting point for an examination of the evolution of the fluvial landscape. In undertaking this, it necessary to invert the geological dictum that "the present is the key to the past", for in a very real sense the geological past in this context provides significant keys to an understanding of the present.

The general pattern of rock formations within Scotland is dominated by the influence of the Caledonian orogeny, which produced a NE – SW geological graining. This graining is present both north of the Highland Boundary Fault and south of the Southern Uplands Fault and characterizes the strike of rock units of varying, but typically resistant, lithologies and also the alignment of faults which generate major lines of weakness. Through the country, rocks of these areas are intruded granites and other resistant igneous rocks. The Midland Valley, which lies between these two major faults, is underlain by post-Caledonian rocks of varying resistance, from durable lavas in the west to much weaker coal-bearing successions further east.

During the late Cretaceous the highest sea-level known on earth occurred, with seas perhaps as much as 300 m above their present position (Vail *et al.*, 1977). The sea flooded across Scotland including the Highlands, which were temporarily lowered by tectonic activity prior to the opening of the North Atlantic. The volcanic activity during the early Tertiary (63–52 million years ago) was contemporaneous with the opening of the northernmost Atlantic, separating Greenland from Norway. The crustal rifting through the line of the Hebrides was a minor part of this activity, but nevertheless permitted the development of a series of major volcanic centres along the western margins of mainland Scotland (Emeleus and Gyopari, 1992). The assemblages of volcanic rocks and associated dyke swarms were the last significant rock units to form before the onset of glaciation. Offshore, to the east, the Tertiary is marked by substantial deposits of oil-and gas-bearing sands, largely eroded from the Scottish mainland.

Pre-glacial patterns of landscape development

As early as 1901 Geikie had identified south-eastward tilted high level plateaux within the Highlands, and noted substantial erosion subsequent to the Tertiary vulcanicity. Several discrete pre-glacial land surfaces preserved as concordant plateau summits and ridges and high level benches have been identified in the Scottish Highlands by different researchers (Peach and Horne, 1910, 1930; Fleet, 1938; Bremner, 1942; Soons, 1958; Rice, 1962). The origin of these ancient landscape relicts is a matter of debate (Linton, 1951a; George, 1965; Sissons, 1967; Hall, 1987, 1991), and they have been attributed to both marine planation and sub-aerial processes during the Tertiary, and possibly earlier. However, it would appear that the severe entrenchment, which fixed the drainage pattern, probably occurred either during the exceptionally low sea-levels (−200 m) for 10 million years during the late Oligocene or the less extreme lowering of sea-level (−100 m) in the late Miocene (Vail *et al.*, 1977; Figure 5.1).

Eastward or south-east tilting of the landmass (probably contemporaneous with the final opening of the North Atlantic) generated the east–west trends to be found in the major drainage systems (Figure 5.2). Linton (1951a) demonstrated that these

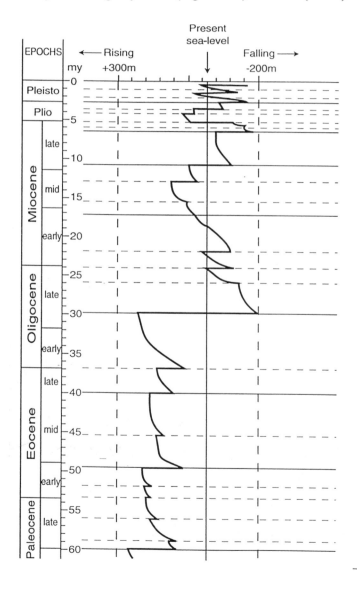

FIGURE 5.1. Geological timescale and Cenozoic sea-level changes (after Vail *et al.*, 1977)

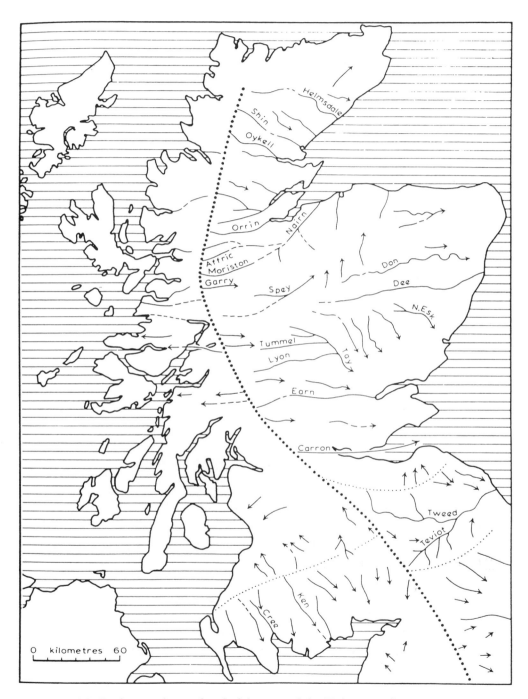

FIGURE 5.2. Drainage prior to the glacial stages of the Pleistocene (from Sissons, 1967)

early rivers originated close to the present-day west coast and drained east, cutting courses transcurrent to the geological structures. This probably involved superimposition of initial parallel streams draining across essentially uniform rocks, which covered the structural basement. The remnants of these ancient rivers comprise high altitude features (often open structures) which could have originated during the Oligocene low stand of sea-level which lasted 10 million years (Vail *et al.*, 1977; Figure 5.1). More recently (possibly in the Miocene) adjustment to lithological and structural controls occurred in most watercourses, this being accomplished before the onset of glaciation. Thus, prior to the glacial stages of the Pleistocene, the Tay basin streams had been initiated and flowed into the sea via the present estuary (McManus, 1967); the Angus and eastern Tayside glens already drained south-eastwards into Strathmore; the Teviot and Tweed carried waters from the Southern Uplands into the North Sea; and the rivers north of the Cairngorms drained into the Moray Firth (Figure 5.2).

Quaternary glaciations and the Holocene

Glaciation during the Quaternary has had an important impact on the development and characteristics of the freshwater resource through the effects of both glacial erosion and deposition (Figure 5.3). Glacial erosion has been responsible for shaping valley forms, particularly where ice streams drained the main centres of ice accumulation, producing steep, overdeepened glacial troughs (Linton, 1957, 1959). The floors of many of these troughs were deeply scoured by the ice, forming rock basins (Sissons,

FIGURE 5.3. Upper Glen Feshie, looking south towards the "glacial breach", the upper braided reach of the river and associated Holocene terraces. Photograph: Vanessa Brazier

1967). Many pre-existing watersheds were breached by powerful ice streams, modifying the earlier drainage patterns particularly in western Scotland (Sissons, 1967, 1976). Striking examples of glacial diversion of drainage also occur in the eastern Grampians, as in the valleys of the Rivers Feshie and Avon and elsewhere in the Cairngorms (Linton, 1949, 1951b, 1954; Sugden, 1968). In other cases, diversion of drainage was initiated through the infilling of pre-existing river courses by glacial deposits, as in the middle River Clyde. Small-scale rock basins were also produced in areas extensively scoured by warm-based ice sheets, forming the distinctive "knock and lochan" topography of north-west Scotland (Linton, 1959).

Glacial meltwaters have also contributed significantly to the character of the Scottish landscape. There is the extensive legacy of glacio-fluvial landforms; for example, eskers and meltwater channel systems (Sutherland, 1984, 1991). Also, as the Late Devensian ice sheet melted, massive spreads of glacio-fluvial outwash deposits infilled the floors of many valleys (Sutherland and Gordon, 1993). As discharge declined, these valley floor fills became terraced (Robertson-Rintoul, 1986; Maizels and Aitken, 1991), with local kettle hole development where the deposits included buried ice. Subsequently, as these deposits have been reworked by Holocene and present-day rivers, they have provided the fundamental sedimentary controls on river behaviour.

In suitable topographic localities, ice-dammed lakes formed during the melting of the Late Devensian ice sheet and also during the subsequent Loch Lomond Readvance (Sutherland and Gordon, 1993). Among the most spectacular effects are the shorelines, alluvial fans and deltas in Glen Roy (Figure 5.4) (Sissons and Cornish, 1983; Peacock, 1986) and the delta terraces at Achnasheen (Sissons, 1977; Benn, 1992).

Rapid warming of Scotland's climate hastened the wastage of the Loch Lomond Readvance glaciers about 10 000 years BP. Unconsolidated glacial and glacio-fluvial deposits were reworked by mass-movement processes and running water. Debris flows and avalanches reworked sediment-covered hillsides, and cones of debris accumulated at the foot of many rock and drift-cut gullies (Figure 5.5). Rivers reworked their valley floors by repeated phases of cutting and filling, producing further flights of river terraces. There is evidence that suggests a decrease in the magnitude of post-glacial valley-floor modifications since the Early to Mid Holocene (e.g. Brazier *et al.*, 1988).

Lochs and estuaries: sediment sinks and stores

Recognized by the Geological Survey of Scotland as significant landforms, the lochs were first surveyed bathymetrically by Wilson (1888), with systematic scientific examination undertaken in the major investigations of Murray and Pullar (1910). Over 560 lochs were charted, leading to the first systematic discussion of loch origins (Peach and Horne, 1910).

Of widely differing scales and storage capacities, many lochs undoubtedly originated during the retreat phases of the glaciers, kettle lakes – both small and large – abounding (e.g. Loch Leven). Moraine-dammed water bodies such as the Lake of Menteith are not uncommon, although the best known features are probably the large, linear lochs in the Northern and Grampian Highlands and in the Southern

FIGURE 5.4. The Parallel Roads of Glen Roy, the shorelines of ice-dammed lakes. Photograph:
Vanessa Brazier

FIGURE 5.5. Active debris slope processes reworking sediment-covered hillsides in Glencoe.
Photograph: Vanessa Brazier

Uplands. Some, such as Loch Muick, certainly were present before the Loch Lomond Stadial for their floors bear sedimentary deposits from the terminal moraines of the ice (Lowe *et al.*, 1991).

In many of the larger lochs, layered sequences of muds line the floors, and pollen analysis of cores has demonstrated uninterrupted deposition throughout post-glacial times (Pennington *et al.*, 1972). No evidence of any pre-glacial deposits on the bed of any of the lochs is currently known. Indeed, during the height of glaciation the majority of the basins were occupied by great thicknesses of ice several hundreds of metres thick, especially in deep loch basins such as Loch Ness and Loch Morar. During glacial retreat, very large volumes of sediment were released, filling many former valley floors and rock basins.

Most rivers enter the sea by way of estuarine reaches which are commonly fjordic on the west coast but more evidently drowned valleys in the south and east of the country. In many of the larger estuaries substantial sequences of clays bearing an Arctic fossil fauna overlie the glacial materials, but are buried beneath later estuarine successions, including peats, which originated as marsh deposits (McManus, 1968, 1972). Today, lowland estuaries are essentially sites of sediment accumulation, with land-derived muds and sands supplemented by incoming marine sands to generate tidal flats and channel margin sandbanks (Fleming, 1970; Al-Ansari and McManus, 1979; Al-Jabbari *et al.*, 1980; McManus, 1986; Reid and McManus, 1987).

Where continued isostatic uplift exceeds the rate of sea-level rise, estuaries show evidence of rejuvenation, with headward-migrating rapids forming within the main channels, as seen in the Eden, Tay and Ythan estuaries. The geomorphic importance of estuaries to the freshwater systems stems largely from the variations in the level of tidal waters which enter from the sea. These salt waters serve to dam up the effluent fresh water, preventing its free egress from the fluvial reaches. During periods of high river discharge this may lead to temporary backing up and flooding in areas above the tidal limit.

Controls on the operation of fluvial processes

The three major controls which have determined the geomorphology of Scotland's rivers, lochs and estuaries are climate, geology and time, often working together rather than separately. Climate determines the hydrological setting, with a marked west–east rainfall gradient (>3000 mm in Glen Quoich and <700 mm in Aberdeen, Fife and Berwick). This pattern arises because of the westerly origin of most of the cyclones reaching the British Isles and the rainfall triggered by orographic uplift of moist air masses in the north and west. This, when combined with generally low evapo-transpiration losses, results in parts of the North West Highlands converting more than 75% of its rainfall into run-off and the majority of Scotland exceeding 50%. Not surprisingly, this rainfall-controlled pattern of run-off for the River Tay makes it the largest river in Britain in terms of average flow (167 m^3 s^{-1} at Perth), a value which can be augmented to over 2000 m^3 s^{-1} by snowmelt, as demonstrated by the catastrophic floods in January 1993.

Given this pattern of run-off one would anticipate that the largest and most powerful rivers would flow to the north and the west. This does not arise because of the geological control which has produced an asymmetric location for the main east

–west watershed (Figure 5.2). The geological evolution of Scotland in the late Tertiary and the size and direction of flow of the major ice-streams during the Pleistocene have jointly produced this result. Thus, west of the present-day watershed, deeply incised, steep but relatively short rivers flow to the Atlantic, often with tributary hanging valleys (e.g. Glen Coe), whereas the largest rivers in the Highlands (Rivers Tay, Spey and Dee) flow to the east. It is only in the Southern Uplands that the watershed between the Rivers Clyde and Tweed is more symmetrically located.

The impact of geology is registered in the calibre of the bed material supplied to many of the upland rivers in Scotland, with many of the large rivers having gravel beds to their marine limits (e.g. the Rivers Tay, Spey, Findhorn and Tweed). This occurs, not because such material is continuously transported, as if on a conveyor belt from source to mouth, but because lateral migration constantly reworks the Late Quaternary deposits adjacent to these rivers on their valley floors. This combination of geology and former climate also serves to explain the location and origin of the gorges cut by glacial meltwaters, producing within many large rivers a stepped long profile in which alluvial reaches occupy a series of basins separated from each other by steeper bedrock reaches. The precise pattern of such alternating alluvial and bedrock channels owes much to differential glacial erosion during the Pleistocene and is especially well developed in the middle reaches of the Tay–Tummel–Garry river system. Another direct result of selective glacial erosion is the presence of many lochs within river courses, a striking example of which is the Tay drainage system with four lochs with volumes >0.1 km^3 (Murray and Pullar, 1910).

The role of time as a controlling factor is different since it is only through the passage of time that climate and geology register their effects. The important point arising from this is that the geomorphological freshwater resources of Scotland owe their origin to groups of processes operating within contrasting timescales (Schumm, 1977). Thus within "geological" time (10^6 years) the geological controls of structure and lithology have been dominant in generating the overall pattern for Scotland's rivers. Within "graded" time (10^2–10^3 years) local features adjacent to valley floors will have been formed (e.g. floodplains, terraces and alluvial fans), whilst in "steady" time (10^0–10^1 years) channels migrate and generate temporary bars from the products of bank erosion. These latter elements are clearly a form of "geomorphological embroidery" superimposed on a fluvial system that owes its fundamental delineation to processes operating over timescales of thousands and millions of years and often within drainage basins covering hundreds of square kilometres.

Within these last two timescales ("graded" and "steady") other significant controls on Scotland's river systems can also be identified. These include changes in land use and human action which sometimes involve unplanned effects (e.g. the impact of afforestation and gravel extraction) and sometimes planned interventions (e.g. hydroelectric power, flood protection and river training). In conservation terms, both types of human intervention often constitute a threat to the continued natural behaviour and development of specific river systems (Werritty and Brazier, in press). However, at the scale of Scotland as a whole, these threats are often site-specific, with the result that most of the larger geomorphic features referred to in this chapter are controlled by climate, geology and time in the manner described above.

THE GEOMORPHOLOGICAL RESOURCE

The nature of the resource

The freshwater features in Scotland are remarkable for their geomorphological diversity, the physical basis of which is explained above. This diversity encompasses fluvial, lacustrine and upper estuarine systems, the principal elements of which comprise relict landforms, active processes and sedimentary records of Pleistocene and Holocene palaeo-environmental changes. The nature of these elements is well exemplified in the selection of key fluvial sites for the Geological Conservation Review (GCR) (Werritty and McEwen, in press) and this work provides a useful context within which to review the nature of the resource and its special significance. This network of 28 fluvial sites (Table 5.1, Figure 5.6) reflects the fundamental scientific interest of Scottish river systems and their underlying controls. Two important factors were considered in the selection of these sites: first, variations in channel typology, and second, the principal characteristics which make Scottish river channels geomorphologically significant. Channel typology includes both bedrock features and alluvial channels, the latter being classified into a range of types based on sinuosity and degree of channel division. Significant characteristics of Scottish rivers, with examples, are summarized in Table 5.2.

While the network of sites chosen for the GCR reflects the fundamental characteristics of the geomorphology of Scotland's rivers, it represents only a small part of the total resource. Many additional sites and reaches are of regional or local importance, while others provide the wider spatial or temporal contexts for the GCR site network. The latter, however, have not been systematically assessed or documented. Moreover, standing water bodies and upper estuary localities generally lay outside the scope of the GCR. Thus although an important start has been made through the work of the GCR, compilation of a comprehensive inventory of the geomorphology of Scotland's freshwater resources remains outstanding. The need for such an audit is underscored both by the importance of the resource and the management requirements necessary to maintain or enhance the value of an integral part of Scotland's natural heritage.

The importance of the resource

The importance of the resource lies in three principal aspects: scientific research and education, applied research and education, and landscape heritage.

Research in geomorphology has an essential field basis, so that an adequate resource of field sites is crucial for the development of the science – for example, through process investigations or in testing theoretical models of stream dynamics. Some of the principal themes in fluvial research in Scotland have been outlined by McEwen (in press). This research emphasizes the dynamics and adjustment of fluvial systems over different timescales (e.g. Werritty and Ferguson, 1980; Maizels, 1988; McEwen, 1989; Maizels and Aitken, 1991). Field sites also provide an invaluable archive of information on landscape evolution and environmental change during the Pleistocene and Holocene. This information is preserved both in landforms and in terrestrial and lacustrine sedimentary records (e.g. Pennington *et al.*, 1972;

TABLE 5.1. Fluvial geomorphology Geological Conservation Review sites in Scotland

No.	Name	Description
1.	Glencoe	Glencoe has nationally important examples of highly active mountain river types and hillslope modifying processes.
2.	Abhain an t-Strath Chuileannaich	An excellent example of an actively meandering upland river, where local environmental controls have influenced channel platform.
3.	Strathglass	Irregularly meandering channel and well-defined palaeofeatures. Run-off artificially controlled.
4.	Lower Spey	The lower braided gravel-bed reach of the River Spey so close to the coast is unique in Scotland.
5.	Randolph's Leap	An impressive slot gorge cut into schist bedrock by glacial meltwaters. The gorge has several large potholes. 1829 flood stage rose 16m above normal level.
6.	Allt a' Choire	An excellent example of a complete geomorphic system of actively eroding gullies and aggradation of an alluvial fan.
7.	Findhorn Terraces	Exceptionally high (approx. 70 m above the present channel) and numerous terrace levels cut into thick drift deposits in Streens Gorge.
8.	Upper River Nairn and Allt Mor	An excellent example of the interface of contrasting fluvial environments: the Allt Mor is a highly active boulder-bed mountain torrent, and the Nairn has a low slope and sinuous planform.
9.	Dorback Burn	A typical example of a wandering gravel-bed stream in an upland environment. Also an important research site for the study of channel adjustment to floods of different magnitudes and frequencies.
10.	Allt Mor	An excellent example of a steep boulder-bed mountain torrent, whose planform adjustment over the last 40 years has been reconstructed.
11.	Eas na Broige	The stratigraphy and chronology of this fluvially modified debris cone provides an important indication of the pattern of hillslope evolution since deglaciation in upland Britain.
12.	Allt Coire Gabhail	Catastrophic change in base level following a large landslide has resulted in the formation in the enclosed alluvial basin of a range of stream channel types from mountain torrent, low sinuosity channels to braided channel patterns.
13.	Allt Dubhaig	This site provides an informative example of the impact of a markedly concave long profile on sediment size and channel type downstream.
14.	Derry Burn	This site provides an excellent example of a river system adjusting to planform controls (low slope, gravel to sand sediment sizes) within a small upland alluvial basin. The reach is close to the threshold separating braiding from meandering streams.
15.	Glen Feshie	This is an internationally important fluvial geomorphology site, with four distinctive areas: A. Braided channel pattern where the highest rates of bank erosion and channel change have been recorded in Scotland. B. Well-preserved outwash terraces and post-glacial cut and fill sequences.

TABLE 5.1. (*Continued*)

No.	Name	Description
		C. A highly active braided reach reworking glacio-fluvial outwash deposits.
		D. A large active alluvial fan marking the confluence of the Rivers Feshie and Spey. Unusual in Europe as it has not been heavily engineered.
16.	Quoich Water Fan	A small active alluvial fan that debouches from a rock-controlled section. The whole surface of the fan was disrupted by a flood in 1829, and subsequent readjustment resulted in a reticulate channel planform.
17.	Luibeg Burn	The Luibeg Burn provides an excellent example of a steep, boulder-bed mountain torrent which has a documented history of large-scale sediment mobilization during extreme floods.
18.	Falls of Dochart	This is a good example of a wide unconfined bedrock reach which exhibits good examples of pot holes.
19.	Allt Coire Chailein	The site provides a compact example of a sediment transfer system encompassing deeply incised drift gullies, and a complex fan of early Holocene age.
20.	River Endrick	The River Endrick is an excellent example of a highly sinuous, lowland sand and gravel-bed river with tortuous meanders. The site is particularly noteworthy for its record of channel and floodplain sedimentary facies, and suite of floodplain landforms.
21.	River Balvag Delta	This delta is prograding out into Loch Lubnaig and has an unusually straight channel.
22.	Oldhamstocks Gullies	Debris flow erosion during an intense rainstorm in 1948 resulted in large gullies on a scale that is rare in upland Scotland.
23.	Falls of Clyde	This site provides an excellent and unusual example of a large-scale sequence of waterfalls and rapids in a gorge in a lowland river.
24.	River Clyde Meanders	This highly active meandering river and its tributary the Medwin Water provide excellent examples of channel migration, cutoffs and cutoff infills that have been documented over a period of 150 years.
25.	Grey Mare's Tail	This spectacular waterfall (over 200 m) comprises a series of cascades of varying sizes which fall over protruding bedrock benches into plunge pools.
26.	River North Esk Palaeosandur	An excellent example of an extensive area of Late-Glacial outwash sandur sediments which have been dissected to form four main terrace systems.
27.	Glen Roy	Glen Roy is an internationally important area for glacio-lacustrine and glacio-fluvial landforms. Fluvial features include well-developed and large alluvial fans/deltas and flights of terraces. The development of these features is closely related to events associated with ice-dammed lake drainage.
28.	Corrieshalloch Gorge	This site is an impressive slot gorge cut through Moine Schists to a depth of 61 m. It is unusually long (1098 m) and narrow at the lip (only 23 m). The gorge may have been rapidly cut by meltwater during ice sheet wastage.

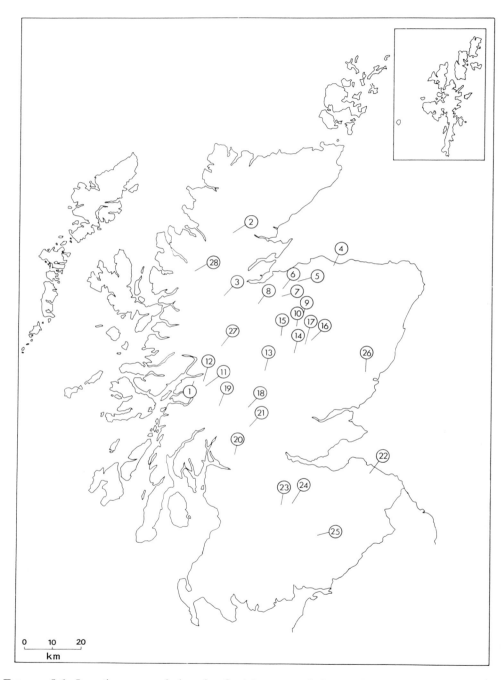

FIGURE 5.6. Location map of sites for fluvial geomorphology selected for the Geological Conservation Review. Site numbers refer to Table 5.1

TABLE 5.2. Summary of significant geomorphological characteristics of Scottish rivers

	Characteristics	Examples	
1.	Classic sedimentary structures	River Endrick (20) Allt Choire Chailein (19)	Allt Coire Gabhail (12)
2.	Downstream changes in fluvial controls	Allt a' Choire (6) Allt Choire Chailein (19)	Allt Mor (8 Nairn) Allt Mor (10 Glenmore)
3.	Interfaces between different types of geomorphic activity	Allt a' Choire (6) Glen Feshie (15) River Quoich (16)	Allt Mor (8 Nairn) Allt Mor (10 Glenmore) Allt Coire Chailein (19)
4.	Evidence of the geomorphic impact of extreme floods	River Feshie (15) Allt Mor (10 Glenmore)	River Quoich (16)
5.	Types and rates of fluvial adjustment over historic time	River Clyde (24) River Endrick (20)	Abhainn an t-Strath Chuileannaich (2)
6.	Late-glacial and Holocene fluvial adjustment	Glen Roy (27) Glen Feshie (15)	Findhorn Terraces (7) River North Esk (26)

Source: Werritty and McEwen (in press)
Note that the numbers refer to GCR sites in Table 5.1 and Figure 5.6

Robertson-Rintoul, 1986; Birks, 1988; Huntley, 1991). A strong scientific resource base, with adequate representation of the current range of landforms and process domains, also serves an important educational function, particularly where the sites have been studied in some detail.

In an applied context, an understanding of freshwater systems is fundamentally important in such areas as landscape management, hazard prediction, water resources planning and engineering design. Such understanding is based on the need for sound scientific underpinning, particularly of the dynamics and sensitivity to change of freshwater systems, either through the effects of natural processes or human modifications to the natural environment. In the field of environmental monitoring, the record of past changes in geomorphological processes – for example, in sediment movements or river channel changes – includes vital baseline information not only for evaluating present-day changes, but also for developing predictive models for possible changes in the future. Sites such as lakes and bogs provide an invaluable source for assessing human impact on the environment through pollution, land-use changes and enhanced soil erosion (e.g. Battarbee *et al.*, 1989; Jones *et al.*, 1989; Duck and McManus, 1990; Stevenson *et al.*, 1990).

The significance of the resource in terms of landscape heritage involves three issues. First, the character and variety of the scenery of Scotland strongly reflect the imprint of geomorphological processes, the landforms and deposits providing much of the detail of the present landscape. They form part of Scotland's recent geological history and are an integral part of the landscape heritage. At one extreme, there are many distinctive landform landmarks, including examples identified in the GCR. However, much of the more subtle detail of landscape form at a local scale is a function of fluvial systems, reflecting both current processes and relict features from earlier in the Quaternary. Second, the science of geomorphology addresses the evolution of the landscape and the physical processes that continue to shape its development. The study of geomorphology can thus provide a valuable vehicle in helping to understand and interpret the landscape heritage and the changes that are currently taking place. This heritage may be decoded from the subtleties of the landforms or sediments or from the environmental archives contained in lake sediments or peat bogs. Third, the physical characteristics and history of the landscape are also significant for the manner in which they interact with biological and socio-economic systems. Landforms and surface deposits provide the foundations for soils, vegetation, habitats and energy pathways. They can also provide a resource for socio-economic exploitation (e.g. recreation, hydro-electric power). Rivers and lochs may also represent a hazard to human activity (flooding) or they may facilitate cultural and economic exchange along valleys or waterways.

PRESENT PROBLEMS AND FUTURE CONSERVATION MANAGEMENT STRATEGIES

Threats to the stability of the drainage basin

Scotland's geomorphological freshwater resources are threatened by many potentially damaging human activities and developments (see examples in Table 5.3 and Figure 5.7), the cumulative effects and interactions of which are poorly documented and difficult to predict. From an earth science conservation perspective, effective river basin management must seek to balance and minimize the conflicting demands made on the natural environment. However, this challenge is complicated by uncertainty about the effects of climatic change. During the Holocene (the last 10 000 years since the glaciers melted) several major fluctuations in Scotland's climate altered the behaviour of river systems and the nature of geomorphic processes in their catchments (e.g. Robertson-Rintoul, 1986; Brazier and Ballantyne, 1989; Ballantyne, 1991a, b). There is also a growing body of evidence for a significant and widespread change in Scotland's weather during the last 20 years, which has resulted in an increase in winter precipitation of up to 15% in the north and west. The longer-term implications of such a change may herald an increased incidence of major floods, which could have implications for the nature of river process response and river management. The Holocene landform record of the lowlands also provides evidence for the impact of changing sea-levels on estuarine and lowland river processes. The potential outcome of the combined impact of "natural" environmental change and human activities within a drainage basin is therefore hard to predict, but must be considered if we are to attempt to manage our freshwater geomorphological heritage. Conservation management of this heritage falls into two separate approaches: conservation of the relict or static features and conservation of active or dynamic environments.

TABLE 5.3. Principal threats to the freshwater geomorphic heritage of Scotland

	Threat	Generalized examples of principle impacts
1.	Mineral extraction (sand and gravel resources, mining and large-scale quarrying)	• Destruction of relict landform assemblages and stratigraphic and sedimentary records. • Reduction of sediment supply to active process systems, leading to various responses such as channel scour. • Interference with, and potential disruption of, drainage network, with potential impacts on run-off behaviour.
2.	Agriculture (intensive cultivation methods, land drainage)	• Landform damage through ploughing, ground levelling, drainage. • Episodic increases in soil eroded from fields, leading to increased sedimentation in lochs and lowland river systems. • Changes in run-off response times as a result of drainage.
3.	Other land management (dumping, drainage, disruption of active processes, construction of tracks, storage of materials)	• Degradation of landforms. • Changes in watercourse and water-body turbidity. • Changes in sediment availability – for example, temporary increases in soil erosion following track construction. • Changes in run-off response time as a result of interference with natural drainage pattern.
4.	Afforestation/ deforestation	• Temporary increases in sediment yield and run-off. • Loss of landform visibility.
5.	River management and engineering	• Destruction of active and relict landforms. • Disruption of active processes. • Potential for fundamental change in process regime (see text).
6.	Recreation	• Localized direct damage; for example, along paths and within ski fields. • Snow fences on ski fields increase localized snow accumulation which could increase meltwater potential.
7.	Commercial and industrial developments	• Large-scale damage and disruption of surface and sub-surface features. • Specific impacts may include reduced flood peak and therefore certain channel processes in rivers downstream of major abstraction facilities.

Conservation management of relict landforms

In many respects the conservation of relict landforms, such as glacio-fluvial outwash terraces, kettle holes and kames, is relatively straightforward (Gordon and Campbell, 1992). For example, Scottish Natural Heritage must be consulted about developments requiring planning consent on Sites of Special Scientific Interest (SSSIs), and also by the owner/occupier of land designated for its conservation interest, when activities identified as "potentially damaging operations" are proposed. Not all developments

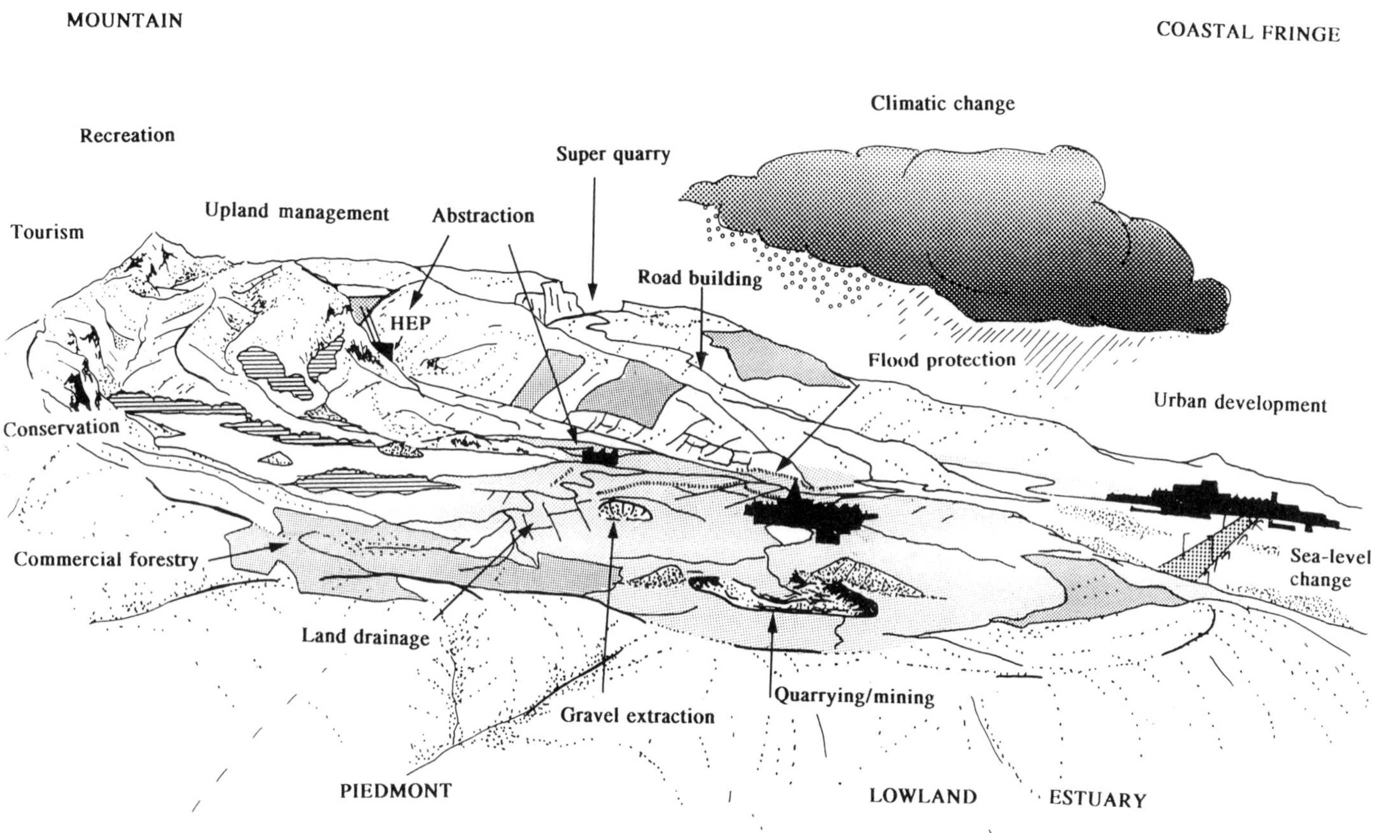

82

FIGURE 5.7. Potential threats and natural changes affecting the geomorphological interest of the freshwater resources of Scotland (modified after Newson and Sear, in press)

TABLE 5.4. Scale for use in assessing potential impacts on relict landform assemblages

Scale of increasing impact	Description of the degree of impact of potentially damaging operations on individual relict landforms and relict landform assemblages (from Werritty and Brazier, 1991a, Table 2.5).
1.	The operation is not generally applicable.
2.	The operation would obscure or mask the surface and stratigraphic exposures of the landform.
3.	The operation would cause localized disruption or destruction of part of the landform.
4.	The operation would cause general disruption to either the surface or stratigraphy of the landform.
5.	The operation would either disrupt or destroy the landform surface, stratigraphy and the relationship with other components of the (designated) area.

will damage or destroy relict geomorphological features, even though the landforms in question constitute a non-renewable resource developed under different environmental conditions. Assessing the vulnerability of individual landforms and landform assemblages is dependent on the type of development proposed. A useful approach is that of Werritty and Brazier (1991a) who developed a table of rankings (Table 5.4) for worst-case scenarios of developments such as land drainage, afforestation, deforestation, and constructing roads, walls and buildings. However, it will be difficult to develop swiftly from a reactive approach based around the conservation of designated sites to a proactive approach set within the wider remit of conservation of landscape. A national database on Scotland's geomorphological and stratigraphic heritage is required, together with further documentation of the range and scale of impacts associated with different types of development on landform and stratigraphic integrity. Further research and the compilation of an inventory is therefore needed to enable both informed and sensitive planning of developments in the landscape and effective conservation management of our relict geomorphic heritage.

Conservation management of dynamic environments

Conservation management of dynamic landforming environments is more complex, and faces several problems ranging from the development of process-response models to public relations. However, the central problem is one of a history of piecemeal river basin management in Britain (Table 5.1; Figure 5.7). On an individual basis some of the activities listed in Table 5.3 may only pose a relatively minor threat to geomorphic stability, but the potential impacts of cumulative stresses on river and lacustrine dynamics are neither well understood by researchers nor fully appreciated by water resource managers.

The development of appropriate management strategies to ensure the survival of the character and behaviour of dynamic process environments (but not necessarily the preservation of individual ephemeral landforms) is a central theme of earth science conservation. The concept of geomorphic sensitivity of dynamic river systems, based on qualitative models of river metamorphosis (Schumm, 1977), is still at a formative stage (Figure 5.8). Geomorphic sensitivity denotes the ability of a landform assemblage to withstand externally imposed change. Such changes include the effects of climatic change, and changes in the nature and degree of human interference, either directly in the river system or indirectly in the wider catchment area. In contrast to the case of relict landforms described above (Table 5.4), the nature of the active geomorphic system and its limiting thresholds (Figure 5.8) determine whether the system absorbs the externally imposed change or is sensitive to it (Werritty and Brazier, 1991b, in press). If the system is sensitive, then the initial process regime may cross an extrinsic threshold into a new process regime in which a very different assemblage of landforms is likely to develop. Such changes could be manifest by an aggrading reach of river becoming deeply entrenched as a result of sediment depletion upstream, or in a once braided river becoming increasingly sinuous as a result of changes in sediment type or river flow control. Conservation management is usually concerned with the protection of species and habitats (biological conservation) and river processes and the physical environments in which these processes operate (earth science conservation). In order to be effective, conservation management of Scotland's dynamic fluvial heritage requires further applied research to establish both the

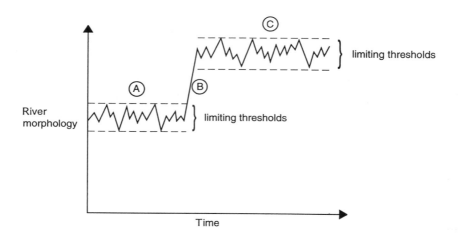

A, C **robust behaviour** - river repeatedly crossing intrinsic thresholds, but overall response stable within limiting thresholds. Negative feedback regulates change. Landforms retain stable identity as they form and reform.

B **sensitive behaviour** - in response to externally imposed change river moves across extrinsic threshold to new process regime. Landforms in original regime A destroyed and replaced by new landforms created in regime C.

FIGURE 5.8. The distinctions between robust and sensitive behaviour, the two types of geomorphic threshold and stable and unstable behaviour (from Werritty and Brazier, in press)

properties and characteristics that determine geomorphic sensitivity across a wide range of fluvial environments, and further development of methods for identifying aberrant river behaviour indicative of externally imposed change, as distinct from natural variability in river behaviour (Figure 5.8).

The way ahead

The dynamic behaviour of Scottish rivers (e.g. flooding, bank erosion and channel pattern change) constitutes a hazard when river changes impinge on human activities. Society's demand for safe and permanent solutions to these hazards means that effective approaches that are sympathetic to dynamic processes are often ignored. This conflict of interest is compounded when there is a statutory responsibility for a government department or local administrative body to take action by repairing old, or implementing new, hazard mitigation programmes. Effective conservation of rivers and water bodies is therefore faced with a considerable challenge in determining and managing the balance between continued natural environmental change and the ever increasing demands of urban and rural development on river basins.

River management will be effective only if the whole drainage basin is considered, and long-term management plans implemented that regulate the demands made throughout the river system. River management consortia are needed where all river users are represented (see chapter 31), and through which promotion of the benefits of sound conservation practice can be marketed (e.g. through making available information on river management practices that provide viable alternatives to excessively interventionist river engineering schemes where hazard mitigation is deemed necessary). Within this context the development of applied models of geomorphic sensitivity and detailed environmental sensitivity monitoring programmes need to be urgently developed for sound and holistic conservation management practice.

REFERENCES

Al-Ansari, N. A. and McManus, J. (1979). "Fluviatile sediments entering the Tay Estuary: sediment discharge from the River Earn", *Scottish Journal of Geology*, **15**, 203–216.

Al-Jabbari, M. H., McManus, J. and Al-Ansari, N. A. (1980). "Sediment and solute discharge into the Tay Estuary from the river system", *Proceedings of the Royal Society of Edinburgh*, **78B**, 15–32.

Ballantyne, C. K. (1991a). "Late Holocene erosion in upland Britain: climatic deterioration or human influence?", *The Holocene*, **1**, 81–85.

Ballantyne, C. K. (1991b). "Holocene geomorphic activity in the Scottish Highlands", *Scottish Geographical Magazine*, **107**, 84–98.

Battarbee, R. W., Stevenson, A. C., Rippey, B., Fletcher, C., Natkanski, J., Wik, M. and Flower, R. J. (1989). "Causes of lake acidification in Galloway, south-west Scotland: a palaeoecological evaluation of the relative roles of atmospheric contamination and catchment change for two acidified sites with non-afforested catchments", *Journal of Ecology*, **77**, 651–672.

Benn, D. I. (1992). "Scottish landform examples – 5. The Achnasheen terraces", *Scottish Geographical Magazine*, **108**, 128–131.

Birks, H. J. B. (1988). "Long-term ecological change in the British uplands", in *Ecological Change in the Uplands* (Eds M. B. Usher and D. B. A. Thompson), pp. 37–56, Blackwell Scientific Publications, Oxford.

Bluck, B. J. (1971). "Sedimentation in the meandering River Endrick", *Scottish Journal of Geology*, **7**, 93–138.

Bluck, B. J. (1976). "Sedimentation in some Scottish rivers of low sinuosity", *Transactions of the Royal Society of Edinburgh*, **69**, 425–456.

Brazier, V. and Ballantyne, C. K. (1989). "Late Holocene debris cone evolution in Glen Feshie, western Cairngorm Mountains, Scotland", *Transactions of the Royal Society of Edinburgh: Earth Sciences*, **80**, 17–24.

Brazier, V., Whittington, G. and Ballantyne, C. K. 1988 "Holocene debris cone evolution in Glen Etive, Western Grampian Highlands, Scotland", *Earth Surface Processes and Landforms*, **13**, 525–531.

Brazier, V., Kirkbride, M. and Werritty, A. (1993). "Scottish landform examples: the River Clyde–Medwin-Meanders", *Scottish Geographical Magazine*, **109**, 45–49.

Bremner, A. (1942). "The origin of the Scottish river system", *Scottish Geographical Magazine*, **58**, 15–20, 54–59, 99–103.

Duck, R. W. and McManus, J. (1990). "Relationships between catchment characteristics, land use and sediment yield in the Midland Valley of Scotland", in *Soil Erosion on Agricultural Land* (Ed. J. Boardman), pp. 284–299, John Wiley, Chichester.

Emeleus, C. H. and Gyopari, M. C. (1992). *British Tertiary Volcanic Province, Geological Conservation Review Series*, Chapman and Hall, London.

Fleet, H. (1938). "Erosion surfaces in the Grampian Highlands of Scotland", *Rapport de la Commission pour la Cartographie des Surfaces d'Aplanissement Tertiares*, Union Geographique Internationale, Paris, 91–94.

Fleming, G. (1970). "Sediment balance of the Clyde Estuary", *Proceedings of the American Society of Civil Engineers, Hydraulics Division*, **96**, HY11, 2219–2230.

Geikie, A. (1865). *The Scenery of Scotland Viewed in Connection with its Physical Geology*, Macmillan, London.

Geikie, A. (1901). *The Scenery of Scotland Viewed in Connection with its Physical Geology*, Macmillan, London, 3rd edition.

George, T. N. (1965). "The geological growth of Scotland", in *The Geology of Scotland* (Ed. G. Y. Craig), pp. 1–48, Oliver and Boyd, Edinburgh.

Gordon, J. E. and Campbell, S. (1992) "Conservation of glacial deposits in Great Britain: a framework for assessment and protection of Sites of Special Scientific Interest", *Geomorphology*, **6**, 89–97.

Hall, A. M. (1987) "Weathering and relief development in Buchan, Scotland", in *International Geomorphology 1986* Part II, (Ed. V. Gardiner), pp. 991–1005, John Wiley, Chichester.

Hall, A. M. (1991). "Pre-Quaternary landscape evolution in the Scottish Highlands", *Transactions of the Royal Society of Edinburgh: Earth Sciences*, **82**, 1–26.

Huntley, B. (1991). "Historical lessons for the future", in *Scientific Management of Temperate Communities for Conservation* (Eds I. F. Spellerberg, F. B. Goldsmith and M. G. Morris), pp. 473–503, Blackwell Scientific Publications, Oxford.

Jones, V. J., Stevenson, A. C. and Battarbee, R. W. (1989). "The acidification of lakes in Galloway, south-west Scotland: a diatom and pollen study of the post-glacial history of the Round Loch of Glenhead", *Journal of Ecology*, **77**, 1–23.

Linton, D. L. (1949). "Some Scottish river captures re-examined", *Scottish Geographical Magazine*, **65**, 123–132.

Linton, D. L. (1951a). "Problems of Scottish scenery", *Scottish Geographical Magazine*, **67**, 65–85.

Linton, D. L. (1951b). "Watershed breaching by ice in Scotland", *Transactions of the Institute of British Geographers*, **15**, 1–15.

Linton, D. L. (1954). "Some Scottish river captures re-examined. III. The beheading of the Don", *Scottish Geographical Magazine*, **70**, 64–78.

Linton, D. L. (1957). "Radiating valleys in glaciated lands", *Tijdschrift van het Koninklijk Nederlandsch Aardrijkskundig Genootschap*, **74**, 297–312.

Linton, D. L. (1959). "Morphological contrasts between eastern and western Scotland", in *Geographical Essays in Memory of Alan G. Ogilvie* (Eds R. Miller and J. W. Watson), pp. 16–45, Nelson, Edinburgh.

Lowe, P. A., Duck, R. W. and McManus, J. (1991). "A bathymetric reappraisal of Loch Muick, Aberdeenshire", *Scottish Geographical Magazine*, **107**, 110–115.

McManus, J. (1967). "Pre-glacial diversion of drainage through the Perth Gap", *Scottish Geographical Magazine*, **83**, 138–139.

McManus, J. (1968). "The hydrology of the Tay Basin", in *Dundee and District* (Ed. S. J. Jones), pp. 107–124, British Association for the Advancement of Science, Dundee.

McManus, J. (1972). "Estuarine development and sediment distribution with particular reference to the Tay", *Proceedings of the Royal Society of Edinburgh*, **71B**, 97–115.

McManus, J. (1986). "Land derived sediment and solute transport in the Forth and Tay estuaries", *Journal of the Geological Society of London*, **143**, 927–931.

McManus, J. and Duck, R. W. (1988). "Scottish freshwater lochs and reservoirs: a physical perspective", *Scottish Geographical Magazine,* **104**, 97–107.

McEwen, L. J. (1989). "River channel changes in response to flooding in the upper River Dee catchment, Aberdeenshire, over the last 200 years", in *Floods: Hydrological, Sedimentological and Geomorphological Implications* (Eds K. Bevan and P. Carling), pp. 219–238, John Wiley, Chichester.

McEwen, L. J. (in press). "Site assessment criteria for the conservation of fluvial systems: the Scottish experience", in *Conserving our Landscape: Evolving Landforms and Ice-Age Heritage*, English Nature, Peterborough.

McEwen, L. J. and Werritty, A. (1988). "The hydrology and long-term geomorphic significance of a flash flood in the Cairngorm Mountains, Scotland", *Catena*, **15**, 361–377.

Maizels, J. K. (1988). "Sediment size and channel changes in braided and meandering gravel-bed streams, upper Deeside, Scotland", in *International Conference on River Regime* (Ed. W. R. White), pp. 215–230, John Wiley, Chichester.

Maizels, J. K. and Aitken, J. F. (1991). "Palaeohydrological change during deglaciation in upland Britain: case study from northeast Scotland", in *Temperate Palaeohydrology* (Eds L. Starkel, K. J. Gregory and J. B. Thornes), pp. 105–145, John Wiley, Chichester.

Murray, J. and Pullar, L. (1910). *Bathymetrical Survey of the Fresh Water Lochs of Scotland*, Challenger Office, Edinburgh.

Newson, M. D. (1981). "Mountain streams", in *British Rivers* (Ed. J. Lewin), pp. 59–89, Allen & Unwin, London.

Newson, M. and Sear, D. (in press). "River conservation, river dynamics, river maintenance: contradictions?", in *Conserving our Landscape: Evolving Landforms and Ice-Age Heritage*, English Nature, Peterborough.

Peach, B. N. and Horne, J. (1910). "The Scottish lochs in relation to the geological features of the country", in *Bathymetrical Survey of the Freshwater Lochs of Scotland, vol. 1.* (Eds J. Murray and L. Pullar), pp. 439–513, Challenger Office, Edinburgh.

Peach, B. N. and Horne, J. (1930). *Chapters on the Geology of Scotland*, Oxford University Press, London.

Peacock, J. D. (1986). "Alluvial fans and an outwash fan in upper Glen Roy, Lochaber", *Scottish Journal of Geology*, **22**, 347–366.

Pennington, W., Haworth, E. Y., Bonny, A. P. and Lishman, J. P. (1972). "Lake sediments in northern Scotland", *Philosophical Transactions of the Royal Society of London*, **264B**, 191–294.

Reid, G. and McManus, J. (1987). "Sediment transport paths in the Moray Firth, Scotland", *Journal of the Geological Society of London*, **144**, 179–186.

Rice, R. J. (1962). "The morphology of the Angus coastal lowlands", *Scottish Geographical Magazine*, **78**, 5–14.

Robertson-Rintoul, M. S. E. (1986). "A quantitative soil–stratigraphic approach to the correlation and dating of post-glacial river terraces in Glen Feshie, western Cairngorms", *Earth Surface Processes and Landforms*, **11**, 605–617.

Schumm, S. A. (1977). *The Fluvial System*, John Wiley, New York.

Sissons, J. B. (1967). *The Evolution of Scotland's Scenery*, Oliver and Boyd, Edinburgh.

Sissons, J. B. (1976). *The Geomorphology of the British Isles: Scotland*, Methuen, London.

Sissons, J. B. (1977). "Former ice-dammed lakes in Glen Moriston, Inverness-shire, and their significance in upland Britain", *Transactions of the Institute of British Geographers*, n.s. **4**, 12–29.

Sissons, J. B. and Cornish, R. (1983). "Fluvial landforms associated with ice-dammed lake drainage in upper Glen Roy, Scotland", *Proceedings of the Geologists' Association*, **94**, 45–52.

Soons, J. M. (1958). "Landscape evolution in the Ochil Hills", *Scottish Geographical Magazine*, **74**, 86–97.

Stevenson, A. C., Jones, V. J. and Battarbee, R. W. (1990). "The cause of peat erosion: a palaeolimnological approach", *New Phytologist*, **114**, 727–735.

Sugden, D. E. (1968). "The selectivity of glacial erosion in the Cairngorm Mountains, Scotland", *Transactions of the Institute of British Geographers*, **45**, 79–92.

Sutherland, D. G. (1984). "The Quaternary deposits and landforms of Scotland and the neighbouring shelves: a review", *Quaternary Science Reviews*, **3**, 157–254.

Sutherland, D. G. (1991). "Late Devensian glacial deposits and glaciation in Scotland and the adjacent offshore region", in *Glacial Deposits in Great Britain and Ireland* (Eds J. Ehlers, P. L. Gibbard and J. Rose), pp. 53–59, Balkema, Rotterdam.

Sutherland, D. G. and Gordon, J. E. (1993). "The Quaternary in Scotland", in *The Quaternary of Scotland, Geological Conservation Review Series* (Eds J. E. Gordon and D. G. Sutherland), pp. 11–47, Chapman and Hall, London.

Vail, P. R., Mitchum, R. M. Jr, Thompson, S., III, Sangree, J. R., Dubb, J. N. and Haslid, W. G. (1977). "Sequence stratigraphy and global changes of sea level", in *Seismic Stratigraphy – Applications to Hydrocarbon Exploration* (Ed. C. E. Payton), pp. 49–205, Memoirs of the American Association of Petroleum Geologists, **26**.

Werritty, A. and Brazier, V. (1991a). *The Geomorphology, Conservation and Management of the River Feshie SSSI*, Nature Conservancy Council Report, Peterborough.

Werritty, A. and Brazier, V. (1991b). *Geomorphological Aspects of the Proposed Strathspey Flood Alleviation Scheme*, Report to the Institute of Hydrology, Wallingford.

Werritty, A. and Brazier, V. (in press). "Geomorphic sensitivity and the conservation of fluvial geomorphology SSSIs", in *Conserving our Landscape: Evolving Landforms and Ice-Age Heritage*.

Werritty, A. and Ferguson, R. I. (1980). "Pattern changes in a Scottish braided river over 1, 30 and 200 years", in *Timescales in Geomorphology* (Eds R. A. Cullingford, D. A. Davidson and J. Lewin), pp. 247–259, John Wiley, Chichester.

Werritty, A. and McEwen, L. J. (in press). "The fluvial geomorphology of Scotland's rivers", in *The Fluvial Geomorphology of Britain*, (Ed. K. J. Gregory), Chapman and Hall, London.

Wilson, J. S. G. (1888). "A bathymetrical survey of the chief Perthshire Lochs and their relation to the glaciation of that district", *Scottish Geographical Magazine*, **4**, 251–258.

6

Water Chemistry

R. HARRIMAN

Freshwater Fisheries Laboratory, Faskally, Pitlochry, PH16 5LB, UK

and

K. B. PUGH

North East River Purification Board, Greyhope Road, Aberdeen, AB1 3RD, UK

INTRODUCTION

The quality and quantity of its fresh waters is one of Scotland's greatest assets. Although it is unlikely that any surface waters in Scotland have completely escaped man's influence (see Chapter 7), the quality, by most European standards, is considered to be excellent for over 90% of the area.

To give a complete and detailed description of the chemical characteristics of Scottish fresh waters is clearly an impossible task as water from many remote lochs and streams has probably never been analyzed. Despite this drawback there has undoubtedly been a significant expansion of the Scottish freshwater database during the past decade resulting from environmental concerns, such as acidification and afforestation, and the need for stricter chemical controls on pollutant discharges. New instrumentation and rapidly developing analytical techniques have allowed chemists to identify and measure hitherto undetectable organic pollutants. At the same time it has also been recognized that continuous chemical surveillance to cover all pollution incidents is not a feasible proposition; therefore, the recent introduction of a complementary biological classification by the Scottish River Purification Boards (SRPBs) has been designed to fill this gap. This subtle change in emphasis has also altered the classification of rivers from a "chemical" basis to a "quality" basis.

While an assessment of the "well-being" or "drinkability" of fresh water has normally been determined on the basis of a few key chemical criteria, i.e. Biochemical Oxygen Demand (BOD), oxygen content, ammonia, etc., the current biological classification uses aquatic biota (fish, macroinvertebrates) to integrate day-to-day and season-to-season changes in chemistry.

The Fresh Waters of Scotland: A National Resource of International Significance
Edited by P. S. Maitland, P. J. Boon and D. S. McLusky. © 1994 John Wiley & Sons Ltd

In the useful ecological booklet by Calow *et al.* (1990), it is emphasized that water "chemistry" and water "quality" are not synonymous; the former simply represents a wide range of chemical constituents while the latter reflects a wider-based assessment of the "fitness for a specified use" of fresh water based on chemical limits, biological integrity and a management-based classification. A major assumption with this type of quality index is that the relationship between selected chemical criteria and biological response is well established. The evolution of this concept of Environmental Quality Objectives (EQOs) and Environmental Quality Standards (EQSs) in relation to pollution control is covered later in this volume (see Chapter 20) while in this chapter we consider freshwater chemistry both in terms of distribution patterns and classification.

HISTORICAL PERSPECTIVE

According to Smith and Lyle (1979) there are about 3800 lochs of >4 ha in Scotland and a similar number of burns (streams). In terms of the UK freshwater resource about 69% of standing waters can be classed as "lochs" and 66% of running waters as "burns" (see also Chapters 2 and 3). Murray and Pullar (1910) calculated that one quarter of all standing water in Scotland is held in Loch Ness while over one half (by volume) is contained in the five largest lochs – Ness, Lomond, Morar, Tay and Awe. In their classic study, the above authors determined many geophysical characteristics of Scottish lochs but the unfortunate omission of any systematic chemical sampling has deprived scientists of a chemical database which would now be considered as a unique environmental snapshot of historical water chemistry. In fact, remarkably few studies of the chemistry of these large lochs, or smaller, remote upland lochs and streams, have been attempted. These studies include Bailey-Watts and Duncan (1981) for five of Scotland's largest lochs, Gorham (1957) for Cairngorm lochs, and Harriman *et al.* (1987) for remote lochs and burns in Galloway. More recent and extensive databases are described later and in greater detail.

Early chemical data for Scottish rivers were predominantly linked to concerns over human health. For example, a paper by Smith (1852) describes investigations into the action of River Dee water on lead pipes and cisterns. It provides an interesting insight into the chemical methodology used in the mid and late 19th century, especially in the context of trace metals such as lead. Many gallons of water were evaporated down to dryness so that concentrations down to 200 μg L^{-1} could be detected. A few ecological studies also included chemical information (e.g. Traquair, 1892) which was generally provided by city analysts. An example of data from these early studies is given in Table 6.1.

One of the first attempts to set limits on certain chemical and physical constituents of Scottish rivers was published by The Rivers Pollution Commission (1872). This report identified sewage and industrial discharges as the major polluting sources in rivers and recommended maximum allowable levels of many chemicals. Although many of these recommendations never reached the statute book, some (e.g. suspended solids) were adopted and are still in use today.

Systematic sampling of major rivers on a national scale began in earnest in the 1950s with the setting up of the SRPBs, which established Scottish sites within the

TABLE 6.1. Historical chemical data for Loch Enoch (Traquair, 1892) and the Aberdeenshire Dee and Don (1850 data from Smith, 1852). Data as grains per imperial gallon (1 grain per gallon = 14.3 mg L^{-1}

Determinand	Enoch	Dee	Don
Carbonate of lime	0.04	0.85	2.18
Sulphate of lime	0.08	0.121	0.17
Sulphate of magnesia	0.15	0.323	1.00
Chloride of sodium (plus potassium)	1.01	0.67	1.32
Phosphate of lime and iron	–	0.08	0.38
Silica	–	0.14	0.60
Loss on ignition (organic matter)	0.54	1.82	3.00

UK Harmonised Monitoring (HM) network. During the past decade many smaller river catchments have been sampled under the SRPB network.

DATABASES

For the purpose of this chapter two databases have been used to describe the general chemical characteristics of Scottish fresh waters. Firstly, for running waters, a dataset covering all major rivers and many minor streams has been collected by the SRPBs. Together, the SRPBs regularly monitor over 2000 sampling sites, 60% of which are used to determine the impact of point source discharges. The remaining 40% are strategic sites (i.e. on unpolluted stretches or at the confluent end of tributaries) to provide baseline data for chemical characterization. Most of the major river systems are sampled just upstream of any tidal influence and these sites form part of the HM network. Many of these chemical and biological data are compiled by the Civil Engineering and Water Services unit of the Scottish Office Environment Department to produce approximately quinquennial reports on the quality of Scottish rivers (e.g. Scottish Office Environment Department, 1992). This valuable database is available in the SRPB public registry.

For standing waters, the only extensive database covering both upland and lowland sites is that collected by the Freshwater Group of the UK Critical Loads Advisory Committee. This study, sponsored by the Department of the Environment, provides information on more than 750 of those waters most sensitive to acidification, each representing a 10 km grid square. While the SRPB database covers the four major chemical groups of constituents (i.e. major ions, trace metals, organics and nutrients), the Critical Load database is currently limited to major ions and some nutrients.

Data from other reports and papers, already referred to, have also been considered and we recognize that many individual sites have been investigated in much greater detail by universities and research institutes. Extensive databases are also held by Regional Water Authorities for compliance with drinking water directives, whilst large Scottish industries, such as the whisky distillers and Scottish Hydro-Electric, hold chemical information on streams and large reservoirs respectively. This information will obviously extend the size of the database used, but general chemical relationships are unlikely to be significantly altered by its inclusion. Stringent quality control procedures are now applied to most routine chemical analyses whereas the datasets of 30–40 years ago would have few, if any, control procedures. Consequently, data collected during the past two decades at laboratories located throughout the UK can be compared with a great degree of confidence even when different methods and procedures are employed.

FACTORS AFFECTING FRESHWATER CHEMISTRY

One of the most common problems associated with assessing environmental damage in fresh water is the lack of background information on the chemical and biological status before the onset of a specific pollutant input. Consequently, any attempt to predict the behaviour and fate of even the most common pollutants has proved to be extremely difficult. To some extent this problem was addressed by the establishment of the SRPB monitoring sites in all the major river catchments during the 1950s. In recent years this network has been updated and modified, both in terms of the improved range and detectability of chemical determinands and the use of biological indicators, and now provides a valuable baseline against which "ecosystem" trends can be measured.

For Scottish waters the terms "pristine" and "natural" are probably misnomers as it is unlikely that any waters are free from some evidence of anthropogenic pollutants, especially those derived from emissions of sulphur and carbonaceous particles (see Chapter 7). Nevertheless, the majority of lochs and rivers still retain "natural" chemical "fingerprints" which are derived from two major sources – soil/bedrock contributions and marine inputs.

Soil/bedrock contributions

The dissolution and weathering of rocks and soils determines the acid/base status of most Scottish fresh waters, especially those located in upland areas. The extent of these processes is reflected in pH, alkalinity and base cation levels (Ca and Mg) which are generally well correlated ($r > 0.9$). Unlike many other countries (e.g. Norway) there is a large spatial variability in the acid/base status of Scottish waters which is due to the exceptional diversity of the geological environment (Craig, 1983). Despite this great diversity, many of the common geological types produce waters of similar quality. A comparison of the major acid/base components for four of the major rock types in Scotland is shown in Table 6.2. Only where limestone, or other fast-weathering rocks, intrude into catchments does the chemistry change to a great extent. Because of this feature the distribution of alkalinity and calcium levels in Scottish waters is skewed towards the lower range. Thus, while calcium levels in the Critical Loads Survey ranged between 12 and 6045 μeq L^{-1}, the mean value of 386 μeq L^{-1} was more than double the median value of 165 μeq L^{-1}. On a regional basis the waters of the Tweed basin probably reflect the greatest geological influence in Scotland with calcium levels consistently exceeding 1000 μeq L^{-1} (Figure 6.1). Local limestone beds and dykes are scattered throughout Scotland (Rock, 1989) and are often surrounded by granitic type rocks overlain with acid peaty soils. The famous Durness limestone lochs – Croispol, Borralie and Caladail – are good examples of

TABLE 6.2. Water chemistry derived from major Scottish rock types (modified from Webb and Walling (1992). All units as μeq L^{-1} except pH

Parameter	Rock type			
	Granite	Gneiss	Sandstone	Limestone
pH	6.6	6.6	6.8	7.9
HCO$_3$	128	136	125	3195
Ca	39	60	88	2560
Mg	31	57	63	640
Na	88	80	51	34
K	8	10	21	13
Cl	0	0	0	–
SO$_4$	31	56	95	85

isolated calcium-rich waters, having calcium concentrations in the range 1500 – 2000 μeq L^{-1}. On a river catchment scale, the Kirkton Burn at Balquhidder provides a rare example of a limestone outcrop at the head of the catchment producing high alkalinity water in the headwater reaches (Ca *ca* 1000 μeq L^{-1}) which is subsequently neutralized by more acid waters in the lower reaches to produce calcium levels of around 250 μeq L^{-1}. Many other biogeochemical processes operate in fresh waters, especially in standing waters (see Stumm and Morgan, 1970; Stumm, 1985), but consideration of their effects on acid/base status is outside the scope of this chapter.

Marine inputs

For the majority of fresh waters in Scotland marine salts constitute the highest proportion of the total ion content. Concentrations of sodium and chloride can reach 5000 μeq L^{-1} in the Western Isles compared with 40 μeq L^{-1} in the small, remote Cairngorm lochs (Figure 6.2). Inputs of marine salts are random and episodic and predominantly associated with westerly and south-westerly gales. Levels of marine salts (Na, Cl, Mg and SO$_4$) increase by two- to three-fold in every freshwater system after major storms such as those recorded during 1986, 1989 and 1993. The impact of such episodes has attracted considerable interest, especially in the context of surface water acidification, because pH levels can decline considerably during these events, causing concern for the survival of aquatic biota.

The mechanism by which this acid response is produced has been described by Harriman and Wells (1985) as a simple ion-exchange process whereby soil exchange sites are saturated by the excess Na$^+$ ions and consequently release an equivalent quantity of other cations, including H$^+$; hence the reduction in pH. In catchments where soils are acidified by atmospheric pollutants the effect on surface water pH appears to be more intense.

The biological implications of sea-salt-generated acid episodes are not yet clear (see Chapter 24) because base cations such as calcium, which are known to protect biota from acid stress, also increase in concentration, thus mitigating the toxic effects of lower pH.

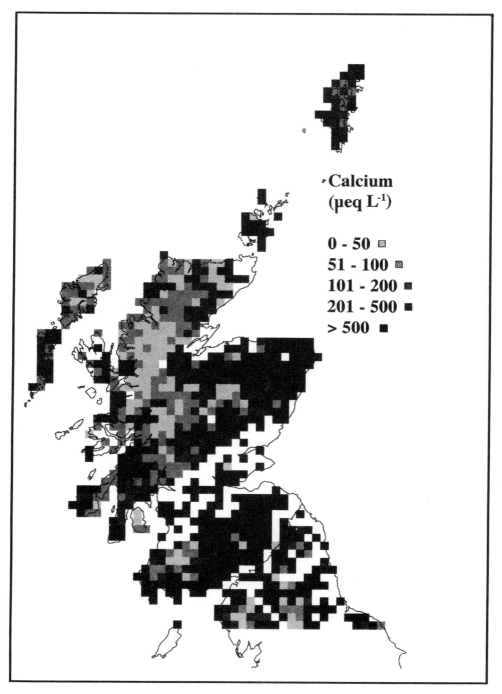

FIGURE 6.1. Distribution of calcium in Scottish standing waters based on one site per 10 × 10 km square. White squares indicate no sample

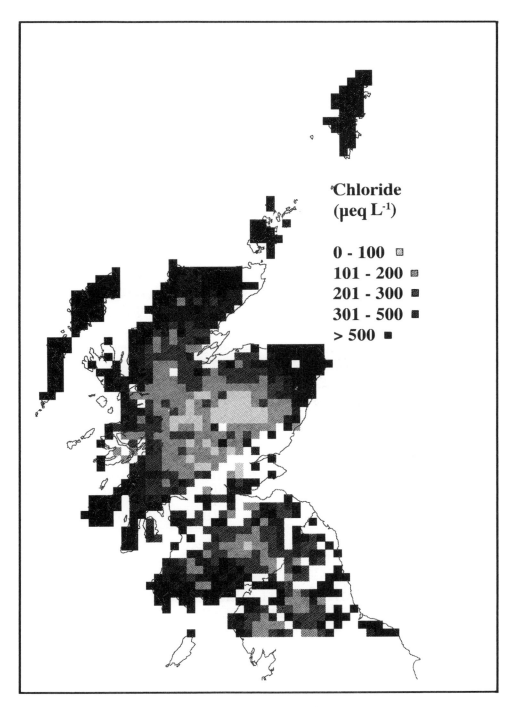

FIGURE 6.2. Distribution of chloride in Scottish standing waters based on one site per 10 × 10 km square. White squares indicate no sample

To separate the marine ions from those derived from catchment sources the ratios of ions to chloride in sea-salts are used: e.g. $SO_4/Cl = 0.104$ $Mg/Cl = 0.2$ on an equivalent basis. Chloride is generally preferred to sodium because in some areas of Scotland (e.g. the Cairngorm region) sodium is released as a result of catchment weathering and is therefore associated with alkalinity generation rather than sea-salt inputs. The effects of sea-salt inputs are most evident not, as might be expected, in coastal regions but 20–50 km inland where the relative change in the chloride gradient is greatest.

POLLUTANT SOURCES

Superimposed on these natural chemical imprints are man-made pollutant sources which are perceived to cause a deterioration in water quality. These types of pollutants are continually changing and this inevitably creates difficulties in their detection and measurement. Pollutants which enter watercourses from point sources are, in theory, more easy to detect and treat than diffuse sources. However, in most cases it is the intermittent nature of the discharges that creates difficulties in designing appropriate sampling strategies.

A summary of the major pollutant sources in Scottish waters is given in Table 6.3 with some indication of the source type and chemical pollutant.

TABLE 6.3. Major pollutant sources in Scotland and their chemical impact

	Source[a]	Type[b]	Increased levels of
1. Agricultural fertilizers	(C)	(D)	N, P, K
2. Crop spraying	(I)	(D)	Pesticides, herbicides
3. Sewage treatment works	(C)	(P)	BOD, N, P, organics, etc.
4. Urban stormwater discharges	(I)	(D)	Potentially all pollutants
5. Industrial discharges	(C)	(P)	Potentially all pollutants
6. Silage and farm wastes	(I)	(P/D)	BOD, N, P, NH_4
7. Mining	(I)	(P)	Trace metals
8. Fish farming	(C)	(D)	N, P, BOD
9. Atmospheric deposition	(C)	(D)	N, S
10. Forestry practices	(C)	(D)	N, P, K, herbicides, pesticides

a (C) Continuous, (I) Intermittent
b (D) Diffuse, (P) Point

CLASSIFICATION AND CHEMICAL CHARACTERISTICS OF SCOTTISH FRESH WATERS

Classification

In the previous section the natural constituents of Scottish fresh waters are classified in terms of geochemical characteristics and marine inputs. Other classification systems based on physical criteria (e.g. depth, elevation, water retention index) have been described in Chapters 2 and 3. For chemical and quality purposes three examples are described below.

Quality criteria

The basic chemical classification system used by RPBs in Scotland has remained relatively unchanged for the past 15 years. While modifications to both the chemical and biological systems are likely in the future, the retention of the same system does allow direct comparisons to be made between previous surveys. The present chemical classification is heavily biased towards organic pollutants, which accentuates the key role of BOD and dissolved oxygen in determining which quality band any water should occupy (Scottish Office Environment Department, 1992). Recently an equivalent four-class biological classification has been developed which is based on the

TABLE 6.4. Comparison of river water quality in Scotland using chemical (c) and biological (b) classification (Scottish Office Environment Department, 1992)

| RPB | % of total monitored river length in each class | | | |
	Class 1/A	Class 2/B	Class 3/C	Class 4/D
Clyde	c 93.4	5.8	0.6	0.2
	b 68.2	24.9	3.0	3.9
Forth	c 84.5	9.8	4.4	1.3
	b 66.5	23.3	5.9	4.3
Highland	c 99.6	0.4	0	0
	b 81.2	18.8	0	0
North East	c 99.4	0.5	0.1	0
	b 75.0	20.5	3.2	1.3
Solway	c 98.3	1.4	0.2	0.1
	b 88.2	10.8	1.0	0
Tay	c 99.0	1.0	0	0
	b 87.4	10.9	1.7	0
Tweed	c 99.7	0.3	0	0
	b 86.6	11.4	2.0	0
All	c 97.0	2.4	0.5	0.1
	b 78.5	18.1	2.1	1.3

median of three predictive Ecological Quality Indices (EQIs). Although the chemical and biological classes are not directly comparable, and the length of rivers sampled for each index is different, there are clear indications that the biological classification system produces a lower quality status than the chemical system (Table 6.4).

The finding is not unexpected as biota integrate the "whole" chemical climate including short-term pollutant discharges which could be missed during weekly or monthly chemical sampling. Other chemical indices have been developed; for example, the Water Quality Index (WQI) incorporates a much wider range of chemical parameters which are subjectively ranked in order of their biological importance (Scottish Development Department, 1976).

Nutrient-based criteria

Nutrient enrichment and associated effects on biota, commonly termed eutrophica-tion, has been recognized as a major environmental problem in Scotland for many decades. Scientific interest probably peaked in the late 1960s to early 1970s during which period the major International Biological Programme (IBP) on Loch Leven was completed (see Chapter 22). Despite the movement towards more pressing environmental problems such as freshwater acidification and afforestation, there still remain many uncertainties associated with nutrient enrichment and removal. Classifi-cation of waters in terms of their nutrient status is well established. While nitrogen and phosphorus have been identified as the key limiting nutrients, other elements such as silica, carbon, potassium and molybdenum are known to influence biological production under certain circumstances. Typical trophic bands associated with a range of phosphorus and nitrogen levels are presented in Table 6.5.

TABLE 6.5. Trophic state classification by total P and N of Vollen-weider (1968)

Trophic classification	Total P (μg L^{-1})	Inorganic-N (μg L^{-1})
1. Ultra-oligotrophic	<5	<200
2. Oligo-mesotrophic	5–10	200–400
3. Meso-eutrophic	10–30	300–650
4. Eu-polytrophic	30–100	500–1500
5. Polytrophic	>100	>1500

Attempts to use catchment inputs to predict phosphorus (P) concentrations and phytoplankton production in lochs have resulted in the development of various models (Vollenweider, 1968; Dillon and Rigler, 1974) which incorporate estimates of phosphorus retention coefficients based on aerial P loading and sedimentation rate coefficients. Nutrient levels are routinely obtained for many of the major Scottish rivers (see Table 6.6) but data on small upland lochs are extremely sparse.

A more extensive discussion of nutrient/phytoplankton interactions is given in Chapter 22.

Acidification-based criteria

During the past 20 years the ecological effects of acidic deposition in Scotland have received considerable attention culminating in the government sponsored symposium in Edinburgh during 1988 (Scottish Development Department, 1989), and an interna-tional conference in Glasgow in 1990 (see, for example, Billet and Cresser, 1992). Patterns of surface water acidification are described by Harriman (1989). More recently the UK Government has publicly announced its intention to reduce sulphur dioxide emissions by 30% by 1995, 60% by 2003 and 80% by 2010, relative to 1980 levels. The cornerstone of this abatement policy is the Critical Load concept which essentially classifies surface waters in terms of their sensitivity to acidification. Thus

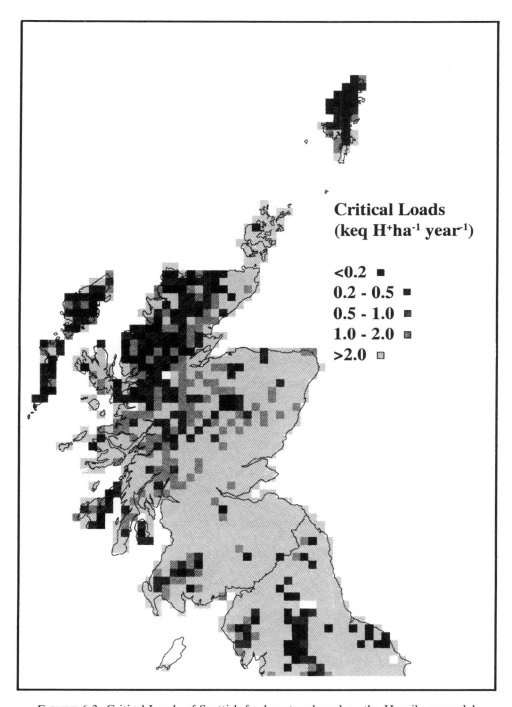

FIGURE 6.3. Critical Loads of Scottish fresh waters based on the Henriksen model

the Critical Load is the deposition threshold above which damage to the freshwater ecosystem may occur.

As would be expected, the most sensitive regions (lowest Critical Loads) are located in upland regions of central and western Scotland (Figure 6.3) where slow-weathering, siliceous rocks predominate. Details of Critical Load methodology and sites where Critical Loads are exceeded are given by Harriman and Christie (1993).

Other classification systems may be developed in the future using the Critical Load concept – for example, trace metals and pesticides – but the sources, fate and distribution of such substances have still to be established.

Chemical characteristics

Running waters

Table 6.6 summarizes the mean concentrations of chemical determinands measured during 1991 at Harmonised Monitoring sites on 10 of the major river catchments in Scotland. The data reflect the net effects of all catchment and atmospheric inputs upstream of tidal influences. Table 6.6 includes parameters used to describe quality indices (e.g. BOD, dissolved oxygen (DO) and ammonia); major ions (e.g. Cl, SO_4, Ca, Na), and nutrient status (NO_3, NO_2 and PO_4). These data are compared with environmental quality standards or limit values obtained from a variety of sources (Gardiner and Zabel, 1991).

The results indicate extremely good quality in most of these river systems with only the Clyde and Don showing significant departures from the best WQI score of 100. On the Clyde the lower index is mainly due to high BOD and reduced oxygen levels, while the low index on the Don is predominantly caused by elevated nutrient levels – especially nitrate and ammonia. This situation is not entirely unexpected as the sampling locations on both these rivers are within the conurbations of Glasgow and Aberdeen respectively, where major discharges of sewage and industrial effluents are present.

Table 6.7 summarizes the available data on trace metal concentrations. It should be noted that a range of EQSs are given which are hardness-related. Again these rivers are notable for their low trace metal content; in fact, only a few minor tributaries have elevated trace metal content, associated with mine drainage problems.

A more recent requirement is the estimation of "Red List" trace organics as part of the EC "Dangerous Substances" directive. Of the 19 individual or groups of substances listed in Table 6.8 only the concentration of DDT in the Clyde exceeds the limit values and most are below the analytical detection limit. Other toxic, persistent and bioaccumulating organics include chloroform, carbon tetrachloride, and tri- and tetra-chloroethylene, but the levels of all these substances are below the detection limit at all sites. The only known locations where the EQSs are exceeded are at sites where timber preserving agents are used.

Standing waters

Using the Critical Loads database the mean concentration of major ions for 643 standing waters is given in Table 6.9. The sources of different ion groups can be

TABLE 6.6 Water quality of the major Scottish rivers 1991 – major chemical and physical components. Determinands as mg L^{-1} unless otherwise stated

	Clyde	Ness	Spey	Dee (Grampian)	Don	Tay	Forth	Tweed	Annan	Dee (Solway)	Environmental Quality Standards[e]
River NGR	NS 595 644	NH 664 446	NJ 341 596	NJ 859 004	NJ 926 093	NO 122 234	NS 775 955	NT 890 473	NY 191 704	NX 733 642	
LTA[d] flow (m³ s⁻¹)	47	87	64	46	20	173	50	78	28	42	
DO (%)	76	96	99	95	94	98	85	105	102	99	93–109[c]
DO	9.0	11.2	11.6	11.4	11.0	11.4	9.4	11.9	11.9	11.2	9.0[b]
BOD	4.4	1.1	0.9	0.8	2.0	1.4	1.4	2.2	2.8	2.2	3[a], 0[b], 1[c]
SS	11	1	3	2	9	4	6	8	6	3	25[a], 10[b]
NH₄-N	0.72	<0.01	0.03	0.04	0.30	0.03	0.06	0.07	0.05	0.05	0.1[c]
TON	2.56	0.19	0.32	1.04	3.06	0.48	0.50	2.09	1.50	0.35	11.3[a], 0.5[c]
NO₂-N	0.21	<0.01	<0.01	<0.01	0.04	<0.02	0.01	0.02	0.03	0.01	–
PO₄-P	0.47	<0.01	<0.01	<0.01	0.11	0.03	0.02	0.06	0.04	0.01	0.065[b], 0.03[c]
SiO₂-Si	–	–	2.63	2.71	5.0	–	3.0	–	1.52	1.26	–
SO₄	–	1.4	17	–	–	15	11.0	–	12.4	5.0	150[a]
Alk	86	5	9	13	42	6	25	18	51	5	–
Cl	53	9	–	12	26	–	–	–	14	10	200[a]
Cond(µS cm⁻¹)	392	45	84	99	247	76	93	245	171	57	1000[a], 50–190[c]
pH (units)	7.5	6.8	6.5	6.4	6.9	7.5	7.2	8.0	7.6	6.6	6–9[b], 6.5–8.0[c]
Na	–	4.3	5.1	7.7	13.0	–	7.0	–	8.0	5.6	–
K	–	0.3	0.6	1.1	1.6	–	0.8	–	1.6	0.6	–
Ca	–	3.9	5.3	7.1	16.0	6.9	10.4	–	22.9	3.3	–
Mg	–	1.2	2.3	1.9	4.3	1.3	2.4	–	5.2	1.4	–
Total hardness	125	12	–	–	–	–	39	97	72	17	–
Total N	2.6	–	–	–	–	–	0.7	–	–	–	1.0[a]
Total P	0.5	–	0.02	0.02	0.15	–	0.04	–	–	–	0.065[a]
Water Quality Index[c]	33	95	100	95	67	95	91	79	86	95	

[a]EC Directive 75/440/EEC
[b]EC Directive 78/659/EEC
[c]Water Quality Index (Scottish Development Department, 1976)
[d]LTA = long-term average
[e]EC Directive 76/464/EEC

TABLE 6.7. Water quality of the major Scottish rivers 1991 – trace metals. Determinands as total metals in mg L^{-1}

River NGR LTA[d] flow (m³ s⁻¹)	Clyde NS 595 644 47	Ness NH 664 446 87	Spey NJ 341 596 64	Dee (Grampian) NJ 859 004 46	Don NJ 926 093 20	Tay NO 122 234 173	Forth NS 775 955 50	Tweed NT 890 473 78	Amman NY 191 704 28	Dee (Solway) NX 733 642 42	Environmental Quality Standards[e]
Iron	–	–	176	120	387	–	590	274	207	201	1000[b]
Zinc	29.5	16.9	4.9	11.4	11.8	7.6	15.0	10.8	2.1	7.3	30–500[b]
Copper	7.4	1.2	4.4	2.0	5.3	3.7	3.8	5.1	2.6	4.3	1–28[b]
Lead	15.2	1.2	0.6	2.9	1.3	3.0	1.1	1.6	6.1	5.1	4–20[b]
Manganese	–	–	13.3	15.0	41.3	–	–	–	18.4	66.1	50[a]
Cadmium	0.12	<0.5	0.02	0.01	0.03	<0.1	0.06	<0.5	–	–	5[c]
Nickel	3.2	0.5	<1	<1	1.2	1.0	1.0	0.5	–	–	50–200[b]
Chromium	22.1	0.2	<0.5	0.6	0.7	<0.5	<0.8	0.8	–	–	5–50[b]
Aluminium	–	–	87	.58	208	–	–	–	120	152	–
Mercury	0.017	0.02	<0.1	<0.1	<0.1	<0.06	0.012	<0.1	–	–	1[c]
Arsenic	–	2.6	<1	<1	<1	–	<0.5	0.3	–	–	10[a], 50[b]

[a] EC Directive 75/440/EEC
[b] EC Directive 78/659/EEC
[c] 76/464/EEC
[d] LTA = long-term average
[e] EC Directive 76/464/EEC

TABLE 6.8. Water quality of the major Scottish rivers 1991 – Red List. Determinands in mg L^{-1}

River NGR LTA[b] flow (m³ s⁻¹)	Clyde NS 595 644 47	Ness NH 664 446 87	Spey NJ 341 596 64	Dee (Grampian) NJ 859 004 46	Don NJ 926 093 20	Tay NO 122 234 173	Forth NS 775 955 50	Tweed NT 890 473 78	Annan NY 191 704 28	Dee (Solway) NX 733 642 42	Environmental Quality Standards[a]
Lindane	8.8	1.8	3	2	6	20.2	1.5	2	<2	<2	100
DDT	63	2.5	1	<9	<9	<1	<1	<1	<2	<2	10
PCP	115	13	17	<5	17	<1	<20	40	<200	<200	2000
HCB	1.9	3.7	<2	<2	<2	<1	<0.5	<2	<2	–	30
HCBD	3	1	<2	<2	1	–	<1	<2	<2	<2	100
Aldrin	<2	<1	<2	<2	<2	1	<1	<1	<2	<2	10
Dieldrin	2.2	3.6	<5	1.0	1.0	<1	<1	<1	<5	<5	10
Endrin	11.3	3.6	<5	<5	<5	<1	<2	<2	<5	<5	5
PCBs	–	<1	–	–	–	<1	<1	<1	–	–	
Dichlorvos	–	–	<5	<5	<5	–	<5	4.4	–	–	
1,2 dichloroethane	–	–	–	–	–	–	<1	–	–	–	
Trichlorbenzene	–	–	–	–	–	–	<9	–	–	–	
Atrazine	156	–	–	–	–	–	<10	16	–	–	
Simazine	405	–	–	–	–	–	<10	32	<2	<2	
Trifluralin	<50	–	<1	<1	<1	–	<1	2.1	–	–	
Fenitrothion	<50	–	–	–	–	–	3	1.4	–	–	
Azinphos-Me	<100	–	–	–	–	–	<10	<1	–	–	
Malathion	<50	–	–	–	–	–	3	4.2	–	–	
Endosulfan	5.4	<1	<1	<1	<1	–	<1	<1	–	–	

[a]EC Directive 76/464/EEC
[b]LTA = long-term average

TABLE 6.9. Means, standard deviations (SD), minimum (Min.) and maximum (Max.) values for Scottish standing waters ($n = 643$). Values as meq L^{-1} unless stated otherwise

	Mean	SD	Min.	Max.
pH	6.47	0.940	4.09	9.19
Alkalinity	310	501	−69.00	4004
Conductivity ($\mu S\ cm^{-1}$)	106	102	11.00	1094
Na	414	376	43.00	4635
K	26	53	0	955
Ca	386	613	9	6045
Mg	183	300	9	5435
Cl	478	498	21	6622
SO$_4$	178	653	0	14750
NO$_3$	33	129	0	1498
Al-tm[a] ($\mu g\ L^{-1}$)	28	47	0	825
Abs-250[b] (nm)	0.244	0.235	0.002	2.17
TOC[c] (mg L^{-1})	4.78	3.8	0.2	39.1

[a]Al-tm = Total soluble monomeric aluminium
[b]Abs-250 = Absorbance units as a measure of soluble organic matter
[c]TOC = Total organic carbon.

clearly identified using a correlation matrix for the 13 measured variables (Table 6.10). Sea-salt components (Na, Mg, Cl) are highly correlated as are those from geochemical sources (alkalinity and Ca), while acidification indicators such as Al are negatively correlated with pH and alkalinity. Absorbance measurements at 250 nm are an effective surrogate for total organic carbon (TOC) with an *r* value of 0.88. There is no evidence of a link between pH and TOC; however, many of the acidified sites in south-west Scotland with pH < 5 exhibit low TOC values whereas relatively unpolluted sites in north-west Scotland with pH < 5 have relatively high TOC values. The pH distribution generally reflects catchment geology (Figure 6.4). Most of the missing squares designated as white are in non-sensitive areas and would be expected to be represented as black or dark grey squares.

The major patterns of variation in standing water chemistry can be summarized using Principal Component Analysis (PCA). Nearly 50% of the ionic variability can be explained along the first major PCA axis which reflects the total ion gradient. The second PCA axis embraces sites with high TOC, aluminium (Al) and absorbance–250 with high pH and alkalinity values, which explains a further 20.5% of the total variance. Overall, the four major axes account for about 90% of the total major ion variation (Table 6.11).

SCOTTISH FRESH WATERS – AN INTERNATIONAL PERSPECTIVE

In a global context the fresh waters of Scotland are predominantly of low ionic strength, of excellent drinking quality and support a wide diversity of flora and fauna. For example, most of the rivers support runs of Atlantic Salmon (*Salmo salar*) and Sea Trout (*S. trutta*). Average ion concentrations in major rivers are similar to those of standing waters but generally lower than world average values except for marine

TABLE 6.10. Pearson product-moment correlations between the 13 chemical determinands (transformed data) for Scottish standing waters ($n = 643$)

	pH	Alk	Cond	Na	K	Ca	Mg	Cl	SO$_4$	NO$_3$	Al	Abs	TOC
pH	–												
Alk	0.85	–											
Cond	0.28	0.53	–										
Na	−0.01	0.15	0.86	–									
K	0.24	0.47	0.83	0.70	–								
Ca	0.73	0.87	0.70	0.34	0.63	–							
Mg	0.41	0.67	0.93	0.71	0.77	0.79	–						
Cl	−0.07	−0.08	0.81	0.94	0.66	0.28	0.64	–					
SO$_4$	0.26	0.48	0.81	0.61	0.75	0.69	0.81	0.58	–				
NO$_3$	0.22	0.42	0.47	0.26	0.58	0.56	0.54	0.27	0.62	–			
Al	−0.50	−0.36	−0.03	0.03	0.02	−0.18	−0.06	0.03	0.05	0.13	–		
Abs	−0.19	−0.01	0.20	0.17	0.27	0.19	0.20	0.18	0.20	0.18	0.52	–	
TOC	−0.02	0.20	0.38	0.28	0.41	0.39	0.37	0.29	0.35	0.25	0.42	0.88	–

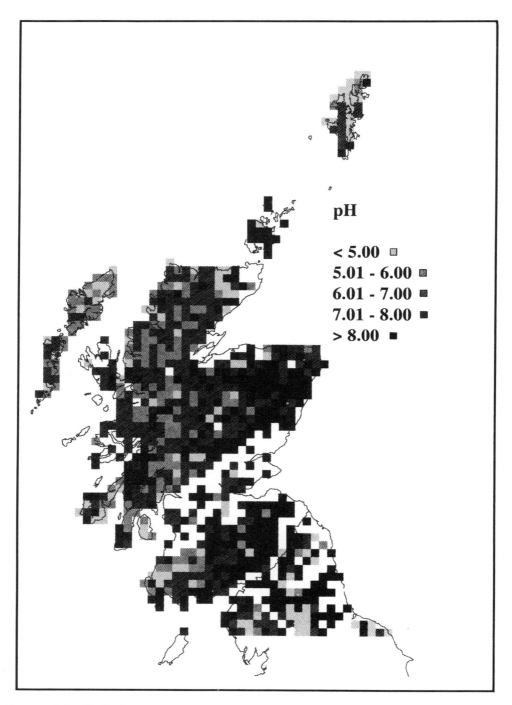

FIGURE 6.4. pH distribution in Scottish standing waters based on one site per 10 × 10 km square. White squares indicate no sample

TABLE 6.11. Results of Principal Component Analysis of the transformed water data (13 determinands × 643 grid-squares)

Eigenvalue	0.493	0.205	0.132	0.066
Percentage variance	49.3	20.5	13.2	6.6
Variable loadings (correlations)				
pH	0.42	−0.78	0.27	−0.18
Alkalinity	0.66	−0.61	0.33	−0.08
Conductivity	0.95	0.07	−0.02	−0.07
Na	0.75	0.31	−0.53	−0.17
K	0.88	0.11	−0.10	0.09
Ca	0.84	−0.37	0.33	−0.02
Mg	0.94	−0.07	−0.06	−0.19
Cl	0.70	0.35	−0.54	−0.16
SO_4	0.87	0.04	−0.05	0.25
NO_3	0.63	−0.01	0.21	0.66
AL-tm	−0.03	0.76	0.31	0.30
Abs-250	0.31	0.66	0.58	−0.25
TOC	0.50	0.53	0.56	−0.31

salts (Table 6.12). However, in terms of standing water volume the ionic content of Loch Ness, which holds 25% of this total, is only about one fifth of the Scottish average. Even when the five largest lochs, representing 50% of the standing water, are considered this fraction only increases slightly.

On a European scale the chemistry of Scottish fresh waters probably bears the closest resemblance to Scandinavian waters, particularly those of Sweden (see Henriksen, 1980).

TABLE 6.12. Comparison of mean concentrations of major ions in Scottish fresh waters with world average values

Determinands	Loch Ness	A	B	C	D
pH	6.55	7.1	6.47	–	–
Alkalinity	59	580	310	850	957
Na	166	313	414	225	274
K	8	23	26	33	59
Ca	81	475	386	670	749
Mg	45	206	183	275	337
SO_4	37	156	178	172	233
Cl	187	507	487	162	220
NO_3	7	86	33	7	–
DOC (mg l^{-1})	3.0	–	4.8	5.8	–
PO_4-P (μg l^{-1})	2	80	–	10	–

All values as μeq L^{-1} except where stated
A – major Scottish rivers: 1991
B – Scottish standing waters: 1990–1991
C – world average, unpolluted running waters (Meybeck and Helmer, 1989)
D – world average, unpolluted standing waters (Henriksen, 1980)

SHORT-TERM CHANGES IN WATER CHEMISTRY

It has long been recognized that short-term chemical variations (hours, days) can be as great as monthly or seasonal changes and certainly greater than variations in annual mean values. Interest in hydrochemical processes at plot and catchment scale has intensified during the past decade due to concern over episodic acidification and associated biological effects. Scotland has been at the forefront of such investigations (e.g. Reid *et al.*, 1981; Harriman *et al.*, 1990a), and a major component of the joint UK/Scandinavian Surface Water Acidification Programme (SWAP) was conducted in Scotland (see Harriman *et al.*, 1990b; Jenkins *et al.*, 1990). Predicting short-term chemical responses is understandably difficult because of the key role of soil/water pathways and the varying responses of different ions to changes in flow. For major ions (except sea-salts), concentrations generally decline with flow while organic anions and pH-dependent trace metals tend to increase.

Nutrient concentrations can also vary considerably with flow but seasonal variations tend to be greater, resulting in peak levels of nitrate and phosphate during winter/spring and minimum levels during peak biological activity in the summer. For other point source pollutants the major concern over water quality is during low flow conditions when dilution is at a minimum. It is during these circumstances that quality standards for BOD, dissolved oxygen and ammonia may be exceeded.

Routine sampling may fail to detect short-term pollutant discharges, thereby emphasizing the need to incorporate a biological component to quality indices.

LONG-TERM CHANGES IN WATER CHEMISTRY

In recent times the most obvious changes in the chemistry of Scottish fresh waters have come as a result of pollution control and prevention measures introduced by the SRPBs during the past few decades. The quinquennial reviews by the Scottish Office of the chemical quality of surface water show a gradual improvement with time, the number of kilometres of river in classes 4 and 2 decreasing consistently (Table 6.13).

The curbing of polluting discharges has developed in stages (see Chapter 20), with attention being focused at first on the polluting sewage and industrial effluents from the major conurbations, thereafter on lesser point source discharges in the middle and lower populated reaches of the rivers. As these improvements have occurred, the

TABLE 6.13. Changes in the quality, by chemical classification, of Scottish rivers between 1980 and 1990

	% of total monitored length in each class		
Class	1980	1985	1990
1	94.9	95.5	97.0
2	4.3	3.6	2.4
3	0.5	0.6	0.5
4	0.3	0.3	0.1

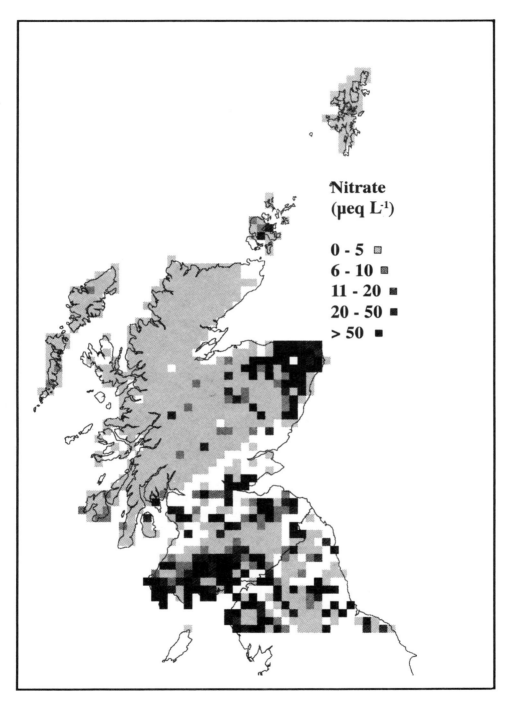

FIGURE 6.5. Distribution of nitrate in Scottish standing waters based on one site per 10 × 10 km square. White squares indicate no sample

effects of non-point source, diffuse inputs – for example from agriculture, forestry, land-use changes, the atmosphere – in the middle and upper reaches of the catchments have increased in importance.

At the same time, recovery from acidification in the Galloway area is now evident (see Chapter 24), as a result of recent reductions in sulphur deposition. This relatively short response time has encouraged government support for additional emission reductions which should result in further improvements to aquatic ecosystems. A difficulty in predicting the timescale of such improvements is the extent to which present and future afforestation and clearfelling will delay the recovery process. Removal of mature trees can certainly produce short-term (three to five years) acidification pulses due to nitrate leaching, while old plantations can significantly increase the quantity of sulphur and nitrogen deposited into catchments (Chapter 23).

Information on long-term trends in the phosphorus status of the majority of Scottish waters is not available. Nevertheless, eutrophication still remains a major concern in certain localities (e.g. Loch Leven) and a number of previously oligotrophic lochs are now enriched as a result of fish farming practices. Unlike phosphorus, nitrate leaching patterns are much clearer (Figure 6.5) because more spatial and temporal data are available. A recent examination of data from major rivers in the North East RPB area suggests little change in nitrate run-off during the past decade, although on a longer timescale nitrate levels have increased considerably during the past century due to agricultural practices. Perhaps the greatest area of concern over nitrogen is the extent to which nitrate and ammonia deposition is causing elevated nitrogen levels in remote upland lochs and streams. In response to these concerns the Department of the Environment has set up an advisory group to assess the consequences of increasing nitrogen deposition. Many remote upland waters in the UK have elevated nitrate levels in association with high nitrogen deposition.

In conclusion, the general chemical quality of running and standing waters is improving and will probably continue to do so as stricter UK and EC regulations are applied. As analytical methodology continues to progress, so will the ability to detect lesser known groups of pollutants (e.g. pesticides, trace elements) and thereby quantify their biological effects.

Concern remains over the spatial expansion of nutrient enrichment to remote regions resulting from atmospheric deposition and water-based industries. Continuing vigilance will be required to maintain and extend the positive improvements in water quality over the past two decades.

ACKNOWLEDGEMENTS

The authors wish to acknowledge all the RPB scientists who contributed to the Scottish rivers database. The chemical data for Scottish standing waters was derived from the Critical Loads database sponsored by the Department of the Environment.

REFERENCES

Bailey-Watts, A. E. and Duncan, P. (1981). "Chemical characterisation. A one year comparative study", in *The Ecology of Scotland's Largest Lochs: Lomond, Awe, Ness, Morar and Shiel* (Ed. P. S. Maitland), pp. 67–89, Junk, The Hague.

Billet, M. F. and Cresser, M. S. (1992). "Predicting stream-water quality using catchment and soil chemical characteristics", *Environmental Pollution*, **77**, 263–268.

Calow, P., Armitage, P., Boon, P., Chave, P., Cox, E., Hildrew, A., Learner, M., Maltby, L., Morris, G. and Whitton, B. (1990). *River Water Quality*, Ecological Issues No. 1, British Ecological Society, London.

Craig, G. Y. (Ed.) (1983). *Geology of Scotland*, Scottish Academic Press, Edinburgh.

Dillon, P. J. and Rigler, F. H. (1974). "The phosphorus – chlorophyll relationships in lakes", *Limnology and Oceanography*, **19**, 767–73.

Gardiner, J. and Zabel, T. (1991). "United Kingdom Water Quality Standards arising from European Community Directives – an update", Report PRS 2287 – M, Water Research Centre, Medmenham.

Gorham, E. (1957). "The chemical composition of some natural waters in the Cairngorm – Strathspey district of Scotland", *Limnology and Oceanography*, **3**, 143–154.

Harriman, R. (1989). "Patterns of surface water acidification in Scotland", in *Acidification in Scotland*, pp. 72–79, Scottish Development Department, Edinburgh.

Harriman, R. and Christie, A. E. G. (1993). "Evaluation of the steady state water chemistry method for surface waters", in *Critical Loads: Concept and Applications* (Eds M. Hornung and R. A. Skeffington), ITE Symposium 28, pp. 103–108, HMSO, London.

Harriman, R. and Wells, D. E. (1985). "Causes and effects of surface water acidification in Scotland", *Journal of Water Pollution Control Federation*, **84**, 215–224.

Harriman, R., Morrison, B. R. S., Caines, L. A., Collen, P. and Watt, A. W. (1987). "Long-term changes in fish populations of acid streams and lochs in Galloway, south west Scotland", *Journal of Water, Air and Soil Pollution*, **32**, 89–112.

Harriman, R., Gillespie, E., King, D., Watt, A. W., Christie, A. E. G., Cowan, A. A. and Edwards, T. (1990a). "Short-term ionic responses as indicators of hydrochemical processes in the Allt a Mharcaidh catchment, western Cairngorms, Scotland", *Journal of Hydrology*, **116**, 267–285.

Harriman, R., Ferrier, R. C., Jenkins, A. and Miller, J. D. (1990b). "Long- and short-term hydrochemical budgets in Scottish catchments", in *The Surface Waters Acidification Programme* (Ed. B. J. Mason) pp. 31–45, Cambridge University Press, Cambridge.

Henriksen, A. (1980). "Acidification of freshwaters – a large scale titration", in *Ecological Impact of Acid Precipitation* (Eds D. Drablos and A. Tollan), pp. 68–74, SNSF Project, Oslo.

Jenkins, A., Harriman, R. and Tuck, S. J. (1990). "Intregrated hydrochemical responses on the catchment scale", in *The Surface Waters Acidification Programme* (Ed. B. J. Mason) pp. 47–55, Cambridge University Press, Cambridge.

Meybeck, M. and Helmer, R. (1989). "The quality of rivers: from pristine stage to global pollution", *Palaeogeography, Palaeoclimatology, Palaeoecology (Global and Planetary Change Section)*, **75**, 283–309.

Murray, J. and Pullar, L. (1910). *Bathymetrical Survey of the Fresh Water Lochs of Scotland*, Challenger Office, Edinburgh.

Reid, J. M., MacLeod, D. A. and Cresser, M. S. (1981). "Factors affecting the chemistry of precipitation and river water in an upland catchment", *Journal of Hydrology*, **50**, 129–145.

Rivers Pollution Commission (1872). *Rivers of Scotland Report IV*, HMSO, London.

Rock, N. M. S. (1989). "The limestones of Scotland: an information update for limestones within the Moine and Lewisian outcrops of the Highlands and Islands", *British Geological Survey Report*, **16**, 1–27.

Scottish Development Department (1976). "Development of a Water Quality Index", *Report ARD3*, Edinburgh.

Scottish Development Department (1989). *Acidification in Scotland*, Edinburgh.

Scottish Office Environment Department (1992). *Water Quality Survey of Scotland, 1990*, HMSO, Edinburgh.

Smith, I. and Lyle, A. (1979). *Distribution of Freshwaters in Great Britain*, Institute of Terrestrial Ecology, Cambridge.

Smith, J. (1852). "On the composition of the waters of the Dee and Don, at Aberdeen, with an investigation into the action of Dee water on lead pipes and cisterns", *The Quarterly Journal of the Chemical Society*, **IV** (XIV), 123–133.

Stumm, W. (1985). *Chemical Processes in Lakes*, John Wiley, New York.
Stumm, W. and Morgan, I. J. (1970). *Aquatic Chemistry*, Wiley Interscience, New York.
Traquair, R. H. (1892). "On malformed trout from Scottish waters", *Annals of Scottish Natural History*, **2**, 92–103.
Vollenweider, R. A. (1968). "Water management research: scientific fundamentals of the eutrophication of lakes and flowing waters with particular reference to nitrogen and phosphorus as factors in eutrophication", OECD, Paris, Technical Report DAS/CS1/68.27.
Webb, B. W and Walling, D. E. (1992). "Chemical characteristics", In *The Rivers Handbook*, Vol. 1, pp. 73–100, Blackwell Scientific Publications, Oxford.

7

Palaeolimnology

R. W. BATTARBEE and T. E. H. ALLOTT

Environmental Change Research Centre, University College London, 26 Bedford Way, London, WC1H 0AP, UK

INTRODUCTION

Most Scottish lochs were formed following deglaciation approximately 14 000 years ago. However, some lochs, mainly in the north-west Highlands, were re-covered by ice as deglaciation was abruptly halted by renewed glaciation (the "Loch Lomond Re-advance") between 11 000 and 10 000 years ago.

The sediments accumulated in deep-water areas of lochs since deglaciation are usually highly organic and contain a rich fossil record of material derived not only from the lake, but also from the lake catchment and the atmosphere. Palaeolimnology is the study of this record. It involves sediment coring, sediment dating and the analysis and interpretation of the physical, chemical and biological stratigraphy of sediment cores.

In Scotland, studies have been concerned with the very early history of lakes following deglaciation (14 000 to 10 000 years ago), the long-term development of lakes during the post-glacial period (over the last 10 000 years) and with problems of recent change and pollution (over the last 200 years).

In this chapter we review published work relating to these different time periods and environmental themes.

THE LATE-GLACIAL: 14 000–10 000 BP

Environmental changes affecting Scottish lake history in the three to four millennia following initial deglaciation were both rapid and dramatic, relating to major changes of land and sea level, climatic change and ecological succession.

Marine influences

At the opening of the late-glacial period sea level was considerably depressed. However, the Scottish coastline was higher than at present because the land mass was even more depressed due to the weight of ice. As ice melted, the land rose by isostatic

The Fresh Waters of Scotland: A National Resource of International Significance
Edited by P. S. Maitland, P. J. Boon and D. S. McLusky. © 1994 John Wiley & Sons Ltd

114

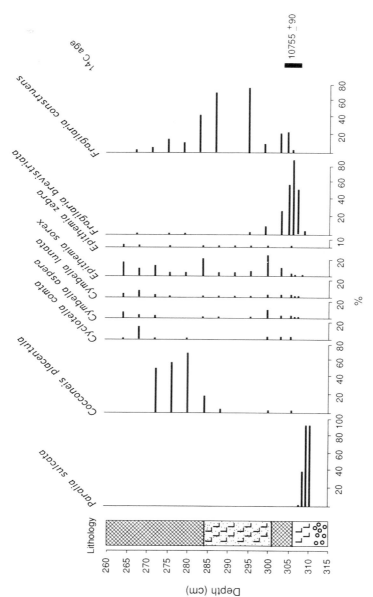

FIGURE 7.1. A diatom diagram from Rumach Iodar, Arisaig, showing a transition from marine to freshwater species in the Late-glacial. The lithological column shows basal deposits of gravel grading into a clay layer. This clay is overlain by organic mud (306–301 cm) followed by a sandy clay layer (301–284 cm) and then a second organic mud unit in the upper section of the core. Modified from Shennan et al. (1993)

rebound more rapidly than sea level rose from meltwater inflow, and the relative height of the coastline fell, causing low-lying coastal sea lochs to be isolated from the sea.

Evidence for these changes is clear from the sediments of coastal lochs. Shennan *et al.* (1993) have studied a series of basins between 4 and 20 m OD in the Arisaig region of Western Scotland. The basins with sills above about 9.2 m OD register a relative fall in sea level prior to the Loch Lomond stadial. Figure 7.1 shows a diatom diagram from one site, Rumach Iodar. The basal clays are dominated by the marine diatom *Paralia sulcata*. This is replaced by freshwater species as the basin is isolated some time before about 11 000 BP.

Catchment influences

For lochs not affected by land/sea-level changes, the main influence on their chemistry and biology during the Late-glacial was the characteristics of their catchments. Following deglaciation, lake catchments were initially unvegetated with newly exposed minerogenic soils. As climate improved vegetation cover developed and soils became more organic, until about 11 000 BP when ice re-advanced and the climatic deterioration of the Loch Lomond stadial signalled a return to Arctic tundra conditions for 1000 years or so.

The first major study explicitly concerned with the character of Scottish lochs during this period was that of Vasari and Vasari (1968). Of the five sites they studied using pollen and macrofossil analysis, the Loch of Park in Aberdeenshire provided the best material. Samples from this site were consequently also analyzed for diatoms (Alhonen, 1968).

In the earliest sediments of the Loch of Park, macrofossil remains of both submerged aquatic macrophytes (principally *Chara*, *Nitella*, *Potamogeton berchtoldii* and *Naias flexilis*) and emergent species (*Equisetum fluviatile*, *Hippuris vulgaris* and *Carex rostrata*) were found, and the pollen record showed high quantities of *Myriophyllum alterniflorum*. The presence of these taxa indicated a flora characteristic of an Arctic, alkaline lake, a conclusion supported by Alhonen's diatom analysis.

Later studies of late-glacial loch conditions at other sites throughout Scotland (Pennington *et al.*, 1972; Birks, 1973; Haworth, 1974, 1976; Birks and Mathewes, 1978) also indicated that lochs were more base-rich during this period than at present. At Loch Sionascaig – an acid, oligotrophic loch in north-west Scotland – Atkinson and Haworth (1990) used diatom-based pH reconstruction techniques to show that this site in the Late-glacial was well over pH 7, compared with present-day values of *ca* pH 6.5.

Although this early phase of lake history after deglaciation is usually the most alkaline, the degree of alkalinity between sites probably varied according to catchment conditions. For the Round Loch of Glenhead lying on the Loch Doon granite in Galloway, a detailed diatom study by Jones (Jones *et al.*, 1989) showed that these early stages were acidic from the beginning with a diatom assemblage dominated by *Fragilaria virescens*, *Cymbella perpusilla* and *Brachysira vitrea*, indicating a water pH of about 5.5 to 6.0. In contrast, the basal clays of Linton Loch in the Borders Region, studied by Mannion (1978), are dominated by alkaliphilous taxa indicating a water pH significantly above 7.0, and reflecting the calcareous nature of the glacial tills in the catchment of this lowland site.

THE POST-GLACIAL PERIOD: 10 000 BP–1800 AD

Following the final ice retreat at the end of the Loch Lomond stadial about 10 000 years ago, changes in the character of Scottish lochs occurred more gradually, influenced by minor changes in climate, by changes in the characteristics of the soils and vegetation of the catchments, and in the case of some coastal, low-altitude sites by marine influences.

Early soil/vegetation changes

The differences between lochs in the early post-glacial period are related to the extent to which the relatively base-rich conditions of the Late-glacial were maintained. At Loch Sionascaig pH declined rapidly from pH 7.7 to 6.5 between 10 000 and 8000 BP as soils weathered and became more organic (Atkinson and Haworth, 1990). At the Round Loch of Glenhead an early acidification is also apparent but to a much lesser extent, presumably reflecting the much lower initial alkalinity at this site. In contrast, the high pH of Linton Loch is maintained throughout the early Holocene (Mannion, 1978), reflecting the alkaline nature of the catchment soils and the speed with which cations lost through leaching can be replaced by primary weathering.

Marine transgression

For a small number of lochs in low-lying coastal locations the post-glacial development of flora and fauna was interrupted by a further marine transgression, similar to the one that had previously occurred in the Late-glacial.

In the early Holocene, world sea level rose rapidly as a result of the melting of major ice-sheets after 10 000 BP. By about 7000 BP the rate of sea-level increase became greater than the rate of land uplift in Scotland and the Scottish coastline was again submerged. This marine transgression lasted approximately 2000 years with affected sites returning to freshwater conditions as sea-level rise slowed down and land uplift continued.

The most visible features in the Scottish landscape of this marine transgression are an abandoned raised shoreline up to 15 m OD and the raised estuarine mud-flats (or "carselands"), especially in the Firth of Forth, most recently studied by Robinson (1993).

The most notable loch to be affected at this time was Loch Lomond. From a 4.94 m core (Figure 7.2) taken in 24 m of water in the southern basin, Dickson *et al.* (1978) described the presence of a marine layer between 3.05 and 3.75 m, characterized by very low magnetic susceptibility and intensity values and by cysts of planktonic marine dinoflagellates, especially *Operculodinium centrocarpum* and *Bitectatodinium tepikiense*. From radiocarbon dating the authors estimated that the marine phase lasted from 6900 BP to 5450 BP.

Later analysis of this core by MacKenzie *et al.* (1983) showed that this marine stage was characterized by very high iodine and bromine levels (Figure 7.2). The presence

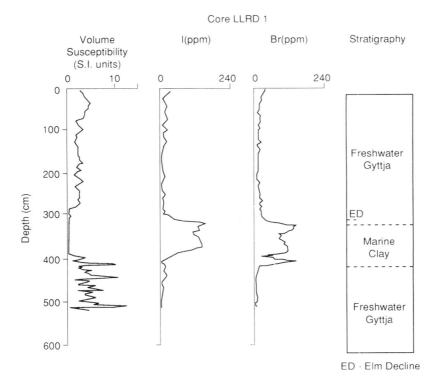

FIGURE 7.2. Plots of volume susceptibility, concentrations of iodine and bromine, and major stratigraphic horizons against depth for Loch Lomond core LLRD1. Redrawn from Snowball and Thompson (1990). Reproduced by permission of the American Geophysical Union

of this marine layer, trapped between two freshwater layers, has been used by MacKenzie and co-workers as an historical analogue to study the extent to which halogens diffuse in clays (MacKenzie *et al.*, 1990), an issue of importance with respect to the storage of low-level radioactive waste (MacKenzie *et al.*, 1983).

Additional sedimentary evidence for marine transgression during the Holocene has been provided for Loch Shiel (Thompson and Wain-Hobson, 1979) and sites in the Arisaig region (Shennan, personal communication).

Paludification

For many upland lakes in Scotland during the mid-Holocene the most important change was probably the replacement of forest vegetation by blanket peatland. For the catchment of the Round Loch of Glenhead, Jones (1987) showed that peat accumulation began in wet hollows or pools as early as 9000 BP and gradually spread outwards over the next few thousand years. However, the more rapid expansion of peat throughout the catchment, replacing forest, occurred after 5000 BP, a change most clearly seen in the pollen diagram from the lake (Figure 7.3).

118

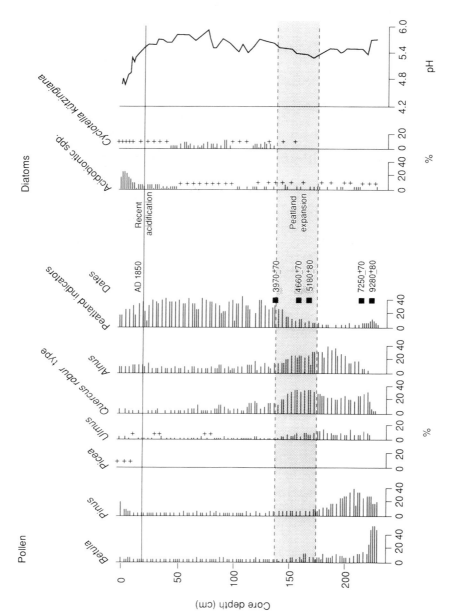

FIGURE 7.3. Composite pollen and diatom diagram for a core from the Round Loch of Glenhead, including ^{14}C and ^{210}Pb dates and pH reconstruction. Redrawn from Jones *et al.* (1986). Reproduced with permission from *Nature* Vol. 322, pp. 157–158. Copyright (1986) Macmillan Magazines Limited

FIGURE 7.4. Scanning electron micrograph of *Cyclotella kützingiana*, a planktonic diatom associated with circumneutral waters. This species has been found to decline in abundance following increased loch-water turbidity associated with peat erosion (Stevenson *et al.*, 1990)

At this site the spread of blanket peat, perhaps surprisingly, did not cause acidification of the loch (Jones, 1987; Jones *et al.*, 1989). In fact, at this point in the sediment core (Figure 7.3) the first appearance of the planktonic diatom *Cyclotella kützingiana* (see Figure 7.4) occurs, suggesting that some amelioration of the toxic effects of acidity was taking place, possibly owing to an increase in the supply of dissolved organic carbon to the loch (cf. Birks *et al.*, 1990).

For Loch Sionascaig (Pennington *et al.*, 1972) catchment peat began to form about 6000 BP and extended considerably in the following millennia, accelerating from about 3500 BP. The diatom assemblages in the loch sediment during this time were dominated by acidophilous species, but, as in the case of the Round Loch, there was no coincidental acidification of the loch water, the acidification period having occurred earlier whilst forest rather than peatland still dominated the catchment.

Peat erosion

Peat erosion in the Scottish uplands is a major problem for nature conservation. The history of erosion is recorded by loch sediments and can be shown especially by the changing percentage of organic matter in cores, measured by "loss on ignition".

The effect on lake ecosystems is to increase sediment accumulation, and increase water colour and turbidity. So far, detailed evidence is available only for one site, the Round Loch of Glenhead, where at precisely the same level that "loss on ignition" increases there is a decrease in the spores of the aquatic macrophyte *Isoetes* and a decline in the proportion of the planktonic diatom *Cyclotella kützingiana* (Figure 7.4); (Stevenson *et al.*, 1990). Although the evidence is not recorded in the sediments, such increased erosion is likely to have also disrupted benthic invertebrate and fish communities.

RECENT POLLUTION: 1800 AD – PRESENT

In the last 200 years human factors have been clearly dominant in changing the ecology of Scottish lochs. No site in Scotland has escaped some impact from pollution.

Many of these pollutants, such as acid deposition, have had severe biological consequences; some, such as radioactive isotopes, are present only as contaminants causing, as yet, no discernible problem. Evidence for all is usually present in the recent sediments.

Recent acidification

Over the last two decades lake acidification has become an environmental problem of international significance, and Scotland has become a focus of acidification research (see Chapter 24). The first region to be studied in detail using palaeolimnological techniques was Galloway (e.g. Flower and Battarbee, 1983; Battarbee *et al.*, 1985a; Jones *et al.*, 1986; Flower *et al.*, 1987).

The recent diatom record of one of the Galloway sites, the Round Loch of Glenhead, is shown in Figure 7.5. Before 1850, the record is dominated by circumneutral or acidophilous diatoms such as *Achnanthes minutissima* and *Brachysira vitrea*, and the diatom-inferred pH was stable at values above 5.5. In the last 150 years the profile shows circumneutral taxa being replaced by more acidophilous species such as *Eunotia incisa*. In the uppermost sediments acidobiontic species such as *Tabellaria quadriseptata* and *Tabellaria binalis* (Figure 7.6) become dominant. The pH reconstruction demonstrates that the loch has acidified by approximately one pH unit over the last 150 years.

Over 40 lochs throughout Scotland have now been examined for evidence of recent lake acidification using these techniques, and, consequently, the extent of acidification is now well established (Battarbee *et al.*, 1988a; Battarbee, 1989). The most strongly affected areas are Galloway, Arran (Battarbee *et al.*, 1988a), the Trossachs (Kreiser *et al.*, 1990), and Rannoch Moor (Flower *et al.*, 1988). In the Trossachs study, Kreiser *et al.* (1990) concluded that the acidification of Loch Chon was exacerbated by recent afforestation.

Acidified lochs have also been identified in the Cairngorms (Jones *et al.*, 1993), and Morvern and Strontian (Jones *et al.*, 1990; Kreiser *et al.*, 1990). In the north and north-west of Scotland levels of acid deposition are low, and the problems of acidification less severe (Flower *et al.*, 1993). However, even in this area the most sensitive lochs have suffered slight acidification (Kreiser *et al.*, 1990; Allott, unpublished data).

The spatial pattern of acidification corresponds approximately to that of the loading of acid deposition and to the flux of fly-ash particles (Rose, 1991), and these correlations, based on palaeolimnological data, substantiate the hypothesis that recent acidification is primarily due to acid deposition from fossil fuel combustion (Battarbee, 1990).

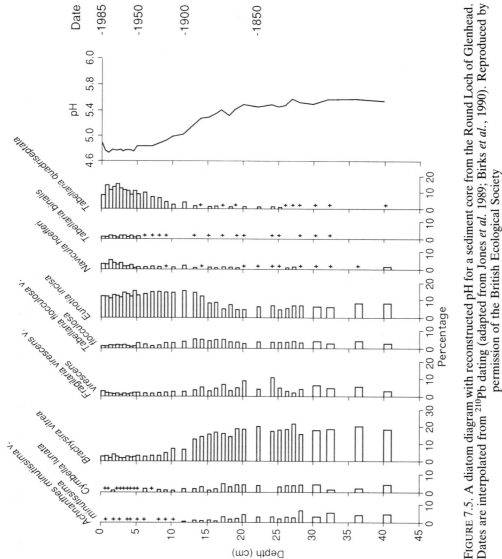

FIGURE 7.5. A diatom diagram with reconstructed pH for a sediment core from the Round Loch of Glenhead. Dates are interpolated from ^{210}Pb dating (adapted from Jones et al. 1989; Birks et al., 1990). Reproduced by permission of the British Ecological Society

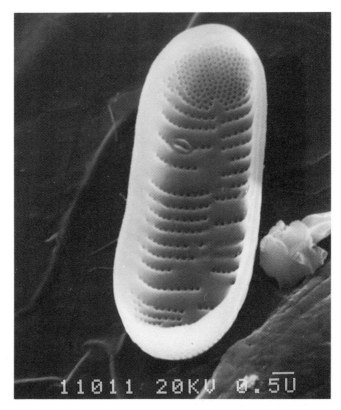

FIGURE 7.6. Scanning electron micrograph of *Tabellaria binalis*, a diatom tolerant of strongly acid water. This species increases in abundance in the uppermost sediments of recently acidified lochs, such as the Round Loch of Glenhead

Palaeolimnological studies have also shown that the process of lake acidification is reversible. Since 1970, UK sulphur dioxide (SO_2) emissions have fallen by approximately 40%, and in south-west Scotland this has been reflected in a decrease in acid deposition. Battarbee *et al.* (1988b) demonstrated recent diatom recovery from acidification in two of the Galloway lochs, and this was supported by a further study at the Round Loch of Glenhead by Allott (1991) and Allott *et al.* (1992).

In some Scottish lochs liming has been used to ameliorate the effects of acidification. Cameron (1990) and Flower *et al.* (1990) used palaeolimnological techniques to study the effects of liming on the algal communities of Loch Fleet, Galloway. They found that although liming successfully raised the pH of the loch water, the pre-acidification diatom flora did not re-establish itself. Instead a new flora appeared that included taxa that had not previously occurred in the loch. They concluded that the pH of the loch had been raised to unnaturally high levels by liming, and that liming was not suitable as a method of managing the ecological recovery of acidified waters.

Eutrophication

In lowland lochs the emphasis of palaeolimnological research has been on the extent of eutrophication. Nutrient enrichment of lochs can take place both through increased inputs of effluent from urban areas and by nutrient inputs from agriculture and forestry.

Despite the importance of this problem there has been only one published palaeolimnological study of a eutrophic loch in Scotland. Haworth (1972) analysed the sediment of a short core from Loch Leven and showed that major changes in the loch were represented by changes in the diatom assemblages in the uppermost sediment, indicated especially by increases in the proportion of *Stephanodiscus tenuis*, *S. hantzschii* and *Diatoma elongatum*.

The symptoms of eutrophication are often obvious at very productive lowland sites, such as Loch Leven. However, a growing problem is the impact of nutrient inputs to large oligotrophic and ultra-oligotrophic lochs in the Highlands as a result of fish farming, fertilizers from forestry and sewage effluent disposal. Even Loch Ness, a loch which had been considered more at risk from acidification than eutrophication, is becoming slightly enriched. Diatom analysis of a core from this site (Jones *et al.*, unpublished) has shown an increase in the abundance of the planktonic diatoms *Asterionella formosa* and *Aulacoseira subarctica* in the uppermost sediments, probably representing increasing nutrient inputs over the last 40 years, a conclusion in agreement with the earlier arguments of Maitland (1981).

Afforestation

A major environmental change in Scotland over the past 70 years or so has been the extensive afforestation of large areas of the uplands. Afforestation can affect lake ecosystems in several ways: enhanced acidification through scavenging, nutrient enrichment through the use of fertilizers, and soil erosion and inwash through catchment ploughing (see Chapter 23).

The first two of these have already been mentioned. The last, however, may be the most severe, at least in the short term. At sites with catchments being prepared for afforestation, sediment accumulation rates are often massively enhanced (Appleby *et al.*, 1985; Battarbee *et al.*, 1985b). An example is provided by Loch Fleet where part of the catchment was ploughed and planted in 1961. Sediment cores taken from the loch show an increase in the organic matter content of the loch sediment, and a major increase in sediment accumulation rate after 1961, reaching 10 cm yr^{-1} at its peak (Anderson *et al.*, 1986).

Trace metal contamination

Analysis of recent sediments at sites throughout Scotland (Battarbee *et al.*, 1988a; Rippey, 1990) shows that concentrations of trace metals, such as lead (Pb), copper (Cu) and zinc (Zn), are high in the south and central areas of the country but decrease towards the north. Pb shows the earliest contamination, often dated to the beginning of the 19th century, reaching a maximum in the mid-20th century. Cu and Zn follow similar, but not identical, historical patterns.

It is apparent from the widespread nature of trace metal contamination, and from the fact that remote upland lakes (Figure 7.7) are as contaminated as lowland sites, that these metals are derived from atmospheric pollution sources. Sugden *et al.* (1991), in their study of Loch Lomond sediments, confirm this inference, and they demonstrate from a decline in the isotopic ratio ^{206}Pb:^{207}Pb in the sediments that lead from heavy industry and coal combustion has declined and lead from car exhausts has increased since the 1930s. The overall decline in lead suggests that vehicles are less important sources of lead pollution in lochs than earlier heavy industry.

However, high levels of some trace elements in Loch Lomond surface sediments are not always caused by pollution. Lovell and Farmer (1983) and Farmer and Lovell (1986) have shown that very high arsenic (As) values (up to 675 mg kg^{-1}) are found in surface or near-surface sediments. Because there are no obvious industrial sources of As in the catchment, the authors attributed the profiles to natural processes of post-depositional enrichment, a hypothesis they confirmed by showing how such an effect can be produced by diagenetic remobilization of As under reducing conditions, upward migration in pore-water, and re-precipitation or re-adsorption on iron oxides and hydroxides in the surface sediment aerobic zone.

Fly-ash particles and polycyclic aromatic hydrocarbons

Conclusive evidence that Scottish lochs have experienced a long history of acid deposition from fossil fuel combustion came from the work of Natkanski (Battarbee *et al.*, 1989), Rippey (1990) and Rose (1991), who showed that the recent sediments of Scottish lochs were contaminated by spheroidal carbonaceous particles and poly-cyclic aromatic hydrocarbons (PAHs) derived from the combustion of coal and oil. The carbonaceous particles are typically 5–50 μm in diameter, and are mainly derived from coal (Rose, 1991). Figure 7.7 shows a carbonaceous particle curve for Loch Laidon, a remote upland loch in the southern Highlands (Flower *et al.*, 1988).

Rose (Rose and Juggins, 1994) has also recently completed a detailed study of surface sediments throughout Scotland that has enabled the concentration of these particles to be mapped. The results show that there are especially high levels near sources of industrial activity, but, as for trace metal distribution, there is a general decline towards the north. Despite their abundance, however, there is no evidence that these particles have interfered with loch ecology. Rather they are unambiguous indicators of other forms of more potent pollution, such as acid deposition.

Further evidence of contamination of Scottish lochs from fossil fuel combustion comes from the record of PAHs in recent sediments. Rippey (1990) examined the PAH stratigraphy of cores from five Scottish lochs and showed that high levels of benzo [a] pyrene occurred especially in the uppermost sediments of lochs Tinker and Chon (in the Trossachs) in an area of high acid deposition, in contrast to Loch Doilet, Lochan Dubh (near Strontian) and Lochan Uaine in the Cairngorms, where acid deposition is significantly lower.

Radio-isotopes

A more recent contaminant of Scottish lochs has been radioactive fallout, both from nuclear weapons testing in the 1950s and 1960s and from the Chernobyl nuclear power station accident in 1986.

Atmospheric weapons testing caused global contamination, recorded in lake sediments by clear spikes of radioactive isotopes (Figure 7.8). Many short-lived fission products decayed rapidly but other isotopes with longer half-lives, such as ^{137}Cs and ^{241}Am, are still present. In sediments with rapid accumulation rates and little

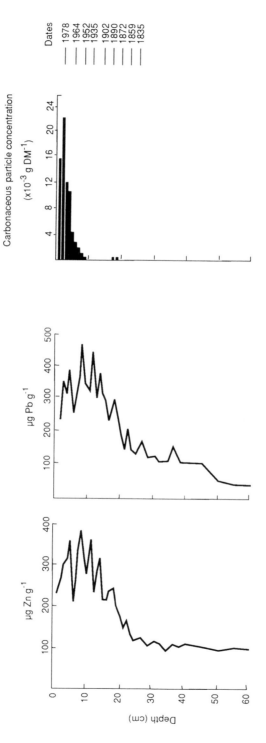

FIGURE 7.7. Sediment profiles of zinc, lead and carbonaceous particles from Loch Laidon (adapted from Flower *et al.*, 1988). Metal concentrations are in $\mu g\ g^{-1}$ dry weight of sediment and sediment dates are extrapolated from ^{210}Pb dating. Reproduced by permission of the British Ecological Society

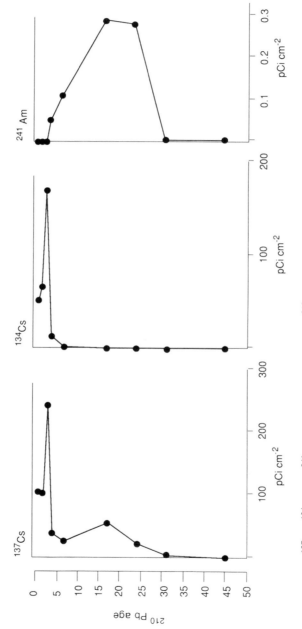

FIGURE 7.8. [137]Cs, [134]Cs and [241]Am concentrations against ^{210}Pb age in years for a sediment core taken from Loch Ness in 1990 (Appleby, unpublished data)

bioturbation, peaks of activity representing fallout maxima in the years 1959 and 1963 can be differentiated, but in most cores only a single peak, usually ascribed to 1963, can be resolved. In acid waters there is evidence of post-depositional mobility of Cs. Whereas [241]Am appears stable and picks out the 1963 horizon clearly, ^{137}Cs is often found in deep, pre-1800 sediments and sometimes has a maximum in the surface sediments, maintaining contact with the lake water and the benthic food chain.

CONCLUSIONS

Palaeolimnological studies have made a major contribution to our knowledge of Scottish lochs. The approach provides a mechanism for effectively placing the contemporary chemistry and biology of lochs in a temporal perspective, and evaluating whether, how fast, where and why changes are taking place.

Although only a small fraction of potential sites have been studied it is apparent that, despite their relative remoteness from major industrial and urban centres, few have been uninfluenced by human activity over the last century. Some lowland lochs have been severely enriched, many upland sites have been strongly acidified, and a few have suffered from massive soil inwash associated with poor forestry management. All have been contaminated by air pollutants of various kinds.

Such recent changes are made all the more clear when set against the much slower and less extreme changes that have occurred in Scottish lochs during the post-glacial period and since the dramatic events at the end of the last Ice Age.

ACKNOWLEDGEMENTS

We thank all those who helped us with this chapter by providing advice and unpublished data: especially Peter Appleby, Hilary Birks, John Birks, John Dearing, John Farmer, Elizabeth Haworth, Viv Jones, Gus MacKenzie, Antoinette Mannion, Marie Robinson, Ian Shennan, Richard Tipping, Roy Thompson and all members of the Environmental Change Research Centre.

REFERENCES

Alhonen, P. (1968). "On the Late-glacial and early Post-glacial diatom succession in Loch of Park, Aberdeenshire, Scotland", *Memoranda Societatis Pro Fauna et Flora Fennica*, **44** 13–20.

Allott, T. E. H. (1991). "The reversibility of lake acidification: a diatom study from the Round Loch of Glenhead, Galloway, Scotland", Unpublished PhD thesis, University of London, London.

Allott, T. E. H., Harriman, R. and Battarbee, R. W. (1992). "Reversibility of lake acidification at the Round Loch of Glenhead, Galloway, Scotland", *Environmental Pollution*, **77**, 219–225.

Anderson, N. J., Battarbee, R. W., Appleby, P. G., Stevenson, A. C., Oldfield, F., Darley, J. and Glover, G. (1986). "Palaeolimnological evidence for the recent acidification of Loch Fleet, Galloway", Research Paper No. 17, Palaeoecology Research Unit, University College London, London.

Appleby, P. G., Dearing, J. A. and Oldfield, F. (1985). "Magnetic studies of erosion in a Scottish lake catchment, 1. Core chronology and correlation", *Limnology and Oceanography*, **30**, 1144–1153.

Atkinson, K. M. and Haworth, E. Y. (1990). "Devoke Water and Loch Sionascaig: recent environmental changes and the post-glacial overview", *Philosophical Transactions of the Royal Society of London*, **327B**, 349–355.

Battarbee, R. W. (1989). "Geographical research on acid rain. I. the acidification of Scottish lochs", *The Geographical Journal*, **155**, 353–377.

Battarbee, R. W. (1990). "The causes of lake acidification, with special reference to the role of acid deposition", *Philosophical Transactions of the Royal Society of London*, **327B**, 339–347.

Battarbee, R. W., Flower, R. J., Stevenson, A. C. and Rippey, B. (1985a). "Lake acidification in Galloway: a palaeoecological test of competing hypotheses", *Nature*, **314**, 350–352.

Battarbee, R. W., Appleby, P. G., Odell, K. and Flower, R. J. (1985b). "^{210}Pb dating of Scottish lake sediments, afforestation and accelerated soil erosion", *Earth Surface Processes and Landforms*, **10**, 137–142.

Battarbee, R. W., Anderson, N. J., Appleby, P. G., Flower, R. J., Fritz, S. C., Haworth, E. Y., Higgitt, S., Jones, V. J., Kreiser, A., Munro, M.A.R., Natkanski, J., Oldfield, F., Patrick, S. T., Richardson, N. G., Rippey, B. and Stevenson, A. C. (1988a). *Lake Acidification in the United Kingdom 1800–1986*, ENSIS Publishing, London.

Battarbee, R. W., Flower, R. J., Stevenson, A. C., Jones, V. J., Harriman, R. and Appleby, P. G. (1988b). "Diatom and chemical evidence for reversibility of acidification of Scottish lochs", *Nature*, **322**, 530–532.

Battarbee, R. W., Stevenson, A. C., Rippey, B., Fletcher, C., Natkanski, J., Wik, M. and Flower, R. J. (1989). "Causes of lake acidification in Galloway, south-west Scotland: a palaeoecological evaluation of the relative roles of atmospheric contamination and catchment change for two acidified sites with non-afforested catchments", *Journal of Ecology*, **77**, 651–672.

Birks, H. H. and Mathewes, R. W. (1978). "Studies in the vegetational history of Scotland. V. Late Devensian and early Flandrian pollen and macrofossil stratigraphy at Abernethy Forest, Inverness-shire", *New Phytologist*, **80**, 455–484.

Birks, H. J. B. (1973). *Past and Present Vegetation on the Isle of Skye – a Palaeoecological Study*, Cambridge University Press, Cambridge.

Birks, H. J. B., Juggins, S. and Line, J. M. (1990). "Lake-surface water chemistry reconstructions from palaeolimnological data", in *The Surface Waters Acidification Programme* (Ed. B. J. Mason), pp. 301–315, Cambridge University Press, Cambridge.

Cameron, N. G. (1990). "Representation of diatom communities by fossil assemblages in Loch Fleet, Galloway, Scotland", Unpublished PhD Thesis, University of London, London.

Dickson, J. H., Stewart, D. A., Thompson. R., Turner, G., Baxter, M. S., Drndarsky, N. D. and Rose, J. (1978). "Palynology, palaeomagnetism and radiometric dating of Flandrian marine and freshwater sediments of Loch Lomond", *Nature*, **274**, 548–553.

Farmer, J. G. and Lovell, M. A. (1986). "Natural enrichment of arsenic in Loch Lomond sediments", *Geochemica et Cosmochimica Acta*, **50**, 2059–2067.

Flower, R. J. and Battarbee, R. W. (1983). "Diatom evidence for recent acidification of two Scottish lochs", *Nature*, **305**, 130–133.

Flower, R. J., Battarbee, R. W. and Appleby, P. G. (1987). "The recent palaeolimnology of acid lakes in Galloway, south-west Scotland: diatom analysis, pH trends, and the role of afforestation", *Journal of Ecology*, **75**, 797–824.

Flower, R. J., Battarbee, R. W., Natkanski, J., Rippey, B. and Appleby, P. G. (1988). "The recent acidification of a large Scottish loch located partly within a National Nature Reserve and Site of Special Scientific Interest", *Journal of Applied Ecology*, **25**, 715–724.

Flower, R. J., Cameron, N. G., Rose, N., Fritz, S. C., Harriman, R., and Stevenson, A. C. (1990). "Post-1970 water-chemistry and palaeolimnology of several acidified upland lakes in the UK", *Philosophical Transactions of the Royal Society of London*, **327B**, 427–433.

Flower, R. J., Jones, V. J., Battarbee, R. W., Appleby, P. G., Rippey, B., Rose, N. L. and Stevenson, A. C. (1993). "The extent of regional acidification in north-west Scotland: palaeoecological evidence", Research Paper No. 8, Environmental Change Research Centre, University College London, London.

Haworth, E. Y. (1972). "The recent diatom history of Loch Leven, Kinross", *Freshwater Biology*, **2**, 131–141.

Haworth, E. Y. (1974). "Some problems of diatom taxonomy in Scottish lake sediments", *British Phycology Journal*, **9**, 47–55.

Haworth, E. Y. (1976). "Two Late-glacial (Late Devensian) diatom assemblage profiles from northern Scotland", *New Phytologist*, **77**, 227–256.

Jones, V. J. (1987). "A palaeoecological study of the post-glacial acidification of the Round Loch of Glenhead and its catchment", Unpublished PhD thesis, University of London, London.

Jones, V. J., Stevenson, A. C. and Battarbee, R. W. (1986). "Lake acidification and the land-use hypotheses: a mid-post-glacial analogue", *Nature*, **322**, 157–158.

Jones, V. J., Stevenson, A. C. and Battarbee, R. W. (1989). "Acidification of lakes in Galloway, south-west Scotland: a diatom and pollen study of the post-glacial history of the Round Loch of Glenhead", *Journal of Ecology*, **77**, 1–23.

Jones, V. J., Kreiser, A. M., Appleby, P. G., Brodin, Y. -W., Dayton, J., Natkanski, J., Richardson, N., Rippey, B., Sandoy, S. and Battarbee, R. W. (1990). "The recent palaeolimnology of two sites with contrasting acid-deposition histories", *Philosophical Transactions of the Royal Society of London*, **327B**, 397–402.

Jones, V. J., Flower, R. J., Appleby, P. G., Natkanski, J., Richardson, N., Rippey, B., Stevenson, A. C. and Battarbee, R. W. (1993). "Palaeolimnological evidence for the acidification and atmospheric contamination of lochs in the Cairngorm and Lochnagar areas of Scotland", *Journal of Ecology*, **81**, 3–24.

Kreiser, A. M., Appleby, P. G., Natkanski, J., Rippey, B. and Battarbee, R. W. (1990). "Afforestation and lake acidification: a comparison of four sites in Scotland", *Philosophical Transactions of the Royal Society of London*, **327B**, 377–383.

Lovell, M. A. and Farmer, J. G. (1983). "The geochemistry of arsenic in the freshwater sediments of Loch Lomond", *Proceedings of the Fourth International Conference on Heavy Metals in the Environment*, **2**, 776–779.

MacKenzie, A. B., Scott, R. D., McKinley, I. G. and West, J. M. (1983). "A study of the long term (10^3–10^4 Y) elemental migration in saturated clays and sediments", *Institute of Geological Sciences Report*, FLPU 83–86.

MacKenzie, A. B., Shimmield, T. M., Scott, R. D., Davidson, C. M. and Hooker, P. J. (1990). "Chloride, bromide and iodine distributions in Loch Lomond sediment interstitial water", *British Geological Survey Technical Report* WE/90/2.

Maitland, P. S. (1981). "Introduction and catchment analyses", in *The Ecology of Scotland's Largest Lochs: Lomond, Awe, Ness, Morar and Shiel*, (Ed. P. S. Maitland), pp. 1–27, Junk, The Hague.

Mannion, A. M. (1978). "Late Quaternary deposits from southeast Scotland. II. The diatom assemblage of a marl core", *Journal of Biogeography*, **5**, 301–318.

Pennington, W., Haworth, E. Y., Bonny, A. P. and Lishman, J. P. (1972). "Lake sediments in northern Scotland", *Philosophical Transactions of the Royal Society of London*, **264B**, 191–294.

Rippey, B. (1990). "Sediment chemistry and atmospheric contamination", *Philosophical Transactions of the Royal Society of London*, **327B**, 311–317.

Robinson, M. (1993). "Microfossil analyses and radiocarbon dating of depositional sequences related to Holocene sea-level change in the Forth valley, Scotland", *Transactions of the Royal Society of Edinburgh: Earth Sciences*, **84**, 1–60.

Rose, N. L. (1991). "Fly ash particles in lake sediments: extraction, characterisation, and distribution", Unpublished PhD thesis, University of London, London.

Rose, N. J. and Juggins, S. (1994). "A spatial relationship between carbonaceous particles in lake sediments and sulphur deposition", *Atmospheric Environment*, **28**, 177–183.

Shennan, I., Innes, B. J., Long, A. J. and Zong, Y. (1993). "Late Devensian and Holocene relative sea-level changes at Rumach, Arisaig Bay north-west Scotland", *Norsk Geologisk Tiddsskrift*, 73.

Snowball, I. and Thompson, R. (1990). "A stable chemical remanence in Holocene sediments", *Journal of Geophysical Research*, **95**, 4471–4479.

Stevenson, A. C., Jones, V. J. and Battarbee, R. W. (1990). "The cause of peat erosion: a palaeolimnological approach", *New Phytologist*, **114**, 727–735.

Sugden, C. L., Farmer, J. G. and Mackenzie, A. B. (1991). "Isotopic characterisation of lead inputs and behaviour in recent Scottish freshwater loch sediments", *Proceedings of the Eighth International Conference on Heavy Metals in the Environment*, **1**, 511–514.

Thompson, R. and Wain-Hobson, T. (1979). "Palaeomagnetic and stratigraphic study of the Loch Shiel marine regression and overlying gyttja", *Journal of the Geological Society*, **136**, 383–388.

Vasari, Y. and Vasari, A. (1968). "Late- and Post-glacial macrophytic vegetation in the lochs of northern Scotland", *Acta Botanica Fennica*, **80**, 1–20.

8

Algae

A. J. BROOK

Department of Life Sciences, University of Buckingham, Buckingham, MK18 1EG, UK

INTRODUCTION

The earliest reference to the occurrence of any freshwater alga in Scotland, and also probably the earliest reference to an algal water bloom in Britain, comes from what used to be Wigtownshire (now Dumfries and Galloway). The 12th century Abbey of Soulseat, near Stranraer, was described as the "monasterium viridis stagnii" (Griffiths, 1939; Brook, 1957a). The abbey, situated on a peninsula in a small lake, was all too frequently affected by odorous blooms. Its Latin description has been translated in a Victorian visitor's guide as "The Monastery of the Green Stank"! There then appears to be a very long gap in our knowledge of Scottish freshwater algae until some records appear in Greville's *Flora Edinensis* (1824). The *Scottish Cryptogamic Flora*, which Greville started in 1823, was continued in monthly parts and eventually extended to six volumes (e.g. Greville, 1827; 1828). He also contributed Diatomaceae to Dr Hooker's *British Flora*, Vol. II (Greville, 1833), as well as an individual paper on diatoms from the Braemar district (Greville, 1855).

A major figure in the history of British cryptogamic botany was the surgeon, turned mycologist and algologist, John Ralfs. He is recognized internationally for his major contribution to the study of desmids with the publication of the first monograph on these exclusively freshwater algae, *The British Desmidiae* (1848). Some of his earliest publications on desmids appeared in the *Transactions of the Botanical Society of Edinburgh* (Ralfs, 1843; 1846). There are interesting references to Scottish desmids in his monograph from Professor Dickie of Aberdeen University and Mr P. Grant of Banff. Both must have collected fairly extensively in what are even now remote areas of the Grampian Region, for there are records of *Euastrum binale* (Turp.) Ehr. ex Ralfs from Moss Hagg, between Tomintoul and Loch Avon at 1097 m and of *Staurastum orbiculare* (Ehr.) Ralfs at 1060 m on Ben Macdui.

DESMIDS UNIQUE TO SCOTLAND

Ralfs' monograph was a great stimulus to the study of British desmids, and it soon became clear that the bogs and peaty pools of the highlands and islands of Scotland

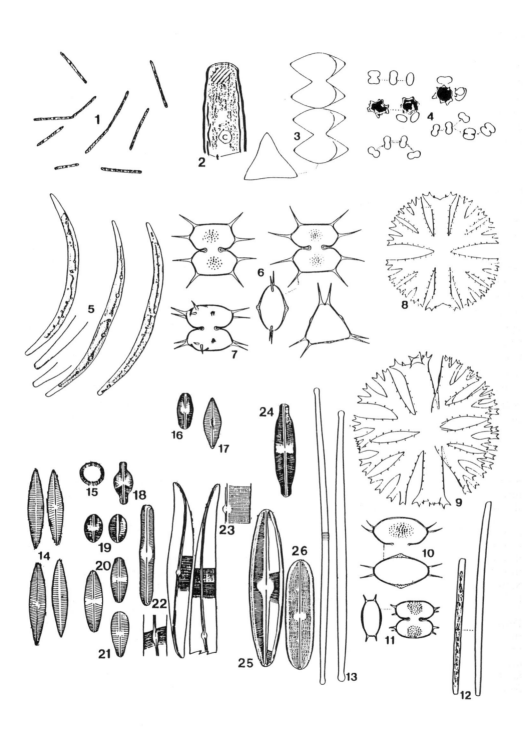

provided rich gathering grounds. One result was that Dr John Roy, headmaster of an Aberdeen school, contributed papers to Scottish natural history journals on desmids from Perthshire (1877), the island of Mull (1883) and East Fife (1892), as well as producing an interesting historical sketch of the freshwater algae of the east of Scotland (1887). With J. P. Bisset he wrote a series of papers in which a number of new desmids from Scotland were described (Roy and Bisset, 1894). It is of particular interest to note that on at least one occasion Roy accompanied the eminent Swedish desmidiologist, Professor C. F. O. Nordstedt, to Sutherland to study the algae in some of the area's shallow freshwater lochs. Although Nordstedt published on desmids from virtually all over the world, unfortunately no papers resulted from his Scottish visit. Two species with connections to Roy and Bisset, and of current interest, are the desmids *Closterium scoticum* and *C. balmacarense*. They were first described by Turner (1893) from material collected by A. W. Wills from Balmacara, near the Kyle of Lochalsh, in 1881 and then redescribed, using Turner's illustrations, by Roy and Bisset (1894).

A search in 1985 for these two essentially Scottish desmids which have never been reported from any other part of the world was unsuccessful. However, in October of 1992, Alan Joyce sent samples collected in Glen Drynoch on Skye. In one of the samples was an unmistakeable specimen of *C. scoticum* (Figure 8.1(13)); in another, several specimens which concur in several respects with the brief, original and only description of *C. balmacarense*. The latter, however, can almost certainly be referred to as *C. subscoticum*, which should now be declared its synonym. So far, 216 desmid taxa have been identified from these recent collections; some are new to the British Isles, and several are new to Scotland (Brook, in preparation).

Because of the apparent inability of the majority of desmids to resist desiccation, which thus limits their dispersal, many populations, especially of phytoplankters, are probably clones which may have propagated themselves by purely vegetative means

---

FIGURE 8.1. Some freshwater algae, mainly desmids and diatoms, which to date have only been recorded from Scotland. 1. *Synecococcus capitatus* (Cyanobacteria) from Loch Leven, Kinross, showing individual cells and cells about to divide. 2. Electron micrograph section of cell of *S. capitatus* (from Bailey-Watts and Komarek, 1991). 3. *Staurodesmus angulatus* var. *planctonicum* from Loch Shin, Inverness. 4. *Cosmocladium perissum* from Aberdeenshire and Glen Clova. 5. *Closterium arcus* from Sutherland. 6. *Xanthidium controversum* from north-west Scotland, Skye and the Hebrides. 7. *X. subhastiferum* var. *murrayi* facies *triquetra*, restricted to the plankton of Loch Lomond. 8. *Micrasterias murrayi* from the plankton of Loch Ruar, Sutherland, and from Loch an Eilean, Skye. 9. *M. murrayi* facies *triquetra* from the plankton of Loch Doon, Ayrshire. 10. *Xanthidium tetracentrotum* fo. *protuberans* from the plankton of Loch Laxdale, Isle of Harris. 11. *X. tetracentrotum* var. *quadricornutum* from a pool near Durris Bridge, Kincardine (after Roy and Bisset, 1894). 12. *Roya cambrica* fo. *limnetica* from the plankton of Loch Katrine, Perthshire. 13. *Closterium scoticum* from Balmacara, Inverness, and Glen Drynoch, Isle of Skye. 14. *Achnanthes exiloides* from Shetland. 15. *Cyclotella delicatissima* from Shetland. 16. *Navicula pseudoclamans* from Shetland. 17. *N. pseudomeniscu-lus* from Shetland. 18. *N. glomus* from Shetland. 19. *Cocconeis confusa* from Shetland. 20. *Navicula scirpus* from Shetland. 21. *Gomphoneis olivaceoides* from Shetland. 22. *Navicula caenosus* from Shetland. 23. *Gyrosigma algoris* from Shetland. 24. *Navicula menda* from Shetland. 25. *Neidium juba* from Shetland. 26. *N. testa* from Shetland.
(Figures 8.1 (14–26) are all from Carter and Bailey-Watts, 1981)

over periods of thousands of years (Brook, 1959a). Such isolated populations are of interest in evolutionary terms with reference to Mayr's "Founder Principle". As a consequence, quite distinctive local races may arise in a particular locality. Indeed, there is good evidence that several planktonic desmid taxa have quite restricted distributions. Distinctive forms of a particular species have thus been described from different lakes within a comparatively small geographic area, such as Scotland. Depending on the predilections of their discoverer, these have been named as distinct varieties, or have even been given specific rank (Brook, 1959a). Examples are *Xanthidium controversum* var. *planctonicum* (Figure 8.1(6)) which is restricted to the north-west of Scotland and lochs in Skye and the Hebrides; *Staurastrum cingulum* var. *affine*, confined to Caithness, the Orkney and Shetland Islands; and *X. subhastiferum* var. *murrayi* facies *triquetra* (Figure 8.1(7)) found only in the plankton of Loch Lomond. The species *Staurodesmus angulatus* var. *planctonicum* (Figure 8.1(3)) seems to be unique to the plankton of Loch Shin. The colonial *Cosmocladium perissum* (Figure 8.1(4)) seems to be restricted to the Grampians and the Clova Mountains. Of non-planktonic desmids, *Staurastrum retusum* var. *boreale* has been recorded only from the Orkneys and Shetlands (see Williamson (1993) for the most recent survey of Shetland desmids), *X. teracentrotum* var. *quadricornutum* has been recorded from Kincardine (Figure 8.1(11)) and a new species, *Closterium arcus* (Figure 8.1(5)) has recently been described from a Sutherland bog (Brook and Williamson, 1988). The Wests described 690 species and 450 varieties of desmids from the British Isles, and 90 taxa have been added subsequently (Brook and Williamson, 1991). A very considerable proportion of these taxa occur in Scotland.

THE DIATOM FLORA

It is not known exactly how many diatoms have been recorded from Scottish fresh waters, but the figure is probably in excess of 4000 taxa (John Carter, personal communication). Two indications of the diversity of this component of the freshwater flora can be gauged from just two papers. According to Whitton (1974), a Natural History Museum survey of all groups of plants on the Isle of Mull listed *ca* 400 species of freshwater diatoms (Ross and Simms, 1978), while from 58 pools and lochs in the Shetland Islands 603 species and varieties of diatoms were recorded, of which 21 (e.g. Figure 8.1 (14–23)) were reported as new to science (Carter and Bailey-Watts, 1981). Although there is very little understanding of the ecology of these largely attached and benthic diatoms, the ecology of numerous species of diatoms in the phytoplankton is much better known and some valuable contributions to their biology have been made in recent investigations of a few Scottish lochs. These include, in particular, Loch Leven (Bailey-Watts *et al.*, 1989a; b) and Coldingham Loch (Bailey-Watts, 1987) and, to a lesser extent, studies on Lochs Awe, Lomond, Morar, Ness and Shiel (Bailey-Watts and Duncan, 1981), Loch Lomond and the Lake of Menteith (Maulood and Boney, 1978; 1980; 1981) and Loch Kinardochy (Brook and Holden, 1957).

   Diatom analyses of Scottish lake sediment cores and lake surface sediments have made important contributions to recent investigations that have been concerned with the well-publicized problems of acid rain and freshwater acidification (see Chapter

7). In this connection it is of interest to note that, resulting from these studies, a diatom species new to science, *Acnanthes scotica* has been described from Lochnagar in the Cairngorms (Flower and Jones, 1989).

PHYTOPLANKTON OF SCOTTISH LOCHS

A major impetus to the study of the Scottish freshwater phytoplankton was the Bathymetric Survey of Scottish Lochs (Murray and Pullar, 1910) and the investigations associated with it by West and West (1903; 1905a). From a limnological point of view, a later paper (West and West, 1909) on the British freshwater phytoplankton proved to be a significant contribution to the biological classification of lakes. In this, the Wests concluded that desmid-rich phytoplankton corresponded geographically with pre-Carboniferous, granitic rocks, which give rise to waters poor in dissolved minerals. Although the Wests did not formulate, in any precise way, biological lake types, it was partly on the basis of their work and the researches of Lemmermann (1904), and Wesenberg-Lund's (1905) comparison of the lakes of Scotland and Denmark, that Teiling (1916) applied the terms Caledonian and Baltic, respectively, to lakes poor and rich in nutrients (see also Bachmann, 1906; 1907). Naumann (1917; 1919) substituted the now much used ecological terms oligotrophic and eutrophic to poor and rich lake waters. Pearsall (1922; 1930; 1932) introduced the concept of lake evolution, and it was his chemical investigations, coupled with phytoplankton studies in the English Lake District, that provided some insight regarding the factors that were probably responsible for the appearance of distinctive phytoplankton types.

Pearsall (1924) concluded that it was the ratio of monovalent to divalent cations, $(Na^+ + K^+)/ (Ca^{2+} + Mg^{2+})$, that was the determining factor in the occurrence of distinctive phytoplankton assemblages. Thus, ratios less than 1.0 would be found in lakes most likely to support diatom/blue-green algae (Cyanobacteria) assemblages, while lakes with ratios greater than 1.0 would have a plankton dominated by desmids. From data pertaining to net-collected phytoplankton distribution in 99 Scottish lochs, ranging from distinctly eutrophic and productive to oligo-dystrophic lochs (Brook, 1954; 1957a; b; 1958a; 1959a; 1964; 1965), and the relevant data on their water chemistry, statistical associations were determined between phytoplankton assemblages as represented by phytoplankton quotients (Nygaard, 1949; Brook, 1981), and the levels of Ca^{2+}, Mg^{2+}, Na^+ and K^+, and the ratio $(Na^+ + K^+)/(Ca^{2+} + Mg^{2+}$ (Shoesmith and Brook, 1983). The resulting analysis suggested that the observed strong correlation between phytoplankton types and Pearsall's widely accepted monovalent/divalent ratio was a spurious one. It did, however, confirm that there is a strong correlation between phytoplankton type and divalent cation concentrations, and especially Ca^{2+}. These divalent cation concentrations may be acting as "proxies" for other features of the aquatic chemical environment which are more important in a causal sense. One such may be bicarbonate ions which are intimately associated with Ca^{2+} in the chemistry and biology of fresh waters. Much still remains to be learned about the chemical conditions which determine the occurrence and distribution of widely differing phytoplankton types (Moss, 1972; 1973a; b) such as exist in Scotland's great diversity of lochs.

Prior to and associated in part with their important studies of Scottish freshwater phytoplankton, the Wests were assembling a major monograph on the British desmid flora (West and West, 1904; 1905b; 1908; 1912; West *et al.*, 1923). In these, 690 species and 450 varieties of desmids are described and beautifully illustrated; for the great majority of these taxa there are references to their occurrence in Scotland. Noteworthy in the detailed records of occurrence is the area around Rhiconich, in Sutherland, which is still a desmid collector's paradise and without question one of the most prolific desmid areas in the world.

NUTRIENT ADDITIONS AND THE PHYTOPLANKTON

Except for a paper on the net phytoplankton of some lochs on the island of Raasay, Inner Hebrides (Griffiths, 1939), in which some attempt was made to relate distribution of the algae in the 22 lochs sampled to the island's fairly complex geology and to the pH and hardness of their waters, the study of the freshwater algae of Scotland appears to have been completely neglected for almost 50 years. After the Second World War, however, a new impetus was applied to algal studies with the establishment of the Brown Trout Research Laboratory (see Chapter 1). A major aspect of the research initiated here was an investigation of the effects of mineral fertilizer additions – initially phosphorus and later NPK – on the growth of Brown Trout (*Salmo trutta*) in Scottish hill lochs. The research was designed to look not just at the effects on the trout, but to follow in as much detail as possible changes brought about on the various components of the food chain. This led to the detailed weekly sampling (for the first time in Scotland) of several lochs, and importantly this sampling was integrated with the measurement of relevant physical and chemical parameters (Brook and Holden, 1957; Brook, 1958b). The sampling was begun in the summer of 1951, a year before the addition of the fertilizer calcium superphosphate, and continued until 1956.

In addition to providing further understanding of some of the problems (as well as raising new questions) regarding phytoplankton periodicity, these first quantitative studies of Scottish freshwater phytoplankton revealed how important were algae of nannoplankton size. Also of special interest were the observations relating to the late winter and early spring dominance of the chrysophytes *Dinobryon cylindricum* and *D. crenulatum* and the very small cryptophyte *Chroomonas acuta* – especially their occurrence under ice. In early January 1953 when ice and packed snow on Loch Kinardochy was over 30 cm thick, some 2250 individuals mL^{-1} of *C. acuta* were present and reached a peak of 3500 mL^{-1}, still under ice, in the following month. Observations on the periodicity of *Dinobryon* species in relation to the spring diatom maxima following fertilization appeared to conflict with the findings of Rodhe (1948). He suggested that *D. divergens* was limited by high phosphorus concentrations (between 100 and 200 μg P L^{-1}) and that this chrysophyte's normal maximum occurrence, which was after the spring diatom outburst, could be correlated with the utilization of phosphorus by the diatom population and the consequent fall in phosphorus to concentrations below the value which inhibits the growth of *Dinobryon*. The size of the spring (and autumn) maxima of chrysophytes declined progressively in Loch Kinardochy in the four years following phosphate enrichment. These maxima were mostly dominated by *D. bavaricum*, or sometimes by *D.*

divergens. The periodicity of the colonial chrysophyte *Stichogloea doederleinii*, which is fairly widespread in oligotrophic Scottish lochs, was also studied. Each of the five seasons of weekly sampling of Loch Kinardochy confirmed it as having late summer maxima.

The phytoplankters which responded most immediately to the phosphate additions were the diatoms *Asterionella formosa* and *Synedra acus* var. *radians*. The green tetrasporine *Gemellicystis neglecta* which had not previously been recorded in Scotland but was subsequently found to be widespread, dominated the phytoplankton community from the late summer of 1953 through to March 1954. It had a maximum of 2600 cells mL^{-1} in November 1953 and a smaller maximum of 1500 cells mL^{-1} in March. The latter maximum fell rapidly, however, and the tetrasporine's final disappearance by the end of March was associated with a devastating infection of its cells by the fungal parasite *Rhizophydium fulgens*.

A further series of fertilization experiments were initiated in 1954 in small lochs in the Scourie district of Sutherland (Holden, 1959). However, because of the considerable distance between these experimental sites and the Pitlochry laboratory, their phytoplankton could not be studied in the same detail as in the Loch Kinardochy experiment.

THE USE OF ALGAE IN LAKE CLASSIFICATION

The relative dominance of the major groups of planktonic algae recognized by West and West (1909) and Teiling (1916) as significant for the classification of lakes, was extended when Thunmark (1945), and Nygaard (1949) suggested that such algae might be used as indicators of the trophic status of lakes. Thunmark (1945) indicated that the ratio of the number of species of Chlorococcales to Desmidiaceae in a net collection of phytoplankton was "eloquently expressive" of the trophic status of several Swedish lakes. Nygaard (1949) elaborated Thunmark's so-called "Chlorophycean Quotient" and devised, in particular, a Compound Quotient. Its numerator included not only the numbers of Chlorococcales but also Cyanobacteria + centric diatoms + Euglenophyta, all of whose species tend to have eutrophic tendencies, while the denominator was represented only by Desmidiaceae. Quotient values of less than 1.0 were said to indicate oligotrophy, with values of 0.3 or less signifying dystrophy. Values greater than 1.0 suggested eutrophy, while values of 5.0 or more indicated hypertrophic conditions.

With chemical and various biological parameters being available from various researches conducted at the Freshwater Fisheries Laboratory, it was possible to test in some detail the validity of Nygaard's quotient hypothesis. One of the major problems recognized in using phytoplankton quotients is to distinguish between true (euplankter) and chance (tychoplankter) populations. The inclusion of the latter, especially in the denominator when calculating quotients, can lead to very considerable errors. An analysis was made of the desmid populations in almost a hundred lochs. Using the criteria that euplankters are: (1) rarely, if ever, found in habitats other than the plankton, and (2) that a significant number of individuals of a species have been found undergoing division in the open water of the deepest lochs, the results suggested that only about 30 desmids can be considered as euplanktonic (Brook, 1959a). Data from 18 lochs of diverse character ranging from acid, dystrophic lochs in Sutherland to the very productive, eutrophic Loch Leven near Kinross, showed reasonable agreement in their ranking based on pH, alkalinity and quantitative assessments of their bottom faunas, in relation to assessments of their Compound Phytoplankton Quotients. Moreover, in the fertilization experiments of the Sutherland lochs mentioned above, in those lochs where blooms of Chlorococcales and Cyanobacteria developed, Compound Quotients increased from between 0.3 and 0.7 (oligotrophic) to between 5.0 and 11.0 (distinctly eutrophic). The values for the controls over the same period showed no significant changes when their quotients were assessed (Brook, 1958b; 1965).

There are examples in the literature of rapid eutrophication of lakes with corresponding dramatic changes in the composition of their phytoplankton, such as the Zurichsee and to a lesser extent Windermere. Increasing urban development within the lakes' catchment areas has been held to be a major cause. Loch Leven, undoubtedly Scotland's most famous fishing loch, although eutrophic by the nature of its morphology and underlying geology, has been enriched by agricultural fertilizers and urban and industrial development over the past 100 years or so. Blooms of the cyanobacterium *Anabaena* were reported by Wesenberg-Lund (1905) and Bachmann (1906), while Rosenberg (1937) reported a dramatic reduction of trout catches from a previous 10-year average of 43 000 fish per annum to only 23 538 for 1937. The massive decline in fishing success was attributed to a bloom of 10 000 filaments ml^{-1} of the cyanobacterium *Oscillatoria bornetii*, which was said to be obscuring the fishermen's lures. Catches recovered to normal levels once the bloom dispersed. In 1954, some 20 000 filaments ml^{-1} of the significantly smaller *O. limnetica* were counted and in 1963 17 000 ml^{-1} of *Aphanizomenon flos aquae* (Brook, 1965). This latter bloom appeared as the ice broke up in April of that year following the severe winter of 1962/63 when ice covered the loch for six weeks. The bloom persisted until June 1964 (Holden and Caines, 1974). An irregular succession of blooms involving a range of phytoplankters has occurred until the present time (Bailey-Watts *et al.*, 1990; see also below).

Bachmann's (1907) data from Loch Leven also indicate that, despite the blooms of *Anabaena* in the early years of this century, 10 desmid species were present in the loch's plankton. A Compound Quotient determined from his data is 19/10 = 1.9, and samples of phytoplankton collected by the Wests in 1904 (and found in the basement of the Royal Scottish Museum exactly 50 years later), revealed on re-examination a quotient of 1.6. Analyses of samples collected in the summers of 1954 and 1955 showed a marked increase in the numbers of Chlorococcales present while the numbers of desmids had diminished. The Compound Quotient of Loch Leven as determined from these samples had increased in 50 years to 7.2, a value clearly indicative of marked eutrophy (Brook, 1965). The desmid species are, in contrast to most Desmidiaceae, amongst those that not only survive, but on occasions thrive in enriched and even markedly alkaline waters (Brook, 1981).

In an account of the dominant phytoplankters in five nutrient-poor Scottish lochs – Lomond, Awe, Ness, Morar and Shiel (Bailey-Watts and Duncan, 1981) – it is pointed out that although desmids are well represented, so also are other green algae and Cyanobacteria. Moreover, it is emphasized that Cryptophyceae and/or Chrysophyceae constitute the bulk of the summer maxima in terms of numbers of cells per unit volume. Many more contributions need to be made to the taxonomy of these undoubtedly important but "difficult" taxonomic groups in Scottish fresh waters (see Brook, 1954; 1955; 1957b; 1958a). Bailey-Watts and Duncan (1981) review concepts concerning the phytoplankton of oligotrophic lakes and indicator species. They point out that the very existence of species which indicate oligotrophic conditions has been questioned by Rawson (1956), and that both he and Brook (1965) have discussed the relative merits of dominant and rare forms as indicators.

Phytoplankton ecologists also recognize that individual species from groups of organisms, such as desmids, that are supposed to be indicative of oligotrophy, or Cyanobacteria generally assumed to be almost exclusively associated with eutrophy, may thrive in oligotrophic waters. For example, in Scottish lochs, the desmids *Staurastrum chaetoceras* and *S. pingue* are most commonly associated with productive, alkaline waters (Brook, 1965). Desmids can even produce significant populations in such waters, and there are at least two reports of them becoming very abundant in enriched Scottish lochs. Thus in the small, eutrophic Coldingham Loch, Berwick, late winter and early spring phytoplankton assemblages contained significant numbers of *Closterium acutum.*, *C. limneticum* and *S. chaetoceras*. A large population of *C. acutum*, estimated in the region of 1000 cells mL^{-1} and with a chlorophyll *a* biomass of 3.5 μgL^{-1}, developed in September (Bailey-Watts, 1987). In the shallow, Lower Faedaire Loch, Tayside (alkalinity *ca.* 25 mg $CaCO_3$ L^{-1}), the highest density of a desmid ever recorded (91.4×10^3) was present in October 1991 (Bailey-Watts, unpublished). The desmid is a very small *Cosmarium* ($7.0–8.5 \times 6.0–7.0$ μm) which has tentatively been assigned to *C. asphaerosporum* var. *dissectum*. On the other hand, it should be noted that the large, complex cyanobacterial filaments of various *Scytonema* and *Stigeonema* species can be common in peaty pools and lochans (Brook, 1954), as can species of *Chroococcus*, *Gomphosphaeria*, *Merismopedia*, etc. (Brook, 1955). These fascinating cyanobacterial components of the Scottish freshwater flora have been virtually neglected and are well worthy of detailed study.

LOCH LEVEN PHYTOPLANKTON AND THE INTERNATIONAL BIOLOGICAL PROGRAMME

As indicated above, several isolated, short-term studies were carried out on the phytoplankton of Loch Leven from the early years of this century to the end of the 1950s. It was the appearance of frequent and extensive blooms of Cyanobacteria that led to the first detailed and regular chemical analyses being carried out in 1963. In the following year it was proposed that an extensive programme of research on the loch should be developed as one of the United Kingdom's contributions to the International Biological Programme (IBP). In 1967, regular monitoring of Loch Leven's phytoplankton populations was initiated (Figure 8.2). A year later these studies were enhanced by regular measurements of the loch's primary production (Morgan, 1974). Although the IBP officially came to an end in 1971, the results of the Loch Leven phytoplankton studies proved to be of such fundamental interest (being the first to have been carried out in such detail on a large, shallow lake which rarely became stratified) that they have continued to the present time. As pointed out by Bailey-Watts (1974), the features of the loch of particular limnological interest are its unusual area/depth ratio, the abundant sources of dissolved inorganic nutrients

FIGURE 8.2. A Ruttner bottle being lowered to sample algae in Loch Leven, Kinross, during the International Biological Programme (1967–1971). Photograph: Peter Wakely

which are delivered by way of several measurable inflows and from bottom sediments, the relative unimportance of the macrophytic vegetation, and the differing feeding strategies of the loch's dominant zooplankters.

Bailey-Watts *et al.* (1990), reviewing the phytoplankton studies carried out over an 18-year period, emphasize that there are marked seasonal and annual differences in species composition and population densities. Approximately 300 species of algae and Cyanobacteria have now been recorded from the loch of which some 150 are listed in Bailey-Watts (1974). However, only about 50 species are said to have assumed any aspect of importance and many of these only for short periods. In spite of the complex and somewhat erratic kaleidoscope in species succession, an interesting and original aspect of Bailey-Watts *et al.*'s long-term research has been the identification of seasonal patterns in the size distribution of the loch's phytoplankton assemblages. Thus it has been shown (Bailey-Watts, 1986a; b; Bailey-Watts *et al.*, 1990) that in recent years the winter to spring chlorophyll *a* maxima are invariably dominated by small cells (< 15 m). In contrast, the summer chlorophyll *a* maxima (and minima) are largely composed of populations of significantly larger species. Of particular interest amongst the very small cells was a cyanobacterium new to science, *Synecococcus capitatus* (Bailey-Watts and Komarek (1991)), which dominated the summer plankton prior to 1971. It had two major maxima of abundance, one in 1968 of *ca.* 5×10^6 cells mL^{-1} and another in 1970 of *ca.* 1.5×10^6 cells mL^{-1}. Other small phytoplankters present in the summer of the earlier study years were, in 1969, the filamentous cyanobacterium *Oscillatoria redeki* with 0.8×10^4 trichomes mL^{-1}, and a May – June maximum of the small green alga *Steiniella* (near *gravenitzii*). The virtual disappearance of small forms (picoplankton) from the summer plankton after 1971 coincided with an explosive increase in the numbers of the zooplankter *Daphnia hyalina* which has attained maxima of 50–100 individuals L^{-1} in most years since 1971. Another consequence of the increase in *D. hyalina* numbers was a marked increase in water clarity and a corresponding decrease in the levels of chlorophyll *a*. In the winter of 1971 the very small centric diatom *Cyclotella pseudostelligeria* became dominant in the plankton with a maximum of 250×10^5 cells mL^{-1}.

Since 1971, the observed maxima of *Synecococcus*, *O. redeki* and *Steiniella* and other green algae such as *Micractinium pusillum* and *Dictyosphaerium pulchellum*, have been about 1/1000th of their greatest maxima. Also *Diatoma elongatum* was never more than one tenth of its greatest 1968–71 maximum abundance. However, *Asterionella formosae* and various unicellular centric diatoms continued to thrive while *Cyclotella glomerata* was the main component of the 1973–74 mid-winter plankton maximum.

One of the most difficult problems to be solved in phytoplankton dynamics is the identification of the centric diatoms. Because the diversity of forms, many as abundant as 10^4–10^6 cells mL^{-1}, were difficult to identify during the long-term Loch Leven studies, the examination of their frustules by scanning electron microscopy was resorted to. It was then found that the major genus was *Stephanodiscus* and included, in the main, *S. parvus*, *S. hantzschii* and *S. hantzschii* fo. *tenuis*. Other specimens resembled *S. invisitatus*, *S. oreganica*, *S. alpina* and *S. makarovae*. The genus *Cyclotella* was represented mainly by forms of *C. pseudostelligera*, but on one occasion there was a virtually pure population of C. *radiosa*. Cells tentatively assigned to the new genus *Cyclostephanos* were also recorded (Bailey-Watts, 1986b).

Most of the Loch Leven algal studies have explored the dynamics of phytoplankton populations in relation to physical factors (light and temperature regimes) and nutrient cycles (phosphorus, nitrogen and silica; see Bailey-Watts *et al.*, 1989a; b) which are known to determine production. Elsewhere most studies of phytoplankton periodicity have been of thermally stratifying, dimictic temperate lakes and, as pointed out by Round (1971), it is the development and subsequent stratification that are cardinal points in the annual cycles observed in such lakes; it is these events that provide a degree of regularity to phytoplankton periodicity. The lack of well-defined temperature cycles may explain, at least in part, the absence of any clear seasonality in phytoplankton succession in Loch Leven (Bailey-Watts, 1978).

Useful contributions have also been made by the Loch Leven studies to our understanding of the influence of fungal parasites and of some of the effects of grazing by protozoa, rotifers and planktonic crustaceans on phytoplankton. Fungal studies include parasitism by chytrids on *Dictyosphaerium pulchellum* and *Ankyra judayi* (Bailey-Watts and Lund, 1973; Bailey-Watts, 1988). With regard to protozoa, a vampyrellid has attacked *D. pulchellum* while another, *Asterocaelum algophilum* has affected centric diatom populations. May (1980) has provided quantitative data relating to the grazing of the rotifer *Notholca squamula* on the diatom *Asterionella formosa*. Changes in the abundance of *Daphnia hyalina* have been associated with changes in the mean lengths of *Oscillatoria agardhi* trichomes, while changes in filament lengths of species of the diatom *Melosira* have been attributed to changes in the abundance of *Cyclops* spp. (Bailey-Watts and Kirika, 1981). Parasitism and grazing have been considered as a possible cause for the rarity of many of the less common phytoplankters in the loch (Bailey-Watts *et al.*, 1990) though the major impact of parasites and micro-grazers is that they probably accelerate the decline of those populations which are already under the stresses brought about by nutrient limitation.

One other aspect of phytoplankton dynamics which has been highlighted by the Loch Leven studies is the importance of the variable oceanic climate of Scotland on this large, exposed, shallow body of water. The effects of weather have thus been explored, especially insofar as it affects the residence of water in the loch (flushing rates) (Bailey-Watts *et al.*, 1990). Flushing rates would seem to have a considerable effect on temperature regimes and on nutrient dynamics. These in turn control major features of phytoplankton succession which may then determine the success or demise of the zooplankters which graze on these algae.

The many and varied aspects of the Loch Leven study have provided important contributions to general knowledge of phytoplankton population dynamics and have attracted back to Scotland international interest almost forgotten since the days of Murray and Pullar (1910). In particular, these studies have increased our understanding of the biology of large shallow lakes, a limnological category which previously had been virtually ignored. The results also have relevance to the much better studied, stratifying lake systems of classical limnology (Hutchinson, 1957; 1967), and confirm how vital it is to engage in long-term studies if one is to gain more than a superficial understanding of the dynamics of any highly complex community.

CONCLUDING COMMENT

In reviewing the 170 years or so since it became obvious to Greville (1824) that the fresh waters of Scotland had much to offer the cryptogamic botanist, or the 100 years since Turner (1893) described *Closterium scoticum*, it is fair to conclude that considerable progress has been made in the study of the country's freshwater algae. Undoubtedly much awaits to be achieved even from a purely floristic standpoint, for there are great gaps in our knowledge of such "unpopular" taxonomic groups as Chrysophyceae, Cryptophyceae and Xanthophyceae (there are no recognized British experts for any of them), which are undoubtedly abundant in upland areas of the country. With regard to the Cyanobacteria it is understandable that it is those species that proliferate to become nuisance organisms that have received considerable attention. However, much remains to be discovered about the occurrence and ecology of the many species that are known to occur in peaty, acid waters. How much will be achieved in the next 100 years, or even between now and the celebration of the 100th meeting of the Scottish Freshwater Group, will undoubtedly depend on how much both young professional scientists, and amateur microscopists (Brook, 1993) can be encouraged to enter this important field of freshwater science.

REFERENCES

Bachmann, H. (1906). "Le plankton des lacs écossais", *Archives Scientifique et Physique Naturelle*, **20**, 1–24.

Bachmann, H. (1907). "Vergleichende Studien über das Phytoplankton von Seen Schottlands und der Schweiz", *Archiv für Hydrobiologie,* **3**, 1–37.

Bailey-Watts, A. E. (1974). "The algal plankton of Loch Leven," *Proceedings of the Royal Society of Edinburgh*, **74 B**, 135–156.

Bailey-Watts, A. E. (1978). "A nine-year study of the phytoplankton of the eutrophic and non-stratifying Loch Leven, Kinross, Scotland", *Journal of Ecology*, **6**, 741–771.

Bailey-Watts, A. E. (1986a). "Seasonal variation in size spectra of phytoplankton assemblages in Loch Leven, Scotland", *Hydrobiologia*, **138**, 25–42.

Bailey-Watts, A. E. (1986b). "The abundance, size distribution and species composition of unicellular Centrales assemblages at late Winter–early Spring maxima in Loch Leven (Kinross, Scotland) 1968 – 1985", *9th Diatom Symposium 1986*, 1–16.

Bailey-Watts, A. E. (1987). "Coldingham Loch, S. E. Scotland. II. Phytoplankton succession and ecology in the year prior to mixer installation", *Freshwater Biology*, **17**, 419–428.

Bailey-Watts, A. E. (1988). "Studies on the control of the early spring diatom maximum in Loch Leven, 1981", in *Algae and the Aquatic Environment* (Ed. F. E. Round), pp. 53–87, Biopress Bristol, and Koeltz, Koenigstein.

Bailey-Watts, A. E. and Duncan, P. (1981). "The phytoplankton", in *The Ecology of Scotland's Largest Lochs: Lomond, Awe, Ness, Morar and Shiel* (Ed. P. S. Maitland), pp. 91–118, Junk, The Hague.

Bailey-Watts, A. E. and Kirika, A. (1981). "The assessment of size variation in Loch Leven phytoplankton: methodology and some of its uses in the study of factors influencing size", *Journal of Plankton Research*, **3**, 261–282.

Bailey-Watts, A.E and Komarek, J. (1991). "Towards a formal description of new species of Synechococcus (Cyanobacteria/Cyanophyceae) from the freshwater picoplankton", *Algological Studies*, **61**, 5–19.

Bailey-Watts, A. E. and Lund, J. W. G. (1973). "Observations of a diatom bloom in Loch Leven, Scotland", *Biological Journal of the Linnean Society*, **5**, 235–253.

Bailey-Watts, A. E., Smith, I. R. and Kirika, A. (1989a). "The dynamics of silica in a shallow, diatom-rich stream I: Stream inputs of the dissolved nutrient", *Diatom Research*, **4**, 179–190.

Bailey-Watts, A. E., Smith, I. R. and Kirika, A. (1989b). "The dynamics of silica in a shallow, diatom-rich Scottish loch II: The influence of diatoms on an annual budget", *Diatom Research*, **4**, 191–205.

Bailey-Watts, A. E., Kirika, A., May, L. and Jones, D. H. (1990). "Changes in phytoplankton over various time scales in a shallow, eutrophic lake: the Loch Leven experience, with special reference to the influence of flushing rate", *Freshwater Biology*, **23**, 85–111.

Brook, A.J. (1954). "Notes on some uncommon algae in the Tummel–Garry catchment area", *Transactions of the Botanical Society of Edinburgh*, **36**, 207–214.

Brook, A. J. (1955), "Notes on some uncommon algae from lochs in Kinross, Perthshire and Caithness", *Transactions of the Botanical Society of Edinburgh*, **36**, 309–316.

Brook, A. J. (1957a). "Water blooms", *New Biology*, **23**, 86–101.

Brook, A. J. (1957b). "Notes on some uncommon algae from lochs in Perthshire and Sutherland", *Transactions of the Botanical Society of Edinburgh*, **37**, 112–114.

Brook, A. J. (1958a). "Notes on algae from the plankton of some Scottish freshwater lochs", *Transactions of the Botanical Society of Edinburgh*, **37**, 175–181.

Brook, A. J. (1958b). "Changes in the phytoplankton of some Scottish hill lochs resulting from their artificial enrichment", *Verhandlungen der Internationalen Vereiningung für theoretische und angewandte Limnologie*, **13**, 298–305.

Brook, A. J. (1959a). "*Staurastrum paradoxum* Meyen and *S. gracile* in the British freshwater plankton, and a revision of the *S. anatinum*-group of radiate desmids", *Transactions of the Royal Society of Edinburgh*, **63**, 589–628.

Brook, A. J. (1959b). "The status of desmids in the phytoplankton and the determination of phytoplankton quotients", *Journal of Ecology*, **47**, 429–445.

Brook, A. J. (1964). "The phytoplankton of the Scottish freshwater lochs", in *The Vegetation of Scotland* (Ed. J. H. Burnett), pp. 290–300, Oliver and Boyd, Edinburgh.

Brook, A. J. (1965). "Planktonic algae as indicators of lake types, with special reference to the Desmidiaceae", *Limnology and Oceanography*, **10**, 403–411.

Brook, A. J. (1981). *The Biology of Desmids*, Botanical Monograph 16, Blackwell, Oxford.

Brook, A. J. (1993). "Mainly for pleasure; or the amateur microscopist as a contributor to science", *Quekett Journal of Microscopy*, **37**, 1–6.

Brook, A. J. and Holden, A. V. (1957). "Fertilization experiments on Scottish freshwater lochs. I. Loch Kinardochy", *Scientific Investigations of the Freshwater Fisheries of Scotland*, No. 17.

Brook, A. J. and Williamson, D. B. (1988). "*Closterium arcus* sp. nov., a new British desmid", *British Phycological Journal*, **23**, 391–394.

Brook, A. J. and Williamson, D. B. (1991). "*A Check-list of Desmids of the British Isles*, Occasional Publication No. 28, Freshwater Biological Association, Ambleside.

Carter, J. R. and Bailey-Watts, A. E. (1981). "A taxonomic study of diatoms from standing water in Shetland", *Nova Hedwigia*, **33**, 513–629.

Flower, R. J. and Jones, V. J. (1989). "Taxonomic descriptions and occurrence of new *Achnanthes* taxa in acid lakes in the U.K.", *Diatom Research*, **4**, 227–239.

Greville, R. K. (1824). *Flora Edinensis*, Blackwood, Edinburgh.

Greville, R. K. (1827). *Scottish Cryptogamic Flora*, Vol. V, MacLachlan and Stewart, Edinburgh.

Greville. R. K. (1828). *Scottish Cryptogamic Flora*, Vol. VI, MacLachlan and Stewart, Edinburgh.

Greville, R. K. (1833). "Div. IV, Diatomaceae", in *British Flora* (Ed. W. Mooker), Vol. II, pp. 401–415, Longman, Orme, Brown, Green and Longman, London.

Greville, R. K. (1855). "Report on a collection of Diatomaceae made in the district of Braemar by Professor Balfour and Mr George Lawson", *Annals and Magazine of Natural History*, Series 2, **15**, 252–261.

Griffiths, B. M. (1939). "The free-floating microscopic plant life or phytoplankton of the lakes of the Isle of Raasay, Inner Hebrides, Western Scotland", *Proceedings of the University of Durham Philosophical Society*, **10**, 71–87.

Holden, A. V. (1959). "Fertilization experiments in Scottish freshwater lochs. II. Sutherland 1954. 1. Chemical and botanical observations", *Freshwater Salmon Fisheries Research Scotland*, **24**, 1–42.

Holden, A. V. and Caines, L. A. (1974). "Nutrient chemistry of Loch Leven", *Proceedings of the Royal Society of Edinburgh*, **74B**, 101–121.

Hutchinson, G. E. (1957). *A Treatise on Limnology*, Vol. I, John Wiley, New York.

Hutchinson, G. E. (1967). *A Treatise of Limnology*, Vol. II, John Wiley, New York.

Lemmerman, E. (1904). "Das Plankton schwedischer Gewasser", *Arkiv für Botanik*, **2**, 1–209.

Maulood, B. K. and Boney, A. D. (1978). "Diurnal variation of the phytoplankton in Loch Lomond", *Hydrobiologia*, **58**, 99–117.

Maulood, B. K. and Boney, A. D. (1980). "A seasonal and ecological study of the phytoplankton of Loch Lomond", *Hydrobiologia*, **71**, 239–259.

Maulood, B. K. and Boney, A. D. (1981). "Phytoplankton ecology of the Lake of Menteith", *Hydrobiologia*, **79**, 179–186.

May, L. (1980). "On the ecology of *Notholca squamula* Müller in Loch Leven. Kinross, Scotland", *Hydrobiologia*, **73**, 177–180.

Morgan, N. C. (1974). "Historical background to the International Biological Programme project at Loch Leven, Kinross", *Proceedings of the Royal Society of Edinburgh*, **74B**, 45–55.

Moss, B. (1972). "The influence of environmental factors on the distribution of freshwater algae. An experimental study. I. Introduction and Ca concentration", *Journal of Ecology*, **60**, 917–932.

Moss, B. (1973a). "The influence of environmental factors on the distribution of freshwater algae. II. The role of pH and the carbon dioxide–bicarbonate system", *Journal of Ecology*, **61**, 157–177.

Moss, B. (1973b). "The influence of environmental factors on the distribution of freshwater algae. IV. Growth of test species in natural lake waters, and conclusion", *Journal of Ecology*, **61**, 193–211.

Murray, J. and Pullar, L. (1910). *Bathymetrical Survey of the Fresh Water Lochs of Scotland*, Challenger Office, Edinburgh.

Naumann, E. (1917). "Undersokningar ofver Fytoplankton och uber deb pelagiska regionen forsiggaende gyttjeoch dybildingar inom vissa sydoch mellansvenska urbergavatten", *Kungliga Svenska Vetenskaps-Akadamiens Handlinger*, **56**, 1–165. English translation by Freshwater Biological Association.

Naumann, E. (1919). "Nagra synpunkter angaende Limnoplanktons Ökologie med sarskild hansyn till fytoplankton", *Svenska Botanika Tidskrift*, **13**, 129–161.

Nygaard, G. (1949). "Hydrobiological studies of some Danish ponds and lakes. Part II. The Quotient Hypothesis, and some new or little known phytoplankton organisms", *Det Kogelige Danske Videnskabernes Selskab Biologiske Skrifter*, **7**, 1–293.

Pearsall, W. H. (1922). "A suggestion as to the factors influencing the distribution of free-floating vegetation", *Journal of Ecology*, **9**, 241–253.

Pearsall, W. H. (1924). "Phytoplankton and environment in the English Lake District", *Revue Algologique*, **1**, 54–67.

Pearsall, W. H. (1930). "Phytoplankton of the English Lakes. I. The proportions in the water of some dissolved substances of biological importance", *Journal of Ecology*, **18**, 306–320.

Pearsall, W. H. (1932). "Phytoplankton of the English Lakes. II. The composition of the phytoplankton in relation to dissolved substances", *Journal of Ecology*, **20**, 241–263.

Ralfs, J. (1843). "Remarks of the species of *Desmidium*", *Transactions of the Botanical Society of Edinburgh*, **2**, 5–9.

Ralfs, J. (1846). "On the British Desmidieae", *Transactions of the Botanical Society of Edinburgh*, **2**, 119–169.

Ralfs, J. (1848). *British Desmidieae*, Reeve, Benham and Reeve, London.

Rawson, D. S. (1956). "Algal indicators of lake types", *Limnology and Oceanography*, **1**, 18–25.

Rodhe, W. (1984). "Environmental requirements of freshwater algae. Experimental studies in the ecology of phytoplankton", *Symbolae Botanicae Upsaliensis*, **10**, 1–149.

Rosenberg, M. (1937). "Algae and Trout. A biological aspect of the poor trout season in 1937", *Salmon and Trout Magazine*, Dec. 1937, 1–11.

Ross, R. and Sims, P. (1978). "Notes on some diatoms from the Isle of Mull, and other Scottish localities", *Bacillaria*, **1**, 151–168.

Round, F. E. (1971). "The growth and succession of algal populations in freshwaters",

Mitteilungen der Internationalen Vereinigung für theoretische und angewandte Limnologie, **19**, 70–99.

Roy, J. (1877). "Contributions to the desmid flora of Perthshire", *Scottish Naturalist*, 1877, 68 –74.

Roy, J. (1883). "List of the desmids hitherto found in Mull", *Scottish Naturalist*, **1**, 37–40.

Roy, J. (1887). "Historical sketch of the freshwater algae of the east of Scotland", *Scottish Naturalist*, **18**, 148–159.

Roy, J. (1892). "The Desmidieae of East Fife", *Annals of Scottish Natural History*, 192–197.

Roy, J. and Bisset, J. P. (1894). "On Scottish Desmidieae", *Annals of Scottish Natural History*, 100–105; 167–178; 241–256.

Shoesmith, E. and Brook, A. J. (1983). "Monovalent–divalent cation ratios and the occurrence of phytoplankton, with special reference to the desmids", *Freshwater Biology*, **13**, 151–155.

Teiling, E. (1916). "En Kaledonisk fytoplankton-formation", *Svensk Botaniska Tidskrift*, **10**, 506–519.

Thunmark, S. (1945). "Zur Sziologie des Süsswasserplankton. Eine methologische-ökolgische Studie", *Folia Limnological Scandinavica*, **3**, 5–66.

Turner, W. B. (1893). "Desmid notes", *The Naturalist*, 343–347.

Wesenberg-Lund, C. (1905). "A comparative study of the lakes of Scotland and Denmark", *Proceedings of the Royal Society of Edinburgh*, **25**, 401–408.

West, W. and West, G. S. (1903). "Scottish freshwater plankton. No. I", *Journal of the Linnean Society (Botany)*, **35**, 519–556.

West, W. and West, G. S. (1904). *A Monograph of the British Desmidiaceae*, Vol. I, Ray Society, London.

West, W. and West, G. S. (1905a). "A further contribution to the freshwater plankton of the Scottish lochs", *Transactions of the Royal Society of Edinburgh*, **41**, 477–518.

West, W. and West, G. S. (1905b). "A Monograph of the British Desmidiaceae, Vol. I, Ray Society, London.

West, W. and West, G. S. (1908). *A Monograph of the British Desmidiaceae*, Vol. II, Ray Society, London.

West, W. and West, G. S. (1909). "The British freshwater phytoplankton, with special reference to the desmid-plankton and the distribution of British desmids", *Proceedings of the Royal Society of London*, **81B**, 165–206.

West, W. and West, G. S. (1912). *A Monograph of the British Desmidiaceae*, Vol. IV, Ray Society, London.

West, W., West, G. S. and Carter, N. (1923). *A Monograph of the British Desmidiaceae*, Vol. V, Ray Society, London.

Whitton, B. A. (1974). "Changes in the British freshwater algae," in *Systematics Association Special Volume No. 6* (Ed. D. L. Hawksworth), pp. 115–141, Academic Press, London.

Williamson, D. B. (1993). "A contribution to our knowledge of the desmid flora of the Shetland Islands", *Botanical Journal of Scotland*, **46**, 233–285.

9

Macrophytes

M. A. PALMER

Joint Nature Conservation Committee, Monkstone House, City Road, Peterborough, PE1 1UA, UK

N. T. H. HOLMES

Alconbury Environmental Consultants, The Almonds, 57 Ramsey Road, Warboys, PE17 2RW, UK

and

S. L. BELL

Cobham Resource Consultants, 7 Mentone Gardens, Edinburgh, EH9 2DJ, UK

INTRODUCTION

Aquatic macrophytes include a range of flowering plants (Angiospermae), ferns and their allies (Pteridophyta), mosses (Bryopsida and Sphagnopsida), liverworts (Hepaticae), lichens (Eumycota) and larger algae such as stoneworts (Charophyceae). Aquatic species are regarded as plants which spend the majority of time submerged in water, floating on the surface, or rooted beneath the water but with shoots emerging from it. Some plants, especially pondweed *Potamogeton* and water crowfoot *Ranunculus* spp, have leaves of two types – submerged and floating. Other species, for example Amphibious Bistort *Persicaria amphibia*, have two very different forms – aquatic and terrestrial. The distinction between aquatic and terrestrial species is subjective, especially in wetland habitats with fluctuating water levels, but the check-list in Palmer and Newbold (1983) is used here, with the omission of the genera *Spartina* and *Zostera*, which grow in saline situations.

FACTORS INFLUENCING THE AQUATIC FLORA OF SCOTLAND

Because it lies on the Atlantic fringe of the northern half of Europe, Scotland is subject to a number of biogeographical influences. It is particularly important

The Fresh Waters of Scotland: A National Resource of International Significance
Edited by P. S. Maitland, P. J. Boon and D. S. McLusky. © 1994 John Wiley & Sons Ltd

internationally for the Atlantic elements of its bryophyte and lichen floras. Although many of Scotland's aquatic plants are cosmopolitan, the northern element is strong. This is represented, for instance, by the lawns of Shore-weed *Littorella uniflora* and Water Lobelia *Lobelia dortmanna* typical of shallow water in upland lochs. These species extend from north of the Arctic Circle through Northern Europe, with *Lobelia dortmanna* penetrating locally to south-west France (Clapham *et al.*, 1987). The moss *Schistidium agassizzi* is associated with melt waters in Scandinavia and occurs in Scottish rivers such as the Dee, which rise at high altitudes. Conversely, some species are near their northern limit in Scotland. These include Great Pond-sedge *Carex riparia*, which occurs in north Africa, Asia and through Europe to 62°N in Finland (Clapham *et al.*, 1987). A number of species are at the western limit of their distribution in Scotland and Ireland: Shining Pondweed *Potamogeton lucens* and Shetland Pondweed *P. rutilus*, for instance, occur in western Asia as well as in Europe. A few North American plants have naturally colonized areas on the Atlantic seaboard of Europe. These include Pipewort *Eriocaulon aquaticum*, which occurs in a few sites in western Scotland and Ireland, and American Pondweed *Potamogeton epihydrus*, which is known as a native in Europe only from the Outer Hebrides (Clapham *et al.*, 1987).

There are about 190 species (excluding hybrids) of fresh and brackish water vascular plants in Britain. Of these, 15 native and eight recently introduced alien species have not been recorded in Scotland. Twenty-eight native species which are either included in the *British Red Data Book* of vascular plants (Perring and Farrell, 1983) or are nationally scarce (i.e. occur in 16 to 100 10 × 10 km squares in Great Britain) occur in Scotland. These species are listed in Table 9.1. Four of them are confined to Scotland and a number of others, including Slender-leaved Pondweed *Potamogeton filiformis*, Least Yellow Water-lily *Nuphar pumila* and Slender Naiad *Najas flexilis*, occur almost exclusively in Scotland. Britain has an obligation, both under the Bern Convention and the European Union *Directive on the conservation of natural and semi-natural habitats and of wild fauna and flora*, to conserve *Najas flexilis*. This Directive requires member states not only to protect certain species from taking, destruction and sale, but to designate and manage sites for them (Chapter 29).

Table 9.2 shows species which are common in Britain as a whole but are uncommon either north or south of the Scottish border. Distribution patterns for the two groups are exemplified by *Lobelia dortmanna*, which occurs in northern and western Scotland, north Wales and the English Lake District, and *Potamogeton lucens*, which is common only in south, east and midland England (Perring and Walters, 1982). The distribution of these two groups of species can be related partly to the geographical influences already discussed and partly to the nutrient levels of the waters in which they are found. Palmer *et al.* (1992) identified ranges of tolerance of aquatic macrophytes to waters of different nutrient status. From this information, given in Table 9.2, it is apparent that the species rarer in Scotland are generally those confined to nutrient-rich waters, but the species rarer in the south are associated with nutrient-poor situations.

Table 9.3 lists alien species, a number of which (notably the antipodean Swamp Stonecrop *Crassula helmsii* and the North American pondweeds *Elodea canadensis* and *E. nuttallii*) pose a threat to native species through competition. *E. canadensis* first appeared on mainland Britain in 1842 in lochs near the River Tweed. By 1850 the Tweed was so invaded that the growth was a serious hindrance to salmon fisheries (Siddall, 1885) and the plant had spread rapidly south to many waters in England. The first British record of *E. nuttallii* was from Oxfordshire in 1966 and the first Scottish record was from near Inverness in 1978 (Institute of Terrestrial Ecology Biological Records Centre, personal communication). The ease with which propagules of aquatic plants can be transported by boats or animals from one water body to another may account for much of the expansion in range of alien plants, but dumping of unwanted material from aquaria has also been implicated in their spread.

TABLE 9.1 Native aquatic vascular plants which are rare or scarce in Great Britain and occur in Scotland

	No. of 10 × 10 km square records (1970 onwards)	
	GB	Scotland
Callitriche brutia[a]	20	3
Carex appropinquata	21	4
Cicuta virosa	62	27
Crassula aquatica	1	1
Elatine hexandra	94	40
E. hydropiper	19	11
Eriocaulon aquaticum	9	9
Hydrocharis morsus-ranae	90[b]	4 (naturalized)
Isoetes echinospora	75	51
Juncus alpinoarticulatus	28	24
Limosella aquatica	56	19
Luronium natans[c]	33[b]	3 (naturalized)
Lysimachia thyrsiflora	27[b]	25[b]
Myosotis stolonifera	75	10
Najas flexilis[c]	15	14
Nuphar pumila	34	31
Nymphoides peltata	16[b]	12 (naturalized)
Pilularia globulifera	89	22
Potamogeton coloratus	67	12
P. compressus	35	1
P. epihydrus	1[b]	1
P. filiformis	85	84
P. rutilus	11	11
P. trichoides	84	4
Rumex aquaticus	3	3
Ruppia cirrhosa	33	7
Sium latifolium	60	Only pre-1970 records
Stratiotes aloides	19[b]	Only pre-1970 records (introductions)

[a]Species under-recorded because of taxonomic difficulties
[b]Native records only; introduced elsewhere
[c]Species requiring protection within their natural range under the Bern Convention and the EU "Habitats and Species" Directive
"Rare" species occur in 15 or fewer 10×10 km squares in Great Britain, according to data held by the Joint Nature Conservation Committee
"Scarce" species are those recorded from 1970 onwards from 16 to 100 10×10 km squares in Great Britain, according to data held by the Biological Records Centre, Institute of Terrestrial Ecology

TABLE 9.2 Native aquatic vascular plants common in Great Britain but regionally uncommon

(a) Species uncommon[a] in Scotland

	No of 10 × 10 km square records (1950 onwards)		DOME code[b]
	GB	Scotland	
Berula erecta	759	40	E
Butomus umbellatus	508	22[c]	E
Callitriche obtusangula	369	7	ME
Carex acuta	498	30	E
C. elata	207	6	ME
C. pseudocyperus	500	1	E
C. riparia	920	33	E
Ceratophyllum demersum	521	19	E
Hottonia palustris	270	1	–
Lemna gibba	391	10	E
L. trisulca	839	39	E
Oenanthe aquatica	296	1	E
O. fistulosa	547	12	–
Potamogeton lucens	252	26	E
Ranunculus circinatus	326	7	E
R. fluitans	312	34	–
Rorippa amphibia	395	5[c]	–
Rumex hydrolapathum	728	19	E
Sagittaria sagittifolia	509	4	–
Spirodela polyrhiza	294	4	–
Typha angustifolia	482	23	E
Veronica catenata	667	27	–

(b) Species uncommon[d] in England and Wales but common in Scotland

	No. of 10 × 10 km square records (1950 onwards)		DOME code[b]
	GB	England and Wales	
Carex limosa	261	57	O
Isoetes lacustris	368	53	Om
Lobelia dortmanna	470	46	Om
Sparganium angustifolium	417	55	dO
Subularia aquatica	228	22	O
Utricularia intermedia[e]	260	21	O

[a]"Uncommon" species are here defined as those recorded from 1950 onwards from 40 or fewer 10×10 km squares in Scotland, according to data held by the Biological Records Centre, Institute of Terrestrial Ecology
[b]DOME codes represent the tolerance of species to nutrient levels (Palmer *et al.*, 1992): d = weakly associated with "dystrophic" waters; O = strongly associated with "oligotrophic" waters; M/m = strongly/weakly associated with "mesotrophic" waters; E = strongly associated with "eutrophic" waters
[c]Doubtfully native in Scotland
[d]"Uncommon" species are here defined as those recorded from 1950 onwards from 60 or fewer 10×10 km squares in England and Wales, according to data held by the Biological Records Centre, Institute of Terrestrial Ecology
[e]*Utricularia ochroleuca* and *U. stygia* have recently been recognized in Scotland. As they have previously been confused with *U. intermedia*, the figures refer to *U. intermedia sensu lato*

TABLE 9.3. Aquatic vascular plants introduced to Great Britain
and recorded in Scotland

	No. of 10 × 10 km square records (1950 onwards)	
	GB	Scotland
Acorus calamus[a]	288	15
Aponogeton distachyos	10	2
Azolla filiculoides[b]	294	3
Calla palustris	12	1
Crassula helmsii[b]	185	4
Elodea canadensis[b]	1289	231
E. nuttallii[b]	329	15
Iris versicolor	11	5
Lagarosiphon major[b]	107	3
Lemna minuta	107	1
Nuphar advena	6	3

[a]Ancient introduction
[b]Aggressive species which threaten native flora, at least in part of their
range in Great Britain

SURVEY AND CLASSIFICATION OF BRITISH STANDING WATERS

Standing water vegetation was studied intensively in the Lake District by Pearsall (1920) and in Scotland by West (1910) and Spence (1964). A limited nationwide survey was carried out for *A Nature Conservation Review* (Ratcliffe, 1977), but a more comprehensive survey of British standing waters was initiated in 1975 by the former Nature Conservancy Council (NCC). One objective of the latter survey was to identify areas worthy of protection as Sites of Special Scientific Interest (SSSIs). The process of SSSI selection (Nature Conservancy Council, 1989) involves carrying out a comparison between sites and setting them in a national and local context. In order to do this it is necessary to erect site classifications. This process was accomplished for standing waters through the analysis of data collected by the NCC between 1975 and 1987 from 1124 lakes, reservoirs, ponds, pools, gravel pits and canals, over half of which are in Scotland. The analysis was carried out using the TWINSPAN program (Hill, 1979). Table 9.4 shows the floating and submerged species which characterize the 10 "Standing Water Types" which were recognized (Palmer *et al.*, 1992).

Site Types 1 to 7 lie predominantly in the north and west of Britain. Type 1 includes *Sphagnum* pools and small lochs on blanket bog in northern Scotland and a few acid pools in southern Britain. Type 2 sites are mainly upland tarns in the English Lake District and peaty lochs in Scotland. Type 3 sites tend to be larger and rockier than Type 2 sites and they occur in base-poor areas in Scotland (e.g. Loch Awe: Figure 9.1), north west England (e.g. Wastwater), Wales (e.g. Llyn Idwal) and occasionally elsewhere (e.g. Oak Mere in Cheshire). Type 4 sites contain species (e.g. Alternate-flowered Water-milfoil *Myriophyllum alterniflorum*) typical of Type 3 sites, and also a number of plants (e.g. Spiked Water-milfoil *M. spicatum*) characteristic of Types 7 and 10. Type 4 sites are typified by coastal freshwater lochs of the Scottish islands,

TABLE 9.4. Submerged and floating macrophyte species characteristic of Standing Water Types in Great Britain (Palmer et al., 1992)

	Standing Water Type											
	1	2	3	4	5 A	5 B	6	7	8	9	10 A	10 B
Potamogeton polygonifolius	II	IV	III									
Utricularia intermedia		II										
Lobelia dortmanna		IV	III		II							
Sparganium angustifolium		II	III									
Isoetes lacustris			III									
Subularia aquatica			II									
Myriophyllum alterniflorum		III	IV	IV	V*							
Sparganium natans					II							
Juncus bulbosus	V*	IV	V*	II	III							
Eleogiton fluitans		II		II								
Sphagnum spp.	IV											
Nymphaea alba		III		III	III	V*				IV		
Potamogeton alpinus					II							
Nitella spp.		II	II		IV*							
Callitriche hamulata		II	II	V*	V*		II					
Littorella uniflora		IV	V*	II	V*	IV*	II	III				
Apium inundatum			II	II	III							
Potamogeton natans		IV	III	III	III	IV*		III	II	II	III	
Glyceria fluitans			III	III	III			III	II			
Potamogeton gramineus			III	II	II			III		II		
Fontinalis antipyretica			II	IV	III			III		II		
Potamogeton perfoliatus					III			II			II	
Potamogeton obtusifolius					III			II			II	
Potamogeton berchtoldii				II	IV			II	IV	II	III	
Callitriche stagnalis			II	II				II	IV	II	II	

Species	48	192	322	72	52	34	15	127	70	28	73	85
Elodea canadensis		IV*										II
Nuphar lutea		II			II				II	II	IV*	
Lemna minor									III	V*	II	
Lemna trisulca									IV	III	IV	
Elodea nuttallii										III	II	III
Potamogeton lucens												II
Sparganium emersum											II	II
Persicaria amphibium		II							IV		III	II
Zannichellia palustris								II	III			II
Enteromorpha spp.							II					
Myriophyllum spicatum	II		II	II	II			III			II	III
Potamogeton crispus			II		II		IV*	II			III	
Potamogeton pectinatus	II		II	II	II			III			III	IV
Potamogeton pusillus	II		II	II	II			II			III	III
Callitriche hermaphroditica	II		II	II	III*			II			II	
Chara spp.	III	III*	II	III				III	II		II	IV
Fucoids							III			II		
Ranunculus baudotii	II		II	II				III	II		II	
Ruppia spp.							IV*					
Hippuris vulgaris	II		III	II				IV		II		
Potamogeton filiformis	III		III	III				III				
No. of sites in group	48	192	322	72	52	34	15	127	70	28	73	85
Av. no. spp. per site (submerged and floating)	3	7	9	10	13	4	3	8	7	7	10	6
Av. no. spp. per site (submerged, floating and emergent)	7	14	17	19	24	11	6	16	24	19	22	15

Constancy classes: V = 80+ to 100%; IV = 60+ to 80%; III = 40+ to 60%; II = 20+ to 40%

* = cover value high (frequent to abundant)

"Species" numbers include bryophytes and algae determined to genus only

FIGURE 9.1. Loch Awe – the longest loch in Scotland and a typical Type 3 site. Photograph: Peter S. Maitland

including machair lochs situated on calcareous sand with acid inflows from a peaty hinterland. The mixture of influences often expresses itself in very species-rich assemblages of water plants. Type 5 sites are mainly lakes in Scotland and northern England, often on slightly base-rich rock. Typical examples of the species-rich variant 5A are Bassenthwaite Lake in the English Lake District and the Lake of Menteith in the Central Region of Scotland. Type 6 sites are brackish lochs. Although similar in many ways to Type 4 water bodies, Type 7 sites lack a number of acidophilous species. Lochs with a marine influence on shell sand, limestone and Old Red Sandstone in northern Scotland are typical of Type 7.

Sites of Types 8 to 10 tend to be more southerly. Most Type 8 sites are poor in open water species, but rich in emergents. Many are meres of glacial origin in the West Midlands of England, but there are similar sites elsewhere, including the Orkney Islands. Type 9 sites are dominated by Yellow and White Water Lilies *Nuphar lutea* and *Nymphaea alba*, often in combination. These waters are scattered throughout England and Wales, with few in Scotland (this type is not included in Figure 9.5). Type 10 sites include artificial water bodies such as gravel pits and little-used canals, but also lakes such as Malham Tarn in Yorkshire and Loch Watston in the Central Region of Scotland. The substrate of these water bodies is predominantly fine, the water is frequently calcareous and most of the sites are in southern and eastern England.

During the NCC survey programme, pH and conductivity were routinely recorded, alkalinity was measured at over 40% of sites, but data on other chemical variables were gathered only occasionally. Figures 9.2–9.4 illustrate the ranges of conductivity,

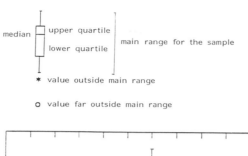

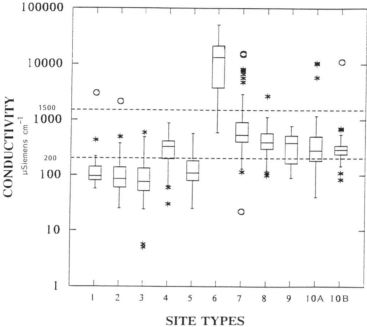

FIGURE 9.2. Ranges of conductivity in Standing Water Site Types (Reproduced by permission from Palmer *et al.*, 1992)

alkalinity and pH for waters in the Standing Water Types. It is obvious that despite considerable overlap there is a general trend from low to high values for all these variables, with the progression from Type 1 to Type 10. Alkalinity, pH and conductivity are generally closely related, but exceptionally low pH values distinguish Type 1 sites from Types 2 and 3, and very high conductivity distinguishes the brackish Type 6 sites from Types 7 to 10. The broad range of conditions evident in Type 4 can be explained by the fact that many of the sites in this group lie in calcareous basins fed by water from acid catchments.

The available data on nitrogen and phosphorus levels generally indicate nutrient-poor conditions where there are low values of alkalinity, conductivity and pH, and nutrient-rich waters where these values are high (see Chapter 6), but there are exceptions, notably for some calcareous sites in Scotland. The Standing Water Types are therefore categorized as follows, in the knowledge that some sites will be misclassified.

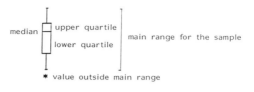

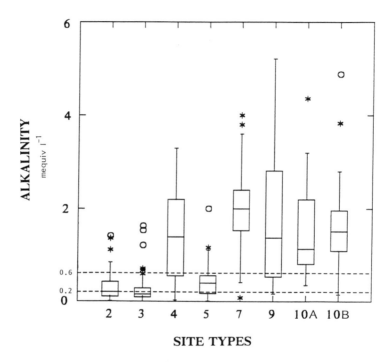

FIGURE 9.3. Ranges of alkalinity in Standing Water Site Types (Reproduced by permission from Palmer *et al.*, 1992). Values for Types 1 and 8 are not included because data are too few. Type 6 is excluded because of its salinity

Type 1   – "dystrophic"/very acid
Types 2 and 3   – "oligotrophic"/base-poor
Type 4   – mixture of influences
Type 5   – "mesotrophic"/moderately rich
Type 6   – brackish
Types 7, 8, 9 and 10 – "eutrophic"/base-rich

The terms "dystrophic", "oligotrophic", "mesotrophic" and "eutrophic" are not closely defined, but are used as convenient terms for recognizable levels in a fertility series.

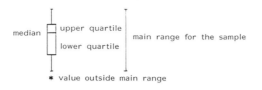

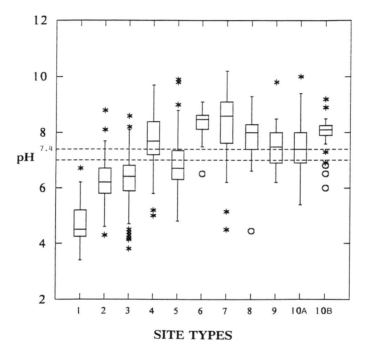

FIGURE 9.4. Ranges of pH in Standing Water Site Types (Reproduced by permission from Palmer *et al.*, 1992)

Spence (1964) sampled the vegetation of over 100 lochs and associated swamps and fens, from Wigtownshire to Shetland, and identified 19 lentic community types dominated by submerged or floating species. The National Vegetation Classification (NVC) covers the whole of Great Britain and recognizes 24 aquatic communities, many of which have sub-communities (Rodwell, in preparation). Spence's and Rodwell's plant community types can be allocated to Standing Water Site Types. For example, the *Littorella uniflora–Lobelia dortmanna* and *Isoetes* communities of the NVC and the *Juncus fluitans–Lobelia dortmanna* association of Spence are found most frequently in sites of Types 2 and 3, whilst the *Ranunculus baudotii* community of the NVC is common in sites of Types 4 and 7. Spence described a *Potamogeton filiformis–Chara* sociation, and in the NVC *P. filiformis* characterizes sub-communities of both *P. pectinatus–Myriophyllum spicatum* and *P. perfoliatus–M.*

alterniflorum communities. *P. filiformis* is characteristic of Scottish examples of Standing Water Types 4 and 7.

SURVEY OF STANDING WATER VEGETATION IN SCOTLAND

One of the most systematic and intensive parts of the NCC's national survey of the flora of standing waters was undertaken in northern Scotland, between 1983 and 1990. The areas surveyed and the number of lochs examined are given in Table 9.5. The objectives of the survey were to:

- determine the range and quality of loch vegetation
- provide a baseline against which to monitor change
- identify sites vulnerable to change (e.g. acidification, eutrophication) and sites already damaged
- identify sites of high conservation value for aquatic flora
- improve knowledge of the distribution of aquatic plants

Lochs were selected for survey within areas based on NCC's administrative boundaries. In some areas, particularly vulnerable or interesting sites were identified and survey was limited to these. In other areas, a synoptic survey approach, based upon that outlined by Maitland (1979), was employed. All standing water bodies marked on Ordnance Survey maps at a scale of 1:50 000 were identified and categorized in a

TABLE 9.5. Number of sites surveyed by the Nature Conservancy Council in each area of northern Scotland

Area	Year	Number of sites surveyed	Proportion of total resource (number of lochs) surveyed in areas where "synoptic survey" method used
Outer Hebrides	1983/84	44	N/A
Spey Valley	1985	52	N/A
Shetland	1986	28	N/A
Orkney	1986	146	N/A
Caithness	1986/87	69	54%
Moray and Nairn	1987	4	N/A
Sutherland	1987/88	546	48%
Inverness	1988	130	26%
Deeside	1988	252	N/A
Skye and Lochalsh	1989	365	52%
South Argyll	1989	68	26%
West Ross and Cromarty	1990	189	19%
North Argyll	1990	20	N/A

N/A = not applicable

three-way matrix based upon size, altitude and geology. Priority sites were identified from this matrix. These included lochs lying within existing or proposed SSSIs, sites known to contain rare plants or an interesting *Potamogeton* flora, and sites of known interest for other groups (e.g. birds) for which botanical data were required. Additional water bodies were then selected from the matrix to cover a minimum of 25% of each category as a target for survey coverage (Table 9.5).

A standard method was used for surveying the aquatic vegetation. This involved walking the perimeter of each loch and recording shoreline and shallow water species. Deeper water was sampled by means of a grapnel thrown from the bank at frequent intervals during the walk. Where possible a boat was used and grapnel samples were obtained from the bottom during transects of the lake. All aquatic plants were recorded on a subjective "DAFOR" abundance scale – dominant; abundant; frequent; occasional; rare. Stands of emergent vegetation were marked on a large-scale map of the site and the distribution of dominant and otherwise notable species in all three vegetation zones was indicated.

Other observations were made on substrate, water colour and clarity, adjacent land use, wetland edges, artificial features, use of or damage to the site, inflows and outflows, and obvious fauna. Water samples collected from the outflow were tested for pH and conductivity at a majority of sites, whilst a more detailed chemical analysis was conducted for about a quarter of the lochs.

The value of the sites for conservation was assessed using a method based on that described in *Guidelines for the Selection of Biological SSSIs* (Nature Conservancy Council, 1989). The lochs were first classified into Standing Water Types. For each area of survey, lochs within each Type were compared and evaluated independently. Two forms of comparison were made: an objective assessment relating to botanical quality (primary criteria) and a more subjective assessment of other factors contributing to diversity and naturalness (secondary criteria). For the primary criteria, sites were ranked on the number of aquatic macrophyte species recorded and the number of nationally and locally rare aquatic plants (Palmer and Newbold, 1983). Secondary criteria included physical diversity (e.g. of substrate), the number of swamp and tall herb fen communities (Rodwell, in preparation), the presence of adjacent wetland, and the absence of man-made modifications (e.g. dams). An account of the work is given in Bell (1989a, b, 1991, 1992), Charter (1989), Charter and van Houten (1989), Butterfield (1992), Butterfield and Bell (1992) and Dalton and Clegg (1992).

Scotland supports the whole range of Site Types present in Britain (Figure 9.5), but as indicated by Spence (1964), nutrient-rich waters are relatively under-represented north of the border. Some areas of Scotland (e.g. Galloway) are particularly subject to acidification, which causes changes in the aquatic plant communities of lochs (Raven, 1988; Battarby *et al.*, 1992). Important and unusual Site Types confined to or best represented in Scotland are brackish lochs and species-rich Type 4 lochs on machair sand. In a few areas, such as the Outer Hebrides, a well-defined series of Site Types can be seen in close proximity. There are pools of Type 2 in the mountains, rocky lochs of Type 3 towards the west at the foot of the hills, Type 2 lochs on the peaty "blacklands" of the coastal plain, Type 4 water bodies where the "blacklands" give way to machair, Type 7 lochs on the sand nearer to the sea, and brackish Type 6 waters on the coast.

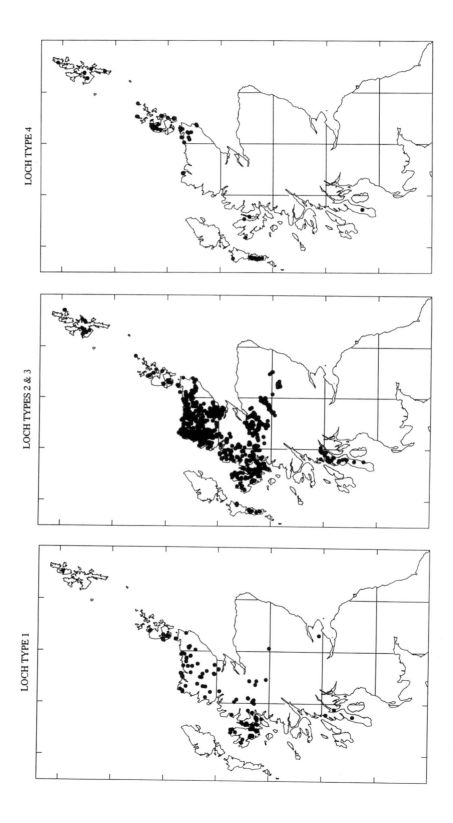

LOCH TYPE 4

LOCH TYPES 2 & 3

LOCH TYPE 1

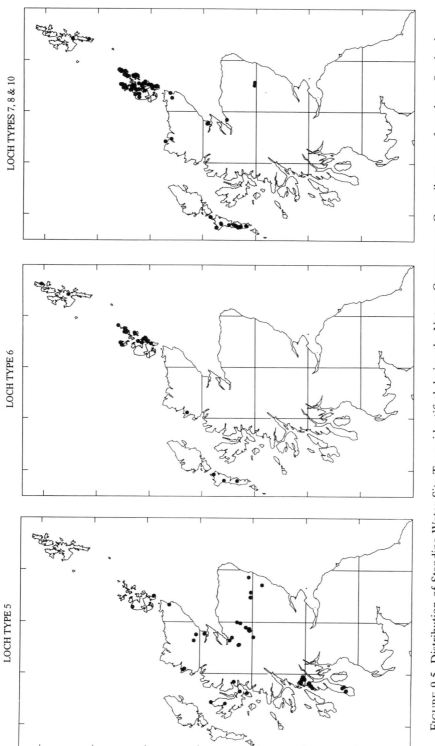

FIGURE 9.5. Distribution of Standing Water Site Types identified during the Nature Conservancy Council survey of northern Scotland

SURVEY AND CLASSIFICATION OF BRITISH RIVERS

The first classification of British rivers based on plants was published by Butcher (1933). He indicated that rivers which traversed certain rock types, rose at similar heights, had comparable water velocities and flowed over beds of similar sediments invariably had similar plant communities. He concluded that geology had a fundamental effect on river plant communities, since it influences, directly or indirectly, altitude, velocity, substrate size and the chemistry of sediments and water. Subsequent surveys by both Haslam (1978) and the NCC (Holmes, 1983; Holmes and Rowell, 1993) have confirmed this, but it is obvious that geographical location is also an important determinand.

The most comprehensive set of data on vegetation in British rivers was gathered by the NCC, with the aim of describing and evaluating the national resource. Between 1978 and 1982 surveys of over 150 rivers in England, Scotland and Wales were carried out. Records were made of macrophytes occurring within the main river channel or at the base of banks inundated for at least 50% of the time. Data from 1055 1 km stretches of river were analysed using TWINSPAN (Hill, 1979), to develop a classification of British rivers (Holmes, 1983; 1989; Department of the Environment, 1987). Fifty-six "communities" were recognized and these were combined to form ten "River Types" (Nature Conservancy Council, 1989). These ten Types were derived from four major "Groups": A, B, C and D.

Since the initial surveys did not cover all regions of Britain, with a particular lack of information from the islands of Scotland, further surveys were undertaken between 1988 and 1991. The additional information enabled the robustness of the classification to be tested through a re-analysis using TWINSPAN. This time the dataset had a more even geographical and geological spread and had 50% more sites. The classification (Holmes and Rowell, 1993) showed exactly the same general distribution of River Types throughout Great Britain and the same associations with rock types, altitude and geographical location as the original system.

Group A rivers are distinctly lowland in character, flowing over soft rocks or drift materials, where the gradient is slight. As a consequence, Group A rivers have substrates of silts, clays, sands and occasionally gravels, with the water rich in both nutrients and bases. At the other extreme is Group D, with opposite characteristics. Typically, rivers classified as D rise at high altitudes, have steep gradients, flow over resistant rocks and are frequently boulder-strewn. However, the key to Group D is the acidic and nutrient-poor nature of the water. As a consequence of this, rivers at low altitude which drain acidic soils will also have Group D plant communities. Group B rivers have intermediate characteristics, with mid-range values for altitude and gradient, but a very close association with sandstone, mudstone and hard limestone. The more basic and nutrient-rich soil and water mean that these rivers are closer to Group A than Group D. Rivers in Group C also have intermediate characteristics, but they tend to flow at higher altitudes than Group B, over resistant shales and other hard rocks which do not produce either basic or nutrient-rich sediments or water chemistry. Some rivers remain in the same category throughout their length, whereas others become more eutrophic as they descend to the sea.

RUNNING WATER VEGETATION IN SCOTLAND

Figure 9.6 shows the distribution of Group A, B, C and D rivers identified in Scotland and indicates a number of important features of Scottish rivers. Firstly, there is a virtual absence of Group A communities. The presence of the occasional site on tributaries of the Tweed and on the lower Annan, both on the English border, suggests that latitude influences river plant communities in Britain. Secondly, the rivers which traverse hard limestone and the extensive bands of sandstone running down the east coast of Scotland are dominated by plant communities in Group B. This is epitomized by the Ugie system in the north and the Tyne in the south. Even the River Don, which rises on acidic uplands, has a Group B plant community for much of its length, where it meanders slowly over sandstone.

Thirdly, most rivers in north and west Scotland, even those in the islands, have mesotrophic or oligotrophic plant communities typical of Groups C and D. Some, such as the Findhorn, have upper reaches with Group D communities and lower reaches with Group C communities. Shorter rivers which flow only over resistant rocks hardly ever develop a community change from source to mouth, remaining oligotrophic Group D rivers throughout. Lastly, Scotland is noteworthy for having large rivers (by British standards) which can exceed 100 km in length but not develop Group A or B communities in their lower reaches. The Dee and Spey are classic examples.

Table 9.6 lists some of the plants commonly found in Scottish rivers and typifying River Groups A to D. Table 9.7 lists plants which are characteristic of particular river habitats and are not uncommon in Scottish rivers (e.g. *Potamogeton polygonifolius*: Figure 9.7). These tables indicate that the most common aquatic plants in Scottish rivers are bryophytes. Several of these form dense cushions on boulders, even in the fastest currents. For them, current velocity is rarely important, but to have a substrate that will not move in a spate is of paramount importance. Truly aquatic vascular plants are not common in fast-flowing rivers, but Alternate-flowered Water-milfoil *Myriophyllum alterniflorum* and several species of water crowfoot *Ranunculus* can live in fast currents. In peaty pools in the uplands, Bulbous Rush *Juncus bulbosus* thrives and may often be found with White Water-lily *Nymphaea alba*.

Some Scottish rivers have notable species or assemblages of plants which are not known or are rare elsewhere in Britain. For instance, in England mare's-tail *Hippuris vulgaris* is typical of chalk streams and occurs extremely rarely in other flowing waters. In Scotland it is not uncommon in many small rivers in the north of the country, where it grows amongst acid-loving mosses and liverworts such as *Fontinalis squamosa* and *Scapania undulata*. It is also extremely rare for the two milfoils, *Myriophyllum spicatum* and *M. alterniflorum*, to occur within the same stretch of river, because the former is associated with basic waters and the latter with neutral or slightly acid ones. In several rivers in Scotland (e.g. Tweed and Teviot) they do grow alongside each other in short stretches, usually where rocks are basic but the water flowing over them is derived from a nutrient-poor catchment (cf. Type 4 standing waters).

Relatively unspoilt small torrent rivers are still fairly common in the remote mountains of England and Wales, but Scotland has a profusion of these. Scotland, unlike other parts of Britain, has large oligo-mesotrophic rivers. The largest, and possibly the best, are the Dee and the Spey. These are of very high quality, the former for its wilderness river flora, virtually from source to mouth, and the latter because of the unique low-gradient flora associated with the Insh Marshes. Both deserve high priority for protection, as recognized by their inclusion in the list of key British sites in *A Nature Conservation Review* (Ratcliffe, 1977).

FIGURE 9.6. Distribution of Group A, B, C and D rivers studied in Scotland (Reproduced by permission of Scottish Natural Heritage from Holmes and Rowell, 1993)

TABLE 9.6. Species typical of Group A, B, C and D rivers
in Scotland

Species	River Group			
	A	B	C	D
Elodea canadensis	F	O		
Amblystegium riparium*	O	O		
Persicaria amphibium	O	O		
Ranunculus penicillatus agg.	O	O		
Potamogeton crispus	O	O		
Ranunculus fluitans agg.	O	F		
Myriophyllum spicatum	O	F		
Lemna minor	R	R		
Carex acuta	R	R		
Glyceria maxima	R	O		
Apium nodiflorum	R	O		
Potamogeton perfoliatus	R	F		
Sparganium erectum	I	I	O	
Nasturtium aquaticum	F	F	R	
Hildenbrandia rivularis****	R	I	O	
Phalaris arundinacea	I	I	F	R
Glyceria fluitans	F	F	F	F
Rhynchostegium riparioides*	F	I	I	F
Juncus effusus	O	O	O	I
Amblystegium fluviatile*	R	I	I	R
Potamogeton natans	R	R		R
Collema fluviatilis***		O		
Cinclidotus fontinaloides*		I	I	
Myriophyllum alterniflorum		F	F	F
Chiloscyphus polyanthos**		F	I	F
Callitriche hamulata		O	F	F
Schistidium alpicola*		O	I	I
Dermatocarpon fluviatilis***		R	F	O
Fontinalis squamosa*		R	F	F
Hygrohypnum spp.*			I	I
Scapania undulata**			F	I
Solenostoma triste**			F	I
Brachythecium plumosum*			F	I
Hyocomium armoricum*			R	I
Marsupella emarginata**				F
Nardia compressa**				F
Blindia acuta*				F
Dicranella palustris*				F
Juncus bulbosus				I

R = rare
O = occasional
F = frequent
I = invariably present
*   = moss
**   = liverwort
***   = lichen
**** = alga

TABLE 9.7. Species characteristic of river habitats in Scotland

Species	River habitats						
	1	2	3	4	5	6	7
Nasturtium aquaticum agg.	F						
Sparganium erectum	I	R					
Eleocharis palustris	F	O					
Potamogeton natans	O	O					
Potamogeton perfoliatus	O	R					
Elodea canadensis	F	R	R				
Myriophyllum alterniflorum	R	I	F				
Potamogeton crispus	O		R				
Ranunculus fluitans agg.	R		F				
Ranunculus penicillatus agg.	R		F				
Potamogeton polygonifolius		I					
Glyceria fluitans		I					
Ranunculus flammula		I					
Juncus bulbosus		I					
Sphagnum spp*.		F					
Carex rostrata		O					
Hydrocotyle vulgaris		O					
Littorella uniflora		R			O	R	
*Rhynchostegium riparioides**			R	I			R
*Fontinalis antipyretica**			R	I			R
*Thamnobryum alopecurum**				F			
*Cinclidotus fontinaloides**				F			
*Amblystegium fluviatile**				O			
*Collema fluviatile****				O			
*Hildenbrandia rivularis*****				O			
*Chiloscyphus polyanthos***				F			R
Juncus effusus					O	O	
*Calliergon cuspidatum**					O	O	
*Philonotis fontana**					O	F	
*Brachythecium rivulare**					O	F	
Carex nigra						O	
*Bryum pallens**						F	
*Bryum alpinum**						F	
*Polytrichum commune**						I	
*Dichodontium pellucidum**						R	O
*Hyocomium armoricum**						R	F
*Schistidium agassizzi**							R
*Blindia acuta**							O
*Nardia compressa***							F
*Marsupella emarginata***							F
*Fontinalis squamosa**							F
*Scapania undulata***							F
*Racomitrium aciculare**							F
Hygrohypnum spp*							I

Rivers habitats:

1 = lowland slacks	6 = upland shingles	I = invariably present
2 = upland slacks	7 = rapids and rockfalls	* = moss
3 = riffles	R = rare	** = liverwort
4 = lowland boulders	O = occasional	*** = lichen
5 = mid-river shingles	F = frequent	**** = alga

FIGURE 9.7. *Potamogeton polygonifolius* (Table 9.7), a typical plant of River Habitat 2 (upland slacks). Photograph: Peter S. Maitland

THE EUROPEAN DIMENSION

Haslam (1987) gives descriptions of river types for all the countries of the European Community and provides a great deal of information on the distribution of aquatic plants in relation to physical factors.

In order to fulfil obligations to designate and protect sites under the EU *Directive on the conservation of natural and semi-natural habitats and of wild fauna and flora*, it will be necessary to select sites referable to the European CORINE classification (Devillers *et al.*, 1991). This system is an amalgam of narrow vegetation types and broad habitat types, some of which are equivalent to the Standing Water Types and River Groups described here. Aquatic habitats of importance in the European Community and listed in this Directive include "dystrophic lakes", "oligotrophic waters of Atlantic sandy plains with amphibious vegetation *Lobelia, Littorella* and *Isoetes*", "natural eutrophic lakes with *Magnopotamion*-type vegetation", "hard oligo-mesotrophic waters with benthic vegetation of *Chara* formations" and "floating vegetation of *Ranunculus* of plain and sub-mountainous rivers". All these types are represented in Scotland and some of the best examples may become part of a European network of protected sites.

REFERENCES

Battarbee, R. W., Logan, N. A., Murphy, K. J., Raven, P., Aston, R. J. and Foster, G. N. (1992). "Other aquatic biology: flora and fauna", in *Restoring Acid Waters: Loch Fleet 1984 –1990* pp. 289–330, Elsevier Scientific Publishers, Berking.

Bell, S. L. (1989a). *An Evaluation of the Aquatic Macrophyte Interest of Some Argyll Lochs 1989*, Internal report, Nature Conservancy Council, Edinburgh.

Bell, S. L. (1989b). *Freshwater Macrophyte Survey of Caithness Lochs 1986–1987*, Contract Surveys No. 19, Nature Conservancy Council, Peterborough.

Bell, S. L. (1991). *Freshwater Macrophyte Survey of Selected Sutherland Lochs 1987–1988*, Contract Surveys No. 34, Nature Conservancy Council, Peterborough.

Bell, S. L. (1992). *Freshwater Macrophyte Survey of Inverness 1988*, Contract Surveys No. 35, Nature Conservancy Council, Peterborough.

Butcher, R. W. (1933). "Studies on the ecology of rivers I. On the distribution of macrophytic vegetation in the rivers of Britain", *Journal of Ecology*, **21**, 58–91.

Butterfield, I. (1992). *Freshwater Macrophyte Survey of Deeside 1988*, Contract Surveys No. 36, Nature Conservancy Council, Peterborough.

Butterfield, I. and Bell, S. L. (1992). *Freshwater Macrophyte Survey of Skye and Lochalsh 1989*, Contract Surveys No. 85, Nature Conservancy Council, Peterborough.

Charter, E. (1989). *Survey of Four Lochs in Moray and Nairn Districts 1987*, Contract Surveys No. 17, Nature Conservancy Council, Peterborough.

Charter, E. and van Houten, A. (1989). *Survey of Orkney Lochs*, Contract Surveys No. 18, Nature Conservancy Council, Peterborough.

Clapham, A. R., Tutin, T. G. and Moore, D. M. (1987). *Flora of the British Isles*, 3rd edition, Cambridge University Press, Cambridge.

Dalton, R. A. and Clegg, E. M. (1992). *Freshwater Macrophyte Survey of West Ross and Cromarty 1990*, Contract Surveys No. 124, Nature Conservancy Council, Peterborough.

Department of the Environment (1987). *Methods for the Use of Aquatic Macrophytes for Assessing Water Quality 1985–86*, HMSO, London.

Devillers, P., Devillers-Terschuren, J. and Ledant, J-P. (1991). *CORINE Biotopes Manual. Habitats of the European Community. Data Specifications Part 2*, Commission of the European Communities, Luxembourg.

Haslam, S. M. (1978). *River Plants*, Cambridge University Press, Cambridge.

Haslam, S. M. (1987). *River Plants of Western Europe*, Cambridge University Press, Cambridge.

Hill, M. O. (1979). *TWINSPAN – A Fortran Program for Arranging Multivariate Data in an Ordered Two-way Table by Classification of the Individuals and Attributes*, Ecology and Systematics, Cornell University, Ithaca, New York.

Holmes, N. T. H. (1983). *Typing British Rivers According to their Flora*, Focus on Nature Conservation No. 4, Nature Conservancy Council, Peterborough.

Holmes, N. T. H. (1989). "British rivers – A working classification", *British Wildlife*, **1**, 20–36.

Holmes, N. T. H. and Rowell, T. A. (1993). *Typing British Rivers According to their Flora – 1993 Up-date*, A report to Scottish Natural Heritage, Edinburgh.

Maitland, P. S. (1979). *Synoptic Limnology. The Analysis of British Freshwater Ecosystems*, Institute of Terrestrial Ecology, Cambridge.

Nature Conservancy Council (1989). *Guidelines for the Selection of Biological SSSIs*, Nature Conservancy Council, Peterborough.

Palmer, M. A. and Newbold, C. (1983). *Wetland and Riparian Plants in Great Britain*, Focus on Nature Conservation No 1, Nature Conservancy Council, Peterborough.

Palmer, M. A., Bell, S. L. and Butterfield, I. (1992). "A botanical classification of standing waters in Great Britain: applications for conservation and monitoring", *Aquatic Conservation: Marine and Freshwater Ecosystems*, **2**, 125–143.

Pearsall, W. H. (1920). "The aquatic vegetation of the English Lakes", *Journal of Ecology*, **8**, 163–201.

Perring, F. H. and Farrell, L. (1983). *British Red Data Book 1: Vascular Plants*, 2nd edition, Royal Society for Nature Conservation, Lincoln.

Perring, F. H. and Walters, S. M. (Eds) (1982). *Atlas of the British Flora*, 3rd Edition, Botanical Society of the British Isles, Nelson, London.

Ratcliffe, D. R. (Ed.) (1977). *A Nature Conservation Review*, Cambridge University Press, Cambridge.

Raven, P. J. (1988). "Occurence of *Sphagnum* in the sublittoral of several small oligotrophic lakes in Galloway, south west Scotland", *Aquatic Botany*, **30**, 223–230.

Rodwell, J. S. (in preparation). *British Plant Communities: Volume 4. Swamps, Tall Herb Fens and Aquatic Communities*, Cambridge University Press, Cambridge.

Siddall, J. D. (1885). "The waterweed *Anacharis alsinastrum* Bab.: its structure and habitat; with some notes on its introduction into Great Britain and the causes affecting its rapid spread at first and apparent present diminution", *Proceedings of Chester Society for Natural Science*, **3**, 125–133.

Spence, D. H. N. (1964). "The macrophytic vegetation of lochs, swamps and associated fens", in *The Vegetation of Scotland* (Ed. J. H. Burnett), pp. 306–425, Oliver and Boyd, Edinburgh.

West, G. (1910). "A further contribution to a comparative study of the dominant phanerogamic and higher cryptogamic flora of aquatic habit in Scottish lakes", *Proceedings of the Royal Society of Edinburgh*, **30**, 65–81.

10

Invertebrates

I. R. FOZZARD

Forth River Purification Board, Avenue North, Riccarton, EH14 4AP, UK

C. R. DOUGHTY

Clyde River Purification Board, Murray Road, East Kilbride, G75 0LA, UK

and

B. E. CLELLAND

Tay River Purification Board, 1 South Street, Perth, PH2 8NJ, UK

INTRODUCTION

Scotland's fresh waters support an invertebrate fauna of relatively restricted richness. Nevertheless, this brief account cannot present a comprehensive review but instead considers the communities associated with recognizable habitat types. Although this approach will inevitably leave gaps where particular taxonomic groups or unusual water bodies are overlooked it still allows the special character, functional role and intrinsic value of Scotland's freshwater invertebrate fauna to be emphasized.

Most work on Scottish freshwater invertebrates has been carried out over the last 100 years, commencing with the first systematic surveys of Scottish lochs by Scott (1890–1899) and Murray and Pullar (1910). Since the 1940s, there has been a great upsurge in research and monitoring activities, resulting largely from the setting up of Glasgow University's Field Station by Loch Lomond, the Freshwater Fisheries Laboratory at Pitlochry and the formation of statutory bodies concerned with the management of fresh waters, such as the River Purification Boards (RPBs) and the Nature Conservancy and its successors (see Chapter 1). With greater public awareness of the need to conserve and protect Scotland's freshwater resources, this trend seems set to continue.

The Fresh Waters of Scotland: A National Resource of International Significance
Edited by P. S. Maitland, P. J. Boon and D. S. McLusky. © 1994 John Wiley & Sons Ltd

Origins

The origins of Scotland's freshwater invertebrate fauna can be traced back 10 000 years to the end of the last major glaciation, which eliminated most existing biota. As the ice retreated, invertebrates colonized the newly formed freshwater habitats. The pioneer colonizers of streams were probably insects – in particular Chironomidae – followed by Ephemeroptera and Plecoptera (Milner, 1987). Subsequent marine incursions and regressions would have facilitated colonization by euryhaline species. The further development of freshwater invertebrate communities would have been strongly influenced by the rapid post-glacial establishment of mixed woodland and the later transition to moorland and bog which is believed to have been accelerated by human activities.

The relatively short period since glaciation, allowing little time for speciation, and Scotland's status as part of an island group, have restricted the diversity of its freshwater invertebrate fauna. The fauna is characterized by widely distributed species with good dispersal abilities and some relict species. The latter include boreoalpine species (e.g. the dragonfly *Somatochlora arctica* and the chironomid *Parametriocnemus boreoalpinus*) with strongholds in Scotland, and southern forms (e.g. the water beetle *Noterus crassicornis*) which colonized Scotland at a time when the climate was warmer. For certain less mobile species (e.g. the common lake-dwelling triclads), post-glacial colonization of northern areas is still proceeding. However, colonization may also be rapid. For example, the euryhaline gastropod *Potamopyrgus jenkinsi*, first recorded from the River Tay in 1906, spread through the central lowlands to the west coast within 50 years (Hunter and Warwick, 1957).

STANDING WATERS

Lochs

The invertebrate fauna of lochs may be conveniently categorized as zooplankton, and profundal, sub-littoral and littoral zoobenthos. In reality, however, some species may be part of more than one such assemblage, occupying complex and sometimes ill-defined habitats.

Zooplankton

The zooplankton are mainly species of Cladocera, Copepoda and Rotifera which typically frequent the open waters of lakes. They fulfil a vital role in transferring energy from phytoplankton, bacteria and organic detritus to higher trophic levels. Zooplankton also play an important part in nutrient recycling. Most species are grazers, but some are predatory. Zooplankton are in turn an important food for fish, so that the intensity of fish predation may largely determine the composition of the zooplankton community. Probably the most important controlling factor is the availability of food in the form of planktonic algae. Abiotic factors such as lake morphometry and water chemistry are usually of secondary importance.

Zooplankton communities worldwide are generally composed of relatively few species, with only one species from each of the major groups likely to be dominant at any one time (Pennak, 1957). In Scottish lochs, species of general occurrence include the copepods *Eudiaptomus gracilis* and *Cyclops strenuus abyssorum*, the cladocerans *Diaphanosoma brachyurum, Holopedium gibberum, Daphnia hyalina, Bosmina coregoni var. obtusirostris, Polyphemus pediculus, Bythotrephes longimanus* and *Leptodora kindti*, and the rotifers *Conochilus unicornis, Asplanchna priodonta, Polyarthra* spp., *Keratella cochlearis* and *Kellicottia longispina* (Murray and Pullar, 1910).

The Scottish zooplankton is characterized by common European species with Arctic and sub-alpine elements, the latter being especially prevalent in the north and west – a pattern particularly evident among the calanoid copepods (Murray, 1905). The most widespread species on the mainland, *Eudiaptomus gracilis*, is replaced by *Arctodiaptomus wierzejskii* on the islands of the north and west. A third species, *Mixodiaptomus laciniatus*, is found sporadically in central, western and northern Scotland. *Mixodiaptomus laciniatus, Arctodiaptomus laticeps* and *A. wierzejskii* have typically relict distributions in the British Isles and tend to be found in areas with a low maximum summer temperature. It is thought that at the end of the last Ice Age these species followed the retreating ice northwards, with populations in the south and east dying out as temperatures rose (Fryer and Joyce, 1981).

Although richer lochs would be expected to support a more abundant zooplankton, there also appear to be differences in species dominance between lochs of different trophic status. The crustacean zooplankton of oligotrophic lochs tends to be dominated by *Eudiaptomus gracilis* but dominance shifts towards *Daphnia* spp. and then to *Cyclops strenuus abyssorum* as trophic status increases (Table 10.1). Harper (1986) found a similar shift in dominance among the Rotifera of three lochs in Angus and Tayside. *Keratella cochlearis* dominated the mesotrophic Loch of the Lowes, while *K. quadrata* was dominant in the hypertrophic Forfar Loch. The two species were co-dominant in the eutrophic Balgavies Loch.

Studies in Scandinavia and North America have shown a number of effects of acidification on zooplankton communities, including a reduction in the number of crustacean species and a decline in the importance of *Daphnia* species (Brett, 1989). In Scotland, the absence of *Daphnia* has been noted in the acidified Loch Dee and Loch Grannoch in Galloway (Burns *et al.*, 1984) and Loch Chon in the Trossachs (Forth RPB, unpublished). The recent appearance of *Daphnia* in Loch Dee may be due to declining acidity (Scottish Office Agriculture and Fisheries Department, 1990). Although Loch Doon, Galloway, has undergone recent acidification (Maitland *et al.*, 1991; Clyde RPB, unpublished data) it has retained its *Daphnia* population. Here, perhaps, the effects of acidification have been ameliorated by its humic nature (Brett, 1989). The rotifer *Keratella serrulata*, a species restricted to humic acid waters and which frequently dominates the zooplankton of Scandinavian acid lakes, was noted in Loch Doon in 1987.

Zoobenthos

The profundal zoobenthos of lakes inhabits sediments below the thermocline and beyond the depth of light penetration. Energy requirements depend upon organic deposition from the plankton and allochthonous inputs. In Scotland, this sparse fauna has been the subject of comparatively little study, partly due to the difficulty of

TABLE 10.1. Dominant crustacean zooplankton in lochs of different trophic status

	Eudiaptomus gracilis	*Daphnia spp.*	*Cyclops strenuus abyssorum*
Oligotrophic			
Awe	+		
Laidon	+		
Lomond	+		
Lyon	+	+	
Morar	+		
Ness	+		
Shiel	+		
Mesotrophic			
Earn		+	
Lintrathen	+	+	
Lowes	+		
Menteith	+	+	
Eutrophic			
Balgavies		+	
Leven		+	+
Hypertrophic			
Forfar			+

Data from: Maitland *et al.* (1981), Jones (1984), Harper (1986), Fozzard and Marsden (1990)

obtaining good samples from the considerable depths which are typically encountered. Thirteen of the 16 largest lochs listed by Maitland (1981) exceed 100 m at their deepest.

The profundal habitats of large, deep lochs have low and relatively stable temperatures, fine-grained substrata and no primary production. This results in broad similarities between profundal faunas which typically include oligochaete worms, chironomid larvae and *Pisidium* spp. The number of species encountered is usually small (Smith *et al.*, 1981b).

Weerekoon (1956) found that *Tubifex tubifex, Stylodrilus heringianus* and *Spirosperma ferox* were the worms most likely to be encountered at depth in Loch Lomond. Species of *Pisidium* are the most common molluscs in its profundal, and of particular interest is *P. conventus*, considered by Slack (1965) to be a glacial relict dependent on low temperatures (5–8°C). It is restricted to the northern trough, *P. lilljeborgi* and *P. nitidum* dominating in the south.

In more productive waters, larvae of the dipteran *Chaoborus* may also be present as well as high densities of oligochaete worms. Samples of the profundal fauna of the Lake of Menteith, for example, were dominated by tubificid worms, including *Tubifex tubifex* (Fozzard and Marsden, 1990) with estimated densities of several thousand per m^2 in late summer. This, together with an abundance of *Chaoborus flavicans*, was associated with moderately high productivity.

The relationship between the productivity of a lake and its profundal zoobenthos has provided a basis for a number of lake classification schemes as discussed by Wiederholm (1980). That of Lundbeck, which depends on the dominant profundal species of chironomid larvae to assign a trophic status to a lake, has been applied to lochs in the Trossachs area of Central Scotland (Forth RPB, unpublished data) and to Loch Earn (Tay RPB, unpublished data). Table 10.2 compares the resulting classifications with those produced by reference to annual mean concentrations of chlorophyll *a* and total phosphorus (OECD, 1982). For these lochs, the trophic classes inferred from profundal benthos are at variance with those based on lake chemistry, although similar rankings result. Significant inputs of allochthonous plant material are believed to be supplementing the rain of planktonic detritus and enriching the profundal sediments. Weerekoon (1956) found similar anomalies in the benthic chironomid fauna of Loch Lomond where the profundal sediments of the northern trough are strongly influenced by organic matter from its steep, tree-lined shores. Evidently, benthic Chironomidae reflect the nature of the benthic environment without necessarily typifying the loch as a whole.

The littoral and sub-littoral zones of lochs provide a more complex and subtle variety of habitats than is found in the profundal, and invertebrate species richness is often high. Poorer, oligotrophic lochs generally have a fauna dominated by insects, while more productive alkaline waters may also contain leeches, molluscs and crustaceans (Maitland and Holden, 1983).

The macrobenthos of machair lochs in the Outer Hebrides is particularly rich among the sub-littoral weed beds (Waterston *et al.*, 1979). The leeches present may include *Haemopsis sanguisuga* and, ectoparasitic on wildfowl, *Theromyzon tessulatum*. The most abundant insects are the mayflies *Caenis luctuosa* and *C. macrura*, but many species of caddis, corixids, beetles, chironomid midges and dragonflies also occur.

Slack (1957) found that in Loch Lomond, too, the most diverse fauna was associated with the shallow margins and their dense swards of *Littorella uniflora*, where 98 invertebrate taxa were collected. The majority were nymphs and larvae of insect species, most of which are commonly found in lotic habitats. Of some 20 trichopteran genera recorded, for example, only three, *Phryganea*, *Lepidostoma* and *Oxyethira*, were regarded as typically lacustrine and rarely found in the burns and rivers of the loch catchment. Turbulence at the margins of lochs is sufficient to maintain the well-oxygenated water which many lotic species require. In more sheltered bays, where fine sediments and plant detritus accumulate, such species were absent. *Sialis lutaria*, agrionid dragonflies, *Caenis* spp. and corixid bugs characterize these less turbulent areas.

In shallow non-stratifying lochs the benthos throughout the entire loch may resemble a sub-littoral fauna. Gartmorn Dam, Clackmannan, for example, has *Caenis horaria*, *Asellus aquaticus*, *Gammarus pulex*, *Sialis lutaria* and *Mystacides* sp. at even its deepest (5 m) part. (Forth RPB, unpublished data).

Loch Leven, Kinross, Britain's largest natural eutrophic lake, is relatively shallow (mean depth 3.9 m) and wind action prevents stratification other than for brief intervals in the two deepest regions. Progressive anthropogenic enrichment this century changed the ecology of the loch dramatically (Morgan, 1970). The formerly diverse community of insects, molluscs and crustaceans was replaced by an impoverished benthic fauna. In the sub-littoral this was dominated by the tubificid *Pota-*

TABLE 10.2. Trophic classification of some Scottish lochs using indicator genera of profundal chironomid larvae and mean 1991 concentrations of total phosphorus and chlorophyll *a* (OECD, 1982)

	Indicator genera	Classification (after Lundbeck)*	P (μg L^{-1})	Chl *a* (μgL^{-1})	Classification (OECD, 1982)
Loch Ard	*Stictochironomus*	mesotrophic A	7	1.2	oligotrophic
Loch Achray	*Stictochironomus + Sergentia*	mesotrophic B	7	1.6	oligotrophic
Loch Earn	*Stictochironomus + Sergentia*	mesotrophic B	13	3	mesotrophic
Loch Lubnaig	*Sergentia*	mesotrophic B	11	1.7	oligotrophic
Lake of Menteith	*Sergentia + Chironomus*	eutrophic A	19	4.3	mesotrophic

*(Cited in Wiederholm, 1980)

mothrix hammoniensis, and chironomid larvae, particularly *Chironomus plumosus* and *C. anthracinus*. Maitland and Hudspith (1974) found that the composition of the littoral invertebrate fauna was influenced by substrate texture. Nematoda, Naididae, Enchytraeidae, Orthocladiinae, *Cryptochironomus*, *Stictochironomus*, Tanytarsini and Ceratopogonidae were more common in sandy areas. *Hydra*, *Asellus*, *Pentaneura*, *Procladius*, *Chironomus* and *Polypedilum* preferred mud. Tubificidae and Mollusca (mainly *Valvata*, *Anodonta* and *Pisidium*) were also present and, in 1968, the density of the macro-invertebrate fauna was around $58\,000\ m^{-2}$. Annual zoo-benthos production was estimated in this study to be about $46.5\ g\ m^{-2}$ of which $40\ g\ m^{-2}$ were contributed by *Glyptotendipes* larvae. Recent observations suggest improving conditions, with the reappearance of some Ephemeroptera, Plecoptera and Trichoptera (Forth RPB, unpublished data).

The range of Cladocera and Copepoda found in the inshore waters of lakes far exceeds that of the plankton, owing to the greater variety of habitats and niches available. Species richness is often related to the size of the water body, larger lakes tending to possess a greater range of habitats than small ones. However, this is not always the case. Fryer and Forshaw (1979), for example, found that three of the largest lochs on Rum, which had very uniform littoral zones, supported only 10–12 species. Most of the waters investigated were acidic and oligotrophic or dystrophic in character. The composition of microcrustacean assemblages was strongly correlated with pH and calcium concentrations, although it was not possible to determine whether these factors acted directly or indirectly. Jones (1986) was unable to establish a link between microcrustacean species composition and catchment land use in Tayside lochs.

Several of the Scottish littoral microcrustaceans are boreoalpine species with northern and western distributions in Britain. Among these are the cladocerans *Latona setifera*, *Rhynchotalona falcata*, *Alonopsis elongata*, *Alona intermedia*, *A. rustica* and *Chydorus ovalis*, and the harpacticoid copepod *Bryocamptus rhaeticus* (Fryer and Forshaw, 1979). As few areas have been intensively sampled, it is difficult to define rare species with certainty. However, the chydorid cladoceran *Eurycercus glacialis* is a national rarity, the only two known British sites being in Shetland and Easter Ross (Duigan, 1991).

The shallowest margins of lochs may be subject to significant wave action and develop coarse substrata of gravel, stones or boulders. The associated fauna may closely resemble that of an eroding river. In the study by Smith *et al.* (1981a) of the littoral zoobenthos of Lochs Lomond, Awe, Ness, Morar and Shiel, the major faunal constituents common to all were Oligochaeta, Ephemeroptera, Plecoptera, Coleoptera, Trichoptera and Diptera. Most species encountered were commonly considered to prefer lotic habitats. The steep, rocky shores of Loch Ness, for example, favour nymphs of stoneflies and the mayfly *Ameletus inopinatus*. Similarly, *Ecdyonurus venosus*, usually associated with flowing waters, was recorded from the steeper and more exposed banks of the northern half of Loch Lomond. On the gently sloping shores of the southern basin only the more widespread *E. dispar* occurred (Calow, 1974).

Further parallels between littoral zoobenthos and river invertebrate communities were drawn by Harper (1986). Increasing degrees of anthropogenic enrichment of some Angus and Tayside lochs have modified their faunas in a pattern commonly encountered in organically polluted rivers. Plecoptera, Ephemeroptera and Trichoptera are eliminated progressively and *Gammarus lacustris* is replaced by *Asellus aquaticus* in the most enriched lochs.

Clearly, the littoral benthos is vulnerable to exposure by low water levels. Smith *et al.* (1987) investigated 27 lochs and found that the littoral zoobenthos of 12 was of low richness (fewer than 10 taxa) and low abundance (fewer than 250 individuals per 10-minute collection). All 12 water bodies were hydro-electric reservoirs, 11 having major water-level fluctuations. Oligochaete worms, baetid mayflies, a species of dytiscid beetle and chironomid midge larvae seemed most tolerant of fluctuating levels.

Ponds

A useful definition of a pond is a water body of small size such that wave action exerts no influence on the marginal habitat. Ponds are highly individual, relatively temporary habitats whose faunas vary widely. Several factors have been identified as important in determining their invertebrate assemblages, including age, isolation, stability, habitat diversity, water chemistry, adjacent land use, and presence of fish (Macan, 1965; Friday, 1987; Jeffries, 1989a, 1991). Conditions within ponds fluctuate greatly; for example, temperature and dissolved oxygen concentration, and flushing rates during rainstorms may be very high.

Scotland has both base-poor, often acidified ponds, and circumneutral ponds, typical of lowland agricultural areas. The former group includes small dubh lochans, forestry ponds and acid bog-pool complexes, which are an important habitat in Scotland for Hemiptera, Coleoptera, and Odonata such as *Aeshna caerulea, Somatochlora arctica* and *Leucorrhinia dubia*. Undisturbed, sheltered lochans may contain *Somatochlora metallica, Cordulia aenea, Brachytron pratense* and *Coenagrion pulchellum*, the latter two species restricted to neutral or slightly alkaline waters. A threatened species, *Coenagrion hastulatum*, is confined to shallow waters of a few weedy pools in three small areas of Scotland (Shirt, 1987; E. M. Smith, personal communication).

Jeffries (1989b, 1991) surveyed circumneutral and naturally acid forestry ponds, in addition to some made acid by mining activity. These latter waters were the most acid studied, with pH values of 3.3 and 3.8, yet 20 and 15 taxa respectively were recorded – in the middle range for the ponds surveyed. Their fauna included *Pyrrhosoma nymphula, Aeshna* sp., *Gerris odontogaster, Notonecta glauca, Hydroporus* sp. and *Helophorus* sp. Rare Scottish Odonata like *Aeshna caerulea* and *Leucorrhinia dubia* appeared to be restricted to old (> 500 years) acid ponds on a peat substratum. The most alkaline ponds in this survey (pH 7.5–8.3) contained Odonata, including *Pyrrhosoma nymphula*, the mayfly *Cloeon dipterum*, Hemiptera, *Gammarus pulex*, Mollusca and flatworms.

Jeffries' (1987, 1989a) work at Aberlady Bay, East Lothian, also provides data on small, circumneutral, base-rich ponds. These were 25 years old and in all over 100 invertebrate taxa were recorded, including 10 Hemiptera, 28 Coleoptera and 28 Diptera. Their common fauna included *Bathyomphalus contortus, Cloeon dipterum, Limnephilus rhombicus, Asellus meridianus* and *Simocephalus vetulus*. This latter species was also the common cladoceran in all but the most acid of Jeffries' forestry ponds. The water spider *Argyroneta aquatica*, uncommon in southern Scotland, also occurs at Aberlady Bay.

Two threatened species are recorded from temporary seasonal pools in Scotland (Bratton, 1991). *Lymnaea glabra* is typically found in small, muddy, soft-water puddles and ditches and is declining throughout Scotland as such habitats are lost. The Tadpole Shrimp *Triops cancriformis*, which completes its life cycle within two to three weeks in seasonal pools, has been recorded from Preston Merse in Kirkudbright but has not been found for over 30 years and may now be extinct at this site. Another threatened species, *Hirudo medicinalis* (the Medicinal Leech), is recorded from Islay and Sutherland. This leech is typically found in weedy, eutrophic ponds. It needs warm conditions for the completion of its life cycle and this may restrict it to shallow water bodies which warm rapidly.

Canals

Knowledge of the invertebrate communities of Scotland's canals is largely restricted to those of the Forth and Clyde Canal and the Union Canal. The Forth and Clyde Canal, in keeping with its productive status, supports an abundant and varied macroinvertebrate fauna dominated by Mollusca, Oligochaeta and *Asellus aquaticus* (Fowler, 1972; Clyde RPB, unpublished data) and a rich cladoceran fauna (Doughty, 1983). This diversity reflects the variety of available habitats provided particularly by a rich aquatic and marginal flora and the generally good water quality. In some areas, however, invertebrate diversity has been reduced, apparently in response to pollution. Near Kirkintilloch, for example, a feeder burn containing treated sewage effluent has encouraged massive growths of duckweed (*Lemna* spp.), resulting in serious habitat degradation (Ross *et al.*, 1986). Information on the Union Canal suggests that macroinvertebrate communities are similar to those in the Forth and Clyde Canal (Forth RPB, unpublished data).

Although limited in extent, the Scottish canal system is thought to have been instrumental in the east to west spread of *Potamopyrgus jenkinsi* (Hunter and Warwick, 1957). The Forth and Clyde Canal also holds several invertebrate species of note. The triclad *Bdellocephala punctata*, for which there are only scattered records in Britain (Adams, 1981), is not uncommon. The euryhaline calanoid copepod *Eurytemora velox* has been found at several locations in the western half of the canal. The nationally rare cladoceran *Alona weltneri* and the leech *Piscicola geometra*, rare in the west of Scotland, were recorded near Kirkintilloch (Doughty, 1980; Fraser, 1981; Clyde RPB, unpublished data).

RUNNING WATERS

Rivers and burns present a diverse mosaic of macro- and micro-habitats. Invertebrates are associated with these specific biotopes but the complex relationships are incompletely understood. Current, acting largely via the substrate, is generally considered to be the primary factor of the many determining invertebrate distribution, with water chemistry of secondary importance (Ratcliffe, 1977).

The distribution of sources of organic carbon, both spatially along a river system and temporally through the seasons, also affects invertebrate community composition. Fallen leaves are of prime importance (Egglishaw, 1964), supplemented to some degree by autochthonous production of algae. Plankton from lentic waters and eroding peat may be locally significant sources. "Life history omnivory" has been proposed as a general model for many stream insects (see Williams and Feltmate, 1992); that is, as immature stages grow they become capable of ingesting different food items and may proceed, for example, from particle collection to detritus shredding to carnivory.

The degree of complexity of a habitat will determine the number of biotopes present and therefore the diversity of the invertebrate fauna. As a general rule faster flowing waters will contain more biotopes, produced by variations in flow in different areas of the channel and, through this, substratum heterogeneity.

Headwater streams are an important habitat for a number of species – for example, the mayfly *Ameletus inopinatus*, the stoneflies *Protonemura montana* and *Diura bicaudata*, and the flatworm *Crenobia alpina*, all typical of high altitude riffles. Backwaters and pools are important biotopes for Odonata and other invertebrates normally associated with lentic waters or slow-flowing streams. The Monachyle Burn in Central Region, typical of many in Scotland, contains near its source at an altitude of 460 m a variety of habitats in addition to riffles. Peat development has produced a range of depths, current velocities and particle abundances providing suitable conditions for a diverse chironomid fauna. In riffles, Orthocladiinae such as *Tvetenia calvescens* and *Eukiefferiella* spp. dominate. In particle-rich backwaters, Tanytarsini such as *Micropsectra atrofasciata* reach very high densities, and Chironominae such as *Microtendipes* sp., *Phaenopsectra* sp. and *Stempellinella* sp. are common in the soft organic sediments of pools.

Despite the complexities of habitat it is possible to generalize about the distribution of invertebrates along a river system. For example, Langton (personal communication) has identified chironomid species typical of various reaches of Scottish rivers (Table 10.3). The distribution of invertebrates shows a downstream "transition of associations", a term used by Maitland (1966) in his study of the River Endrick. Maitland's findings clearly indicated a relationship between species and habitats, but produced little evidence of any distinct zonation when considered collectively. More relevant, perhaps, is the frequency of occurrence of specific biotopes along a river's course.

A similar spatial distribution was demonstrated for the oligotrophic River Dee, Grampian Region (Davidson *et al.*, 1985). *Polycelis felina*, for example, was present throughout the main river and some smaller tributaries whilst *Crenobia alpina* was restricted to the upper part of the main river and upland tributaries. Gradient, current speed, water temperature and competition are believed to be the significant factors controlling distribution of these species (Reynoldson, 1978). The differences in habitat preference between species of the same genus was also clearly demonstrated by the data from the Dee. *Hydropsyche siltalai* and *H. pellucidula* had similar distributions and were widespread throughout the catchment. *H. instabilis* was restricted to a number of tributaries and *H. contubernalis* to the middle and lower main river. *H. angustipennis* was found at only three sites, downstream of the eutrophic Loch of Skene.

The longitudinal distribution of biota along watercourses has been widely recognized and has fostered schemes of classification based on discrete zones, often related

TABLE 10.3. Transition of chironomid associations in Scottish rivers. (Records based on exuviae collected by Dr P.H. Langton)

	streams (1st and 2nd order)	rivers		
		Upper reaches	Middle reaches	Lower reaches
Thienemanniella spp.	+			
Corynoneura spp.	+			
Eukiefferiella brevicalcar	+			
Micropsectra bidentata	+			
Heterotrissocladius marcidus	+	+	+	+
Nilotanypus dubius		+	+	+
Synorthocladius semivirens		+	+	+
Tvetenia calvescens		+	+	+
Cricotopus bicinctus		+	+	+
Eukiefferiella coerulescens		+		
Cricotopus similis		+		
Rheotanytarsus pentapoda		+	+	
Krenosmittia camptophleps		+	+	
Cricotopus annulator			+	
Cricotopus albiforceps			+	
Tvetenia verralli			+	+
Orthocladius rubicundus				+
Eukiefferiella clypeata				+
Tanytarsus eminulus				+

to fish distribution. These have generally proved too inflexible to gain wide acceptance (Maitland, 1966). Illies (see reviews by Hynes, 1970a, and Hawkes, 1975) proposed a primary division of rivers into two zones, *rhithron* and *potamon*, which have some ecological validity and are useful descriptors of major habitats.

Rhithron

The running waters of Scotland fall predominantly into the rhithron zone (Figure 10.1), having cool, fast, turbulent water, an eroding substratum of boulders, cobbles and gravels, and dissolved oxygen near to saturation. The rhithron fauna is dominated by insects, including several ancient groups, and shows strong similarities worldwide (Hynes, 1970b). The Scottish invertebrate riffle fauna is generally dominated by members of the Ephemeroptera, Plecoptera, and Trichoptera. Some Diptera, Mollusca, Oligochaeta, Crustacea and Coleoptera may also be present, but usually in lower abundances.

Baetis rhodani is probably the most widespread and abundant ephemeropteran and Morgan and Egglishaw (1965) found it to be the most abundant species in 103 burns in the Highlands. It can be multivoltine (see Elliott *et al.*, 1988), tolerates organic enrichment and many other forms of pollution, and rapidly recolonizes affected streams and rivers. However, it is excluded from acidified sites (pH < 5.5) and has been proposed as an indicator of acidification (Doughty, 1990). Nymphs of *Rhithrogena semicolorata* and *Ephemerella ignita* are also common and widespread, the former being most conspicuous in winter whilst the latter are restricted to the summer months. The differences in their life histories are due to rapid hatching of *Rhithrogena* eggs and delayed hatching of *Ephemerella* eggs until spring.

Plecoptera are generally sensitive to poor water quality, particularly organic enrichment, but relatively tolerant of surface water acidification, *Leuctra* spp., *Capnia vidua* and *Amphinemura sulcicollis* all being recorded from the most acidified streams in the Loch Ard Forest (Harriman and Morrison, 1982).

Trichoptera are rarely found in abundance except the filter-feeding *Hydropsyche* spp., below loch outlets and in organically polluted waters – situations providing comparably rich particulate feeding. *Hydropsyche pellucidula* and *H. siltalai* are the most frequently recorded species. Two other caseless caddis – *Rhyacophila dorsalis* and *Polycentropus flavomaculatus* – are both very widespread, the former often associated with moss.

Gammarus pulex is the most frequently recorded macrocrustacean but was not found in Highland burns with less than 400 μeq L^{-1} cations (Morgan and Egglishaw, 1965). *Gammarus pulex* is replaced in the west and north by *G. duebeni* (Spirit, 1986; Sutcliffe, 1991) and in lochs and loch outlets by *G. lacustris*. Gammarids generally are not present in acidified waters and are typically associated with leaf accumulations and other coarse particulate organic matter.

FIGURE 10.1. The Rhithron. River Dee at Linn of Dee. The habitat of *Rhyacophila dorsalis* (left) and *Ecdyonurus venosus* (right). Photograph: North East River Purification Board

Of the Mollusca, *Ancylus fluviatilis* is a grazer on epilithic algae found wherever there is a stable substratum and some alkalinity. The Freshwater Pearl Mussel *Margaritifera margaritifera* is widespread but declining in Scotland and is absent from the sandstone area of Caithness and the Tweed system. *Margaritifera* requires a stable coarse-sand substratum and is sensitive to enrichment and pearl fishing (Young, 1991; Young, personal communication).

Potamon

The potamon zone (Figure 10.2), downstream of the rhithron, has higher temperatures, slower, laminar flows, and a depositing substratum of sand, mud and silt. Habitat of this type is relatively rare in Scotland but most likely to be encountered in rivers of the east coast and central lowlands, such as the Forth, Earn, Clyde and Endrick. Data on invertebrates of the potamon are scarce, principally due to sampling difficulties. These lower reaches contain fewer biotopes than those upstream due to the greater uniformity of current velocity and substratum, although submerged aquatic macrophytes may diversify the habitat available for invertebrate colonization. Insects are still well represented in this zone although often by different families, especially dipteran. Molluscs and oligochaetes are more abundant and more diverse.

FIGURE 10.2. The Potamon. River Forth at Gargunnock. The habitat of *Sialis nigripes* (left) and *Aphelocheirus aestivalis* (right). Photograph: Ian R. Fozzard

The development of an alternating pool and riffle sequence, extensive in most Scottish rivers, becomes pronounced in the transition from rhithron to potamon. Many of the "pools", however, do not acquire a permanent accumulation of fine sediments due to frequent scouring during spates, and their fauna resembles that of adjacent riffle areas (Logan and Brooker, 1983).

The lower River Forth below Flanders Moss comprises some relatively short, shallow sections with other, more extensive reaches resembling the potamon. The fauna of these slower reaches with their muddy sand substratum differs markedly from that of the stony riffles. It includes the burrowing mayfly *Ephemera danica*, *Sialis nigripes*, the caseless caddis *Cyrnus trimaculatus*, and the large bivalve *Anodonta* sp. Most filter feeders, *Taeniopteryx nebulosa*, Ecdyonuridae, the chironomids *Eukiefferiella* spp, and Baetidae are restricted to the riffles. Invertebrates associated with both the faster and slower flowing areas include many Mollusca and Oligochaeta, the leeches *Glossiphonia complanata* and *Erpobdella octoculata*, the Crustacea *Gammarus pulex* and *Asellus aquaticus*, and Insecta such as *Aphelocheirus aestivalis*, *Sialis lutaria* and the chironomid *Microtendipes* sp.

THE RESOURCE

In functional terms, invertebrate animals are the secondary producers in aquatic food webs, utilizing detritus, plants or other animals for their energy requirements. Cummins (1975) stated that the role of stream invertebrates is "conversion of reduced carbon compounds derived principally from the surrounding land, supplemented by in-stream carbon fixation, into temporary storage in their own tissues, and into carbon dioxide". Fish and some birds are the ultimate consumers of this resource. Invertebrates provide the principal food for most species of freshwater fish, including the commercially important salmonids. The impact of fish predation is well established for lentic waters but there is little evidence that macroinvertebrate populations and community structure are particularly sensitive to changes in predation pressure in flowing waters (see Williams and Feltmate, 1992).

Many birds will feed on the aerial stages of aquatic insects during the summer months (see Chapter 13), particularly wagtails, martins, swallows and flycatchers. The Dipper, *Cinclus cinclus*, feeds almost exclusively on aquatic invertebrates, particularly caddis larvae.

Pollution control authorities in Scotland have made use of the sensitivity of many freshwater invertebrates to various forms of pollution for over 30 years. A sample of the benthos of a river, for example, provides a valuable and convenient indication of the river's condition, when related to previous observations or to other comparable rivers. The rhithron community typical of most Scottish rivers is well suited to the standard kick-sampling technique. Simple biotic indices for summarizing rhithron data have been devised to produce readily accessible information. Current work on RIVPACS, a prediction and classification package for invertebrate communities (Wright *et al.*, 1989), promises to overcome some of the difficulties of assessing sites with differing physical characteristics.

The value of freshwater invertebrates as an educational and research resource should not be overlooked. The relative ease and low cost of sampling, the availability of simple keys for identifying major groups and the easy access to freshwater habitats in Scotland make them ideal for teaching purposes. Despite the evident interest shown by ecologists in Scottish freshwater invertebrates, our knowledge and understanding of most species and habitats are far from complete. Scotland's wealth of standing water communities, in particular, has been inadequately studied.

Human interactions

A number of non-native invertebrate species are believed to have been either introduced directly to Scotland, or spread from other parts of Britain by human activities. Of the 12 British species of freshwater flatworms, three were probably introduced to Scotland in this way. Scottish records of *Planaria torva* are concentrated in the Forth – Clyde area, and Reynoldson and Piearce (1979) suggested that it was introduced from Scandinavia via the timber trade. The American amphipod *Crangonyx pseudo-gracilis* is suspected to have been introduced to Scotland from Canada by similar means (Warwick, 1959). *Dugesia tigrina*, an American triclad presently restricted in Scotland to the River Tweed, was probably introduced through the aquarium trade (Wright, 1987). Another American triclad, *Phagocata woodworthi*, is thought to have been introduced to Loch Ness on equipment brought from America by scientists searching for the Loch Ness Monster (Reynoldson *et al.*, 1981). The impact of these introductions is unknown.

Scotland's rivers and lochs remain relatively unpolluted compared with fresh waters elsewhere in Britain. A national survey of river water quality in 1990 concluded that 96% of rivers were biologically Class A or B (good or moderate quality) and that there was evidence of continuing improvement compared with earlier surveys (Scottish Office Environment Department, 1992). This suggests that, on a national scale, pollution is exerting only a minor impact on Scotland's freshwater invertebrate communities. For the more obvious forms of pollution, such as discharges of treated sewage, trade effluent and farm waste, this is undoubtedly the case, but recently attention has been increasingly focused on the more subtle, long-term effects on freshwater communities of acidification, eutrophication, land-use changes and global warming.

Acidification of surface waters in upland areas of Scotland resulting from acid deposition from the atmosphere and exacerbated by coniferous afforestation has been well documented (see Chapters 23 and 24). Although most attention has been focused on Galloway and the Trossachs, effects on invertebrate communities have been recorded from other areas, including the Cairngorms, Arran and parts of Argyll. Acid waters generally have fewer invertebrate species than those of neutral pH. Invertebrate groups such as the mayflies, caddis flies and water beetles are less well represented. Gastropod molluscs and *Gammarus* are absent, and *Daphnia* may be eliminated from the zooplankton of lochs. The effects on invertebrate communities are probably both direct (e.g. through low pH or high aluminium concentrations) and indirect, acting through food supply or predation (Sutcliffe and Hildrew, 1989; Herrmann, 1990).

There is increasing concern about the prospect of global climate change – in particular, the warming effect associated with the release of "greenhouse gases". The mechanisms by which a rise in average air temperature may affect freshwater invertebrates are complex and difficult to predict, particularly as the ecological

requirements of many species are poorly known. Although the temperature toler-
ances and optima of different species, and the effects of temperature on their rates
of development may be determined experimentally, possible changes in other factors
such as food availability, competition, predation and susceptibility to disease may be
important. Associated climatic changes could affect river flow regimes and wind-
driven mixing in lochs. Likely consequences of these various interactions are changes
in the composition of freshwater communities and in the distributions of individual
species by, for example, a contraction in the range of boreoalpine species with a
corresponding advance northwards of southern forms. Aquatic insects of running
waters have been identified as potentially useful indicators of climate change (Elliott,
1991). In order to make use of the indicator value of these and other groups of
freshwater invertebrates, there must be a firm commitment to the long-term monitoring of the status of sensitive species and sites.

Conservation

The conservation of aquatic invertebrates is a relatively recent development in
Scotland and the rest of Europe. The broad approaches employed are the legal
protection of individual species and the maintenance and management of defined
habitat. The latter, involving such issues as land use, continuity of habitat and site
management, is seen to be the key to the conservation of freshwater invertebrates
(Shirt, 1987). Until much more is known about their ecological requirements, conservation will depend upon the maintenance of present habitat conditions.

The main instrument offering legal protection to individual species in Scotland is
the Wildlife and Countryside Act 1981 (see Chapter 29). Species designated for
varying degrees of protection are listed in schedules which are periodically reviewed.
The Freshwater Pearl Mussel, *Margaritifera margaritifera*, is probably the best known
inclusion from the Scottish invertebrate fauna.

"Red Data Books" produced by the International Union for the Conservation of
Nature and the Nature Conservancy Council list rarer species in Britain in categories
based on the degree of threat. The freshwater invertebrates of Scotland are a small
minority of the total listed. For example, in the *Red Data Book No. 2: Insects* (Shirt,
1987), 1800 of the 22 500 insect species in Britain are listed, but less than a dozen of
these are likely to be found in Scottish fresh waters. Species which are listed include
Coenagrion hastulatum, a damselfly from shallow, well-vegetated pools; *Hagenella
clathrata*, a caddis from raised bogs and mosses; *Hydroporus rufifrons*, a water beetle
of temporary marshes; *Ochthebius lenensis*, a water beetle of grassy pools; and
Limonia omnissinervis, a cranefly found in alluvial river banks. The range of species
listed reflects to some degree the expertise available. Only eight orders are covered,
excluding Plecoptera, Ephemeroptera and most of the Diptera.

Movement and migration are important features of the ecology of many insects
(Dempster, 1989). Insect populations are spatially and temporally dynamic and their
persistence may owe more to repeated colonization after extinction than any internal
population regulation. The beetle *Ochthebius lenensis*, for example, is confined to
saltmarsh pools in north-eastern Scotland which are utilized by the beetle for only a
limited period in their cycle of formation and degradation. Consequently, the species
requires large areas of saltmarsh for its conservation. Similar considerations may hold

for other freshwater invertebrates, implying that the protection of small isolated fragments of habitat will be inadequate. For riverine species this would seem particularly likely and suggests that for many species of freshwater invertebrate the maintenance of whole catchments or sub-catchments will be necessary for their effective conservation (see Chapter 31).

ACKNOWLEDGEMENTS

The authors are indebted to Mrs E. M. Smith for information on Odonata, Dr P. H. Langton (Chironomidae), Dr M. Jeffries and Dr O. Lassière (ponds), Dr L. May (Rotifera), Dr M. Young (Mollusca) and to their fellow RPB biologists. Dr J. F. Wright's constructive criticism of the draft text was much appreciated. Mr B. E. Clelland drew the insects in Figures 10.1 and 10.2.

REFERENCES

Adams, J. (1981). "The influence of environment and competition on the distribution of *Bdellocephala punctata* (Turbellaria, Tricladida) in Britain", *Journal of Natural History*, **15**, 971–980.

Bratton, J. H. (Ed.) (1991). *British Red Data Books: 3. Invertebrates other than Insects*, Joint Nature Conservation Committee, Peterborough.

Brett, M. T. (1989). "Zooplankton communities and acidification processes (a review)", *Water, Air and Soil Pollution*, **44**, 387–414.

Burns, J. C., Coy, J. S., Tervet, D. J., Harriman, R., Morrison, B. R. S. and Quine, C. P. (1984). "The Loch Dee project: a study of the ecological effects of acid precipitation and forest management on an upland catchment in south west Scotland. 1. Preliminary investigations", *Fisheries Management*, **15**, 145–167.

Calow, P. (1974). "Ecological notes on mayfly larvae (Ephemeroptera) in Loch Lomond", *Glasgow Naturalist*, **19**, 123–130.

Cummins, K. W. (1975). "Macroinvertebrates", in *River Ecology* (Ed. B. A. Whitton), pp. 70–198, Blackwell, Oxford.

Davidson, M. B., Owen, R. P. and Young, M. R. (1985). "Invertebrates of the River Dee", in *Proceedings of the Biology and Management of the River Dee Symposium*, pp. 64–82, Institute of Terrestrial Ecology, Banchory.

Dempster, J. P. (1989). "Fragmentation, isolation and mobility of insect populations. Conservation of insects and their habitats", *Proceedings of the 15th Symposium of the Royal Entomological Society of London*, Academic Press, London.

Doughty, C. R. (1980). "A species of water-flea new to Scotland (*Alona weltneri*)", *Glasgow Naturalist*, **20**, 25–28.

Doughty, C. R. (1983). "The Cladocera (water fleas) of the Forth and Clyde Canal", *Glasgow Naturalist*, **20**, 361–367.

Doughty, C. R. (1990). *Acidity in Scottish Rivers. A Chemical and Biological Baseline Survey*, Scottish River Purification Boards and the Department of the Environment, East Kilbride.

Duigan, C. A. (1991). "The rediscovery of the cladoceran *Eurycercus glacialis* Lilljeborg, 1887 (Brachiopoda, Chydoridae) in Scotland", *Freshwater Forum*, **1**, 184–194.

Egglishaw, H. J. (1964). "The distributional relationship between the bottom fauna and plant detritus in streams", *Journal of Animal Ecology*, **33**, 463–476.

Elliott, J. M. (1991). "Aquatic insects as target organisms for the study of effects of projected climate change in the British Isles", *Freshwater Forum*, **1**, 195–203.

Elliott, J. M., Humpesch, U. H. and Macan, T. T. (1988). *Larvae of the British Ephemeroptera: A Key with Ecological Notes*, Scientific Publication No. 49, Freshwater Biological Association, Ambleside.

Fowler, A. R. (1972). *A Biological Survey of the Forth and Clyde Canal*, Nature Conservancy Council, Edinburgh.

Fozzard, I. and Marsden, M. (1990). "The Lake of Menteith, some aspects of its ecology", *The Scottish Naturalist*, **102**, 97–129.

Fraser, S. M. (1981). "Additional records of freshwater leeches", *Glasgow Naturalist*, **20**, 179.

Friday, L. E. (1987). "The diversity of macroinvertebrate and macrophyte communities in ponds", *Freshwater Biology*, **18**, 87–105.

Fryer, G. and Forshaw, O. (1979). "The freshwater Crustacea of the island of Rhum (Inner Hebrides) – a faunistic and ecological survey", *Biological Journal of the Linnean Society*, **11**, 333–367.

Fryer, G. and Joyce, A. (1981). "The distribution of some freshwater copepods and its bearing on the history of the flora and fauna of the British Isles", *Journal of Biogeography*, **8**, 281–291.

Harper, D. M. (1986). "The effects of artificial enrichment upon the planktonic and benthic communities in a mesotrophic to hypertrophic loch series in lowland Scotland", *Hydrobiologia*, **137**, 9–19.

Harriman, R. and Morrison, B. R. S. (1982). "Ecology of streams draining forested and non-forested catchments in an area of central Scotland subject to acid precipitation", *Hydrobiologia*, **88**, 251–263.

Hawkes, H. A. (1975). "River zonation and classification", in *River Ecology* (Ed. B. A. Whitton), pp. 312–374, Blackwell, Oxford.

Herrmann, J. (1990). "Physiological, foodchain and ecological effects among benthic invertebrates exposed to low pH and associated metal concentrations", in *The Surface Water Acidification Programme* (Ed. B. J. Mason), pp. 383–396, Cambridge University Press, Cambridge.

Hunter, W. R. and Warwick, T. (1957). "Records of *Potamopyrgus jenkinsi* (Smith) in Scottish fresh waters over fifty years (1906–56)", *Proceedings of the Royal Society of Edinburgh*, **66**, 360–373.

Hynes, H. B. N. (1970a). *The Ecology of Running Waters*, Liverpool University Press, Liverpool.

Hynes, H. B. N. (1970b). "The ecology of stream insects", *Annual Review of Entomology*, **15**, 25–42.

Jeffries, M. (1987). "The freshwater fauna from the Yellow Mires marsh, Aberlady Bay, Long Niddry, East Lothian", *Glasgow Naturalist*, **21**, 283–286.

Jeffries, M. (1989a). "Measuring Talling's 'element of chance in pond populations' ", *Freshwater Biology*, **21**, 383–393.

Jeffries, M. (1989b). *Forest Ponds Survey, 1989*, Newcastle upon Tyne Polytechnic, Newcastle.

Jeffries, M. (1991). "The ecology and conservation of forestry ponds in Scotland, United Kingdom", *Biological Conservation*, **58**, 191–211.

Jones, D. H. (1984). "Open-water zooplankton from five Tayside freshwater lochs", *Scottish Naturalist*, 1984, 65–91.

Jones, D. H. (1986). "The effect of afforestation on freshwaters in Tayside, Scotland. Zooplankton and other microfauna", *Hydrobiologia*, **33**, 223–235.

Logan, P. and Brooker, M. P. (1983). "The macroinvertebrate faunas of riffles and pools", *Water Research*, **17**, 263–270.

Macan, T. T. (1965). "Predation as a factor in the ecology of water bugs", *Journal of Animal Ecology*, **34**, 691–698.

Maitland, P. S. (1966). *Studies on Loch Lomond 2. The Fauna of the River Endrick*, Blackie, Glasgow.

Maitland, P. S. (Ed.) (1981). *The Ecology of Scotland's Largest Lochs: Lomond, Awe, Ness, Morar and Shiel*, Junk, The Hague.

Maitland, P. S. and Holden, A. V. (1983). "Inland waters in the Inner Hebrides", *Proceedings of the Royal Society of Edinburgh*, **83B**, 229–244.

Maitland, P. S. and Hudspith, P. M. G. (1974). "The zoobenthos of Loch Leven, Kinross, and estimates of its production in the sandy littoral area during 1970 and 1971", *Proceedings of the Royal Society of Edinburgh*, **74B**, 219–239.

Maitland, P. S., Smith, B. D. and Dennis, G. M. (1981). "The crustacean zooplankton", in

The Ecology of Scotland's Largest Lochs: Lomond, Awe, Ness, Morar and Shiel (Ed. P. S. Maitland), pp. 135–154, Junk, The Hague.

Maitland, P. S., May, L., Jones, D. H. and Doughty, C. R. (1991). "Ecology and conservation of Arctic charr, *Salvelinus alpinus* (L), in Loch Doon, an acidifying loch in southwest Scotland", *Biological Conservation*, **55**, 167–197.

Milner, A. M. (1987). "Colonization and ecological development of new streams in Glacier Bay National Park, Alaska", *Freshwater Biology*, **18**, 53–70.

Morgan, N. C. (1970). "Changes in the fauna and flora of a nutrient enriched lake", *Hydrobiologia*, **35**, 545–553.

Morgan, N. C. and Egglishaw, H. J. (1965). "A survey of the bottom fauna of streams in the Scottish Highlands. Part 1. Composition of the fauna", *Hydrobiologia*, **25**, 181–211.

Murray, J. (1905). "On the distribution of the pelagic organisms in Scottish lochs", *Proceedings of the Royal Physical Society of Edinburgh*, **16**, 51–62.

Murray, J. and Pullar, L. (1910). *Bathymetrical Survey of the Fresh Water Lochs of Scotland*, Challenger Office, Edinburgh.

OECD (1982). *Eutrophication of Waters. Monitoring, Assessment and Control*, Organisation for Economic Co-operation and Development, Paris.

Pennak, R. W. (1957). "Species composition of limnetic plankton communities", *Limnology and Oceanography*, **2**, 222–232.

Ratcliffe, D. A. (1977). *A Nature Conservation Review*, Cambridge University Press, Cambridge.

Reynoldson, T. B. (1978). *A Key to the British Species of Freshwater Triclads*, Scientific Publication, No. 23, Freshwater Biological Association, Ambleside.

Reynoldson, T. B. and Piearce, B. (1979). "Predation on snails by three species of triclad and its bearing on the distribution of *Planaria torva* in Britain", *Journal of Zoology*, **189**, 459–484.

Reynoldson, T. B., Smith, B. D. and Maitland, P. S. (1981). "A species of North American triclad new to Britain found in Loch Ness, Scotland", *Journal of Zoology*, **193**, 531–539.

Ross, S. L., Doughty, C. R. and Murphy, K. J. (1986). "Cause, effects and environmental management of a *Lemna* problem in a Scottish canal", *Proceedings of EWRS/AAB 7th Symposium on Aquatic Weeds*, pp. 277–283, European Weed Research Society, and association of Applied Biologists, Loughborough.

Scott, T. (1890–1899). "The invertebrate fauna of the inland waters of Scotland", *Annual Reports of the Fishery Board for Scotland*.

Scottish Office Agriculture and Fisheries Department (1990). *Freshwater Fisheries Laboratory Pitlochry Annual Review 1989–90*, HMSO, Edinburgh.

Scottish Office Environment Department (1992). *Water Quality Survey of Scotland, 1990*, HMSO, Edinburgh.

Shirt, D. B. (Ed.) (1987). *British Red Data Books: 2 Insects*, Nature Conservancy Council, Peterborough.

Slack, H. D. (1957). *Studies on Loch Lomond 1*, Blackie, Glasgow.

Slack, H. D. (1965). "The profundal fauna of Loch Lomond", *Proceedings of the Royal Society of Edinburgh*, **69**, 272–297.

Smith, B. D., Maitland, P. S., Young, M. R. and Carr, M. J. (1981a). "The littoral zoobenthos", in *The Ecology of Scotland's Largest Lochs: Lomond, Awe, Ness, Morar and Shiel* (Ed. P. S. Maitland), pp. 155–203, Junk, The Hague.

Smith, B. D., Cuttle, S. P. and Maitland, P. S. (1981b). "The profundal zoobenthos", in *The Ecology of Scotland's Largest Lochs: Lomond, Awe, Ness, Morar and Shiel* (Ed. P. S. Maitland), pp. 205–222, Junk, The Hague.

Smith, B. D., Maitland, P. S. and Pennock, S. M. (1987). "A comparative study of water level regimes and littoral benthic communities in Scottish lochs", *Biological Conservation*, **39**, 291–316.

Spirit, M. G. (1986). *Freshwater Invertebrates of Caithness*, Caithness and Sutherland District Council's Community Programmes Agency, Wick.

Sutcliffe, D. W. (1991). "British freshwater malacostracan 'shrimps' ", *Freshwater Forum*, **1**, 225–237.

Sutcliffe, D. W. and Hildrew, A. G. (1989). "Invertebrate communities in acid streams", in

Acid Toxicity and Aquatic Animals (Eds R. Morris, E. W. Taylor, D. J. A. Brown and J. A. Brown), pp. 13–29, Cambridge University Press, Cambridge.

Warwick, T. (1959). "*Crangonyx pseudogracilis* Bousfield, an introduced freshwater amphipod, new to Scotland", *Glasgow Naturalist*, **18**, 109–110.

Waterston, A. R., Holden, A. V., Campbell, R. N. and Maitland, P. S. (1979). "The inland waters of the Outer Hebrides", *Proceedings of the Royal Society of Edinburgh*, **77B**, 329–351.

Weerekoon, A. C. J. (1956). "Studies on the biology of Loch Lomond 1. The benthos of Auchentullich Bay", *Ceylon Journal of Science*, (*C*), **7**, 1–94.

Wiederholm, T. (1980). "Use of benthos in lake monitoring", *Journal of the Water Pollution Control Federation*, **52**, 537–547.

Williams, D. D. and Feltmate B. W. (1992). *Aquatic Insects*, CAB International, Oxon.

Wright, J. F. (1987). "Colonization of rivers and canals in Great Britain by *Dugesia tigrina* (Girard) (Platyhelminthes: Tricladida)", *Freshwater Biology*, **17**, 69–78.

Wright, J. F., Armitage, P. D., Furse, M. T. and Moss, D. (1989). "Prediction of invertebrate communities using stream measurements", *Regulated Rivers: Research and Management*, **4**, 147–155.

Young, M. (1991). "Conserving the freshwater pearl mussel (*Margaritifera margaritifera*, L.) in the British Isles and Continental Europe", *Aquatic Conservation: Marine and Freshwater Ecosystems*, **1**, 73–77.

11

Fish

P. S. MAITLAND

Fish Conservation Centre, Easter Cringate, Stirling, FK7 9QX, UK

INTRODUCTION

There are many historical references to the fish fauna of Scotland – several of them from as far back as the 17th century (Franck, 1658; Sibbald, 1684). Most of these older works refer to the fish of one geographic area only (e.g. Brown, 1891) or to the status of just one or two species – sometimes only in a single water (e.g. Parnell, 1838). Two exceptions to this are found in the *Statistical Account of Scotland* (Sinclair, 1791) and in the *Ordnance Gazetteer of Scotland* (Groome, 1884).

The most recent review of fish distribution in Scotland (Maitland, 1992a) updates in a computerized form a previous survey (Maitland, 1972). The database relies on records from specific sites which are identified by name and National Grid Reference. As well as provision for fish species names there is also an allowance within the database for specified physical and chemical information about each site. The data can be interrogated and analyzed in various ways and both textual and graphical output are possible.

For most parts of the British Isles, the history of the freshwater fish begins during the final stages of the last Ice Age, about 13 000 to 15 000 years ago, when the great ice cap that had covered all of Scotland and all but the most southern parts of England, Wales and Ireland was melting and retreating northwards. At that time, and for about the next 3000 years, a land connection existed between England and the Continent, from just north of the River Humber southwards to the River Thames. Both humans and much of the British terrestrial wildlife recolonized the country, sterilized by the ice cap, via this land bridge. Through it flowed rivers which were either tributaries of the River Rhine, or at least shared a common floodplain with this large continental river, giving them a shared fish fauna.

ORIGIN OF SCOTTISH FISH FAUNA

The freshwater fish fauna of Scotland is substantially impoverished compared with the communities found further south in Britain and elsewhere in Europe. Neverthe-less, 42 out of the 55 species recorded from the British Isles as a whole are found

The Fresh Waters of Scotland: A National Resource of International Significance
Edited by P. S. Maitland, P. J. Boon and D. S. McLusky. © 1994 John Wiley & Sons Ltd

TABLE 11.1 Check-list of the freshwater fish of Scotland

LAMPREYS Family PETROMYZONIDAE
  Sea Lamprey *Petromyzon marinus* Linnaeus 1758
  River Lamprey *Lampetra fluviatilis* (Linnaeus 1758)
  Brook Lamprey *Lampetra planeri* (Bloch 1784)
STURGEON Family ACIPENSERIDAE
  Common Sturgeon *Acipenser sturio* Linnaeus 1758
SHADS Family CLUPEIDAE
  Allis Shad *Alosa alosa* (Linnaeus 1758)
  Twaite Shad *Alosa fallax* (Lacepede 1803)
SALMON, TROUT AND CHARR Family SALMONIDAE
  Atlantic Salmon *Salmo salar* Linnaeus 1758
  Brown Trout *Salmo trutta* Linnaeus 1758
  Rainbow Trout *Oncorhynchus mykiss* (Walbaum 1792)
  Pink Salmon *Oncorhynchus gorbuscha* (Walbaum 1792)
  Arctic Charr *Salvelinus alpinus* (Linnaeus 1758)
  Brook Charr *Salvelinus fontinalis* (Mitchill 1815)
WHITEFISH Family COREGONIDAE
  Powan *Coregonus lavaretus* (Linnaeus 1758)
  Vendace *Coregonus albula* (Linnaeus 1758)
GRAYLING Family THYMALLIDAE
  Grayling *Thymallus thymallus* (Linnaeus 1758)
SMELT Family OSMERIDAE
  Sparling *Osmerus eperlanus* (Linnaeus 1758)
PIKE Family ESOCIDAE
  Pike *Esox lucius* Linnaeus 1758
CARP Family CYPRINIDAE
  Common Carp *Cyprinus carpio* Linnaeus 1758
  Crucian Carp *Carassius carassius* (Linnaeus 1758)
  Goldfish *Carassius auratus* (Linnaeus 1758)
  Gudgeon *Gobio gobio* (Linnaeus 1758)
  Tench *Tinca tinca* (Linnaeus 1758)
  Common Bream *Abramis brama* (Linnaeus 1758)
  Minnow *Phoxinus phoxinus* (Linnaeus 1758)
  Rudd *Scardinius erythrophthalmus* (Linnaeus 1758)
  Roach *Rutilus rutilus* (Linnaeus 1758)
  Chub *Leuciscus cephalus* (Linnaeus 1758)
  Orfe *Leuciscus idus* (Linnaeus 1758)
  Dace *Leuciscus leuciscus* (Linnaeus 1758)
LOACH Family COBITIDAE
  Stone Loach *Noemacheilus barbatulus* (Linnaeus 1758)
EELS Family ANGUILLIDAE
  European Eel *Anguilla anguilla* (Linnaeus 1758)
STICKLEBACKS Family GASTEROSTEIDAE
  Three-spined Stickleback *Gasterosteus aculeatus* Linnaeus 1758
  Nine-spined Stickleback *Pungitius pungitius* (Linnaeus 1758)
BASS Family SERRANIDAE
  Sea Bass *Dicentrarchus labrax* (Linnaeus 1758)
PERCH Family PERCIDAE
  Perch *Perca fluviatilis* Linnaeus 1758
  Ruffe *Gymnocephalus cernuus* (Linnaeus 1758)
GOBIES Family GOBIIDAE
  Common Goby *Pomatoschistus microps* (Kroyer 1840)
MULLETS Family MUGILIDAE
  Thick-lipped Mullet *Chelon labrosus* (Risso 1826)
  Thin-lipped Mullet *Liza ramada* (Risso 1826)
  Golden Mullet *Liza aurata* (Risso 1810)
SCULPINS Family COTTIDAE
  Bullhead *Cottus gobio* Linnaeus 1758
FLATFISH Family PLEURONECTIDAE
  Flounder *Platichthys flesus* (Linnaeus 1758)

here (Table 11.1, where all common and scientific names are listed), and the number is very gradually increasing as more species appear from the south. Taking the starting point of the fish communities of Scotland as the closing stages of the last Ice Age, it is clear that euryhaline fishes, many of which come into fresh water to spawn, would have had no difficulty in invading new waters as the ice receded (Table 11.2). Thus Common Sturgeon, shads, Sparling, Sea Bass, gobies and mullets must have occurred in Scottish estuaries for thousands of years (Maitland, 1974). The only fish which were able to colonize truly fresh waters as the ice receded were also those with marine affinities and capable of existing in the ice lakes and glacial rivers which prevailed at that time. At most there were then probably only about 12 species, most notable among which were lampreys, Atlantic Salmon, Brown Trout, Arctic Charr, Powan (Figure 11.1), Vendace, European Eel, sticklebacks and Flounder.

Moving into the period of recorded history (Table 11.2), it is known from the *Statistical Account of Scotland* and other sources that by about 1790 only another five species had been added to the Scottish fauna – Pike, Minnow, Roach, Stone Loach and Perch (Figure 11.2) (Maitland, 1977). How they did so is uncertain; some probably came by natural means (eggs on the feet of wildfowl, or carriage within water spouts) but others may have been transported by humans. Ninety years later (1880) another six species were known to occur in Scotland – Brook Charr (from North America), Grayling, Crucian Carp, Tench, Common Bream and Chub. The

TABLE 11.2. Scottish freshwater fish and their occurrence at different times since the last Ice Age

Original colonizers (euryhaline spp.)	Land bridge (by 1790)	Introductions		
		By 1880	By 1970	By 1990
Sea Lamprey	Pike	Brook Charr	Rainbow Trout	Ruffe
River Lamprey	Minnow	Grayling	Pink Salmon	
Brook Lamprey	Roach	Crucian Carp	Common Carp	
Common Sturgeon	Stone Loach	Tench	Goldfish	
Allis Shad	Perch	Common Bream	Gudgeon	
Twaite Shad		Chub	Rudd	
Atlantic Salmon			Orfe	
Brown Trout			Dace	
Arctic Charr			Bullhead	
Powan				
Vendace				
Sparling				
European Eel				
Three-spined Stickleback				
Nine-spined Stickleback				
Sea Bass				
Common Goby				
Thick-lipped Mullet				
Thin-lipped Mullet				
Golden Mullet				
Flounder				

FIGURE 11.1. Two adult Powan from Loch Lomond. An original colonizer, this is one of Scotland's rarest freshwater fish and occurs only in Lochs Lomond and Eck. Photograph: Peter S. Maitland

main agents of dispersal during this period (and subsequently) were humans and there are numerous records of introductions of these and other species around this time. This was a most intensive period of introduction and movement of fish and many landowners introduced new fish, several from North America, to waters on their estates (Maitland, 1887).

By 1970 another eight species (Rainbow Trout, Common Carp, Goldfish, Gudgeon, Rudd, Orfe, Dace and Bullhead) were known to have established viable populations in Scotland and humans appear to have been responsible for the introduction of all of them. Pink Salmon started appearing around our coasts as vagrants from Russian introductions to the White Sea. The latest species in this saga is the Ruffe, a small perch-like fish which appeared in Loch Lomond in 1982 (probably introduced there by anglers from the south). This has since burgeoned in the loch and is one of the commonest fish there now (Maitland and East, 1989).

Many other fish have been introduced unsuccessfully over the last 200 years (Table 11.3), including Largemouth and Smallmouth Bass (introduced to Loch Ba by the Duke of Argyll in 1881) and Cutthroat Trout to a small loch on Shetland. Between 1920 and 1930 a number of foreign species were introduced to ponds on an estate in Fife (Dr J. Berry, personal communication), including the American Lake Charr, Dolly Varden, Mudminnow, Bleak, Bitterling, Danube Catfish, Brown Bullhead and Pumpkinseed. None of these species is known to exist in the wild in Scotland today.

Thus the present freshwater fish fauna of Scotland is a mixture of natural immig-

FIGURE 11.2. A young Perch from Loch Leven. This species, though entirely freshwater, has become widely distributed since the last Ice Age. It now occurs north of the Great Glen and is still dispersing northwards. Photograph: Kenneth H. Morris

rants from the sea and from further south, along with many more recent fish which have been brought in by humans from England, continental Europe and even North America. The situation is by no means a stable one even yet and other arrivals can be expected in future years. These will certainly add to the diversity of fish communities but may bring with them threats in the form of diseases, competition and predation on more sensitive indigenous fish species.

TABLE 11.3. Fish which are known to have been introduced to waters in Scotland (after Maitland, 1977) but have never become established. Those marked*, however, are native to* or have become established** in England

---

Cutthroat Trout *Oncorhynchus clarkii* Richardson 1836
American Lake Charr *Salvelinus namaycush* (Walbaum 1792)
Dolly Varden *Salvelinus malma* (Walbaum 1792)
Mudminnow *Umbra krameri* (Walbaum 1792)
Bleak* *Alburnus alburnus* (Linnaeus 1758)
Bitterling** *Rhodeus sericeus* (Bloch 1782)
Danube Catfish** *Silurus glanis* Linnaeus 1758
Brown Bullhead *Ictalurus nebulosus* (Le Sueur 1819)
Largemouth Bass** *Micropterus salmoides* (Lacepede 1802)
Smallmouth Bass *Micropterus dolomieu* Lacepede 1802
Pumpkinseed** *Lepomis gibbosus* (Linnaeus 1758)

While the above introductions can all be classed as intentional, humans have, of course, been responsible for many unintentional introductions. In England, Wales and Ireland and to a lesser extent in Scotland, the construction of navigational canals has been a major factor in the redistribution of species from one river system to another. In Scotland, relatively recently, previously separate catchments have been linked by tunnels for hydro-electric generating purposes and it is known that Arctic Charr, Pike, Minnow, Three-spined Stickleback and Perch have all been redistributed in this way.

CURRENT THREATS

Humans have been involved and interacting with fish populations for many thousands of years, and it is often difficult to separate the effects of human impact from changes which have taken place due to more natural processes. Over the last 200 years and particularly the last few decades various new and intense pressures have been applied to fresh waters and very many species have declined in range and in numbers. Some of the more important of these pressures are reviewed below and summarized in Table 11.4; inevitably many of them are interlinked, the final combination often resulting in a complex and sometimes unpredictable situation.

The pollution of fresh waters is probably the single most significant factor in causing major declines in the populations of many fish species in Europe, North America and elsewhere. Most pollution comes from domestic, agricultural or industrial wastes and can be lethal, killing all the fish species present, or selective, destroying a few sensitive species or so altering the environment that some species are favoured and others not. However, considerable research has been carried out in this area and suitable water quality criteria are now available in relation to freshwater fish. Pollutants present at sub-lethal levels can raise the susceptibility thresholds of fish to other threats, such as heated effluents. Eutrophication is sometimes thought of as a mild form of pollution whilst the recent acidification from atmospheric pollution of many waters in Scandinavia and elsewhere (Maitland *et al.*, 1987) has shown that even waters far away from urbanization are not necessarily safe.

The impact of various forms of land use on many species of fish can be considerable. Land drainage schemes can totally alter the hydrology of adjacent river systems and, in addition, lead to problems of siltation. The type of crop grown on the land can also have a major effect; for instance, the recent development of extensive mono-culture forests of non-indigenous conifers has led to concern about excessive water loss from catchments through evapo-transpiration together with increased acidification of runoff to the streams. A serious problem in lowland areas is the drainage or filling in of many ponds which were formerly important sites for various species of fish.

River and lake engineering have been responsible for the immediate elimination of various fish species. Migratory species are particularly threatened by weirs, dams and other obstructions on watercourses and, if they are unable to reach their spawning grounds, may become extinct in these systems in just a few years. Stretches of severe pollution in river systems can act in the same way to such species by blocking migration routes. Engineering works can also completely destroy the habitat for some fish, often by dredging or siltation of the river or lake bed, or by exposing the fish to intolerable fluctuations in water level. The technology of fish-pass design and other ways of ameliorating the impact of such works has improved in recent years and most problems can now be solved at the project planning stage if the will or appropriate legislation is there.

The impact of fisheries (both sport and commercial) on the populations which they exploit can range from extinction (e.g. the elimination of coarse fish by the use of rotenone) to the more or less stable relationship of recruitment and cropping on a sustainable basis which existed in many old established fisheries (e.g. that for Brown Trout in Loch Leven (Thorpe, 1974)). The essence of success in such management is to have a well-regulated fishery where statistics on the catch are consistently monitored and used as a basis for future management of the stock.

Apart from physical and chemical habitat alterations created by humans, there are also various biological perturbations. Of major importance among these is the introduction of new fish species, discussed above. If these establish themselves they can alter the community structure radically and lead to the extinction of sensitive native species. The introduction of Ruffe to Loch Lomond is an example. It should

TABLE 11.4. A summary of the main pressures facing freshwater fish and their habitats in Scotland

Pressure	Effect
Industrial and domestic effluents	Pollution, poisoning, blocking of migration routes
Acid deposition	Acidification, release of toxic metals
Land use (farming and forestry)	Eutrophication, acidification, sedimentation
Industrial development (including roads)	Sedimentation, obstructions, transfer of species
Warm-water discharge	Deoxygenation, temperature gradients
River obstructions (dams)	Blocking of migration routes, sedimentation of spawning beds
Infilling, drainage and canalization	Loss of habitat, shelter and food supply
Water abstraction	Loss of habitat and spawning grounds, transfer of species
Fluctuating water levels (reservoirs)	Loss of habitat, spawning and food supply
Fish farming	Eutrophication, introductions, diseases, genetic changes
Angling and fishery management	Elimination by piscicides, diseases, introductions
Commercial fishing	Overfishing, genetic changes
Introduction of new species	Elimination of native species, introduction of diseases, parasites
Global warming	Loss of some southern or low altitude populations. Movement north of southern species

be emphasized that such introductions, unlike pollution which can be eliminated and the habitat restored, are likely to be permanent, for most fish species are virtually impossible to eliminate, once established.

On the positive side, some new types of habitat have been created by humans, notably numerous reservoirs of a variety of sizes and, in lowland areas, canals. Most of these have provided extremely suitable habitats for fish communities.

RESOURCE VALUE

The careful commercial harvesting of native freshwater fish can have relatively little harmful influence on the waters concerned. Indeed, because it is in their interests to avoid contamination, fishermen can act as a strong force against pollution and other threats. However, harm can be done to fish populations by overfishing and poor management, and efficient sustainable cropping should always be the long-term conservation and economic objective.

Superficially at least, the Atlantic Salmon is economically the most important of the three native salmonids and it is certainly the one which receives most attention politically. Wild fish were formerly the most important component, but nowadays less than 1000 tonnes a year are caught by angling and commercial netsmen. However, with the rapid development of Salmon farming the wild catch has been rapidly overtaken and the production of farmed fish is currently many times that of wild fish (see Chapter 18). Partly because the price of farmed fish has depressed that of wild fish some netsmen have gone out of business, but more important in the last few years has been the buying out of netting rights by so-called "charitable" angling interests. This trend seems likely to continue and eventually most wild fish will be taken by rod and line.

Trout farming, like that for Salmon, has also burgeoned in Britain in recent years and the production in 1987 was 10 750 tonnes. Most of the production is Rainbow Trout for the table, but there are also significant numbers of Rainbow and Brown Trout sold for stocking angling waters. There have been few attempts to estimate the value of the resident Brown Trout fisheries of Scotland, but because of their number and extensive usage it is possible that their value may exceed that of Atlantic Salmon or Sea Trout. Certainly there are many more Trout anglers than Salmon anglers in Scotland.

Though of commercial value in other parts of the world, the Arctic Charr is of little economic importance in Scotland. There are a few small local angling fisheries, such as that on Loch Lee, and recent interest in developing small commercial net fisheries in some highland lochs. In addition, there are tentative experiments and proposals to farm Arctic Charr in floating cages. Such systems are likely to be successful technically for they are already operating commercially in Canada and Norway. However, if the numerous ecological mistakes which were made during the over-rapid development of the Salmon farming industry in Scotland are to be avoided, then a conservation-oriented policy should be drawn up now by the relevant authorities.

Apart from the salmonids, few other freshwater fish are of commercial importance in Scotland at present. There is a small fishery for Eels, based mainly on fyke nets in lochs and occasionally on traps in rivers. Attempts at farming Eels have largely been unsuccessful. There has been a recent move to develop a commercial fishery for Eels and Pike in lochs in the highlands, but this is still at a very early stage. Clearly it is important that such fisheries are established carefully and on a sustainable basis.

RESEARCH

Substantial research has been carried out on freshwater fish in Scotland and only a selection can be mentioned in this short review. Most of the effort has been directed at salmonids, especially Atlantic Salmon and Brown Trout, and relatively little work has been carried out on other species. A bibliography of the latter has recently been prepared by Treasurer and Mills (1993).

Apart from the studies by MacDonald (1959a, b), about which there is some controversy (Potter and Osborne, 1975; Schoonoord and Maitland, 1983), lampreys were virtually ignored until the review of their ecology in Europe (Maitland, 1980a) and the recent work on populations in Loch Lomond (Maitland, 1980b; Morris, 1989) and in the Firth of Forth (Maitland *et al.*, 1984b).

Estuarine species such as Common Sturgeon, shads, Sea Bass and mullets have been relatively little studied in Scotland, though there is significant information from other countries. Some work has been carried out on Sparling (Hutchinson, 1983), Common Goby (Healey, 1972) and Flounder (Summers, 1979), and currently both Allis and Twaite Shad are being investigated by the author in the Solway area.

The Atlantic Salmon has been the subject of more studies than any other fish species in Scotland and there is an enormous literature on this species worldwide, which is reviewed regularly (e.g. Pyefinch, 1955; Mills, 1971; 1989). There is also a significant amount of ongoing research on this species, much of which is of importance both internationally and commercially (e.g. Thorpe, 1977b; Buck and Hay, 1984). Brown Trout, too, have been much studied in Scotland in the past (Pyefinch, 1960; Campbell, 1971; Pemberton, 1976; Treasurer, 1976; Campbell, 1977; Pratten and Shearer, 1983) and there is also some current research. Arctic Charr, previously a neglected species (Maitland *et al.*, 1984a) is now a focus of interest with several recently published studies (e.g. Barbour and Einarsson, 1987; Walker *et al.*, 1988; Maitland *et al.*, 1991; Hartley *et al.*, 1992,) and some ongoing ones.

The biology of the Powan has now been studied in some detail (Slack *et al.*, 1957; Maitland, 1969; Scott, 1975; Brown and Scott, 1987; 1990; Brown *et al.*, 1991) but less is known about the Vendace (Maitland, 1966; 1967) which is now believed to be extinct in Scotland. The Grayling is the focus of attention of the Grayling Society (Gardiner, 1991), though only a few studies of its biology in Scotland are available (Mackay, 1970).

The Pike is one of the few non-salmonid Scottish species to have been studied in some detail. Apart from the comprehensive study of a whole population by Munro (1957), work has also been done by Shafi and Maitland (1971a), Treasurer (1980) and others.

Although 12 members of the carp family are now established in Scotland, few studies of their biology have been carried out here, exceptions being Gudgeon (Radforth, 1940), Minnow (Maitland, 1965), Roach (Mills, 1969) and Dace (Starkie, 1976). Little information apart from the study by Maitland (1965) is available on the Stone Loach in Scotland, but the European Eel has been researched in a few waters (Shafi and Maitland, 1972). The Three-spined Stickleback has also been studied by several authors (Maitland, 1965; Giles, 1983; Campbell, 1985) but little is known of the biology of the Nine-spined Stickleback in Scotland (Campbell, 1979b).

The Perch is another non-salmonid fish which has received considerable research attention and its biology has been studied in a number of waters (Campbell, 1955; Shafi and Maitland, 1971b; Thorpe, 1977a; Treasurer, 1981). The recent invasion of Loch Lomond by Ruffe has merited attention and several studies are now available (Maitland and East, 1989; Adams and Tippett, 1991).

Finally, the Bullhead, probably introduced to Scotland only within the last century, has been studied in both river systems in which it occurs – the Clyde and the Forth (Morris, 1978).

As well as studies of individual species there have been several studies of inter-specific relationships (Egglishaw, 1967; Morrison, 1976; Campbell, R. N., 1979a; Campbell, R. N. B., 1982; 1984).

CONSERVATION

Threatened fish

A recent review of rare species of fish and their conservation in the British Isles (Maitland and Lyle, 1991) showed that 10 species are regarded as under threat, but three of these (Houting *Coregonus oxyrinchus*, Pollan *Coregonus autumnalis* and Burbot *Lota lota*) do not occur in Scotland. The seven species occurring in Scotland (Table 11.5) all need a variety of conservation measures if their future is to be secured. Four are anadromous species which live mostly in the sea but spawn in fresh

TABLE 11.5. Rare and extinct species of native freshwater fish in Scotland

Fish	Occurrence
Common Sturgeon *Acipenser sturio*	An increasingly rare vagrant around all coasts
Allis Shad *Alosa alosa*	Now uncommon around British coasts. No certain breeding sites
Twaite Shad *Alosa fallax*	Less common than formerly around all coasts. Breeds in only a few rivers. Landlocked race in Lough Leane (Killarney)
Arctic Charr *Salvelinus alpinus*	Fewer populations than formerly. Many in Scotland and Ireland, a few in Wales and England
Powan *Coregonus lavaretus*	Only seven populations altogether. Two in Scotland, four in England, one in Wales
Vendace *Coregonus albula*	Only two populations left (in England). Two others (in Scotland) extinct this century
Sparling *Osmerus eperlanus*	Much less common than formerly in most estuaries. Far fewer breeding stocks left. The single landlocked population (in England) now extinct

water: Common Sturgeon (now rare in British waters), Allis Shad (very rare and no known spawning sites), Twaite Shad (a declining species with only a few known spawning sites all south of the border) and Sparling (formerly known to have at least 11 stocks in Scotland of which only three remain). Three are purely freshwater species: Arctic Charr (still found in many lochs in the north-west of Scotland but in a decreasing number of sites in the south (Maitland, 1992b), Powan (found only in Lochs Lomond and Eck) and Vendace (occurring formerly in only two sites – the Castle and Mill Lochs (Figure 11.3) near Lochmaben; it is now extinct in both waters).

The isolation of many freshwater systems and the strong homing instinct at spawning time in migratory species has meant that many populations have evolved a stock individuality over the last few thousand years (Stephen, 1984). In some species (e.g. Atlantic Salmon and Brown Trout) it is likely that this is being substantially interfered with due to indiscriminate stocking or other careless management practices. However, there are still important stocks of these and several other species which are of particular note and worthy of special conservation measures. Several of these are considered below, but it is likely that there may be others which will be found worthy of attention once further research has been carried out on the stock individuality of freshwater fish in Scotland.

There are several distinct stocks of common native species which have unusual characteristics and require special conservation measures. These fish include a purely freshwater race of the normally anadromous River Lamprey in Loch Lomond, a dwarf form of Brook Lamprey in the Inner Hebrides, spineless Three-spined Sticklebacks

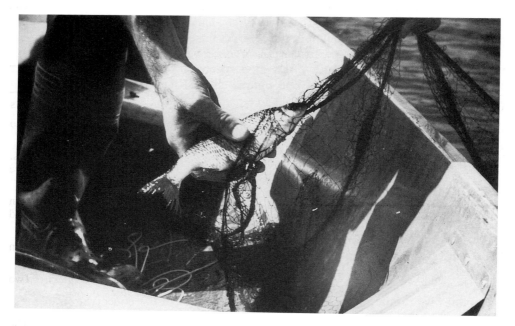

FIGURE 11.3. A Roach being gill-netted from the Mill Loch, Lochmaben. The introduction of coarse fish (such as Roach and, more recently, Bream) into the Mill Loch is probably one of the factors responsible for the extinction of Vendace there: Photograph: Kathleen Maitland

in the Outer Hebrides and a number of races of Brown Trout (and perhaps other species) which are important because of distinctive features of form or behaviour.

Rare fish communities in the British Isles have also been considered by Maitland (1985) and Maitland and Lyle (1991). Many of the original fish communities in Scotland have been eliminated by pollution or habitat destruction and others have been altered by the introduction of foreign species. However, there are still several interesting and valuable communities left and all of these are worthy of conservation measures. Their value can relate to a variety of combinations of fish species reflecting pristineness, simplicity, diversity, uniqueness and classical community structures. Probably the most important of these is in Loch Eck which has a unique fish community found nowhere else in the British Isles.

Protection

Current protection for British freshwater fish exists mainly through legislation, but this is inadequate in some respects and tends to focus mainly on sport and commercial species (Maitland and Lyle, 1992). There are also many protected areas, of various designations, for native flora and fauna, but very few have been established because of their fish. A recent survey of fresh waters and fish in 68 National Nature Reserves (NNRs) throughout Scotland (Lyle and Maitland, 1992) revealed that although no NNRs have been declared for fish interests, 91% of NNRs included fresh waters, and of these only 9% had no fish. Of the 42 Scottish fish species, 24 (60%) were recorded in NNRs during the survey. As might be expected, the majority of these fish are common species and there is little immediate concern for their conservation. Of the seven threatened species in Scotland, only Arctic Charr and Powan (Figure 11.1) are present in NNRs. Although a number of reserves have diverse fish communities, only four are regarded as having particular conservation value. Outstanding among these is Loch Lomond NNR because of its high species diversity (15 native and four introduced), rare species (Powan), a unique race (River Lamprey) and unusual species combinations.

There is considerable scope through the management of waters in existing NNRs to enhance fish conservation there and the acquisition of new reserves for threatened species should be considered. There is no similar information for fish for the many other protected areas, such as Sites of Special Scientific Interest, Local Nature Reserves, etc. A study of the status of fish and fresh waters in such reserves would be a worthwhile project.

The main future options for fish conservation in Scotland are habitat management and restoration, stock transfer to new sites, captive breeding and cryopreservation (Maitland and Lyle, 1992). The first two of these are the most useful for the long-term conservation of threatened species. Improved legislation would also help, especially in relation to preventing the import and transfer of potentially harmful species.

Habitat restoration and management is a major goal in the conservation of most species and communities. Obviously enormous damage has been done to many fish habitats and the situation is often not easy to reverse. However, there are a number of important examples of habitat restoration in temperate areas and it should be emphasized that habitat restoration, protection and management are the principal long-term means through which successful fish conservation will be achieved. An example in Scotland is the River Clyde which is now far less polluted than 50 years ago when it was virtually fishless in its lower reaches. However, salmonid fish are conclusive evidence of high water quality and the return of the Atlantic Salmon to this river after an absence of more than 100 years is a tribute to decades of work by the local River Purification Board.

As well as promoting the importance of habitat management and conservation at specific sites, trial programmes of translocation for Arctic Charr and Powan have been implemented to create new safeguard populations (Maitland and Lyle, 1990). Specific criteria have been developed in planning such translocations (Maitland and Lyle, 1992). For example, the translocation activities must pose no threat to the parent stock, nor to the ecology or scientific interest of the introduction site, which clearly must be ecologically suitable.

In addition to the implementation of conservation management programmes for rare fish, research and monitoring studies are also needed to aid such management and to maintain an awareness of the status of important species.

DISCUSSION

Every year, changes take place in the distribution of freshwater fish in Scotland, for the situation has never reached equilibrium during the 10 000 years or so since the last Ice Age. In addition to the slow rate of natural dispersal northwards by many native fish species (especially, the cyprinids), humans have caused many changes few of which have been beneficial.

In spite of existing legislation, casual introductions continue to occur – sometimes with potentially disastrous consequences. The introduction of Ruffe to Loch Lomond (Figure 11.4) in recent years is an example of this and the more recent establishment there of Gudgeon, Dace and Chub has presented additional threats to the native fish community – especially the endangered Powan and the unique race of River Lamprey. As well as tightening the legislation to prevent such introductions, a change of philosophy is needed among those involved in carrying out such transfers – in the majority of cases, anglers. With many thousands of lakes and streams in this country is there any justification at all for moving relatively common species (in the south of the country at least) into additional waters further north, just because they do not occur there? The rare local fish in some of these waters are under enough threats without those posed by the indiscriminate introductions of unwanted species.

The present situation with regard to the management of fish and fisheries in Scotland is, and has been for centuries, very unsatisfactory and is discussed in Chapter 26. It was thought formerly that many fish, especially cyprinids, in Britain had already reached their northern limits and were unlikely to disperse much further. This is clearly not the case as the successful moves made recently by several species (e.g. Gudgeon, Chub, Dace and Ruffe) have resulted in thriving new populations north of their previous areas of distribution. All of these new stocks appear to have resulted from deliberate introductions by humans – either intentionally to initiate new populations or by discarding excess livebait at the end of fishing.

Although present controls on the movement of fish are probably adequate in England and Wales, this is not the case in Scotland. The Wildlife and Countryside

FIGURE 11.4. Loch Lomond, Scotland's largest loch by surface area (71 km^2), has a larger number of native fish than any other loch (15 species). Since 1980, another four species have been introduced from England and become established here. Photograph: Peter S. Maitland

Act 1981 covers exotics but not fish native to Great Britain. If the introduction of fish (like Ruffe) native to England but not to Scotland is to be controlled, then they need to be specified by the Secretary of State under Section 1 of the Import of Live Fish (Scotland) Act 1978. This should be done now for the species concerned, including Barbel, Silver Bream, Bleak and Spined Loach. There are, of course, a number of exotic species already established in England (but not in Scotland) and these include Bitterling, Danube Catfish, Largemouth Bass and Pumpkinseed (all of which have been introduced unsuccessfully to Scotland: see Table 11.3), Rock Bass *Ambloplites rupestris* and Pikeperch *Stizostedion lucioperca*. Movement of these species should be controlled by the Wildlife and Countryside Act 1981.

A further problem, of course, relates to the movement of fish within Scotland. The southern species which have managed to get a foothold relatively recently can now be moved around the country without hindrance. The recent population explosions of four of these species in the River Endrick within a few years of their introduction shows how quickly they can establish themselves.

Finally, even with appropriate legislation, statutory provisions can easily be thwarted. For example, at the moment in Edinburgh (and most other large cities in Scotland) it is possible to buy stocks of several non-native (mostly North American) fish species (e.g. Fathead Minnow *Pimephales promelas*, Black Bullhead *Ictalurus melas*, Channel Catfish *Ictalurus punctatus*), which might well become established, and introduce them virtually anywhere in the country – illegally but without hindrance. Thus as well as legislation, it is important to give advice and guidance to the public through as many channels as possible. Most of the problems at the moment are being created by anglers (especially coarse fishermen) and these should be targeted with a booklet and/or one or more articles in their magazines pointing out the hazards of introducing new species.

The main difficulty is that there is really no adequate organization for freshwater fish/fisheries in Scotland comparable to that in England and Wales and in most other western countries (see Chapter 26).

However, there is still relatively little information about the population biology of most species in Scotland and the factors controlling their numbers. Information of this kind is vital to stock management, but unfortunately is difficult to acquire because of the difficulties of obtaining exact counts of entire fish populations and the complexity of factors involved. Nonetheless, some useful studies have already been made and, with the advances in modern technology related to echo sounding, revolutionary new fish counters and new methods of tagging, the future looks bright.

ACKNOWLEDGEMENT

I am grateful to Dr David Scott for helpful comments on an early draft of this text.

REFERENCES

Adams, C. E. and Tippett, R. (1991). "Powan ova (*Coregonus lavaretus* (L.)) predation by newly introduced Ruffe (*Gymnocephalus cernuus* (L.)) in Loch Lomond", *Aquaculture and Fisheries Management*, **22**, 261–267.

Barbour, S. E. and Einarsson, S. M. (1987). "Ageing and growth of Charr *Salvelinus alpinus* (L.) from habitat types in Scotland", *Aquaculture and Fisheries Management*, **18**, 1–13.

Brown, A. (1891). "The fishes of Loch Lomond and its tributaries", *Scottish Naturalist*, **10**, 114–124.

Brown, E. A. R. and Scott, D. B. C. (1987). "Abnormal pelvic fins in Scottish Powan, *Coregonus lavaretus* (L.) (Salmonidae, Coregoninae)", *Journal of Fish Biology*, **31**, 443–444.

Brown, E. A. R. and Scott, D. B. C. (1990). "Anabolic adaptiveness in the two Scottish populations of *Coregonus lavaretus* (L.) (Salmonidae, Coregoninae)", *Journal of Fish Biology*, **37A**, 251–253.

Brown, E. A. R., Finnigan, N. and Scott, D. B. C. (1991). "A life table for Powan, *Coregonus lavaretus* (L.) in Loch Lomond, Scotland: a basis for conservation strategy. *Aquatic Conservation: Marine and Freshwater Ecosystems*, **1**, 183–187.

Buck, R. J. G. and Hay, D. W. (1984). "The relation between stock size and progeny of Atlantic Salmon, *Salmo salar* L., in a Scottish stream", *Journal of Fish Biology*, **23**, 1–12.

Campbell, J. S. (1977). "Spawning characteristics of Brown Trout and Sea Trout *Salmo trutta* L. in Kirk Burn, River Tweed, Scotland", *Journal of Fish Biology*, **11**, 217–230.

Campbell, R. N. (1955). "Food and feeding habits of Brown Trout, Perch and other fish in Loch Tummel", *Scottish Naturalist*, **67**, 23–27.

Campbell, R. N. (1971). "The growth of Brown Trout, *Salmo trutta* L., in northern Scotland with special reference to the improvement of fisheries", *Journal of Fish Biology*, **3**, 1–28.

Campbell, R. N. (1979a). "Ferox Trout (*Salmo trutta* L.) and Charr (*Salvelinus alpinus* (L.)) in Scottish lochs", *Journal of Fish Biology*, **14**, 1–29.

Campbell, R. N. (1979b). "Sticklebacks (*Gasterosteus aculeatus* (L.) and *Pungitius pungitius* (L.)) in the Outer Hebrides, Scotland", *Hebridean Naturalist*, 1979, 1–3.

Campbell, R. N. (1985). "Morphological variation in the Three-spined Stickleback (*Gasterosteus aculeatus*) in Scotland", *Behaviour*, **93**, 161–168.

Campbell, R. N. B. (1982). "The food of Arctic Charr in the presence and absence of Brown Trout", *Glasgow Naturalist*, **20**, 229–235.

Campbell, R. N. B. (1984). "Predation by Arctic Charr on the Three-spined Stickleback and its nest in Loch Meallt, Skye", *Glasgow Naturalist*, **20**, 409–413.

Egglishaw, H. J. (1967). "The food, growth and population structure of Salmon and Trout in two streams in the Scottish highlands", *Freshwater Salmon Fisheries Research Scotland*, **38**, 1–32.

Franck, R. (1658). *Northern Memoirs, calculated for the Meridian of Scotland*, London.

Gardiner, R. W. (1991). "Scottish Grayling: history and biology of the populations", *Proceedings of the Institute of Fisheries Management Annual Study Course*, **22**, 171–178.

Giles, N. (1983). "The possible role of environmental calcium levels during the evolution of phenotypic diversity in Outer Hebridean populations of Three-spined Sticklebacks, *Gasterosteus aculeatus*", *Journal of Zoology, London*, **199**, 535–545.

Groome, F. M. (1884). *Ordnance Gazetteer of Scotland: A survey of Scottish topography: Statistical, Biographical and Historical*, Jack, Edinburgh.

Hartley, S. E., McGowan, C., Greer, R. B. and Walker, A. F. (1992). "The genetics of sympatric Arctic Charr (*Salvelinus alpinus* (L.)) populations from Loch Rannoch, Scotland", *Journal of Fish Biology*, **41**, 1021–1031.

Healey, M. C. (1972). "On the population ecology of the Common Goby in the Ythan Estuary", *Journal of Natural History*, **6**, 133–145.

Hutchinson, P. (1983). "Some ecological aspects of the Smelt, *Osmerus eperlanus* (L.), from the River Cree, southwest Scotland", *Proceedings of the British Freshwater Fish Conference*, **3**, 1–13.

Lyle, A. A. and Maitland, P. S. (1992). "Conservation of freshwater fish in the British Isles: the status of fish in National Nature Reserves", *Aquatic Conservation: Marine and Freshwater Ecosystems*, **2**, 19–34.

MacDonald, T. H. (1959a). "Identification of ammocoetes of British lampreys", *Glasgow Naturalist*, **18**, 91–95.

MacDonald, T. H. (1959b). "Estimates of length of larval life in three species of lamprey found in Britain", *Journal of Animal Ecology*, **28**, 293–298.

Mackay, D. W. (1970). "Populations of Trout and Grayling in two Scottish rivers", *Journal of Fish Biology*, **2**, 39–45.

Maitland, J. R. G. (1887). *A History of Howietoun*, Guy, Stirling.

Maitland, P. S. (1965). "The feeding relationships of Salmon, Trout, Minnows, Stone Loach and Three-spined Sticklebacks in the River Endrick, Scotland", *Journal of Animal Ecology*, **34**, 109–133.

Maitland, P. S. (1966). "Present status of known populations of the Vendace, *Coregonus vandesius* Richardson, in Great Britain", *Nature*, **210**, 216–217.

Maitland, P. S. (1967). "Echo sounding observations on the Lochmaben Vendace, *Coregonus vandesius* Richardson", *Transactions of the Dumfries and Galloway Natural History and Antiquarian Society*, **44**, 29–46.

Maitland, P. S. (1969). "The reproduction and fecundity of the Powan, *Coregonus clupeoides* Lacepede, in Loch Lomond, Scotland", *Proceedings of the Royal Society of Edinburgh*, **70B**, 233–264.

Maitland, P. S. (1972). "A key to the freshwater fishes of the British Isles", *Scientific Publication* No. 27, Freshwater Biological Association, Ambleside.

Maitland, P. S. (1974). "The conservation of freshwater fishes in the British Isles", *Biological Conservation*, **6**, 7–14.

Maitland, P. S. (1977). "Freshwater fish in Scotland in the 18th, 19th and 20th centuries", *Biological Conservation*, **12**, 265–277.

Maitland, P. S. (1980a). "Review of the ecology of lampreys in northern Europe", *Canadian Journal of Fisheries and Aquatic Sciences*, **37**, 1944–1952.

Maitland, P. S. (1980b). "Scarring of Whitefish (*Coregonus lavaretus*) by European River Lamprey (*Lampetra fluviatilis*) in Loch Lomond, Scotland", *Canadian Journal of Fisheries and Aquatic Sciences*, **37**, 1981–1988.

Maitland, P. S. (1985). "Criteria for the selection of important sites for freshwater fish in the British Isles", *Biological Conservation*, **31**, 335–353.

Maitland, P. S. (1992a). "A database of fish distribution in Scotland", *Freshwater Forum*, **2**, 59–61.

Maitland, P. S. (1992b). "The status of Arctic Charr, *Salvelinus alpinus* (L.), in southern Scotland: a cause for concern", *Freshwater Forum*, **2**, 212–227.

Maitland, P. S. and East, K. (1989). "An increase in numbers of Ruffe, *Gymnocephalus cernua* (L.), in a Scottish loch from 1982 to 1987", *Aquaculture and Fisheries Management*, **20**, 227–228.

Maitland, P. S. and Lyle, A. A. (1990). "Practical conservation of British fishes: current action on six declining species", *Journal of Fish Biology*, **37A**, 255–256.

Maitland, P. S. and Lyle, A. A. (1991). "Conservation of freshwater fish in the British Isles: the current status and biology of threatened species", *Aquatic Conservation: Marine and Freshwater Ecosystems*, **1**, 25–54.

Maitland, P. S. and Lyle, A. A. (1992). "Conservation of freshwater fish in the British Isles: proposals for management", *Aquatic Conservation: Marine and Freshwater Ecosystems*, **2**, 165–183.

Maitland, P. S., Greer, R. B., Campbell, R. N. and Friend, G. F. (1984a). "The status of the Arctic Charr, *Salvelinus alpinus* (L.), in Scotland", *International Symposium on Arctic Charr, Winnipeg*, **1**, 193–215.

Maitland, P. S., Morris, K. H., East, K., Schoonoord, M. P., Van der Wal, B. and Potter, I. C. (1984b). "The estuarine biology of the River Lamprey, *Lampetra fluviatilis*, in the Firth of Forth, Scotland, with particular reference to size composition and feeding", *Journal of Zoology*, **203**, 211–225.

Maitland, P. S., Lyle, A. A. and Campbell, R. N. B. (1987). *Acidification and Fish Populations in Scottish Lochs*, Institute of Terrestrial Ecology, Grange-over-Sands.

Maitland, P. S., May, L., Jones, D. H. and Doughty, C. R. (1991). "Ecology and conservation of Arctic Charr, *Salvelinus alpinus* (L.), in Loch Doon, an acidifying loch in southwest Scotland", *Biological Conservation*, **55**, 167–197.

Mills, D. H. (1969). "The growth and population densities of Roach in some Scottish waters", *Proceedings of the British Coarse Fish Conference*, **4**, 50–57.

Mills, D. H. (1971). *Salmon and Trout: A Resource, Its Ecology, Conservation and Management*, Oliver & Boyd, Edinburgh.

Mills, D. H. (1989). *Ecology and Management of Atlantic Salmon*, Chapman and Hall, London.

Morris, K. H. (1978). "The food of the Bullhead (*Cottus gobio* L.) in the Gogar Burn, Lothian, Scotland", *Forth Naturalist and Historian*, **7**, 31–44.

Morris, K. H. (1989). "A multivariate morphometric and meristic description of a population of freshwater-feeding River Lampreys, *Lampetra fluviatilis* (L.), from Loch Lomond, Scotland", *Zoological Journal of the Linnean Society*, **96**, 357–371.

Morrison, B. (1976). "The coarse fish of the Lake of Menteith", *Fisheries Management*, **7**, 89.

Munro, W. R. (1957). "The Pike of Loch Choin", *Freshwater Salmon Fisheries Research Scotland*, **16**, 1–16.

Parnell, R. (1838). "Observations on the Coregoni of Loch Lomond", *Annals and Magazine of Natural History*, **1**, 161–165.

Pemberton, R. (1976). "Sea Trout in North Argyll sea lochs: II. diet", *Journal of Fish Biology*, **9**, 195–208.

Potter, I. C. and Osborne, T. S. (1975). "The systematics of British larval lampreys", *Journal of Zoology, London*, **176**, 311–329.

Pratten, D. J. and Shearer, W. M. (1983). "The migrations of North Esk Sea Trout", *Fisheries Management*, **2**, 99–113.

Pyefinch, K. A. (1955). "A review of the literature on the biology of the Atlantic Salmon (*Salmo salar* Linn.)", *Freshwater Salmon Fisheries Research Scotland*, **9**, 1–24.

Pyefinch, K. A. (1960). *Trout in Scotland*, HMSO, Edinburgh.

Radforth, I. (1940). "The food of the Grayling (*Thymallus thymallus*), Flounder (*Platichthys flesus*), Roach (*Rutilus rutilus*) and Gudgeon (*Gobio gobio*), with special reference to the Tweed watershed", *Journal of Animal Ecology*, **9**, 302–318.

Schoonoord, M. P. and Maitland, P. S. (1983). "Some methods of marking larval lampreys", *Fisheries Management*, **14**, 33–38.

Scott, D. B. C. (1975). "A hermaphrodite specimen of *Coregonus lavaretus* (L.) (Salmoniformes, Salmonidae) from Loch Lomond, Scotland", *Journal of Fish Biology*, **7**, 709.

Shafi, M. and Maitland, P. S. (1971a). "Comparative aspects of the biology of Pike *Esox lucius* in two Scottish lochs", *Proceedings of the Royal Society of Edinburgh*, **71B**, 11–60.

Shafi, M. and Maitland, P. S. (1971b). "The age and growth of Perch *Perca fluviatilis* in two Scottish lochs", *Journal of Fish Biology*, **3**, 39–57.

Shafi, M. and Maitland, P. S. (1972). "Observations on a population of Eels – *Anguilla anguilla* – in the Dubh Lochan, Rowardennan, Stirlingshire", *Glasgow Naturalist*, **19**, 17–20.

Sibbald, R. (1684). *Scotia Illustrata, sive Prodromus Historiae Naturalis Scotiae*, Edinburgh.

Sinclair, J. (1791). *The Statistical Account of Scotland*, Creech, Edinburgh.

Slack, H. D., Gervers, F. W. T. and Hamilton, J. D. (1957). "The biology of the Powan", *Glasgow University Publications: Studies on Loch Lomond*, **1**, 113–127.

Starkie, A. (1976). "Some aspects of the ecology of the Dace, *Leuciscus leuciscus* L., in the River Tweed", PhD thesis, University of Edinburgh.

Stephen, A. B. (1984). "Electrophoretic evidence for population variation in Brown Trout (*Salmo trutta*) and the implications for management", *Proceedings of the Institute of Fisheries Management, Annual Study Course*, **15**, 119–127.

Summers, R. W. (1979). "Life cycle and population ecology of the Flounder *Platichthys flesus* (L.) in the Ythan Estuary, Scotland", *Journal of Natural History*, **13**, 703–723.

Thorpe, J. E. (1974). "Estimation of the number of Brown Trout *Salmo trutta* (L.) in Loch Leven, Kinross, Scotland", *Journal of Fish Biology*, **6**, 135–152.

Thorpe, J. E. (1977a). "Daily ration of adult Perch, *Perca fluviatilis* L., during summer in Loch Leven, Scotland", *Journal of Fish Biology*, **11**, 55–68.

Thorpe, J. E. (1977b). "Bimodal distribution of length of juvenile Atlantic Salmon (*Salmo salar* L.) under artificial rearing conditions", *Journal of Fish Biology*, **11**, 175–184.

Treasurer, J. W. (1976). "Age, growth and length–weight relationship of Brown Trout *Salmo trutta* (L.) in the Loch of Strathbeg, Aberdeenshire", *Journal of Fish Biology*, **8**, 241–253.

Treasurer, J. W. (1980). "The occurrence of duck chicks in the diet of Pike", *North East Scotland Bird Report*, 1979, 1–3.

Treasurer, J. W. (1981). "Some aspects of the reproductive biology of Perch, *Perca fluviatilis* L. Fecundity, maturation and spawning behaviour", *Journal of Fish Biology*, **18**, 729–740.

Treasurer, J. W. and Mills, D. H. (1993). "An annotated bibliography of research on coarse and salmonid fish (excluding Salmon and Trout) found in fresh water in Scotland", *Freshwater Forum*, **3**, 202–236.

Walker, A. F., Greer, R. B. and Gardiner, A. S. (1988). "Two ecologically distinct forms of Arctic Charr (*Salvelinus alpinus* (L.)) in Loch Rannoch, Scotland", *Biological Conservation*, **43**, 43–61.

12

Amphibians

M. J. S. SWAN

Amphibian Habitat Advisory Services, 19 St Judith's Lane, Sawtry, Huntingdon, Cambridgeshire, PE17 5XE, UK

C. P. CUMMINS

Institute of Terrestrial Ecology, Abbots Ripton, Huntingdon, PE17 2LS, UK

and

R. S. OLDHAM

Department of Applied Biology and Biotechnology, De Montfort University, Leicester, LE7 9SU, UK

INTRODUCTION

All six species of Amphibia native to Great Britain breed in fresh waters in Scotland. These are the three anuran species – *Rana temporaria* (Common Frog), *Bufo bufo* (Common Toad) and *B. calamita* (Natterjack Toad); and the three urodeles – *Triturus vulgaris* (Smooth Newt), *T. helveticus* (Palmate Newt) and *T. cristatus* (Great crested Newt).

In this chapter we report and discuss the distributions of the six species and assess their status, as revealed by recent surveys. The types of water bodies in which each species has been recorded to breed, and actual and potential threats to their habitats are also described.

RECENT AMPHIBIAN RECORDING IN SCOTLAND

Herpetofaunal recording in Britain has been undertaken mainly by volunteers, and much of the information presented here was collected during the Nature Conservancy Council's National Amphibian Survey (NAS), co-ordinated from Leicester Polytechnic between 1983 and 1992 (Swan and Oldham, 1993). Other important sources of information were recent surveys of Tayside and Central Regions by Taylor (1990) and Lassière (1993), respectively, the survey of the Clyde area (Gibson, 1976, 1982, 1988), the Biological Records Centre (BRC) (Arnold, 1983) and the Natterjack Toad Site Register (Beebee, 1989).

Scotland suffers two main disadvantages in respect of amphibian recording: firstly,

The Fresh Waters of Scotland: A National Resource of International Significance
Edited by P. S. Maitland, P. J. Boon and D. S. McLusky. © 1994 John Wiley & Sons Ltd

low human population densities over large areas provide a relatively small pool of potential surveyors – Scotland comprises 34% of the land area of mainland Britain yet fielded only 10% of the NAS recorders. Secondly, Scotland's extensive areas of remote and difficult terrain are inaccessible to many would-be recorders – a point of particular relevance to the recording of amphibians whose nocturnal behaviour favours torchlight surveys (Swan and Oldham, 1989). However, in spite of their small numbers, Scotland's recorders were more productive individually than their southerly counterparts, returning a median of three records each to the NAS – three times the median for England and Wales.

SPECIES DISTRIBUTIONS

Common Frog *Rana temporaria*

The Common Frog occurs throughout north-western, central and eastern Europe, its range extending north of the Arctic Circle. It is, however, absent from most of the Mediterranean area.

The species has been recorded throughout Scotland including several offshore islands. Post-1960 BRC records (Arnold, 1983) include Shetland, the Outer Hebrides, Skye, Eigg, Mull and Jura, and Gibson (1976, 1982) reported post-1969 records from Arran, Holy Island, Bute, Inchmarnock, the Burnt Islands, Sanda and Davaar (Figure 12.1 (a)). There is an absence of records from some high-relief areas of the Highlands and the Southern Uplands (Arnold, 1983; Swan and Oldham, 1993) but this may simply reflect low recording effort. High altitude does not preclude frog breeding in the UK: Aston *et al.* (1987) recorded frog breeding sites above 600 m in Weardale in the north of England, and Lassière (1993) observed frogspawn at 900 m on Beinn Dubhchraig in Central Region.

Common Toad *Bufo bufo*

The Common Toad has a more southerly global distribution than the Common Frog, occurring throughout the Mediterranean as well as much of central and Northern Europe. It is not, however, found north of the Arctic Circle and is absent from Ireland (Frazer, 1983).

Toads are also widely distributed in Scotland being more selective in their choice of breeding sites than frogs, but are found in fewer sites overall (Swan and Oldham, 1993). They have been reported relatively frequently in the Central Lowlands and in coastal areas throughout Scotland but there are few records from high altitudes. Islands where the toad has been recorded since 1960 include Skye, Orkney, Raasay, Eigg, Mull and Jura (Arnold, 1983), and Arran, Holy Island, Bute, Sanda and Davaar (Gibson, 1982), (Figure 12.1 (b)).

Taylor (1990) and Lassière (1993) reported that the toad exhibited a more lowland distribution than the frog in Tayside and Central Regions, respectively. However, the toad is the more difficult species to census; it does not obligingly leave a large clump of visible spawn on the water surface, but winds strands of eggs around submerged vegetation and other structures, where they are difficult to detect during a daylight pond inspection. A nocturnal head-count of breeding animals by torchlight is the recommended survey method (Swan and Oldham, 1989), so the species may be even more under-recorded in remote and inaccessible areas than the frog.

(a) Common Frog (*Rana temporaria*)

(b) Common Toad (*Bufo bufo*)

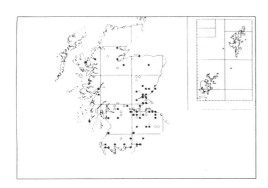

(c) Smooth Newt (*Triturus vulgaris*)

(d) Palmate Newt (*Triturus helveticus*)

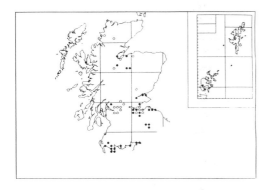

(e) Great Crested Newt (*Triturus cristatus*)

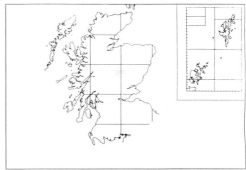

(f) Natterjack Toad (*Bufo calamita*)

FIGURE 12.1. Distribution of the six species of amphibian in Scotland, by 10 km square. ○: pre-1970 records; ●: 1970 onwards. Maps reproduced with the kind permission of the Biological Records Centre, Monks Wood

Smooth Newt *Triturus vulgaris*

This species has been divided into seven sub-species globally (Macgregor *et al.* 1990), *T. vulgaris vulgaris* being the sub-species occurring in Scotland and northern Europe. *T.v. vulgaris* has a more restricted European distribution than the common anurans, extending neither as far to the east nor to the south as either species. The sub-species is absent from southern France, the Iberian peninsula and southern Italy.

In Scotland, the Smooth Newt has a patchy distribution, but one which extends from Dumfries and Galloway Region to the Highland and Grampian Regions. The species is recorded on Skye (Arnold 1983) and Gibson (1976, 1982) reported it to be present locally in small numbers on Arran and Bute (Figure 12.1 (c)).

The overall distribution pattern for the species in Scotland suggests that the Smooth Newt is a lowland species, generally absent from high altitude areas. Gibson (1976, 1982) described the Smooth Newt as well-distributed throughout the former lowland counties of Ayrshire, Renfrewshire and Lanarkshire and occurring in small numbers in the south of the Loch Lomond area, but absent from much of present Strathclyde Region. Lassière (1993) reported a narrower and lower altitudinal range for *T. vulgaris* than for *T. helveticus* (the Palmate Newt) within Central Region, but the difference was not statistically significant. In Great Britain the distributions of these two small newt species show limited overlap: the Smooth Newt has a lowland and eastern distribution, the centre of its range being the English Midlands, while the Palmate Newt predominates in upland habitats or far western counties. Their ranges tend to overlap either in areas transitional between upland and lowland, or in acidic lowlands such as the heathland of south-east England (Swan and Oldham, 1993). The Smooth Newt has been recorded in proportionately fewer surveyed localities in Scotland than in Great Britain as a whole, and is only the fourth most common amphibian in Scotland. This contrasts with the situation in England, where it is the most common of the newt species and the second most frequently reported amphibian (Swan and Oldham, 1993).

Palmate Newt *Triturus helveticus*

The European range of *T. helveticus* is relatively small compared with those of the other five British amphibians. It is predominantly a north-western European species, its range confined to Great Britain, northern Spain, France, the low countries and western Germany.

The Palmate Newt is, however, the commonest newt species in Scotland and is distributed throughout the country, including the central mass of the North West Highlands, the Grampians and the Southern Uplands. *T. helveticus* has been recorded on the islands of Skye, Rum, Mull (Arnold, 1983), Arran, Holy Island, Bute, Inchmarnock, Ailsa Craig, Great and Little Cumbrae and Sanda (Gibson, 1976, 1982) (Figure 12.1 (d)).

Great Crested Newt *Triturus cristatus*

The Great Crested Newt exhibits a mainly northern European distribution, similar to that of *T. vulgaris* but latitudinally narrower – *T. cristatus* does not occur south of either the Alps or the Carpathians.

Within Great Britain the Great Crested Newt has a predominantly lowland and eastern distribution, again similar to that of *T. vulgaris*. In Scotland, the species has been recorded mainly within lowland farming areas (Figure 12.1 (e)) (Arnold, 1983; Swan and Oldham, 1993). Gibson (1976, 1982) stated that the species had previously been recorded in Argyllshire, Ayrshire, Lanarkshire and Renfrewshire, but not since the 1950s. Gibson (1986) described the species' former distribution as always "local" in the Clyde area, but reported that by the 1980s it had declined virtually to extinction. There are also a few recent records from around the Moray Firth (Swan and Oldham, 1993), where the species was allegedly introduced onto highland estates in the 19th century (NAS recorders, external communications). Predominantly, though, this is a species of agricultural lowlands.

Natterjack Toad *Bufo calamita*

The Natterjack Toad is widely distributed across western and central Europe; it occurs throughout the Iberian peninsula and is found in parts of Scandinavia (Beebee, 1983; Frazer, 1983; Garcia Paris, 1985).

Within the British Isles, the species survives in small, scattered populations in sandy coastal habitats and lowland heath in England, Scotland and the west of Ireland. *Bufo calamita* is the rarest amphibian in Britain, and in Scotland is known to breed at only four sites, all of which are on the Solway coast (Beebee, 1989) (Figure 12.1 (f)).

LIMITATIONS OF SPECIES DISTRIBUTIONS WITHIN SCOTLAND

Three of the six amphibian species apparently reach the northern edge of their British geographic ranges within Scotland. The Smooth Newt is found in very few localities north of the Highland Boundary Fault, the Great Crested Newt is virtually absent from the north-west of the country, and the Natterjack Toad is found only on the Solway coast. Although this is suggestive of a climatic limitation, all three species are found at higher latitudes in Scandinavia (Dolmen, 1982; Andrén and Nilson, 1988). Further-more, although Smooth and Great Crested Newts have not been recorded above 450 m in the UK, both are known to occur above 600 m in Scandinavia (Dolmen, 1982). However, a detailed analysis of climatic requirements, which would need to take account of the diversity of climatic conditions observed within Scotland (associated with latitude, oceanicity, topography and the influence of the Gulf Stream), is beyond the scope of this chapter. Furthermore, present-day species distributions may also reflect historical limitations, such as opportunities for the recolonization of northern Britain after the last Ice Age.

Within the area in which climate is suitable, and which the species have had the opportunity to colonize, distributions may still be limited by the availability of fresh waters suitable for breeding and the structure of the intervening terrestrial land use. For example, typical Great Crested Newt breeding sites are small (less than 1000 m^2) well-vegetated ponds in lowland agricultural settings, a habitat seldom recorded in northern Scotland (Swan and Oldham, 1993).

Most British Natterjack Toad populations are found on sand dunes, yet, despite the fact that Scotland contains many relatively undisturbed coastal dune and machair systems (Dargie, 1993), the species occurs no further north than the Solway (Beebee,

1989). Notwithstanding possible climatic constraints, the species is said to avoid acid habitats (Beebee and Griffin, 1977); the acidity of many Scottish sand dune systems might therefore render them unsuitable (Dargie, 1993).

SCOTTISH FRESH WATERS SURVEYED FOR AMPHIBIANS

During the NAS, the most frequently recorded types of water body, both in Scotland and in Great Britain, were field or farm ponds. In Scotland, however, this type comprised only 27% of records, compared to 49% in Britain as a whole (Figure 12.2). Garden ponds also comprised a lower percentage of Scottish than British sites overall – 6% of Scottish records compared to 14% of British. On the other hand, lochs and reservoirs (the "large" category), woodland and moorland ponds, and mineral extraction sites were all represented more frequently among Scottish records than among British records overall. There is, however, considerable variation within Scotland: in

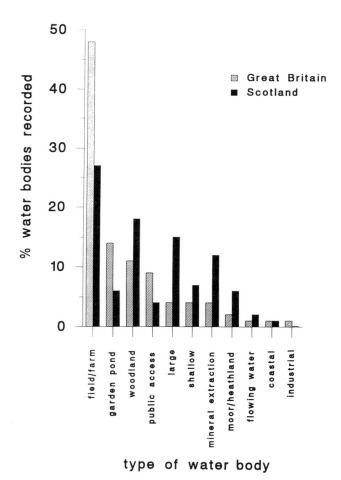

FIGURE 12.2. Types of water bodies surveyed for amphibians during the National Amphibian Survey, 1987 to 1992, in Scotland and throughout Great Britain. (See text for explanation of water-body categories)

a survey of ponds in Lothian Region, Hamilton (1978) recorded a much higher percentage of "industrial" ponds (water bodies associated with factories, mills, railway-lines, etc.) than were recognized in Scotland as a whole (28% of the Lothian survey sites cf. 0.2% of all NAS Scottish survey sites). The percentage of garden ponds within Lothian Region (11%) was also greater than for Scotland generally. These differences illustrate the diversity of wetland habitats within Scotland – ranging from the garden, field and industrial ponds characteristic of the lowland central belt to the lochs, forest and peat ponds of the uplands.

AMPHIBIAN BREEDING SITES WITHIN SCOTLAND

Common Frogs breed in a wide variety of water bodies in Scotland without, apparently, exhibiting significant preference for any of the site categories identified by NAS recorders (Figure 12.3). Although the highest frequencies of occupation were

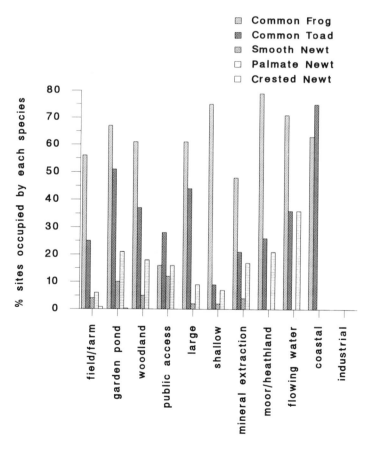

FIGURE 12.3. Percentages of each water-body type reported to contain populations of the five widespread amphibian species in Scotland during the National Amphibian Survey, 1987 to 1992. (See text for explanation of water-body categories)

reported for moorland ponds, over 70% of "shallow" (marsh, ditch, flooded field, etc.) and flowing waters surveyed also contained frogspawn (Swan and Oldham, 1993). Lassière (1993) also reported that frogs bred in many different types of water body, forest ditches and marshy areas being the most frequently recorded spawning sites in Central Region. Scottish "industrial" sites were not used by any of the species.

Common Toads bred in a relatively high proportion (44%) of the Scottish lochs and reservoirs surveyed during the NAS (Figure 12.3), exhibiting a preference for large sites also noted by Lassière (1993) in Central Region. Over one third of garden and woodland ponds, "coastal" sites (dune slack, coastal marshes and scrapes) and flowing waters also supported toad populations (Swan and Oldham, 1993).

The newt species each occupied a different range of water-body types: Smooth Newts were most frequently recorded in "public access" sites (park, school and hospital ponds) and garden ponds (Figure 12.3). Palmate Newts, however, were found most often in flowing water, garden, moorland and woodland ponds (Figure 12.3). They were found in comparatively few field or farm ponds (6%) (Swan and Oldham, 1993). Of the four Great Crested Newt records for which site descriptions were supplied, three were field ponds and one a garden pond. All were located in lowland situations.

The four Scottish Natterjack toad sites comprise shallow pools in fields or grazed heath inland of sandy coastal areas, and coastal marshes at the edge of farmland (Beebee, 1989).

AMPHIBIAN STATUS WITHIN SCOTLAND

The status of amphibians in Britain was assessed during the NAS from systematic surveys of all water bodies within discrete areas of the country (Swan and Oldham, 1989). Data thus collected allows calculation of the percentage of available water bodies used by amphibians as breeding sites and the estimation of breeding site densities (number of breeding populations km^{-2} – standardized information which is comparable between different parts of the country).

The study revealed that the status of amphibians in Scotland was different from that pertaining in Great Britain overall. Amphibians were found in a greater percentage of available water bodies in Scotland, but the densities of breeding sites were considerably lower than in the UK as a whole (Swan and Oldham, 1993) (Table 12.1).

Within Scotland, Common Frogs were found in a median (rather than a mean) of 73% of systematically surveyed ponds, compared to 47% in the whole of Great Britain (Table 12.1(a)). Similarly, Common Toads, found in 23% of ponds in Britain as a whole, were present in 41% of Scottish sites. Correspondingly high proportions of ponds were reported to support frogs and toads in the 1978 Lothian Region survey – 74% and 40%, respectively (Hamilton, 1978). The median percentage of ponds in which Palmate Newts were found nationally was zero, compared to 6% in Scotland. The two other newt species had lower status in Scotland: Smooth Newts were found in 17% of ponds nationally, but in only 0.5% within Scotland. Great Crested Newts occurred in only one systematically surveyed area within Scotland (within Highland Region), compared to over half of those within Britain as a whole (Swan and Oldham, 1993).

However, breeding site densities of all the species except the Palmate Newt, were

TABLE 12.1. Status of the five widespread amphibian species in Scotland and throughout mainland Britain, calculated from data received during the National Amphibian Survey (1987 to 1992): (a) percentage of water bodies reported to support amphibian populations; (b) density of breeding sites of each species

	(a) Median % occupancy of water bodies		(b) Median breeding site density (no. sites km^{-2})	
	Scotland	Great Britain	Scotland	Great Britain
Common Frog	73	47	0.20	0.70
Common Toad	41	23	0.10	0.20
Smooth Newt	0.5	17	0.02	0.20
Palmate Newt	6	0	0.02	0.00
Great Crested Newt	0	2	0.00	0.00
Number of surveys	14	99	12	75
Area covered (km^2)	–	–	1313	5688

lower in Scotland than in the rest of Britain (Table 12.1(b)). The median common frog breeding site density, for example, was 0.2 km^{-2} in Scotland compared to 0.7 km^{-2} nationally (Swan and Oldham, 1993).

The Natterjack Toad breeds in so few sites, both in Scotland and south of the border, that its overall status is generally better understood than those of the five other species. However, even though the four Scottish natterjack sites are regularly monitored, the status of two of the populations is uncertain. At one of those, site security is apparently doubtful, and at the second, loss of ponds has probably precipitated a decline in toad numbers; the future of these populations is regarded as precarious. The other two breeding sites are described as "safe," and their toad populations as stable (Beebee, 1989).

THREATS TO AMPHIBIANS AND THEIR BREEDING SITES IN SCOTLAND

An overall net loss of mapped Scottish ponds (i.e. potential amphibian breeding sites) has occurred since the 1950s, according to 14 systematic pond surveys undertaken in six Scottish Regions during the NAS (Table 12.2). The median percentage loss per survey in Scotland was 7%, indicating a lower rate of habitat disappearance than for Great Britain as a whole (17%). Upland areas of Great Britain have suffered lower levels of water-body loss than the agricultural lowlands in recent decades (Swan and Oldham, 1993). Within Scotland, greatest losses were reported from surveys in the Lothian Region and Fife (42 and 57%, respectively), but losses were also reported from Grampian and Highland Regions. Significant increases were recorded in forest surveys in Strathclyde and Dumfries and Galloway Regions, the rise in numbers due to the creation of fire ponds.

In general, perceived threats to fresh waters and amphibians in Scotland were similar to those reported for the whole of Great Britain (Swan and Oldham, 1993) (Figure 12.4). The most commonly cited "threats" were agricultural practices, mismanagement (neglect or inappropriate clearance), and infilling. "Forestry activities"

TABLE 12.2. Percentage change in pond numbers in Scotland and throughout Great Britain since the 1950s, calculated from data received during the National Amphibian Survey (1987 to 1992)

	Number of surveys	Median change in numbers	Percentage change in pond numbers	
			Maximum loss	Maximum gain
Scotland	13	−7.0	42.1	76.9
Great Britain	93	−17.0	88.0	380.0

were recorded as potential threats to more Scottish than British sites overall (4% c.f 1%, respectively). Within Lothian Region, Hamilton (1978) recorded drainage, domestic and industrial waste dumping and pollution as other important causes of pond loss, and Gibson (1986) specifically implicated land drainage in the marked decline of the Common Frog observed in the Clyde area in the 1970s.

Scotland's Natterjack Toad populations have been adversely affected by the proximity of agricultural land. Cattle trampling, and excessive eutrophication from

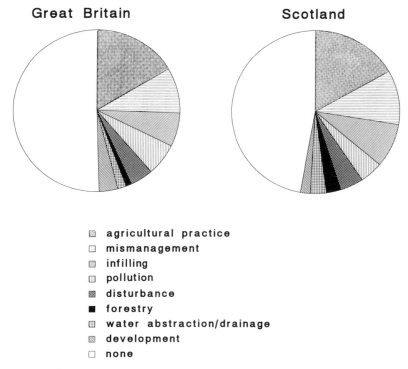

Great Britain   **Scotland**

- ▨ agricultural practice
- ▤ mismanagement
- ▨ infilling
- ▥ pollution
- ▨ disturbance
- ■ forestry
- ▦ water abstraction/drainage
- ▨ development
- ▢ none

FIGURE 12.4. Threats to amphibians and their breeding sites as perceived by National Amphibian Survey recorders, 1987 to 1992, in Scotland and throughout Great Britain

animal dung, silage and agricultural chemicals have all been listed by Beebee (1983) as factors known to have had deleterious effects on the species' breeding ponds. Recent additional damaging activities reported have been the dumping of vegetable waste into one pond and the digging of a drainage ditch adjacent to others (Beebee, 1989).

HABITAT ACIDIFICATION

Surface water acidification may pose a significant threat to amphibians in certain areas, particularly those with high precipitation, base-poor soils and slowly weathering bedrock. The potential threat to European amphibians from habitat acidification has been recognized since the late 1970s, and damage to Common Frog spawn in acid waters has been reported in the Netherlands (Strijbosch, 1979; Leuven *et al.*, 1986), Sweden (Hagström, 1981), Germany (Gebhardt *et al.*, 1987) and England (Aston *et al.*, 1987), as well as in south-west Scotland (Cummins and Ross, 1986). Recent studies of the Natterjack Toad have implicated pond acidification in the loss of the species from its heathland sites in England (Beebee *et al.*, 1990), but there is probably little risk to populations in non-acid coastal habitats.

Cummins and Ross (1986) observed extensive frog embryo mortality during a study of frogspawn deposition and survival on the Cairnsmore of Fleet National Nature Reserve (NNR) and surrounding conifer plantations (Dumfries and Galloway Region). The surface waters surveyed spanned a wide range of acidity (pH 3.4–6.3), and embryo mortality which reached 100% in some sites, showed a strong inverse correlation with pH in the breeding site ($P>0.001$). The levels of pH and embryo mortality observed in the field were consistent with laboratory estimates of acid toxicity to this species (Leuven *et al.*, 1986; Gebhardt *et al.*, 1987; Cummins, 1988, 1989).

Exposure of frogspawn to low pH was exacerbated by frogs' tendency to spawn shortly after periods of snow-melt and heavy rain, when surface waters were at their most acid. These "acid events" were due largely to the flushing of acid soil water, rather than the acid content of the rain, although the acid input from airborne pollutants may well influence soil acidity in the longer term. It is notable that the most acid pools were within areas of coniferous forest. Although the timing of most frogs' breeding put their eggs at risk from short-term depressions of pH, other aspects of their behaviour reduced the risk. In particular, communal spawning produced masses of spawn in which the pH was considerably higher than in the surrounding water.

Very high levels of labile monomeric aluminium were also found in several clear waters – up to 740 μg L^{-1}. Similar aluminium concentrations have been associated with frog embryo mortality in some laboratory experiments (Leuven *et al.*, 1986; Tyler-Jones *et al.*, 1989; cf Olsson *et al.*, 1987), but aluminium did not appear to be a major cause of mortality among frog embryos in the Scottish sites (Cummins, 1990). Nevertheless, labile aluminium concentrations lower than 800 μg L^{-1} have caused mortality among Common Frog tadpoles in laboratory and mesocosm studies (Cummins, 1986, 1990).

It has been suggested that Palmate Newts are more tolerant than Smooth Newts of even mildly acid conditions (Cooke and Frazer, 1976) – a potential explanation of the prevalence of *T. helveticus* in upland areas. However, recent studies comparing the effects of low pH on *T. helveticus* and *T. vulgaris* revealed no interspecific difference in the sensitivity of embryonic survival or larval growth rate to low pH – both species were affected equally (Griffiths *et al.*, 1993).

Beattie *et al.* (1993) have suggested that lethal and sub-lethal effects of low pH, high aluminium concentration and low temperature could reduce adult Common Frog recruitment in upland areas of Britain. As yet, however, there has been no study following the effects of acid conditions through the terrestrial phase of any amphibian's life cycle. Clearly, such studies are necessary if the full impact of surface water acidification is to be understood.

CONSERVATION OF AMPHIBIANS AND THEIR HABITATS IN SCOTLAND

Each of the six species breeding in Scotland is listed under Schedule 5 of the Wildlife and Countryside Act 1981 (WCA), and it is illegal intentionally to sell any of them (HMSO, 1985). Additionally, the Great Crested Newt and the Natterjack Toad are afforded total protection under the Act, making it an offence to kill or injure them, to damage or destroy their habitats or to prevent access to them by these species. It is also illegal to handle the animals without a licence. As well as its protection under the WCA, the Great Crested Newt is listed in Appendix II of the Bern Convention and has recently been included in Annexes II and IV (a) of the 1992 EC Habitats and Species Directive. The Natterjack Toad is also listed in Appendix II of the Bern Convention and Annexes II and IV (a) of the EC Habitats and Species Directive. The Great Crested Newt is officially classed as a "vulnerable" species in Britain and the Natterjack Toad as "rare".

In Great Britain, amphibian breeding sites assessed as being of exceptional conservation value may be afforded the status of "Site of Special Scientific Interest" (SSSI), which confers, potentially, a level of protection. Three criteria are currently used to assess the amphibian conservation value of individual water bodies (Nature Conservency Council, 1989). These are:

(1) the presence of a large population of Great Crested Newts,
(2) the presence of an exceptional species assemblage (i.e. a site supporting at least four of the widespread species in significant numbers), and
(3) the presence of Natterjack Toads

In Scotland, although some species exhibit high status throughout the country, very few individual water bodies qualify for designation as SSSIs on amphibian grounds. Of the 184 sites throughout Britain currently listed as qualifying for SSSI status under criteria (1) or (2) above, only three are found in Scotland. Two are located in Lothian Region and one is in Fife (Swan and Oldham, 1993). The four Natterjack Toad sites, however, should all receive some statutory protection as two are at least partly situated on SSSIs, the third is a proposed SSSI and the fourth is on an NNR.

Most of Scotland, though, does not qualify for any form of amphibian habitat protection, despite the fact that parts of the country may represent national strongholds for species which are currently under pressure from land development and "improvement" in the rest of Britain (Figure 12.5). The effective conservation of

FIGURE 12.5. Moorland ditches and ponds are an important spawning habitat for Common Frogs in Scotland. Photograph: Peter S. Maitland

Scotland's amphibians (particularly the widespread species) could be achieved with the development of conservation criteria recognizing not only the significance of individual breeding sites, but also the conservation value of areas, regions or specific habitat types where species' status is particularly high. Furthermore, habitat protection centred on individual breeding sites will probably fail to address widespread and insidious impacts such as acidification.

ACKNOWLEDGEMENTS

The authors would like to acknowledge that the National Amphibian Survey was funded firstly by the Nature Conservancy Council and latterly by English Nature, and to thank English Nature for allowing the use of the data for this chapter. For information we thank Olivia Lassière of Stirling University, Michael Taylor of the Perth Museum and J. A. Gibson of the Scottish Natural History Library. Special thanks are due to Henry Arnold of BRC who prepared the Scottish species distribution maps. For their contributions to the National Amphibian Survey we should like to thank all the volunteers who participated, in Scotland and throughout Great Britain. In particular we acknowledge the extensive surveys undertaken by Stewart Pritchard, Pat Batty, and the Forestry Commission rangers of forest districts throughout Scotland. Finally, for their useful and constructive criticism of the text we thank J. A. Gibson, Olivia Lassière and Stewart Pritchard.

REFERENCES

Andrén, C. and Nilson, G. (1988). "Island populations of the natterjack toad *Bufo calamita* on the Swedish west coast", *Memoranda Societatis Fauna Flora Fennica*, **64**, 112.

Arnold, H. R. (1983). "Distribution maps of the amphibians and reptiles of the British Isles", Biological Records Centre, Huntingdon.

Aston, R. J., Beattie, R. C. and Milner, A. G. P. (1987). "Characteristics of spawning sites of the common frog (*Rana temporaria*) with particular reference to acidity", *Journal of Zoology*, **213**, 233–242.

Beattie, R. C., Tyler-Jones, R. and Baxter, M. J. (1993). "The effects of pH, aluminium concentration and temperature on the embryonic development of the European common frog, *Rana temporaria*", *Journal of Zoology*, **228**, 557–570.

Beebee, T. J. C. (1983). *The Natterjack Toad*, Oxford University Press, Oxford.

Beebee, T. J. C. (1989). *Natterjack Toad* (Bufo calamita) *Site Register for the UK. Volume 1: 1970–1989*, Report to English Nature, Peterborough.

Beebee, T. J. C. and Griffin, J. R. (1977). "A preliminary investigation into natterjack toad (*Bufo calamita*) breeding site characteristics in Britain", *Journal of Zoology*, **181**, 341–350.

Beebee, T. J. C., Flower, R. J., Stevenson, A. C., Patrick, S. T., Appleby, P. G., Fletcher, C., Marsh, C., Natkanski, J., Rippey, B. and Battarbee, R. W. (1990). "Decline of the natterjack toad *Bufo calamita* in Britain: paleaoecological, documentary and experimental evidence for breeding site acidification", *Biological Conservation*, **53**, 1–20.

Cooke, A. S. and Frazer, J. F. D. (1976). "Characteristics of newt breeding sites", *Journal of Zoology*, **178**, 223–236.

Cummins, C. P. (1986). "Effects of aluminium and low pH on growth and development in *Rana temporaria* tadpoles", *Oecologia*, **69**, 248–252.

Cummins, C. P. (1988). "Effect of calcium on survival times of *Rana temporaria* embryos at low pH", *Functional Ecology*, **2**, 297–302.

Cummins, C. P. (1989). "Interaction between the effects of pH and density on growth and development in *Rana temporaria* tadpoles", *Functional Ecology*, **3**, 45–52.

Cummins, C. P. (1990). "The impact of acid conditions on the common frog *Rana temporaria* L.", PhD thesis, Leicester Polytechnic.

Cummins, C. P. and Ross, A. (1986). *Effects of Acidification of Natural Waters upon Amphibia*, Final report to the Commission of the European Communities, Institute of Terrestrial Ecology, CEC/NERC Contract EV3V.0907.UK.(H).

Dargie, T. (1993). *Sand Dune Vegetation Survey of Great Britain – Part 2 Scotland*, Joint Nature Conservation Committee, Peterborough.

Dolmen, D. (1982). "Zoogeography of *Triturus vulgaris* (L.) and *T. cristatus* (Laurenti) (Amphibia) in Norway, with notes on their vulnerability", *Fauna Norvegica*, **3**, 12–25.

Frazer, J. F. D. (1983). *Reptiles and Amphibians in Britain*, Collins New Naturalist Series, London.

Garcia Paris, M. (1985). *Los Amphibios de España*, Publicaciones de Extension Agraria, Madrid.

Gebhardt, H., Kreimes, K. and Linnenbach, M. (1987). "Untersuchungen zur Beeinträchtigung der Ei- und Larvalstadien von Amphibien in sauren Gewassern", *Natur und Landschaft*, **62**, 20–23.

Gibson, J. A. (1976). "The reptiles and amphibians of the Clyde area", *Western Naturalist*, **5**, 53–66.

Gibson, J. A. (1982). "Reptiles and amphibians of the Clyde faunal area" *Glasgow Naturalist*, **20**, 211–227.

Gibson, J. A. (1986) "Recent changes in the status of some Clyde vertebrates", *Proceedings of the Royal Society of Edinburgh*, **90B**, 451–467.

Gibson, J. A. (1988). *A regional bibliography of the reptiles and Amphibians of the West of Scotland*, Scottish Natural History Library, Kilbarchan.

Griffiths, R. A., de Wijer, P. and Brady, L. (1993). "The effect of pH on embryonic and larval development in smooth and palmate newts, *Triturus vulgaris* and *T. helveticus*", *Journal of Zoology*, **230**, 401–409.

Hagström, T. (1981). "Reproductive strategy and success of amphibians in waters acidified by atmospheric pollution", in *Proceedings of the European Herpetological Symposium 1980*, pp. 55–57, Cotswold Wildlife Park, Oxfordshire.

Hamilton, E. (1978). *Ponds in the Lothians*, Scottish Wildlife Trust, Edinburgh.

HMSO (1985). *Wildlife and Countryside Act 1981*, London.

Lassière, O. (1993). "The distribution of amphibians in Central Region, Scotland", *Glasgow Naturalist*, **22**, 221–238.

Leuven, R. S. E. W., den Hartog, C., Christiaans, M. M. C. and Heijligers, W. H. C. (1986). "Effects of water acidification on the distribution pattern and reproductive success of amphibians", *Experientia*, **42**, 495–503.

Macgregor, H., Sessions, S. K. and Arntzen, J. W. (1990). "An integrative analysis of phylogenetic relationships among newts of the genus *Triturus* (family Salamandridae), using comparative biochemistry, cytogenetics and reproductive interactions", *Journal of Evolutionary Biology*, **3**, 329–373.

Nature Conservancy Council (1989). *Guidelines for Selection of Biological SSSIs*, Peterborough, pp. 265–268.

Olsson, M., Hogstrand, C., Dahlberg, A. and Berglind, S.-A. (1987). "Acid-shock, aluminium, and presence of *Sphagnum aurantiacum*: effects on embryological development in the common frog, *Rana temporaria* and the moor frog, *Rana arvalis*", *Bulletin of Environmental Contamination and Toxicology*, **39**, 37–44.

Strijbosch, H. (1979). "Habitat selection of amphibians during their aquatic phase", *Oikos*, **33**, 363–372.

Swan, M. J. S. and Oldham, R. S. (1989). *Amphibian Communities*, final report to the Nature Conservancy Council, Contract No. HF3–03–332, Peterborough.

Swan, M. J. S. and Oldham, R. S. (1993) *Herptile Sites. Volume 1: National Amphibian Survey*, final report to English Nature, Research Report No. 38, Contract No. F72–15–04, Peterborough.

Taylor, M. A. (1990). *Report of the 1989 Amphibian Survey*, Perth Museum and Art Gallery, Perth.

Tyler-Jones, R., Beattie, R. C. and Aston, R. J. (1989). "The effects of acid water and aluminium on the embryonic development of the common frog (*Rana temporaria*)", *Journal of Zoology*, **219**, 355–372.

13

Birds

D. W. Minns

Royal Society for the Protection of Birds, 17 Regent Terrace, Edinburgh, EH7 5BN, UK

R. W. Summers

Royal Society for the Protection of Birds, Etive House, Beechwood Park, Inverness, IV2 3BW, UK

and

C. A. Galbraith

Joint Nature Conservation Committee, Monkstone House, City Road, Peterborough, PE1 1UA, UK

INTRODUCTION

This chapter reviews the current status of some water bird species in Scotland (Table 13.1). Many which breed on fresh waters spend the winter on the sea, leaving the migrant wildfowl from further north as the main users of fresh waters in winter. In this chapter the main freshwater sites in each region of Scotland are listed and the role of birds in aquatic food webs and as importers of nutrients into freshwater systems are described. Finally, the international and national measures which cover the conservation of fresh waters and their associated bird life are reviewed.

In her account of birds in Scotland, Thom (1986) considered freshwater habitats as falling into three groups: standing open waters, running waters and mires. The open water habitat is diverse, ranging from dystrophic hill lochans to large eutrophic lowland lochs, each with its characteristic suite of birds (Fuller, 1982; Fox *et al.*, 1989). Scotland is particularly rich in oligotrophic lochs. Many of the larger lochs have been increased in size by damming for hydro-electricity and some are wholly man-made (e.g. Loch Faskally in Tayside). In contrast to England there are few gravel pits.

The major rivers in Scotland generally flow east (e.g. the Spey, Dee, Tay, Forth and Tweed) and only one major one flows west – the Clyde – which is also the most

The Fresh Waters of Scotland: A National Resource of International Significance
Edited by P. S. Maitland, P. J. Boon and D. S. McLusky. © 1994 John Wiley & Sons Ltd

TABLE 13.1. Check-list of birds regularly associated with
fresh water in Scotland

Gaviidae
Red-throated Diver   *Gavia stellata*
Black-throated Diver   *Gavia arctica*

Podicipedidae
Little Grebe   *Tachybaptus ruficollis*
Great Crested Grebe   *Podiceps cristatus*
Slavonian Grebe   *Podiceps auritus*
Black-necked Grebe   *Podiceps nigricollis*

Phalacrocoracidae
Cormorant   *Phalacrocorax carbo*

Ardeidae
Grey Heron   *Ardea cinerea*

Anatidae
Mute Swan   *Cygnus olor*
Bewick's Swan   *Cygnus columbianus*
Whooper Swan   *Cygnus cygnus*
Bean Goose   *Anser fabalis*
Pink-footed Goose   *Anser brachyrhynchus*
White-fronted Goose   *Anser albifrons*
Greylag Goose   *Anser anser*
Barnacle Goose   *Branta leucopsis*
Mandarin   *Aix galericulata*
Wigeon   *Anas penelope*
Gadwall   *Anas strepera*
Teal   *Anas crecca*
Mallard   *Anas platyrhynchos*
Pintail   *Anas acuta*
Garganey   *Anas querquedula*
Shoveler   *Anas clypeata*
Pochard   *Aythya ferina*
Tufted Duck   *Aythya fuligula*
Scaup   *Aythya manila*
Common Scoter   *Melanitta nigra*
Goldeneye   *Bucephala clangula*
Red-breasted Merganser   *Mergus serrator*
Goosander   *Mergus merganser*
Ruddy Duck   *Oxyura jamaicensis*

Accipitridae
Marsh Harrier   *Circus aeruginosus*

Pandionidae
Osprey   *Pandion haliaetus*

Rallidae
Water Rail   *Rallus aquaticus*
Spotted Crake   *Porzana porzana*
Moorhen   *Gallinula chloropus*
Coot   *Fulica atra*

TABLE 13.1 (*Continued*)

Haematopodidae
Oystercatcher   *Haematopus ostralegus*

Charadriidae
Ringed Plover   *Charadrius hiaticula*
Lapwing   *Vanellus vanellus*
Golden Plover   *Pluvialis apricaria*

Scolopacidae
Dunlin   *Calidris alpina*
Snipe   *Gallinago gallinago*
Whimbrel   *Numenius phaeopus*
Curlew   *Numenius arquata*
Redshank   *Tringa totanus*
Greenshank   *Tringa nebularia*
Wood Sandpiper   *Tringa glareola*
Common Sandpiper   *Actitis hypoleucos*
Red-necked Phalarope   *Phalaropus lobatus*

Laridae
Black-headed Gull   *Larus ridibundus*
Common Gull   *Larus canus*
Lesser Black-backed Gull   *Larus fuscus*
Herring Gull   *Larus argentatus*

Sternidae
Common Tern   *Sterna hirundo*

Apodidae
Swift   *Apus apus*

Alcedinidae
Kingfisher   *Alcedo atthis*

Hirundinidae
Sand Martin   *Riparia riparia*
Swallow   *Hirundo rustica*
House Martin   *Delichon urbica*

Motacillidae
Yellow Wagtail   *Motacilla flava*
Grey Wagtail   *Motacilla cinerea*
Pied Wagtail   *Motacilla alba*

Cinclidae
Dipper   *Cinclus cinclus*

Sylviidae
Grasshopper Warbler   *Locustella naevia*
Sedge Warbler   *Acrocephalus schoenobaenus*

Emberizidae
Reed Bunting   *Emberiza schoeniclus*

polluted in Scotland. Thus, the riparian habitat available to birds is greater in the east of the country. Through its course, a river can change from a fast-flowing, rocky stream to a slow-moving muddy river, and there are consequent changes in the bird communities (Fuller, 1982).

Mires (marshes, bogs and swamps) can be associated with the margins of lochs or the floodplains of rivers, or occur separately in their own right. Soil conditions and geography determine the type of flora associated with these. For example, in the hills of north-west Scotland the peaty bogs are largely composed of sedges and mosses. In contrast, the margins of eutrophic lochs may have dense stands of reeds (*Phragmites australis*). Marshy areas can also occur on farmland and attract waders and ducks.

The freshwater birds of Scotland (Table 13.1) include a number of major groups, ranging from divers to passerines, though the dominant group is the wildfowl (ducks, geese and swans). The distribution of water birds is well known from "atlas" work done both in the breeding season (Sharrock, 1976) and in the winter (Lack, 1986). In addition, the status of many of our water birds is well known from survey work, and all the rarer species have been reviewed by Batten *et al*. (1990). At the bird community level, Fuller (1982) gives detailed descriptions of the suites of water birds occurring on the different types of lochs and rivers.

The role that birds play in freshwater systems has received little study, the only detailed work in Scotland being carried out at Loch Leven (Morgan and McLusky, 1974). The general biology of water birds has been covered in detail by Cramp and Simmons (1977–1983).

Conservation of water birds is achieved through legislation, both national (e.g. the Wildlife and Countryside Act) and international (e.g. the EC Directive on the Conservation of Wild Birds), and through the use of nature reserves, mainly owned or leased by Scottish Natural Heritage, the Scottish Wildlife Trust and the Royal Society for the Protection of Birds (RSPB).

THE STATUS OF FRESHWATER BIRDS

Divers and grebes

The Black-throated Diver breeds primarily on large oligotrophic lochs in north and west Scotland. The only total count, in 1985, showed there were about 150 territorial pairs (Campbell and Talbot, 1987). There is a possibility, however, that there may be some recent range contraction (Mudge *et al*., 1991). Most losses of nests are due to flooding and predation (Mudge and Talbot, 1993).

The Red-throated Diver occurs over much the same range as the Black-throated Diver, but on much smaller lochs. It also occurs in Orkney and in Shetland where there has been long-term monitoring of its breeding success (Gomersall, 1987). It is a much commoner species than the Black-throated Diver with over 1200 breeding pairs (Batten *et al*., 1990).

The Slavonian Grebe is also a typical highland bird, having colonized Scotland in 1908. The population comprised 74 pairs in 1990 and is increasing slowly (Crooke *et al*., 1993). The Great Crested Grebe is a less recent colonist. Recorded first in 1877, it reached a population of about 340 adults by 1975 (Hughes *et al*., 1979) with most found in Tayside. The Black-Necked Grebe is the rarest grebe in Scotland and is particularly associated with eutrophic lochs in eastern Scotland. The population in 1992 was 13 breeding pairs (RSPB, unpublished data). The Little Grebe is locally common, nesting in a variety of water bodies from oligotrophic to eutrophic.

Heron

The Grey Heron is largely associated with fresh water throughout Scotland though birds from some colonies forage on the coast. In 1985 there were about 3800 pairs of herons in Scotland. Breeding density varied from less than 0.3 pairs per 100 km^2 in inland Caithness and Sutherland to over 15 pairs per 100 km^2 in North Uist and Benbecula (Marquiss, 1989).

Wildfowl

The Mute Swan occurs throughout the lowland parts of Scotland including Orkney and the Uists. There has been no complete census, but at least 1100 breeding birds and 1800 non-breeders were counted in 1983 (Brown and Brown, 1985). Some freshwater bodies are also important as moulting sites; for example Loch Bee, South Uist, where 400 birds moult, and Loch of Harray, Orkney, where 200 occur. The Whooper Swan is largely known as a wintering bird in Scotland but there have been occasional breeding records.

The status of the wintering swans, as with all the wildfowl, has been well described from counts organized and published by the Wildfowl and Wetlands Trust (e.g. Owen *et al.*, 1986). The total Scottish wintering populations of Mute and Whooper Swans are about 3750 and 4000 respectively.

The Greylag Goose is the only wild species of goose breeding in Scotland, and is confined to the Western Isles and the north-west of the mainland, although feral birds breed elsewhere. The current population is about 2500–3000 birds, which represents the remains of a formerly widespread indigenous population (Owen *et al.*, 1986). Greylag and Pink-footed Geese also have wintering populations which normally use fresh waters for roosting (Figures 13.1–13.4, 13.6). Both species originate from Iceland and their current populations are about 100 000 (Owen *et al.*, 1986).

The status of breeding ducks in Scotland is poorly known since there have been no comprehensive studies, particularly for the commoner ones. It is estimated that 75% of the approximately 500 pairs of Wigeon recorded as the UK population occur in Scotland (Thom, 1986), while the estimates for Mallard and Tufted Duck are 19 000 pairs respectively (Thom, 1986). There are better estimates of the wintering numbers, some of which occur on estuaries as well as fresh waters. For example, there are 130 –40 000 wintering Wigeon, 45–75 000 Mallard, 6–14 000 Pochard and 8–12 000 Tufted Duck (Owen *et al.*, 1986; Thom, 1986).

For the rarer species there has been more of an attempt to census the breeding populations. The Gadwall's strongholds are Tayside (particularly Loch Leven) and also North Uist. The Scottish population is 200–300 birds. The Pintail is found largely on the eutrophic lochs of Orkney with a total population of only about 20 pairs (Thom, 1986). There are an estimated 50 pairs of Pochard and about 100 pairs of Shoveler. The Common Scoter is associated with small peat lochs and large oligotrophic lochs of the Highlands and west of Scotland where about 100 pairs nest (Thom, 1986).

The Goldeneye has been a recent colonist whose establishment has been encouraged by the provision of nest boxes (Dennis and Dow, 1984). The population nests almost entirely in Strathspey. In 1989 there were 85 occupied nest boxes, 22 of which occurred on the ŔSPB reserve at the Insh Marshes (Bhatia, 1992).

The Red-breasted Merganser and Goosander have both expanded substantially throughout the rivers and lochs of Scotland in recent years, so that their current breeding populations are 1200–1700 and 740–950 pairs respectively (Meek and Little, 1977; Owen *et al.*, 1986).

Osprey

The Osprey has been a success story for conservation. Once hunted to extinction, it recolonized Scotland in 1954 (Brown and Waterston, 1962). The population has increased steadily and there were 76 occupied sites in the highlands in 1992 (Dennis *et al.*, 1993).

Waders

A number of wader species can be classed as freshwater birds since they feed along the banks of rivers and lochs and nest in surrounding marshes and wet pastures. The Common Sandpiper is regularly found along the banks of upland rivers and lochs, at about one pair per km in good habitat (Nethersole-Thompson and Nethersole-Thompson, 1986). During a survey of agricultural land in 1982 and 1983, 30 000 pairs of Lapwings and 2700 pairs of Redshanks were found breeding on rough grazing and pasture (Galbraith *et al.*, 1984). Several of these wader species found in marshland and wet fields are showing declines in numbers as a result of drainage and changed farming practices. A repeat survey of these lowland waders is currently being organized (O'Brien, 1992).

The upland breeding waders such as Golden Plover, Greenshank, Wood Sandpiper and Dunlin have been the subject of long-term studies by Nethersole-Thompson and Nethersole-Thompson (1986). Recently, wider ranging surveys have been initiated as a result of threats to their northern nesting habitats by afforestation (Bainbridge *et al.*, 1987; Stroud *et al.*, 1987; Avery and Haines-Young, 1990).

Gulls and terns

Gulls and terns regularly breed on freshwater localities. The Black-headed Gull is the most numerous, nesting in the marshes surrounding eutrophic lochs (e.g. Loch of Kinnordy) and hill lochans. The Common Gull is usually associated only with upland lochs and rivers (e.g. River Tay). The Lesser Black-backed Gull and Herring Gull have several inland colonies, the largest being at Flanders Moss (Thom, 1986). The Common Tern penetrates well up rivers and nests on shingle banks and occasionally loch shores.

Passerines

A number of passerines are associated with fresh water. These include Swallows, martins and Swifts that hunt insects over lochs and rivers and wagtails that forage along banks. The Dipper, however, is entirely dependent on rivers or lochs, and actively hunts invertebrates under water. They occur at densities of four to nine pairs per 10 km of river (Thom, 1986). There has been a great deal of research on Dippers in Wales where there are concerns that the birds are being affected by acid rain (Ormerod *et al.*, 1985). Only recently have similar studies started in Scotland (Vickery, 1991). The Kingfisher is a relatively uncommon member of the freshwater bird assemblage in Scotland, being largely confined to parts of the central lowlands.

IMPORTANT FRESHWATER SITES

Systematic counts organized each winter by the Wildfowl and Wetlands Trust provide the essential basis for assessing the importance of freshwater sites for birds. More recently their importance has been recognized by the publication of a definitive book on Important Bird Areas in the United Kingdom (Pritchard *et al.*, 1992).

Western Isles

The main islands in this archipelago are scattered with lochs of various sizes, from fresh water through brackish water to sea lochs. As well as the water bodies themselves, many of the water birds also occur on the peatlands and the machair.

In South Uist, lochs such as Druidibeg, Hallan, Bee and others, and the machair grassland and marshes around them, support high densities of breeding waders such as Oystercatcher, Ringed Plover and Dunlin, together with some of Scotland's wild population of Greylag Geese. In winter, Loch Bee is renowned for its wintering Mute Swans (200–400 birds).

The largest freshwater body in North Uist is Loch Scadavay, which holds breeding Red-throated Divers and Black-throated Divers together with native Greylag Geese. Loch nam Feithean and the surrounding marshes and machair at Balranald support over 100 pairs of breeding Dunlin and up to 120 pairs of Ringed Plover, as well as high densities of Oystercatcher, Lapwing, Snipe and Redshank.

Although best known for their extensive sand dune systems, the islands of Baleshare and Kirkibost off the south-west coast of North Uist also have freshwater interest in small lochs and associated marshes. As well as breeding waders, in winter they also hold internationally important numbers of Greylag Geese (900) and Barnacle Geese (600).

The lochs and lochans scattered over much of Lewis are used by large numbers of Red- and Black-throated Divers, and waders such as Golden Plover, Dunlin and Greenshank.

Shetland

One of the richest areas in Shetland for breeding birds is the island of Fetlar, with its upland mires and heaths overlying relatively base-rich serpentine rock. These are the main UK areas for such northern species as Whimbrel and Red-necked Phalarope, together with Red-throated Divers.

The UK stronghold of the Red-throated Diver, however, is the northern part of the Shetland mainland known as North Roe which has a multitude of scattered freshwater lochans and pools. This held some 67 pairs of divers in 1983 (Gomersall *et al.*, 1984), 5% of the British and EC population. Lochans on Yell and Unst are also important for Red-throated Divers.

At the southern end of the Shetland mainland, the adjoining eutrophic lochs of Spiggie and Brow support large numbers of wintering and passage Whooper Swans. The average peak of 180 birds between 1985/86 and 1989/90 is 1% of the world population, and 3% of the British wintering numbers.

Orkney

The most important freshwater sites on mainland Orkney are the interconnected Lochs of Harray and Stenness. The Loch of Harray is a shallow eutrophic freshwater loch, but the adjoining Loch of Stenness has a saline gradient between the inflow from the Loch of Harray and the outflow to the sea. Their importance for wintering wildfowl can be seen in Table 13.2.

TABLE 13.2. Average counts of wildfowl at Loch of Stenness and Loch of Harray between 1985/86 and 1989/90 in winter

Species	Number	% of British population
Mute Swan	520	3
Whooper Swan	490	8
Wigeon	4370	2
Pochard	1310	3
Tufted Duck	1610	3
Scaup	190	5
Goldeneye	290	2

The Lochs of Isbister and Banks, together with the adjoining marshy areas of the Loons, form Orkney's best wetland for breeding birds, supporting in recent years some 20% of Britain's small population of breeding Pintail. In winter they hold Greenland White-fronted and Greylag Geese, Wigeon and Teal. Other lochs and wetlands in Orkney's west mainland are also important. For example, the Loch of Boardhouse holds over 1000 wintering Pochard (2% of the British population).

The man-made Mill Dam on Shapinsay is also important for breeding Pintail (5% of the British population) and wintering Whooper Swans (2%). The group of small wetlands on Stronsay is also important for breeding Pintail (12% of the British population).

Highland

Blanket bog is rare in world terms and, at least in summer, has a wild and open beauty. East Sutherland and Caithness still have the most extensive areas of "flow country", despite large losses to forestry in the last decade, and these support distinctive bird communities of international importance.

Around lochs and lochans, Red-throated and Black-throated Divers nest (11% and 20% respectively of the British and EC populations in Sutherland and Caithness as a whole), as well as 20% of the British Wigeon, 30% of the British and EC Common Scoter and small numbers of nesting Greylag Geese. Black-throated Divers and Scoters prefer lochs with islands and with high pH/conductivity, whilst Red-throated Divers occur on lochs which are less rich (Fox *et al.*, 1989). The rolling peatlands are the British stronghold of the Greenshank (an estimated 630 pairs, 41% of the British population), as well as supporting large numbers of Dunlins and Golden Plovers (Bainbridge *et al.*, 1987; Stroud *et al.*, 1987). Although afforestation has declined here because of the removal of tax relief in 1988, and Scottish Natural Heritage has designated large areas as Sites of Special Scientific Interest (SSSIs) the flows remain vulnerable to peat extraction, which, like all developments subject to planning control, can go ahead on SSSIs if the Secretary of State approves.

On the low-lying Caithness plain, lochs such as Heilen, Winless, Mey, Watten, Scarmclate and Toftingall provide roosting and feeding areas for important numbers of wintering Greenland White-fronted Geese and Whooper Swans, as well as smaller numbers of Greylag Geese, Mute Swans and other wildfowl.

Large oligotrophic lochs are extremely important for breeding Black-throated Divers. Their breeding success on many lochs is low, mainly because nests are flooded when there is a rise in water level (Campbell, 1988). Conifer afforestation can aggravate this problem for divers. Increased runoff from ploughing and drainage can cause sudden rises in water levels and increased turbidity following heavy rain (Maitland *et al.*, 1990). Further, mature plantations exacerbate the acidification of lochs, with possible deleterious effects on the birds' food supplies (Maitland *et al.*, 1990). One possible solution is to have buffer zones between plantations and lochs and watercourses. This would be appropriate in many areas of the highlands.

Loch Maree, like the West Sutherland lochs, is one of the most important for Black-throated Divers, with some 10 pairs breeding regularly. In contrast, Loch Eye is a shallow eutrophic loch near the Moray Firth and is a major roost for Greylag Geese and Whooper Swans.

The British population of Slavonian Grebes is centred on a number of shallow, mesotrophic lochs to the north and south of the Great Glen. Like divers, their nests are vulnerable to changes in water level. However, it is hoped their vulnerability to human disturbance has been reduced by the provision of a public observation hide overlooking the RSPB reserve at Loch Ruthven, their main breeding site.

The lochs and marshes of the Spey catchment support nationally important numbers of breeding wildfowl and waders. The Insh Marshes, in particular, form the largest remaining semi-natural floodplain system in Scotland, and RSPB/Scottish Ornithologists Club surveys in 1992 found 59 pairs of Oystercatcher, 95 pairs of Lapwing, 221 pairs of Snipe, 129 pairs of Curlew and 155 pairs of Redshank in 8.5 km^2. The catchment also supports significant proportions of the British breeding

Wigeon and Goldeneye, and in winter the flooded marshes are used regularly by a flock of about 140 Whooper Swans (2% of the British population). The river and its surrounding lochs are also important feeding sites for Ospreys.

Grampian

Most of the ornithological interest of the fresh waters of Grampian Region is centred on the lowland lochs, several of which are of major importance for wintering wildfowl (See Figures 13.1 and 13.2). Some also have breeding bird interest, depending on their surrounding vegetation and land use.

The Loch of Strathbeg, at the north-eastern corner of Grampian, attracts huge numbers of wintering geese, particularly Pink-footed Geese, as well as important numbers of Whooper Swans, Wigeon, Teal, Tufted Ducks, Goldeneye and Goosanders. Breeding bird interest includes Common Terns and waders.

Loch Spynie in Moray is a shallow, eutrophic loch, formed originally from a tidal inlet. It supports a range of breeding wildfowl and internationally important numbers of wintering Greylag Geese and passage Pink-footed Geese.

Meikle Loch, near the Ythan estuary north of Aberdeen, is another important goose roost, especially for Pink-footed Geese, with around 6% of the world population using this area. Further west, Loch of Skene held an average of 9% of the Icelandic population of Greylag Geese in the winters between 1985/86 and 1989/90, as well as up to 4200 Wigeon and large numbers of Whooper and Mute Swans, Goldeneye and Goosander. For these and related reasons it has been designated under both the Ramsar Convention and the EC Birds Directive (see later sections in this chapter).

Tayside

As with Grampian Region, wintering wildfowl are the most significant birds using fresh water in Tayside, with the major roosts of grey geese being the most obvious. Figures 13.3 and 13.4 show winter counts of major roost sites in Tayside between 1982 and 1990 for Greylag and Pink-footed Geese. The increase in Pink-footed Geese is thought to be linked with the increase in area of cereals being grown, particularly winter barley, together with reduced hunting.

As well as being a major goose roost, Loch Leven is also famous for its breeding ducks, with nationally important numbers of Wigeon, Gadwall, Mallard, Shoveler and Tufted Ducks, while the Loch of Kinnordy holds one of the largest colonies of Black-headed Gulls in the UK (7000 pairs) and much smaller numbers of Gadwall, Shoveler and Pochard. Loch Leven is a long-established National Nature Reserve (NNR) and designated Ramsar Site, while the Loch of Kinnordy is an RSPB reserve. The Loch of Lintrathen, with its important goose roost, is a Scottish Wildlife Trust reserve and also a Ramsar Site.

Fife

In Fife, Cameron Reservoir registers on a national scale for wintering geese (7% of the world's Pink-footed Geese), whilst Kilconquhar Loch is important for grebes, Shovelers, Tufted Duck and Goldeneye.

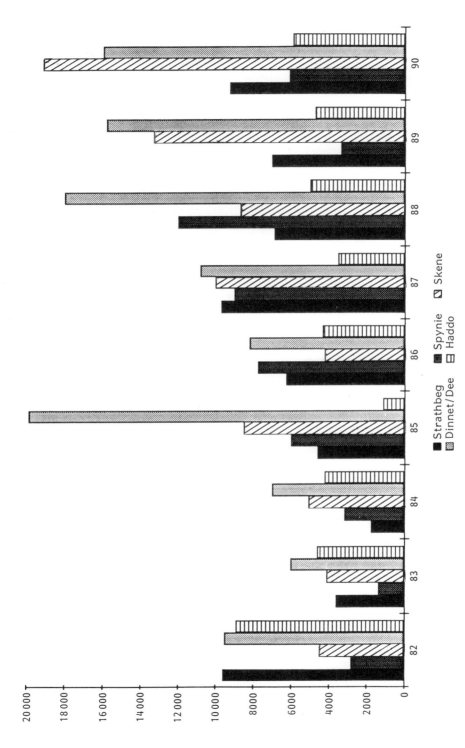

FIGURE 13.1. Winter counts of Greylag Geese at five sites in Grampian Region from 1982 to 1990

236

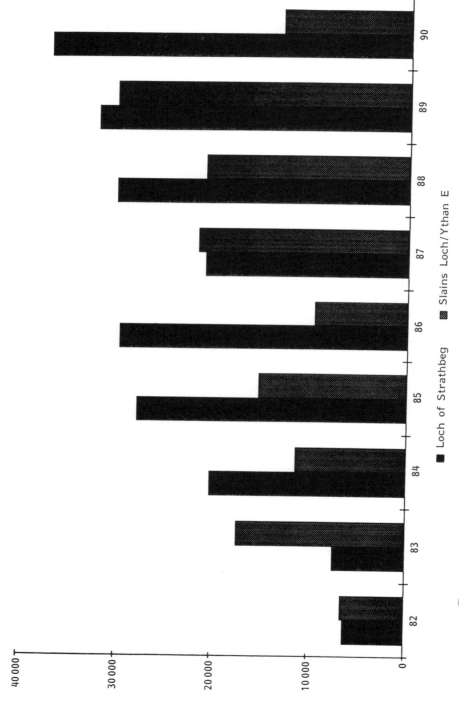

FIGURE 13.2. Winter counts of Pink-footed Geese at two sites in Grampian Region from 1982 to 1990

■ Loch of Strathbeg   ▨ Slains Loch/Ythan E

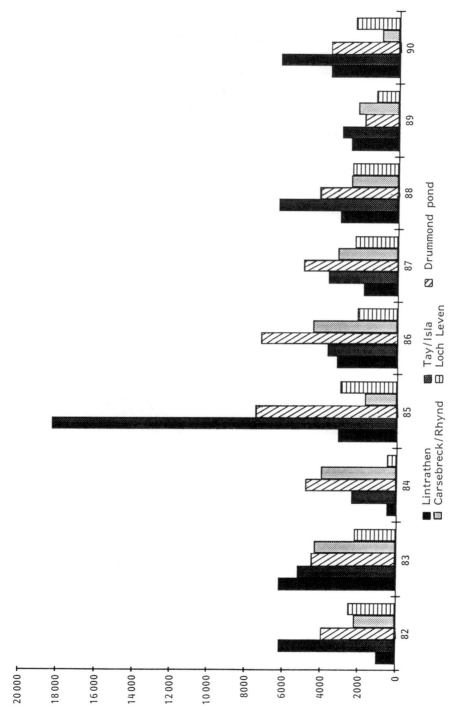

FIGURE 13.3. Winter counts of Greylag Geese at five sites in Tayside Region from 1982 to 1990

238

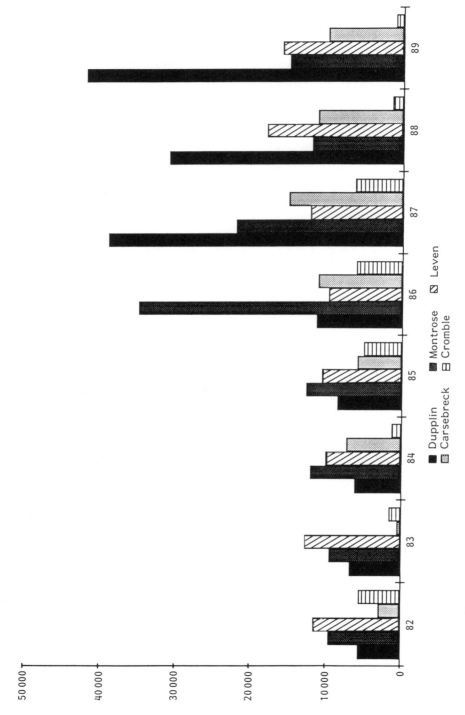

FIGURE 13.4. Winter counts of Pink-footed Geese at five sites in Tayside Region from 1982 to 1990

FIGURE 13.5. The lower reaches of the River Endrick, near the National Nature Reserve which is internationally important for several species of breeding and wintering birds. Photograph: Peter S. Maitland

Strathclyde

The most famous freshwater site in Strathclyde, if not Scotland, is Loch Lomond. It is also the largest freshwater loch in Britain, and one of the most heavily used, particularly for recreation. Freshwater bird interest is mostly in the winter, and is centred around the mouth of the River Endrick (Figure 13.5). This area, part of which is an NNR, supports internationally important numbers of both Greylag and Greenland White-fronted Geese, as well as smaller numbers of wintering Whooper Swans, Wigeon, Teal and Shoveler.

On the Argyll islands, mention must be made of Duich Moss on Islay, an internationally important roost and feeding site for Greenland White-fronted Geese, and now protected by designation as an NNR, Ramsar site and Special Protection Area (SPA). Tiree and Coll support important numbers of breeding Red-throated Divers, Greylag Geese and Pintail, as well as wintering Greenland White-fronted, Greylag and Barnacle Geese and Whooper Swans, and large numbers of breeding waders.

On the Argyll mainland, Tangy Loch and the nearby fields around Machrihanish support internationally important numbers of wintering Greenland White-Fronted Geese.

Central

In the Carse of Stirling, Flanders Moss is the largest remaining lowland raised mire in the UK, and in winter some 1700 Pink-footed Geese feed here and on surrounding fields. They roost on the nearby Lake of Menteith, together with other wildfowl.

Flanders Moss is also the site of the largest inland colony of Lesser Black-backed Gulls in Scotland (4000 pairs in 1982).

Lothian

In Lothian Region, freshwater bird interest is again concentrated on major goose roosts such as Gladhouse Reservoir which, together with the alternative roost at Fala Flow, supports some 3% of the world's Pink-footed Geese in winter (Figure 13.6). Whiteadder Reservoir in the Lammermuir Hills supports up to 2000 Greylags, and Threipmuir Reservoir is also an important roost for this species.

Borders

In the Borders, wintering geese are again the most numerous birds (see Figure 13.6), with the largest roost at Westwater Reservoir in the Pentlands Hills, where the average peak count between 1985/86 and 1989/90 was over 20 000 Pink-footed Geese (about 19% of the world population). Hule Moss is also important for Pinkfeet, and both Pinkfeet and Greylags occur at Hoselaw Loch.

Dumfries and Galloway

Loch Ken and the River Dee Marshes in the Stewartry form one of the most important wetlands in south Scotland, with breeding ducks and wintering Greenland White-fronted Geese. The latter are joined by Whooper Swans and Mute Swans and a range of other wildfowl.

Greenland White-fronted Geese also roost at Lochinch (White Loch) and at Torrs Warren at the head of Luce Bay.

Castle Loch is a eutrophic loch near the village of Lochmaben, which is important for wintering Greylag and Pink-footed Geese and Goosander.

THE ROLE OF BIRDS IN AQUATIC FOOD WEBS

General accounts of freshwater communities and food webs usually mention birds only in passing, since they are regarded by many as a minor component (e.g. Burgis and Morris, 1987; Maitland, 1990).

Birds exploit a wide range of food in aquatic systems, and operate at more than one trophic level. Dabbling ducks and swans are primarily vegetarian, feeding on water plants either at the surface (e.g. *Lemna* spp.) or growing on the bottom (e.g. *Potamogeton* spp.). All parts of plants may be eaten. Some species will eat starch-rich rhizomes or tubers, leaves and fat-rich seeds. Ducks have bills adapted for these different diets. Dabbling ducks have lamellae which line the inner sides of their bills for filtering out small seeds and invertebrates. The Shoveler shows the greatest specialization for this method of feeding.

Diving ducks which feed on invertebrates tend to have relatively smaller bills than dabbling ducks and they too have lamellae to filter their food. The fish-eating species (divers, grebes, Cormorant, sawbill ducks, Grey Heron and Osprey) all show adaptations for catching and holding their prey. The divers, grebes and Grey Heron have

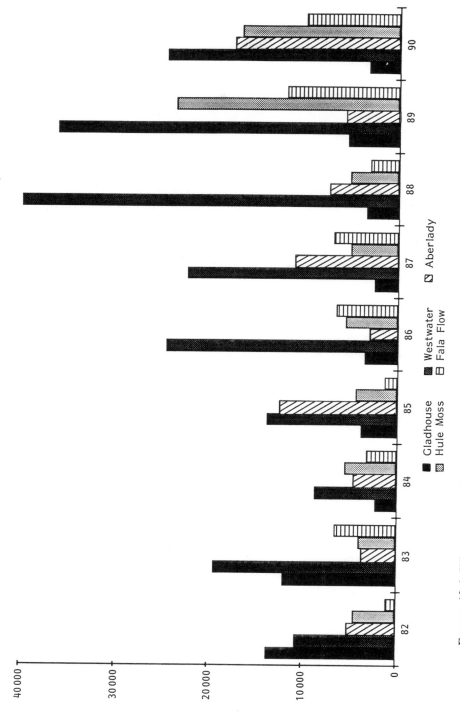

FIGURE 13.6. Winter counts of Greylag Geese at five sites in Lothian and Borders Regions from 1982 to 1990

pointed sharp-edged bills, whilst the Cormorant has a sharp hook to its bill tip. The Red-breasted Merganser and Goosander, as their collective name suggests, have serrated edges to their bills. The Osprey's bill is not particularly specialized but the scales on the soles of its feet help to grip fish. Geese sometimes feed in aquatic systems and their bills have a sharp cutting edge to the tip which enables them to bite into underwater tubers or rhizomes (Cramp and Simmons, 1977).

In addition to those birds that take food within the water column, or at its surface, there are several species that feed on flying insects close to water. Thus, Swallows, martins and Swifts catch insects over water, whilst wagtails and Common Sandpipers hunt along the banks of lochs and rivers. The Dipper, which tends to occur on rivers rather than lochs, is the only passerine to hunt under water, taking primarily the larvae of caddis flies and mayfly nymphs in fast-moving water.

The feeding areas or habitats in which birds feed are determined by the bird's food supply and feeding technique. Thus, the depth at which dabbling ducks feed is usually limited by the length of their necks as they mostly forage by up-ending. The Mute Swan, by virtue of its long neck, can reach down to about a metre to obtain water plants. Although dabbling ducks can dive they rarely do so. Coots, however, regularly dive to reach water plants. Diving ducks will dive several metres to the bottom of lochs to eat benthic invertebrates; as some of this feeding takes place at night they must rely on touch. Herons feed only in shallow margins of lochs and rivers whilst wading, whereas the osprey plunge-dives for fish close to the surface. Divers, grebes, sawbill ducks and the Cormorant hunt fish at all depths by direct pursuit (Cramp and Simmons, 1977).

The aquatic food webs and role of birds will vary depending on the type of loch. Thus webs in eutrophic lochs will tend to be more complex than in oligotrophic or dystrophic lochs, or in those deep lochs with a relatively narrow photic zone. In this respect, the only freshwater loch which has been well studied in Scotland is Loch Leven (Figure 13.7) (Morgan and McLusky, 1974). It became part of the International Biological Programme during 1967–1972, at a time of major human influences on the loch: increased nutrient input from agricultural run-off and sewage, and dieldrin input from a woollen mill. Despite these influences, there were large numbers of breeding and wintering ducks and swans. The energy flow through part of the food web (phytoplankton – chironomids – fish and Tufted Ducks) was quantified. If the Tufted Ducks fed on chironomids alone they would have consumed only 4% of chironomid production, whereas if Perch and Trout fed on chironomids alone, they would have consumed more than the total production (Morgan and McLusky, 1974). Clearly, in this case, the birds were likely to have had little impact in comparison to the fish (see also below).

Although there are few detailed studies of food chains, the numerical and functional responses of water birds to their food supply can sometimes be observed where there has been a gross change. The colonization and spread of the invasive water plant *Elodea canadensis* into Loch of Harray on Orkney led to a marked increase in the numbers of Whooper and Mute Swans and Wigeon (Sinclair *et al.*, 1992). The Whooper Swans rarely visited the loch before the arrival of *Elodea* but now feed exclusively in the loch. The Wigeon used to feed by grazing the grassy banks and now feed largely on scraps of *Elodea* brought to the surface by the swans. The impact that swans have on this food supply is unknown but there was a visible decline in the

FIGURE 13.7. Loch Leven, a National Nature Reserve of international importance for breeding and wintering wildfowl. Photograph: Peter S. Maitland

abundance of *Elodea* in 1991 resulting in the starvation and death of 130 swans. It is not known, however, if the swans depleted their food through over-grazing or if the decline in *Elodea* was due to another factor such as the weather (Sinclair *et al.*, 1992).

The relationship between birds and their food supply can be affected by acid rain. Acidification has been most acute in south-west Scotland (see Chapter 24). Dippers in Galloway are at a lower density where streams have a low pH, but Grey Wagtails and Common Sandpipers that live on terrestrial insects by river banks have been unaffected (Vickery, 1991). The impact of acidification on birds of Scottish lochs has not been investigated, but elsewhere there have been correlative studies. For example, in Scandinavia more species of water birds were found on less acid lakes (Nilsson and Nilsson, 1978). Also, where insect populations have declined due to acidification, Swallows and flycatchers have been forced to feed elsewhere (Magnuson, 1983).

Not all the effects of acidification have been detrimental to birds. The losses of fish from lochs may be beneficial to water birds in some cases where there is competition for invertebrate food. Enhanced populations or breeding success have been noted in Mallard (Pehrsson, 1984), Long-tailed Duck (Pehrsson, 1974), Goldeneye (Eriksson, 1979) and Black-throated Diver (Eriksson, 1984) on acidified lakes. The mechanism for this increase is not always clear. For example, the improved production by Black-throated Divers may have been due to reduced numbers of Pike (*Esox lucius*), which prey on young water birds (Lehtonen, 1970).

THE ROLE OF WATER BIRDS AS IMPORTERS OF NUTRIENTS INTO FRESHWATER SYSTEMS

Lochs are used by water birds as safe roosts as well as feeding and breeding areas. In Scotland, large numbers of Greylag Geese and Pink-footed Geese flock to some of the larger lochs to roost at night. These include the Lochs of Strathbeg, Kinnordy, Leven and Eye. Having fed on surrounding agricultural land by day, they return to the night roosts with a full gut, which is gradually evacuated during the course of the night. This amounts to about 25 droppings per night (Ebbinge *et al.*, 1975) and, as the dry mass of Greylag Goose and Pink-footed Goose droppings are 0.94 and 0.78 g respectively (Kear, 1963), there is the possibility of nutrient enrichment if the roosting population is large.

Detailed work has been carried out at Loch of Strathbeg, a shallow dune loch on the north-east coast of Grampian. Here, there are indications that fish and fresh-water mussels may have declined as a result of nutrient enrichment (Pritchard, 1990). The main avian importers of nutrients are Greylag Geese, whose average winter population during the 1980s was 2000 – 5000, and Pink-footed Geese which have been steadily increasing in numbers (Raffaelli *et al.*, 1991). Not all the geese roost on the water, with many on shallow flooded areas in fields adjacent to the loch, but there have been sufficient numbers of geese for the total annual input of phosphorus to be over one tonne in recent years (Raffaelli *et al.*, 1991). However, this is believed to represent, at most, some 15–20% of the total phosphorus budget, the remaining 80–85% coming in as run-off from agricultural land where increased fertilization is now practised (Pritchard, 1990). Thus, even with very large numbers of geese, it appears that man's impact is much greater (see Chapter 22).

THE CONSERVATION OF FRESHWATER BIRDS

Some protection has been offered, at least to some sites, by designation as Sites of Special Scientific Interest (SSSIs) since as early as 1949. The 1981 Wildlife and Countryside Act gave further protection to SSSIs, partly to fulfil obligations under the EC Directive on Conservation of Wild Birds agreed in 1979. Under this Directive sites of EC importance for migratory and rarer species must be designated as Special Protection Areas (SPAs). Some 238 sites in the UK which qualify as SPAs have been listed by the Joint Nature Conservation Committee (JNCC) (137 in Scotland), but by April 1993 only 72 of these (27 in Scotland) had been designated by the Government. Failure to designate has been the subject of several complaints to the European Commission, some of which have almost resulted in cases at the European Court of Justice. The freshwater SPAs designated in Scotland, while including some areas under threat of damage, tend to be already in conservation ownership or otherwise uncontroversial (Table 13.3)

International recognition is also given to wetlands under the Convention on Wetlands of International Importance especially as Waterfowl Habitat (the Ramsar Convention), which was set up in 1971 in the town of Ramsar in northern Iran. Sites which regularly hold 1% of a species or sub-species of waterfowl or at least 10 000 ducks, geese and swans or 10 000 Coots or 20 000 waders qualify for designation as Ramsar sites. The UK signed the Convention in 1973 and ratified it in 1976. By 1993 some 70 countries had signed, and 570 sites had been designated as internationally important wetlands, covering nearly 36×10^6 ha. A total of 154 sites (56 in Scotland) have been listed by the JNCC as qualifying for designation. Once again designation has been slow, with only 65 designated (23 in Scotland) in the 20 years since the UK signed the Convention. The designated Scottish freshwater sites are listed in Table 13.4.

TABLE 13.3 Designated freshwater Special Protection Areas (SPAs) in Scotland

Site	District/Islands Area	Date designated
Loch Druidibeg and Loch a 'Machair	Western Isles	Aug. 1982
Loch Eye	Ross & Cromarty	Oct. 1986
Loch of Skene	Kincardine & Deeside	Oct. 1986
Bridgend Flats, Islay	Argyll & Bute	Jul. 1988
Eilean na Muice Dubhe, Islay	Argyll & Bute	Jul. 1988
Gladhouse Reservoir	Midlothian	Jul. 1988
Gruinart Flats, Islay	Argyll & Bute	Jul. 1988
Hoselaw Loch	Berwick	Jul. 1988
Laggan Peninsula, Islay	Argyll & Bute	Jul. 1988
Fala Flow	Midlothian	Apr. 1990
Feur Lochain, Islay	Argyll & Bute	Apr. 1990
Glac na Criche, Islay	Argyll & Bute	Apr. 1990
Loch Ken/River Dee Marshes	Stewartry	Aug. 1992
Loch of Lintrathen	Angus	Aug. 1992
Loch Spynie	Moray	Aug. 1992
South Tayside Goose Roosts	Perth & Kinross	Apr. 1993

TABLE 13.4. Designated freshwater Ramsar sites in Scotland

Site	District/Islands Area	Date designated
Loch Druidibeg, Loch a'Machair and Loch Stilligarry	Western Isles	Jan. 1976
Loch Leven	Perth & Kinross	Jan. 1976
Loch Lomond	Stirling, Dumbarton	Jan. 1976
Rannoch Moor	Stirling	Jan. 1976
Cairngorm Lochs	Grampian/Highland	Jul. 1981
Claish Moss	Argyll & Bute	Jul. 1981
Loch of Lintrathen	Angus	Jul. 1981
Silver Flowe	Stewartry	Jul. 1981
Loch Eye	Ross & Cromarty	Oct. 1986
Loch of Skene	Kincardine & Deeside	Oct. 1986
Bridgend Flats, Islay	Argyll & Bute	Jul. 1988
Eilean na Muice Duibhe, Islay	Argyll & Bute	Jul. 1988
Gladhouse Reservoir	Midlothian	Jul. 1988
Gruinart Flats, Islay	Argyll & Bute	Jul. 1988
Hoselaw Loch	Berwick	Jul. 1988
Fala Flow	Midlothian	Apr. 1990
Feur Lochain, Islay	Argyll & Bute	Apr. 1990
Glac na Criche, Islay	Argyll & Bute	Apr. 1990
Loch an Duin	Western Isles	Apr. 1990
Loch Ken/River Dee Marshes	Stewartry	Sep. 1992
Loch Spynie	Moray	Sep. 1992
South Tayside Goose Roosts	Perth & Kinross	Apr. 1993

Another international agreement which will affect the conservation of freshwater habitats and species is the EC Directive on the Conservation of Natural Habitats and of Wild Fauna and Flora. This was passed in June 1992 and EC Member States have until 1995 to ensure that their legislation enables them to comply with it. Its principal provision is for the setting up of a network of protected sites, to be called "Natura 2000", covering the most important areas of habitat types listed in Annex I of the Directive. There will be overlap between sites designated under this Directive and SPAs under the Birds Directive.

Several of Scotlands' prime sites for freshwater birds are also nature reserves, owned or leased by Scottish Natural Heritage or voluntary bodies such as the Royal Society for the Protection of Birds and the Scottish Wildlife Trust.

CONCLUSIONS

Scotland has a wealth of freshwater habitats and a diverse community of waterbirds. Being some of the more visible of birds, they are amenable to study and there are now satisfactory data on the distribution and numbers of many species. The status of wintering wildfowl continues to be assessed by the Wildfowl and Wetlands Trust, whilst the British Trust for Ornithology provides a population index for the commoner species on rivers. Less well known are the factors that determine distribution and numbers. Such studies would require knowledge of diet, feeding and breeding habitat, coupled with information on productivity and mortality. Such ecological and population studies have been applied to only a few water birds in Scotland such as Black-throated Diver (Mudge and Talbot, 1993), Slavonian Grebe (RSPB study in progress), Red-breasted Merganser (Marquiss and Duncan, 1993) and the Grey Heron (Marquiss, 1989). Clearly, there is much to learn. Equally, there have been few studies of the role that birds play in the energy transfer through systems. The study of Tufted Ducks feeding on invertebrates suggests their role is small (Morgan and McLusky, 1974) but this may not apply to birds higher in the food chain (e.g. divers).

Freshwater systems are vulnerable to abuse and threats to sites escalate as man makes continual demands, either directly or indirectly. Current threats still include water abstraction, and this is likely to increase. Although it is unlikely that there will be much further expansion of hydro-electric schemes, they cause a chronic disruption of sites by influencing water levels on lochs and flow rates in rivers. The leisure industry poses a threat by disturbing nesting, feeding and roosting birds. Waste pollution is not an acute threat apart from in a few rivers (e.g. the River Clyde), but runoff from agricultural land is increasing and this could affect some lochs.

Acid rain has had a marked affect on lochs and rivers in south-west Scotland (Battarbee, 1989) but lochs in the north-west have been largely unaffected. Many lochs are now being used as fish farms where pollution from waste food and faeces may cause problems. Marshes are vulnerable to drainage, and in the drive to maximize agricultural production many of the lowland marshes and their birds have gone. The North American Mink (*Mustela vison*) is now well established in Scotland after escaping from fur farms, and is known to take the eggs and young of water birds and to kill adult birds. There is concern that it may be affecting some populations (see Chapter 14).

Many freshwater sites and their birds and other associated wildlife remain vulnerable. International agreements and subsequent national legislation are slowly improving the protection of key sites, but many remain undesignated. Further research is needed to improve our understanding of each species' needs. Most importantly, as part of the means of reducing agricultural surpluses, further reform of agricultural subsidies must ensure that no more freshwater sites are lost, and that a start is made replacing those removed. Measures such as Environmentally Sensitive Areas and "set-aside" have a vital role to play in restoring Scotland's countryside.

REFERENCES

Avery, M. and Haines-Young, R. (1990). "Population estimates for the Dunlin *Calidris alpina* derived from remotely sensed satellite imagery of the Flow country of northern Scotland", *Nature*, **344**, 860–862.

Bainbridge, I. P., Minns, D. W., Housden, S. D. and Lance, A. N. (1987). *Forestry in the Flows of Caithness and Sutherland*, Royal Society for the Protection of Birds, Sandy.

Battarbee, R. W. (1989). "Geographical research on acid rain. 1. The acidification of Scottish lochs", *The Geographical Journal*, **155**, 353–377.

Batten, L. A., Bibby, C. J., Clement, P., Elliott, G. D. and Porter, R. F. (1990). *Red Data Birds in Britain*, Poyser, London.

Bhatia, Z. (1992). *Insh Marshes Nature Reserve Goldeneye Newsletter 1991*, Royal Society for the Protection of Birds, Sandy.

Brown, A. W. and Brown, L. M. (1985). "The Scottish Mute Swan Census 1986", *Scottish Birds*, **13**, 140–148.

Brown, P. and Waterston, G. (1962). *The Return of the Osprey*, Collins, London.

Burgis, M. J. and Morris, P. (1987). *The Natural History of Lakes*, Cambridge University Press, Cambridge.

Campbell, L. H. and Talbot, T. R. (1987). "Breeding status of black-throated divers in Scotland", *British Birds*, **80**, 1–8.

Campbell, L. M. (1988). "Loon conservation in the British Isles," in *Proceedings of 1987 Conference on Common Loon Research and Management* (Ed. P. I. V. Strong), pp. 78–85, North American Loon Fund.

Cramp, S. and Simmons, K. E. L. (1977–1983). *The Birds of the Western Palearctic*, Volume I, Oxford University Press, Oxford.

Crooke, C., Dennis, R., Harvey, M. and Summers, R. (1993). "Population size and breeding success of Slavonian grebes in Scotland", in *Britain's Birds in 1990–1991* (Eds J. Andrews and S. P. Carter), pp. 135–138, British Trust for Ornithology, Thetford, and the Joint Nature Conservation Committee, Peterborough.

Dennis, R., Broad, R., Brockie, K., Crooke, C. and Duncan, K. (1993). *Ospreys in Scotland*, Royal Society for the Protection of Birds, Sandy.

Dennis, R. H. and Dow, H. (1984). "The establishment of a population of goldeneye (*Bucephala clangula*) breeding in Scotland", *Bird Study*, **31**, 217–222.

Ebbinge, B., Canters, K. and Drent, R. (1975). "Foraging routines and estimated daily food intake in barnacle geese wintering in the northern Netherlands", *Wildfowl*, **26**, 5–19.

Eriksson, M. O. G. (1979). "Competition between freshwater fish and goldeneye *Bucephala clangula* (L.) for common prey", *Oecologia*, **14**, 99–107.

Eriksson, M. O. G. (1984). "Acidification of lakes: effects on waterbirds in Sweden", *Ambio*, **13**, 260–262.

Fox, A. D. (1988). "Breeding status of the Gadwall in Britain and Ireland", *British Birds*, **81**, 51–66.

Fox, A. D., Jarret, N. J., Gitay, H. and Paynter, D. (1989). "Late summer habitat selection by breeding waterfowl in northern Scotland", *Wildfowl*, **40**, 106–114.

Fuller, R. J. (1982). *Bird Habitats in Britain*, Poyser, Calton.

Galbraith, H., Furness, R. W. and Fuller, R. J. (1984). "Habitats and distribution of waders breeding on Scottish agricultural land", *Scottish Birds*, **13**, 98–107.

Gomersall, C. H. (1987). "Breeding performance of the red-throated diver *Gavia stellata* in Shetland", *Holarctic Ecology*, **9**, 227–284.

Gomersall, C. H., Morton, J. S. and Wynde, R. M. (1984). "Status of breeding Red-throated Divers in Shetland, 1983", *Bird Study*, **31**, 223–229.

Hughes, S. W. M., Bacon, P. and Flegg, J. J. M. (1979). "The 1975 census of the great crested grebe in Britain", *Bird Study*, **26**, 213–226.

Kear, J. (1963). "The agricultural importance of wild goose droppings", *Wildlife Trust Annual Report*, **14**, 72–77.

Lack, P. (1986). *The Atlas of Wintering Birds in Britain and Ireland*, Poyser, Calton.

Lehtonen, L. (1970). "Zur Biologie des Prachttauchers, *Gavia a. arctica* (L.)", *Annales Zoologica Fennici*, **7**, 25–60.

Magnuson, J. J. (1983). "Effects on aquatic biology", in *The Acidic Deposition Phenomenon and its Effects* (Ed. A. P. Altshuller and R. A. Linthurst), Vol. II, Section 5, pp. 1–203, Draft document of US Environmental Protection Agency/North Carolina State University Acid Precipitation Programme.

Maitland, P. S. (1990). *Biology of Fresh Waters*, 2nd edition, Blackie, Glasgow.

Maitland, P. S., Newson, M. D. and Best, G. A. (1990). *The Impact of Afforestation and Forestry Practice on Freshwater Habitats*, Focus on Nature Conservation No. 23, Nature Conservancy Council, Peterborough.

Marquiss, M. (1980). "Grey herons *Ardea cinerea* breeding in Scotland: numbers, distribution and census techniques", *Bird Study*, **36**, 181–191.

Marquiss, M. and Duncan, K. (1993). "Variation in the abundance of red-breasted mergansers *Mergus serrator* on a Scottish river in relation to season, year, river hydrology, salmon density and spring culling", *Ibis*, **135**, 33–41.

Meek, E. R. and Little, B. (1977). "The spread of the goosander in Britain and Ireland", *British Birds*, **70**, 229–237.

Morgan, N. C. and McLusky, D. S. (1974). "A summary of the Loch Leven IBP results in relation to lake management and future research", *Proceedings of the Royal Society of Edinburgh*, **74**, B, 408–416.

Mudge, G. P. and Talbot, T. R. (1993). "The breeding biology and causes of nest failure of Scottish black-throated divers, *Gavia arctica*", *Ibis*, **135**, 113–120.

Mudge, G. P., Dennis, R. H., Talbot, T. R. and Broad, R. A., (1991). "Changes in breeding status of black-throated divers in Scotland", *Scottish Birds*, **16**, 77–84.

Nethersole-Thompson, D. and Nethersole-Thompson, M. (1986). *Waders, their Breeding Haunts and Watchers*, Poyser, Calton.

Nilsson, S. G. and Nilsson, I. N. (1978). "Breeding bird community densities and species richness in lakes", *Oikos*, **31**, 214–221.

O'Brien, M. (1992). "1992/93 survey of breeding waders on Scottish agricultural land", *Scottish Bird News*, **28**, 1–3.

Ormerod, S. J., Tyler, S. J. and Lewis, J. M. S. (1985). "Is the breeding distribution of dippers influenced by stream acidity?", *Bird Study*, **32**, 32–39.

Owen, M., Atkinson-Wilkes, G. L. and Salmon, D. (1986). *Wildfowl in Great Britain*, 2nd edition, Cambridge University Press, Cambridge.

Pehrsson, O. (1974). "Nutrition of small ducklings regulating breeding area and reproductive output in the long-tailed duck, *Clangula hyemalis*", *Proceedings of the International Congress of Game Biology*, **11**, 259–264.

Pehrsson, O. (1984). "Relations of food to spatial and temporal breeding strategies of mallards in Sweden", *Journal of Wildlife Management*, **48**, 322–339.

Pritchard, D. E., Housden, S. D., Mudge, G. P., Galbraith, C. A. and Pienkowski, M. W. (Eds) (1992). *Important Bird Areas in the UK including the Channel Islands and the Isle of Man*, Royal Society for the Protection of Birds, Sandy.

Pritchard, J. S. (1990). *Freshwater Macrophyte Survey of Loch of Strathbeg, Meikle, Sand and Cotehill Lochs, Banff and Buchan and Gordon Districts*, Nature Conservancy Council, Aberdeen.

Raffaelli, D., Warbrick, S. and Young, M. (1991). *Long-term Trends in Wildfowl Counts and Land-use Relevant to the Nutrient Status of the Loch of Strathbeg, Aberdeenshire, Scotland*, University of Aberdeen, Aberdeen.

Sharrock, J. T. R. (1976). *The Atlas of Breeding Birds in Britain and Ireland*, Poyser, Berkhamsted.

Sinclair, A. H., Armstrong, G., Young, M., Ford, M. A. and Raffaelli, D. (1992). *The Impact of Agriculture on Water Quality in Loch of Harray and Feeder Burns*, Scottish Agricultural College/Aberdeen University, Aberdeen.

Stroud, D. A., Reed, T. M., Pienkowski, M. W. and Lindsay, R. A. (1987). *Birds, Bogs and Forestry. The Peatlands of Caithness and Sutherland*, Nature Conservancy Council, Peterborough.

Thom, V. M. (1986). *Birds in Scotland*, Poyser, Calton.

Vickery, J. (1991). "Breeding density of dippers *Cinclus cinclus*, grey wagtails *Motacilla cinerea* and common sandpipers *Actitis hypoleucos* in relation to the acidity of streams in south-west Scotland", *Ibis*, **133**, 178–185.

14

Mammals

J. GREEN and R. GREEN

Vincent Wildlife Trust, Barjarg, Barrhill, Girvan, KA26 0RB, UK

INTRODUCTION

Only four mammal species in Scotland are intimately associated with fresh water although various mammals, from deer to harvest mice, exploit waterside habitat to some degree.

WATER SHREW

At 12–18g, the Water Shrew, *Neomys fodiens*, is the largest of the British shrews, but by far the smallest aquatic mammal in Great Britain. It is widely distributed across northern Europe, as far south as northern Spain and Italy, and eastwards through Russia to central Asia. There are also isolated populations on Sakhalin Island, the adjacent Asian coast and in Korea. In Scotland it is widespread, but patchily distributed, on the mainland and on the islands of Raasay, Skye, Pabbay, Mull, Kerrera, the Garvellachs, Shuna, Islay, Arran and Bute (Figure 14.1). Three records on Hoy from 1847 to 1964 have not been recently confirmed. The species is undoubtedly under-recorded and many records are derived from cat kills or raptor pellets which reveal little about the species' habitat requirements or preferences. In southern England Water Shrews are said to favour fast-flowing, clean streams and watercress beds (Churchfield, in Corbet and Harris, 1991). They have been recorded from a wide range of Scottish habitats, including rocky seashores and mountain burns (known altitudes in Scotland range to 230 m and in Wales to 420 m). They can also live an entirely terrestrial life.

Some differences in size and pelage, particularly coloration of the underparts, have been detected in specimens from Scottish islands (Corbet, 1966). Little is known about the significance of this and there is no recognized Scottish variant.

Adaptations for aquatic life include a vascular plexus in the interscapular adipose tissue resembling the *retia mirabilia* of diving mammals. This is thought to assist in the process of gaseous exchange. Fringes of stiff hair on the margins of the feet aid swimming. Water Shrews can dive to around 1 m, but their rounded shape together with air trapped in the short, dense fur creates buoyancy which restricts foraging time

The Fresh Waters of Scotland: A National Resource of International Significance
Edited by P. S. Maitland, P. J. Boon and D. S. McLusky. © 1994 John Wiley & Sons Ltd

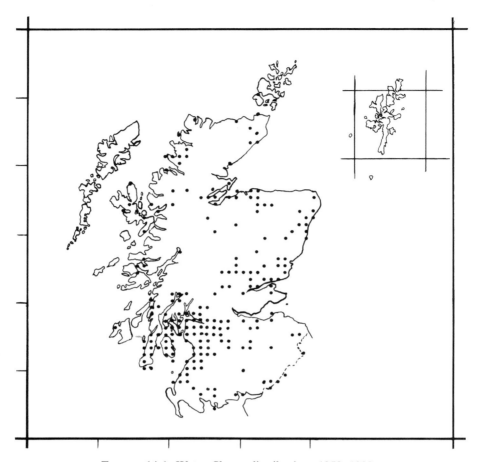

FIGURE 14.1. Water Shrew distribution, 1950–1992

at this depth. Hunting in shallow water is more successful, but foraging under water is still energy consuming. At most, 67% of prey is aquatic (mean 50%) and some Water Shrews subsist entirely on terrestrial food, overlapping the prey range of the Common Shrew, *Sorex araneus*. Churchfield (1986) suggests that aquatic hunting avoids competition with sympatric species. It also provides access to larger prey items such as amphibians, small fish and large invertebrates. Large prey is immobilized using venom from the submaxillary glands.

Water Shrews have a high metabolic rate, a year-round activity cycle and a short life span (14–19 months). The breeding season extends from April to September, involving one to three litters per season and a mean litter size of six young.

WATER VOLE

Scotland's other aquatic small mammal, the Water Vole, *Arvicola terrestris*, is rather better known than the Water Shrew. Worldwide it has a similar distribution to that

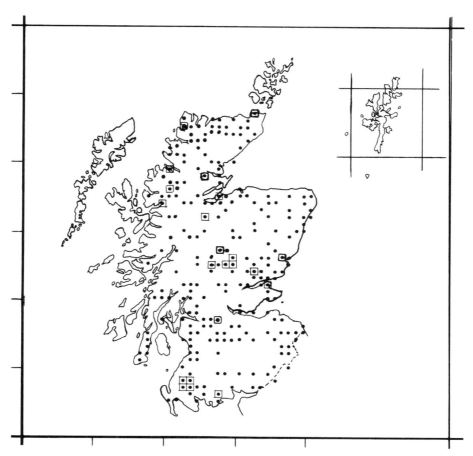

FIGURE 14.2. Water Vole distribution, 1970–1992. Black variant ▣

of the Water Shrew, but extends into the Middle East and does not range as far east in northern Asia. It is widely but thinly spread over the Scottish mainland but has only been recorded from the inshore islands of Bute, Eilean Gamhna and Eilean Creagach (Figure 14.2). Both Gibson (1990) and Strachan and Jefferies (1992) report their recent failure to find Water Voles in these former island ranges. Jefferies *et al.* (1989) suggested a countrywide decline since 1900, but produced few hard data, whilst Gibson (1986) reported a decline in the Clyde area from the 1970s. Strachan and Jefferies' systematic British survey confirmed the decline after 1900, with a sudden increase in site loss in the last 20 years. This was based on a survey of 730 sites of which 32% were positive. The authors demonstrate a significant negative correlation between the distribution and density of Water Voles and Mink, attributing the decline of Voles to the spread of feral mink, together with habitat loss and pollution. This inverse relationship is less marked in Scotland, where the main difference in distribution is that Mink have not yet reached the north-west (Figures 14.2 and 14.4). Elsewhere in Scotland Mink appear to have expanded without apparent contraction of the vole range, but current records are too incomplete to permit analysis of population trends.

A Scottish race of the Water Vole *A. amphibius reta* was proposed early this century but is not now considered to represent a discrete sub-species. It was said to be smaller and darker with a higher frequency of melanism occurring in northern Scotland, where black animals were the norm (Boyce, in Corbet and Harris, 1991). However, black Water Voles also occur in lowland England as well as throughout Scotland (Figure 14.2) and black fur may be an adaptation to peat soils (R. Strachan, personal communication). Populations in south-west Scotland and Torridon contain black, brown and brindled animals (personal observations and Strachan and Jefferies, 1992).

Water Voles are found in most freshwater habitats in Scotland, ranging from headstreams (to 620 m) to slow-flowing lowland ditches. Recent work (personal observations and unpublished records) has shown that they are more numerous in upland and peatland habitats than formerly thought.

Unlike the Water Shrew, the Water Vole shows no morphological adaptation for an aquatic life and some live entirely terrestrially, burrowing like Moles. Waterside populations may migrate seasonally to avoid flooding.

Male Water Voles are about 5% larger than females with adult body weights ranging from 225–386 gm. The species is predominantly vegetarian and consumes about 80% of body weight daily, often selecting the most nutritious portions of food plants. Breeding ocurs from April to September with up to five litters, averaging six young.

OTTER

In contrast to both preceding species, Scottish Otters are relatively well researched. Since 1977 their status has been monitored systematically every seven years whilst local Otter populations in Tayside and on Deeside have been subjected to detailed ecological research using radio-telemetry and radio-isotopes.

Lutra lutra has a worldwide distribution extending from Ireland to Japan. Within this range few sub-species have been proposed and in Scotland only the isolated Otter population of Shetland shows any apparent racial characteristics.

Otters have declined throughout Europe in the past 30 years, but markedly less in Scotland than elsewhere. Green and Green (1980) showed a population split into a fragmented southern and a more robust northern distribution by 1979, with 73% of 4636 survey sites used by Otters. The Northern and Western Isles, the Inner Hebrides, the west coast and south-west Scotland supported good populations, but central and eastern Scotland showed reductions or local extinctions. Only Ireland, with 92% of sites occupied (Chapman and Chapman, 1982), had a wider distribution. Together these countries remain the stronghold of the species in Europe. By 1985 there was an 8% increase in Otter distribution in southern Scotland (Green and Green, 1987), whilst the current survey (Green and Green, in preparation) shows substantial increases in distribution, particularly in the central and eastern lowlands (Figure 14.3). The national population now includes a significant urban component, most markedly within Greater Glasgow. Improvements in water quality and a good baseline population are probably the major contributors to the species' recovery.

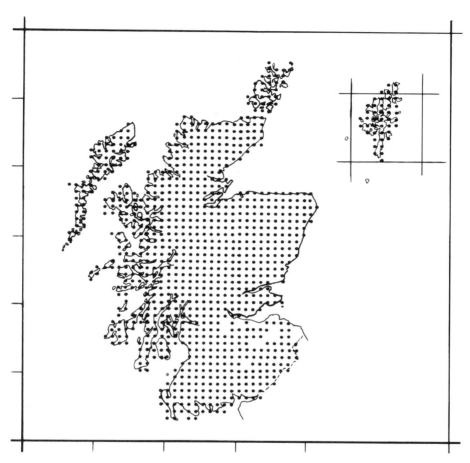

FIGURE 14.3. Otter distribution, 1977–1992.

Locally, Glasgow Planning Department's policy of conserving river corridors and a network of wildlife habitats has also played a part in this process.

Otters remain scarce throughout much of central, southern and eastern England whilst elsewhere in western Europe populations have continued to decline, in some cases to extinction (e.g. The Netherlands). The use of persistent organochlorine pesticides, beginning in the 1950s, provides the most plausible overall explanation for the Otter's decline in the UK (Chanin and Jefferies, 1978), but local impacts from polychlorinated biphenyls (PCBs) may also have been influential (Mason *et al.*, 1992). PCBs are thought to have had a more significant impact on the Continent. Otters throughout Scotland continue to accumulate a range of pollutants but generally at modest levels. Reductions in direct pollution are perhaps being offset by the impacts of indirect pollution since there are indications that acidification may be restricting the distribution of Otters in the heavily afforested uplands of south-west Scotland.

Otters inhabit all types of aquatic habitat in Scotland, from the coast to mountain lochans (0–730 m) but show a preference for sheltered sea lochs, lowland fresh waters and slow-flowing watercourses. Although commonly associated in the public mind with large water bodies they will exploit small stream systems intensively wherever these remain undegraded. Home ranges are large (e.g. 40 km for males; 20 km for females) and overlapping, apparently both between and within sexes (Green *et al.*, 1984).

Otters possess various adaptations for an aquatic life including webbed feet, a dense pelt, powerful hindquarters and tail, ears and nostrils which can be closed when diving, and tactile whiskers. Sexual dimorphism is pronounced, with male Otters, at 8–10 kg, weighing 30% more than females.

Otters are predominantly piscivorous, but will also take large invertebrates, birds, mammals and amphibians. Their food supply varies seasonally in a more complex manner than that of other British predators. According to habitat, it may include or combine a variety of peaks of prey availability; for example, spawning salmonids in winter, spring-spawning amphibians, or in summer spawning cyprinids. Consequently Otters breed throughout the year, though with a more pronounced winter cub mortality. The mean size of the single yearly litter is two.

The recent history of Otter populations throughout Europe suggests that they are capable of rapid decline but, at best, only slow recovery. Internationally, the species is protected by the Bern Convention and by CITES whose provisions in Great Britain are empowered through the Wildlife and Countryside Act 1981. The Act protects both Otters and their holts and prohibits trade in otter products. The forthcoming EC Habitats and Species Directive will also require Community members to designate Special Areas of Conservation for the Otter (see also Chapter 29).

MINK

The American Mink, *Mustela vison*, is a relative newcomer to Europe, deriving from animals escaping from fur farms. Translocations associated with fur farming have resulted in feral populations in Ireland, Great Britain, Iceland, France, Spain, Russia, Germany, and all of Scandinavia. Over much of this range it is sympatric with the European Mink, *M. lutreola*.

The first Scottish mink farm opened in 1938 and in that same year the first Mink escaped. Fur farming expanded rapidly in the 1940s and 1950s, peaking at about 100 farms but declining from the 1960s (Cuthbert, 1973). Most farms were situated in eastern and central Scotland. Breeding was recorded on the Rivers Ugie, Deveron, Urr, Teviot and Tweed between 1962 and 1964 and this feral population expanded such that by 1969 Arran, where mink were never farmed, had been colonized. By the end of the 1970s mink were widely dispersed throughout mainland Scotland south of the Great Glen. Since then expansion appears to have slowed but the species is gradually spreading northwards up the east and west coasts (Figure 14.4). An isolated record of Mink at Kinlochbervie, in north-west Scotland, may be associated with an observation of an individual leaving a trawler which had travelled from the Isle of Lewis (D. O'Driscoll, personal communication). In the Western Isles Mink have colonized all of Lewis and Harris but have yet to extend significantly further southwards. In the Inner Hebrides Mink have been recorded on Mull since 1990. A small population appears to have become established on Islay since 1987 and there have been unconfirmed reports of Mink on Jura. The rutting migration in spring and the dispersal of young in autumn, with animals moving 10–45 km, facilitate their spread.

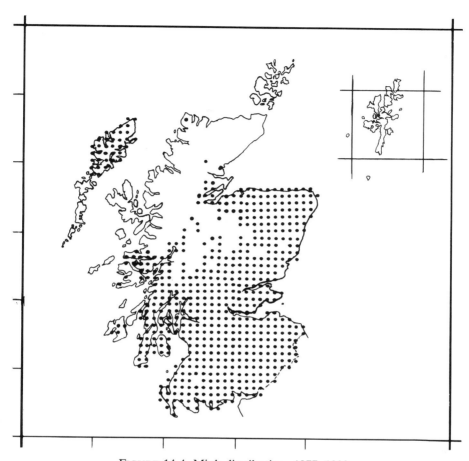

FIGURE 14.4. Mink distribution, 1977–1992

Resident adults exploit home ranges of 1–6 km with little intersexual overlap. Breeding occcurs in late winter and the four to six young are born in the spring after a variable period of delayed implantation.

Mink are opportunistic feeders exploiting a wide range of aquatic and terrestrial prey. Their marked dimorphism (males *ca* 1.1 kg; females *ca*. 0.6 kg) enables the sexes to exploit different habitats and food supplies. Male Mink, in particular, may spend long periods away from water hunting large prey such as rabbits. In Scotland they range from sea lochs and estuaries to high mountain burns and lochans (0–717 m; Green and Green, 1987). Most are dark brown, but small numbers of Mink showing the fancy colours bred for the fur trade still occur.

Despite predictions of ecological disaster, the impact of Mink on indigenous species has been mixed. Craik (1990) reported predation of breeding seabirds in Argyll and Woodroffe *et al.* (1990) believed that Mink threatened the survival of Water Voles in Yorkshire, but Birks (1986) considered that mink have not caused a significant decline in the numbers of any prey species. The impact of Mink upon Water Voles in Scotland is uncertain (Strachan and Jefferies, 1992). It had been suggested that Mink were a factor in the decline of the Otter, but this pre-dated the expansion of Mink while the Otter's present recovery parallels the continuing growth of the Mink population. Wise *et al.* (1981) considered that interspecific competition for food was unlikely and Green *et al.* (1984) showed that dens may be shared by both species. Observations of a Mink attempting to steal food from an Otter family (P. Collin, personal communication) or eating scraps dropped by Otter cubs (personal observation) also suggest a relatively relaxed interrelationship.

For better or worse, the Mink is now an established member of the Scottish fauna since trapping has proved to be effective only at a local level. Britain is unusual, in Europe, in not possessing a native Mink species and this has undoubtedly contributed to the speed and completeness of its assimilation.

ACKNOWLEDGEMENTS

We are grateful to Henry Arnold of the Biological Records Centre, Dr J. Gibson of the Clyde Branch, Scottish Wildlife Trust, the Royal Museum of Scotland, the curators of the museums of Perth, Inverness, Dundee, Kelvingrove and Hawick, the staff of Forest Enterprise, members of the Scottish Wildlife Trust and all the individuals who have sent us records used in compiling distribution maps. Murray Welsh of the Scottish Natural Heritage Maps Office assisted in the preparation of the diagrams.

REFERENCES

Birks, J. (1986). *Mink*, Anthony Nelson, Oswestry.
Chanin, P. R. F. and Jefferies, D. J. (1978). "The decline of the otter *Lutra lutra* in Britain: an analysis of hunting records and discussion of causes", *Biological Journal of the Linnean Society*, **10**, 305–328.
Chapman, P. J. and Chapman, L. L. (1982). *Otter Survey of Ireland*, The Vincent Wildlife Trust, London.
Churchfield, S. (1986). *Shrews*, Anthony Nelson, Oswestry.
Corbet, G. B. (1966). "Records of mammals and their ectoparasites from four Scottish islands", *Glasgow Naturalist*, **18**, 426–434.
Corbet, G. B. and Harris, S. J. (Eds) (1991). *The Handbook of British Mammals*, 3rd edition, Blackwell Scientific Publications, Oxford.
Craik, J. C. A. (1990). "The price of mink", *Scottish Bird News*, **3**, 4–5.
Cuthbert, J. H. (1973). "The origin and distribution of feral mink in Scotland", *Mammal Review*, **3**, 97–103.
Gibson, J. A. (1986). "Recent changes in the status of some Clyde vertebrates", *Proceedings of the Royal Society of Edinburgh*, **90B**, 415–467.
Gibson, J. A. (1990). "Some recent notes on Bute mammals", *Transactions of the Buteshire Natural History Society*, **23**, 65–79.
Green, J. and Green, R. (1980). *Otter Survey of Scotland 1977–1979*, The Vincent Wildlife Trust, London.
Green, J. and Green, R. (1987). *Otter Survey of Scotland 1984–1985*, The Vincent Wildlife Trust, London.
Green, J., Green, R. and Jefferies, D. J. (1984). "A radio-tracking survey of otters *Lutra lutra* on a Perthshire river system", *Lutra*, **27**, 85–145.
Jefferies, D. J., Morris, P. A. and Mulleneux, J. E. (1989). "An enquiry into the changing status of the water vole *Arvicola terrestris* in Britain", *Mammal Review*, **19**, 111–131.
Mason, C. F., Macdonald, S. M., Bland, D. H. and Ratford, J. (1992). "Organochlorine pesticide and PCB contents in otter (*Lutra lutra*) scats from Western Scotland", *Water, Air and Soil Pollution*, **64**, 617–626.

Strachan, R. and Jefferies, D. J. (1992). *The Water Vole Arvicola terrestris in Britain 1989–1990: Its Distribution and Changing Status*, The Vincent Wildlife Trust, London.

Wise, M. H., Linn, I. and Kennedy, C. (1981). "A comparison of the feeding biology of mink *Mustela vison* and otter *Lutra lutra*", *Journal of Zoology*, **195**, 181–213.

Woodroffe, G. L., Lawton, J. H. and Davidson, W. L. (1990). "The impact of feral mink *Mustela vison* on watervoles *Arvicola terrestris* in the North Yorkshire Moors National Park", *Biological Conservation*, **51**, 49–62.

15

Archaeology

T. N. DIXON

Scottish Trust for Underwater Archaeology, Department of Archaeology, University of Edinburgh, Edinburgh, EH8 9JZ, UK

INTRODUCTION

Exploitation of the freshwater environment has been taking place since Scotland was first inhabited about 10 000 years ago. Inland waters have been an important resource serving as habitat, food source, refuge, means of trade and transport, and source of water for power and for consumption. Much of the evidence for these activities can be seen around the edges of lochs and along the banks of rivers but even more evidence, particularly from the earlier periods, is preserved beneath the waters. Underwater archaeological techniques need to be employed to examine fully and record these submerged remains.

There is a significant gap in the archaeological record of Scotland. The Royal Commission on the Ancient and Historical Monuments of Scotland has, since the 19th century, systematically surveyed archaeological remains on land and produced the results in the form of Inventories. Unfortunately, due to the problems of working under water in the past no such survey of submerged remains has been carried out and it is not possible to quantify the number and range of types of submerged sites and scattered artefacts.

Underwater archaeology is not a new concept within the discipline of archaeology but it is only just beginning to receive serious consideration by the profession. An "out of sight, out of mind" attitude may be attributed not only to the different parameters associated with working under water, but also to different laws pertaining to some classes of material remains, particularly those in the marine environment. These differences and a general lack of awareness have resulted in the disparate handling of archaeological remains found on land and under water. Despite these differences, important archaeological material found under water should receive no less attention and protection than such material found on land. This chapter seeks to outline the submerged freshwater archaeological resource and threats to it in Scotland and to demonstrate the need for better protection and management.

The Fresh Waters of Scotland: A National Resource of International Significance
Edited by P. S. Maitland, P. J. Boon and D. S. McLusky. © 1994 John Wiley & Sons Ltd

ARCHAEOLOGICAL INTEREST

Unfortunately, archaeology has traditionally neglected latter periods of the more modern past and some of the most massive modifications to freshwater bodies, such as hydro-electric power schemes and reservoir construction, have taken place in the last 200 years. The situation is changing with the rise in interest of post-mediaeval and industrial archaeology, but still there has been insufficient support to record and analyze most remains of this kind in the Scottish landscape. Many important structures in the form of mills, canals and other waterside facilities are being demolished or filled in as being of no importance.

Evidence of early use of lochs often came to light when later work was being carried out. In the 19th century lochs were often dredged for marl extraction, drained to create more pasture land, or lowered and raised for the improvement of fishing and the building of mills. During this work the remains of crannogs, canoes, fish traps and many hoards and artefacts were discovered and recorded. The remains of the 19th century developments are now of archaeological interest and are being both discovered and destroyed by modern exploitation of lochs.

THE USE OF FRESH WATERS

Lochs as refuges

It is not surprising that the lochs of Scotland were used as refuges in times of trouble. There are early references by Roman writers to "natives who disappeared into the bogs where they stayed up to the neck in water for days until the enemy left". It is more likely that they hid on artificial islands.

Loch Ternait near Arisaig, Inverness-shire, has the remains of an artificial island which is referred to in later history:

> Those accused of crimes from Lismore or Mull or neighbouring places, if they got permission from the Chief of Ardtornish to reside forty-eight hours on the island, were free from any liability to punishment. The island was thus a sanctuary – hence name Tearnait or Tearneach Inaid, "place of safety". (Blundell, 1913).

On the Isle of Bute there is a small loch which was noted as early as 1812 as being a refuge. MacKinlay in 1860 referred to events from his past:

> There is a small mossy lake, called Dhu-Loch, situated in a narrow valley in the middle of that strong tract of hill-ground extending from the Dun-hill of Barone to Ardscalpsie Point, to which valley, it is said, the inhabitants of Bute were wont to drive their cattle in times of danger. (MacKinlay, 1860).

In this loch he discovered the remains of a crannog (see later section) with substantial numbers of structural timbers similar to hundreds of other sites discovered throughout Scotland during the 19th and 20th centuries.

Canals

The most important period of canal construction in Scotland was in the 18th century (Butt, 1967). While the Caledonian, Crinan, Forth and Clyde and Union Canals are

FIGURE 15.1. The so-called "Viking Canal" which joins the small Loch na h-Airde to the sea.
Photograph: T. N. Dixon

well known, there were many much smaller canals built and planned throughout the country. Many of them were not economically viable and eventually almost all of them gave way to cheaper road transport. Evidence of canalization from an earlier period is seen on the Isle of Skye where there is a structure known as the Viking Canal (Figure 15.1). The canal is only about 200 m long and joins a small loch to the sea. The canal is reputed to have been built by the MacAskills who lived nearby but there is no direct evidence that they constructed it. The area is relatively isolated now but there is evidence in the vicinity of burial monuments and settlements from the Neolithic, Bronze and Iron Ages.

River crossings

The number, type and antiquity of river crossings in Scotland is not known since there has never been a complete survey of them. Many bridges were built in the 18th century for military purposes, but the Romans are assumed to have constructed bridges across a number of major rivers 1500 years earlier (Martin, 1992). The Roman fort at Carpow on the south shore of the Tay near Newburgh, Fife, was possibly the south end of a pontoon bridge, and the remains of a Roman bridge could still be seen in the River Tweed near Melrose during the 18th century.

Before the construction of bridges, many rivers had fording places. These can often still be seen near bridges that superseded them. A good example is a well-constructed ford beside the bridge in the main street of Aberfeldy, Perthshire. Fords would have been constructed from the earliest periods but dating them is difficult.

Water-powered mills in Scotland

Many mills utilized water as a power source in Scotland and the subject is adequately covered by Shaw (1984). He covers the period 1550–1870, which includes the times of greatest impact of water power, and he considers the complete range of functions from grain and textile mills to the use of water wheels in the drainage of mines and in other industries.

It is worth considering horizontal mills and their use before the period covered by Shaw's work. Shaw points to the lack of evidence for the dating of the introduction of these early horizontal mills in Scotland although he refers briefly to an Irish reference which suggests that they may be as early as the 3rd century AD. Horizontal mills are found in large numbers in the Western Isles but they have not been systematically surveyed or examined archaeologically. Often more than one mill is supplied by the same loch and in the case of Loch Bharabhat, Cnip, Isle of Lewis, there are the remains of five mills in the ravine leading from the loch to the beach below. The loch outlet has been altered in the past with the original outflow being dammed and another cut through bedrock so that the flow of water could be regulated by a sluice.

Evidence from the excavation of an island dun in the loch (see below) suggests that an ancillary building to the dun was partly drowned by rising water level which could be accounted for by the alterations to the outlet. However, radiocarbon dates from the submerged structure place it in the first centuries BC/AD which is the traditional period of such structures. Horizontal mills, on the other hand, have not been dated to such an early period in Scotland or Ireland. While more work is required to clarify fully the situation in Loch Bharabhat it seems likely that the mills originated in the first half of the first millennium AD.

In some cases the mills fed by Loch Bharabhat still have the stones *in situ* and local tradition, referring to the last century, talks of a noise like thunder coming from the ravine when the mills were operating. Such continuity of use is probably not surprising in the Western Isles where traditions are long-standing. It is interesting that the remains of a hand-operated rotary quern were discovered in the submerged structure, representing the small-scale methods used before the development of the horizontal mills.

Fishing stations

The remains of fish traps can be seen at the sea end of many rivers, for example in the Western Isles, where they are manifested as lines of walling leading from both banks to the middle of the river with a narrow gap left where the walls would otherwise join. The antiquity of such features is not clear but the method is so simple that it is likely to have been employed from the earliest times (see Chapter 26).

Fish netting stations for salmon are currently used on a number of rivers, such as the Tay, and were more important in the past before salmon farming developed. The right to net fish in Loch Tay goes back at least to the 16th century. A tack of 1568, between Sir Colin Campbell of Glenorchy and Patrick Campbell, recording the rental of an area of land including an artificial island near Killin, states:

> And farther he [Sir Colin Campbell] sets to the said Patrick, his isle called Ilan Puttychan, lying in Loch Tay, opposite his lands of Finlarig, with power to build a stable upon the port of the said isle, for yearly payment of a sheaf of arrows, if they be required, also with power to set six small nets upon the loch ewis to the said isle . . . (Gillies, 1938).

In Loch Tay, fishing for salmon with nets was finally abolished, in favour of sport fishing, by the Sixth Earl of Breadalbane sometime between 1867 and 1871 (Gillies, 1938).

A different method of catching salmon, reminiscent of the river fish traps of the Western Isles and elsewhere (see above), has been reported:

> 2. *The McNab Salmon Trap*. – As has been said, the southern channel of the Dochart at Killin bridge usually passes but little water. It is rather narrow, and across its upper end has been built a wall of very large blocks of stone, some of them secured by iron bars. The result of this arrangement is that when the river is in spate any salmon that are then able to ascend the southern channel are stopped by the wall, and can easily be caught when the spate is over. (Cash, 1912).

It is interesting that the excavations at the Late Bronze/Early Iron Age site of Oakbank Crannog in Loch Tay (see below) have not produced fish bones or indisputable evidence of fishing, although a number of roughly circular stones with holes through the middle may be net weights.

Hunting lodges

A number of islands are marked on maps, or are referred to in documents, as Hunting Lodges. An example can be seen in Loch Laggan. In some cases the islands had been the major residence of wealthy families in unsettled periods, but when times became more peaceful they moved to larger more comfortable houses on shore and kept the island as a summer home or hunting lodge. This was the case with an island in the Loch of Kinellan, Dingwall, which was the home of the MacKenzies (Fraser, 1917) and with Priory Island, Loch Tay, which was the Campbell stronghold prior to the construction of Balloch Castle on the shore nearby (Gillies, 1938).

Transport and trade

Before the development of effective roads the lochs and rivers of Scotland were extensively used as routes for transport and trade. Major river systems such as the Clyde and the Forth were navigable by river boats into the hinterland. In the case of the River Forth, boats could proceed further than the town of Stirling. Several years ago a number of large pots were recovered from the River Forth near the village of Gargunnock some miles upstream from Stirling. An examination of the river bed, by Dr Colin Martin of St Andrews University and the author, brought to light more pots and potsherds indicating that a boat carrying wine, probably ultimately from France via Leith, was plying the river taking full wine jars to the farms, hamlets and castles along the river and picking up empty jars in return. Apparently the boat had capsized, losing some of its cargo in the process. The pots were dated to the 17th century and clearly the river was regularly used for transport at that time. It seems more than likely that it would have been used for similar purposes prior to that period.

Steamships were used for passenger transport, as well as freight, on the lochs throughout the 19th century and well into the 20th century. Numerous piers and docking facilities can be seen on the shores of larger lochs and the remains of steamships are still lying on the bottom of many.

Evidence of use of Scottish rivers and lochs for transport in the past comes from the large number of dugout canoes which have been discovered. There are records of 150 examples (Mowat, personal communication).

Ritual

In some cases the canoes indicate purposes other than mere transport. For example, a single-piece dugout canoe 45 feet (13.7m) long was discovered in the 19th century in Loch Arthur (also called Loch Lotus), Kirkcudbright (Gillespie, 1874). The canoe had an animal head prow. Loch Arthur is very small now and, according to the height above water of a crannog in the loch, it does not seem to have been much bigger in the past. The form of the boat and its length suggest that it may have been used for ritual purposes as it would have been of little use for mundane transport in a small loch.

Other evidence of ritual comes from Carlingwark Loch, near Castle Douglas, where an iron cauldron was discovered (Stuart, 1865). It contained a large number of iron utensils and tools which are considered to have been a ritual deposit as scrap iron is not re-usable in the same manner that bronze is. Another hoard, this time of bronze, was discovered in Duddingston Loch in Edinburgh in the 19th century and this is also believed to have been a ritual deposit (Chambers, 1851). While it is not possible to outline clearly the ritual practices of the prehistoric past it is apparent from the evidence of bog bodies which have been mutilated and deliberately killed before being deposited in bogs that watery rituals were relatively common in the Iron Age some 2000 years ago.

THE SUBMERGED CULTURAL HERITAGE

The submerged archaeological resource includes all cultural material under water. Scotland's underwater heritage is as diverse as it is widespread, making it one of the richest in the world. The range of material remains in the freshwater environment is outlined below.

Submerged cultural material is found in the inland waters of rivers and lochs and includes features such as wells, reservoirs and bodies of water created by damming. Artefacts and sites may have been deliberately deposited, accidentally lost, inundated, abandoned, constructed in the water or eroded from the loch shores or river banks. Means of discovery are often fortuitous and include observations by walkers, finds by fishermen and reports by divers. Less often, they are the results of deliberate search and survey projects.

Where search and survey is carried out it is not necessarily for the benefit of the archaeological record or for the public good. Treasure hunting and salvage are a growing concern in Scotland and have caused considerable problems in Ireland where crannogs have produced very rich finds.

Submerged structures and other features

Artificial islands were constructed in Scotland in the first millennium BC and the first millennium AD, and some sites were inhabited until the 17th century AD. There is evidence that island sites, totally artificial or modified natural features, were constructed as early as the Neolithic period (Armit, 1991). Few lochs have been systematically surveyed to establish the presence or quantity of sites. Loch Awe and Loch Tay, the only two which have been fully surveyed, produced the remains of 38 sites (McArdle and McArdle, 1972; Dixon, 1982; Morrison, 1985) and there are references to more than 400 others throughout the country.

Submerged settlement sites were first examined in the 19th century and since then they have all been considered under the name "crannog". However, given the range in type and date of artificial islands and submerged structures, the term requires further consideration. Overall site remains range in size from less than 10 m to more than 100 m in diameter. Survey, and possibly excavation, of these sites is required in order to formulate a meaningful classification system and to determine settlement patterns. Research undertaken by the Scottish Trust for Underwater Archaeology (STUA) and the Department of Archaeology at Edinburgh University is contributing to an inventory and classification of such sites, but the programme is hampered by a lack of funds and trained personnel.

Crannogs

Crannogs may be categorized as artificial islands originally built of timber, utilizing driven piles to create a platform above the water supporting a house or settlement. The Late Bronze Age site of Oakbank Crannog in Loch Tay (Dixon, 1981; 1982; 1991) is one example of this type of crannog. The site was inhabited for as much as 400 years and contains the remains of at least six phases of building and rebuilding. Some time after the site was abandoned, the mound of organic debris, which had built up around the piles supporting the dwelling, was systematically covered with stones. It is still unclear when the boulders were placed in position and by whom. Seventeen additional crannogs in Loch Tay and many others throughout the Highlands are also covered with stones.

Early references to crannogs

Crannogs and artificial islands have been studied in Scotland since the 19th century and even before then they were recorded in the Old and New Statistical Accounts. The earliest references from the OSA are merely observations made by local clergy but even these make it clear that the sites were recognized as the dwelling places of ancient people. Most of the descriptions are cursory but occasionally it is clear that the observer took to the water to visit the site. It was noted that timbers could be seen in the water around a site in Lochrutton and, since the site is some 200 m from the loch shore, it must have been visited by the observer (Sinclair, 1791).

Many crannogs came to light throughout the 19th century as this was a time of land improvements when small lochs were drained to create new pastures. The second half of the 19th century was the most productive time for crannog research. The impetus for this work in Scotland came mainly from the considerable interest generated in Switzerland, where numerous lake dwellings came to light when the lakes in that country were unnaturally low due to a particularly cold winter in 1853/54 (Keller, 1866).

Oakbank Crannog, Loch Tay 1980–1992

In Loch Tay there are the remains of 18 artificial island dwellings which were inhabited by the people who lived in this area over the last 3000 years (Dixon, 1982). The sites are in a superb state of preservation because they are submerged in the cold peaty waters of the loch. One of these sites, Oakbank Crannog, has set a precedent as the first in Britain to be excavated under water.

At Oakbank Crannog, the remains of a Bronze Age house floor have been discovered. It is preserved with the bracken and ferns that the crannog dwellers laid down to make the house a comfortable place to live in. Around the floor are the upright stakes and piles, still complete with their bark, that supported the walls and roof of the house. Forty oak stumps mark the remains of a walkway which led to the shore.

In the bracken and ferns are many of the objects that the people used in their everyday life. There is pottery with burnt food still sticking to the inside, remains of the only pot discovered so far. It is clear that the inhabitants relied heavily upon wood to make their domestic utensils. Wooden plates and dishes, remains of a wooden cup for drinking, a wooden spoon, and a butter dish with remains of butter still sticking to the inside, have all been recovered. Agricultural practice is indicated by the discovery of a unique cultivation implement, and the presence of *Triticum spelta*, an early form of wheat, 500 years earlier than previously discovered in the north. Animal bones, food remains and sheep droppings with parasite eggs still preserved in them have been found, as well as a fragment of fine textile not suspected from this early date in Scotland. The stratigraphy of the site is clear and shows that it was initially constructed as a free-standing pile dwelling with open water underneath the platform.

The methods employed to excavate Oakbank Crannog were developed experimentally in the early years but they are now well established. Other sites are now being investigated using these methods and survey work is being undertaken throughout Scotland.

Island brochs and duns

Island brochs and island duns are widely distributed throughout the highlands and islands of Scotland. They consist of man-made and modified natural islands with a foundation of stones and the remains of a dun or broch on top, usually connected to shore by a stone causeway. They may have fulfilled the same function as crannogs but were constructed in stone in response to the relatively treeless landscape in which they are located. Examples of this site type are found on the Isle of Lewis in Loch an Duin, Shader; Loch an Duna, Bragar; and in Loch Bharabhat, Cnip (Dixon and Topping, 1986). It is possible that many of these island brochs and duns overlie the remains of earlier habitation.

Loch Bharabhat, Cnip, Isle of Lewis 1985–1990

Only one island site of this type has been excavated under water, and this was undertaken in conjunction with the land excavations at Dun Bharabhat on the Isle of Lewis (Harding and Topping, 1986; Dixon and Harding, 1988; Dixon, 1989a). The loch is situated at the top of a steep, 100 m high, rocky ravine which is reached by crossing a marshy plain. The remains of five horizontal mills (also known as Norse mills) are situated in the ravine between the loch at the top and the floodplain at the bottom. Underwater excavation has taken place on the remains of an Iron Age island dun in Loch Bharabhat for five seasons (Figure 15.2). This work has been undertaken in conjunction with dry land excavations of the dun itself with the ultimate aim of tying in, chronologically and spatially, the underwater and surface remains and structures.

Visibility in the loch did not, at first, seem to be suitable for serious, large-scale archaeological work under water. The water is only about 1.5 m deep and the bottom silts are so fine that they are easily disturbed (Harding and Topping, 1986). These conditions contrast with the deeper, clear water of Loch Tay, with its coarse, firm silts. The problem in Loch Bharabhat was overcome by moving carefully around the

FIGURE 15.2. Two diving archaeologists working in shallow water on the Iron Age island dun in Loch Bharabhat, Isle of Lewis. Photograph: T. N. Dixon

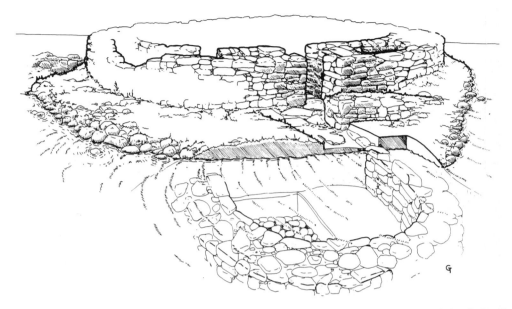

FIGURE 15.3. The relationship of the submerged structure and the Iron Age island dun in Loch
Bharabhat, Isle of Lewis. Drawing: G. Thomas

site, by using scaffold poles for supporting divers and equipment, and by laying a floor
made from corrugated roofing sheets on the loch bed near the working area.

The initial aim of the underwater work was to add the extra dimension of organic
material to the results of the dry excavation on the island dun. However, removal of
the bottom silts exposed another circular stone structure submerged in the shallow
water beside the island (Figure 15.3).

This building was complete with straw, heather and peat floors still intact and with
wood, bone, antler and metal objects *in situ* on the floors. It served several functions
in a series of phases, including use as a byre and a workshop. Unlike Oakbank
Crannog, a great deal of decorated and undecorated pottery has been recovered
(Dixon, 1989a).

Analysis of material from Bharabhat has supplied important information about
the way of life of the Iron Age inhabitants of the region and their exploitation of
the environment. They kept cattle, sheep and pigs but they also hunted Red Deer.
Surprisingly, the number of Red Deer bones surpasses that of the other species.
A small number of Grey and Common Seal bones were also recovered and exploitation of the nearby seashore is further demonstrated by a wide range of marine
molluscs including oyster, mussel, scallop, Common Limpet, Edible Periwinkle, Flat
Periwinkle and Dogwhelk.

Stone mounds

In areas where island duns and brochs are widely distributed, there are a number of
submerged mounds that do not support dun or broch structures. The two types are
sometimes found in the same small loch such as at Loch an Duin (Figure 15.4) and

FIGURE 15.4. Aerial view of Loch an Duin, Shader, Isle of Lewis, showing the well-developed island dun and the remains of a submerged stone structure near by. Photograph: D. W. Harding

Loch an Duna in Lewis where substantial island duns both have submerged stone mounds nearby. The relationship between the two groups is of considerable importance to our understanding of the development of settlement types and patterns in the region.

There is a clear impression in the two examples mentioned above that the substantial island dun/broch sites were preceded by the submerged mounds. Elsewhere, such mounds are the only site in a loch; for example, in Loch Airigh na Lic, near Stornoway. As there are no remains of stone buildings on the mounds it may be that they supported turf or timber buildings, or none at all. Alternatively, stone associated with buildings may have been robbed for the larger island dun/broch sites. Superficially, the mounds are similar to the remains of mainland crannogs.

Other submerged and partly submerged sites

Island mounds superficially resembling brochs and duns but of earlier or later date must be considered, as there is often associated material in the water. This proved to be the case at the 5000-year-old Neolithic site of Eilean Domnhuill, Loch Olabhat,

North Uist, where the STUA carried out test excavations under water and encountered a well-preserved hurdle, timber piles, animal bones, straw rope, and other organic remains below the levels reached in the land excavations. A segment of walling is submerged nearby in the shallow water off the island and suggests a complex sequence of occupation (Dixon, 1989b).

THREATS TO THE RESOURCE

All submerged cultural material in Scotland is at risk from a wide range of commercial, mechanical, chemical and biological threats. The preservation of sites in inland waters is challenged by fish farms, water sports, agricultural run-off, pollution and acidification.

Fish farms are a potential source of both mechanical and chemical damage. The infrastructure associated with fish farms, including boats and fish cages, can cause significant erosion and direct damage through collision. Raised nutrient levels and chemical additions for the prevention of diseases in fish can cause environmental damage to cultural as well as natural resources. Impact studies should be implemented in lochs known to contain submerged archaeological material.

The increase in water sports as a leisure activity is a growing threat to sites through collision and the effect of wave action created by jet-skis, water skiers and powerful motor boats. The general availability of water transport of all forms allows easy access to the island sites where campers and picnickers can inadvertently or deliberately cause damage. A crannog in Barean Loch, Kirkcudbright, provides one example of such a problem. Timbers at the water's edge and in the shallows were deliberately kicked out, damaging the timbers and exposing a section of organic material to erosion. Local residents attributed the damage to young campers (Dixon, 1989c).

The effect of raised nutrient levels from agricultural and forestry run-off of fertilizers now appears to be having a significant impact on the fragile timber and organic deposits of many crannogs. Historic Scotland launched a project in 1989 to examine this effect in lochs in south-west Scotland. Twenty timber samples were taken from six crannogs in Lochrutton, Milton Loch, Loch Arthur and Barean Loch. The timbers were visibly suffering attack from a wide range of micro-organisms (Dixon, 1989c). In Milton Loch, piles and other timbers, from a crannog excavated in 1950 (Piggott, 1953), were riddled with holes and damage caused by freshwater plants, snails and wood-borers. The laboratory results from the survey have not yet become available but provide important evidence of the need to carry out further survey and analysis of this nature.

The effects of pollution and acidification have not yet been quantified, but problems such as the severe algal blooms discovered in Loch Leven and other lochs may be as damaging to cultural resources as they are to aquatic and human life. At the time of writing, archaeological impact assessments have not yet been implemented for submerged freshwater areas of potential exploitation in Scotland, although this is beginning to be addressed in a limited manner. It is therefore not possible to quantify the destruction that has already occurred, and that which may be currently taking place.

Regional archaeologists are employed in only nine of Scotland's 12 Regions and their remit and expertise does not include the management of underwater remains. It is not clear that UK legislation, existing or forthcoming, will rectify this situation.

PROTECTION OF THE RESOURCE

Legislative background

It is not within the scope of this chapter to cover in detail the inconsistencies and failure of the legislation to protect our underwater heritage. The Ancient Monuments and Archaeological Areas Act 1979 applies to Scotland's inland waters and a significant number of crannogs have now been scheduled. However, few of these sites have been properly examined as there is no underwater team attached to Historic Scotland or to the Royal Commission on the Ancient and Historical Monuments of Scotland.

Submerged monuments record

Scotland's lack of an inventory of underwater archaeological remains serves to highlight the vulnerability of this aspect of the nation's heritage. Damage and potential dangers to the submerged cultural resource in the freshwater environment cannot be quantified until the resource itself can be identified and quantified. A survey of Scotland's inland waters is important to enhance the existing record of crannogs and other features. The size of the resource must be established to allow appropriate protection measures to be set in motion where required. The financial constraints imposed by the current recession may require the phasing of such programmes, but they could begin immediately. Remotely-operated vehicles (ROVs) and remote sensing equipment can be deployed in lochs where visibility is reduced by high peat content, while aerial photography is effective in the shallows of relatively clear lochs. The techniques of low technology survey based on snorkelling and diving practice are simple, inexpensive, and well-established (Dixon, 1982; Dean *et al.*, 1992).

Underwater excavation, whether motivated by research or rescue, will enhance a monuments record with information on site identification and interpretation. Material remains from underwater archaeological sites are normally very well-preserved due to the anaerobic conditions in which they are found. Excavations, therefore, almost can be guaranteed to produce valuable archaeological data in the form of structure, artefacts and environmental evidence. Underwater excavation, particularly in shallow water, need not be expensive; however, the costs of conservation and laboratory analysis of rich organic deposits is high. While the physical constraints imposed by diving and working in an alien environment may seem daunting, working under water has many distinct advantages over working on, for example, a drained waterlogged site (Dixon, 1991).

Raising awareness

Education and raising awareness are major themes for the development of underwater archaeology and the protection of the underwater heritage. Only by raising public awareness of the need to protect the increasingly vulnerable heritage will it eventually become socially unacceptable to damage, pollute, sell off, or otherwise dispose of archaeological material.

The Scottish Trust for Underwater Archaeology is an independent charitable organization formed to promote the research, recording, and protection of Scotland's underwater heritage. Towards realizing these aims, the Trust carries out surveys and excavations, provides advice and expertise, and tries to increase awareness of the underwater heritage through education, publication and exhibition. The STUA also liaises with statutory and other organizations, including environmental groups, in an attempt to ensure that underwater archaeology is considered in management and conservation strategies. Introductory and familiarization courses in underwater archaeology are offered at all levels.

Archaeology practised underwater should need no more justification than archaeology practised on land. The submerged cultural resource is an immensely rich and important aspect of the nation's heritage, yet legislation is severely limited and has been shown to be inadequate for the protection of a large part of the resource. The National Monuments Record of Scotland and regional Sites and Monuments Records allow land-based rescue surveys and excavations to be carried out in areas where known or suspected archaeological material may be jeopardized by development. Recognizing that an unquantified but well-preserved range of cultural material lies throughout Scottish fresh waters, the charting of the underwater heritage must be considered a priority and incorporated into current strategies outlining the way forward in Scottish archaeology.

Archaeologists and environmentalists share many common concerns, for instance in the areas of conservation and protection of the natural heritage. It is important that they work together to form national and regional strategies for freshwater management, where the interests of all freshwater users are represented.

REFERENCES

Armit, I. (1991). "Loch Olabhat", *Current Archaeology*, **127**, 284–287.
Blundell, Rev. F. O. (1913). "Artificial islands in the Highland Area", *Proceedings of the Society of Antiquaries of Scotland*, **47**, 257–302.
Butt J. (1967). *Industrial Archaeology of Scotland*, David and Charles, Newton Abbot.
Cash, C. G. (1912). "Archaeological gleanings from Killin", *Proceedings of the Society of Antiquaries of Scotland*, **46**, 264–285.
Chambers, R. (1851). "On ancient terraces of cultivation, commonly called daisses", *Proceedings of the Society of Antiquaries of Scotland*, **1**, 132–133.
Dean, M. *et al.* (1992). *Archaeology Underwater; The NAS Guide to Principles and Practice*, Archetype Books and the Nautical Archaeology Society, London.
Dixon, T. N. (1981). "Preliminary excavation of Oakbank Crannog, Loch Tay: Interim Report", *The International Journal of Nautical Archaeology and Underwater Exploration*, **10**, 15–21.
Dixon, T. N. (1982). "A survey of crannogs in Loch Tay", *Proceedings of the Society of Antiquaries of Scotland*, **112**, 17–38.
Dixon, T. N. (1989a). "Loch Bharabhat, the underwater excavations", in *Annual Report*, **35**, 19–20, Department of Archaeology, University of Edinburgh, Edinburgh.
Dixon, T. N. (1989b). "Eilean Domhnuill, Loch Olabhat; underwater excavations", in *Annual Report*, **35**, 21–22, Department of Archaeology, University of Edinburgh, Edinburgh.
Dixon, T. N. (1989c). "Crannogs in Southwest Scotland", in *Annual Report*, **35**, 28, Department of Archaeology, University of Edinburgh, Edinburgh.
Dixon, T. N. (1991). "The history of crannog survey and excavation in Scotland", *The International Journal of Nautical Archaeology and Underwater Exploration*, **20**, 1–8.
Dixon, T. N. and Harding, D. W. (1988). "Loch Bharabhat, Cnip, Isle of Lewis", in *Annual Report*, **34**, 19–20, Department of Archaeology, University of Edinburgh, Edinburgh.
Dixon, T. N. and Topping, P. G. (1986). "Preliminary survey of later prehistoric artificial

islands on the Isle of Lewis, Outer Hebrides", *The International Journal of Nautical Archaeology and Underwater Exploration*, **15**, 189–194.

Fraser, H. (1917). "Investigation of the artificial island in Loch Kinellan, Strathpeffer", *Proceedings of the Society of Antiquaries of Scotland*, **51**, 48–98.

Gillespie, J. E. (1874). "Notice of a canoe found in Loch Lotus, Parish of New Abbey, Kirkcudbrightshire", *Proceedings of the Society of Antiquaries of Scotland*, 1874, 21–23.

Gillies, W. A. (1938). *In Famed Breadalbane*, reprinted in 1980 by Clunie Press, Strathtay, Perthshire.

Harding, D. W. and Topping, P. G. (1986). "Callanish Archaeological Research Centre", *Annual Report*, **1**, Department of Archaeology, University of Edinburgh, Edinburgh.

Keller, F. (1866). *The Lake Dwellings of Switzerland*, 1878 translation, Longmans, Green & Co., London.

McArdle, C. M. and McArdle, T. D. (1972). "Loch Awe Crannog Survey", *Discovery and Excavation in Scotland*, 1972, 11–12.

MacKinlay, J. (1860). "Notice of two 'crannoges,' or pallisaded islands, in Bute, with plans", *Proceedings of the Society of Antiquaries*, **3**, 43–46.

Martin, C. J. M. (1992). "Water transport and the Roman occupations in north Britain", in *Scotland and the Sea* (Ed. T. C. Smout), pp. 1–34, John Donald, Edinburgh.

Morrison, I. (1985). *Landscape with Lake Dwellings*, Edinburgh University Press, Edinburgh.

Piggott, C. M. (1953). "Milton Loch Crannog I", *Proceedings of the Society of Antiquaries of Scotland*, **87**, 134–152.

Shaw, J. P. (1984). *Water Power in Scotland 1550–1870*, John Donald, Edinburgh.

Sinclair, J. (1791). *The Statistical Account of Scotland*, Edinburgh.

Stuart, J. (1865). "Notices of a group of artificial islands in the Loch of Dowalton, Wigtownshire, and of other artificial islands or 'crannogs' throughout Scotland", *Proceedings of the Society of Antiquaries of Scotland*, **6**, 114–178.

SECTION II
USING THE RESOURCE

16

Water Supply

T. D. MACDONALD

Scottish Office Environment Department, 27 Perth Street, Edinburgh, EH3 5RB, UK

INTRODUCTION

Fresh water is essential to successful modern societies, and a useful way to compare living standards of different nations is to examine the per capita consumption of water. Countries with a high standard of living show a high requirement for potable fresh water compared with poor countries. The ever-increasing standards of living in most countries and the increase in human population can make heavy demands on freshwater resources, and result in conflicting interests in available water.

The quantity of water required for domestic and industrial (including agricultural) purposes has shown no sign of lessening in recent years, making it necessary to consider the whole question of water resource and supply on a more integrated basis. Water conservation means the preservation, control and development of water resources (by storage, prevention of pollution or other means) to ensure that adequate and reliable supplies are available for all purposes in the most suitable and economic way, whilst safeguarding legitimate interests.

Precipitation is, of course, the initial source of water, and a study of the rainfall and hydrological cycle is a necessary preliminary to assessing the water supply potential of any area. Only a relatively small proportion of the total rainfall in a large geographic area is readily available for water supply; major losses occur from evaporation during precipitation, from the ground or open water and from transpiration from vegetation. Colossal amounts of water flow into the sea directly. Utilization of this available rainfall can involve collecting it as surface water (by intakes or pumping from rivers, or by piping from suitable lakes or reservoirs) or as groundwater (by utilizing springs, or by sinking wells).

Mountainous regions such as much of Scotland, where natural systems are oligotrophic, are the most suitable areas for utilizing existing lakes or establishing reservoirs. Waters in highland areas are especially suitable for domestic supplies in that there is less pollution than in lowlands. Also, the initial rainfall is higher in highland than lowland areas. Oligotrophic waters contain little suspended matter (especially algae) and require little filtration. Though the geographic regions most suitable for water supply bodies are often far from areas where water is most needed, the altitude

The Fresh Waters of Scotland: A National Resource of International Significance
Edited by P. S. Maitland, P. J. Boon and D. S. McLusky. © 1994 John Wiley & Sons Ltd

of such systems means that water will readily pass by gravity, obviating the need for expensive pumping.

THE EARLY YEARS

The development of water supplies in Scotland has a long history. Before they became a significant element, private rights to water were important as evidenced by the well-established principles of Scottish Common Law dealing with water and its use for a variety of purposes. In 1621, Edinburgh Town Council obtained powers from the Scots Parliament to take water from Comiston Springs four miles into the city. This was an isolated instance which nonetheless demonstrated a number of key factors which characterize public supplies.

(1) Water requires to be taken a significant distance to consumers.
(2) Water is taken using specific Parliamentary powers.
(3) Public supply requirements can affect existing rights to water.
(4) Public water supply can involve works on land owned by third parties.

Private enterprise did at times play its part in supplying water for public use. In 1804 Mr W. Gibb delivered treated water to the centre of Paisley whence it was distributed to consumers at a cost of one halfpenny a gallon. This was not an isolated example of private enterprise in this field and various private water companies operated in the second half of the 19th century. The main impetus to improvement came from the growing recognition that hygiene standards were necessary for public health reasons. In Glasgow, for instance, major epidemics of typhus (1847) and cholera (1848–49, 1853–54) led to the Glasgow Corporation Water Works Act of 1855 and thus to the taking over of two private water companies and the promotion of the Loch Katrine scheme. The challenges presented by the rapidly growing urban population at the time were many, but successive Acts of Parliament in 1833, 1892 and 1897 conveyed to local authorities wide powers to arrange for public water supplies for the consumers in their areas. These powers were not always exercised, as evidenced by court proceedings taken against councils in Pittenween and Galashiels (1874), Forfar (1876), Lochmaben (1893) and Dunbar (1913) for failure to provide a water supply.

Frequently the general powers available from these Acts were seen as insufficient and authorities sought private legislation to promote major schemes. Important aspects concerned the power to acquire water rights, the laying of mains and systems of charging.

By 1914, inhabitants of cities and towns generally had good public water supplies and about one third of those in the more rural landward areas were also served. Most local authorities acted independently but some combined, using Parliamentary powers, to form such bodies as the East Lothian Water Board and the Irvine and District Water Board in order to discharge their duties jointly.

Up to 1939 there had been little attention paid by central government to the quantity or quality of supplies but, during the war, security of supply became a major issue and it was decided that all supplies should be capable of chlorination. Surveys carried out by the Department of Health for Scotland brought to light a number of less than satisfactory features – some administrative and some operational. The kinds of problem encountered included parallel mains belonging to different authorities with no co-ordination of supplies, inadequate small supplies – in terms of both quantity and quality – and untrained staff. Following a White Paper in 1944 (Department of Health for Scotland, 1944), the Rural Water Supplies and Sewerage Act of 1944 established a grants system to assist the provision of supplies in rural areas. Then came the Water (Scotland) Act of 1946 which laid the foundations for existing arrangements.

During the next 20 years, much was achieved by authorities in expanding and improving the water supplies in their areas. By the early 1960s it had become clear that further improvements were limited by the large number of authorities involved and the lack of funds. The Scottish Water Advisory Committee considered the arrangements for water supply throughout Scotland and reported in 1966 (Scottish Development Department, 1966). This report incorporated recommendations based not only on this study but on three earlier reports on Central Scotland (1963), Ayrshire (1964) and Renfrewshire (1966). There were three principal recommendations. First, there was a need to reform completely the administration of water supply authorities; many were too small with inadequate financial resources. At that time there were 199 water authorities, 13 of which served less than 1000 people. The solution recommended was to establish autonomous water boards made up of elected councillors from authorities in their areas.

The second recommendation was aimed at addressing a particular problem perceived for Central Scotland where there was an urgent need for a major water source to be developed on a scale beyond the scope of even the new regional boards. Here a Water Development Board was proposed as a vehicle through which such a system could be delivered. The Central Scotland Water Development Board (CSWDB) was the outcome of this recommendation and, with its two major sources at Loch Turret and Loch Lomond, is the sole surviving product of the Committee's deliberations.

The third main recommendation was for the new arrangements to be put in place by major primary legislation rather than reliance on the rather indirect powers of the Secretary of State to require authorities to combine.

The work of the Scottish Water Advisory Committee in the 1960s had a profound effect on the shape of the industry and the institution of the new Regional Water Boards was seen as very successful. With their independent sources of finance and focused duties they were able to bring improved management and professionalism to water supply, particularly in the remoter parts of the country. However, the success of the regional boards was to be short-lived, as was the respite of the Scottish Water Advisory Committee which was called into existence again in 1970 to consider the implications for the newly established boards of the Wheatley Report on the structure of local government.

In practice, the Committee's remit was constrained to a consideration of any problems likely to be caused by incorporating water supply back into the local government structure as one of the strategic functions of the new top-tier authorities. Two particular problem areas were identified in Fife/Kinross and South Stirlingshire/ East Dunbarton. In those areas supply arrangements paid scant regard to the new regional boundaries. Although a majority of the Committee favoured addressing this problem by creating an *ad hoc* water authority for the whole of Central Scotland, others felt a solution based on "added areas" would be preferred. This was the solution adopted, allowing one authority to supply part of another's area (Scottish Development Department, 1972).

During the late 1960s, with the establishment of water boards and greater integration of supplies, assessments were made of the resources developed for Scotland as a whole. At the end of 1968, for instance, it was estimated that there were 2273 ML d^{-1} available from water undertakings and that 2090 ML d^{-1} were taken in supply. Growth was thought to be taking place at about 2½% per annum.

This rate of increase was close to that generally manifest throughout the UK at the time, and implies a doubling of supplies in 30 years. The general rate of growth anticipated in the report by the Water Resources Board's Northern Technical Working Party in 1970 was 2% (Water Resources Board, 1970). Such growth was a common theme in the Board's reports on regional studies in England and Wales published over the next few years. The anticipated additional consumption was to come from an increased industrial demand together with further growth of water-using devices in the home.

"A MEASURE OF PLENTY"

A Measure of Plenty (Scottish Development Department, 1973) was the first comprehensive general survey of Scottish water resources. This report provides a useful general picture of water supplies at the time and, unusually, makes estimates of the scale of other water uses. The aim was to plan for the year 2001 when it was felt necessary to allow for a consumption throughout Scotland of some 4414 ML d^{-1}. Subsequently the Scottish Development Department (SDD), with the new regional authorities, established a regular system of update for the information on supplies. Initially this was done on a two-year basis but since 1975 information has been collected and reported on an annual basis. The questions posed in *A Measure of Plenty* were looked at again in 1984 and a further full scale survey was carried out in 1993.

It is worth recording here some of the salient features of the water services in 1971 as recorded in *A Measure of Plenty*. The wide disparity of incident rainfall and of population distribution throughout Scotland were highlighted. The average annual rainfall varies from 600 mm to 3800 mm while 85% of the population lived in the central belt with 5% living in the 50% of the country which made up the Highland counties. In so far as problems had either manifested themselves or could be anticipated, these were felt to concern the populous central belt.

In 1973, public water supplies were drawn almost exclusively from surface sources – natural lochs, artificially impounded reservoirs and intakes on burns and rivers (Figure 16.1). Springs made a contribution but wells and boreholes provided relatively little. The major resources were located in the upland areas which were relatively unpolluted. It was estimated that non-industrial consumption ranged from 185 litres per head per day (L h^{-1} d^{-1}) in the North East to 366 L h^{-1} d^{-1} in Argyll with an average of 266 L h^{-1} d^{-1}. This is almost one third higher than the corresponding estimate for England and Wales. To this had to be added the estimate for metered consumption averaging 141 L h^{-1} d^{-1} compared with 100 L h^{-1} d^{-1} for England and Wales. All this amounted to a total consumption of 2129.5 ML d^{-1} against an assessed

FIGURE 16.1. The abstraction point on the upper reaches of the River Endrick, below Wester Cringate, where water is diverted to Carron Valley Reservoir – a major public water supply for Central Region. Photograph: Peter S. Maitland

total safe yield from all sources of some 2622.5 ML d^{-1}. This margin of some 23% took no account of the lack of flexibility of supplies which means that, in general, surpluses in one area could not always be transferred to meet deficits in another. A major contribution to improving overall flexibility was to be made by the CSWDB's Loch Lomond Scheme (Figure 16.2) which came on stream shortly before the survey was published.

Assessments were made of private abstraction and these were characterized as "gross" or "net" depending on whether or not the volumes abstracted were returned locally to the system from which they had been taken. The gross total was 10 441.8 ML d^{-1} while the net total was 132.5 ML d^{-1}. Electricity Boards used about 90% of the gross total for cooling and hydro-electric generation. These are the most recent all-Scotland assessments of such uses.

In the conclusions to *A Measure of Plenty* a number of pertinent questions were asked:

(1) Why was the unit consumption in Scotland so much higher than it was in England and Wales?
(2) Why was there such a wide variation in the consumption between areas with apparently similar characteristics?
(3) Is the measurement of supplies adequate to enable authorities to obtain accurate information about supplies in their areas?

FIGURE 16.2. Looking north up the River Leven to the barrage which now controls the level of Loch Lomond, from which water is abstracted for public supply. Scotland's largest loch is now a regulated reservoir. Photograph: Barbara D. Smith

(4) Should not potential schemes be identified well before they are needed?
(5) Is the balance of interest between water supply and fisheries properly struck so as to pay due regard to the requirements of both interests?

The main conclusion of the report was that local sources generally supplied and would continue to supply ample water for all uses – thus fully justifying the title.

THE ADMINISTRATIVE ARRANGEMENTS AFTER 1975

The Local Government (Scotland) Act of 1973 gave effect to the current administrative arrangements for water supply and in 1975 the new Councils assumed responsibility. As mentioned earlier, water supply, with other strategic services, became the responsibility of nine Regional and three Islands Councils, together with the CSWDB. The information presented in the tables in this chapter is based on the areas of these Councils.

The importance of the water supply function in the new Councils depended to some extent on the circumstances of the time. With the availability of the Loch Lomond scheme in the central belt, the development of Loch Bradan in Ayrshire, Phase 1 of the River Deveron scheme in the North East, and the Loch Glass scheme in Highland all being completed by the time the Councils took over, water supply was generally not a major priority for action. That is not to say that everywhere things were regarded as satisfactory; Tayside and Lothian energetically pursued developments at Backwater and Megget respectively.

The Councils continued the process of integration of supplies initiated by the Regional Water Boards. The average yield of individual supply sources in 1971 was 3.23 ML d^{-1} compared with 4.21 ML d^{-1} in 1991. In addition, Councils have continued to improve services and with the introduction of more comprehensive treatment systems there has been a growth in automatic control and telemetry systems.

NEW DEMANDS ON NEW AUTHORITIES

There were new pressures also coming to bear on Councils in regard to water supply. Just as the period 1962–1973 had seen a concentration on water resource planning and development in England and Wales, the period 1973–1983 saw a switch of emphasis to the quality of supplies. Scotland was not immune to these changes and the new Councils found themselves particularly concerned with the quality of supplies, their adequacy in quantitative terms having been well demonstrated. This new concern took two particular forms.

By its nature, the unpolluted upland water so favoured by Scottish authorities was known to have one characteristic acknowledged to be undesirable: it was plumbosolvent. As recently as the late 1950s lead pipe had been the normal material used in domestic plumbing although it was abandoned about that time. Expert committees met at national level to consider this issue and recommended that authorities survey and identify levels of lead to which their consumers were exposed. Authorities, having identified by survey the areas where high lead levels merited attention, were to address the problem by dosing supplies with lime to increase pH, and where this proved inadequate, by further dosing with orthophosphate. The ultimate solution was seen as lead pipe removal. This task has been tackled by authorities in a systematic way and results to date suggest that the campaign has been very successful in reducing exposure of consumers to lead in supplies, most of which are now able to meet the standard set in Regulations. This is not the end of the story, however, since there are now suggestions of a major reappraisal and tightening of the standard which could not be addressed by treatment of supplies but only by wholesale lead pipe removal. Such matters extend well beyond the concern of supply authorities but their success in reducing exposure should not be forgotten.

The other major issue which dominated the Councils' agenda in the early years was the impact of EC legislation. While the so-called Surface Water Directive (European Council, 1975) addressed the quality of raw water and the degree of treatment to be given in order to produce drinking water, the Drinking Water Directive (European Council, 1980) had a much more significant effect. The Directive came into effect on 15 July 1985. Hitherto there had been only a requirement for drinking water to be "wholesome", supported by the kind of guidance given in such publications as Report 71 (Department of Health and Social Security, 1935 *et seq.*). Until the beginning of 1990 the terms of the Drinking Water Directive were implemented in the UK by administrative means but the Water Supply (Water Quality) (Scotland) Regulations 1990 (HMSO, 1990) imposed for the first time a statutory code for the sampling and analysis of supplies, as well as setting a number of new standards not covered by the Drinking Water Directive. Councils were required to open public registers and produce annual reports on the quality of supplies in their areas. The Scottish Office Environment Department (successors to SDD) published a summary of the first set of reports in 1992 and a more comprehensive review of the second set in 1993.

DEMAND AND RESOURCES IN 1984 AND IN 1993

In May 1985 SDD, with the co-operation of water authorities, published a reassessment of *A Measure of Plenty* entitled *An Assessment of Demands and Resources at*

1984 (Scottish Development Department, 1985). This showed that in 1983 the total consumption was estimated at 2233 ML d^{-1} compared with 2129 ML d^{-1} in 1971. These supplies were drawn from resources with safe yields estimated at 3359 ML d^{-1} in 1983 compared with 2622 ML d^{-1} in 1971. This implies a reduction in the Resource Deployment ratio of 15% over the period. The growth in consumption of almost 5% fell far short of that planned for in 1971 as the upper limit. This was shown to be due, to a large extent, to a shortfall in metered demand associated with the industrial recession which had taken place over the period of the review. The whole question of demand prediction is discussed in the 1985 report in some detail and the drawbacks of extrapolation of trends were noted, particularly where no consideration was given to what particular use was to be made of additional water put into supply.

Reference is also made in the 1985 report to a study of domestic water consumption published by SDD reporting on a joint research project carried out with Councils in 1982 and aimed at answering the first three of the questions in *A Measure of Plenty*. The report, *Unmetered Domestic Water Consumption in Scotland* (Scottish Development Department, 1984) concluded that the median domestic water consumption was 120 L h^{-1} d^{-1} ± 15 L h^{-1} d^{-1} compared with per capita unmetered demand of some 304 L h^{-1} d^{-1}. The difference was taken to be "unaccounted for" water. Thus it emerged that the domestic consumption in Scotland was broadly similar to that in England and Wales at that time. A repeat study carried out in 1991 confirms this with a revised estimate of unmetered domestic consumption of 148 L h^{-1}d^{-1} ± 5 L h^{-1} d^{-1} in 1991 compared with per capita unit demand of 313 h^{-1} d^{-1}. Similarly the study established that there was no consistent variation in consumption due to area, type of housing or pressure of supply. The main part of variability was explained by the variations in the structure of households. Both studies also looked at individual components of use and thus established that the Scottish pattern did not vary significantly from that elsewhere in the UK.

This report on demands and resources addressed for the first time the levels of waste inherent in the assessment of supplies. Thus metered plus domestic supplies deducted from total demand gives unaccounted for water. From this, some 5% of total demand was to be deducted to give a general allowance for such matters as operational use, fire fighting and so forth. The remainder, in general the largest component of supply, was seen as leakage. This is taken to provide the answer to the second question in *A Measure of Plenty*; variations in demand in similar situations are to a large extent explained by differences in levels of leakage. This is thought to depend on such matters as the extent and state of the distribution system and pressure. The official guidance on levels of leakage which may be expected are given in *Report 26* (Department of the Environment and National Water Council, 1980). This weighs acceptable levels of leakage against the marginal cost of water in the supply under consideration. Given that the supply of water in Scotland is generally not limited by volume, then marginal costs tend to be low. Accordingly, the extensive operational survey and subsequent renovation recommended in *Report 26* found relatively little acceptance, although it does seem that levels of wastage are generally high.

In the course of assessments of future demand the report took the opportunity to look at individual components of consumption separately. Thus metered, domestic consumption and leakage were projected separately to give upper and lower values

TABLE 16.1. Public water supplies: average daily demand

(a) Total, potable (unmetered and metered) and non-potable supply 1971–1990 (ML d^{-1})

Year	Total demand	Potable			Non-potable
		Total	Unmetered	Metered	
1971	2129	2129	1389	741	0
1973	2196	2196	1402	795	0
1975	2212	2155	1424	731	57
1976	2245	2194	1464	730	51
1977	2279	2223	1470	753	56
1978	2294	2243	1493	750	51
1979	2301	2248	1495	753	53
1980	2237	2191	1533	657	47
1981	2262	2218	1588	630	44
1982	2246	2219	1568	651	27
1983	2236	2210	1601	609	23
1984	2199	2172	1537	635	27
1985	2198	2169	1540	629	29
1986	2243	2214	1602	612	30
1987	2194	2172	1553	619	22
1988	2205	2189	1576	613	16
1989	2248	2225	1571	654	23
1990	2301	2281	1645	636	19

(b) 1991 by authority

	Total demand	Potable			Non-potable
		Total	Unmetered	Metered	
Borders	35.7	35.7	24.4	11.3	0.0
Central	225.2	223.9	132.4	91.5	1.3
Dumfries & Galloway	74.0	74.0	49.6	24.4	0.0
Fife	139.8	139.8	96.5	43.3	0.0
Grampian	168.3	168.3	114.6	53.7	0.1
Highland	94.5	88.0	73.2	14.8	6.5
Lothian	278.5	278.5	205.9	72.7	0.0
Orkney	9.7	9.7	5.7	4.0	0.0
Shetland	12.4	12.4	9.7	2.7	0.0
Strathclyde	1059.9	1051.2	782.2	269.1	8.7
Tayside	128.0	128.0	90.8	37.3	0.0
Western Isles	12.7	12.7	11.2	1.6	0.0
1991 total	2238.7	2222.1	1596.0	626.1	16.5

Source: The Scottish Office Environment Department

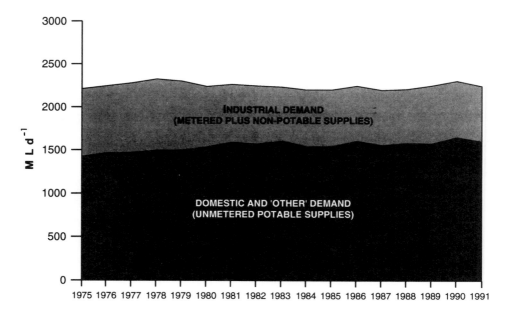

FIGURE 16.3. Scotland's average daily demand 1975–1991

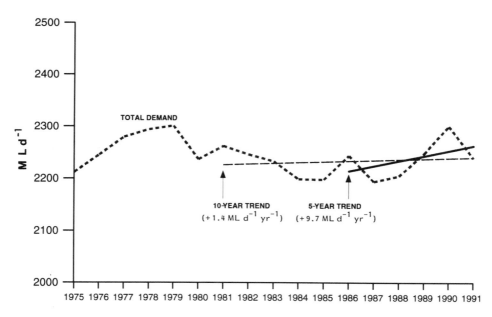

FIGURE 16.4. Scotland's total demand, 1975–1991, and trends in demand, 1981–1991

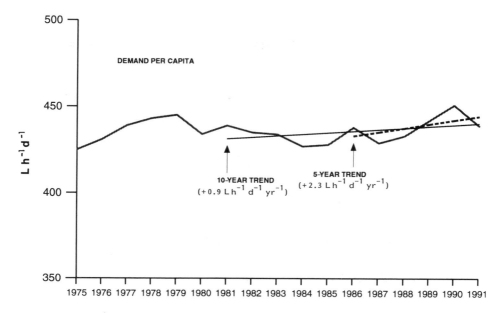

FIGURE 16.5. Demand per capita, 1975–1991 and trends in demand per capita, 1981–1991 (L h^{-1} d^{-1}: litres per head per day)

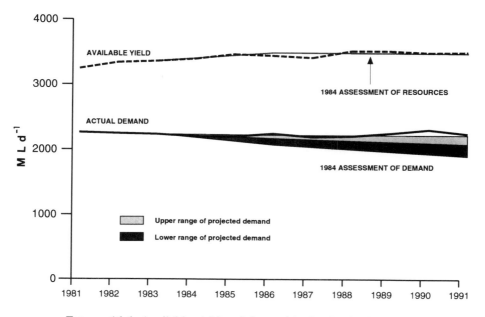

FIGURE 16.6. Available yield and demand in Scotland, 1981–1991

TABLE 16.2. Developed water resources in Scotland

(a) Number and yield (ML d^{-1}) of sources in each category 1971–1990

| Year | Reservoirs | | | River intakes | | Underground sources | | | | Total supply sources | | Total incl compensation reservoirs |
| | All[a] (yield) | Res[c]/lochs[b] (no) | Feed int (no) | Yield | No | Boreholes | | Springs | | Yield | No | No |
						Yield	No	Yield	No			
1971	2257	380		259	212	22	22	84	199	2622	813	
1977	2793	383		249	214	12	19	68	178	3222	794	
1978	2921	386		257	223	13	19	65	175	3256	803	
1979	2912	366	25	262	227	12	18	67	166	3253	802	
1981	2906	365	28	262	223	15	21	63	159	3246	796	
1982	2992	356	28	264	225	19	28	63	157	3338	794	
1983	2993	368	28	262	222	37	28	67	154	3359	800	
1984	3031	358	29	258	236	36	28	68	162	3393	813	
1985	2973	360	29	409	248	36	29	44	156	3462	822	
1986	2954	345	30	401	238	47	30	41	148	3443	791	
1987	2932	345	31	386	237	56	39	37	161	3411	813	831
1988	2988	345	27	415	252	51	40	61	169	3516	833	852
1989	2993	355	30	405	247	55	49	62	165	3515	846	864
1990	2971	357	30	403	246	55	51	57	160	3486	844	862

(b) 1991 by authority

| | Reservoirs | | | River intakes | | Underground sources | | | | Total supply sources | | Total incl compensation reservoirs |
| | | | | | | Boreholes | | Springs | | | | |
	All[a] (yield)	Res[c]/lochs[b] (no)	Feed int (no)	Yield	No	Yield	No	Yield	No	Yield	No	No
Borders	24	5	4	16	13	8	15	2	12	50	49	50
Central	189	15	0	4	11	0	1	1	1	195	28	30
Dumfries & Galloway	91	14	0	5	9	14	6	2	2	112	31	31
Fife	162	14	3	0	0	14	6	0	0	176	23	25
Grampian	18	5	1	213	13	12	2	16	84	260	109	109
Highland	138	61	3	110	119	1	2	6	34	254	219	219
Lothian	348	17	9	0	0	1	0	25	3	373	29	38
Orkney	18	10	0	0	0	1	10	0	2	18	22	22
Shetland	26	23	0	1	6	0	0	0	3	28	32	32
Strathclyde	1273	138	8	13	48	1	4	3	11	1290	209	215
Tayside	136	7	0	39	15	5	2	0	1	179	25	25
Western Isles	20	42	2	1	8	0	0	0	0	21	52	52
Central Scotland Water Development Board	540	2	0	0	0	0	0	0	0	540	2	2
1991 TOTAL	2982	353	30	402	242	55	52	56	153	3495	830	850

[a]Column 2 gives yield from reservoirs, lochs, feeder intakes and regulating reservoirs
[b]Column 3 is a count of reservoirs, lochs and regulating reservoirs (feeder intakes are counted in column 4)
[c]Compensation reservoirs are excluded except in the extreme right-hand column where they are included in the count.
Source: The Scottish Office Environment Department

as well as a principal projection. For 2001 the three forecasts for total demand were 2229, 1994 and 1712 ML d^{-1} compared with the estimate in *A Measure of Plenty* of 4414.2 ML d^{-1}. The average daily demand on supplies for the period 1971 to 1991 is shown in Table 16.1 and Figure 16.3. The lower part of Table 16.1 gives a breakdown of water put into supply by each regional authority. The trend in total demand is shown in Figure 16.4 and demand on a per capita basis in Figure 16.5. In both cases the 10-year trend is rather less than that in the last five years. Returns in the next two years or so will indicate whether or not there has been an increase in the growth of demand recently.

Available yield and actual demand for the last 10 years are shown in Figure 16.6. Also shown is the single projection made in *A Measure of Plenty* and the more sophisticated ranges of projected demand produced in 1984. Actual total demand in 1991 of 2238.7 ML d^{-1}is at the boundary of the upper range of the latter projection. A further assessment will be made in the 1993 report.

THE NATURE OF SUPPLIES

The individual sources of supply which Councils have at their disposal to meet demands vary very greatly in their nature and scale. Table 16.2 shows the breakdown of sources by safe yield and number as between reservoirs and lochs, river intakes and boreholes and springs. Since detailed records began in 1971 there has been little change in the relative contributions of these types of source. During the first 10 years of the period there was a decline in the total number of sources but, since 1984, there has been an increase which more than matches the decline. In terms of overall yield, there has been growth of a third in the total yield of all sources.

The lower part of Table 16.2 shows the most recent data, for 1991, by Council area. These indicate that the distribution of type of source is highly varied (Figures 16.7, 16.8). The reservoirs and loch sources tend to serve the more urban areas while the more rural areas frequently draw their supplies from simple stream intakes by gravity to basic treatment works, which provide little more than disinfection. In 1991 there were 830 sources of supply in Scotland, of which almost 90% have yields of less than 5 ML d^{-1} and about 66 have yields of less than 1 ML d^{-1}. In contrast, the 10 largest sources account for almost half of the total available yield. Details of these sources are set out in Table 16.3. As described earlier, many are based on augmentation of historic sources first exploited in the last century. Others, such as Loch Lomond, are entirely new. Whatever their age, the sources have been the subject of considerable investment in recent years in order to provide for efficient running with a high level of automation and a minimum of manned sites.

Details of water treatment and the nature of distribution systems are not given here but may be found in standard texts such as the Water Practice Manuals published by the Institution of Water and Environmental Management (IWEM, 1979 *et seq*).

THE WAY AHEAD

In 1992 the Secretary of State published a consultation paper on the future of water supplies entitled *Investing for our Future* (Scottish Office Environment Department, 1992). Responses to the paper were to be provided by 29 January 1993. The theme

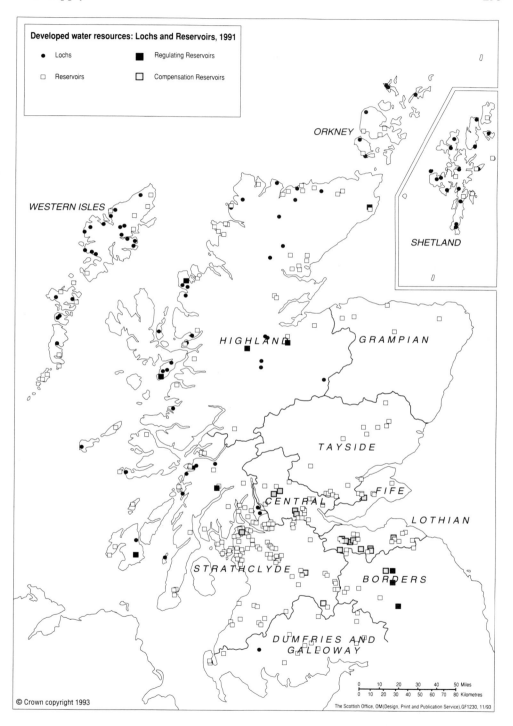

FIGURE 16.7. Developed water resources: lochs and reservoirs (1991)

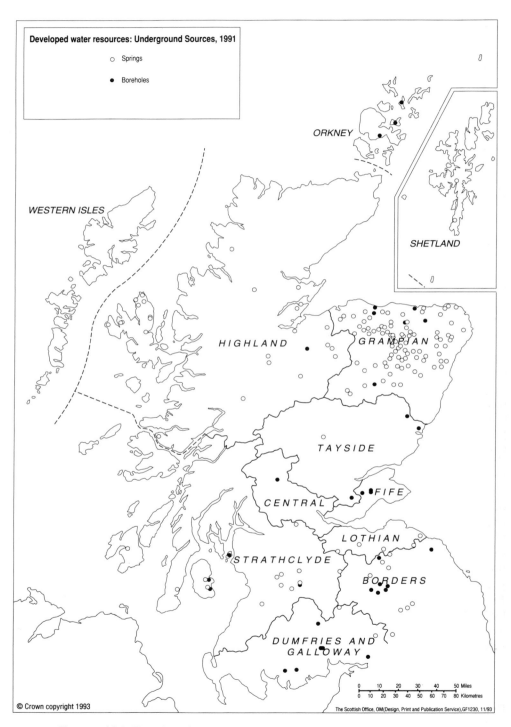

FIGURE 16.8. Developed water resources: underground sources (1991)

TABLE 16.3. Details of the 10 largest water supply sources in Scotland

Source (construction period)	Type	Authority	Area served	Yield (ML d^{-1})	Typical distance taken (km)
Loch Lomond (1969–1971)	Loch	Central Scotland Water Development Board	Central Scotland	455	50
Loch Katrine (1855–1926)	Reservoir	Strathclyde	Greater Glasgow	343	60
Daer (1948–1953)	Reservoir	Strathclyde	Lanark	129	46
Carron Valley (1935–1938)	Reservoir	Central	Central Region	125	20
Megget (1976–1982)	Reservoir	Lothian	Edinburgh	102	45.5
Loch Bradan (1970–1973)	Reservoir	Strathclyde	Ayr	91	54
Loch Turrett (1958–1968)	Reservoir	Central Scotland Water Development Board	Tayside, Grangemouth and Clackmannan	85	45
Glen Finglas (1958–1965)	Reservoir	Strathclyde	Greater Glasgow	82	60
River Dee Inchgarth (1980–1985)	Intake	Grampian	Aberdeen	75	2.5
River Dee Cairnton (1884–1886)	Intake	Grampian	Aberdeen	70	27

of the paper is that the proposed local government reform will lead to single-tier councils which are likely to be smaller than the existing water and sewerage authorities. Additionally, the demands for capital investment in water, and more particularly sewerage services, make it necessary to consider a range of specific options aimed at promoting the involvement of private capital. Decisions have yet to be taken but the years ahead seem to offer much in the way of change to Scottish water authorities. In carrying out their task the existing authorities have been aided in no small measure by Scotland's relatively favourable position as regards resources and supplies. Whatever form the successors to the present water authorities take, the new undertakings will find a service which is generally in very good shape.

REFERENCES

Department of the Environment and National Water Council (1980). *Leakage Control Policy and Practice*, Standing Technical Committee Report No. 26, National Water Council, London.

Department of Health for Scotland (1944). *A National Water Policy*, Command Paper Cmd 6515, HMSO, Edinburgh.

Department of Health and Social Security (1935 *et seq.*). *The Bacteriological Examination of Water Supplies*, Report on Public Health and Medical Subjects No. 71, HMSO, London.

Institution of Water Engineers and Scientists (1979). *Water Practice Manual*, IWES, London.

Scottish Development Department (1966). *The Water Services in Scotland*, Command Paper Cmnd 3116, HMSO, Edinburgh

Scottish Development Department (1972). *Local Government Reform: The Water Service in Scotland*, HMSO, Edinburgh.

Scottish Development Department (1973). *A Measure of Plenty*, HMSO, Edinburgh.

Scottish Development Department (1984). *Unmetered Domestic Water Consumption in Scotland*, ARD 14, Edinburgh.

Scottish Development Department (1985). *An Assessment of Demand and Resources at 1984*, Edinburgh.

The Scottish Office Environment Department (1992). *Investing for Our Future*, Edinburgh.

Water Resources Board (1970). *Water Resources in the North*, HMSO, Edinburgh.

17

Hydro-electric Generation

F. G. JOHNSON

Mott MacDonald, 15 Cadogan Street, Glasgow G2 6NW, UK

INTRODUCTION

Great Britain as a whole has relatively little hydro-electric power, compared with leading hydro-power countries, due to the absence of very mountainous regions and the fact that most of its rivers are small with modest flows and low gradients. However, Scotland has the most favourable conditions for hydro-power in Britain and over the past 100 years these limited resources have been well exploited. This was particularly true in the 20 years following the 1939–45 war, when a wide range of schemes and many interesting designs were developed and constructed.

TOPOGRAPHY, GEOLOGY AND CLIMATE

Topography, geology and climate have all encouraged development of hydro-power in Scotland, particularly in the Highlands. The topography of the Highlands is generally only suitable for low to medium head schemes but its deep valleys generally fall sufficiently slowly to offer good reservoir sites. Geologically impervious rocks mostly underlie the schemes and the virtual absence of limestone has led to little difficulty in finding watertight reservoir sites, although the U-shaped valleys and the prevalence of considerable depths of morainic drift have increased the cost of some dams. There are one or two recognized earthquake zones, such as the vicinity of Comrie, but seismic intensities are, on the whole, low.

The climate is favourable for hydro-power. Temperatures are moderate and evaporation losses generally small and reasonably constant from year to year. Rainfall is fairly even, with more in the winter than the summer months, varying considerably from up to 4600 mm at Loch Quoich in the west of Highland Region, to as little as 600 mm per year in the east, and generally matching the changing electricity demand over the year. The humid, prevailing south-west winds moderate the influence of winter and usually ensure an immediate availability of run-off, beneficially affecting generation output and an important influence in planning the reservoir storage to be provided for power production. The annual diversity of rainfall in Scotland is considerable, varying from about 70% of the long-term average for a dry year to

The Fresh Waters of Scotland: A National Resource of International Significance
Edited by P. S. Maitland, P. J. Boon and D. S. McLusky. © 1994 John Wiley & Sons Ltd

about 150% in a wet year. Such large differences made it almost impossible to provide, at reasonable cost, storage large enough to average out dry and wet years and instead reservoirs have been provided to accommodate seasonal variations.

A distinct characteristic of Scottish schemes is the necessity to divert the maximum quantity of water from other catchments into the main storage reservoirs, to make the schemes economically viable. Run-off is carried by free-flowing surface pipelines, open aqueducts and tunnels augmenting power production and resulting in very extensive networks of collecting waterways and diverted catchments on the schemes. In all, about one third of the total energy generated is produced in this way with the marginal cost of this additional output often being modest.

HISTORY OF HYDRO-DEVELOPMENT IN SCOTLAND

The first significant hydro-scheme in Scotland was commissioned in 1896 at Foyers on Loch Ness for the production of aluminium; it had a capacity of 4 MW (MW = 10^3 kW of power) and ran until 1967. The next two major stations were also built for the manufacture of aluminium and comprised the 23 MW Kinlochleven Scheme, commissioned in 1909, and the 80 MW Lochaber Scheme, near Fort William, which followed in 1928.

In the early 1930s, the building of the high voltage grid made possible large-scale transmission of hydro-power. The 100 MW Galloway Scheme on the River Dee, Kirkcudbright, and the 80 MW Grampian Scheme on the River Tummel, were built in the 1930s by private companies for public supply. However, no less than six schemes were rejected during the inter-war years.

In 1941, the Cooper Committee (1942) was set up to examine the utilization of Highland water resources for public use and reported that further hydro-power development could amount to about 4000 GWh yr^{-1} (1 GWh = one million units or kWh of energy); the total is equivalent to about half the output per year from the Torness Nuclear Power Station near Dunbar.

The North of Scotland Hydro-Electric Board (NSHEB) was constituted in 1943 and published its *Development Scheme* in 1944 (Figure 17.1) in which 102 sites were listed for possible investigation with a preliminary estimated output of 6274 GWh yr^{-1}. Between 1945 and 1965, some 28 conventional hydro-schemes were constructed comprising 66 dams, 51 power stations, 171 miles of tunnels and 103 miles of aqueducts (Figure 17.2). During this same period the South of Scotland Electricity Board (now Scottish Power plc) was established, but has developed very little hydro-power. There are also now a number of small Independent Power Producers involved in hydro-power generation.

In 1961, the Mackenzie Committee (1962) was set up to review electricity in Scotland. It reported that improvements in technology in thermal stations had tended to offset the rise in fuel costs, making thermal power more attractive than hydro-power. The Committee believed that hydro-power potential might amount to as much as 7250 GWh yr^{-1} with up to a further 1000 MW of installed capacity, of which some 400 MW might be developed. Although recognizing that water power was an inexhaustible asset, it considered that the economic argument should prevail.

With the change of economic criteria, and especially the rise in interest rates, no further conventional hydro-schemes were put forward after the rejection of two in

FIGURE 17.1. The "Development Scheme" prepared by the North of Scotland Hydro-Electric Board in 1944

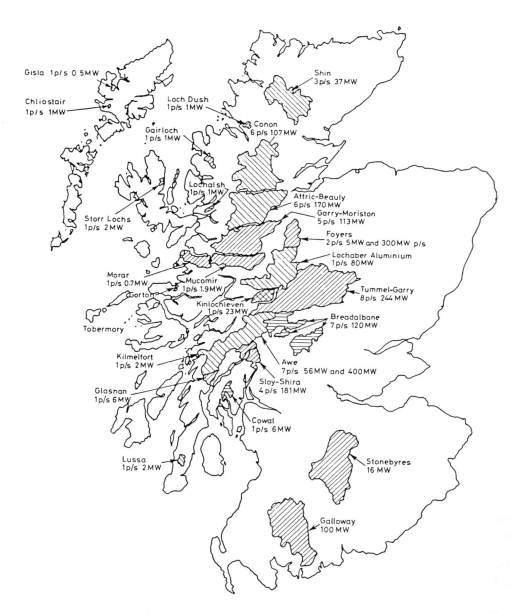

Gisla 1p/s 0 5MW

Chliostair
1p/s 1MW

Loch Dush
1p/s 1MW

Shin
3p/s 37MW

Gairloch
1p/s 1MW

Conon
6 p/s 107 MW

Lochalsh
1p/s 1MW

Affric-Beauly
6p/s 170 MW

Garry-Moriston
5p/s 113MW

Foyers
2p/s 5MW and 300MW p/s

Lochaber Aluminium
1p/s 80MW

Storr Lochs
1p/s 2MW

Morar
1p/s 0.7MW

Mucomir
1p/s 1.9MW

Gorton

Kinlochleven
1p/s 23MW

Tummel-Garry
8p/s 244 MW

Breadalbane
7p/s 120MW

Tobermory

Kilmelfort
1p/s 2MW

Awe
7p/s 56MW and 400MW

Sloy-Shira
4 p/s 181MW

Glasnan
1p/s 6MW

Cowal
1p/s 6MW

Stonebyres
16 MW

Lussa
1p/s 2MW

Galloway
100 MW

FIGURE 17.2. Developed hydro-electric schemes in Scotland, indicating the number of power stations (p/s) and their maximum output in megawatts (MW)

1965, until 1983 when the Grudie–Talladale Scheme in Wester Ross promoted by the North of Scotland Hydro-Electric Board (1983) was unsuccessful due to the pressure on the Public Sector Borrowing Requirement at the time.

An excellent and detailed account of the development of hydro-power in Scotland is given by Payne (1988).

TYPES OF HYDRO-SCHEME INCLUDING PUMPED STORAGE

For aluminium production, a scheme must produce approximately the same output every day, necessitating large storage reservoirs.

For public power supply, however, more output was originally required during daytime than at night, on weekdays than at weekends, and in winter than in summer. The NSHEB developed three, essentially different, types of schemes. Firstly, those sites in the south, near the industrial belt, were designed for peak demand loads, requiring modest reservoirs. Secondly, in the north, intermediate 30–50% load factor stations were built to serve the more local and mainly domestic and agricultural consumers via the expanding 132 kV grid and distribution system. These schemes required reservoirs storing typically 30–40% of annual run-off to cater for seasonal variations of rainfall and for the inadequacies of the grid at that time. Thirdly, small isolated hydro-stations were constructed, supplying remote areas in the north-west and the Islands, usually with back-up from existing diesel stations instead of expensive reservoir storage.

The existing Scottish schemes are generally of the storage type, in which water flowing from the catchment is regulated by a reservoir. Since the late 1970s, there has been a surplus of firm generating capacity from large fossil and nuclear power stations on the Scottish system, and this has allowed the simpler "run-of-river" type of scheme to be considered in which the output is related directly to the unregulated flow of a river. No large reservoir is required for seasonal storage, leading to major savings in capital cost. The schemes are simple in design, utilizing short steep falls in rivers and generally comprising an intake weir and headpond with very limited storage, a short underground pipeline and a small power station housing one or more turbines.

By the mid-1960s, most of the more economically attractive catchments had been developed, marking the end of the conventional hydro-power era and a switch to larger-scale pumped storage schemes. A major objective of these schemes was to improve the overall generation efficiency of the large thermal and nuclear stations which were then under construction.

Since the annual output of conventional hydro-schemes is relatively small, most of the schemes were designed for operation in daytime and, unless there is a heavy run-off, the stations do not generate at night, apart from minimum duties to provide compensation flows. The generating capacity can be increased if the machines run for a shorter period each day and the available water is used over a shorter period. This led to the development of pumped storage schemes where the natural flow is augmented by pumping during off-peak periods and the generation increased in peak periods (energy transfer), thereby greatly increasing the capacity of the station. Relatively small storage capacities are required in the upper and lower reservoirs amounting typically to 5–20 hours full load running.

FIGURE 17.3. Aerial view of Loch Awe (itself controlled for conventional hydro-electric production), with Cruachan Reservoir high in the hills above – the upper reservoir of the pumped storage scheme. Photograph: North of Scotland Hydro-Electric Board.

The area of catchment and run-off are not important for pumped storage schemes although advantageous if available. Topography and geology and not hydrology are the key aspects and the designer is no longer constrained by the flow from the natural catchment. The early stations were primarily designed for energy transfer to match in output the very large thermal and nuclear stations which are now the backbone of the electricity supply in Britain. Pumped storage plant is inherently more flexible than fossil or nuclear plant and later stations were designed to provide peak load and spinning reserve which enables the machines to be brought on to full load in as little as 10 seconds compared with thermal plant which takes hours from cold. However, without supplementary water from their own on diverted catchments, they use more energy than they produce.

The 400 MW Cruachan (Figure 17.3) and 300 MW Foyers Pumped Storage Schemes were primarily designed for energy transfer purposes. In the early years, a weekly operating cycle was adopted, with the upper reservoirs being partially refilled by pumping overnight to replace some of the water used for generation during the day and with complete refilling over the weekends (Figure 17.4). Both these schemes are really combined hydro/pumped storage schemes with considerable natural flow to their upper reservoirs, amounting to 12% and 30% respectively of their average annual generation.

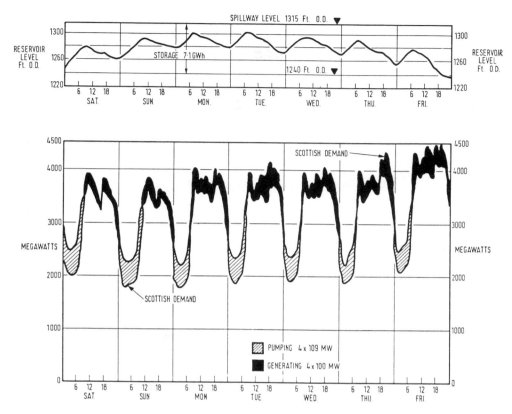

FIGURE 17.4. Typical weekly operating regime for Cruachan Pumped Storage Scheme in December 1969

Today, a weekly cycle still operates although the pattern of use has changed because (a) electricity demand now peaks around midnight during the winter months, and (b) a substantial proportion of electricity production comes from "must take" contracts.

HYDRO-POWER GENERATION IN RELATION TO OTHER FORMS OF GENERATION

Hydro-power and pumped storage are particularly valuable forms of generation because of their very rapid response and flexibility as well as the high availability and reliability of plant. In the late 1960s, immediately after the intense period of hydro-power development in the Highlands, some two-thirds of all generation by the North of Scotland Hydro-Electric Board was derived from hydro-power with the remainder generated using coal and oil. With the cessation of further development of conventional hydro-power, the proportion of hydro-generation delivered by Scottish Hydro-Electric has fallen until in 1991/92 it was only 25%, with 36% provided from oil and gas, 24% from nuclear and 15% from coal and other sources.

At the present time, the hydro and pumped storage plants meet, as far as possible, the day period load fluctuations, leaving the thermal and nuclear plants delivering as high and constant an output as possible through the day. During the day, the hydro-generation programme may need to change at short notice due to differences between actual and estimated conditions (e.g. breakdown of other generating plant, higher than anticipated run-off, weather colder or warmer than forecast, etc. (Figure 17.5).

The development and strengthening of the national grid, particularly in the north of Scotland, over the last 30 years, and the great flexibility of hydro-power plant has led to the hydro-schemes being run more and more for meeting peak demand,

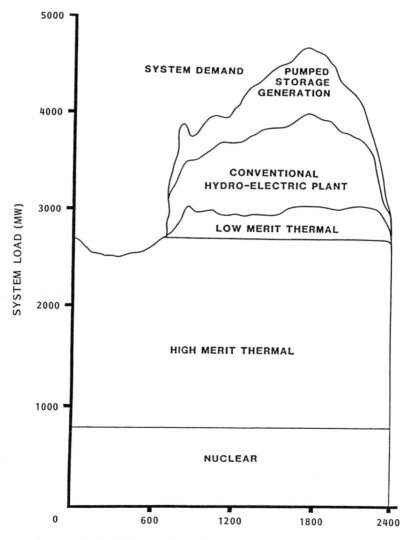

FIGURE 17.5. All Scotland Load Demand on a typical winter day

particularly in the breakfast and evening periods, rather than running them continuously over the whole day to serve the demands of the local area, as was the case when they were constructed.

An increasing amount of this flexible hydro and pumped storage generation is now being very profitably exported south of the Border. The wide mix of type of plant in both the recently privatized Scottish Electricity companies (Scottish Hydro-Electric and Scottish Power) results in a robust and flexible system producing the cheapest electricity in the UK.

WATER MANAGEMENT AND OPERATION OF SCHEMES

It is fortunate that the operational requirements for flood relief coincide broadly with those for optimum generation. For the main storage reservoir, procedures to optimize output have been developed based on the reservoir levels and the expected run-off from the catchments. These target storage curves make provision for both unusually dry and wet spells of weather. Under drought conditions, it is necessary that sufficient water is retained in storage to meet statutory compensation water and essential system requirements. Additionally, under conditions of heavy run-off, the aims are: to provide sufficient storage to ameliorate the impact of the storm, to spill as little water as possible, and to maximize generation. As a routine, the current reservoir levels are compared with the target levels and the projected generation for each reservoir computed accordingly. On a daily basis, the generation of each Hydro Group, which contains a number of schemes, is further refined by taking into account the estimated run-off depending upon the weather, the forward forecast, generation on the system and system requirements.

High run-off presents a different set of problems from those of normal system operation. Flood control takes priority over economic operation of the Power System. Each storage reservoir is assigned a "full generation level" which is aimed at maintaining sufficient freeboard to absorb heavy run-off without spill. Typically, the operation of a scheme is changed in a number of stages:

Stage 1 – Normal operation of the reservoir following the predicted run-off. If the reservoir level rises and reaches the full generation level, continuous 24-hour running of the generating plant is initiated, even if this incurs economic penalties.

Stage 2 – Continuous generation in an effort to reduce the reservoir level to maintain sufficient freeboard to absorb heavy run-off, although some adjustment may be made for prevailing and forecast conditions.

Stage 3 – If high run-off conditions persist and the levels continue to rise with maximum generation, before the spillway level is reached, diverted catchments are generally turned back into their original natural watercourses.

Stage 4 – During large floods, gate-controlled reservoirs are manned to give a further guarantee that the flood gates follow the correct sequence of operation, although in recent years, sophisticated remote monitoring has been introduced. Normally, an on-site automatic control system adjusts gate positions to produce the appropriate discharge.

TABLE 17.1. Operating levels (metres above sea level) for main reservoirs of Northern Group

Reservoir	Spillway level	Full generation level	% Storage at full generation level	Flood release level
Shin	93.88	91.44	75	93.42
Fannich	256.11	252.38	90	
Glascarnoch	251.69	246.50	68	
Orrin	255.96	250.55	65	
Monar	224.93	222.49	78	224.33
Mullardoch	249.02	247.80		247.80
Cluanie	213.97	211.50	85	
Quoich	201.20	198.00	85	

As a result of the experience gained over the past 45 years, it was found advantageous generally to operate reservoirs some metres below spillway level (Table 17.1). Although this results in slightly less head at the turbines, there is a much reduced spill and overall a much greater output from the scheme. In general, the aim is to retain storage at each reservoir capable of accommodating the run-off from 150 mm of rain falling on its catchment. At a number of the major reservoirs, which are critical with respect to flood flows downstream, an additional stage known as "flood release level" has been instituted in which the ground sluice of the dam is opened to maintain the necessary freeboard to provide the requisite flood retention capacity.

Compensation water releases are an important aspect of hydro-power development and are of two forms. Firstly, there are individual schemes where minimum flows are released and these vary for particular seasons of the year depending upon the time of the run of migratory fish. In addition, water is released in the form of freshets over periods of one to three days, in close collaboration with the local District Salmon Fishery Boards. Secondly, there are schemes in cascade where compensation water is released from the dams in an increasing flow down the valley. In these situations, endeavours are made to operate the lowest reservoir in the cascade in such a way as to even out the daily fluctuations from generation and compensation flows from the upstream reservoirs. Examples of this are Pitlochry Dam, on the Tummel–Garry Scheme, Torr Achilty Dam on the Conon Scheme, and Kilmorack Dam on the Beauly Scheme.

Compensation flows range between 5 and 40%, averaging about 10% of the long-term average annual flow, which is generally considerably more than the dry weather flow. On a number of schemes, the minimum flow requirement is a combination of compensation and generation flows. In these circumstances, the flow averages about 20% with the highest flow up to 45%. To meet compensation requirements it is quite often necessary in drought periods to cut down the running of the plant to conserve water by reverting to a "minimum duties" regime. It has also been found difficult at times to provide compensation flows during low run-off periods on a number of the schemes, and in later schemes provisions were negotiated to reduce the compensation releases to not less than the natural run-off into the reservoir; for example, discharge from the Awe Barrage during the summer.

FLOOD STUDIES AND MANAGEMENT

By the early 1970s, some 20 years of operational experience were available for many of the schemes and it was decided to undertake detailed appraisals of the flood magnitudes in relation to the operational and flood management procedures in force (Johnson and Cooke, 1975). Safety criteria were established for each reservoir and river basin and a general flood routing computer programme developed incorporating the techniques of the *Flood Studies Report* (Natural Environment Research Council, 1975) but refined to take account of conditions in the Highlands derived from actual operating experience. Some of the interesting results (Johnson *et al.*, 1980) of these studies were:

(1) Very long storm durations of several days were found to be critical in relation to reservoir levels for very large reservoirs with restricted discharge channels. In these situations, the volume of inflow is more significant than the peak inflow; for example, at Loch Lochy on the Caledonian Canal and at Loch Morar. In both these cases, prolonged wet spells are more severe than the shorter, more intense storms of comparable return period.
(2) The weather conditions leading to the most severe floods in the Highlands are typically those arising in the winter when heavy accumulations of snow build up over a few weeks, often accompanied by hard frost, and are followed by a deep depression with heavy rain over two or three days and a large and rapid rise in temperature. A recent notable example is the January 1993 Perth flood. This type of storm is much more severe than thunderstorms which normally give rise to the critical conditions for floods in other parts of Britain.
(3) Estimates in the *Flood Studies Report* (Natural Environment Research Council, 1975) for the return periods of very severe storms have been questioned in the light of the greater frequency of the comparatively rare events which have been experienced in the Highlands over the past 40 years and especially in the last few years.

More recently apparent abnormal rainfalls have been experienced. The possibility of climatic change, due to the "greenhouse effect", may be an important cause of the increased flooding which has arisen in this decade, for severe floods have been experienced in the Highlands in 1983, 1989, 1990, 1992 and 1993. Assessments of the January to March 1989 floods over the north of Scotland are striking. In January, twice the average January rainfall was recorded – equivalent to a 50-year return period. In February, it was three times the February average with a 1000-year return period; in March, it was four times the March average. Over the three-month period the rainfall was three times average and quite unprecedented.

The application of the refined flood management procedures has led to improved operational efficiency and flood control. This is borne out by the handling of the floods which occurred on the hydro-power schemes during January and February of 1989, 1990, 1992 and 1993. The schemes were operated in accordance with these procedures and peak flows at critical locations were below pre-scheme levels; thus the schemes played a significant role in impounding and controlling flows which otherwise would

TABLE 17.2. Comparison of peak flows (cu ft sec^{-1}) in Conon Valley during February 1989 storm with and without hydro-schemes

Location	Flow with schemes	Flow without schemes	% higher without schemes
Vaich Dam	720	1860	157
Glascarnoch Dam	4100	5490	34
Contin	7400	9920	34
Orrin Dam	3960	4640	17
Comrie Bank	15 370	15 440	0.5
Moy Bridge	24 570	27 810	13

have exacerbated the situation in the north; for example, the flooding of Inverness by the River Ness and in the Conon Scheme in 1989 (Table 17.2).

PERFORMANCE OF SCHEMES

Hydrology

With up to 50 years of operation of the main schemes, it is now possible to make an accurate assessment of their performance. Outputs have been closely in line with the original estimates for the schemes, as will be seen from Table 17.3, although there is now some evidence of outputs increasing in the last few years due to increased rainfall.

An aspect which is now having a significant effect on outputs from some schemes is afforestation of their catchments which may give rise to the following effects:

TABLE 17.3. Comparison of estimated and actual outputs of schemes

Scheme	Reservoirs in scheme	Original estimate of output (GWh yr^{-1})	Actual Average output (GWh yr^{-1})
Shin	2	137	158
Conon	9	438	438
Affric/Beauly	6	492	487
Garry/Moriston	12	379	389
Tummel	11	635	663
Breadalbane	7	377	340
Sloy/Shira	9	220	215
Awe	6	183	187
Others	14	56	63
Total	76	2917	2940

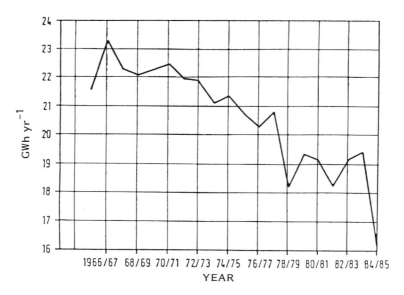

FIGURE 17.6. Fall in output with time of the Tarsan Scheme

(1) Water yields from some catchments have been reduced by 15 to 20%, probably due to the greater evaporation and transpiration losses from mature trees. This effect is illustrated by the fall in the output of the Tarsan Scheme with time (Figure 17.6). Yields from the Galloway and Glashan Schemes have also been reduced in this way.

(2) The deep ploughing which takes place prior to planting results in a higher run-off, greater floods and increased spill, along with lower drought flows which require increased discharges of water from reservoir storage to meet compensation flow requirements.

(3) Ploughing can cut through the vegetation/peat cover of catchments into the subsoil beneath, leading to the transport of much gravel and sand into aqueducts, thereby choking intakes, requiring more frequent cleaning, and resulting in greater losses of water and increased maintenance costs. This problem has recently been addressed by the Forestry Commission (1993) in their *Forests and Water Guidelines*.

Fishery aspects

Most of the rivers in the Highlands carry migratory salmonid fish; their presence and value (particularly Atlantic Salmon) and the statutory requirement to maintain stocks have profoundly influenced hydro-power development.

Fishery aspects are affected in at least four important ways:

(1) Dams obstruct the ascent of the fish to their spawning gravels and nursery areas, necessitating the construction of fish ladders or Borland fish locks.

(2) Reservoirs may inundate spawning gravels and nursery areas and increase habitat for Pike and other predators. On several schemes, fish hatcheries have been established to provide eggs and fry for planting out on alternative catchments and in streams not containing migratory fish (due to inaccessible falls) to compensate for spawning and nursery areas lost by flooding. The experience of these practices is mixed and their value uncertain.

(3) The regime of the river downstream is changed because of intermittent generation and, in some cases, by the diversion of catchments. This has led to compensation and freshet flows on rivers. Although there has been no proper evaluation to substantiate their use, it is believed that it has been of benefit on the Rivers Tummel and Conon.

(4) Dams present an obstruction to the smolts and kelts of salmonids descending to the sea and this has required extensive smolt screening to station intakes (required only at high-head stations) as well as the provision of special structures to facilitate their seaward migration.

Overall, the creation of fish passes (Figure 17.7), structures and screens has complicated the design of dams and power stations, adding considerable cost (e.g. 25% at Orrin Dam) as well as requiring a fairly high level of compensation water. However, fish counts although varying widely from season to season, as in nature, indicate that the development of hydro-power has in many cases not had significant deleterious effects on salmon stocks.

FIGURE 17.7. An adult Atlantic Salmon moving upstream passes salmon parr moving down through the viewing chamber of the fish pass round Faskally Dam on the River Tummel.
Photograph: North of Scotland Hydro-Electric Board

A recent study by Maitland *et al.* (1990, unpublished report to NSHEB) assessed the effects of hydro-power development on salmon stocks in the Awe System. Fish counts by electrical resistivity counter have been recorded at Awe Barrage from 1965 and there are rod catch data, for above and below the barrage, from 1920. Analysis of the data produced the following conclusions:

(1) The counter data are reliable and provide a good approximation to the true numbers of salmon passing through the barrage into Loch Awe. Over the study period (1965–86), an accuracy of over 90% was achieved.
(2) The rod catch data are limited in value because of the absence of information on angling effort and efficiency.
(3) There is no evidence that the Awe Barrage has had a detrimental impact on local salmon fisheries. Catches indicate that, on average, the numbers taken in the two decades after the construction of the barrage are approximately the same as the two decades before it.
(4) In the period 1965–86, there was no positive or negative trend in abundance of salmon.

The fish counts at Awe Barrage and Aigas Dam on the River Beauly are shown in Figures 17.8 and 17.9 and illustrate two typical schemes where fish stocks do not

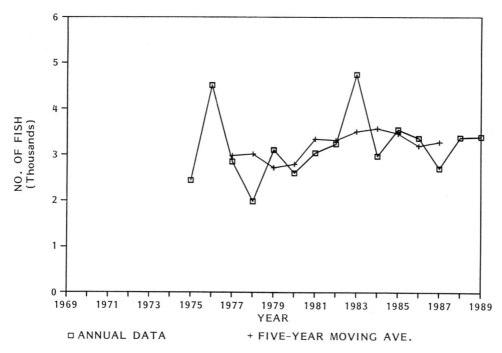

FIGURE 17.8. Fish counts at Awe Barrage on Loch Awe

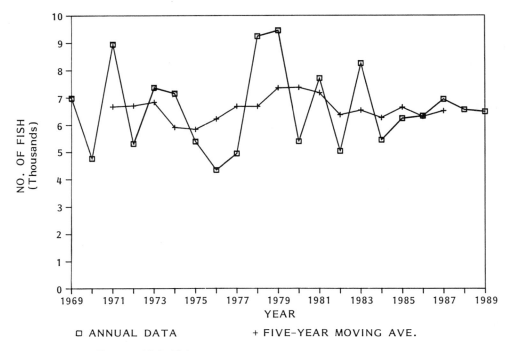

FIGURE 17.9. Fish counts at Aigas Dam on the River Beauly

appear to have diminished. However, it should be pointed out that counts on other systems (e.g. Lochy, Lairg, Morar) have declined – for reasons which are uncertain.

Environmental aspects

During the late 1930s and 1940s, there were real fears about the effects of hydro-power development on the environment (e.g. visual impact, new roads, drawdown, etc.), particularly since nearly all the schemes were located in Areas of Outstanding Natural Beauty (AONBs). To address these fears, statutory Fisheries and Amenity Committees were set up to advise the NSHEB and the Secretary of State on these aspects and much was achieved. The Amenities Committee was disbanded in 1982.

The first two schemes – Sloy and Tummel–Garry – were the subject of Public Inquiries, but thereafter the Board managed to reach agreement with the objectors on most schemes and only two further Public Inquiries were held. As a result of this policy, many of the schemes are not designed for optimum electricity production, but necessarily incorporate compromises to meet fishery and amenity requirements.

Over the last 40 years, environmental guidelines have gradually evolved for application on schemes, viz;

(1) Development of schemes is aimed at ensuring that the main flows of rivers remain in their natural catchment and flow direction. Local diversions and re-routing of

flows may be necessary to augment the output of schemes to make them economically viable.

(2) The effects of large intermittent flows, especially from peak load stations, on river regimes downstream can be reduced or virtually eliminated by siting the stations as far as practicable on lochs; for example, Clunie Power Station on Loch Faskally.

(3) Storage reservoirs, where considerable variation of water level is unavoidable, are located wherever possible in the less environmentally sensitive and more remote and higher regions. Where there is more than one reservoir in cascade as much storage as possible is concentrated on the highest of these reservoirs (e.g. Lochs Monar and Mullardoch in the Beauly scheme).

(4) For lower reservoirs, situated in outstanding scenic areas, the range of variation of water level has been kept within very strict narrow limits. Two classic examples of the care taken in implementing this guideline are Loch Faskally at Pitlochry, where the variation in level of the Loch is normally kept within a range of about one metre, and Loch Benevean in Glen Affric, which is in an AONB.

(5) Apart from the earlier, smaller and remote schemes, tunnels and shafts have been increasingly adopted to convey the pressure water from reservoirs to power stations rather than surface pipelines which are more obtrusive in the environment.

(6) Later schemes have tended to be based on underground stations to reduce environmental intrusion. A typical example of this is Glen Farrar which has been left more or less untouched by development apart from the Monar Dam and a low dam at Beannachran. The two stations in Glen Farrar – Deanie and Culligran – are both underground and, apart from the tunnel entrance to these stations, there is little evidence of development in the Glen.

Recently, Scottish Hydro-Electric has issued an Environment Policy Statement (1992) defining its commitment to environmental responsibilities.

Life of schemes

There has been little deterioration of the dams, apart from some superficial damage due to frost, etc., and this can be repaired. There has been no appreciable silting up of reservoirs. Overall, there would appear to be no limiting feature of the dams which will prevent them from lasting hundreds of years.

The performance of tunnels and shafts of conventional hydro-schemes has been good and, even after 40 and 50 years of service, they are still in a condition which has not required major maintenance. Relining them is practicable but will be expensive.

Many of the overland concrete piped aqueducts have suffered serious deterioration due to the climatic conditions to which they are subjected, particularly in the winters, and major maintenance work has had to be undertaken. It is difficult to see many of them lasting their planned life of 60 years without further major maintenance and/or partial replacement.

Performance of conventional hydro-power plant has been good and lends itself to refurbishing or even replacing without major difficulty. Earlier machines are being refurbished and higher efficiencies and outputs achieved (e.g. Luichart Power Station where the output has been raised from 28 to 34 MW) Power stations were well built, mostly in masonry, and these should be good for a life of 100 years or more with regular maintenance.

In a typical conventional hydro-scheme, plant and equipment costs might amount to 10–20% of the total cost compared with 80–90% for civil engineering and building works. It will be necessary to carry out major refurbishment of the plant every 30 to 50 years, but the cost of this work is small compared with the overall capital and potential life of the schemes.

Economics

The overall generation cost from a hydro-scheme is very largely made up of capital charges with only a few per cent for operation and maintenance. Therefore capital costs, amortization periods and interest charges are paramount.

When most of the hydro-schemes were promoted, interest rates varied from 2.5 to 4% per annum, coal was cheap but in short supply and difficulties were experienced in making an economic case for the schemes. A fact which was not taken into account at all was the devaluation of money over time, and this has had a beneficial effect on the cost of power produced by schemes in recent years. The schemes have therefore been very good investments and continually appreciate in value with reducing generation costs.

FUTURE DEVELOPMENT OF HYDRO-POWER

Until 1983, the NSHEB had not attempted to promote any conventional hydro-schemes since 1965 when two were rejected on the grounds that fossil-fuelled stations could be built more economically. As stated in the Mackenzie Report (1962), there is still, theoretically, 1000 MW of potential hydro-power undeveloped in the Highlands, capable of producing some 3000–4000 GWh yr^{-1}. However, the potential which is economically viable and at the same time environmentally acceptable and promotable is very much less (Vernon, 1986).

In order to provide guaranteed output, many existing hydro-schemes had to have sufficient storage to allow seasonal fluctuations to be accommodated and (as noted above) this necessitated the creation of large reservoirs holding typically 30–40% of the annual run-off and resulting in substantial dams. With the present surplus generating capacity on the Scottish system, run-of-river schemes are attractive, for no major reservoir is required, leading to major savings in capital cost.

There are a considerable number of sites which would be suitable for run-of-river schemes, mostly located in the north-west of the mainland where comparatively minor rivers with high catchments run steeply to the sea and inland lochs. The Grudie-Talladale Scheme (1983) is an example of this but, as noted above, it was put forward by the NSHEB in 1983 and was unsuccessful.

The terrain in the Highlands is also particularly suitable for large pumped storage schemes and a number of good sites for future development have been identified including Craigroyston, on Loch Lomond, which has the potential for an ultimate development of up to 3000 MW although there is no immediate prospect of such a scheme proceeding.

It is likely that there will be increasing pressure to develop the unexploited hydro-power resources where they are economic and environmentally acceptable since they produce "Green Electricity" and are likely to qualify for the Renewable Energy Obligation (REO), as advocated in the recent Report by the Renewable Energy Advisory Group (1992). The recent Scottish Office proposals for Scottish Renewables Obligation will stimulate hydro-electric development through subsidies. The most likely type of hydro-scheme to be developed in the immediate future is the "run-of-river" scheme without significant dams. Pumped storage will always be attractive as more nuclear plant and renewable resources are commissioned.

There will be increasing competition within catchments for water supply, afforestation, fisheries, fish farming, agriculture, hydro-power generation, recreation and sporting pursuits, requiring an integrated approach to their use (see Chapter 31). The public are becoming increasingly concerned with the protection of the environment, especially in the many Areas of Outstanding Natural Beauty found in the Highlands, and greater opposition can be expected to the development of new hydro-power schemes.

CONCLUSIONS

Hydro-power is a fully renewable, benign and proven source of indigenous power. It is a continually appreciating asset lasting in perpetuity, with many beneficial effects for the communities and amenities of the area. The probable steady increase in the real costs of fossil and nuclear fuels in the longer term and the high cost of other renewable forms of generation should, in the medium and long term, improve the viability of those resources not yet developed in the Highlands. The record and performance of the existing schemes have been outstanding and justify the further exploitation of the undeveloped resources at the appropriate time, provided that careful attention is paid to conservation of the environment in each case.

ACKNOWLEDGEMENT

The author has used a considerable amount of information gathered during his career with the North of Scotland Hydro-Electric Board. He is indebted to Scottish Hydro-Electric plc for consent to use this information. The opinions expressed are those of the author and independent of Scottish Hydro-Electric plc.

REFERENCES

Cooper Committee (1942). *Hydro-Electric Development in Scotland*. Command Paper Cmd 6406, HMSO, Edinburgh.

Forestry Commission (1993). *Forests & Water Guidelines*, 3rd edition, Edinburgh.

Johnson, F. G. and Cooke, W. (1975). "Operation of the Reservoirs of the North of Scotland Hydro-Electric Board", *Symposium on Inspection, Operation and Improvement of Existing Dams*, University of Newcastle-on-Tyne and BNCOLD.

Johnson, F. G., Jarvis, R. M. and Reynolds, G. (1980). "Use made of the Flood Studies Report for Reservoir Operation in Hydro-Electric Schemes", Conference on the *"Flood Studies Report – Five Years On"*, Institution of Civil Engineers, Manchester.

Mackenzie Committee (1962). *Electricity in Scotland (Report on the Generation and Distribution of Electricity in Scotland)*. Command Paper Cmnd 1859, HMSO, Edinburgh.

Natural Environment Research Council (1975). *Flood Studies Report*, London.

North of Scotland Hydro-Electric Board (1944). *Development Scheme*, North of Scotland Hydro-Electric Board (Prepared, approved and confirmed as required under Section 4 of the Hydro-Electric Development (Scotland) Act, 1943), Edinburgh.

North of Scotland Hydro-Electric Board (1983). *Constructional Scheme No. 79, Grudie–Talladale Scheme*, Edinburgh.

Payne, P. L. (1988). *The Hydro*, Aberdeen University Press, Aberdeen.

Renewable Energy Advisory Group (1992). Report to the President of the Board of Trade, *Energy Paper Number 60*, London.

Scottish Hydro-Electric (1992). *Hydro-Electric and the Environment*, Perth.

Vernon, K. R. (1986). "Future Prospects for Hydro Electricity and Wind Power", *Proceedings of the Royal Society of Edinburgh*, **92B**, 107–117.

18

Fisheries and Aquaculture

R. B. WILLIAMSON

Scottish Office Agriculture and Fisheries Department, Pentland House, 47 Robbs Loan, Edinburgh, EH14 1TW, UK

and

M. C. M. BEVERIDGE

Institute of Aquaculture, University of Stirling, Stirling, FK9 4LA, UK

INTRODUCTION

Conceptually, aquaculture is as different from freshwater fisheries as agriculture is from hunting or sea fisheries; the subjects are therefore described separately in the first two sections of this chapter. Clearly, however, both activities exploit the capacity of fresh waters to support stocks of fish and there are interactions between them – the third section therefore discusses both.

Economically, the most important species for Scottish aquaculture and for fishing in Scottish rivers is the Atlantic Salmon (*Salmo salar*). When considering the exploitation and culture of this anadromous species in fresh water, it is necessary also to make some reference to salmon fisheries and salmon farming in the sea.

FISHERIES

Fishing rights

The right to fish in the fresh waters of Scotland is a private right originally derived from the Crown under feudal charter. For Salmon, it is a separate heritable right which can be held independently of the adjacent land. (There is an exception in Orkney and Shetland where fishing rights may be under udal tenure, a relic from the days when the islands belonged to Norway.) The right to fish for Salmon in the open sea is also a private right; this has had an important effect on the management of salmon fisheries in fresh water. The salmon fishing right includes the exclusive right to fish for Sea Trout (migratory *Salmo trutta*), which is classed with Salmon for almost

The Fresh Waters of Scotland: A National Resource of International Significance
Edited by P. S. Maitland, P. J. Boon and D. S. McLusky. © 1994 John Wiley & Sons Ltd

all legal and administrative purposes in Scotland. The right to fish for freshwater fish other than Salmon or Sea Trout is a pertinent of ownership of land, and although the right can be leased, it cannot be sold separately from the land (unless, as at the Lake of Menteith, the two have been separated by Act of Parliament). The fisheries based on these rights are often categorized as "commercial" (netting) and "recreational" (angling). The terms, however, can mislead, because some recreational fisheries are managed for commercial profit and some net fisheries are recreational; in Scotland, the law does not distinguish between the two purposes.

Administration

Because the fisheries are privately owned, administration is principally by the owner or tenant of each fishery. For salmon fisheries, the legislation provides that the owners may establish a local District Salmon Fishery Board with statutory powers to protect and develop the salmon fisheries in the district (which includes the sea out to the three-mile limit). A Board has the power to levy a fishery rate on the owners of salmon fisheries in its district. It can employ water bailiffs to enforce the fisheries law, may operate hatcheries for restocking and may promote other improvements. These arrangements, first formally established under an Act of 1828, were re-enacted in modern form in the 1986 Salmon Act. There are no statutory arrangements for the co-ordinated local administration of fisheries for trout or other freshwater fish. However, in some areas, local angling clubs manage several fisheries and there are also regional associations of clubs which cover larger areas. The historic reason for the different arrangements is that the management of Salmon required formal co-operation among the owners of the rights; it was necessary to find a mechanism whereby money raised mainly from the valuable fisheries in the lower reaches of the river, and on the coast, could be used to fund improvements or protection anywhere in the district. Fisheries for sedentary stocks could more easily be managed by the individual proprietors. The difference persists because, by and large, the arrangements worked.

Regulation

The exercise of the fishing right is constrained by common law and by regulations made by Parliament or by Ministers empowered by Parliament. Subject to the statutory regulations, individual fishery owners may make their own more restrictive rules, and many do.

The existence of the private right has had a significant effect on the development of the regulatory regime: there is no licensing of fishermen or of fishing equipment and no direct control of fishing effort; access to the fisheries is through the marketable fishing right. The exploited stock is conserved by prohibiting detrimental methods of fishing and by the interest of the owners in managing their fisheries in a sustainable way. This has several advantages, but there is concern that some management practices may have an adverse effect on the characteristics of the stock or on other species. The system is sometimes criticised as *laissez faire* but it has, without bureaucratic control, kept Scottish Salmon stocks in better shape than those in many other countries.

Net fisheries and traps

Salmon and Sea Trout

The legislation of the late middle ages reflected the significance and importance of the salmon fisheries. They generated important exports and earned hard currency (a Scottish Parliamentary Act of 1431 required that half the proceeds be remitted in English silver or gold). Records of the late 18th century show Salmon being fished for in all parts of Scotland, and barrelled up for shipment to England and continental ports. It is interesting to note that fish from different rivers were distinguished on grounds of quality – for example, those from the Shin rather coarse, those from Aberdeen the best (Haldane, 1981).

The main fishing method used then was much the same as that used now: a beach seine net operated under restrictive rules that prevent obstruction to the passage of fish. The same method is used for both Salmon and Sea Trout. At most stations Sea Trout is a relatively small proportion of the catch and may be treated as a bycatch. The minimum mesh size for the nets, 90 mm stretched mesh, is such that Sea Trout less than about 0.5 kg are not caught. The use of fixed nets or any passive catching method (except cruives, see below) is not allowed in inland waters.

The development of stake and bag nets for salmon fishing on the sea coast (Figure 18.4) in the early 19th century led to a series of Commissions and Reports on Scottish salmon fisheries which contain much information about salmon fisheries in the rivers (Select Committee, 1836, 1860; Departmental Committee, 1890; Commission on Salmon Fisheries, 1902). The development of a drift-net fishery for Salmon in Scottish coastal waters in the early 1960s prompted an inquiry which produced descriptions of the salmon and freshwater fisheries at that time (Departmental Committee, 1965).

Until the early 1980s there were net fisheries in the estuary or lower reaches of most of the main salmon fishing rivers of Scotland. However, the increase in the production of farmed Salmon in the 1980s resulted in a drop in the price of the fish and, in 1988, an increase in the weekly close time for salmon netting further adversely affected profitability. These factors, together with the creation of a trust to purchase salmon fishing rights with the intention of extinguishing them, resulted in a decrease in the number of stations operated; for example, there are now no net fisheries on the Dee and the Don, rivers long famed for the high quality of their Salmon (Haldane, 1981). The most important remaining fisheries are on the big rivers of the east coast – the Tay, Tweed and North Esk – but even they are much reduced.

The netting season is set by regulation; it varies from district to district and runs from February or March through to August or September.

There are now no salmon traps – *cruives* – operated in Scottish rivers. These were weirs or dykes across a river, with several gaps occupied by wooden-framed fish traps. They obstructed the passage of fish but there were successive laws about leaving free gaps: "It is enjoined that on Saturdays the trellis barriers be removed to let the salmon run freely . . ." – but, as ever, there were ways round the law – "to keep them from going through, we put, just there, a horse's skull, its bones gleaming whiter than midwinter snow" (Johnstone, 1637). The cruive fishery which operated on the River Don until the 1960s is described by Summers (1989).

The Scottish Office has collected statistics of salmon and sea trout catches since

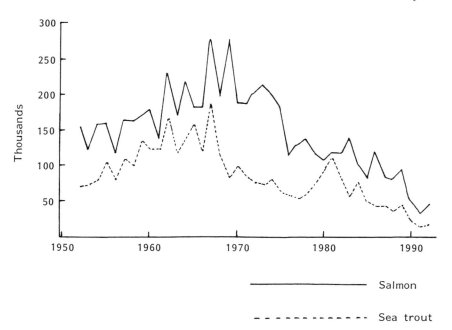

FIGURE 18.1. Numbers of Salmon and Sea Trout reported caught by net and coble in Scotland, 1952–1992 (source: SOAFD).

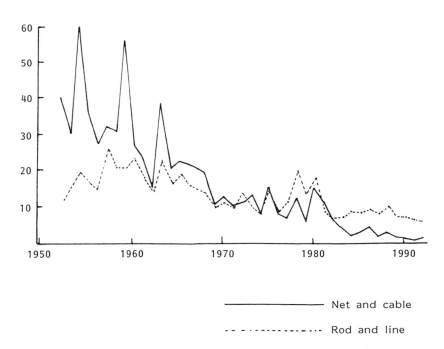

FIGURE 18.2. Numbers of Salmon reported caught in the spring (February to April) by rod and line and net and coble in Scotland, 1952–1992

1952 and summaries are now published annually (e.g. Scottish Office Agriculture and Fisheries Department, 1993a). Statistics are also available for some individual rivers and fisheries for earlier years – some of these are reviewed by Shearer (1992). The total net and coble catches for the years 1952–92 are shown in Figure 18.1. Sea trout catches are also shown; they are not so accurate but are probably indicative of the trend in catch from year to year. The record of salmon catches can, roughly, be divided into four periods: 1952–1961, when about 150 000 fish were caught; 1962–1975, average about 200 000; 1976–1983 about 125 000; and the period since 1984 when catches declined to less than 50 000. The changes which occurred around 1962 and 1976 cannot be explained by changes in fishing effort in Scotland or elsewhere, although part of the difference between the years 1952–1961 and 1976–1983 was due to increased catches of Scottish Salmon in other countries during the later period (Williamson, 1991). The decrease since 1984 can be attributed in part to the decrease in fishing effort in Scotland and, especially in 1990 and 1991, to an apparent scarcity of Salmon during the fishing season.

The catch of Salmon taken by the nets in the "spring", has declined fairly steadily over the past 40 years (Figure 18.2) such that the number taken by net and coble is now much less than that taken by rod and line.

There is concern about a decrease in sea trout catches, by nets and rods, in the west of Scotland (Picken, 1990). An analysis of catches (all methods) in each statistical region confirms that, in contrast to the east coast, catches in the north-west are lower than at any time since 1952 when the official record began (Scottish Office Agriculture and Fisheries Department, 1992).

Trout and charr

In practice, there is no net fishery for Brown Trout (non-migratory *Salmo trutta*) though the law allows such fishing in lochs if all proprietors agree. There have in the past been net fisheries for Arctic Charr (*Salvelinus alpinus*), most famously on Loch Leven, where the species was exterminated in the 1830s (either by the fishery or, more likely, by a combination of that and the lowering of the level of the loch (see Day, 1887)). There is some renewed interest in the possibility of local commercial fisheries for Charr and other freshwater fish in some Scottish lochs.

Eels

The Eel (*Anguilla anguilla* L.) has not been much exploited in Scotland (one is tempted to believe that this is due to a cultural aversion to Eels). There are, however, some small), long-standing fisheries for migrating silver Eels on streams in the fertile east of Scotland, for example, on the Lunan Burn in Tayside and the Lunan Water in Angus. There is also a history of itinerant fishermen for yellow Eels. Recently there has been an increase in the number of fishermen from England and continental Europe using fyke nets to catch Eels.

Coarse fish

Gill nets are sometimes set for Pike (*Esox lucious*) and traps for Perch (*Perca fluviatilis*) – usually as management measures in relation to salmon or trout fisheries (see Chapter 26). There have been some attempts to market Pike and, as with Charr, there is some new interest in small-scale fisheries.

Angling

Salmon and Sea Trout

Scotland's salmon fishing rivers are world famous, and in recent centuries that fame has been based on angling as much as, or more than, netting. There is a vast angling literature (see Colbey (1979) for a check-list). The rivers and lochs, viewed from a salmon angling perspective, were described by Grimble (1899) and Calderwood (1909) and, for the present day, by Mills and Graesser (1992).

The value of Scottish Salmon and Sea Trout angling is difficult to assess. Mackay Consultants (1989) estimated that it generated expenditure of £50 million a year; Radford *et al.* (1991) that the total capitalized economic rent was £255 million. One has to be careful in making comparisons on the basis of these figures alone, but it is clearly a significant business, important to the economy of some rural areas.

The reported angling catch has been steadier than that from the nets and has generally been above average during the last 15 years (Figure 18.3). It is thought there are now more salmon anglers than previously but levels of effort are not easy to judge because statistics are not available and because of difficulties in distinguishing between qualitative and quantitative effects.

The type of bait or lure used varies from river to river, and often within rivers, mainly at the discretion of the owner. In the rivers of the north it is mainly fly-fishing only and the same is true for parts of other rivers. There is increased pressure in some areas for anglers to adopt the practice of catch-and-release.

Some of the fishing is exclusive and very expensive, some is more accessible and relatively cheap; prices range from £10 a day to over £1000 a week. Recently, some

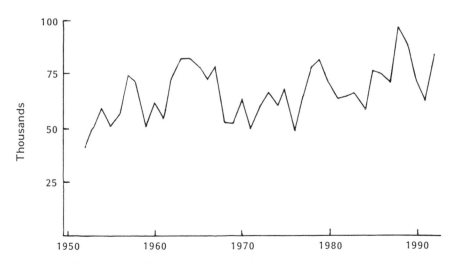

FIGURE 18.3. Numbers of Salmon reported caught by rod and line in Scotland, 1952–1992

fisheries have been marketed on a time-share basis. The purchaser buys only a small fraction of the whole fishery (or the whole fishery is vested in a trustee) but also receives a certificate which entitles him to the exclusive right of fishing during one or more weeks of the season – much like holiday time-share, but with added complications because of potential changes in the length of the fishing season.

Other salmonids

Brown Trout are almost ubiquitous in Scottish lochs and rivers. In contrast to salmon fisheries, the fishing right was not considered especially valuable and anyone could, almost anywhere, get access to trout fishing if they wanted (as a consequence some think the right to be a public one, which it is not). There have been angling tourists for more than three centuries (Franck, 1694) but there was a great increase in the 19th century with improvements to roads and the development of the railways. Large numbers of Brown Trout were taken by guests at various fishing hotels in the 1880s and 1890s (Fishery Board for Scotland, 1891). This led to pressure for a close season which was introduced in 1902. There was a further increase in pressure on trout fisheries in the 1950s and 1960s which led to recommendations for statutory protection of the fishing right so that owners and tenants could manage the fisheries more effectively.

In 1976, in an attempt to maintain a balance between public access and effective management, Parliament provided that the Secretary of State could make Orders which would create a statutory offence of fishing without permission in areas for which acceptable proposals for access had been made (Freshwater and Salmon Fisheries (Scotland) Act 1976). This has led to a series of Protection Orders for the Rivers Tweed, Tay, Upper Spey and some other waters.

Grayling

Traditionally not much fished for in Scotland, there was an increase in interest in winter angling for Grayling (*Thymallus thymallus*) in the late 1980s. This initially gave rise to concern among those responsible for the salmon fishings (worries about poaching and damage to salmon redds) but it is now an established element of angling in many rivers from the Tay system southwards.

Coarse fish

The distribution of fish species dictates that coarse fishing is concentrated in the southern part of Scotland. Even there it is less popular than in England (and the Scottish legislation does not take account of some coarse fishing practices nor are there any close seasons or other special management measures). There is no significant angling for the smallest species but an increasing interest in waters with natural populations of the larger cyprinids. There are also now some artificially stocked fisheries for Carp *Cyprinus carpio* and other cyprinids. The large Pike present in some Scottish lochs, notably Loch Lomond and Loch Ken, have long attracted anglers from England – especially during the close season there. The use of Ruffe (*Gymnocephalus cernuus*) as a live bait for pike fishing in Loch Lomond has allowed the establishment of a large population of Ruffe in that loch.

Pearl fishing

There are river pearls in the crown of Scotland and records of trade in Scottish river pearls in the 14th century. Pearls were fished for in many rivers; the River Tay was the most important and Perth the centre of the trade. It is arguable that the fishing right is private, but it has not been much protected. Until quite recently several itinerant professional pearl fishers made a precarious living. Goodwin (1985) gives an account of pearl fishing in the 1970s and concludes that there is no longer a living to be made from it. In the 1970s and 1980s there was an increase in amateur recreational fishing. The Freshwater Pearl Mussel (*Margaritifera margaritifera*) is now protected by law: it is an offence to kill a mussel, but it is lawful to take a pearl provided the mussel is not injured (see Chapter 29).

AQUACULTURE

The development of aquaculture in Scotland

Although fish farming was probably introduced to Scotland by monks during the middle ages, this had little influence on the subsequent development of the industry. As in North America, modern fish farming in Scotland developed initially out of a desire to improve recreational fisheries through stocking (Wilkins, 1989). During the 19th century rapid developments in the biological sciences and the zeal of prominent scientists such as Frank Buckland provided the tools and the impetus (Buckland, 1863). Early pioneers in Scotland included Shaw, the first to propagate salmon artificially (Shaw, 1840), Armistead (Armistead, 1870) and Maitland (Maitland, 1887; Lannon, 1989). Salmon hatcheries were established on several rivers including the Tay (Day, 1887) and the Leven, although many were short-lived (Williamson, 1991). A somewhat interventionist approach to the development of recreational fisheries was apparent among fish farmers of this period who, in addition to Trout and Salmon, sold a variety of aquatic plants and invertebrates (e.g. *Asellus*, *Gammarus*). Markets for Brown Trout included not only Scotland and England, but also cold waters throughout the British Empire (Maitland, 1887; Worthington and Worthington, 1933). Similar pond-based fish farms could be found in France and Germany around the same time (Wilkins, 1989). Of the early ventures in Scotland, however, only Howietoun and Solway Fisheries are still in existence.

Rainbow Trout farms which supplied food for the table began to appear in Scotland in the mid-1960s and were initially modelled on the well-established Danish trout industry. Salmon farming developed a few years later. Much research had been carried out on salmonid biology and culture by the Scottish scientific community, particularly at the Freshwater Fisheries Laboratory, Pitlochry, and the University of Stirling, and this was to prove important in the development of the industry. Eel farming, which took advantage of industrial heated waste water, was established at Tomatin Distillery and by Coates at Paisley and Hunterston in the mid-1970s, but both ventures proved to be comparatively short-lived, closing in the early 1980s due to a combination of technical and financial difficulties.

Today, freshwater fish farming, including the production of Atlantic Salmon smolts, is worth an estimated £25 million to the Scottish economy. It directly employs some 410 full-time and 160 part-time staff (Scottish Office Agriculture and Fisheries Department, 1993b), mostly in rural areas, and supports probably half as many again in ancillary industries (feed manufacture, transport, equipment supply, training, etc.

Present-day aquaculture practices

Fish farming involves rearing animals throughout their life cycle, from egg to mature adult (for details of current fish farming practices see Roberts and Shepherd, 1986; Laird and Needham, 1987; Drummond Sedgwick, 1992). The facilities required consist of a system for holding and maturing broodstock and a hatchery and nursery system in which fertilized eggs can be kept until the young emerge and are sufficiently large to be transferred to a "grow-out" facility where they are reared until ready for sale. Not all facilities, however, are found on all farms. Until recently, fish farming was treated like agriculture and there was no statutory requirement for planning permission. However, since 1990, all new farms and extensions to existing farms have required planning permission. Interested parties who may be consulted include River Purification Boards (RPBs), Scottish Natural Heritage (SNH), Scottish Office Department of Agriculture and Fisheries (SOAFD), council departments of Roads and Transport, Environmental Health, Water and Sewerage and, where appropriate, the local District Salmon Fishery Board (see Nature Conservancy Council, 1990 and Burbridge *et al.*, 1993, for reviews). Farms must also register with SOAFD under the 1983 Diseases of Fish Act and, under the provisions of the 1974 Control of Pollution Act (COPA) as amended by the 1989 Water Act, obtain a Consent to Discharge from the appropriate RPB (Nature Conservancy Council, 1990; Burbridge *et al.*, 1993).

Both land-based and cage systems are used to rear Trout and Salmon. The former comprises a range of designs of tanks, raceways and ponds, choice depending upon circumstances. Surface and/or groundwater supplies may be used and something in the order of 25 litres per kilogram of fish per hour is required for grow-out. Water may have to be filtered or treated to improve pH or temperature prior to use, particularly for hatcheries. Effluent may also be treated before discharge using settlement or filtration systems to remove suspended solids. Cage-based systems (Figure 18.5), in which fish are reared in floating net enclosures in lochs, are inexpensive compared with land-based systems. Most cages are of the "Kames" design with a wooden and polystyrene frame supporting a net bag of 100–250 m^3 capacity and are sited in sheltered sites in depths of 10–50 m (Beveridge, 1987).

Since 1979, SOAFD has published comprehensive statistics on farmed Rainbow Trout and Atlantic Salmon production on an annual basis. Although the data collected have changed over the years, it is one of the most comprehensive sets of statistics available from any country.

Rainbow Trout

Production of Rainbow Trout (*Oncorhynchus mykiss*) in Scottish fresh waters increased by a factor of 10 between the early 1970s and mid-1980s (Figure 18.6), a situation which occurred in many other trout-producing countries. Recent increases,

FIGURE 18.4. A stake net fisherman on the Solway Firth. Photograph: Peter S. Maitland

FIGURE 18.5. Floating cages for rearing Rainbow Trout on a Loch in southwest Scotland.
Photograph: Peter S. Maitland

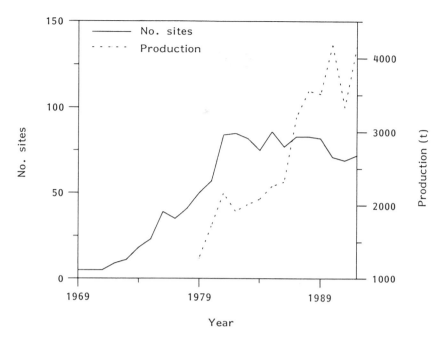

FIGURE 18.6. Numbers of Rainbow Trout farms and farmed Rainbow Trout production in Scotland (source: SOAFD)

however, have been by expansion at existing sites rather than by development of new farms; indeed, the number of sites has fallen from a peak of 86 in 1985 to 72 in 1992 whilst production per site has risen from 26 to 58 tonnes (t). For the moment, production appears to have stabilized at around 3500–4200 t and, in global terms, Scotland is ranked about 10th.

In 1992, Trout production increased somewhat surprisingly by 25% over the previous year to reach its highest figure, 4162 t, with an estimated value of £6 million. For reasons part historic and part economic, most farms are located in Dumfries and Galloway and Highland Regions. Production is divided among freshwater cages (41%), ponds and raceways (39%), and tanks (20%). Although farms range in size from those producing less than 1 t to more than 400 t yr^{-1}, the bulk of production is from a few, large farms, such as Kames Fish Farm in Argyll. Forty percent of sites produce less than 10 t yr^{-1}, largely for local markets.

The proportion of imported eggs varies from year to year but currently accounts for just over half of all used in the industry. The technology for mass production of faster growing, sex-reversed, all-female fish was developed in the early 1980s and since then the proportion of production accounted for by all-female stock has increased to almost 85%. Sterile, triploid fish account for a further 4% of fish.

Production in fresh water is now largely geared towards 350–450 g fish. In Scotland much production for the table is marketed through Scot Trout Ltd, a highly successful producers' co-operative which has introduced a measure of stability into the industry.

Numbers of Rainbow Trout released into the wild for restocking purposes, principally into put-and-take fisheries, increased throughout the 1980s from 74 t in 1980 to 706 t in 1992 and at present accounts for 17% of production by weight although somewhat higher in terms of value.

Brown Trout

There are around half-a-dozen Brown Trout farms situated in central and southern Scotland, mostly supplying fish for restocking angling waters. Many are well established and although there are no reliable production statistics annual production is probably around 100 t, worth in excess of £1 million. Brown Trout tend to be reared less extensively in earth ponds at low stocking densities so that they are in excellent condition and are predisposed towards natural food on release into the wild.

Atlantic Salmon

Atlantic Salmon smolt production in Scotland is geared exclusively towards supplying the indigenous salmon farming industry. Smolt production increased slowly during the 1970s, but accelerated dramatically in the mid-1980s to a peak of 26 million in 1989. Since then, however, annual production has fallen to around 21 million (Figure 18.7), worth an estimated £17.5 million. The number of sites producing Atlantic Salmon smolts has also fallen, from a peak of around 180 in the late 1980s to 137 or

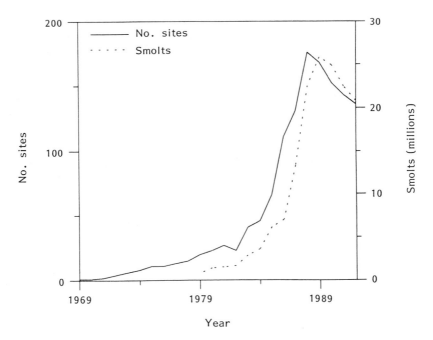

FIGURE 18.7. Numbers of Atlantic Salmon smolt production sites and numbers of smolts produced in Scotland (source: SOAFD)

so in 1992 (Figure 18.7). Those sites that have remained in production, however, are considerably larger, producing on average somewhere in excess of 150 000 smolts compared with less than 50 000 a decade ago. Some 40% of sites are cage-based and 60% tank-based.

In the early years, eggs from a variety of Scottish rivers were used. There were substantial imports from Norway in the 1980s but since 1987 the industry has, with few exceptions, used eggs produced in Scotland. Although in the early 1980s almost a third of ova were from wild fish, this figure has declined in both real and relative terms to around 0.3 million, equivalent to 0.5% of total requirements.

In recent years there has been a considerable amount of vertical integration in the Atlantic Salmon farming industry with the result that many of the hatcheries and smolt-producing sites are now owned by the companies farming Salmon in the sea. Current information (Scottish Office Agriculture and Fisheries Department, 1993b) indicates that production per smolt stocked into the sea is increasing, so that some stability in terms of freshwater production should also become apparent.

DISCUSSION

The structures and mechanisms which have evolved for the administration and management of freshwater fisheries and aquaculture in Scotland face many new pressures. Some of these arise as a result of membership of the European Community or through other international constraints. There are new risks of spread of disease, of overfishing and of environmental degradation; and there are also requirements to comply with new standards. There is some direct pressure on the Scottish arrangements just because they differ from those of England and Wales or other countries. While there is scope for improvement, and there are ideas that could usefully be adopted from elsewhere, there is also much of value in the Scottish arrangements which need to be well understood and preserved where appropriate.

It is arguable that the stocks of Salmon should be able to sustain a significant net fishery on most large Scottish rivers as well as the current angling pressure, but it seems likely that the salmon net fishing industry will continue to decline for economic and social reasons.

The development of the practice of catch-and-release in salmon angling is interesting. It does not have many whole-hearted converts in Scotland, but is a simple and attractive idea and may grow. It may, however, pose more questions than it answers – fishing for Salmon with the intention of releasing them all may be difficult to justify in argument with advocates of animal rights. In contrast to English coarse fishing, a significant element of game fishing in Scotland has been that the quarry is edible and eaten.

The development of time-share fishing has also been disturbing. It inflated the capital values of salmon fisheries to record levels (as much as £15 000 for each fish in the average annual catch) and, while it has made some of the fisheries less exclusive, it has also, by increased commercialization, reduced the amount of casual or preferential local access. The increased commercialization of angling management may result in further tension between angling and net-fishing interests.

There are conflicts, too, between fishery interests and fish farming, and concern about the effects that escaped farmed fish may have on wild stocks. Escaped Salmon are known to breed in the wild and to interbreed with wild Salmon and Trout (Scottish Office Agriculture and Fisheries Department, 1993c; Webb *et al.*, 1993). The number of escaped Salmon is sufficient to affect catch statistics and the management of fisheries on the west coast. Fish farm wastes have an effect on water quality and may thus affect wild fish stocks; this is considered in Chapter 21.

Until the mid-1990s at least we can expect a period of stability in the fish farming industry in Scotland, with trout production continuing at a level of 3500–4200 t and salmon farming at around 38 000–42 000 t. Any growth is likely to be largely through expansion of existing sites, thereby capitalizing on labour (trout production per fish-farm worker, for example, has doubled from 12 to 24 t over the past decade) and equipment. Although small-scale, Eel, Tilapia and Charr farms may materialize from time to time, significant new industries based on novel species are unlikely in Scottish fresh waters. Instead, we can expect to see an increasing divergence in the genotypes of farmed and wild fish in terms of growth, nutritional quality and disease resistance potential, although whether such developments will continue to rely upon conventional selection techniques or utilize the already well-established techniques of genetic engineering is a moot point.

At present, control of planning and management of fish farming is based upon a cumbersome system of permits which differs from region to region. Procedures for obtaining permits are not standardized among agencies or even within agencies at regional level. Although the EC Directive on Environmental Assessment (85/337/ EEC) may be applied to fish farming, the guidelines with respect to fish farming are poorly developed and there is a lack of trained staff to review statements. According to a recent survey (Burbridge *et al.*, in press) no Environmental Statements have been submitted by any of the 446 registered businesses operating 721 sites in Scotland. The problems are widely recognized, however, and increased harmonization of standards and conditions of consents is likely.

Disease is one of the biggest concerns for farmers, wild fishery interests and the general public. There is a two-way traffic of infection: introduced farm stock may carry a new disease and, vice-versa, the introduced stock may pick up an infection from fish in the local water supply. Munro *et al.*, (1976) concluded that the distribution of IPN virus among wild salmonids in the vicinity of an infected Scottish Trout farm was a result of the farming activity. Legislation restricts the movement of live fish, ova and foodstuffs from areas where there is infection with certain specified diseases. Whilst a number of effective vaccines and therapeutants are available, and increasingly being used by farmers, an assured future for the industry (and assurance for the wild fishery interests) depends on a reduced incidence of disease and the key to this is better husbandry.

The conflict between fisheries and aquaculture is balanced by some common interests and interdependence. The continued well-being of each depends on the maintenance of the quality of the fresh waters of Scotland.

ACKNOWLEDGEMENTS

We would like to thank Mr David Dunkley, Mr Ross Gardiner and Dr Alasdair MacVicar and staff at SOAFD for generous provision of information and data; FAO, Rome, for access to their statistical database; Ms Fiona Gavine and colleagues at the University of Stirling for access to unpublished information; Dr James Muir, Institute of Aquaculture, Mr David Scott, Stirling Aquaculture, and Mr Robert Murray, Howietoun Fishery, for information on the Trout and Salmon farming industries of Scotland.

REFERENCES

Armistead, J. J. (1870). *A Short History of the Art of Pisciculture, Shewing its Utility and Some of the Advantages Which May Be Derived From It If Properly Carried On*, Leeds.
Beveridge, M. C. M. (1987). *Cage Aquaculture*, Fishing News Books, Oxford.
Buckland, F. T. (1863). *Fish Hatching*, Tinsley Brothers, London.
Burbridge, P. R., Gavine, F. M. and Kelly, L. A. (1993). "Control and regulation of the environmental impact of fish farming in Scotland", in *Workshop on fish farm effluents and their control in EC countries* (Eds H. Rosenthal and V. Hilge), pp. 146–165, University of Keil, Hamburg.
Calderwood, W. L. (1909). *Salmon Rivers and Lochs of Scotland*, Edward Arnold, London.
Colbey, R. J. W. (1979). *Regional Angling Literature: A Check-list of Books on Angling and the Salmon Fisheries in Scotland, Northern England, Wales and Ireland*, Colbey, Billinghay.
Commission on Salmon Fisheries (1902). *Report of the Commission on Salmon Fisheries*, Command Paper Cd 1188, HMSO, London.
Day, F. (1887). *Salmonidae of Britain*, William and Norman, London.
Departmental Committee (1890). *Report of the Committee on Crown Rights of Salmon Fishing in Scotland*, Command Paper C 6036, HMSO, Edinburgh.
Departmental Committee (1965). *Scottish Salmon and Trout Fisheries*, Command Paper Cmnd 2691, HMSO, Edinburgh.
Drummond Sedgwick, S. (1992). *Trout Farming Handbook*, 5th edition, Fishing News Books, Oxford.
Fishery Board for Scotland (1891). *Ninth Annual Report (for year 1890)*, HMSO, Edinburgh.
Franck, R. (1694). *Northern Memoirs*, 2nd edition, Edinburgh and London, 1821.
Goodwin, P. J. (1985). *The River and the Road*, Robert Hale, London.
Grimble, A. (1899). *The Salmon Rivers of Scotland*, Kegan Paul, London.
Haldane, A. R. B. (1981). *The Great Fishmonger of the Tay*, Abertay Historical Society Publication No. 21, Dundee.
Johnstone, A. (1637). "Apologia piscatoris", in *Delitiae poetarum scotorum*, Blaeu, Amsterdam; English translation in *The Golden Treasury of Scottish Poetry* (Ed. H. MacDiarmid) (1946), pp. 217–230, Macmillan, London.
Laird, L. M. and Needham, T. (1987). *Salmon and Trout Farming*, Ellis Horwood, London.
Lannon, T. (1989). *The Story of Howietoun*, Institute of Aquaculture Publications, University of Stirling, Stirling.
Mackay Consultants (1989). *Economic Importance of Salmon Fishing and Netting in Scotland*, Inverness.
Maitland, J. R. G. (1887). *The History of Howietoun*, J. R. Guy, Howietoun, Stirling.
Mills, D. and Graesser, N. (1992). *The Salmon Rivers of Scotland*, Ward Lock, London.
Munro, A. L. S., Liversage, J. and Elson, K. (1976). "Distribution and prevalence of IPN virus in wildlife in Loch Awe", *Proceedings of the Royal Society of Edinburgh*, **75B**, 223–232.
Nature Conservancy Council (1990). *Fish Farming and the Scottish Freshwater Environment*, Edinburgh.
Picken, M. J. (1990). "The history of west coast sea trout catches", in *The Sea Trout in Scotland* (Eds M. J. Picken and W. M. Shearer), pp. 53–59, Natural Environment Research Council, Oban.
Radford, A. F., Hatcher, A. C. and Whitemarsh D. J. (1991). *An Economic Evaluation of Salmon Fisheries in Great Britain*, Centre for Marine Resource Economics, Portsmouth Polytechnic, Portsmouth.
Roberts, R. J. and Shepherd, C. J. (1986). *Handbook of Trout and Salmon Diseases*, Fishing News Books, Oxford.
Scottish Office Agriculture and Fisheries Department (1992). *Freshwater Fisheries Laboratory Pitlochry Annual Review 1990–1991*, Pitlochry.

Scottish Office Agriculture and Fisheries Department (1993a). *Scottish Salmon and Sea Trout Catches: 1992*, Statistical Bulletin, Fisheries Series, Fis/1993/1, Scottish Office, Edinburgh.

Scottish Office Agriculture and Fisheries Department (1993b). *Report of the Annual Survey of Fish Farms for 1992*, Aberdeen.

Scottish Office Agriculture and Fisheries Department (1993c). *Freshwater Fisheries Laboratory Pitlochry Annual Review 1991–1992*, Pitlochry.

Select Committee (1836). *Report of the Select Committee [Commons] on Salmon Fisheries, Scotland*, 329, London.

Select Committee (1860). *Report from the Select Committee of the House of Lords [on the regulation of fixed nets and engines in fishing for salmon in Scotland]*, 135, London.

Shaw, J. (1840). "Account of experimental observations on the development and growth of salmon-fry, from the exclusion of ova to the age of two years", *Transactions of the Royal Society of Edinburgh*, **14**, 547–566.

Shearer, W. M. (1992). *The Atlantic Salmon*, Fishing News Books, Oxford.

Summers, D. W. (1989). "The cruives of Don", *The Salmon Net*, **21**, 21–27.

Webb, J. H., McLaren, I. S., Donaghy, M. J. and Youngson, A. F. (1993). "Spawning of farmed Atlantic salmon, *Salmo salar* L., in the second year after their escape", *Aquaculture and Fisheries Management*, **24**, 557–561.

Wilkins, N. P. (1989). *Ponds, Passes and Parcs*, Glendale Press, Dublin.

Williamson, R. (1991). *Salmon Fisheries in Scotland*, Atlantic Salmon Trust, Pitlochry.

Worthington, S. and Worthington, E. B. (1933). *Inland Waters of Africa*, Macmillan, London.

19

Tourism and Recreation

S. E. WALKER

Centre for Leisure Research, Heriot-Watt University, Cramond Road North, Edinburgh, EH4 6JD, UK

INTRODUCTION

Water plays a major role in outdoor recreation and tourism, both as a setting for shore-based activities and as a venue for a wide range of water-based activities and sports. Although coastal waters are a key attraction for many people on holiday or a day out, fresh water (or inland water) also acts as a focus for a large number of visits.

This chapter begins by describing the different types of inland water in Scotland and some of the factors which influence its availability for recreation. The nature and scale of activities which take place on or by the water are then described, while the final section discusses some of the current trends in outdoor recreation and their implications for the resource.

THE NATURE AND AVAILABILITY OF THE RESOURCE

Inland water encompasses a wide range of different types of water space. Firstly, there are linear waterways – rivers and canals. Secondly, there are natural lochs, and thirdly, there are man-made water bodies: impounded lochs, purpose-built reservoirs, flooded gravel pits and other flooded mineral workings. One source estimates the area of inland water in Scotland to be just over 1700 km², or about 2% of the total area (Scottish Office, 1990); (see Chapter 3) for comparison, this is over twice the area of inland water in England and Wales (estimated to be around 800 km² – Patmore, 1983).

Not all of this water is available for recreation or the full range of water-based activities. The factors which influence the amount of recreational water space available include:

- The degree of physical access – Tivy (1980), for example, in her study of the effects of recreation on freshwater lochs and reservoirs in Scotland assumed that unless a water body was within easy reach by car (i.e. 100 m from the road) then its recreational use was not likely to be significant; applying this criterion, the 3000

The Fresh Waters of Scotland: A National Resource of International Significance
Edited by P. S. Maitland, P. J. Boon and D. S. McLusky. © 1994 John Wiley & Sons Ltd

water bodies (over 5 ha in extent) identified initially by Tivy were reduced to 760. Further, when the lengths of shore accessible from the road were taken into account, only around 50 water bodies had 1 km or more of their shoreline close to an "A" or "B" road.

- The nature of the water body – its depth and extent, the character of the banks and surrounding land – all influence the range of activities it can accommodate; for example, a minimum depth of 1.2 m is required for sailing and for water skiing the recommended water area is 650–1100 m × 150–180 m (Land Use Consultants, 1991).
- The law governing access – gaining access to inland water is often doubly complicated in that not only does the public have to be able to use the water space, but also the surrounding land has to be accessible at some point. The law for access over water is complex and separate from that for rights of way over land. A public right of navigation is the equivalent to a public right of way, but on most inland waters access for recreation is through permissive or negotiated arrangements, rather than legal entitlement. Access to inland waters can be negotiated by local authorities (and since 1991 by Scottish Natural Heritage (SNH) through *access agreements*, but there are few cases where these powers have been used. A more detailed discussion of the legal framework surrounding access to water can be found in Centre for Leisure Research (1986) and in SNH's recent consultation paper on access (Scottish Natural Heritage, 1992).
- Proprietorial rights – most inland waters are privately owned and riparian owners have the right to control the use of the water. Riparian owners also own the right to fish on non-tidal waters. This right can be sold or leased separately from the land and so may be owned as a proprietary interest independent of the owner of the river bed and banks (Salmon fishing is something of an exception, as it belongs to the Crown which grants rights to individuals and so Salmon fishing also may be owned independently of the land). For the recreational user this can mean having to negotiate access with more than one owner. In addition, because of the economic value of fishing, owners or lessees are often unwilling to restrict their property rights for the benefit of other recreational users.
- Management of the water body – even where the public has access to a water body for recreation, the range of activities which can take place may be limited by the way in which the river or water body is managed; for example, byelaws can be used to set speed limits at a level which effectively excludes water skiing and power boats. Conservation designations may also restrict access to water, if the activity is considered damaging to the conservation interest.

In practice, therefore, the area of inland water accessible for recreation is limited and, as elsewhere in Britain, the demands made on the available water space are considerable, as the next section attempts to demonstrate.

THE NATURE AND SCALE OF TOURISM AND RECREATION

Inland waterways attract a wide range of recreation activities. The river banks, loch or reservoir shore may be used for land-based activities which range from general sightseeing (Figure 19.1) and picnicking to more active forms of recreation such as

FIGURE 19.1. Loch Shiel and the monument to Bonnie Prince Charlie on the "Road to the Isles". Clean and clear lochs and rivers are an integral part of the scenery which attracts so many tourists to Scotland. Photograph: Scottish Tourist Board

walking, cycling and riding. Water recreation includes: swimming, diving, canoeing, rowing, sailing, cruising, power boating, water skiing, jet skiing, wildfowling and coarse and game angling (which can be undertaken from boats or the bank), while both the land and the water may attract people with an interest in bird-watching and nature study. These activities are popular with a large number of people who may be on holiday, on a day trip, or taking part in sport.

Inland water and holiday tourism

At present, around five million holiday trips (i.e. involving an overnight stay) are made to Scotland each year (in 1991, for example, the Scottish Tourist Board (STB, 1992) estimated that 4.3 million trips were made by UK residents and 0.92 million by visitors from overseas). Recent surveys, however, do not record the types of area which holidaymakers visit, and so in order to assess how important inland water is as a holiday destination, it is necessary to go back to the 1981 Scottish Leisure Survey (SLS) (Mackenzie, 1985). The SLS collected information on more than 6000 holidays taken in Scotland over the five summer months May to September by both UK residents and visitors from overseas. Five outdoor activities were overwhelmingly popular with holidaymakers, and visits to loch-sides and river-sides topped the list (Table 19.1).

TABLE 19.1. Activities undertaken by holidaymakers (Mackenzie, 1985)

	% of all holidaymakers
Visits to loch-sides or river-sides	55
Visits to historic buildings, stately homes, museums, and gardens in the countryside	51
Drives, outings and picnics in the countryside	49
Visits to sea coast, beaches and cliff tops	47
Walking and hiking in the countryside (for more than two miles)	33

Many holidaymakers made more than one visit to a river-side or loch shore, resulting in more than seven million visits to these destinations over the period May to September; only drives, picnics and outings generated more visits. Information also was recorded for selected water-based activities including fishing (undertaken by 10% of holidaymakers), river, loch or canal cruises (9%), and rowing, sailing or canoeing (5%).

Inland water and day-trip tourism

Day-trip tourism makes an increasingly important contribution to tourism in Scotland; in 1990, for example, 53% of the Scottish adult population had a "day out" in the countryside during an average month (averaged across the year) and an estimated 22 million trips were made to the countryside – 26% of all day trips (Scottish Tourist Board, 1992). Again, recent surveys do not provide information about visits to inland water and the SLS is the main source of information available. As with holiday trips, SLS shows that water-side locations emerge as the most popular place for day trips (Table 19.2).

Many people reported making more than one visit to a loch-side or river-side in a month and it was estimated that nearly three million trips were made to these destinations in a typical summer month, averaged over May to September. A comparison of the results from SLS with an earlier survey in 1973 also reveals that

TABLE 19.2. Day trips – places where the main stop is made (Mackenzie, 1985)

	% of trips
Loch-sides, river-sides, canal banks, reservoir edges	19
Villages	15
Sea coast, cliff tops (not seaside resort)	11
Country park, gardens, parkland, estate grounds	10
Other destinations	45

both day trips and holiday visits to loch shores and river-sides increased substantially over this period – the proportion of respondents who had visited these locations in the last year increased by 22% (Coppock *et al.*, 1985).

Inland water and outdoor sports

Compared with day trips and holidays in the countryside, individual water recreation activities are minority pursuits. For example, only 2% of the Scottish adult population take part in angling in a typical four-week period and less than 1% take part in sailing and other water sports (ASH Partnership, 1991). Nevertheless, many of these participants take part in their sport on a regular basis and make significant demands of the resource.

The value of inland water as a tourism and recreational resource

While it is easy to describe qualitatively the popularity of inland water and its value in terms of the enjoyment and exercise it provides for users, it is very difficult to quantify the value in economic terms. Holiday visitors to Scotland spent an average of £34 per night, if they were from overseas, and £28 per night if they were from Britain – a total of £1058 million in 1991 – while day-trip visitors spent an average of £12.93 per trip – a total spend of £1100 million. However, the information is not available to assess what proportion of this spending is associated with trips to inland water.

Information about the economic value of some individual water-based activities is available; for example, the contribution of game fishing to the economy – expenditure by game fishermen is estimated to be £77.25 per day and gross expenditure in Scotland in 1988 was £33.6 million (Mackay Consultants, 1989).

Interactions between users, and users and the resource

The variety of activities which takes place on or by inland water appeals to a wide range of people who are often very different in their character and aspirations. Many activities can co-exist but all too often users compete for water space and conflicts of interest arise. The level of incompatibility varies with the nature of the activity, and the feelings of one group of users towards another are not necessarily reciprocated, as Table 19.3 demonstrates.

The popularity of inland water as a tourism and recreation destination also leads to pressures on the landscape and the environment. In a recent study of the Lough Erne system in Northern Ireland, Centre for Leisure Research (1993) identified the following impacts on the environment from shore- and water-based tourism and recreation:

- Visual intrusion into the landscape by some of the developments and facilities – this occurred with both large and small developments, although most of the adverse impacts could be reduced significantly by better siting and design, taking into account that water-side developments are viewed from both the shore and the water.

TABLE 19.3. Compatibility of water sports – the users' view

	Water skiing	Jet skiing	Power boating	Cruising	Angling	Canoeing	Sailing
Water skiing			*	**	***	***	**
Jet skiing	*		*	**	***	***	***
Power boating	*		**	**	***	***	**
Cruising	**		**	***	**	**	*
Angling	*		**	***		*	*
Canoeing	*	*	**	**	***	*	*
Sailing	*		*	*	*	*	

Note: the asterisks in the columns show how the participants in that sport view those who take part in the sport shown in the row: * some competition for water space; ** moderate competition for water space; *** considerable competition for water space. This shows how views vary from one sport to the next – for example, while most anglers consider that they compete with canoeists for water space, the feeling is not reciprocated to the same extent.

- Disturbance to wildlife – this is caused mainly by noise and the presence of people and boats on land and water, but it is very difficult to quantify the degree and extent of disturbance; some disturbance also occurs from wildfowling.
- Loss and alteration of natural habitats through: facility development; boats moored along bank-sides and in reed beds; erosion of the shoreline by recreational users on land and water.
- Impacts on the aquatic environment from boat movement – for example, increased turbidity of the water, damage to aquatic plants, erosion from wash. The extent of damage is related to craft size, hull design and speed.
- Impacts on the aquatic environment by anglers – for example, through discarding lead weights and fishing line and introducing fish species (as live bait).
- Impacts on water quality from sewage effluent from boats (this will be eliminated over time with the introduction of closed systems on boats and sewage disposal stations on shore) and litter.

This list is very similar to that produced by Tivy (1980) in her study of freshwater lochs and reservoirs in Scotland. Other reviews of the impact of recreation on aquatic environments includes Chmura and Ross (1978), Liddle and Scorgie (1980), Adams (1993) and Ward and Andrews (1993). While these effects give cause for concern, relative to other land uses the impacts of tourism and recreation on the environment are not substantial, but locally they can be significant.

The extent to which conflicts between users and impacts on the environment increase in the coming years will depend in part on what happens to the market and in part on the responses from those responsible for planning and managing the resource. The final section, therefore, looks at current market trends and discusses some of the issues which will face planners and managers in the coming years.

CURRENT TRENDS AND THEIR IMPLICATIONS FOR INLAND WATER

While up-to-date information on the scale and nature of tourism and recreation associated with inland water is limited, data on trends are even more difficult to find, either because surveys have not been carried out over a number of years or, where they have, the methods have been inconsistent. Nevertheless, from a general review of market information, the following trends emerge:

- In Scotland, the number of tourism trips fluctuates from year to year but the general trend for some time has been one of declining numbers, largely due to a decline in the domestic tourism market.
- The number of leisure day trips also appears to be declining, and certainly the rapid increase in the popularity of countryside recreation so evident in the 1970s appears to be slowing.
- Some activities, however, have shown considerable growth in recent years and water sports are one such category (Leisure Consultants, 1989), although more recent market assessments suggest that the recession has halted this growth for the present (Mintel, 1992).

However, although these trends tend to suggest that the scale of tourism may not increase substantially, a number of changes in the way in which many activities are pursued may increase pressures on inland waters.

(1) There is a growing interest in active, rather than passive, recreation activities which may mean fewer people sitting in one spot by the water and more people wanting to engage in water-based activities or to make use of more of the shoreline for cycling, walking or other shore-based pursuits.

(2) There is an increasing trend for people to take part in activities on an individual basis, rather than with a club or organization. For example, while club membership of the Royal Yachting Association only increased by 2% from 1980 to 1990, individual membership increased by 64%. Similarly, club membership of the British Water Ski Federation only increased by 10% over this period but individual membership increased by 35% (Centre for Leisure Research, 1991). This tendency means that it is more difficult to manage activities through consensus,

FIGURE 19.2. The east shore of Loch Lomond looking north across the boat moorings beside the village of Balmaha. The recent increase in boating activity on Loch Lomond is one of several current problems created by recreation. Photograph: Stanley V. Mills

as it is not easy to identify representatives for particular activities and sports or communicate effectively with all the participants.

(3) Many users are becoming more mobile, either because like the touring canoeist they want to experience different stretches of water, or because technological advances are making craft easier to move around – light-weight boats, windsurfers and jet skis, for example, are all easy to trail behind, or put on top of, a car. This tendency also makes it more difficult to plan for and manage use at a particular location.

(4) Tourism and recreation is extending more and more out of the summer season and becoming a year-round activity. This is a result partly of technological advances – for example, better and less expensive wet suits – but also due to policies deliberately aimed at encouraging tourism and recreation in the off-peak season to increase the economic benefits.

(5) The water-based activities which are increasing in popularity are those which tend to have the greatest impact on other users and the environment. The motorized water sports are the ones which have seen the most significant growth in recent years (Figure 19.2) and although these are still minority activities in terms of overall participation, the people who take part in these pursuits do so more regularly than other types of user (Table 19.4) and take up a disproportionate amount of water space (Centre for Leisure Research, 1992, 1993; Adams, 1993). This means that other people are more likely to encounter these users at some stage and the impacts of these activities (noise and wash) are likely to increase.

(6) The availability of the resource, especially for motorized water sports, is decreasing, as more managers seek to exclude these activities in the interests of other users and the environment. However, solving one area's problems may increase those elsewhere; for example, there is concern that if the proposed 10 mph speed

TABLE 19.4. Regular sports participants (three or more times in the previous year) (Centre for Leisure Research, 1992)

	% of respondents
Jet skiing	94
Cycling	92
Water skiing	75
Windsurfing	75
Boating/motor boats	71
Canoeing	71
Fishing	71
Sailing	59
Swimming/paddling	42

Note: This information comes from users interviewed in the Loch Lomond Park Authority area. Sports participants were found to be among the most regular visitors but even among this group some types of user visited the area more often

limit is imposed on Windermere, this will increase use by motorized water sports on Loch Lomond – participants in water sports are prepared to travel considerable distances to gain access to water. Water space also may become less generally available, if the water authorities, who manage a substantial area of water, are privatized. There is already evidence in England and Wales of some of the private water companies restricting access or making users pay more (Beskine, 1991).

(7) There is an increasing awareness of environmental issues and an expectation of a high quality environment for leisure and recreation activities. While most users still complain about the weather and in Scotland the midges (Centre for Leisure Research, 1992; 1993), there is a significant minority who are put off by other users, noise, environmental pollution and activities which are not considered in keeping with a natural setting, and over time this may lead to a change in the type of people coming to an area.

CONCLUSIONS

From the review of tourism, recreation and inland water in this chapter, the present situation can best be described as changing and challenging. However, it is important to remember that tourism and recreation are only two of many pressures on inland water and perhaps the challenges will be met most effectively through increased collaboration and cooperation between the many users and interests. There are already examples of this – the Loch Lomond Working Party in Scotland and the Erne Lakeland Management Liaison and Advisory Groups in Northern Ireland – and the success or otherwise of these groups will no doubt be watched with interest. The Erne Lakeland Management Liaison Group has begun its task by substantially improving its information base, and given the lack of up-to-date information about tourism and recreation on inland waters in Scotland evident from this contribution, perhaps this should be an objective of one or more of the Scottish agencies with responsibilities in the leisure and environment sectors.

REFERENCES

Adams, C. E. (1993). "Environmentally sensitive predictors of boat traffic loading on inland waterways. Research Note", *Leisure Studies*, **12**, 71–79.

ASH Partnership (1991). *Sports Participation in Scotland (1987–1989)*. Research Report No. 16, The Scottish Sports Council, Edinburgh.

Beskine, D. (1991). "Water privatisation – the rambler's view", *Ecos*, **12**, 23–27.

Centre for Leisure Research (1986). *Access to the Countryside for Recreation and Sport*, Sports Council, London, and Countryside Commission, Cheltenham.

Centre for Leisure Research (1991). *A Digest of Sports Statistics for the UK*, 3rd edition, The Sports Council, London.

Centre for Leisure Research (1992). *Loch Lomond and Dumbarton Area Visitor Survey, 1991*, Edinburgh.

Centre for Leisure Research (1993). *Erne Lakeland Tourism and Recreation Study*, A report to the Department of the Environment, Northern Ireland, the Northern Ireland Tourist Board, the Department of Agriculture, Northern Ireland and the Northern Ireland Sports Council.

Chmura, G. H. and Ross, N. W. (1978). *The Environmental Impact of Marinas and their Boats*, University of Rhode Island, Marine Memorandum 45.

Coppock, J. T., Munroe, D. M. and Walker, S. E. (1985). *Changes in Outdoor Recreation 1973–1981*, Scottish Leisure Survey Report No. 2, Countryside Commission for Scotland, Battleby, Perthshire.

Land Use Consultants (1991). *Amenity Reclamation of Mineral Workings: Supplementary Fact Sheets*, A report to the Department of the Environment, London.

Leisure Consultants (1989). *Boating and Water Sports in Britain*, Sudbury.

Liddle, M. J. and Scorgie, H. R. A. (1980). "The effects of recreation on freshwater plants and animals: a review", *Biological Conservation*, **17**, 181–206.

Mackay Consultants (1989). *The Economic Importance of Salmon Fishing and Netting in Scotland*. A report to the Scottish Tourist Board and Highlands and Islands Development Board, Inverness.

Mackenzie, S. (1985). *Recreation and Holidays in the Countryside*, Scottish Leisure Survey Report No. 1, Countryside Commission for Scotland, Battleby, Perthshire.

Mintel (1992). "Water Sports", *Leisure Intelligence*, **4**, 1–31.

Patmore, J. A. (1983). *Recreation and Resources*, Blackwell, Oxford.

Scottish Natural Heritage (1992). *Enjoying the Outdoors*, A consultation paper on access to the countryside for enjoyment and understanding, Edinburgh.

Scottish Office (1990). *Scottish Abstract of Statistics, 1990*, Scottish Office, Edinburgh.

Scottish Tourist Board (1992). *Research Handbook*, Edinburgh.

Tivy, J. (1980) *The Effects of Recreation on Freshwater Lochs and Reservoirs in Scotland*, Countryside Commission for Scotland, Battleby, Perthshire.

Ward, and Andrews, (1993).

Ward, D. and Andrews, J. (1993). "Waterfowl and recreational disturbance on inland waters", *British Wildlife*, **4**, 221–229.

SECTION III
PRESSURES ON THE RESOURCE

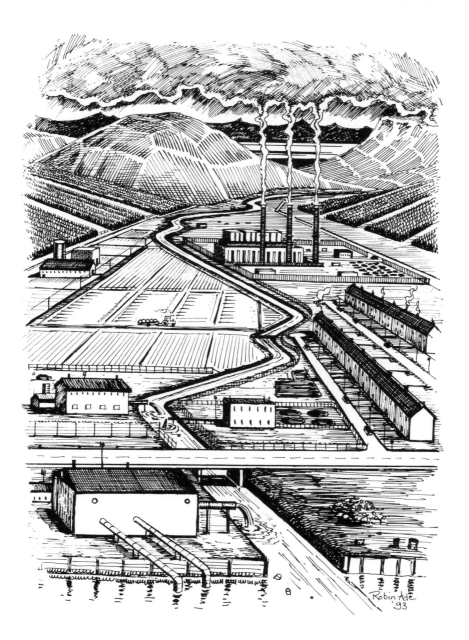

20

Domestic and Industrial Pollution

D. HAMMERTON

Clyde River Purification Board, Murray Road, East Kilbride, G75 0LA, UK

INTRODUCTION

This chapter examines the historical impact of sewage and industrial discharges on Scotland's inland waters and the effectiveness of the relevant Acts of Parliament in bringing water pollution under control. Despite the earliest legislation to control pollution in modern times, in the form of the Rivers Pollution Act 1876, subsequent progress has been painfully slow and successive governments have proved very reluctant to take effective action to bring about environmental improvement (Hammerton, 1983; 1986; 1987). Indeed, it is only since 1965 in Scotland that real progress in restoring polluted waterways has taken place. During the past decade the pace of progress has further quickened under the influence of largely European legislation and most of the blackspots in inland waterways have been eliminated. Now we are about to witness a further tightening of standards and, over the next 12 years, the largest-ever programme of investment in new sewage and industrial effluent treatment plant. In this new phase the main emphasis will move from fresh water to the hitherto neglected bathing beaches and coastal waters.

This account will focus on the history of water pollution control in Scotland up to the last decade while the scope and significance of current UK and European legislation, together with the future outlook for environmental progress, will form the subject of Chapter 27.

THE ONSET OF POLLUTION

Prior to 1800 most rivers and lochs in Scotland were in a clean and healthy condition with relatively few localized stretches affected by sewage and trade wastes. However, during the next five decades a rapid deterioration took place so that, by about 1850, many rivers in the more heavily populated catchments in the central lowlands had become little more than open sewers. Indeed, many rivers throughout Britain and western Europe became heavily polluted during this period. The problem was forcibly brought to the attention of Parliament because the River Thames, which received the untreated sewage from a population of three million, was the worst polluted in Britain

The Fresh Waters of Scotland: A National Resource of International Significance
Edited by P. S. Maitland, P. J. Boon and D. S. McLusky. © 1994 John Wiley & Sons Ltd

and noxious odours from the river during the hot summers of 1858 and 1859 almost brought Parliamentary proceedings to a standstill (Dr William Budd, quoted by Gray, 1940).

Pollution of Scottish rivers in 1872

Eventually the government took action by setting up two Royal Commissions – the first in 1865 and the second in 1868. The latter body – the Rivers Pollution Commission – sat for six years and produced six comprehensive reports on the pollution of rivers by sewage and industrial wastes and on the available methods of treatment. The Commission carried out its work with characteristic Victorian thoroughness: it recorded every source of pollution in the major rivers, listed the factories, the numbers of employees, quantities and nature of raw materials and chemicals in use, and the nature of the effluents discharging to the watercourses. Samples were taken for chemical analysis upstream and downstream of the principal towns and major industries in order to demonstrate the impact of effluents on the rivers. The Commission included, in its minutes of evidence, interviews with a wide range of witnesses comprising councillors, industrialists, landowners, medical officers of health and sanitary inspectors. A key member of the Commission was the distinguished chemist Edward Frankland who, no doubt, did much to ensure the high scientific quality of its reports.

The Fourth Report of this Commission, published in 1872, was devoted to Scotland and provided a remarkably detailed account of the impact of pollution in the principal river basins together with the water supply systems in the major centres of population. What follows is a summary of the principal findings. The Commission reported in succession on the river basins of the Tweed, the Clyde, the Irvine, the Tay and the Dundee, Lothian and northern rivers.

The Tweed Basin

The report stated that the waters of two thirds of the Tweed Basin, comprising grassy uplands and cultivated land and excepting the drainage of peat bogs or "the abrading action of floods" were of exceptional purity. Tables of analyses for organic carbon, organic nitrogen, ammonia, nitrate, nitrite, total combined nitrogen, alkalinity, chloride and hardness confirmed that upstream of the towns, so long as only affected by agricultural industry, the tributaries of the Tweed were remarkably free from pollution.

It is of interest to note here that the Commission drew attention to recent extensive land drainage works which "had the effect of shortening floods and thus intensifying the mischievous effect of a consequently longer period of drought". The comment was added that "A flood in the river channel now begins and ceases almost as abruptly as it begins and leaves off from the clouds".

Serious pollution was noted in the catchment but localized to the immediate downstream vicinity of the towns. The Gala Water, below the woollen manufacturing town of Galashiels to its junction with the Tweed, was singled out as the dirtiest tributary in the whole catchment. The Corporation of Galashiels stated that the principal causes of pollution, which had prevailed for many years and were still getting worse, were town sewage and liquid effluents from the washing and dyeing of wool, animal skin and tanning works and the deposition of solid refuse including ashes and cinders. Apparently no fish could live in the river downstream.

Localized pollution of a similar nature was noted in the Jed below Jedburgh which was described as in a filthy condition and small in volume. Pollution here was due to town sewage and liquid waste from woollen mills, dyeworks, tanyards, skinneries, slaughterhouses, gas works and sheep dip manufactories. At Hawick there was a similar serious impact of pollution on the Teviot and Slitrig although these streams were virtually unpolluted upstream of the town. At Kelso the Commission reported that sewage pollution of the River Tweed gave rise to a most offensive smell.

However, in general the Commission found that the Tweed was not yet "seriously injured" and that, in fact, the value of the fishings was still increasing but that it was most desirable "that remedies be at once applied by which . . . the charm and usefulness of a beautiful river may be retained unspoiled or restored to their original perfection".

The Lothian rivers

As one would expect, the impact of pollution was found to be much more severe here than in the Tweed catchment. In fact, the commissioners suggested that the subject of river pollution "could nowhere be better studied than in the neighbourhood of Edinburgh because of the curiously specific character of the foulness which the streams and running waters of Mid Lothian severally experience".

Thus the North Esk and the Water of Leith exhibited almost exclusively the effect of discharges from paper mills on otherwise clean streams. The River Almond showed, in successive stretches, the effects of flax-steeping followed downstream by drainage from distilleries and finally the impact of paraffin oil due to the distillation of oil-bearing shales. The lower reaches of this river carried a permanent stench of paraffin oil which ranged in concentration from 5.35 parts per 100 000 at Mid Calder to 0.5 parts at Cramond Bridge. The Commission was informed "that the river at Cramond was formerly sweet and clean and much used for making tea but now useless for all purposes".

Finally, the three small streams draining the City of Edinburgh showed exclusively the impact of sewage, there being virtually no trade wastes. Analyses of these streams (the aptly named Foul Burn, the Pow Burn and the Lochrin Burn) showed remarkably high levels of chloride and ammonia – up to 15 parts and 11.6 parts per 100 000, respectively.

Basin of the Clyde

Without any doubt the Clyde was found to be the most polluted river in Scotland and the impact of pollution was described in dramatic terms. "Nowhere", declared the Commission, "is there a greater contrast than that which exists between the unpolluted waters which come down to Lanark, or even as far as Hamilton, and the foul and stinking flood to which they have been changed not twenty miles beyond that point".

The Commission went on to state that this change had all taken place within living

memory and the Clyde, even in the heart of Glasgow, was, until recently, comparatively clean. "Now, its water there is loaded with sewage mud, foul with sewage gas
and poisoned by sewage waste of every kind – from dye works, chemical works,
bleach works, paraffin oil works, tanyards, distilleries, privies and watercloset". The
Commission then went on to explain why these changes had taken place:

> The cause of this change, stated shortly, is to be found in the enormous increase of
> population and of manufacturing industry, which during the past generation has been
> witnessed in Clydesdale. The population of Lanarkshire has been tripled with the past
> fifty years, and that of Glasgow alone is increasing at about the rate of 10 000 annually.
> This, together with the great increase in the water supply of towns, by which their filth
> is more rapidly and perfectly than ever washed into the watercourses, is quite sufficient
> to account for the conditions of the River Clyde.

The report goes on to describe in great detail, with the aid of many chemical
analyses, the appalling state of the lower tributaries, that is, the North and South
Calders, the Kelvin, the Cadzow Burn, the White Cart, the Black Cart and even the
River Leven at Dumbarton. In summer these tributaries were little more than open
sewers conveying sewage and industrial wastes to the main river. It is of interest to
note that the Commission drew particular attention to artificial deepening of the
Clyde through the City which turned the river into a gigantic settlement basin where,
in summer, whenever the water temperature was above 13°C, "putrefactive fermenta-
tion" took place giving rise to sewage gas (methane) and other filthy products, for
example, sulphuretted hydrogen. The Commission showed that experiments carried
out by Professor Anderson of Glasgow University at the time indicated that the river
water caused corrosion to the iron and copper plates of ships moored in the river.

Basin of the River Irvine

This catchment was relatively clean with the notable exception of the Kilmarnock
Water which, in the short space of 25 years, had deteriorated into an open sewer
which had become "a source of discomfort and injurious to health especially in
summer when it emits a very offensive stench".

Basin of the River Tay

This river was found to be virtually unpolluted throughout its length and even the
sewage of Perth (population 26 356) was lost in the immense volume of water.

Northern river basins

In the north of Scotland the Commission found no significant evidence of river
pollution. The Don and the Dee were noted as being relatively clean though the Don,
because of the greater fertility of its catchment and larger area of cultivation,
contained a higher level of nitrogenized organic matter.

Dundee streams

Finally, mention should be made, for the sake of completeness, to the Dighty Burn,
one of the most polluted streams remarkable for the number of linen and jute bleach

works on its banks. In summer almost the whole flow of the stream was diverted into the mill lades and returned downstream as effluent carrying with it the residues of some 4500 tons of chemicals used annually and comprising chloride of lime, soda ash, sulphuric acid and hyposulphite as well as an unknown amount of organic waste.

Chief sources of pollution

Following the reports on the various river basins, the Commission summarized the major pollution problems as being due, first to town sewage (which appears to have been almost entirely untreated at the time) and the following industrial sources: calico dye and print works; flax-steeping, linen and jute bleaching and dyeing; starch works; paper mills; alcohol distilleries; sugar refineries; paraffin oil works; woollen works; chemical works; tanneries.

Recommendations of the Royal Commission on Rivers Pollution

In its Fourth Report the Commission laid great emphasis on the need for legally enforceable effluent standards in order to distinguish between discharges which were polluting and inadmissible to rivers and those which should be permitted (Table 20.1). Great care was taken in framing these standards which, before publication, were submitted for comment to many chemists in Britain and abroad. These included five Fellows of the Royal Society and noted European chemists including Baron von

TABLE 20.1. Standards of purity for effluent proposed by the Royal Commission on Rivers Pollution, Fourth Report 1872

The following standards of purity, of which we have already recommended the enactment, and which we now again submit, represent, in a concentrated form, our experience acquired by the incessant investigation for four years of the chief manufacturing processes carried out in this country.

(a) Any liquid containing, in suspension, more than three parts by weight of dry mineral matter, or one part by weight of dry organic matter in 100 000 parts by weight of the liquid.
(b) Any liquid containing, in solution, more than two parts by weight of organic carbon, or three parts by weight of organic nitrogen in 100 000 parts by weight of the liquid.
(c) Any liquid which shall exhibit by daylight a distinct colour when a stratum of it one inch deep is placed in a white porcelain or earthenware vessel.
(d) Any liquid which contains, in solution, in 100 000 parts by weight, more than two parts by weight of any metal except calcium, magnesium, potassium and sodium.
(e) Any liquid which, in 100 000 parts by weight, contains, whether in solution or suspension, in chemical combination or otherwise, more than 0.05 parts by weight of metallic arsenic.
(f) Any liquid which, after acidification with sulphuric acid, contains, in 100 000 parts by weight, more than one part by weight of free chlorine.
(g) Any liquid which contains, in 100 000 parts by weight, more than one part by weight of sulphur, in the condition either of sulphuretted hydrogen or of a soluble sulphuret.
(h) Any liquid possessing an acidity greater than that which is produced by adding two parts by weight of real muriatic acid to 1000 parts by weight of distilled water.
(i) Any liquid possessing an alkalinity greater than that produced by adding one part by weight of dry caustic soda to 1000 parts by weight of distilled water.
(k) Any liquid exhibiting a film of petroleum or hydrocarbon oil upon its surface, or containing, in suspension, in 100 000 parts, more than 0.05 part of such oil.

Liebig (Munich), Dr Hofmann (Berlin), and M. Dumas, Secretary of the French Institute in Paris. All supported the proposed standards while Monsieur Dumas suggested an additional standard with the following remark: "Even where the cause has not been ascertained by chemical analysis, all water which has become unfit to support the life of fish shall be considered as having received a pollution from which it must be purified". This is the first recorded proposal for a fish toxicity test!

In order to monitor discharges and enforce standards, the Commission proposed the appointment of government inspectors. It also recommended the formation of river conservancy boards with limited powers for river maintenance including the purchase and removal of weirs, straightening and deepening of watercourses and the construction of upland reservoirs.

FIRST LEGISLATION

Rivers Pollution Act 1876

Armed with this report and also backed up by the report of a select committee of the House of Lords, Lord Shaftesbury acted speedily and in the same year introduced a Rivers Pollution Bill incorporating all of these recommendations but, due to the powerful industrial lobby, this was heavily defeated. Further Bills introduced in 1873 and 1875 proposed weaker versions of the recommendations but were also defeated. Finally, in 1876, a Bill was introduced which became the Rivers Pollution Act 1876. This Act – which provided the legal framework for water pollution control for the next 75 years – was, at first sight, a powerful piece of legislation which prohibited virtually all forms of pollution. In fact, it was so seriously flawed that a Scottish MP, Mr Lyon Playfair, declared that it had been so altered in its passage through Parliament that, "so far as Scotland is concerned, the Bill would have far better not been passed into law". In particular, the Act contained a clause which imposed severe restrictions on the circumstances in which the prohibitions could be enforced. A recent study (Richardson *et al.*, 1982) showed that "there can hardly have been a more blatant attempt by Parliament to obstruct the enforcement of a law which by the same enactment it created".

Early attempts at pollution control in Lanarkshire, 1895–1924

Quite apart from the defence clause referred to above, the 1876 Act was also highly deficient in that there were no enforceable standards, no government inspectors and the enforcement was placed in the hands of the local authorities who had little incentive to enforce the Act because they were usually themselves the largest polluters. An attempt was made to remedy this situation by means of the Local Government Scotland Act 1887, which allowed the 1876 Act to be administered by County Councils which, not being responsible for sewerage, were independent of all the polluters. However, as far as can be ascertained, only one authority – Lanark County Council – resolved to make full use of these powers. Under the direction of the Medical Officer of Health, the Council functioned as a river pollution control authority for some 35 years and, within the limitations of the legislation, was remarkably successful (Hammerton, 1983; 1986).

A number of prosecutions were authorized in 1896 and a River Inspector with two assistants and a chemist were appointed. A purpose-built laboratory was opened in 1900. By 1903, when the first report was published, five prosecutions had succeeded against the Burgh of Motherwell, two ammonia works and two coal washeries. As a result of this vigorous campaign three of the seven large burghs in Lanarkshire had sewage treatment works built or under construction in 1903 while 18 out of 29 Special Drainage Districts had sewage treatment works either operating or under construction. Moreover, about 100 industrial dischargers had put in some form of treatment and were regularly inspected.

Reports published in 1909 and 1924 showed that further progress had been made with the construction of industrial and sewage treatment plants, but it is evident from these reports (County Council of Lanark, 1903; 1909; 1924) that the Medical Officer of Health was increasingly frustrated by the serious weakness inherent in the 1876 Act, particularly the inability to enforce standards.

The reports provide a wealth of detail on the pollution problems of the Clyde Basin and some of the more important findings deserve to be recorded here. Firstly, it is clear that despite all the efforts of the County Council in persuading local authorities and industrialists to put in treatment plants which had purification rates ranging from 55% to 90%, the final effluents were seriously polluting by present-day standards (Hammerton, 1983). A survey in 1922–23 showed that in rivers downstream of sewage works the Biochemical Oxygen Demand (BOD) values ranged from 2.6 to 75 ppm with a mean value of 16.7.

Secondly, it is evident that pollution from coal mines (not mentioned in the 1874 report) began to have a serious impact on rivers in the last two decades of the nineteenth century. The 1903 report of Lanark County Council showed that the number of coal washery machines had grown from one or two in 1885 to 68 in 1902 and that in that year some 15 000 tons of coal were being washed daily in the Lanarkshire coal fields. The fine solids entering streams caused severe problems to farmers and industrialists and even interfered with river flows by the siltation of watercourses. One farmer lost many sheep and the post-mortem on one animal revealed the presence of four ounces of coal and solid particles in the stomach. The third report (1924) stated that, after sewage, the discharge of coal solids probably accounted for most of the pollution of the Clyde and its tributaries upstream of Glasgow. The main sources were 74 coal washers at the pit heads, discharging directly to rivers. Although most had silt-recovery tanks, there was no simple legal method of enforcing their proper maintenance.

According to the same report, there was a growing problem of pollution by pit drainage waters which were pumped into the rivers and which were specifically exempt from control under the 1876 Act. These often had high suspended solids and, in an increasing number of cases, iron either in solution or in suspension. The first fish deaths due to ferruginous water took place in Cobbinshaw Loch from Woolfords Colliery. After a successful action for damages the water was diverted to the Dippool Water with disastrous results for fish life. In 1921, closure of two pits for three months led to extensive fish kills in the Douglas Water when pumping resumed. This was the first occasion on which free acid was detected in a pit water.

Thirdly, as a result of 30 years' experience of attempting to administer the defective Rivers Pollution Act, the Medical Officer of Health recommended that early action should be taken by the government to implement the recommendations of the Royal Commission on Sewage Disposal, especially the formation of river boards on a catchment basis with legislative powers to enforce the new standards recommended by that Commission (Royal Commission on Sewage Disposal, 1908; 1912).

Advisory Committee on Rivers Pollution Prevention

A careful study of these and other reports shows that 50 years after the Rivers Pollution Act Scottish rivers were in a worse condition than in 1872. For example, in 1927 the Scottish Board of Health published an "exhaustive" survey of 23 river basins in which it recorded no fewer than 880 established polluting discharges of which only 78 received fairly satisfactory treatment while 539 received no treatment whatsoever. The Clyde Basin was the worst affected with 235 "pollutions" followed by the Forth Basin with 107 and the Tweed in third place with 90.

This report led immediately to the appointment, by the Secretary of State, of the Advisory Committee on Rivers Pollution Prevention. Successive reports by this committee are the best source of information on river pollution in the inter-war years. Reports were produced on the River Tweed (1930), Esk (1931), Ove, Leven and Tyne (1933), and on the Almond and Avon (1935). The latter report again emphasized the seriousness of pollution due to mining. In the Almond Basin, for example, there were 25 collieries and a fireclay pit. Twelve million gallons of pit drainage waters and effluents from coal washeries were discharged daily to the river and its tributaries comprising, in total, a third of the daily flow! A further two million gallons per day reached the lower catchment from shale mines. The report stated that the greatest volume of polluting material in this catchment arose from active and abandoned coal mines.

In 1936 the Advisory Committee produced its final report which confirmed, for Scotland as a whole, what Lanarkshire County Council had stated in 1924, that is the very serious problem of river pollution could not be resolved under the existing legislation. The Committee added its voice to earlier calls and once again proposed the establishment of river boards on a catchment basis to control pollution of inland and tidal waters as had been recommended by the Royal Commission on Sewage Disposal 32 years previously. Unfortunately, the onset of World War II halted all progress and there was a further deterioration of rivers during the ensuing 15 years.

NEW LEGISLATION

Rivers (Prevention of Pollution) (Scotland) Act 1951

Soon after the end of the war the government, now convinced that new legislation was overdue, set up in 1946 a Sub-Committee of the Scottish Water Advisory Committee with a specific brief to consider the amendment of the law with regard to river pollution in Scotland. Its report, published in 1950, provided a comprehensive set of recommendations and, for once, the government acted speedily with the result that the Rivers (Prevention of Pollution) (Scotland) Act received the Royal Assent in August 1951.

This Act marked a major turning point in the history of water pollution control in

Scotland. Firstly, it provided a sound administrative basis for enforcing the law by creating a system of independent, catchment-based River Purification Boards. Secondly, it provided, for the first time, an effective mechanism for controlling pollution whereby it became a criminal offence to make a discharge of sewage or trade effluent without the consent of the river purification authority. The authority could refuse consent or grant consent with such conditions as it thought fit – though such conditions had to be reasonable. If the discharger felt that the conditions were unreasonable he had a right of appeal to the Secretary of State. The Act also provided for a second means of control using local byelaws which had to receive the approval of the Secretary of State.

Altogether nine River Purification Boards were set up between 1953 and 1959 covering 55% of the area of mainland Scotland. The areas varied from 1580 km^2 for the Lothians River Purification Board to 7800 km^2 for the Tay Board and, in population, from 100 000 in the Tweed Board's area to 2 150 000 in the area of the Clyde River Purification Board. In the north of Scotland the new legislation was enforced by 12 River Purification Authorities comprising 10 county councils and two larger burgh councils.

The first task of the new Boards was to appoint River Inspectors (who were required to be Corporate Members of the Royal Institute of Chemistry and Corporate Members of the Institute of Sewage Purification) and supporting staff comprising hydrologists, scientists and administrative staff. In order to carry out an effective control programme it was necessary to establish water quality monitoring systems which, hitherto, were almost non-existent and to build up long-term river flow data so that realistic consent conditions could be determined. There were very few river flow gauging stations and rainfall data were also sparse. The Boards, with financial help and advice from the Scottish Development Department, commenced a long-term programme of establishing a primary network of gauging stations. Routine monitoring of chemical river water quality began in 1955 by the Solway and Tweed Boards and in the following year by the Lothians Board, followed somewhat later by the remaining Boards. The Lothians Board was the first to appoint a biologist and routine biological surveys commenced in 1959. The first routine biological surveys commenced in the Clyde in 1968.

Rivers (Prevention of Pollution) (Scotland) Act 1965

Very soon after their establishment the new River Purification Boards (RPBs) found that there was a serious defect in the 1951 Act. The consent system was undoubtedly an effective means of controlling discharges but it could only be applied to new discharges whereas the major problems of river pollution were caused by a vast number of long-standing discharges which were exempt from the consent system. Originally it was thought that these discharges would eventually come under control by changes in their volume or composition which would enable the Boards to classify them as "new" or "altered" discharges, but this rarely occurred and was very difficult to prove. Moreover, the proposal to control pollution by means of local byelaws was found totally impracticable and was never adopted either in Scotland or in England and Wales. Haigh (1984) has pointed out that "Britain can fairly argue that the idea of emission standards laid down and applied uniformly, over stretches of river or whole rivers, was put to the practical test of being allowed for in legislation for ten years, and failed that test".

These problems were taken up by the Scottish River Purification Boards' Association (SRPBA) and the Scottish River Purification Advisory Committee (SRPAC). It was clear by this time that the Boards had managed to stop the downward trend in river water quality but, without new powers, were unable to carry out the vast programme that their initial surveys had shown to be necessary to restore Scotland's inland waters to a healthy condition.

The Rivers (Prevention of Pollution) (Scotland) Act 1965, by requiring dischargers to apply for consent for all their existing discharges, radically transformed the situation and it is from this point onwards that the restoration of river water quality began in earnest.

One other piece of legislation should be mentioned here. In the drier eastern areas of Scotland – notably East Lothian – abstraction of river water by farmers for crop irrigation became a serious problem. One survey in part of the Tyne catchment showed, theoretically, that farmers had purchased sufficient equipment to extract the whole dry weather flow several times over! As a result, the government promoted the Spray Irrigation (Scotland) Act 1964 under which abstraction was controlled by means of a licensing system.

Progress from 1965 to 1975

The powers to control all discharges to inland waters brought in many thousands of applications for consent for existing discharges and hence a vast increase in workload. To cope with this, the Boards greatly increased the size of their technical staffs and devised long-term programmes for dealing with the applications. Local authorities, especially those with many treatment works, did not have the technical capacity or the finance available to rebuild these works overnight and the Boards also required time to devise suitable consent conditions. As an example, the Clyde Board devised a 10-year programme for dealing with the larger sewage and industrial plants. This programme was based on scientific surveys of water quality and the needs of each river in terms of priority according to the pollution status of each stretch of river. Similar policies were developed by most Boards and dischargers were notified in advance when new, tighter, scientifically based consent conditions would come into force. In some cases interim "relaxed" consent conditions were imposed for specified periods. In retrospect this was perhaps not an ideal solution for it seemed to take the pressure off individual dischargers because samples were then reported as "complying with interim conditions".

Fortunately this period was one of good economic growth, and capital expenditure by local authorities (the biggest polluters) increased steadily to a new peak in 1974 (as a proportion of total local authority capital expenditure). Many blackspots across Scotland were eliminated and overall improvements in river water quality became an increasing feature of the Boards' annual reports.

Around 1969 a new problem developed in the Clyde catchment. In order to avoid control, a growing number of industries started putting their wastes through boreholes or mineshafts into disused underground mine workings in Lanarkshire. In places, this went on for months or years without apparent harm only later to break out into a watercourse remote from the point of discharge. The worst example was the Inverhouse Distillery at Airdrie which discharged a large volume of highly concentrated waste down a local mineshaft. About 12 months later in 1970 a massive break-out occurred through an old day level and 2.3×10^6 L d^{-1} of organic waste turned the North Calder Water black overnight as far downstream as its junction with the Clyde. Unable to control this and other smaller outbreaks, the Board, having failed to persuade the government to introduce legislation, therefore sought and obtained its own in the form of the Clyde River Purification Board Act 1972. The Act gave the Board powers to control and stop underground discharges and also powers for stream clearance, acquiring reservoirs and for controlling the diversion, piping or culverting of rivers. Although largely overtaken by similar powers in the Control of Pollution Act 1974, the CRPB Act proved of great value during a period of 12 years before COPA was implemented.

Progress since 1975

Two pieces of legislation have had a profound impact on the shape and progress of water pollution control in Scotland since 1975. Firstly, mention must be made of the Local Government (Scotland) Act 1973 which, by reforming local government, reduced the number of authorities responsible for the management of water and sewerage from 234 to nine. At a stroke this transformed the consultative and planning procedures and made it far easier for the RPBs to discuss and co-ordinate pollution control programmes in whole river catchments. It also meant that many sewage treatment plants previously belonging to small burgh councils could now benefit from centralized expertise in effluent treatment. The Act also reformed the River Purification Boards into a system of seven Boards covering the whole of mainland Scotland. A prime objective of this reform – as recommended by SRPAC – was to bring major industrial estuaries such as the Forth and Clyde under a single pollution control authority.

The author believes that these areas were essentially right for Scotland, and the track record of the Boards has been vindicated by a Scottish Office report recommending their continuation with the same boundaries but smaller, more streamlined Boards comprising equal numbers of local authority representatives and members nominated by the Secretary of State for Scotland.

Secondly, and of even greater importance, was the passing into law of the Control of Pollution Act in 1974. This Act brought together and reinforced existing controls relating to disposal of solid waste on land, air pollution, water pollution and noise. In doing so it took account of many of the views of the Royal Commission on Environmental Pollution and provided a mechanism for the implementation of EC legislation in accordance with the Community Action Programme on the Environment. The stated aims of this programme were: to prevent or reduce pollution and nuisance; to husband natural resources and the balance of ecological systems; and to improve the quality of life and working conditions. It also provided for the enforcement of international agreements such as the Oslo and Paris Conventions and the North Sea Ministerial Decisions. Part II of the Act relates to water: in so far as fresh water is concerned the main impact has been an end to the secrecy inherent in the previous legislation and the increasingly dominant position of EC Directives which now provide the main controls on all discharges.

TRENDS IN WATER QUALITY

As pointed out earlier in this chapter, real progress in restoring rivers to a healthy condition, after a century of neglect, has only been possible since legislation in 1965 brought all discharges to rivers under control. Moreover, national surveys of water quality by the Scottish Development Department only began in 1975 by which time a considerable number of blackspots had been eliminated as recorded in the annual reports of the River Purification Boards. Strictly comparable survey results are only possible since 1980 and Table 20.2 has been reproduced from the 16th report of the Royal Commission on Environmental Pollution (1992) and Scottish Office Environment Department (1990).

In interpreting this table it is necessary to point out that measuring river quality by length gives a misleadingly favourable impression of the impact of pollution on Scottish rivers. Most of the severe pollution occurs near the mouths of rivers where 1 km, if measured in terms of flow, must be equivalent to many kilometres of a small upland stream. It is pleasing to note that the Royal Commission on Environmental Pollution has recommended that regulatory authorities should move to a system of reporting results volumetrically as well as by length. If this were done it would show the improvements in their true perspective.

Of particular importance is the reduction in grossly polluted (Class 4) rivers by 56% in the 10 year period. The Scottish Office Environment Department (1990) (SOEnD) survey also pointed out that on the basis of biological samples, 80% of sites sampled

TABLE 20.2. Chemical classification of non-tidal rivers, lochs and canals in Scotland, 1980–1990 (Scottish Office Environment Department, 1990) (BOD = Biochemical Oxygen Demand; DO = Dissolved Oxygen)

Class	1980		1985		1990	
	km	%	km	%	km	%
1	45 184	95.0	45 510	95.6	46 111	96.9
2	1981	4.2	1688	3.5	1177	2.5
3	256	0.5	266	0.6	233	0.5
4	162	0.3	131	0.3	70	0.1
Total	47 583		47 595		47 591	

Class 1: BOD < 3 mg L^{-1}, healthy DO, no toxics
Class 2: BOD > 3 mg L^{-1}, healthy though substantially reduced DO, toxics cannot be shown to have any effect
Class 3: BOD > 12 mg L^{-1}, DO $< 50\%$ for considerable periods, suspected toxic levels of substances
Class 4: BOD > 12 mg L^{-1}, completely deoxygenated at times, toxic levels and no fish life

in 1980 recorded an improved biological score in 1990. SOEnD ascribed the improvements to a range of factors including:

- a reduction in the incidence of pollution resulting from agricultural sources;
- an increase in the level of investment by the sewerage authorities, particularly in respect of new and upgraded sewage treatment works;
- improved levels of effluent treatment by some industrial operators;
- the level of vigilance, experience and professionalism of the River Purification Boards' staff;

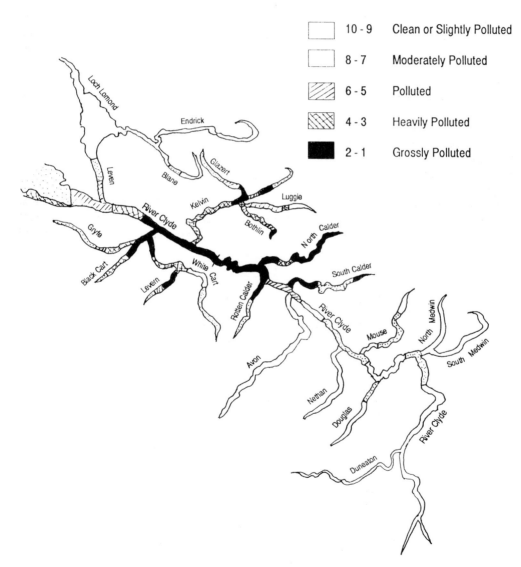

10 - 9	Clean or Slightly Polluted
8 - 7	Moderately Polluted
6 - 5	Polluted
4 - 3	Heavily Polluted
2 - 1	Grossly Polluted

FIGURE 20.1. River Clyde water quality – biological classification 1968

- the increasing awareness that the public has of the benefit of reporting pollution incidents, however small, to the river purification authority.

A further vindication of the substantial improvement in river water quality was provided by the Secretary of State for Scotland in June 1992 when he announced that over 2300 km of Scottish waters had been added to the existing 34 255 km designated in 1980 to meet the quality standards of the European Community Directive on the quality of fresh waters needing protection or improvement in order to support fish life.

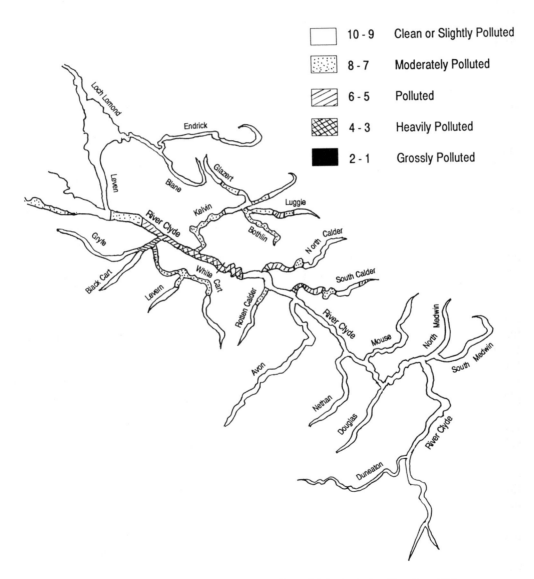

FIGURE 20.2. River Clyde water quality – biological classification 1988

It is perhaps noteworthy that, among the new lengths designated, was the whole length of the White Cart, an urban river on the south side of Glasgow which has suffered substantial sewage and industrial pollution for decades.

An example of the recovery in biological terms of one of the worst polluted river basins in Scotland is given in Figures 20.1 and 20.2. In 1968, when the first biological surveys were carried out, no fish could survive in the Clyde within the Glasgow boundary and none could be found in the lower reaches of the North Calder, South Calder, Kelvin, Black Cart and the White Cart (Hammerton, 1981). It is now more than 10 years since the return of Atlantic Salmon to the Clyde and fish are now found to some degree in all these river stretches. In the same period Salmon and other fish have returned to the Almond and various other rivers in the Forth Board area (Figure 20.3).

SUMMARY AND CURRENT TRENDS

In this necessarily brief account of water pollution in Scotland, what emerges with painful clarity is the recurrent theme of conflict between enlightened scientists and local administrations on the one hand, consistently opposed on the other by the manufacturers, with successive governments in the centre of the argument displaying weakness of intent and delaying tactics at almost every opportunity.

Thus the Victorian forefathers in the Royal Commission on Rivers Pollution of 1868 showed remarkable foresight in their recommendations for enforceable effluent standards, conservancy boards and licensed inspectors. However, in the face of powerful opposition from the industrial lobby the government caved in and produced an Act which had been deprived of all the key recommendations of the Commission and which was actually welcomed by the manufacturers! Gladstone, in the last year of his life, in response to a remark that Parliament had been far too lenient towards the manufacturers retorted: "Say far too cowardly . . ." (Wilson and Calvert, 1913).

There is, of course, a long history of government-appointed commissions and committees, whose recommendations have been left to gather dust, but in no field has this been more apparent than in water pollution control. In this connection no commission has been more highly praised than the Royal Commission on Sewage Disposal. This Commission was so alarmed by the state of British rivers and the total failure of the 1876 Act that it produced a report (1908), which had not originally been planned, in which it urged the government to set up a powerful Central Authority and a nationwide system of river boards each covering one or more catchments and sufficiently large to justify the appointment of a skilled chief inspector at an adequate salary. In its eighth report (1912) the Commission made comprehensive recommendations on the classification of river waters and standards for sewage effluent taking account of both dilution and the quality of the receiving water. These recommendations, as pointed out elsewhere (Hammerton, 1984), were derived from one of the first examples of what is now termed "environmental impact assessment". Because of the thoroughness of that study these recommendations have stood the test of time over the ensuing 80 years and have been applied in almost every country abroad.

Despite the authoritative and comprehensive nature of the Commission's work and the crying need for something to be done, successive governments ignored its recommendations for the next four decades – their only visible action being the setting

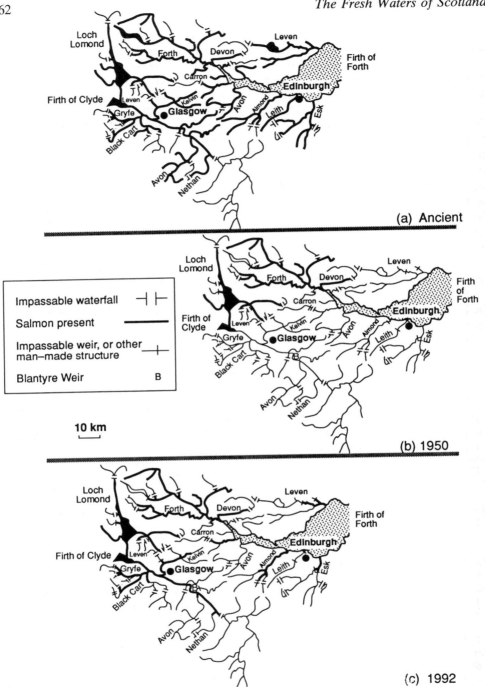

FIGURE 20.3. Maps of the Central Belt of Scotland provided by The Scottish Office (Freshwater Fisheries Laboratory, Pitlochry) showing the likely ancient distribution of salmon (a), and in 1950 (b) and 1992 (c). In general, where there are several impassable waterfalls and weirs (as on the Rivers Leven and Esk in the Firth of Forth) only the furthest downstream is indicated.
Reproduced by permission of The Scottish Office Freshwater Fisheries Laboratory

up of successive advisory committees, all of which supported and vindicated the original recommendations.

Even in 1951 the government showed weakness in that the Rivers (Prevention of Pollution) (Scotland) Act 1951 only enabled new discharges to be controlled so that further legislation was required to rectify matters.

The same reluctance to take firm action was evident almost immediately after the Control of Pollution Act had received the Royal Assent. Firstly, it was apparent, despite promises that this new tough legislation would "make the polluter pay", that the maximum penalty for breach of consent was less in real terms than that enacted in the 1951 law. Secondly, in the face of a recession and a massive lobby by the industrial sector, the government of the day again caved in and delayed implementation of almost the whole of Part II (dealing with water pollution) for over 10 years! This occurred despite a strong plea from the Royal Commission on Environmental Pollution which stated that "expenditure sooner rather than later may be wise economics as well as socially desirable".

Nevertheless, it is pleasing to note that, during the past decade, there has been a very marked change on the part of the government which has promoted or approved a rapidly increasing volume of new environmental legislation both in Parliament and the European Commission. The scope of current legislation and future trends will be dealt with in Chapters 27 and 30.

REFERENCES

County Council of Lanark (1903). "Report on the administration of the Rivers Pollution Prevention Acts by the County Medical Officer", Lanark.

County Council of Lanark (1909). "Second report on the administration of the Rivers Pollution Prevention Acts by the County Medical Officer", Lanark.

County Council of Lanark (1924). "Third report on the administration of the Rivers Pollution Prevention Acts by the County Medical Officer", Lanark.

Gray, H. F. (1940). "Sewerage in ancient and medieval times", *Sewage Works Journal*, **12**, 939–946.

Haigh, N. (1984). *EEC Environmental Policy and Britain*, Environmental Data Services, London.

Hammerton, D. (1981). "The restoration of the river Clyde – 25 years of river quality management", *Environmental Education and Information*, **1**, 197–207.

Hammerton, D. (1983). "The history of environmental water quality management in Scotland", *Journal of the Institute of Water Engineers and Scientists*, **37**, 336.

Hammerton, D. (1984). "Assessing the impact of major development on water resources", in *Planning and Ecology* (Eds R. D. Roberts and T. M. Roberts), pp. 350–363, Chapman and Hall, London.

Hammerton, D. (1986). "Cleaning the Clyde – a century of progress?", *Journal of the Operational Research Society*, **37**, 911–921.

Hammerton, D. (1987). "The impact of environmental legislation", *Water Pollution Control*, **86**, 333–344.

Richardson, G., Ogus, A. and Burrows, P. (1982). *Policing Pollution. A Study of Regulation and Enforcement*, Oxford Socio-Legal Studies, Clarendon Press, Oxford.

Rivers Pollution Commission (1872). *Fourth Report: Pollution of Rivers of Scotland*, HMSO, London.

Royal Commission on Environmental Pollution (1992). *Freshwater Quality*, HMSO, London.

Royal Commission on Sewage Disposal (1901–1914). Nine reports, and final report (1915), HMSO, London.

Scottish Advisory Committee on Rivers Pollution (1936). *Suggested Amendments of the Law on Rivers Pollution Prevention*, Department of Health for Scotland, HMSO, Edinburgh.

Scottish Board of Health (1927). *Annual Report*, HMSO, Edinburgh.

Scottish Office Environment Department (1990). *Water Quality Survey of Scotland*, Edinburgh.

Scottish Water Advisory Committee (1950). *Report of the Rivers Pollution Prevention Sub-Committee*, HMSO, Edinburgh.

Wilson, H. M. and Calvert, H. T. (1913). *Textbook on Trade Waste Waters – their Nature and Disposal*, Griffin, London.

21

Agriculture and Fish Farming

R. ALLCOCK

Tay River Purification Board, 1 South Street, Perth, PH2 8NJ, UK

and

D. BUCHANAN

Highland River Purification Board, Strathpeffer Road, Dingwall, IV15 9QY, UK

INTRODUCTION

In Scotland, as in other parts of Great Britain, post-war changes in agriculture in the latter part of the 20th century have resulted in the agricultural equivalent of the original industrial revolution. Production has far outstripped efforts to conserve and re-use manures and liquid wastes. The result has been an increase in the number of water pollution incidents from agricultural sources – with a deterioration in the quality of some rivers. During the summer months, this is mainly caused by silage liquor discharges and during the winter months is the result of run-off from overloaded, waterlogged fields following the spreading of slurry. Now that the Government has taken action to address the problems of over-production, with schemes such as set-aside and new legislation to combat pollution from the use of slurries, silage and fuel oils from farms, it is anticipated that matters will improve once the new measures begin to make an impact.

Fish farming requires large quantities of good quality water to supply the oxygen needs of the cultured stock and to remove the waste products generated. Intensive fish farming may lead to changes in the concentration of suspended solids, the biochemical oxygen demand, nutrients (particularly nitrogen and phosphorus), bacteria, chemical antibiotics and dissolved oxygen in the water as it passes through a fish farm. Because of the large volumes of water used, the concentration of pollutants produced is generally low. The high volume/low concentration nature of the discharge creates difficulties in treatment and monitoring. Most freshwater fish farms were originally land-based and cage farming is a more recent development. The wastes produced are similar, but different considerations apply, mainly because no treatment

The Fresh Waters of Scotland: A National Resource of International Significance
Edited by P. S. Maitland, P. J. Boon and D. S. McLusky. © 1994 John Wiley & Sons Ltd

of the wastes from cage farming is practicable at present and threats to the environment can only be controlled by limiting the size of any fish farm in relation to the size and nature of the relevant freshwater body, or by preventing any development, where such action can be justified.

This chapter discusses the problems, remedies and initiatives from the point of view of the regulatory authorities with a view to reducing pollution from agriculture and fish farming and protecting the freshwater resources of Scotland.

AGRICULTURE

Agricultural output in Scotland has been increasing steadily over the last 30 years, reaching nearly £1000 million in 1980, when it accounted for more than 3% of the country's Gross Domestic Product (GDP). Since then, there has been some decline and in 1989 agricultural output (including forestry and fishing) accounting for 2.1% of GDP. There has been a decline in the number of people employed directly in agriculture, although the 61 000 wholly or mainly employed still amounts to a bigger workforce than that of any single manufacturing industry in Scotland. The industry is thus vital to the social and economic well-being of many communities.

Agriculture in Scotland is a modern, efficient industry, applying up-to-date technology, with a high level of mechanization and a highly skilled workforce. Livestock and livestock products accounted for 69% of farm output in 1990, with farm and horticultural crops accounting for the remaining 31%. The panorama of farming in Scotland is varied and interesting, ranging from the dairy farms of the south-west to the beef-rearing and feeding farms of the north-east, from the large cropping farms in Lothian, Fife and Tayside to the crofts of the highlands and islands.

Physical background

From even the most cursory glance at a physical map of Scotland, two features are obvious. First, Scotland covers a fairly wide latitudinal range but is narrow, with a long, broken coastline. Second, it is a very hilly country. These two characteristics have a strong influence on Scotland's climate, soils and capability for agricultural production.

Warm ocean currents moderate the climate, the nature of the coastline allowing their effects to penetrate in to the mainland. In general, winters are mild and summers cool, with rainfall normally adequate for crop production; droughts are uncommon. Annual rainfall in the east ranges from 750 to 1250 mm. In the west, excessive rainfall has a depressing effect on agriculture in some areas – mainly the more mountainous regions where annual rainfall is often over 2000 mm.

In the hill regions, the soil is generally peaty, of low fertility and often suffers from impeded drainage. On the upland fringes, acid brown and alluvial soils are more prevalent. The incidence of these more fertile soils increases in the lowlands and, combined with the more level terrain, makes most of this land more suitable for intensive cultivation.

Agricultural production

Altogether, there are some 18 000 full-time farms which display a marked diversity of agricultural types, the predominance of particular farming in different parts of the country being determined principally by the physical factors described above.

Hill sheep farming is common throughout the highlands and islands and upland areas further south. Upland farms number about 5500 and comprise the largest farm group in Scottish agriculture. Farms combining livestock rearing with arable production number about 3200 and are found on the fringes of the upland areas, particularly in the north-east. These farms share many of the characteristics of upland farms, but better soils and climate permit more cropping and more intensive stocking. There are about 900 arable rearing and feeding farms and these are found mainly in the north-east where the quality and extent of the cropping or grassland enables most of the livestock to be reared. Scotland's 3500 cropping farms are located chiefly on the better lands near the east coast. Dairy farms number about 2900 and are situated mainly in the south-west where about 75% of Scotland's cattle are found. However, there are local concentrations elsewhere, notably the north-east and Orkney. Nearly 450 units are engaged in pig or poultry farming – almost half of the Scottish pig production is in the north-east, while most poultry are found in the south-east.

As well as the 18 000 full-time farms in Scotland, there are about 13 000 part-time units contributing significantly to agricultural production (Scottish Office, 1992a).

Farm waste

In Britain as a whole, farms produce more than 200×10^6 t of animal wastes each year, equivalent to the pollution load from 600×10^6 t of human sewage. It is obvious that the capacity of the land and watercourses to absorb this quantity of effluent has been exceeded in many parts of the country. In Scotland, in view of the diversity of farming, it is not surprising that a wide range of point-source pollution problems exist. Slurry and silage liquors, manure heaps, farmyard drainage, disposal of pesticides and herbicides and spent sheep-dip all pose threats.

The intensification of livestock farming has brought about many of these problems. For a long time the emphasis was on increasing production, with the design of structures to contain effluents developing slowly and not keeping pace with production. The trend towards feeding cattle silage rather than hay has meant a considerable increase in the quantity of silage liquor produced and the amount of slurry to be disposed of.

The polluting strengths of silage liquor and slurry are extremely high. In some areas, the capacity of the ground to absorb them has been exceeded, with the subsequent downgrading in the water quality classification of local rivers. Many burns and rivers are badly affected by discharges of silage in summer and autumn and slurry in winter and spring. However, there are also chronic discharges of both pollutants which affect watercourses all year.

Each year, many serious water pollution incidents occur as a direct result of agricultural activities, particularly livestock farming. Between 1985 and 1990 the majority of incidents in Scotland caused by agriculture resulted from silage effluent

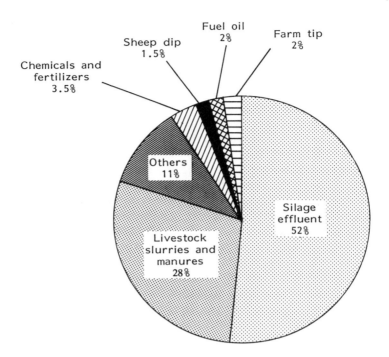

FIGURE 21.1. The percentage of total reported pollution incidents due to the main farm pollution sources (1982–1990).

(52%), slurry (28%) and other sources (20%) (Scottish Farm Waste Liaison Group, 1992: Figure 21.1). There are almost 500 incidents every year (Figure 21.2) with more than 700 recorded in 1985 and in 1987, which were particularly wet years. There is a direct relationship between the number of pollution incidents and the prevailing weather conditions. In a wet winter there is usually an increase in slurry pollution incidents while a wet summer tends to result in an increase in pollution incidents caused by silage effluent.

Water pollution

Thus, the major water pollution problems caused by farm wastes are due to discharges of silage liquor, slurry and milk wastes. All of these can cause rapid deoxygenation of watercourses, frequently resulting in the death of invertebrates and fish. The main reason for these deaths is the very high biochemical oxygen demand (BOD_5) of these farm wastes, which can be 200 times higher than crude sewage (Table 21.1).

Pollution can also result from the specific effects of substances such as ammonia and fuel oil which may be directly damaging or toxic to aquatic life. These pollutants can also affect drinking water where a river is abstracted for water supply as well as water used by farmers for watering stock or for irrigation. Diffuse pollution from any of these sources can also affect groundwater. Even agricultural fertilizers can cause

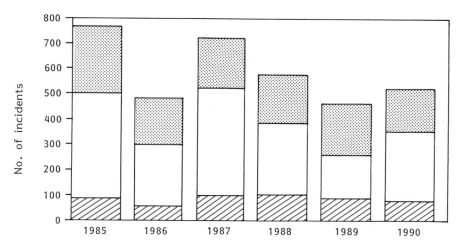

FIGURE 21.2. Farm pollution incidents in Scotland, 1985–1990 (top, slurry; middle, silage; bottom, others)

problems when they find their way into local waters, giving rise to excessive plant growths (see Chapter 22).

The BOD_5 is the most commonly used indicator of the pollution potential of organic wastes and is a measure of the amount of oxygen required by micro-organisms to break down the organic material present. As a Class 1 watercourse normally has a BOD_5 of less than 3 mg L^{-1}, any loading in excess of this can be considered a pollutant, and this threshold places the potential threat from agricultural pollutants in context. The BOD_5 of silage liquor is approximately 200 times more polluting than raw domestic sewage. A clamp containing 500 t of unwilted silage has the same

TABLE 21.1. Examples of typical biochemical oxygen demand (BOD_5) levels

	BOD (mg L^{-1})
Treated domestic sewage	20–60
Raw domestic sewage	300–400
Vegetable washings	500–3000
Dilute dairy parlour and yard washings (dirty water)	1000–2000
Liquid effluent draining from slurry stores	1000–12 000
Liquid sewage sludge	10 000–20 000
Cattle slurry	10 000–20 000
Pig slurry	20 000–30 000
Silage effluent	30 000–80 000
Milk	140 000

TABLE 21.2. Catchment study, 1990–92, for sheep dip concentration (diazinon, propetamphos)

Sample site	Diazinon concentration (ngL^{-1})				propetamphos concentration (ngL^{-1})		
	2–3/10/89	17/10/90	23/10/91	21/10/92	17/10/90	23/10/91	21/10/92
Upper Tweed Catchment							
Tweed at Merlindale	96	33	5	0	77	3	0
Biggar Water upstream STW	137	50	41	0	72	8	0
Lyne Water below Tarth Water	24	65	6	0	140	3	0
Manor Water upstream Kirkton	16	41	6	0	77	3	6
Eddleston Water upstream STW	0	25	3	0	135	4	0
Yarrow Water at General's Bridge	8	39	3	0	135	0	0
Ettrick Water at Tushielaw	96	34	3	0	82	0	10
Gala Water at Fountainhall	40	67	24	1060	260	8	0
Teviot Water Catchment							
Teviot Water at Branxholme Bridge	0	25	0	12	145	0	13
Brothwick Water above Roberton	200	38	3	9	357	0	5
Slitrig Water upstream Stobs Castle	64	30	9	0	87	6	0
Rule Water upstream Bonchester Bridge	56	33	3	0	154	4	6
Ale Water by Castle Side	40	19	3	0	289	3	0
Oxnam Water at Crailinghall	113	14	3	0	116	0	0
Jed Water at Ferniehurst Bridge	40	47	0	0	82	5	0
Kale Water at Linton Burn Foot	64	35	5	0	125	3	0
Lower Tweed Catchment							
Leader Water at Boon Bridge	48	26	4	9	92	5	5
Bowmont Water at Town Yetholm	64	32	12	9	236	3	0
Blackadder Water upstream Greenlaw	137	124	23	0	366	4	0
Whiteadder Water at Ellemford	0	47	5	0	217	3	0
Whiteadder Water at Preston Bridge	NI	NI	20	0	NI	0	0
Eye Water at Gauge	NI	NI	6	0	NI	3	17

Key: NI – Not included
STW – Sewage Treatment Works
Note: Chlorfenvinphos not included as it is widely used in other agricultural applications.

polluting potential as the daily untreated sewage production from a town of about 200 000 people, such as Dundee (Allcock, 1992).

Obvious signs that a water is suffering from pollution include the appearance of "sewage fungus", an aggregation of fungi and bacteria which is visible as grey filamentous strands and can spread for some distance downstream from the source of pollution. In serious cases, sewage fungus blankets the whole stream bed, smothering most species of plants and invertebrates. Farmers are asked by the River Purification Authorities to inspect watercourses around their fields at times when silage is made or slurry is spread on the land. The presence of sewage fungus is a simple sign that something is wrong and that remedial action is necessary.

There are a number of other sources of pollution from agriculture, such as pesticides (Baldock and Bennett, 1991). Annual consumption of pesticides in the UK stands at around 24 000 t of active ingredients, agriculture and horticulture accounting for 91% of sales which are dominated by herbicides and fungicides. The trend has been to use products which are more active biologically at lower dosage rates and so use smaller quantities of active ingredients. Thus, since 1983, consumption of the latter has fallen by about 28%. However, the area of treatment has risen from 15.1 to 23.2×10^6 ha (British Agrochemicals Association, 1990).

Although relatively few incidents of pollution from sheep-dipping have been recorded by the river purification authorities, some have been very serious, causing fish kills and contamination of water supplies. The Tweed River Purification Board has been active in monitoring and evaluating the risk from dipping. An initial study in 1989 revealed that about 40% of Dippers within the Ettrick Water catchment were found to be at risk of causing pollution and an extensive survey confirmed the presence of active ingredients from sheep-dip in 17 out of 20 catchments sampled during the compulsory dipping period. Severe damage to invertebrates was recorded in some places but only two complaints from the public were received – emphasizing the importance of routine inspection and monitoring by Boards (Virtue, 1992). Table 21.2 illustrates the reduction (and in some cases elimination) of sheep-dip chemicals from numerous catchments due to the efforts of the Tweed River Purification Board.

A comparison of three rivers

A simple way of illustrating the effects of agricultural pollution on watercourses is to consider three rivers and their catchments – two in areas where there is intensive agriculture and a third where there is little agricultural activity (Figure 21.3).

On the west of Scotland, the Water of Fail (a tributary of the River Ayr) drains a dairy farming area and is affected by sporadic discharges of silage and slurry from a number of farms, with occasional very serious discharges. The major effects are high BOD_5 levels varying in 1992 at one point (Fail Toll, near the head of the river) from 2 mg L^{-1} in February to 5 mg L^{-1} in March and 9 mg L^{-1} in November. During the same period, elevated ammonia levels were also recorded, at 0.51, 0.33 and 0.80 mg L^{-1} respectively; suspended solids were recorded at 11, 209 and 158 mg L^{-1}. Biological surveys carried out at this point during 1991 and 1992 gave BMWP scores of 85, 117, 68, 116 and 68 and at the next point downstream (Parkmill) of 63, 90, 58, 68 and 58 (Clyde River Purification Board, 1992).

FIGURE 21.3. The river purification authority areas in Scotland and the rivers mentioned in the text

TABLE 21.3. chemical and biological characteristics of three Scottish rivers, 1992

	Mean values (mg L^{-1})			BMWP score
	BOD	Ammonia	Nitrate	
River Tay, Pitnacree	1.28	0.04	0.84	100–143
River Eden, Pitlessie	2.10	0.22	35.0	64–107
Water of Fail, Fail Toll	2.90	0.47	10.0	68–117

In contrast, the River Tay at Pitnacree is little affected by agriculture and has an average BOD of 1.28 mg L^{-1}, an average ammonia level of 0.04 mg L^{-1} and a BMWP score ranging from 150 to 180. BMWP scoring was developed by the UK Biological Monitoring Working Party and is based on the total number and relative sensitivity to pollution of various invertebrate families in a benthos sample.

However, to the south of the River Tay, in north-east Fife, the River Eden drains an intensively cultivated arable farming area and has elevated nitrate levels along much of its length, from Glenfarg to Guardbridge. At Pitlessie, a point sampled regularly and typical of the whole river, the Eden is usually in Class 1 condition, but has an average nitrate level of 35 mg L^{-1}. In comparison, the level in the River Tay at Pitnacree is 0.84 mg L^{-1}. The River Eden is also affected by other diffuse sources of pollution, illustrated by the biological data collected over a number of years; for example, at Pitlessie, the BMWP score is usually about 70 (cf. the River Tay at Pitnacree, Table 21.3).

These examples illustrate the effects of agricultural pollution on watercourses in Scotland and indicate the value of biological survey work in detecting sources of chronic farm waste pollution which are not always so obvious from spot chemical samples, especially at high flows when pollutants are diluted.

Pollution control legislation

Under Section 32 of the Control of Pollution Act (COPA, 1974) it is an offence to cause or knowingly permit any trade or sewage effluent to be discharged to controlled waters without the consent of the river purification authority. Trade effluent is defined as including "any effluent which is discharged from premises used for carrying on any trade or industry, other than surface water and domestic sewage". The river purification authorities (see Chapters 20 and 27) are responsible for enforcing this legislation, but action can only take place after a pollution incident has occurred.

However, with the increasing number of incidents and prosecutions and the limited success of persuasion by the RPAs to obtain improvements by farmers, the Government indicated its determination to reduce pollution from farm wastes by issuing Regulations, their main thrusts being:

(1) to ensure that all installations constructed, substantially reconstructed or enlarged after the Regulations come into effect, meet certain standards; and
(2) to give powers to the RPAs to serve notice requiring action to improve existing installations when there is considered to be a significant risk of pollution of controlled waters.

The importance of the second point is that action can now be taken by an RPA to prevent a discharge and thus avoid water pollution. The maximum penalties on summary conviction have increased and are now imprisonment for a term not exceeding three months or a fine not exceeding £20 000, and, on indictment, two years in prison and/or an unlimited fine.

In order to help farmers carry out their activities in a satisfactory manner with due regard for the environment, a *Code of Good Practice* was launched in 1992 (Scottish Office, 1992b), following preparation by the Scottish Farm Waste Liaison Group. The code is a practical guide for farmers, growers, contractors and others involved in agricultural activities, or where there is a statutory obligation to avoid causing pollution of the environment. The code covers the main agricultural activities which can give rise to pollution of the water, air or soil environments and describes some of the management practices which can be adopted to avoid, or at least minimize, the risk of causing pollution, while enabling economic agricultural practice to continue. This is a valuable document, freely available to all farmers.

Agriculture and conservation

There are increasing pressures on farmers to adopt a more sensitive approach to protecting water quality and enhancing wildlife habitats. Given the losses which the wildlife resource has sustained from agriculture, especially from intensive practices, it is worth considering a number of objectives which could be achieved – especially in view of recent moves towards set-aside and extensification practices. These should aim at:

(1) Protecting existing areas of semi-natural vegetation from any further loss or deterioration in quality.
(2) Protecting and where possible enhancing existing wildlife habitat.
(3) Encouraging the restoration of wildlife habitats in areas where they have disappeared, particularly in intensively farmed districts.
(4) A structured reduction in drainage standards in some areas to reinstate washlands or to create temporary or permanent wetland habitats.

Finally, if current scientific and Government proposals for farmland management are introduced there could be land set-aside to woodland and conservation with some areas farmed less intensively and pesticide-free headlands. More hedges could be planted to prevent soil erosion and provide corridors for wildlife (Natural Environment Research Council, 1992). By very simple means the quality of the landscape could be transformed and the reduction in pollutants from farms by simple land management techniques would mean cleaner waters.

FISH FARMING

Suspended particulate solids from waste food and faeces are a major component of fish farm wastes. Recent improvements in fish diets have been helpful in minimizing pollution but there is still a general lack of understanding of the relationship between feed input and water quality. In general, fish farmers appear to lack adequate

TABLE 21.4. Distribution of freshwater land-based and cage farms

RPA area	No. of cage farms	No. of land-based farms	Treatment	
			S	F
Clyde	16	32	3	0
Forth	4	14	8	2
Highland	33	36	11	5
North East	0	15	6	0
Solway	2	12	9	0
Tay	10	2	5	0
Tweed	0	6	3	0
Orkney Islands	0	4	4	0
Shetland Islands	3	13	3	0
Western Isles	46[a]	16	3	0
Total	114	150	55	7

S – Settlement   F – Filtration
[a]Total consented discharges; only 25 farms in operation in 1992

technical expertise and financial support to ensure that treatment systems are properly designed and operated to achieve appropriate standards; in particular, the importance of sludge removal, treatment and subsequent final disposal does not appear to be generally appreciated.

The discharge of wastes from fish farms may affect water chemistry and the ecology of fresh waters, causing deposition of suspended solids, the outbreak of fungal growths, nutrient enrichment and the introduction of chemicals, many of whose effects are unknown. Because of the high stocking densities and the stressful nature of many of the farm processes, farmed fish are susceptible to a wide range of diseases which may require the use of chemicals for disease treatment or as preventatives of infection.

The present distribution of freshwater land-based and cage farms in Scotland within the river purification authorities is shown in Table 21.4.

Land-based farms

The principal effects of fish farm effluents on running waters are the deposition of organic particulate matter causing siltation and growths of sewage fungus. Reductions in dissolved oxygen are not usually significant. Abstraction of water can lead to problems where there are insufficient flows in the river to dilute the effluent. Typical changes in water quality based on 482 inlet and outlet water samples at 14 fish farms in the Highland River Purification Board area are shown in Table 21.5.

Water abstraction

Normally, water is abstracted from surface water run-off, but groundwater or spring sources may also be used – particularly for hatcheries or as an emergency supply

TABLE 21.5. Typical concentrations of constituents in fish farm effluents (mg L^{-1})

Sample location	n	pH	DO	SS	BOD	COD	NH$_3$ (N)
Inflow							
mean	482	6.50	11.63	1.99	1.48	15.58	0.0145
min		4.50	8.23	0.10	0.20	4.00	0.0020
max		8.25	14.22	82.30	100.00	56.50	0.2990
Outflow							
mean	482	6.38	10.66	5.28	3.92	22.40	0.1944
min		5.00	6.30	0.10	0.30	4.00	0.0025
max		8.10	14.02	211.40	278.20	557.70	8.7500

where surface water is limited. The oxygen requirements of salmonids vary directly with temperature and indirectly with mean fish size. It has been estimated that, in general, the fresh water required to produce 100 000 smolts ranges from 80 to 160 L s^{-1} depending on local circumstances. Assuming a dissolved oxygen level of 5.5 mg L^{-1}, the supply of water needed for 1 t of 200 g trout may increase from 4.3 L s^{-1} at 6°C to 20.9 L s^{-1} at 18°C (Shepherd and Bromage, 1988). Following a survey of fish farms in the UK, Solbe (1982) found that fish production was weakly related to the dry weather flow (DWF) of the receiving water and reported farms with 50 t yr^{-1} production with a DWF of 200 L s^{-1}. Some fish farmers have applied to RPAs for consent for discharges under Section 34 of COPA at maximum flow rates in excess of the 95 percentile flow of the river. This may be possible by operating production patterns such that maximum biomass does not coincide with seasonal periods of low river flows, enhancing supplies by the use of stand-by sources when necessary or regulating river flows by means of controls upstream of the farm.

Experience in the Highland River Purification Board area has shown, however, that dilution of land-based fish farm effluents is essential to avoid pollution problems. Discharges which exceed the 95 percentile flow of the river invariably cause problems either as a result of sedimentation if untreated or the outbreak of sewage fungus or both. As biological treatment of oxidized waste is uneconomic at the flow rates and concentrations normally experienced, partial removal of suspended solids is the only practical treatment available at present. Although the residual BOD after solids removal is normally low, the nature of the dissolved substances present is conducive to the growth of fungus and further dilution with clean water is necessary to maintain satisfactory river conditions.

For an effluent from a land-based farm with treatment to remove solids on a "once through" water system, the minimum dilution necessary with clean river water to avoid pollution appears to be about 1:1 at 95 percentile flow. This, however, still requires the fish farmer to exercise care in discharging chemicals such as malachite green to prevent discoloration and toxicity.

Sedimentation

The deposition of organic matter can blanket a river bed and commonly occurs from the discharge of untreated fish farm effluents where dilution is unlimited. As well as being unsightly, this blanket smothers most plant and invertebrate species – though often invertebrate density may increase (usually pollution-tolerant worms and midge larvae) as diversity decreases. Solbe (1987) reported a decreased loading of 546 kg (dry weight) originating as suspended solids per tonne of fish from a survey of 20 farms compared with a previous survey; he attributed this downward trend to improvements in commercial fish diets.

Organic enrichment

Another common feature of fish farm effluents is the occurrence of heavy growths of sewage fungus. Curtis and Harrington (1970) reported that where pollution was caused by domestic sewage, heavy slime growths were associated with BOD values of 5–30 mg L^{-1} and organic carbon levels of 6–30 mg L^{-1} in the overlying water. Outbreaks which occurred below these values were often associated with effluents containing carbohydrates, organic acids, proteins and amino acids. They also found a strong correlation between inadequacy of treatment and fungus outbreaks. Some outbreaks appear to be associated with poor water quality in terms of ammoniacal nitrogen (0.9–5.0 mg L^{-1}) but not in terms of suspended solids and dissolved oxygen, the latter being in excess of 4.0 mg L^{-1} in 89% of the water samples taken from the sites visited. The role of carbohydrates, proteins and other constituents of fish food in stimulating fungus outbreaks is not well understood.

Treatment of discharges

The current availability of treatment at land-based fish farms in Scotland (Table 21.4) shows that 41% provide treatment to remove solids from their effluents.

Henderson and Bromage (1987) studied 16 settlement ponds on freshwater farms to relate solids removal performance to design and operating parameters. They found that it was difficult to achieve suspended solids (SS) concentrations of less than 6 mg L^{-1} by simple settlement, and that the best results were obtained by maintaining a low water velocity of less than 6.6 cm s^{-1} and preferably below 1.6 cm s^{-1}. A simple settlement pond is the normal method of treating fish farm effluents for the removal of solids as it is the least costly. Effluent quality shows a seasonal trend and normally deteriorates at periods of peak fish biomass in April and May, when suspended solids and BOD levels may rise. In a study of seven treated effluents in the Highland River Purification Board area, six showed a significant correlation between suspended solids and BOD. It was concluded that a properly designed and efficiently operated settlement pond should be capable of achieving a BOD of 4 mg L^{-1} and a suspended solids level of 6 mg L^{-1}. Common defects which are identified at fish farms are:

(1) Insufficient provision for the regular removal of deposited sludge, and inadequate sludge treatment and disposal facilities.
(2) No duplicate pond into which to divert effluents during periods of pond maintenance and sludge removal.
(3) Infrequent removal of sludge, resulting in decomposition and a deterioration in effluent quality due to rising sludge and dissolution of soluble products.
(4) Poorly designed inlet works causing uneven distribution of flow and turbulence resulting in reduced settling efficiency and re-suspension of solids.

(5) Poorly designed outlet works causing increased flow velocities at overflow resulting in a deterioration in effluent quality.

An alternative "high technology" option for solids removal is filtration and there are a number of units now available for this purpose. This technique has the advantage of allowing more rapid removal of suspended solids from waste streams, thus minimizing the potential for dissolution of waste products in the discharge. However, the technological nature of the process increases the risk of operational difficulties caused by breakdowns or malfunctions of equipment and is more costly than settlement ponds. However, an efficient filter system can achieve effluent quality as good as an efficient settling pond, and removal of up to 95% of solids and 80% of phosphorus has been reported for some filters (Kadri, 1988).

The River Polly

Some of the problems in treating fish farm effluents are encapsulated in a pollution problem from a fish farm on the River Polly in north-west Scotland (Figure 21.3). Settlement ponds were installed at the farm in 1986 to improve the quality of the untreated discharge and reduce sedimentation of the river bed. The ponds were designed to give a retention period of 68 minutes at a maximum flow of 800 L s^{-1} for

TABLE 21.6. Organic content of sediments in the River Polly, Sutherland, 1987–90, upstream and downstream of a fish farm

Site	Location	% organic matter[a]			
		1987	1988	1989	1990
1	Upstream farm water intake	0.74	1.10	1.20	1.13
		0.77	1.00	1.30	1.16
2	Upstream old discharge outlet	0.38	0.70	0.90	0.75
		0.72	0.60	0.80	0.66
3	30 m downstream old discharge outlet	39.40	1.10	0.80	0.68
		38.20	0.90	0.80	0.60
4	Upstream new discharge outlet	22.50	1.40	1.00	0.86
		26.30	1.40	1.20	1.16
5	50 m downstream new discharge outlet	15.50	1.60	0.90	0.60
		13.70	1.90	1.00	0.79
				0.80	
				0.80	
6	120 m downstream new discharge outlet	1.90	2.60	1.20	0.74
		1.70	3.10	1.10	0.78
				1.60	
				1.70	

[a] % organic matter measured as loss on ignition at 500°C (2 to 4 replicates at each site)

TABLE 21.7. Biomass and number of oligochaetes at six study sites on the River Polly, Sutherland, 1987–90 upstream and downstream of a fish farm. Site locations are given in Table 21.6

	Number of Oligochaetes				Biomass (damp weight, g)			
Site	1987	1988	1989	1990	1987	1988	1989	1990
1	7	1	6	0	1.09	0.23	0.74	0.35
2	8	0	2	0	0.26	0.26	0.09	0.42
3	157	20	13	4	5.24	0.20	1.04	0.69
4	664	17	33	8	21.03	1.16	1.86	1.56
5	542	111	270	115	24.38	7.31	6.61	10.61
6	448	124	61	60	19.53	7.96	6.32	4.41

Each figure represents one standard 3-minute kick sample

an annual fish production of 40–50 t. The estimated 95 percentile flow of the river was 600 L s^{-1} which needs to be maintained at all times.

Surveys were carried out from 1987 to 1990 at periods of peak fish biomass to assess the impact of the effluent on flora, fauna and sediments. Effluent and river water quality were also measured. All sampling stations were sited on shallow gravelly riffles. Sites 1 and 2 upstream of the old discharge point were "control" sites. Sites 3 and 4 were downstream of the old discharge location and indicate speed of response to full recovery. Site 6 is approximately 120 m downstream of the new effluent discharge.

The results (Tables 21.6, 21.7 and 21.8) show that the settlement ponds succeeded in reducing the suspended solids discharged to the river and resulted in the organic content of the river sediments downstream of the farm recovering to normal levels for highland rivers. Although patches of sewage fungus at Sites 3 and 4 disappeared, a new problem of fungus growths appeared at Sites 5 and 6. This was attributed to the fact that the settlement ponds had not been de-sludged. The maximum BOD and COD (Chemical Oxygen Demand) levels were recorded in April at peak fish biomass, coincident with the prevalence of the fungus. Excessive numbers of large lumbricid worms were still present at Sites 5 and 6 in 1990 although the sediments had returned to normal. There were still good numbers of pollution-sensitive invertebrates present in the downstream fauna (e.g. mayflies and stoneflies), showing that the discharge of chemicals (e.g. malachite green and formalin) was having no effect.

TABLE 21.8. Results from chemical samples taken downstream from the fish farm on the River Polly between March 1989 and February 1990 ($n = 7$)

	Temp (°C)	SS (mg L^{-1})	DO (mg L^{-1})	DO (% sat.)	BOD (mg L^{-1})	COD (mg L^{-1})	NH$_3$ (mg L^{-1})
Mean	6.6	1.8	11.44	93.2	2.4	13.9	0.0381
Min	3.1	0.6	10.57	89.8	0.6	6.9	0.0050
Max	12.9	3.4	12.04	102.1	9.4	23.7	0.0700

Cage farms

The discharge of solid and liquid wastes from cage culture causes reductions in dissolved oxygen, smothers benthic flora and fauna and enriches the water column directly (from fish urine, etc.) and indirectly (by the release of nitrogen and phosphorus from bottom sediments), thus stimulating algal growth. Phillips *et al.* (1986) reported that, for each tonne of trout produced, 292 kg of dry matter (containing 96 kg of carbon, 10.5 kg of nitrogen and 10.3 kg of phosphorus) was deposited below the cage. In addition, the soluble waste carbon, nitrogen and phosphorus amounted to 305, 64 and 9.8 kg t^{-1} respectively. The solids were therefore the more important source of phosphorus accounting for 15.2% of the loss.

Localized reductions in dissolved oxygen are common in the vicinity of cage farms but are not normally significant unless they arise from high organic loadings when they may have a more widespread effect (Stewart, 1985). Of more concern are decreases in dissolved oxygen, due to eutrophication or reductions in the hypolimnion of a loch, which could be damaging to the biota – especially oligotrophic species such as Arctic Charr (*Salvelinus alpinus*) which are sensitive to deoxygenation.

As water movements in freshwater lochs are essentially wind-induced (see Chapter 3), currents are generally of lower velocity than those of sea lochs. Dispersion of solids is therefore much more limited except at shallow exposed sites. Thus, sedimentation at freshwater cages is generally limited to the immediate vicinity of cages (Phillips *et al.*, 1985a).

Nutrient enrichment

As phosphorus is normally the limiting nutrient for primary production in fresh water (see Chapter 22), present pollution control policy is primarily concerned with regulating its concentration in lochs to maintain the appropriate natural trophic conditions. The Royal Commission on Environmental Pollution (1992) has recently expressed concern over the extent of nutrient enrichment in fresh waters and has recommended that, wherever possible, waters should be restored to the original trophic state which obtained prior to significant enrichment from human activities; this is compatible with RPA practice.

For example, in the Highland River Purification Board area where many oligotrophic water bodies are found, modelling is used to restrict the size of cage farms and thus maintain oligotrophy (mean phosphorus <10 μg L^{-1}). The Dillon and Rigler (1985) model is the one most commonly used for this purpose at present and offers a useful management guide for initial assessment of the carrying capacity of lochs to achieve specific water quality standards (Bailey-Watts, 1990). Production may be adjusted in the light of monitoring results after a farm is in operation. The Scotland and Northern Ireland Forum for Environmental Research (SNIFFER) has been instrumental in establishing a study to develop a eutrophication risk model for standing waters. This uses a regression equation approach and may improve present practice for assessing the impact of cage culture in multi-use lochs (SNIFFER, 1992).

Future controls

Although the present approach by the RPAs to controlling pollution by cage culture has been reasonably successful so far, there are important extraneous factors which may cause a change of direction in the future.

Firstly, allowing uncontrolled discharge from cage farms shows preference and discriminates against land-based farms (where, however, it is much easier for treatment to be provided). RPAs have not yet experienced difficulties in obtaining improved treatment at land-based farms, but it is a live issue and could give rise to problems in the future. The Royal Commission on Environmental Pollution (1992) has recently recommended that cage fish farms should be sited in a manner and position consistent with the efficient dispersal of wastes and, where this is not possible, cages should not be permitted until improved methods of waste removal technology have been developed. Adoption of this approach would effectively remove cages from most freshwater lochs in Scotland. Progress in developing cage culture technology to allow for the removal of wastes has been disappointing so far and it is in the long-term interests of the industry that better progress is made in future.

Secondly, there is now substantial evidence that the fertilization of forests by the Forest Authority and private forestry companies (see Chapter 23) gives rise to nutrient enrichment of water bodies due to phosphorus in the run-off from plantations. In many cases the quantities involved far outweigh those from cage farms. This activity is not controlled in any way at present, except on a voluntary basis. There are a number of lochs in Scotland which are affected by the diffuse discharge of phosphorus from forests and some of these lochs support cage farms. If action is necessary in future to reduce the phosphorus loadings in such lochs this can only be carried out by the RPAs by limiting the discharge for the cage farms – even though they may not be the main source. There is provision under Section 31(4) of COPA whereby the application of fertilizers to forests could be controlled by consent procedure by RPAs, but this requires regulations to be made by the Secretary of State which are not available at present. This uneven-handed approach to pollution control therefore undermines current RPA strategy and it cannot be in the interest of the fish farming industry or the RPAs for this situation to continue. The following measures should be taken by the Secretary of State to rectify this deficiency:

(1) Introduce statutory water quality objectives and standards (including phosphorus levels) for rivers and lochs in Scotland.
(2) Make regulations to allow control by RPAs of forest fertilization by consent procedure under Section 31(4) of COPA.

Chemicals and antibiotics

Chemicals and antibiotics are used by fish farmers for the treatment and prevention of disease and other purposes; such medication may be administered in the feed or by immersion treatment. The most widely used chemicals are malachite green, formalin and chloramine T.

Little is known about the persistence of malachite green in the environment but provided it is used properly its effects after discharge should be insignificant due to dilution, conversion to carbinol, adsorption onto organic matter and oxidation – all of which should substantially reduce the amount of free dye present (Alderman, 1985). There are no reported cases of toxicity in Scotland by malachite green but the Scottish Office Agriculture and Fisheries Department is currently undertaking a field study of fish farm sites to assess its ecological effects. Complaints of objectionable discoloration have been received from the public. Aqueous solutions of malachite green can be successfully treated by filtration through a bed of activated carbon (Bills and Marking, 1977) and the Ministry of Agriculture, Fisheries and Food (1982) has also published a code of practice for the use of this chemical on fish farms.

Formalin does not appear to break down rapidly in the environment and filtration by activated carbon does not remove significant amounts. At present, dilution is the only procedure adopted for reducing its toxicity. No cases of damage to freshwater life have been reported, but further information is needed on the toxicity and persistence of formalin and of chloramine T (which has been little studied so far).

The introduction of antibiotics to the environment through fish farm wastes has given rise to concern. SNIFFER (1991) has supported a study into the effects of antibiotics released from fish farms and levels measured so far have been low.

Fisheries

The establishment of fish farms within a watershed can affect fisheries in a variety of ways (Phillips *et al.*, 1985b; Duncan, 1990 (Nature Conservancy Council, 1990; Webb *et al.*, 1991; Williamson, 1991) due to water abstraction, pollution and the construction of physical barriers. Physical impacts can normally be considered at an early stage of development and conflicts resolved then. Nutrient enrichment can affect fisheries in a number of ways and may be detrimental especially to salmonids (Maitland, 1984). Species characteristic of oligotrophic lochs, such as Arctic Charr (Campbell, 1979), are particularly vulnerable.

The escape of farmed fish to the wild is also of widespread concern. Cages are most prone to fish losses (Beveridge, 1987) and large escapes of both Rainbow Trout (*Oncorhynchus mykiss*) and Atlantic Salmon (*Salmo salar*) have been reported (Maitland, 1989; Webb *et al.*, 1991). However, the effects on wild stocks are still uncertain (Williamson, 1991).

The spread of disease from farmed to wild fish is also an area of concern to fishery interests and conservationists (see Chapter 26). Present experience indicates that disease outbreaks at farms are principally caused by high fish densities and there is little evidence that farms are responsible for significant disease transfer to wild fish. However, there are cases of the introduction of disease to farmed and wild stocks from the importation of infected fish, and legislation could be strengthened to minimize this risk.

Birds and mammals

Fish-eating birds (e.g. Heron, *Ardea cinerea*), and mammals (e.g. Otter, *Lutra lutra*) have been reported to prey on fish farm stocks (EIFAC, 1988; Howell and Munford, 1991). As well as eating fish, birds may also cause losses through wounding and transmission of diseases. This creates a problem for fish farmers who may resort to shooting predators to protect their stocks (Ross, 1988), bringing them into conflict with legislation unless they have obtained a licence to do so. The Scottish Salmon Growers Association (1990) has produced a Code of Practice to promote the use of anti-predator netting and other methods of non-destructive control. Additionally, fish farm operations may also cause disturbance to rare species such as Black-throated Divers (*Gavia arctica*) which are protected under the Wildlife and Countryside Act 1981 and the EC Birds Directive. This may mean restriction of fish farming in areas which are designated as Special Protection Areas under the Directive.

ACKNOWLEDGEMENTS

Thanks are due to all our colleagues who have helped with the preparation of this chapter, including Bryan Bellwood, Stuart Brown, Colin Craig, Julian Hunter, Tom Inglis, Andy Rosie and Philip Wright. Malcolm Somerville (SOEnD) helped to collate data.

REFERENCES

Alderman, D. J. (1985). "Malachite green: a review", *Journal of Fish Diseases*, **8**, 289–298.

Allcock, R. (1992). *River Pollution Control in Scotland, The Way Forward*, Scottish Agricultural College, Edinburgh.

Bailey-Watts, A. E. (1990). "Eutrophication: assessment, research and management, with special reference to Scotland's fresh waters", *Journal of the Institution of Water and Environmental Management*, **4**, 285–294.

Baldock, D. and Bennett, G. (1991). "Agriculture and the polluter pays principle", *Institute for European Environmental Policy Paper*, 1991, 186–187.

Beveridge, M. C. M. (1987). *Cage Aquaculture*, Fishing News Books, Farnham.

Bills, T. D. and Marking, L. L. (1977). "Formalin: its toxicity to nontarget organisms, persistence and counteraction", *US Fish and Wildlife Service Investigations in Fish Control*, **73**, 1–7.

British Agrochemicals Association (1990). *Annual Review and Handbook*, London.

Campbell, R. N. (1979). "Ferox Trout, *Salmo trutta* L. and Charr, *Salvelinus alpinus* (L.) in Scottish lochs", *Journal of Fish Biology*, **14**, 1–29.

Clyde River Purification Board (1992). *Annual Report*, East Kilbride.

Curtis, E. J. C. and Harrington, D. W. (1970). "The occurrence of sewage fungus in rivers in the United Kingdom", *Water Research*, **5**, 281–290.

Dillon, P. J. and Rigler, F. H. (1975). "A simple method for predicting the capacity of a lake for development based upon lake trophic status", *Journal of the Fisheries Research Board of Canada*, **32**, 1519–1531.

Duncan, W. M. (1990). "An assessment of the current status of fish communities in Loch Awe, Scotland, with particular emphasis on the interactions between feral Rainbow Trout and indigenous Brown Trout", PhD thesis, University of Stirling.

EIFAC (1988). "Report of the EIFAC Working Party on prevention and control of bird predation in aquaculture and fisheries operations", *EIFAC Technical Paper*, **51**, 1–79.

Henderson, J. P. and Bromage, N. R. (1987). "Optimising the removal of suspended solids from aquaculture effluents in settlement lakes", *Aquaculture Engineering*, **7**, 167–181.

Howell, D. L. and Munford, J. G. (1991). "Predator control on finfish farms", in *Aquaculture and the Environment* (Eds N. De Pauw and J. Joyce), pp. 339–364, European Aquaculture Society Special Publication No. 16, Gent, Belgium.

Kadri, S. (1988). "A study of a screen filter's performance in treating salmonid hatchery effluent," MSc thesis, University of Stirling.

Maitland, P. S. (1984). "Wild salmonids – are they at risk?", *Proceedings of the Institute of Fisheries Management Annual Study Course*, **15**, 100–109.

Maitland, P. S. (1989). *The Genetic Impact of Farmed Atlantic Salmon on Wild Populations*, Nature Conservancy Council, Edinburgh.

Ministry of Agriculture, Fisheries and Food (1982). *Malachite Green: A Code of Practice for its Use in Fish Farming*, Fisheries Notice 72, Lowestoft.

Natural Environment Research Council (1992). *The Land of Britain: Land Use Research for the Future*, Natural Environment Research Council, Swindon.

Nature Conservancy Council (1990). *Fish Farming and the Scottish Freshwater Environment*, Edinburgh.

Phillips, M. J., Beveridge, M. C. M. and Muir, J. F. (1985a). "Waste output and environmental effects of Rainbow Trout culture", *ICES Report*, CM 1985/F, 1–21.

Phillips, M. J., Beveridge, M. C. M. and Ross, L. G. (1985b). "The environmental impact of salmonid cage culture on inland fisheries: present status and future trends", *Journal of Fish Biology*, **27A**, 123–137.

Phillips, M. J., Beveridge, M. C. M. and Stewart, J. A. (1986). "The environmental impact of cage culture on Scottish fresh waters", in *Effects of Land Use on Fresh Waters,* (Ed. J. F. de L. G. Solbe), pp. 504–508, Ellis Horwood, Chichester.

Ross, A. (1988). *Controlling Nature's Predators on Fish Farms*, Marine Conservation Society, Hay-on-Wye.

Royal Commission on Environmental Pollution (1992). *Sixteenth Report, Freshwater Quality*, HMSO, London.

Scottish Farm Waste Liaison Group (1992). *Pollution Review, No. 6*, Perth.

Scottish Office (1992a). *Agricultural Facts and Figures, Scotland*, Edinburgh.

Scottish Office (1992b). *Code of Good Practice: Prevention of Environmental Pollution from Agricultural Activity*, Edinburgh.

Scottish Salmon Growers Association (1990). *Salmon Farming and Predatory Wildlife: A Code of Practice*, Perth.

Shepherd, J. and Bromage, N. (1988). *Intensive Fish Farming*, BSP Professional Books, Oxford.

SNIFFER (1991). *Antibiotics from Fish Farms*, Water Research Centre, Medmenham.

SNIFFER (1992). *Eutrophication Risk Assessment*, Water Research Centre, Medmenham.

Solbe, J. F. de L. G. (1982). "Fish farm effluents: a United Kingdom survey", *EIFAC Technical Paper*, **41**, 29–56.

Solbe, J. F. de L. G. (1987). *EIFAC Working Party on Fish Farms*, Water Research Centre, Medmenham.

Stewart, J. A. (1985). *Third Report on Water Quality and Fish Health at Rothesay Sea Foods Fish Cage Farm, Loch Fad, Bute,* Institute of Aquaculture, Stirling.

Virtue, A. (1992). *A Survey of Sheep Dipping Installations and Practices in the Tweed River Purification Board Area*, Tweed River Purification Board, Galashiels.

Webb, J. H., Hay, D. W., Cunningham, P. D. and Youngson, A. F. (1991). "The spawning behaviour of escaped farmed and wild Atlantic Salmon (*Salmo salar* L.) in a northern Scottish river", *Aquaculture*, **98**, 97–110.

Williamson, R. B. (1991). *Salmon Fisheries in Scotland*, Atlantic Salmon Trust, Pitlochry.

22

Eutrophication

A. E. BAILEY-WATTS

Institute of Freshwater Ecology, Bush Estate, Penicuik, EH26 0QB, UK

INTRODUCTION

This chapter concerns eutrophication (nutrient enrichment) with special reference to Scotland, but in broad historical and geographical contexts. It deals with nutrient loadings, concentrations, the nature and abundance of biota associated with waters of different trophic status, and factors (including the weather) determining the relationship between nutrient inputs and biota. Eutrophication control is discussed and some gaps in our understanding of the eutrophication process in Scotland are identified. Data (some of which have existed hitherto only in unpublished reports) are reviewed with reference to a total of 55 lochs (Figure 22.1). The focus is on standing waters because water "slows down" in loch basins giving more time for nutrients to be used, and for the biomass of planktonic plants and animals to accumulate (Reynolds, 1988). Note also that Chapter 6 reviews the concentrations of nutrients in a wide variety of Scottish rivers included in the Harmonised Monitoring Scheme set up by the Department of the Environment.

Because they are introduced into surface waters in, for example, sewage effluents, fertilizers and certain industrial wastes (Graham, 1968; Millway, 1970; Scottish Agricultural College, 1980; Ellis, 1989), the nutrients of major significance are carbon (C), nitrogen (N) and phosphorus (P). C and N in one form or another can limit the production of particular plant species (Reynolds, 1984). Most algae are affected by nitrate levels falling (in summer in Scotland) to annual minima of ≤ 10 μg N L^{-1} in oligotrophic lochs and $\leq 50\mu$g N L^{-1} in richer systems (Bailey-Watts, 1986a, b; Bailey-Watts *et al.*, 1987b; 1990; 1992; Bailey-Watts and Kirika, 1991; 1993). In rich lochs, the reduction is due as much to denitrifying bacteria as phytoplankton (Johnston *et al.*, 1974; Stewart *et al.*, 1975; 1976). The resulting nitrate-poor environment favours N-fixing species of cyanobacteria (Carr and Whitton, 1982) – a situation existing year-round in the tropics (Payne, 1986; Talling, 1992).

Most of the literature on eutrophication concerns P, either as the sum of the dissolved and particulate fractions (TP) or the soluble reactive fraction (SRP) most immediately available to algae (Harper, 1992). If a chemical, rather than a physical, factor such as light is limiting algal production overall, it is most likely to be P in

The Fresh Waters of Scotland: A National Resource of International Significance
Edited by P. S. Maitland, P. J. Boon and D. S. McLusky. © 1994 John Wiley & Sons Ltd

lochs ——•

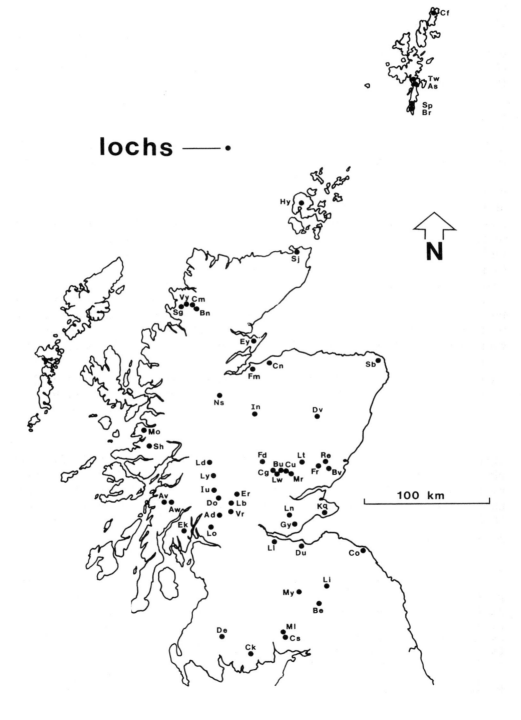

temperate waters (OECD, 1982). Indeed, global food production can be considered as being controlled by P (Porter and Fitzsimmons, 1978). Laboratory enrichment experiments support the P limitation theory (Bailey-Watts, 1973; 1990a; Davidson, 1986; Bailey-Watts *et al.*, 1988), and algal maxima commonly coincide with, or closely follow, the occurrence of low P levels in lochs covering a wide trophic spectrum (Bindloss *et al.*, 1972; Bailey-Watts and Duncan, 1981a, b; Bailey-Watts, 1986a, b; Bailey-Watts *et al.*, 1987a; 1990). Many models (see below) also assume P is the major limiting factor. Nevertheless, levels of nutrients including P remain so high in some systems that phytoplankton maxima are controlled by light and self-shading (Bindloss, 1976).

Silica (SiO_2) is not usually viewed as a major nutrient in eutrophication since its concentrations need not necessarily be elevated by the enrichment process directly. However, waters draining eutrophic, lowland catchments are often rich in this nutrient (Bailey-Watts *et al.*, 1989a), and SiO_2 is utilized by many chrysophycean algae (McGrory and Leadbeater, 1981), higher plants (Lewin and Reimann, 1969) and diatoms (Reynolds, 1986). As long as SiO_2 is available the potential exists for these plants to compete with troublesome cyanobacteria for growth resources. Opaline silica often constitutes >50% of diatom cell dry weight (Bailey-Watts, 1976a). Concentrations of dissolved SiO_2 are commonly reduced to growth-limiting levels (Bailey-Watts, 1976a, b; 1988a; Bailey-Watts *et al.*, 1989b).

Waters are often categorized in terms of trophic status, using the concentrations of forms of C, N and P, plant and animal species composition, organism biomass and productivity, and water clarity (Harper, 1992). OECD (1982) schemes, based on open water concentrations (μg L^{-1}) of TP and chlorophyll$_a$ (chl), provide a simple guide:

ultra-oligotrophic $\rightarrow$ oligotrophic $\rightarrow$ mesotrophic $\rightarrow$ eutrophic $\rightarrow$ hypertrophic
$\leqslant$4 TP $\quad\rightarrow\quad$ $\leqslant$10 TP $\quad\rightarrow\quad$ $\leqslant$35 TP $\quad\rightarrow$ $\leqslant$100 TP $\rightarrow$ $\geqslant$100 TP
$\leqslant$1 chl $\quad\rightarrow\quad$ $\leqslant$2.5 chl $\quad\rightarrow\quad$ $\leqslant$8 chl $\quad\rightarrow$ $\leqslant$25 chl $\rightarrow$ $\geqslant$25 chl

Nutrients are derived from the natural weathering of rocks and the breakdown of organic material (Porter and Fitzsimmons, 1978; House and Casey, 1989); for example, Lochs Sionascaig, Cam and Borralan (Pennington *et al.*, 1972; Haworth, 1976) were richer in the late glacial period than they are now. Gulls may add nutrients naturally to high altitude lochs, as do hippos to certain African lakes (Kilham, 1982). However, atmospheric transport of N oxides and ammonia (UKRGAR, 1990) suggests that few environments are completely unaffected by man.

FIGURE 22.1. The locations of the Scottish lochs referred to in this chapter: Ad Ard; As Asta; Av Avich; Aw Awe; Be Branxholme Easter; Bn Borralan; Br Brow; Bu Butterstone; Bv Balgavies; Cf Cliff; Cg Craiglush; Ck Carlingwark; Cm Cam; Cn Cran; Co Coldingham; Cs Castle; Cu Clunie; Du Duddingston; De Dee; Do Doine; Dv Davan; Ek Eck; Er Earn; Ey Eye; Fd Faedaire; Fm Flemington; Fr Forfar; Gy Gelly; Hy Harray; In Insh; Iu Iubhair; Kq Kilconquhar; Lb Lubnaig; Ld Laidon; Li Lindean; Ll Linlithgow; Ln Leven; Lo Lomond; Lt Lintrathen; Lw Lowes; Ly Lyon; Ml Mill; Mo Morar; Mr Marlee; My St Mary's; Ns Ness; Re Rescobie; Sb Strathbeg; Sg Sionascaig; Sh Shiel; Sj St John's; Sp Spiggie; Tw Tingwall; Vr Venachar; Vy Veyatie

Except for nitrate in some situations (Anonymous, 1989), there is little concern over elevated loadings or concentrations of nutrients in themselves. The main problems stem from biological changes induced by enrichment, and from biomass accumulation rather than production. Indeed, although eutrophication is viewed mainly as a threat, enrichment has been used to enhance fishery production. Biological effects of fertilization were first researched in Scotland many years ago (Brook and Holden, 1957; Brook, 1958; Holden, 1959), and in Continental Europe (Vibert and Lagler, 1961). The results of such work continue to be applied in the tropics (Ghosh *et al.*, 1980; Payne, 1986; Mahmud-ul-Ameen, 1987). Eutrophication has also been used to counteract acidity (Davison, 1986), and nitrate has been added to suppress P releases from lake sediments (Foy, 1986).

THE PROCESS OF ACCELERATED NUTRIENT ENRICHMENT

General considerations

Eutrophication stems initially from the re-distribution of the planet's nutrient resources. Examples on two quite different scales are: the mining of apatite for worldwide P fertilizer and detergent manufacture (Porter and Fitzsimmons, 1978), and the transport of nutrient-rich seaweed and fish gut material to the Western Isles (Thompson, 1976; N. McNeil, personal communication). Eutrophication thus results mainly from food production and the disposal of our metabolic waste, although the production of timber (Bailey-Watts *et al.*, 1988) and certain textiles (Holden and Caines, 1974; Bailey-Watts, 1983) can also result in increased nutrients.

Waste disposal is a major issue in urban Scotland (see Chapter 20) and conventionally treated sewage remains rich in P (Bailey-Watts *et al.*, 1987a). However, this waste often enters surface waters via identifiable pipes so it can be diverted, or the nutrient content can be significantly reduced (Harper, 1992). For example, an alternative manufacturing process was adopted to eliminate P-rich mill effluent at Loch Leven (Bailey-Watts *et al.*, 1991).

Of increasing concern are diffuse, less easily targeted, inputs of animal and human waste derived from agriculture (see Chapter 21). Eutrophication is now increasing in essentially pristine areas, due to afforestation (Harriman, 1978; Bailey-Watts *et al.*, 1988; Greene and Taylor, 1989; Chapter 23), and fish farming (Institute of Aquaculture *et al.*, 1990; Stirling and Dey, 1990; Chapter 21). In areas of outstanding beauty, nutrient inputs from tourist developments can add significantly to the total P loadings of the often nutrient-poor receiving waters (Bailey-Watts *et al.*, 1992; Bailey-Watts and Kirika, 1993). In contrast, population re-distribution since the arrival of people with grain seed and domestic animals in Scotland some 5000 years ago (Grimble, 1985) and up to the "clearances" and emigrations (Lobban, 1974), suggests that some waters in the highlands and islands may have experienced decreases in cultural eutrophication.

Nutrient loadings and concentrations

Loadings assessed by field measurement

Seven Scottish studies (Table 22.1) have employed the close interval sampling and flow recording regimes essential for meaningful estimates of loadings to lochs (Stevens and Smith, 1978). Storm episodes can bring in the majority of the annual loading of P from a stream (Bailey-Watts and Kirika, 1987).

The studies in Table 22.1 estimated that between 3.5 and 35 kg nitrate-N is lost annually per hectare of land, with hill/upland and low intensity agricultural areas giving the lowest values and intensively used land producing the highest figures (see also Cuttle, 1989; Wright *et al.*, 1991). Typical P loss coefficients are listed in Table 22.2 along with a value relating to caged fish production (Institute of Aquaculture *et al.*, 1990).

TABLE 22.1. Loch nutrient loadings obtained by intensive measurements: values are expressed in $t\ yr^{-1}$ and $g\ m^{-2}$ loch surface yr^{-1}: total phosphorus (TP), soluble reactive P (SRP), total nitrogen (TN), total inorganic-N (TIN), nitrate-N (NO_3N), and silica (SiO_2)

Catchment	Loadings			References
	$t\ yr^{-1}$	Deter-minand	$g\ m^{-2}$	
Balgavies (20 ha)	0.26	TP	1.3	Harper and Stewart (1987)
	13.6	TIN	68	
Eye (195 ha)	0.53	TP	0.27	Bailey-Watts and Kirika (1991)
	8.6	NO_3N	4.40	
	20.9	SiO_2	10.7	
Forfar (41 ha)	6.8	TP	16.6	Stewart *et al.* (1975)
	64.5	TIN	157	
	4.1	TP	10.0	Harper and Stewart (1987)
	57	TIN	139	
Leven (1330 ha)	20.6	TP	1.54	Bailey-Watts *et al.* (1987b)
	12.3	SRP	0.92	
	420	NO_3N	31.6	Bailey-Watts (unpublished data)
	1160	SiO_2	87.2	Bailey-Watts *et al.* (1989a)
	6.65–13.3	TP	0.5–1.0	Holden and Caines (1974)
	186–320	TN	14–24	
Lowes (90 ha)	0.23	TP	0.26	Harper and Stewart (1987)
	1.3	TIN	1.44	
Rescobie (86 ha)	0.69	TP	0.80	Stewart *et al.* (1975)
	101	TIN	117	
Strathbeg (206 ha)	5.3	TP	2.57	Hancock (1982)
	2.4	TP	1.16	Raffaelli *et al.* (1990)

Domestic waste contributes considerably to the loadings of both N and P to hypertrophic Forfar Loch, while the majority of the N enters the other lochs in the form of nitrate in diffuse run-off from land (see also Holden, 1976). The relative importance of different sources of P to the other waters varies, however. At Loch Leven, for example, industry, agricultural run-off and treated sewage have each contributed most to the loadings in one year or another (Bailey-Watts *et al.*, 1993). Geese contributed less than 2% of the annual input to Loch Leven (Bailey-Watts *et al.*, 1987a), between 6% and 30% of the loading to the Loch to Strathbeg (Hancock, 1982; Raffaelli *et al.*, 1990), and possibly 60% of the yearly load to Loch Eye (Bailey-Watts and Kirika, 1991).

On the basis of the relationship with loch mean depth, only one of the specific areal loadings (SAL) in Table 22.2 (that of N to the Loch of the Lowes) does not exceed the values considered "dangerous" by Vollenweider (1968), that is, likely to lead to undesirable algal blooms. These values are discussed further below.

Loadings assessed by desk analysis

Water resource managers often require information on nutrient inputs much quicker than a full case study permits, and usually on more than one site. To meet this requirement a desk approach has been tried (Bailey-Watts, 1983; Harper and Stewart, 1987; Bailey-Watts *et al.*, 1992; Bailey-Watts and Kirika, 1993). Harper (1992) gives details, but essentially P loadings are estimated by combining loss coefficients (such as those in Table 22.2) determined by studies of the type listed in Table 22.1, with data on land use, population numbers, caged fish production and wildfowl numbers. Loadings estimated in this way may vary at least three-fold, depending on the nutrient loss coefficients selected and the accuracy of estimates of land areas and numbers of people (Harper and Stewart, 1987; Harper, 1992; M. Marsden, personal communication). However, figures can be revised as more loadings are measured and land-use information is updated. For example, many fish feeds now contain less than one third of previous amounts of P, resulting in the loss coefficient of 20 kg P yr^{-1} t^{-1} (Table 22.2) (Phillips *et al.*, 1988).

Thirty-one catchments ranging considerably in physical and chemical features (Table 22.3), and situated between 54° 56′N in the Borders and 60° 47′N in the Shetland Isles (Figure 22.1), have been analyzed (Bailey-Watts *et al.*, 1992). A few kilogrammes of TP yr^{-1} are likely to enter small, high altitude water bodies such as Lindean Reservoir and Branxholme Easter Loch each year, while annual TP losses from large catchments (e.g. Loch Shiel, 23 000 ha and Insh, 82 000 ha) amount to tonnes. Using the same approach, Bailey-Watts and Kirika (1993) predicted a loading of 0.3 t P yr^{-1} for Loch Dee. A plot of the loadings (expressed as SAL) on loch mean depth (Figure 22.2) suggest that they virtually all exceed Vollenweider's (1968) "dangerous" limits, and the loading of 0.3 g m^{-2} yr^{-1} predicted for Loch Dee (mean depth, 4.2 m) would place this loch in the eutrophic category.

Intensive field measurements are needed to evaluate these predictions, but the results are encouraging. For example, considering the likely errors of estimation, the predicted loadings (in g TP m^{-2} yr^{-1}) of 0.39 for Loch of Lowes, 1.3 for Rescobie Loch, 1.6 for Loch of Strathbeg, and 3.1 for Balgavies Loch do not differ markedly from measured values (see Table 22.1). Desk-predicted annual nitrate-N loads of

TABLE 22.2. Some typical phosphorus loss coefficients

Land types	P loss rate (kg P ha^{-1} yr^{-1})
High ground devoid of agriculture	0.07
Low intensity, non-arable farmland; woodland; rough grazing	0.10
Coniferous forest	0.20 (<15 years)
	0.10 (>15 years)
Arable agriculture	0.25
Improved grassland	0.40

Other sources	
People on septic tank services	1.00 (kg total P per person yr^{-1})
People on main sewerage	0.75 (kg total P per person yr^{-1})
Over-wintering geese	0.04 (kg total P per bird yr^{-1})
Fish cages	20 (kg total P per tonne fish produced yr^{-1})

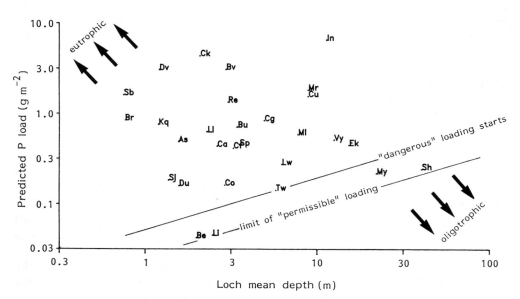

FIGURE 22.2. Annual loadings of total phosphorus to 29 Scottish lochs, predicted by desk analysis and using P loss coefficients, and expressed as specific areal values related to loch mean depth, according to Vollenweider (1968). Codes and loch names are as in Figure 22.1

TABLE 22.3. Basic morphometric and water quality data for the 31 loch catchments used by Bailey-Watts *et al.* (1992) to assess P loadings by desk analysis; ND denotes not determined. Catchments are listed in order of sampling in 1991, from mid-June (Coldingham) to mid-August (Cliff)

Catchment (loch code)	Loch area (ha)	Mean depth (m)	Catchment area (ha)	pH	Conductivity (μS cm^{-1})
Coldingham (Co)	8.4	2.9	33	8.4	455
Lindean (Li)	9.7	2.5	54	7.6	265
Branxholme (Be)	6.4	2.0	41	ND	ND
St Mary's (My)	260.0	22.0	10 600	6.5	61
Kilconquhar (Kq)	38.4	1.2	109	9.1	545
Linlithgow (Ll)	41.7	2.3	480	9.0	515
Balgavies (Bv)	21.0	3.0	2360	7.6	388
Rescobie (Re)	63.9	3.0	2026	8.5	349
Marlee (Mr)	70.8	8.9	7560	8.1	158
Clunie (Cu)	54.2	8.9	5820	7.7	122
Butterstone (Bu)	43.7	3.4	2140	8.0	105
Lowes (Lw)	88.2	6.2	1400	8.9	97
Craiglush (Cg)	28.3	4.9	990	8.0	91
Strathbeg (Sb)	206.0	0.8	5290	9.7	540
Davan (Dv)	59.1	1.2	3470	7.8	150
Eck (Ek)	440.0	15.3	9890	ND	47
Shiel (Sh)	1960	40.5	23 000	ND	37
Mill (Ml)	12.9	7.7	170	ND	ND
Spiggie (Sp)	86.2	3.5	1420	ND	595
Brow (Br)	18.2	0.8	390	10.3	435
Asta (As)	12.9	1.6	410	ND	289
Tingwall (Tw)	43.3	5.8	270	8.5	337
St John's (Sj)	78.9	1.4	440	9.0	376
Veyatie (Vy)	240.0	12.5	11 600	7.2	94
Insh (In)	139.0	11.4	82 000	6.5	54
Cliff (Cf)	104.0	3.3	2930	7.4	316
Duddingston (Du)	8.1	1.6	98	ND	ND
Castle (Ca)	78.1	2.6	690	ND	ND
Carlingwark (Ck)	42.5	2.1	1183	ND	ND
Cran (Cn)	8.1	0.5	820	ND	ND
Flemington (Fm)	16.9	1.5	850	ND	ND

17.3–20.6 g m^{-2} to Loch Leven for 1966 and 1970–72 (Cuttle, 1989) agreed well with the loadings measured by Holden and Caines (1974) although the desk estimates for 1967–69 were considerably lower than those of *ca* 24 g m^{-2} measured.

Loch nutrient concentrations in relation to loadings

In spite of the high loadings, summer TP concentrations in the 25 lochs sampled by Bailey-Watts *et al.* (1992) suggest that only six are eutrophic, and Kilconquhar Loch with 1.2 mg L^{-1} is the only hypertrophic site. Loch Dee, with concentrations of *ca* 5 μg TP L^{-1} (Bailey-Watts and Kirika, 1993) ranks with Lochs Ard, Earn, Lubnaig and Venachar (A. Kirika, personal communication) and oligotrophic Lake Thingval-

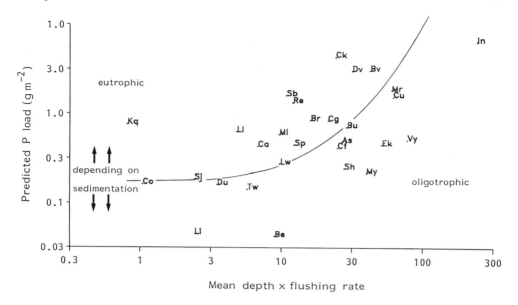

FIGURE 22.3. The specific areal loadings of the 29 lochs in Figure 22.2 related to the product of flushing rate and loch mean depth, according to Vollenweider (1975). The line indicating the boundary between oligotrophic and eutrophic conditions corresponds to an average P sedimentation coefficient of *ca* 0.5. Codes and loch names are as in Figure 22.1

lavatn, Iceland (Jonasson, 1992), and many mountain waters in Europe (Wathne, 1992).

When flushing rate (ρ, in loch volumes yr^{-1}) is accounted for, in accordance with the models of Dillon and Rigler (1974; 1975), Vollenweider (1975; 1976) and OECD (1982), a much smaller proportion of the lochs is classed as eutrophic than when only loch depth is considered (Figure 22.3). This proportion decreases even further if P sedimentation (a function of water throughput rate divided by loch surface area – Kirchner and Dillon, 1975) is higher than the average situation indicated by the line in Figure 22.3.

The contrast between the results in Figures 22.2 and 22.3 emphasizes the role of high ρ values in reducing P concentrations and suppressing some of the potential effects of high P loadings. For example, the SAL predicted for Loch Insh is 6.6 g TP m^{-2} yr^{-1}, which is some four times that measured for Loch Leven (Bailey-Watts *et al.*, 1987a) and comparable to values found for hypertrophic Norfolk Broads (Phillips and Jackson, 1990). However, the input to Loch Insh is attributable to its enormous drainage area rather than any particularly high P loss coefficient. The loch is thus highly flushed (ρ, 21.4 yr^{-1}), and TP concentrations average *ca* 15 μg L^{-1} (Watson, 1991; Bailey-Watts *et al.*, 1992). Its position in Figure 22.3 takes account of these factors and the fact that it has a mean depth of 6.6 m, Loch Dee (mean depth, 4.2 m; ρ, 7 yr^{-1}) would also be placed in this category along with Lochs Iubhair and Doine (author, unpublished), Davan and Cran (Bailey-Watts *et al.*, 1992) – all with ρ values of $\geqslant 20$ yr^{-1}, as well as numerous lochans (Brook and Woodward, 1956).

By no means all oligotrophic systems are rapidly flushed. ρ values of <1 yr^{-1} have been calculated for the large Lochs Lomond, Morar, Ness and Shiel for which Scotland is famed (Smith *et al.*, 1981b). Their oligotrophic status is attributed to the large depths which increase the product of ρ and mean depth. The co-ordinates for the Loch Shiel data in Figure 22.3 (ρ, 0.65 yr^{-1}; mean depth 41 m; SAL, 0.25 g m^{-2} yr^{-1} happen to be very similar to those calculated for the very contrasting Loch Dee.

Rapidly flushed water bodies and deep, poorly flushed lochs can thus sustain relatively high inputs of nutrients without manifesting high levels of P (or plankton – see below), although there are arguments for siting fish cages, for example, in the smaller of any pair of waters with comparable annual flushing volumes (Bailey-Watts *et al.*, 1992). Shallow and poorly flushed water bodies are very different and cannot sustain high nutrient loadings. Much of their plant production can accumulate as biomass. Good examples are Coldingham Loch (ρ, 0.36 yr^{-1}; mean depth 2.9 m – Bailey-Watts *et al.*, 1987b), Kilconquhar (ρ, 0.7 yr^{-1}; mean depth, 1.2 m – Bailey-Watts *et al.*, 1992) and Leven (ρ, *ca* 0.9–2.8 yr^{-1}; mean depth, 3.9 m – Bailey-Watts *et al.*, 1987a).

Data obtained for Loch Leven in 1985 – a year in which rainfall was distributed fairly uniformly and a wet summer suppressed phosphate release from the sediments – fitted very closely to the models referred to above. Co-ordinates based on a SAL of 1.54 g m^{-2} yr^{-1}, a ρ of 2.53 yr^{-1} and the mean depth give a result near that plotted for the Loch of Strathbeg, firmly in the eutrophic sector of Figure 22.3. Field data do not fit the models where SRP is released from the deposits and conditions allow it to accumulate in the water column (Marsden, 1989). This has occurred at Loch

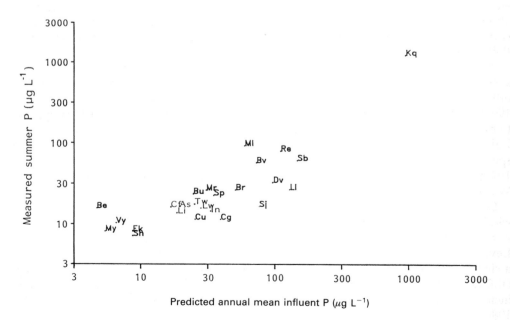

FIGURE 22.4. The predicted loadings of 25 of the lochs in Figure 22.3 expressed as mean influent P concentrations, related to the loch concentrations measured (once) in summer 1991. Codes and loch names are as in Figure 22.1 (Reproduced by permission of the Institute of Freshwater Ecology from Bailey-Watts *et al.*, 1992)

Leven in approximately 50% of the 22 years for which information is available (Holden and Caines, 1974; Bailey-Watts, 1986a; Bailey-Watts *et al.*, 1990; 1991; 1993) and in Coldingham Loch where alternating phases of phosphate release from, and re-adsorption by, the sediments dominate the P dynamics (Bailey-Watts *et al.*, 1987b).

The desk analysis gauged the P status of the lochs reasonably well (Bailey-Watts *et al.*, 1992); a linear regression shows that some 70% of the variation in predicted loads expressed as mean influent concentrations ([P_{in}] of OECD, 1982), was associated with variation in the in-loch P concentrations ([$P_{i/n}$] measured (once) in summer ($r^2 = 0.69$, $n = 25$ – Figure 22.4). The results for many of the individual lochs could also be explained by taking account of (i) the likelihood of the summer P value approximating to an annual mean figure; (ii) P sedimentation predicted from the empirical model of Kirchner and Dillon (1975) to which the detailed data on Loch Leven for 1985 also fitted extremely closely (Bailey-Watts *et al.*, 1987a); (iii) whether the loch flora was dominated by rooted vegetation; and (iv) whether SRP is released from the sediments, as in many rich shallow waters (Holden and Caines, 1974; Harper 1978; Bailey-Watts *et al.*, 1987b; 1990; 1991), or sediment particles are likely to have been re-suspended in windy weather.

BIOLOGICAL EFFECTS OF ACCELERATED NUTRIENT ENRICHMENT

Planktonic algae

The accumulation of biomass of different plants gives rise to the majority of eutrophication-related problems and the cyanobacteria have attracted considerable attention (Reynolds, 1987). "Flowering" of these algae even in oligotrophic waters is by no means a new phenomenon (Wesenberg-Lund, 1905; West, in Murray and Pullar, 1910; Rosenberg, 1938; Chapter 8).

Assuming light and nutrient resources are adequate, the abundance of different species of cyanobacteria is influenced by flushing rate and the interaction with species differing in growth rate potential (Bailey-Watts, 1978; Bailey-Watts *et al.*, 1990; 1993). Large cyanobacteria often follow spells of grazing zooplankton, which appear to prefer the smaller algae (Bailey-Watts and Kirika, 1981; Bailey-Watts, 1982; 1986a; Bailey-Watts *et al.*, 1992). Algal size is also a factor in bloom formation. The larger species buoy up to the surface, although only under calm conditions (Bailey-Watts, 1974; 1978; 1987); small forms remain comparatively uniformly distributed (Bailey-Watts *et al.*, 1968; 1993; Bailey-Watts, 1973).

Diatoms, which can produce much denser, but less noticeable, populations in lake-wide terms than bloom-forming cyanobacteria (Bailey-Watts 1988a, b; Bailey-Watts *et al.*, 1993) favour conditions of good vertical mixing such as those prevailing at Loch Leven (Bailey-Watts, 1976a; Bailey-Watts *et al.*, 1989a). Coldingham Loch produced a significant summer population of *Fragilaria crotonensis* only after artificial mixing (Bailey-Watts, 1986b; 1990b). Even in these waters, however, the populations may incur losses of up to 80% through sinking (Bailey-Watts, 1976b; Bailey-Watts *et al.*, 1989b).

While diatom abundance relies on silica availability, population densities increase more or less in line with trophic status. Approximately 10 cells mL^{-1} of the colonial diatom *Asterionella formosa* were recorded in the largest, oligotrophic lochs including Loch Ness (Bailey-Watts and Duncan, 1981b), while concentrations of >10^4 mL^{-1}

are often achieved in Loch Leven (Bailey-Watts, 1978) where this species was recorded at the beginning of the century (West and West, 1912). The Loch Ness record is significant as, according to the classic research of Lund (1949), the appearance of *A. formosa* indicates mild enrichment. It is thus notable that a population of $ca\ 10^2$ mL^{-1} was recorded in Loch Veyatie which receives fish-farm effluent (Bailey-Watts *et al.*, 1992).

Most desmids are associated with oligotrophic systems (Brook, 1981). The ratio of the sum of the number of species of cyanobacteria, centric diatoms, euglenoids, and chlorococcalean green algae (all essentially eutrophic indicators) to the number of desmids (Nygaard, 1949) correlates strongly with lake trophic status (Brook, 1964; Harper, 1986). However, some desmids can form sizeable crops in eutrophic situations (Brook, 1959; 1964; 1981; Bailey-Watts, 1987). Miss G. Moffet (personal communication) has found what appears to be an undescribed species at a density of 90×10^3 mL^{-1} (!) in a gull-roost lochan, Loch Faedaire, near Pitlochry.

Dense phytoplankton crops can consist very largely of one species, whether it be a green alga, a diatom or a cyanobacterium (Bailey-Watts, 1973; 1974; 1978; 1982; 1986b), but different "forms" or morphotypes of some algae can co-exist (Bailey-Watts, 1973; 1988a, b). Compared to other plant communities in eutrophic waters, however, the phytoplankton is usually very diverse (Bailey-Watts, 1986a; Bailey-Watts and Kirika, 1991).

Annual mean levels and seasonal variation in total phytoplankton biomass (chlorophyll$_a$ concentration) generally increase with trophic status (compare Bailey-Watts and Duncan (1981b) and Bailey-Watts and Kirika (1993) with Bailey-Watts (1978) and Harper (1978)). Chlorophyll$_a$ maxima generally develop earlier in the year in shallow systems than in deeper waters, even where temperatures might be only just above freezing (Bailey-Watts, 1988a, b). The depth of vertical mixing and loch depth (a factor in the "morphometric trophy" of a lake – Rawson, 1955; 1956), as well as daylength, are major determinants of light availability and thus the production of any phytoplankter (Talling, 1971; Bindloss *et al.*, 1972; Bindloss, 1974; 1976; Lyle and Bailey-Watts, 1993). In large oligotrophic lochs the moderate algal maxima of 2.5–3.5 μg chlorophyll$_a$ L^{-1} are not achieved until June or even mid-August (Bailey-Watts and Duncan, 1981b). Only by then have these massive waters warmed up sufficiently to enhance growth processes generally and, perhaps more importantly, to develop a more or less stable, well-illuminated epilimnion which would increase photosynthetic activity. These factors explain the contrasts between the phytoplankton of the deep, northern trench of Loch Lomond (Bailey-Watts and Duncan, 1981a, b), and that of its shallower, mesotrophic southern basin (Maulood and Boney, 1980); however, a catchment analysis suggests that most nutrients enter the loch at its southern end (Bailey-Watts *et al.*, in press).

The degree of spatial variation in phytoplankton abundance within a water body depends rather less than the other features on nutrient status. Of greater importance are water movements, the presence of isolated bays or deep, stratifying "pots", and the size, buoyancy and motility of the algae present (Bailey-Watts, 1973; 1978; Bailey-Watts *et al.*, 1992; 1993).

The observed fluctuations in phytoplankton species abundance reflect the relative abilities of different algae to capitalize on the ever-changing physical, chemical and biotic factors discussed in this chapter. Of prime concern is the net amount of

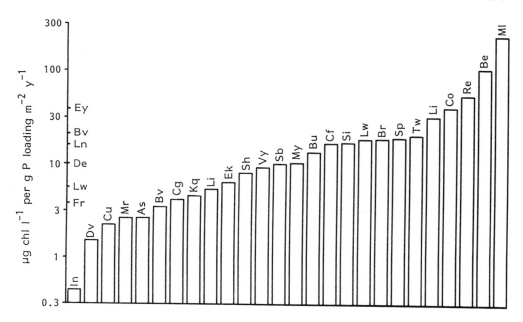

FIGURE 22.5. The efficiency with which the lochs (excluding Coldingham) in Figure 22.4 (vertical bars) and six waters on which more intensive measurements have been made (labelled against the y axis) convert P inputs to phytoplankton biomass, as indicated by the ratios of chlorophyll$_a$ concentration to specific areal P load. Loch codes are as in Figure 22.1

phytoplankton produced in a water body per unit of P loading. Figure 22.5 uses the ratio of chlorophyll concentration to the SAL. The ranking of lochs such as St Mary's, Veyatie, Eck and Shiel, and the Mill Loch, can be explained by the existence of an epilimnion, however temporary, at the time of sampling; the chlorophyll concentrations may have been near or at their annual maxima as a result of this (Bailey-Watts *et al.*, 1992). Turbid water and dense stands of macrophytic vegetation (Harper, 1986) may contribute to the relatively low pigment/SAL ratio of Forfar Loch, while the wet summer can explain the relatively low value of 14 μg chlorophyll$_a$ L^{-1} g^{-1} P m^{-2} yr^{-1} calculated for Loch Leven in 1985; in years with warm summers a value of 50 is more likely (Bailey-Watts *et al.*, 1993). Very high flushing, together with dense growths of benthic algae (Watson, 1991) will have contributed to the extremely low pigment/P loading ratio calculated for Loch Insh.

Attached algae

Dense populations of non-planktonic algae have been associated with eutrophication. Moss (1983) suggests that epiphytic populations may respond before other biota, and that the proliferation of epiphytes as well as that of phytoplankton has led to the decline in macrophytes in many Norfolk Broads. Some of the densest crops of any algae in Loch Leven are produced by 'epipsammic' diatoms on sand grains (Bailey-Watts, 1973; 1974).

Black gelatinous mats on the stony substrates over long stretches of the River Tweed are also dominated by diatoms (Tweed River Purification Board, 1987) although filamentous cyanobacteria are present as well (author, unpublished observations). Growths dominated by filamentous blue-green algae such as Oscillatoriales in Lochs Insh (Watson, 1991), Awe and Avich (Professor G. Codd, personal communication) are of special concern in being toxic to mammals (Codd, 1984; Edwards *et al.*, 1992; Gunn *et al.*, 1992). Thus, even running waters and rapidly flushed lakes can produce dense growths of algae. Eutrophication is likely to be a contributory factor, since nutrients are needed to support the populations.

Growths of filamentous green algae are not a new feature. Carlingwark Loch (for which Bailey-Watts *et al.* (1992) predicted a P loading of 4.4 $gm^{-2} yr^{-1}$ which is some three times that measured for Loch Leven) and Loch Gelly exhibited swathes of filamentous *Oedogonium* and *Spirogyra* at least 80 years ago (West, in Murray and Pullar, 1910).

Higher plants

The status and ecology of aquatic macrophytes in Scotland is discussed in Chapter 9. Problems with overgrowths of higher plants and decreased species diversity are considerable, and enhanced nutrient enrichment is held to be one of the commonest causes (Robson, 1986). Standing waters are the most prone (Murphy, 1990), and these include large systems such as the Loch of Harray (Orkney) and Rescobie Loch, as well as small lochans.

Enrichment, together with associated changes in alkalinity and pH status, contribute to shifts in species composition (Harper, 1992). However, assuming substrates suitable for rooting and nutrient uptake are available, light penetration determines plant depth distribution (Spence, 1964; 1967; 1971; 1975). Light-attenuating humic substances which characterize the majority of Scottish waters play a large role in this (see also Lyle and Bailey-Watts, 1993). As enrichment proceeds, the rapid growth and biomass accumulation rates attainable by phytoplankton lead to reduced water clarity which puts rooted plants at a disadvantage (Jupp *et al.*, 1974; Spence, 1975).

Aquatic macrophytes possibly demonstrate best the reductions in species diversity commonly associated with eutrophication (Harper, 1986; Bailey-Watts and May, 1991). Similar effects are evident in the tropics, from the extensive overgrowths of rooted and floating plants such as *Eichhornia, Pistia* and *Salvinia* in almost pure stand (Denny, 1985; Payne, 1986). These can be considered as invasive plants, but nutrients must be available to support their crops. Heavy fertilizer application for high-yield rice production, for example, is a major factor in countries such as Bangladesh and India.

Species composition and abundance of submerged plants can change long before a water body is what might be termed nutrient-rich. Charophytic algae and isoetids, for example, dominate the vegetation in oligotrophic waters. These are replaced first by species-rich *Potamogeton* assemblages and second by less diverse but denser stands, including invasive forms such as *Myriophyllum spicatum* and *Elodea canadensis* (Harper, 1986). Emergent hydrophytes may respond differently, possibly because they are not in direct competition for nutrients with the rest of the aquatic flora (Harper, 1992). For example, the growth, biomass and efficiency of solar energy conversion of *Phragmites australis* increased during change from mesotrophic to hypertrophic conditions (Ho, 1979).

Invertebrate benthos

Eutrophication-induced changes in plant communities affect the abundance and species composition of the animal communities (e.g. Morgan, 1970; Royal Society of Edinburgh, 1974; Harper, 1986). An individual system is likely to respond with increases in biomass and decreases in species composition. Total invertebrate densities and the proportions of oligochaetes and chironomids are often very much higher in sediments beneath fish cages than elsewhere in oligotrophic lochs (Institute of Aquaculture *et al.*, 1990; Mr I. D. M. Gunn, personal communication). Larval chironomids now dominate the biomass and the production of zoobenthos in both the sandy littoral and the muddy zones of Loch Leven (Charles *et al.*, 1974; Maitland and Hudspith, 1974). Densities in the shallows averaged 10 000 m^{-2} in 1970 and 14 000 m^{-2} in 1971, while a value of 33 000 m^{-2} was obtained for the deeper areas. These populations are considerably less diverse than those recorded in earlier years (Morgan, 1970); declines in the numbers of Coleoptera, Plecoptera, Ephemeroptera and Trichoptera, and increases in the biomass of profundal Chironomidae and Oligochaeta correspond to a reduction in macrophyte diversity and an increase in sedimenting phytoplankton. Harper (1986) recorded 61 invertebrate species in the sandy littoral of mesotrophic Loch of Lowes, 55 species in eutrophic Balgavies Loch and 33 species in hypertrophic Loch of Forfar. Chironomids and tubificids were prominent in all three lochs, but there were more chaoborids in both Lowes and Balgavies than in Forfar, and also more lumbriculids in Balgavies than in the very rich loch. However, the total densities of invertebrates were somewhat similar, with values of 20 000 m^{-2} in Lowes, 31 000 m^{-2} in Balgavies and 27 000 m^{-2} in the Loch of Forfar. While the densities of invertebrates in the oligotrophic Lake Thingvallavatn in Iceland also approximate to 20 000 m^{-2} (Jonasson, 1992), those in the littoral zones of the five largest and less enriched Scottish lochs are likely to be considerably lower than this (Smith *et al.*, 1981a).

Oligotrophic systems with catchments dominated by rough grazing and eutrophic waters surrounded by arable land in Tayside Region, both contained lower numbers of species of inshore and epibenthic microcrustaceans than mesotrophic systems (Jones, 1989). There was, however, a more or less consistent increase in population density with increasing trophic status.

Crustacean zooplankton

Maitland *et al.* (1981) were able to categorize the oligotrophic Lochs Lomond, Awe, Ness, Morar and Shiel on the basis of zooplankton species occurrence and numbers (all <2 L^{-1}) in spite of the limited trophic range represented by these waters. Jones (1984) established a clear pattern of species and abundance from a more varied group of five Tayside lochs. Oligotrophic Lochs Laidon and Lyon contained a diverse assemblage dominated by *Diaptomus gracilis*, while mesotrophic Lochs Earn and Lintrathen contained fewer species and *Daphnia hyalina* was dominant. In the eutrophic Loch Leven where the crustacean populations were some four times as dense as those recorded in the other four waters, diversity was low with *Cyclops strenuus abyssorum* and *D. hyalina* dominating. Total crustacean densities in Loch Leven occasionally approach 100 L^{-1} (Bailey-Watts, 1986a; May *et al.*, 1993b) – similar to summer values recorded by Harper (1986) in Balgavies Loch (*ca* 75 L^{-1}), but more than those found in Loch of Lowes (30 L^{-1}) and less than the populations in the Loch of Forfar (150 L^{-1}).

Harper (1986) found that, with increasing levels of bacteria associated with nutrient enrichment, filter-feeding Cladocera become more prominent. The species involved varied in size according to predation pressure from fish; large *Daphnia magna* thrived where fish populations were low, while smaller *Ceriodaphnia* were more important in lochs where fish were abundant. Bailey-Watts *et al.* (1992) observed very dense swarms of *D. magna* in Kilconquhar Loch which is reputed to be "fishless". In contrast, small *Ceriodaphnia* are prominent in Coldingham Loch which is well-stocked for angling.

Planktonic rotifers

Bailey-Watts *et al.* (1992) found that the majority of 25 lochs sampled in summer 1991 contained the rotifer species expected on the basis of (i) their trophic ranking according to Berzins and Pejler (1989) and (ii) the P content of the waters. Thus, oligotrophic *Kellicottia longispina* and *Gastropus stylifer* were found in low-P waters such as Loch Shiel, St Mary's Loch and Loch Eck. By contrast, the much richer Balgavies Loch, Loch of Strathbeg, Rescobie Loch and Mill Loch contained *Keratella quadrata* and *Filinia longiseta*. No rotifers were recorded in the Kilconquhar Loch samples – not even *Keratella cochlearis* which was found in all of the other lochs except Linlithgow.

The densities of most of the rotifer populations sampled by Bailey-Watts *et al.* (1992) varied from 10 to 100 individuals L^{-1}. Notable exceptions were two records from the Shetland Isles: 2100 *K. cochlearis* L^{-1} in the Loch of Brow and 1100 *Polyarthra vulgaris/dolichoptera* L^{-1} in the Loch of Cliff. There was no consistent relationship between abundance and trophic status in this set of waters. This may be due to the fact that the animal data refer to only one point in time; many rotifers have short lifespans and can change in numbers very rapidly. From seasonal records, however, it appears that maximum rotifer abundance is a good indicator of trophic status. Population densities reviewed by May *et al.* (1993b) range from <10 L^{-1} in oligotrophic Attersee (Austria) to 40 000 L^{-1} in hypertrophic Priest Pot (England). Loch Leven, with 10 600 rotifers L^{-1}, ranked second richest in this series. Most of the species present in Loch Leven are thought to be indicators of eutrophy. However, *Kellicottia longispina*, which is thought to indicate oligotrophy, has recently appeared (May *et al.*, 1993b). This may reflect an effect of the P reduction programmes executed over recent years (Bailey-Watts *et al.*, 1993).

Fish

Nutrient levels, primary production and fish productivity are generally positively correlated (Le Cren and Lowe-McConnell, 1980). However, some fish species are unable to tolerate a wide range of trophic conditions. Eutrophication is considered to have caused the disappearances of the Vendace (*Coregonus albula* from Castle Loch (Lochmaben) and the Arctic Charr (*Salvelinus alpinus* from Loch Leven (Maitland and Lyle, 1991).

Eutrophication-induced algal blooms are implicated in poor fishing returns (Rosenberg, 1938; Bailey-Watts *et al.*, 1993). However, Bailey-Watts and Maitland (1984) suggested that reduced catches are due primarily to reduced angling effort, rather than any direct effect of algae on fish productivity.

THE INFLUENCE OF WEATHER ON NUTRIENT LOADINGS AND BIOLOGY

Eutrophication itself (i.e. nutrient loadings and the concentrations achieved) and the biological responses to these are controlled by weather-driven factors such as flushing rate and temperature, in addition to the effect of temperature on mixing/stratification patterns. A special feature of the Scottish climate is the acute temporal variability in wind, rain and temperature (Smith, 1973; 1974). The effects on flushing rate (Sargent and Ledger, 1992) and winter and summer temperatures (Lyle, 1981; Bailey-Watts, 1990b; Bailey-Watts *et al.*, 1990) are especially marked in shallow waters (which comprise the bulk of eutrophic systems), but calculations suggest that the epilimnia of larger lochs may be similarly affected (Lyle and Bailey-Watts, 1993).

The changeable weather regime ultimately influences factors controlling the production of phytoplankton cells. Included here are: mixing (Bailey-Watts, 1990b) and the associated light climate perceived by planktonic organisms (Bindloss, 1974); loadings of nutrients (Bailey-Watts *et al.*, 1987a, 1993) and concentrations resulting from different types of input (Bailey-Watts and May, 1992); and the fluxes of solutes and particles between sediments and overlying water (Bailey-Watts *et al.*, 1990). The timing of annual phytoplankton maxima is very variable (Bailey-Watts *et al.*, 1990; Bailey-Watts and Kirika, 1993). The vagaries of the weather also impinge on factors which determine the fraction of production that is recorded as biomass. A number of organisms that feed on phytoplankton and thus reduce algal biomass feature here, although losses are also effected by flushing (Bailey-Watts *et al.*, 1990). Scottish research has identified links between temperature and the metabolism of rotifers (May, 1980a; 1983; 1987; May *et al.*, 1993b) and crustaceans (Bailey-Watts and Kirika, 1981; Bailey-Watts, 1986a; May *et al.*, 1993b), and the succession of rotifer species, through its effect on the hatching of resting eggs (May, 1986).

As a result of the interaction between lake morphometry and the weather, many Scottish waters stratify and exhibit clinograde oxygen and temperature profiles only intermittently in summer (Bailey-Watts *et al.*, 1987b; 1990; 1992). Surface sediments as well as the overlying water may thus reach quite high temperatures, and phosphate releases may be enhanced. It is tempting to suggest that Scotland has no truly dimictic systems such as those found on the continent and even in England, on which many limnological principles were founded (Hutchinson, 1957; Ruttner, 1963; Lund, 1965; Reynolds, 1984). Scottish lochs could respond markedly to predicted climate changes (UKCCIRG, 1991; Mitchell and Qingcun, 1992).

Under favourable conditions, many planktonic algae can double in numbers within a few days, and parasitic fungi and grazing protozoa (Canter, 1971; 1973; Bailey-Watts, 1973; 1988a; Bailey-Watts and Lund, 1973) and rotifers (May, 1980b; 1987;

May *et al.*, 1993a) can also reduce the numbers of particular species of algae, over similar timescales. The consequences of weather conditions, enhancing the rates of these loss processes, persisting for a week or so longer in one year than another, may thus be considerable. The formation of a blue-green algal scum could rest on favourable weather lasting for just a few hours longer than usual.

THE STEMMING OF EUTROPHICATION

Much attention is paid to the protection of the high quality waters which drain the majority of the land area of Scotland (Bailey-Watts *et al.*, 1988; 1992; Forestry Commission, 1991; Scottish Office Agriculture and Fisheries Department, 1992). However, for each loch already affected by over-enrichment, a range of restoration strategies needs to be considered, before selecting those most appropriate.

Bailey-Watts *et al.* (1993) considered 33 techniques before deciding on a strategy for suppressing phytoplankton biomass and the incidence of toxic cyanobacterial blooms at Loch Leven. The restorative measures finally selected take account of the conservation status of the loch, the world-famous trout fishery, and the historical interest (Morgan, 1970). In addition, the functioning of downstream paper mills relies on water of reasonable quality.

From a range of possibilities considered for reducing nutrient availability, P-stripping of sewage works effluent remains a firm aim, although the creation of wet meadows is also under review. These techniques are being pursued even though blooms and massive releases of phosphate from the sediments have featured in most summers following an earlier cutback of (mill) effluent which reduced the loading by *ca* 6 t yr^{-1} (Bailey-Watts *et al.*, 1991; 1993). None of five classes of methods for reducing sediment P release, nor any of three procedures for reducing light availability and the photosynthetic potential of phytoplankton, was considered appropriate. In contrast, a mixing technique was used with some success in the suppression of *Aphanizomenon* blooms at Coldingham Loch (Bailey-Watts *et al.*, 1987c).

A number of methods aimed at removing algal biomass by means of the introduction of parasitic or grazing organisms were considered inappropriate at this time. Unfortunately, the option of increasing flushing rates to reduce the time available for biomass to accumulate and to increase washout losses, had to be shelved on logistical grounds; for example, a weekly throughput of some 25×10^6 m^3 of water (half the loch volume) would be required to maintain, at a constant density, the population of an alga capable of doubling in biomass every week.

In view of the unpredictable nature of the weather, the P control options set for Loch Leven assume that conditions will always be such as to maximize the conversion of P supply to phytoplankton biomass; that is, raise the chlorophyll concentration/P loading ratio to *ca* 50:1 in contrast to the ratio of 14:1 calculated for 1985. In common with experiences elsewhere of sediment phosphate releases even after reductions of the external P loadings (Marsden, 1989), the Loch Leven situation emphasizes that "prevention is better than cure".

CONCLUSIONS

There is a reasonable understanding of the factors and processes governing the structure and functioning of Scottish waters in relation to nutrient enrichment. The features that determine what a water body can sustain by way of eutrophication before manifesting algal blooms, for example, have also been identified for a wide variety of lochs. However, there is an urgent need for more case studies of the type done in Northern Ireland (Gibson *et al.*, 1988; 1992), England (Moss, 1983; Moss *et al.*, 1988), continental Europe (Sas, 1989) and the seven Scottish catchments discussed above. Only then can nutrient losses and their effects be properly quantified. There are very few Scottish data on nutrients from septic tanks, for example.

Other gaps in knowledge or areas for which there are few Scottish data, include:

- the influence of the chemical "mix" that is likely to accompany nutrients in many effluents (Scottish Agricultural College, 1980; Ellis, 1989);
- whether the proliferation of bloom-forming cyanobacteria is due primarily to extra (sediment-derived) phosphate or to the accompanying conditions of low flushing and warm, calm weather;
- the quantitative effects of light attenuation and the phosphate binding potential of humic material (Jones et al., 1988; Lyle and Bailey-Watts, 1993);
- the ecology of benthic algal communities with special reference to nutrient utilization in eutrophic waters;
- the biology, ecology and specific identity of picocyanobacteria (cf. Bailey-Watts and Komarek, 1991) in eutrophic waters; and
- the impacts on aquatic food chains (McQueen *et al.*, 1989) and the cycling of P (Carpenter *et al.*, 1992), of losses of fish species due to eutrophication.

ACKNOWLEDGEMENTS

I am very grateful to the departments which have funded much of the research quoted here, and I also wish to record special thanks to my colleagues Mr Iain Gunn, Mr Alex Kirika, Mr Alex Lyle and Dr Linda May, for their encouragement and support over the years. The editors and an anonymous referee made extensive and very useful comments on the original manuscript.

REFERENCES

Anonymous (1989). "The nitrate debate", *Nitrogen*, **182**, 13–17.
Bailey-Watts, A. E. (1973). "Observations on the phytoplankton of Loch Leven", PhD thesis, University of London, London.
Bailey-Watts, A. E. (1974). "The algal plankton of Loch Leven, Kinross", *Proceedings of the Royal Society of Edinburgh*, **74B**, 135–156.
Bailey-Watts, A. E. (1976a). "Planktonic diatoms and some diatom–silica relations in a shallow eutrophic Scottish loch", *Freshwater Biology*, **6**, 69–80.
Bailey-Watts, A. E. (1976b). "Planktonic diatoms and silica in Loch Leven, Kinross, Scotland: a one-month silica budget", *Freshwater Biology*, **6**, 203–213.
Bailey-Watts, A. E. (1978). "A nine-year study of the phytoplankton of the eutrophic and non-stratifying Loch Leven (Kinross, Scotland)", *Journal of Ecology*, **6**, 741–771.
Bailey-Watts, A. E. (1982). "The composition and abundance of phytoplankton in Loch Leven 1977–1979 and a comparison with the succession in earlier years", *Internationale Revue der gesamten Hydrobiologie*, **67**, 1–25.
Bailey-Watts, A. E. (1983). *A Re-assessment of Phosphorus Loadings to Loch Leven, Kinross-shire and their Implications for Eutrophication Control by Phosphorus Removal* (Report to the Nature Conservancy Council), Institute of Terrestrial Ecology, Edinburgh.
Bailey-Watts, A. E. (1985). "Land-use, chemicals and freshwater ecology", *Edinburgh Centre for Rural Economy, Annual Report*, 1985, 1–4.

Bailey-Watts, A. E. (1986a). "Seasonal variation in size spectra of phytoplankton assemblages in Loch Leven, Scotland", *Hydrobiologia*, **138**, 25–42.

Bailey-Watts, A. E. (1986b). "The ecology of planktonic diatoms, especially *Fragilaria crotonensis*, associated with artificial mixing of a small Scottish loch in summer", *Diatom Research*, **1**, 153–168.

Bailey-Watts, A. E. (1987). "Coldingham Loch, S. E. Scotland. II. Phytoplankton succession and ecology in the year prior to mixer installation", *Freshwater Biology*, **17**, 419–428.

Bailey-Watts, A. E. (1988a). "The abundance, size distribution and species composition of unicellular Centrales assemblages at mainly late winter – early spring maxima in Loch Leven (Kinross, Scotland) 1968–1985", in *Proceedings of the 9th International Symposium on Living and Fossil Diatoms*, pp. 1–16, Biopress Bristol and Koeltz, Koenigstein.

Bailey-Watts, A. E. (1988b). "Studies on the control of the early spring diatom maximum in Loch Leven 1981", in *Algae and the Aquatic Environment* (Ed. F. E. Round), pp. 53–87, Biopress, Bristol.

Bailey-Watts, A. E. (1990a). "Eutrophication: assessment, research and management with special reference to Scotland's freshwaters", *Journal of the Institution of Water and Environmental Management*, **4**, 285–294.

Bailey-Watts, A. E. (1990b). "Changes in Loch Leven phytoplankton associated with the warm winter 1988/89. [Abstract]", *Verhandlungen der Internationalen Vereinigung für theoretische und angewandte Limnologie*, **24**, 567.

Bailey-Watts, A. E. and Duncan, P. (1981a). "Chemical characterisation. A one year comparative study", in *The Ecology of Scotland's Largest Lochs: Lomond, Awe, Ness, Morar and Shiel* (Ed. P. S. Maitland), pp. 67–89, Junk, The Hague.

Bailey-Watts, A. E. and Duncan, P. (1981b). "The ecology of Scotland's largest lochs: Lomond, Awe, Ness, Morar and Shiel. 4. The phytoplankton", *Monographiae Biologicae*, **44**, 91–118.

Bailey-Watts, A. E. and Kirika, A. (1981). "The assessment of size variation in Loch Leven phytoplankton: methodology and some of its uses in the study of factors influencing size", *Journal of Plankton Research*, **3**, 261–282.

Bailey-Watts, A. E. and Kirika, A. (1987). "A re-assessment of the phosphorus inputs to Loch Leven (Kinross, Scotland): rationale and overview of results on instantaneous loadings with special reference to runoff", *Transactions of the Royal Society of Edinburgh, Earth Sciences*, **78**, 351–367.

Bailey-Watts, A. E. and Kirika, A. (1991). *Loch Eye, Easter Ross—a case study in eutrophication* (Report to the Nature Conservancy Council), Institute of Freshwater Ecology, Edinburgh.

Bailey-Watts, A. E. and Komarek, J. (1991). "Towards a formal description of a new species of *Synechococcus* (Cyanobacteria, Microcystaceae) from the freshwater picoplankton", *Algological Studies*, **61**, 5–19.

Bailey-Watts, A. E. and Kirika, A. (1993). "Phytoplankton and controlling factors in the rapidly flushed, upland Loch Dee, (Galloway, Scotland)", in *Proceedings of the Loch Dee Symposium: Acidification, forestry and fisheries management in upland Galloway* (Eds T. J. Tervet and F. M. Lees), pp. 83–96, Foundation for Water Research, Medmenham.

Bailey-Watts, A. E. and Lund, J. W. G. (1973). "Observations on a diatom bloom in Loch Leven, Scotland", *Biological Journal of the Linnean Society*, **5**, 235–253.

Bailey-Watts, A. E. and Maitland, P. S. (1984). "Eutrophication and fisheries in Loch Leven, Kinross, Scotland", in *Proceedings of the Institute of Fisheries Management 15th Annual Study Course, 10–13 September 1984*, pp. 170–190, Stirling University, Scotland.

Bailey-Watts, A. E. and May, L. (1991). *A Review of Freshwater Eutrophication Studies Funded by the Nature Conservancy Council: Their Contribution to the Assessment, Control and Prevention of Enrichment Problems in the Future* (Report to the Nature Conservancy Council), Institute of Freshwater Ecology, Edinburgh.

Bailey-Watts, A. E. and May, L. (1992). *Eutrophication Risk Assessment Progress Report for 1991–1992* (Ed. R. Norton), (Report to the Water Research Centre), Institute of Freshwater Ecology, Edinburgh.

Bailey-Watts, A. E., Bindloss, M. E. and Belcher, J. H. (1968). "Freshwater primary production by a blue-green alga of bacterial size", *Nature*, **220**, 1344–1345.

Bailey-Watts, A. E., Sargent, R., Kirika, A. and Smith, M. (1987a). *Loch Leven Phosphorus Loading* (Report to Department of Agriculture and Fisheries for Scotland, Nature Conservancy Council, Scottish Development Department and Tayside Regional Council), Institute of Terrestrial Ecology, Edinburgh.

Bailey-Watts, A. E., Lyle, A. A. and Wise, E. J. (1987b). "Coldingham Loch, S. E. Scotland. I. Physical and chemical features with special reference to the seasonal patterns of nutrients", *Freshwater Biology*, **17**, 405–418.

Bailey-Watts, A. E., Wise, E. J. and Kirika, A. (1987c). "An experiment in phytoplankton ecology and applied fishery management: effects of artificial aeration on troublesome algal blooms in a small eutrophic loch", *Aquaculture and Fisheries Management*, **18**, 259–275.

Bailey-Watts, A. E., Kirika, A. and Howell, D. L. (1988). *The Potential Effects of Phosphate Runoff from Fertilised Forestry Plantations on Reservoir Phytoplankton: Literature Review and Enrichment Experiments* (Report to the Water Research Centre), Institute of Terrestrial Ecology, Edinburgh.

Bailey-Watts, A. E., Smith, I. R. and Kirika, A. (1989a). "The dynamics of silica in a shallow diatom-rich Scottish loch I: stream inputs of the dissolved nutrient", *Diatom Research*, **4**, 179–190.

Bailey-Watts, A. E., Smith, I. R. and Kirika, A. (1989b). "The dynamics of silica in a shallow diatom-rich Scottish loch II: The influence of diatoms on an annual budget", *Diatom Research*, **4**, 191–205.

Bailey-Watts, A. E., Kirika, A., May, L. and Jones, D. H. (1990). "Changes in phytoplankton over various timescales in a shallow, eutrophic loch: the Loch Leven experience with special reference to the influence of flushing rate", *Freshwater Biology*, **23**, 85–111.

Bailey-Watts, A. E., May, L. and Kirika, A. (1991). *Nutrients, Phytoplankton and Water Clarity in Loch Leven following Phosphorus Loading Reduction* (Report to the Scottish Development Department), Institute of Freshwater Ecology, Edinburgh.

Bailey-Watts, A. E., May, L., Kirika, A. and Lyle, A. A. (1992). *Eutrophication Case Studies: Phase II, an assessment based on desk analysis of catchments and summer limnological reconnaissances. Volume I. An analysis of the whole spectrum of waters studied. Volume II. Limnological profiles of the sites with special reference to eutrophication and phosphorus (P)* (Report to the Nature Conservancy Council for Scotland), Institute of Freshwater Ecology, Edinburgh.

Bailey-Watts, A. E., Gunn, I. D. M. and Kirika, A. (1993). *Loch Leven: past and current water quality and options for change* (Report to the Forth River Purification Board), Institute of Freshwater Ecology, Edinburgh.

Bailey-Watts, A. E., Lyle, A. A., Gunn, I.D.M., Traill, I. and Tippett, R. (in press). "Catchment pressures and lake sensitivity factors influencing the nature of the phytoplankton: the Loch Lomond example", *Hydrobiologia*.

Berzins, B. and Pejler, B. (1989). "Rotifer occurrence and trophic degree", *Hydrobiologia*, **182**, 171–180.

Bindloss, M. E. (1974). "Primary productivity of phytoplankton in Loch Leven, Kinross", *Proceedings of the Royal Society of Edinburgh*, **74B**, 157–181.

Bindloss, M. E. (1976). "The light climate of Loch Leven, a shallow Scottish lake, in relation to primary production of phytoplankton", *Freshwater Biology*, **6**, 501–508.

Bindloss, M. E., Holden, A. V., Bailey-Watts, A. E. and Smith, I. R. (1972). "Phytoplankton in relation to nutrient and radiation input at Loch Leven", in *Proceedings of the IBP/UNESCO Symposium on productivity problems of Freshwaters, Kazimierz Dolny, Poland*, pp. 639–659, PWN, Polish Scientific Publishers, Warsaw.

Brook, A. J. (1958). "Changes in the phytoplankton of some Scottish hill-lochs resulting from their artificial enrichment", *Verhandlungen der Internationalen Vereinigung für theoretische und angewandte Limnologie*, **13**, 298–305.

Brook, A. J. (1959). "The status of desmids in the plankton and the determination of phytoplankton quotients", *Journal of Ecology*, **47**, 429–445.

Brook, A. J. (1964). "The phytoplankton of the Scottish freshwater lochs", in *The Vegetation of Scotland* (Ed. J. H. Burnett), pp. 290–305, Oliver and Boyd, Edinburgh.

Brook, A. J. (1981). *The Biology of Desmids*, Blackwell Scientific Publications, Oxford.

Brook, A. J. and Holden, A. V. (1957). "Fertilisation experiments in Scottish freshwater lochs.

I. Loch Kinardochy", *Report of Freshwater and Salmon Fisheries Research*, **17**, 1–30.

Brook, A. J. and Woodward, W. B. (1956). "Some observations on the effects of water inflow and outflow on the plankton of small lakes", *Journal of Animal Ecology*, **25**, 22–35.

Canter, H. M. (1971). "Studies on British Chytrids. XXXI. *Rhizophydium androdioctes* sp. nov. parasitic on *Dictyosphaerium pulchellum* Wood from the plankton", *Transactions of the British Mycological Society*, **56**, 115–120.

Canter, H. M. (1973). "A new primitive protozoan devouring centric diatoms in the plankton", *Zoological Journal of the Linnean Society*, **52**, 63–83.

Carpenter, S. R., Cottingham, K. L. and Schindler, D. E. (1992). "Biotic feedbacks in lake phosphorus cycles", *Trends in Ecology and Evolution*, **7**, 332–336.

Carr, N. G. and Whitton, B. A. (1982). *The Biology of the Cyanobacteria*, Blackwell, Oxford.

Charles, W. N., East, K., Brown, D., Gray, M. C. and Murray, T. D. (1974). "The production of larval Chironomidae in the muds at Loch Leven, Kinross", *Proceedings of the Royal Society of Edinburgh*, **74B**, 241–258.

Codd, G. A. (1984). "Toxins of freshwater cyanobacteria", *Microbiological Science*, **1**, 48–52.

Cuttle, S. P. (1989). "Land use changes and inputs of nitrogen to Loch Leven, Scotland: a desk study", *Agriculture and Water Management*, **16**, 119–135.

Davidson, H. P. B. (1986). *Phytoplankton Studies in Loch Leven, Scotland* (Report on industrial placement with Institute of Terrestrial Ecology).

Davison, W. (1986). "Sewage sludge as an acidity filter for groundwater-fed lakes", *Nature, London*, **322**, 820–822.

Denny, P. (1985). *The Ecology and Management of African Wetland Vegetation*, Junk, Dordrecht.

Dillon, P. J. and Rigler, F. H. (1974). "A test of a simple nutrient budget model predicting phosphorus concentration in lake water", *Journal of the Fisheries Research Board of Canada*, **31**, 1171–1178.

Dillon, P. J. and Rigler, F. H. (1975). "A simple method for predicting the capacity of a lake for development based upon lake trophic status", *Journal of the Fisheries Research Board of Canada*, **32**, 1519–1531.

Edwards, C., Beattie, K. A., Scrimgeour, C. M. and Codd, G. A. (1992). "Identification of anatoxin-a in benthic cyanobacteria (blue-green algae) and in associated dog poisonings at Loch Insh, Scotland", *Toxicon*, **30**, 1165–1175.

Ellis, K. V. (1989). *Surface Water Pollution*, MacMillan, London.

Forestry Commission (1991). *Forests and Water Guidelines*, HMSO, London.

Foy, R. H. (1986). "Suppression of phosphorus release from lake sediments by the addition of nitrate", *Water Research*, **10**, 1345–1351.

Ghosh, A., Rao, L. H. and Saha, S. K. (1980). "Culture of *Sarotherodon mossambicus* in small ponds fertilised with domestic sewage", *Journal of the Inland Fisheries Society of India*, **12**, 74–80.

Gibson, C. E., Smith, R. V. and Stewart, D. A. (1988). "A long term study of the phosphorus cycle in Lough Neagh, Northern Ireland", *Internationale Revue der Gesamten Hydrobiologie*, **73**, 249–257.

Gibson, C. E., Smith, R. V. and Stewart, D. A. (1992). "The nitrogen cycle in Lough Neagh, Northern Ireland", *Internationale Revue der Gesamten Hydrobiologie*, **77**, 73–83.

Graham, T. R. (1968). "Lake enrichment by sewage, detergents and fertilisers. Conclusion", *Effluent and Water Treatment Journal*, **8**, 129–135.

Greene, L. A. and Taylor, J. A. (1989). "Catchment afforestation and water supply in Strathclyde Region", *Journal of the Institution of Water and Environmental Management*, **3**, 288–294.

Grimble, I. (1985). *Scottish Islands*, British Broadcasting Corporation, London.

Gunn, G.J., Rafferty, A. G., Rafferty, G. C., Cockburn, N., Edwards, C., Beattie, K. A. and Codd, G. A. (1992). "Fatal canine neurotoxicosis attributed to blue-green algae (cyanobacteria)", *Veterinary Record*, **130**, 301–302.

Hancock, C. G. (1982). "Sources and Utilisation of Nutrients in the Loch of Strathbeg, Aberdeenshire", PhD thesis, University of Aberdeen.

Harper, D. M. (1978). "Limnological Studies on three Scottish lowland freshwater lochs", PhD thesis, University of Dundee.

Harper, D. M. (1986). "The effects of artificial enrichment upon the planktonic and benthic communities in a mesotrophic to hypertrophic loch series in lowland Scotland", *Hydrobiologia*, **137**, 9–19.

Harper, D. M. (1992). *Eutrophication of Freshwaters: Principles, Problems and Restoration*, Chapman and Hall, London.

Harper, D. M. and Stewart, W. D. P. (1987). "The effects of land use upon water chemistry, particularly nutrient enrichment, in shallow lowland lakes: comparative studies of three lochs in Scotland", *Hydrobiologia*, **148**, 211–229.

Harriman, R. (1978). "Nutrient leaching from fertilised forest watersheds in Scotland", *Journal of Applied Ecology*, **15**, 933–942.

Haworth, E. Y. (1976). "Two late-glacial (Late Devensian) diatom assemblage profiles from Northern Scotland", *New Phytologist*, **77**, 227–256.

Ho, Y. B. (1979). "Shoot development and production studies of *Phragmites australis* (Cav.) Trin. *ex* Steudel in Scottish lochs", *Hydrobiologia*, **64**, 215–222.

Holden, A. V. (1959). *Fertilisation Experiments in Scottish Freshwater Lochs II. Sutherland 1954 I. Chemical and Botanical Observations*, HMSO, Edinburgh.

Holden, A. V. (1976). "The relative importance of agricultural fertilizers as a source of nitrogen and phosphorus in Loch Leven", *Technical Bulletin of the Ministry of Agriculture, Fisheries and Food, London*, **32**, 303–310.

Holden, A. V. and Caines, L. A. (1974). "Nutrient chemistry of Loch Leven, Kinross", *Proceedings of the Royal Society of Edinburgh*, **74B**, 101–121.

House, W. A. and Casey, H. (1989). "Transport of phosphorus in rivers", in *Phosphorus Cycles in Terrestrial and Aquatic Ecosystems. Regional Workshop 1: Europe. Proceedings of a Workshop Arranged by SCOPE and UNEP, Organised by the Department of Agrobiology and Forestry of the Polish Academy of Sciences, May 1–6, 1988* (Ed. T. Holm), pp. 254–288, Czerniejewo, Poland.

Hutchinson, G. E. (1957). *A Treatise on Limnology, Volume 1*, John Wiley, New York.

Institute of Aquaculture, Institute of Freshwater Ecology and Institute of Terrestrial Ecology (1990). *Fish Farming and the Scottish Freshwater Environment* (Report to the Nature Conservancy Council), Nature Conservancy Council, Edinburgh.

Johnston, D. W., Holding, A. J. and McCluskie, J. E. (1974). "Preliminary comparative studies on denitrification and methane production in Loch Leven, Kinross and other freshwater lakes", *Proceedings of the Royal Society of Edinburgh*, **74B**, 123–133.

Jonasson, P. M. (Ed.) (1992). "The ecology of oligotrophic, subarctic Thingvallavatn Iceland", *Oikos*, **64**, pp. 1–440.

Jones, D. H. (1984). "Open-water zooplankton from five Tayside freshwater lochs", *The Scottish Naturalist*, 1984, 65–91.

Jones, D. H. (1989). "The ecology of some microcrustacea from standing waters in Tayside, Scotland", *Journal of Natural History*, **23**, 375–406.

Jones, R. I., Salonen, K. and De Haan, H. (1988). "Phosphorus transformations in the epilimnion of humic lakes: abiotic interactions between dissolved and humic materials", *Freshwater Biology*, **19**, 357–369.

Jupp, B. P., Spence, D. H. N. and Britton, R. H. (1974). "The distribution and the production of submerged macrophytes in Loch Leven, Kinross", *Proceedings of the Royal Society of Edinburgh*, **74B**, 195–208.

Kilham, P. (1982). "The effect of Hippopotamuses on potassium and phosphate ion concentrations in an African lake", *The American Midland Naturalist*, **108**, 202–205.

Kirchner, W. B. and Dillon, P. J. (1975). "An empirical method of estimating the retention of phosphorus in lakes", *Water Resources Research*, **11**, 182–183.

Le Cren, E. D. and Lowe-McConnell, R. H. (1980). *The Functioning of Freshwater Ecosystems*, Cambridge University Press, Cambridge.

Lewin, J. and Reimann, B. E. F. (1969). "Silicon and plant growth", *Annual Review of Plant Physiology*, **20**, 289–304.

Lobban, R. D. (1974). *Scotland*, Batsford, London.

Lund, J. W. G. (1949). "Studies on *Asterionella*. I. The origin and nature of the cells producing seasonal maxima", *Journal of Ecology*, **37**, 389–419.

Lund, J. W. G. (1965). "The ecology of freshwater phytoplankton", *Biological Reviews*, **40**, 231–295.

Lyle, A.A. (1981). "Ten years of ice records for Loch Leven, Kinross", *Weather*, **36**, 116–125.

Lyle, A.A. and Bailey-Watts, A.E. (1993). *I. Effects of light attenuation by humic colouring and turbidity on chlorophyll production. II. Factors controlling lake stratification* (Report to the Water Research Centre), Institute of Freshwater Ecology, Edinburgh.

McGrory, C.B. and Leadbeater, B.S.C. (1981). "Ultrastructure and deposition of silica in Chrysophyceae", in *Silicon and Siliceous Structures in Biological Systems* (Eds T.L. Simpson and B.E. Volcani), pp. 201–230, Springer, New York.

McQueen, D.J., Johannes, M.R.S., Post, J.R., Stewart, T.J. and Lean, D.R.S. (1989). "Bottom-up and top-down impacts on freshwater pelagic community structure", *Ecological Monographs*, **59**, 289–309.

Mahmud-ul-Ameen (1987). *Fisheries Resources and Opportunities in Freshwater Fish Culture in Bangladesh*, DANIDA, Noakhali, Bangladesh.

Maitland, P.S. and Hudspith, P.M.G. (1974). "The zoobenthos of Loch Leven, Kinross, and estimates of its production in the sandy littoral area during 1970 and 1971", *Proceedings of the Royal Society of Edinburgh*, **74B**, 219–239.

Maitland, P. S. and Lyle, A. A. (1991). "Conservation of freshwater fish in the British Isles: the current status and biology of threatened species", *Aquatic Conservation: Marine and Freshwater Ecosystems*, **1**, 25–54.

Maitland, P. S., Smith, B. D. and Dennis, G. M. (1981). "The crustacean zooplankton", in *The Ecology of Scotland's Largest Lochs: Lomond, Awe, Ness, Morar and Shiel* (Ed. P. S. Maitland), pp. 135–144, Junk, The Hague.

Marsden, M. W. (1989). "Lake restoration by reducing external phosphorus loading: the influence of sediment phosphorus release", *Freshwater Biology*, **21**, 139–162.

Maulood, B. K. and Boney, A. D. (1980). "A seasonal and ecological study of the phytoplankton of Loch Lomand", *Hydrobiologia*, **71**, 239–259.

May, L. (1980a). "On the ecology of *Notholca squamula* Müller in Loch Leven, Kinross, Scotland", *Hydrobiologia*, **73**, 177–180.

May, L. (1980b). "Studies on the grazing rate of *Notholca squamula* Müller on *Asterionella formosa* Hass. at different temperatures", *Hydrobiologia*, **73**, 79–81.

May, L. (1983). "Rotifer occurrence in relation to water temperature in Loch Leven, Scotland", *Hydrobiologia*, **104**, 311–315.

May, L. (1986). "Rotifer sampling–a complete species list from one visit?", *Hydrobiologia*, **134**, 117–120.

May, L. (1987). "Culturing freshwater planktonic rotifers on *Rhodomonas minuta var nannoplanktica* Skuja and *Stichococcus bacillaris* Naegeli", *Journal of Plankton Research*, **9**, 1217–1223.

May, L., Bailey-Watts, A. E. and Kirika, A. (1993a). The ecology of *Synchaeta kitina* Rousselet in Loch Leven, Scotland", *Hydrobiologia*, **255/256**, 305–315.

May, L., Gunn, I. D. M. and Bailey-Watts, A. E. (1993b). *Loch Leven Zooplankton* (Report to Scottish Natural Heritage), Institute of Freshwater Ecology, Edinburgh.

Millway, C. P. (1970). *Eutrophication in Large Lakes and Impoundments* (Report on Uppsala Symposium, May 1968), OECD, Paris.

Mitchell, J. F. B. and Qingcun, Z. (1992). "Climate change prediction", in *Climate Change: Science, Impacts and Policy: Proceedings of the Second World Climate Conference* (Eds J. Jager and H. L. Ferguson), Cambridge University Press, Cambridge.

Morgan, N. C. (1970). "Changes in the fauna and flora of a nutrient enriched lake", *Hydrobiologia*, **35**, 545–553.

Moss, B. (1983). "The Norfolk Broadland: experiments in the restoration of a complex wetland", *Biological Reviews*, **58**, 521–561.

Moss, B., Balls, H., Booker, I., Manson, K. and Timms, M. (1988). "Problems in the construction of a nutrient budget for the R. Bure and its broads (Norfolk) prior to its restoration from eutrophication", in *Algae and the Aquatic Environment* (Ed. F. E. Round), pp. 326–353, Biopress, Bristol.

Murphy, K. J. (1990). "Aquatic weeds in Scotland", in *Proceedings European Weed Research Society 8th International Symposium on Aquatic Weeds*, pp. 165–166, European Weed Research Society, Wageningen.

Murray, J. and Pullar, L. (1910). *Bathymetrical Survey of the Fresh Water Lochs of Scotland*, Challenger Office, Edinburgh.

Nygaard, G. (1949). "Hydrobiological studies of some Danish lakes and ponds", *Biologiske Skrifter*, **7**, 1–293.

OECD (1982). *Eutrophication of Waters, Monitoring Assessment and Control*, Organisation for Economic Co-operation and Development, Paris.

Payne, A. I. (1986). *The Ecology of Tropical Lakes and Rivers*, Chapman and Hall, London.

Pennington, W., Haworth, E. Y., Bonny, A. P. and Lishman, J. P. (1972). "Lake sediments in Northern Scotland", *Philosophical Transactions of the Royal Society of London*, **264B**, 191–294.

Phillips, G. and Jackson, R. (1990). "The control of eutrophication in very shallow lakes, the Norfolk Broads", *Verhandlungen der Internationalen Vereinigung für theoretische und angewandte Limnologie*, **24**, 573–575.

Phillips, M. J., Mowat, A. and Clarke, R. (1988). *Phosphorus wastage from a new low phosphorus and traditional freshwater salmon diet*, Unpublished report to Fulmar Feeds.

Porter, R. and Fitzsimmons, D. W. (1978). *Phosphorus in the Environment: Its Chemistry and Biochemistry. CIBA Foundation Symposium 57*, Elsevier, Amsterdam.

Raffaelli, D., Warbrick, S. and Young, M. (1990). *Long-term trends in land-use and wildfowl counts relevant to the nutrient status of the Loch of Strathbeg, Aberdeenshire, Scotland* (Report to the Royal Society for the Protection of Birds), Zoology Department, University of Aberdeen.

Rawson, D. S. (1955). "Morphometry as a dominant factor in the productivity of large lakes", *Verhandlungen der Internationalen Vereinung für theoretische und angewandte Limnologie*, **12**, 164–167.

Rawson, D. S. (1956). "Algal indicators of trophic lake types", *Limnology and Oceanography*, **1**, 18–25.

Reynolds, C. S. (1984). *The Ecology of Freshwater Phytoplankton*, Cambridge University Press, Cambridge.

Reynolds, C. S. (1986). "Diatoms and the geochemical cycling of silicon", in *Biomineralisation in Lower Plants and Animals* (Eds B. S. C. Leadbeater and R. Riding), pp. 269–289, Oxford University Press, Oxford.

Reynolds, C. S. (1987). "Cyanobacterial water-blooms", *Advances in Botanical Research*, **13**, 67–143.

Reynolds, C. S. (1988). "Potamoplankton: paradigms, paradoxes and prognoses", in *Algae and the Aquatic Environment* (Ed. F.E. Round), pp. 285–311, Biopress, Bristol.

Robson, T. O. (1986). "Aquatic plant management problems in Europe", in *Proceedings European Weed Research Society/AAB 7th International Symposium on Aquatic Weeds*, pp. 263–69, European Weed Research Society, Wageningen.

Rosenberg, M. (1938). "Algae and Trout. A biological aspect of the poor trout season in 1937", *Salmon and Trout Magazine*, **89**, 313–322.

Royal Society of Edinburgh (1974). "The Loch Leven IBP Project. A symposium sponsored by the Royal Society of Edinburgh at the University of Stirling on 11–13 June 1973", *Proceedings of the Royal Society of Edinburgh*, **74B**, 45–421.

Ruttner, F. (1963). *Fundamentals of Limnology*, University of Toronto Press, Toronto.

Sargent, R. J. and Ledger, D. C. (1992). "Derivation of a 130 year run-off record from sluice records for the Loch Leven catchment, south-east Scotland", *Proceedings of the Institution of Civil Engineers, Water, Maritime and Energy*, **96**, 71–80.

Sas, H. (1989). *Lake Restoration by Reduction of Nutrient Loading*: Expectations, Experiences, Extrapolations, Academia-Verlag Richarz, St Augustin.

Scottish Agricultural College (1980). *Handling and Utilisation of Animal Wastes*, Edinburgh.

Scottish Office Agriculture and Fisheries Department (1992). *Prevention of Environmental Pollution from Agricultural Activity Code of Good Practice*, Edinburgh.

Smith, B. D., Maitland, P. S., Young, M. R. and Carr, M. J. (1981a). "The littoral zoobenthos", in *The Ecology of Scotland's Largest Lochs: Lomond, Awe, Ness, Morar and Shiel* (Ed. P. S. Maitland), pp. 155–203, Junk, The Hague.

Smith, I. R. (1973). "The assessment of winds at Loch Leven, Kinross", *Weather*, **28**, 202–210.

Smith, I. R. (1974). "The structure and physical environment of Loch Leven, Scotland", *Proceedings of the Royal Society of Edinburgh*, **74B**, 81–100.

Smith, I. R., Lyle, A. A. and Rosie, A. J. (1981b). "Comparative physical limnology", in *The Ecology of Scotland's Largest Lochs: Lomond, Awe, Ness, Morar and Shiel* (Ed. P. S. Maitland), pp. 29–65, Junk, The Hague.

Spence, D. H. N. (1964). "The macrophytic vegetation of lochs, swamps and associated fens", in *Vegetation of Scotland* (Ed. J. H. Burnett), pp. 306–424, Oliver and Boyd, Edinburgh.

Spence, D. H. N. (1967). "Factors controlling the distribution of freshwater macrophytes with particular reference to the lochs of Scotland", *Journal of Ecology*, **55**, 147–170.

Spence, D. H. N. (1971). "Light and freshwater macrophytes", *Transactions of the Botanical Society of Edinburgh*, **41**, 491–505.

Spence, D. H. N. (1975). "Light and plant responses in freshwater" in *Light as an Ecological Factor* (Eds G. C. Evans, R. Bainbridge and O. Rackham), pp. 93–134, Blackwell, Oxford.

Stevens, R. J. and Smith, R. V. (1978). "A comparison of discrete and intensive sampling for measuring the loads of nitrogen and phosphorus in the River Main, County Antrim", *Water Research*, **12**, 823–830.

Stewart, W. D. P., Tuckwell, S. B. and May, E. (1975). "Eutrophication and algal growths in Scottish freshwater lochs", *Symposium of the British Ecological Society*, **15**, 57–80.

Stewart, W. D. P., May, E. and Tuckwell, S. B. (1976). "Nitrogen and phosphorus from agricultural land and urbanisation and their fate in shallow freshwater lochs", *Technical Bulletin of the Ministry of Agriculture, Fisheries and Food, London*, **32**, 276–305.

Stirling, H. P. and Dey, T. (1990). "Impact of intensive cage fish farming on the phytoplankton and periphyton of a Scottish freshwater loch", *Hydrobiologia*, **190**, 193–214.

Talling, J. F. (1971). "The underwater light climate as a controlling factor in the production ecology of freshwater phytoplankton", *Mitteilungen* der *Internationalen Vereinigung für theoretische und angewandte Limnologie*, **19**, 214–243.

Talling, J. F. (1992). "Environmental regulation in African shallow lakes and wetlands", *Revue hydrobiologique tropicale*, **25**, 87–144.

Thompson, F. (1976). *Victorian and Edwardian Highlands from Old Photographs*, Batsford, London.

Tweed River Purification Board (1987). *Annual Report for Year Ending 31 Dec. 1986*, Galashiels.

UKCCIRG (1991). *The Potential Effects of Climate Change in the United Kingdom* (Report for Department of the Environment), United Kingdom Climate Change Impacts Review Group, HMSO, London.

UKRGAR (1990). *Acid Deposition in the United Kingdom, 1986–1988* (Third report for the Department of the Environment), United Kingdom Review Group on Acid Rain, HMSO, London.

Vibert, R. and Lagler, K. F. (1961). *Pêches Continentales; Biologie et Aménagement*, Dunod, Paris.

Vollenweider, R. A. (1968). *Water management research; scientific fundamentals of the eutrophication of lakes and flowing waters, with particular reference to nitrogen and phosphorus as factors in eutrophication* (Technical report DAS/CSI/68.27), OECD, Paris.

Vollenweider, R.A. (1975). "Input – output models with special reference to the phosphorus loading concept in limnology", *Schweizerische Zeitschrift für Hydrobiologie*, **37**, 53–84.

Vollenweider, R. A. (1976). "Advances in defining critical loading levels for phosphorus in lake eutrophication", *Memorie dell' Istituto Italiano di Idrobiologia*, **33**, 53–83.

Wathne, B. M. (1992). "Acidification of mountain lakes: palaeolimnology and ecology. The AL:PE Project", *Documenta dell' Istituto Italiano di Idrobiologia*, **32**, 7–22.

Watson, J. (1991). "Ecological studies on Speyside", MSc thesis, University of Lancaster.

Wesenberg-Lund, C. (1905). "A comparative study of the lakes of Scotland and Denmark", *Proceedings of the Royal Society of Edinburgh*, **25**, 401–448.

West, W. and West, G. S. (1912). "On the periodicity of the phytoplankton of some British lakes", *Journal of the Linnean Society*, **40**, 395–432.

Wright, G. G., Edwards, A. C., Morrice, J. G. and Pugh, K. (1991). "North east Scotland river catchment nitrate loading in relation to agricultural intensity", *Chemistry and Ecology*, **5**, 263–281.

23

Afforestation and Forestry Practice

G. A. BEST

Clyde River Purification Board, Murray Road, East Kilbride, G75 0LA, UK

INTRODUCTION

The landscape of Scotland is currently undergoing a marked change in its appearance. Large areas of moorland are being converted to productive woodland because of the Government's policy to increase substantially the amount of timber that should be home-grown. The UK is the second largest importer of timber products in the world.

In Britain, there are now over 2×10^6 ha of productive woodland. In the 1990s, planted forests account for 10% of the total land area compared with 5.3% in the 1920s. New planting is taking place at a rate of 33 000 ha yr^{-1} and the current target is that the area of afforestation in Britain should increase to 16% by 2025 (Forestry Commission, 1991a). The great majority of new planting is taking place in Scotland where 13.5% of the land area is already occupied by commercial woodland (Figure 23.1). Some regions of Scotland are particularly favoured, such as Galloway where over a quarter of the land area is coniferous forest. In 1990, of the 3314 ha of coniferous forest that were planted, 3275 were in Scotland (Forestry Commission, 1991b). Although it may seem that Scotland has a disproportionate amount of commercial forestry in its area, compared with other European countries the land is under-used. For example, forestry in Italy accounts for 25% of the land area, 28% in France and 30% in Germany (Forestry Commission, 1992).

In 1980, an assessment was made by the Centre for Agricultural Strategy of the area of rough grazing that was available in the UK for planting commercial forests. Of the 6.145×10^6 ha that were considered, only 2.98×10^6 ha were technically suitable. This figure reduced to 1.1×10^6 ha if restriction to planting on water supply catchments and areas of scenic value were taken into account. The Nature Conservancy Council (1986) revised the data for Scotland and Table 23.1 shows their assessment.

The variety of trees that are suitable for planting in upland areas is limited because of high rainfall and wind speeds, and lower temperatures. One tree, imported from North America in 1831, thrives in these conditions – the Sitka Spruce (*Picea sitchensis*). It now dominates the commercial forests; in the period 1951–1960, 29% of the areas planted by the Forestry Commission were with Sitka Spruce but by 1981–90 this

The Fresh Waters of Scotland: A National Resource of International Significance
Edited by P. S. Maitland, P. J. Boon and D. S. McLusky. © 1994 John Wiley & Sons Ltd

FIGURE 23.1. Young Spruce in the foreground with a mature plantation behind. Photograph:
J. Frame

had increased to 68%. The remainder is made up of Lodgepole Pine (10%), Japanese
or hybrid Larch (5%), Scots Pine (3%) other conifers (10.7%) and broad-leaved trees
(5.3%) (Malcolm, 1991).

The usual altitude limit for planting is reckoned to be between 300 m in the north
of Scotland and 450 m in the southern uplands of Scotland. However, in recent years,
planting has been taking place on higher ground (up to 720 m in Galloway) (Nature
Conservancy Council, 1986). There are a number of problems associated with this
activity including increased wind speed at this altitude which can blow trees down
before the usual harvesting size. This problem is countered by felling trees at an
earlier age, 30–35 years after planting, instead of 55–60 years.

The current UK production of wood is 5.6×10^6 m^3 and the aim is to increase this
to 8×10^6 m^3 by 2000 and to 10×10^6 m^3 by 2015. These plans, however, may have

TABLE 23.1. Areas of new and afforested
land in Scotland (ha $\times 10^3$)

Total area of upland	4400
Already afforested	811
Area too high	950
Area unsuitable for other reasons	1050
Plantable area remaining	1589

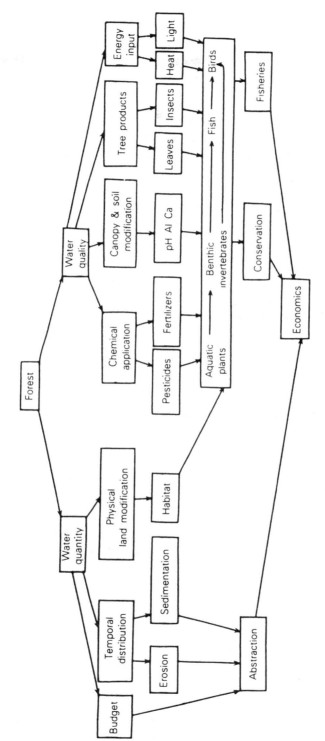

FIGURE 23.2. Selected pathways of forest influence on water utilization and aquatic biota. (Source: Ormerod *et al.*, 1987; copyright: Institute of Terrestrial Ecology)

to be revised because of changes to the grants system for forestry carried out by the private sector. At the moment 38% of forests are in the ownership of the Forestry Commission and 62% are privately owned. Before the 1988 Budget, private individuals were encouraged to invest in afforestation and avoid paying income tax. However this became non-tax deductible by the Finance Act of 1988 and instead the Woodland Grant Scheme came into operation. As a result of this, there has been a marked reduction in new planting by private companies since 1988. For example, in Scotland the planting of new forest by private companies in 1988 amounted to 21.2 $\times$ 10^3 ha but by 1991 this had been halved to 10.6 $\times$ 10^3 ha.

The transformation of open heathland to coniferous forests has a marked impact on freshwater systems in the area. This impact takes place in three stages:

(1) Ploughing/planting phase
(2) When the trees reach canopy closure
(3) Harvesting phase

The main effects are an alteration to the hydrology of the catchment, an increase in the suspended solids of drainage water and a modification to the chemistry of the waters in the afforested catchment. These in turn have a knock-on effect on the aquatic organisms in the receiving waters.

There are also major changes to the habitats of terrestrial species with the change of land use from moorland to forest. However, these are outside the scope of this chapter and have been well described elsewhere by the Nature Conservancy Council (1986).

The overall interactions between the developing forest and aquatic organisms have been described by Ormerod *et al.* (1987) and are summarized in Figure 23.2. There have been a number of useful reviews of the effects of afforestation on aquatic systems including Overrein *et al.* (1980), Stoner and Gee (1985), Horning and Newson (1986), Good (1987), Solbé (1987) and Maitland *et al.* (1990). In this chapter, the topic will be dealt with under three headings – hydrology, water chemistry and biota – followed by the ameliorative measures that can be taken to minimize the effects.

HYDROLOGY

Ground preparation

Before the trees are planted, the ground usually has to be drained and ploughed to provide suitable rooting conditions for the tree crop. The ridges are generally between 2 and 4 m apart and the furrows up to 0.5 m deep. The visual impact of freshly prepared ground can be quite marked (Figure 23.3). Ideally, the drainage ditches should be aligned in a gentle gradient along the contours but in practice this usually cannot easily be done as it is too dangerous a procedure. Ploughing is thus done down the slopes and intercepting ditches need to be created so as to reduce the energy of drainage water as it flows down the slopes.

With the creation of a network of interconnecting ditches and drainage channels, rainfall is transferred relatively rapidly to the nearest stream compared with run-off from an undisturbed slope. This results in a sharpening of the hydrograph of the

FIGURE 23.3. A Scottish hillside which has recently been ploughed and planted with young Spruce. Photograph: J. Frame

catchment and a greater incidence of flooding. There have been a number of studies of the effect of ploughing on hydrology.

Robinson (1980), for example, investigated the response of stream flow to ground preparation in Northumberland and showed that the time to peak flow was reduced from 2.1 hours to 1.6 hours and that peak flow was 40% greater after the creation of drainage ditches (Figure 23.4). Leeks and Roberts (1987) found similar but less marked changes in the flood hydrology in prepared ground in Wales.

There have been unsubstantiated reports of alterations to the low flow regimes after ground preparation. In undisturbed ground, the low flow (base flow) level in streams is prolonged in dry spells by the slow release of water retained in peat and soils. In ploughed land this water drains rapidly resulting in a flow reduction in the drainage streams, which in turn reduces the low flow levels in the larger streams in the catchment.

The network of channels and drains (typically from <10 to >200 km km^{-2} according to Francis (1987)) results in the exposure of large areas of bare earth to the elements. This exposure is usually in upland areas where weather is more extreme (higher rainfall and more frequent frosts) and gives rise to erosion and wash-off at times of heavy rain, a process exacerbated by the increased discharge rates at peak flows.

Erosion is greatest immediately after ground preparation and there have been a number of reported pollution incidents caused by mineral solids as a result of

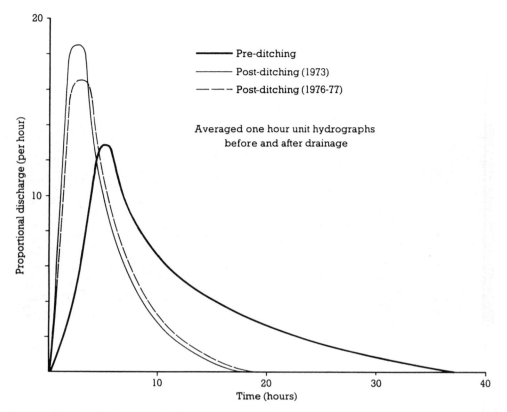

FIGURE 23.4. Unit hydrograph before and after forest ground preparation in the Coalburn catchment, England. (Source: Robinson, 1980; reproduced by permission of the Institute of Hydrology)

ploughing land for tree planting (Austin and Brown, 1982; Stretton, 1984; Clyde River Purification Board, 1985). A study at a forestry development scheme in Coalburn, Northumberland, in 1980 showed that fine sediment was released from ploughed land for five years after the initial work with concentration typically >200 mg L^{-1} compared with pre-ploughing values of about 10 mg L^{-1}. In the example cited by the Clyde River Purification Board, the peak concentration of suspended solids in the drainage water entering a feeder river of Loch Lomond was 1200 mg L^{-1}.

Harvesting

Once the ground has been prepared and the small growing trees become established, the problems of excessive run-off and erosion slowly diminish. The next major hydrological impact occurs some 30 years later when the crop begins to be harvested by thinning and again when the area is clear felled.

Large areas of forest are cleared of trees and fresh surfaces of earth are once again exposed to the weather (Figure 23.5). Leeks and Roberts (1987) calculated that the sediment yield for the Hore catchment in Wales during felling operations increased

FIGURE 23.5. Midway through clear felling a mature plantation. Photograph: J. Frame

from 24.4 t km^{-2} yr^{-1} to 57.1 t km^2 yr^{-1}. Some of this erosion material originates from the roads that are constructed and then used by forestry vehicles. Ferguson *et al.* (1987) monitored the effect of timber harvesting in the Balquhidder experimental forest in Central Scotland and found that 20% of the increased suspended solids could be attributed to the construction of a loading bay.

Interception of water

In between the period of planting and harvesting, the growing trees gradually increase their requirement for water. Some is taken up by the roots and through the needles and used in the growing process (transpiration) whilst some is collected on the needles' surface which then evaporates back into the atmosphere (interception). There is a marked regional variation between the relative amounts of this interception water. In mid Wales interception/evaporation exceeds transpiration by a factor of 2:1 whilst in East Anglia this ratio is reversed. Work carried out by Newson (1985) in Plynlimon in Wales where the annual rainfall is 2350 mm, indicated that 85% of the rainfall falling on grassland reached the streams compared with 65% in an afforested area in the River Severn catchment. In Scotland the interception/evaporation process is most important in the west of the country with transpiration becoming a more important factor in the east. Calder and Newson (1980) predicted a decrease in run-off of 20% for Scottish rivers as a result of afforestation.

This reduction in run-off can have a marked impact in those catchments where the water is used as a resource such as for potable supply or power generation. Pyatt (1984) showed how the amount of run-off can be reduced by varying degrees of afforestation according to the annual rainfall on the catchment (Figure 23.6). This loss can have a direct effect on the exploitation of water resources. For example, calculations by the North of Scotland Hydro-Electric Board have shown that, over a 15-year period, there was a 13% reduction in generating output in the Loch Tarsan scheme as a result of the development of a coniferous forest in the catchment (see Chapter 17).

By synthesizing these data, hydrologists can now predict the extent of water loss from coniferous plantations. In general, it has been estimated that, for each 10% of the catchment that is planted, there will be a 2% reduction in annual run-off (Department of the Environment and Forestry Commission, 1990).

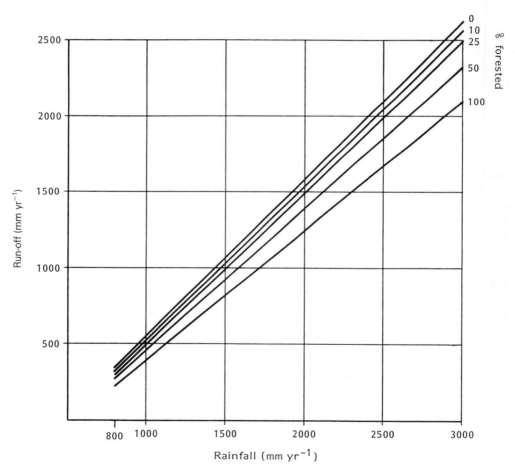

FIGURE 23.6. Annual run-off according to the Calder-Newson formula for a range of annual rainfalls and forest covers. (Source: Pyatt, 1984; copyright: Forestry Commission)

WATER CHEMISTRY

The planting, growth and harvesting of trees can have a marked effect on the chemistry of streams in the planted area, particularly where the soils are deficient in nutrients and base cations. Of particular concern is the effect that the mature forest can have in certain sensitive areas, by increasing the acidity of the soil and water and releasing potentially harmful levels of aluminium into drainage streams.

Nutrient loss

Afforestation to date has usually taken place on marginal upland areas which have little agricultural value. These areas are often lacking in the essential nutrients for tree growth – namely potassium, nitrogen and phosphorus. Furthermore, many forests that were planted at the peak planting period in the 1960s are now growing to maturity and are being harvested. The removal of the trees represents a net loss from the nutrient store because they are not being allowed to fall and release their nutrients during the natural process of decay.

In order to promote the growth of trees in nutrient-poor areas, fertilizer is applied at the time of planting and also when the trees are between six and eight years old if nutrient deficiencies are observed. Usually the ground is most deficient in phosphorus, and rock phosphate is applied at a rate of up to 450 kg ha^{-1} (equivalent to 60 kg P ha^{-1}). Nitrogen and potassium may also be added depending on the nutrient status of the soil. According to Taylor (1986), 56 000 ha yr^{-1} of afforested land in Britain was treated with fertilizer. 25 000 ha were given phosphorus alone, 29 000 ha were treated with both phosphorus and potassium, while 2000 ha were treated solely with nitrogen.

Each of these nutrients is retained by the soils to varying extents in the order P>N>K. Harriman (1978) showed that 73% of applied potassium, the least retained nutrient, was leached from fertilized catchment on the first year after application. For nitrogen, present as nitrate, peak concentrations in drainage water were found two weeks after being applied, with elevated levels existing over the subsequent three years. Phosphorus losses are restricted to between 10% and 16% over a three-year period according to various investigations (Harriman, 1978; Malcolm and Cuttle, 1983; Swift, 1986). Despite these small losses of phosphorus, concentrations in receiving streams reach up to 100 μg P L^{-1} soon after application with values of 15 μg P L^{-1} three years later. Many afforested catchments drain into upland lochs and reservoirs which are usually oligotrophic (phosphate-phosphorus concentrations in the range 5–10 μg L^{-1}). It is estimated that the critical concentration for phosphate-phosphorus in standing waters is 10 μg L^{-1} (see Chapter 22), above which excessive algal growths can arise (Organisation for Economic Cooperation and Development, 1970).

There have been a number of well-documented studies of excessive algal growths occurring in standing water after forest fertilization (Parr, 1984; Richards, 1984).

A further increase in nutrient loading to streams occurs at the time of clear felling; the released nutrients appear to be confined to nitrate and potassium. Studies in Wales have shown that with harvesting there is an increase in the nitrate concentration in the soil which is then leached into streams. The nitrate originates from the bacterial breakdown of felling debris (brash) and, because the forest floor is bare of any other vegetation, atmospheric inputs of nitrate are not taken up by other plants. The increase in light intensity eventually encourages other plants which, along with the newly planted trees, utilize the nitrate (Stevens and Hornung, 1989; Neal et al., 1992). The concentration of nutrients in receiving streams was found to decline about two years after felling. Typical results from these investigations have shown that there is an initial peak of nitrate of up to 14 mg NO_3-N L^{-1} which gradually reduces to 2 mg L^{-1}. The released nitrate anion is accompanied by a cation and, depending on the base cation status of the soil, this is usually calcium, potassium, hydrogen or aluminium.

Acidification of drainage water

From the considerable literature on the role of forests in surface water acidification (see also Chapter 24), five distinct mechanisms have been identified:

(1) Interception of airborne pollutants by the forest foliage.
(2) Ion exchange process on the surface of needles.
(3) Wash-off of components of the reaction in (2).
(4) Chemical reactions in the soil and subsoil.
(5) Wash out of chemicals into drainage streams.

The chemistry of these will be described in turn; the major biological changes are discussed in Chapter 24.

Interception of airborne pollutants

The main acidifying components in the atmosphere are sulphur dioxide (SO_2) and oxides of nitrogen (NOx). SO_2 originates principally from fossil fuel combustion whilst NOx comes mainly from vehicle exhausts. Barrett et al. (1983) showed that in areas remote from sources of pollution, such as the north and west of Scotland, SO_2 constitutes 60–70% of the acidifying gases and NOx from 30–40%. This ratio is changing as reductions in SO_2 emissions are achieved through abatement measures and NOx levels increase because of increased traffic (Agren and Elvingson, 1992). A recent European Community Directive requires that the UK, along with other countries, reduces the emissions from large combustion plants by 20%, 40% and 60% by the years 1993, 1996 and 2003 respectively. For NOx, the agreed reductions are 15% and 30% by 1993 and 1998, all from a 1980 baseline.

Once into the atmosphere, these gases undergo a number of chemical reactions that have been described by Fowler et al. (1991) and ultimately yield SO_4^{2-} and NO_3^-. The sulphate ion is usually present as an aerosol or is in solution in cloud droplets, whilst the nitrate can be in the gas phase as HNO_3 or in particles or droplets.

The pollutants are transported from their point of origin by the wind. For Scotland the prevailing wind is from the south to west quadrant but for about 10% of the time it comes from the south to east quadrant and polluted air is brought in from industrialized areas in England and the near continent. A detailed analysis of acidity in rainfall and weather patterns was carried out by Fowler and Cape (1984) and they

TABLE 23.2. Typical concentration (μeq L^{-1}) (Reproduced by permission from Fowler and Irwin, 1988)

	Cloud droplets	Rain	
		(at 200 m)	(at 800 m)
SO_4^{2-}	100–2000	42	60
NO_3^-	30–2000	45	65
H^+	10–1000	25	40

showed that in Central Scotland 30% of the annual deposition of acidity in rainfall occurred on just five days of rainfall each year.

The variation of rainfall acidity with wind direction and distance from source results in an overall gradient of acidity with the highest values being found in the south-east (pH 4.0–4.3) and lowest values in the north-west (pH 5.0). However, once rainfall amount is taken into account, the areas of Scotland receiving the greatest loading of acidity are in Argyll and the south uplands in Galloway (Fowler and Irwin, 1988). These data were obtained from measurements made on bulk precipitation collected at rainfall measuring stations distributed throughout the country and they give only a broad indication of the acidity arriving in precipitation in a particular area. More detailed work has shown that cloud droplets contain far greater concentrations of major ions, including acidifying anions and cations, than wet deposition at low elevations (Table 23.2). At high altitudes rain is also more acidic than that collected at low altitudes. Similar data have been reported by Crossley and Wilson (1990).

As the cloud water is lifted up hillsides by wind, the size of droplets increases, and these subsequently collect on the leaf surfaces. The efficiency of capture of the droplets is greater on cylindrical shapes such as pine needles than on the flat surfaces that are found on broad-leaved trees (Fowler *et al.*, 1989).

So, taking into account the higher amounts of acidity in clouds and that their impact is on coniferous forests that are usually planted at the high altitudes of the cloud level, the acid loading on forests is considerably greater than that suggested by bulk precipitation measurements taken at low-level rainfall stations.

Chemical exchange on pine needle surfaces and wash-off to the soil

One of the reasons why Sitka Spruce is the favoured species for commercial forestry is because it has adapted to survive in nutrient-poor soils by obtaining nutrients from rainfall by ion exchange on the needle surface. The nitrogen, present in rainfall as nitrate anion and ammonium cation, is exchanged with ions in the needles, such as K^+, H^+, Ca^{2+}, HCO_3^-, Cl^- and organic acid anions. This process is called crown leaching. Smith (1987) found that K^+ plays a major role but that H^+ is also involved. This can result in increased acidity in the water adhering to the pine needles. The exchange of nitrogen is the most important of the ion exchange processes according to Abrahamson (1980) because, relative to calcium, the trees need 35–240 times more nitrogen, 4–15 times more potassium and 1–8 times more sulphur and phosphorus.

The sulphate ion in precipitation thus plays a minor role in the ion exchange processes and, after capture by the trees' needles, is transferred to the soil in wash-off rainfall.

This wash-off water is known as throughfall and, depending on the extent of ion exchange that has taken place on the needle surface, can be more or less acidic than the original rainfall. The factors that determine the acidity of throughfall include the nutrient status of the soil, the age and species of the tree, and the season of the year (Miller *et al.*, 1987).

Once the throughfall water reaches the soil, a further series of chemical reactions take place.

Throughfall effects on soil water chemistry

The planting of coniferous forests on moorland changes the chemical properties of the soil. The initial ground preparation exposes new surfaces of earth to oxidation and erosion whilst the growth of the tree roots results in the deeper earth being penetrated, allowing air and water to enter previously undisturbed layers. The surface of the forest floor develops an acidic mor humus as a result of needle drop and decay. This humus is characterized by having a low nitrogen content and a higher carbon: nitrogen ratio than was in the soil before tree planting. In the soil itself, ion exchange takes place between the throughfall water and the soil particles. The H^+ ions play a major part and it has been estimated that the internal transfer of H^+ ions in soil is at least 10 times greater than that which arrives in the soil from throughfall and rain water. The root uptake of nutrient cations such as Ca^{2+} and NH_4^+ is balanced by a reverse flux of H^+ from the trees, so the H^+ acidity in rain water is relatively unimportant as far as soil acidity is concerned. The NO_3^- uptake is balanced by OH^- which combines with CO_2 from carbonaceous breakdown to form HCO_3^-.

In a natural mixed forest, the uptake of NH_4^+ by the trees is balanced by a release of ammonia from the decay of leaf litter and dead trees. In a commercial coniferous forest, however, the trees are removed before decay and there is a net loss of base cations from the soil and an overall increase in the soil acidity. Ammonia, released into the soil from the decay of tree debris, is oxidized to nitrate which is then leached into streams.

This increased acidity, however, is not necessarily washed out of the soil in drainage water. A number of studies have shown that during dry spells the drainage water originates from deeper layers of the soil and that the naturally generated acidity in the soil is neutralized by base cations in the mineral layers (Bache, 1984; Neal *et al.*, 1992). In wet weather the deeper soils are saturated and stream water originates largely from the shallow organic horizons which contain the acidic cations H^+ and Al^{3+} and the anions NO_3^- and SO_4^{2-}, the amount of the anions being, to a certain extent, dependent upon the extent of pollution in the precipitation.

Much of the afforestation has taken place in upland areas where rainfall is highest and the flow regime of the drainage streams tends to be dominated by surface run-off. For example, Nisbet (1986) found that in an experimental site in Loch Fleet, 90% of the total flow in drainage water came from the surface layers. Similar results were found by Hornung *et al.* (1986) at three different study sites in Wales and northern England. The contribution of groundwater to stream flow varied between 5% and 20%.

Transfer of acidity from soils to streams

Research carried out by Harriman and Morrison (1982) in Scotland, and Stoner and Gee (1985), Reynolds *et al.* (1986) and Hornung *et al.* (1987) in Wales, have all shown that streams draining afforested catchments at times of high flow contain greater concentrations of SO_4^{2-}, H^+ and Al^{3+} than equivalent streams in moorland catchments. Recently, Harriman *et al.* (1987) and Waters *et al.* (1990) have shown that, with increasing maturity of coniferous trees, there is an increase in the acidity of drainage water. The greatest period of change occurs when the trees are approximately 15–20 years old when the canopy closes. The sulphate ion is one of the major pollutants in the atmosphere and has been found to take little part in the ion exchange processes on the tree surface nor is it regarded as an important nutrient. Its capture by the canopy and subsequent transfer to the streams via the surface layers of the soil is regarded as the main factor in causing drainage water acidity. The effect on the stream biota depends upon the accompanying cation that is washed in with the sulphate anion. In those areas where base cations are scarce or depleted and the geology is dominated by resistant rocks such as schists and granite, the accompanying cations are H^+ and Al^{3+}. These effects are also found in moorland areas but the coniferous forests exacerbate the problem because of their interception of cloud droplets and solid particles. Thus the trees do not create the acidity in the streams (though they can increase the acidity in the soil) but they facilitate the passage of greater amounts of sulphate ion from the atmosphere to the streams than the equivalent area of moorland.

As an example of the various studies carried out on this aspect, Harriman and Wells (1985) compared the water chemistry of four streams in an afforested area in Scotland with varying amounts of trees in the catchments. Table 23.3 shows how the acidifying ions increase with increased forest cover.

Reynolds *et al.* (1986) confirmed the effect that high flows have on water chemistry. In their study of two afforested catchments and three moorland streams in mid Wales, there was little difference in water chemistry at times of low flow, but with high

TABLE 23.3. Effects of increasing afforestation on the water chemistry of four drainage streams (Reproduced by permission from Harriman and Wells, 1985)

Stream	% Forest Cover	H^+ (μeq L^{-1})	SO_4^{2-} (μeq L^{-1})	Al^{3+} (total monomeric) (μgL^{-1})
1	0	6 (1–19)	120 (87–156)	42 (7–81)
2	30	35 (16–56)	163 (115–210)	154 (77–219)
3	60	48 (18–79)	166 (119–243)	139 (60–219)
4	90	45 (17–76)	198 (153–311)	171 (86–263)

rainfall the concentrations of aluminium and sulphate were significantly greater on the forest streams compared with the moorland ones. The aluminum can have adverse effects on the stream biota.

EFFECTS ON STREAM BIOTA

During the forest cycle, the effects of sediment release, nutrients and acidification on aquatic biota are many and varied.

Siltation

The increased turbidity in drainage water that results from ground preparation, road construction and clear felling, affects the flora and fauna of the streams. Light penetration is reduced to the detriment of rooted plants whilst the accumulated silt can alter the nature of the stream bed changing it from a stony substrate to one dominated by fine solids. With such a change the burrowing invertebrates, such as midge larvae and worms, replace the mayfly and stonefly nymphs which prefer more varied substrates.

Suspended solids can have a direct effect on the resident fish population. According to Alabaster and Lloyd (1982), concentrations of suspended matter in the range of $100-1000$ mg L^{-1} are harmful to the gills of fish and, for the long-term health of fish, it is suggested that the average concentration should not exceed 80 mg L^{-1}. An indirect effect of increased suspended solids is the clogging of gravel beds used by Salmon for spawning. If eggs have already been laid in the stream bed, the silt can smother them and prevent oxygenated water from reaching them. Maitland *et al.* (1990) have reviewed the effects of turbidity and siltation arising from ground preparation for afforestation.

Nutrients

As described earlier, the essential nutrients – nitrogen, phosphorus and potassium – are retained to varying extents in the soil. The most commonly applied fertilizer to coniferous forests is rock phosphate and this has been shown to leach into drainage water to the extent of about 7–10% of the applied amount in the first year after application (Swift, 1986). Streams in upland areas are usually deficient in nutrients, particularly phosphorus, so the fertilization of commercial forests can have a marked effect on primary productivity in streams and standing waters.

There are many examples in the literature of excessive algae developing in standing water adjacent to afforested areas. However, it has not been possible to attribute the problem unambiguously to forest fertilization (Gibson, 1976; Harriman, 1978; Parr, 1984; Richards, 1984).

An increase in primary productivity after fertilizer addition has a knock-on effect on the secondary production. Higher densities of filter-feeding invertebrates such as blackfly larvae are likely to result.

Of particular concern over forest fertilization is the effect on water supply reservoirs. Much of Scotland's drinking water is taken from upland lochs and reservoirs and, if excessive algae result from phosphorus run-off, there may be financial and technical problems at the treatment works because of clogging of filters. More serious would be the development of certain species of blue-green algae which are known to give rise to toxic by-products.

Acidification

Many studies have been carried out into the effects of acidification on aquatic biota (see Chapter 24). Harriman and Morrison (1982) were the first in Scotland to show that invertebrate diversity was reduced in afforested catchments compared with moorland ones. This was confirmed in Wales by Ormerod *et al.* (1987) with additional evidence from Gee and Smith (1987). Figure 23.7 shows the reduction in the variety of invertebrates found in afforested streams compared with moorland ones. Doughty (1990), after an extensive study of acidic waters in Scotland, summarized the relationship between mean pH values and invertebrate species survival (Table 23.4), though only four of the 145 streams sampled had extensive afforestation (>60%). Adverse effects on fisheries by afforestation have been reported by Egglishaw *et al.* (1986). They assessed the fish catch statistics received from 54 Scottish fisheries districts. Nineteen of the districts reported a decline in catches over the period 1952–81 and

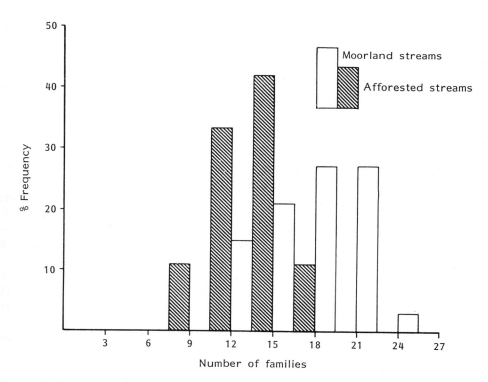

FIGURE 23.7. The percentage frequency distributions of kick-samples with given taxon richness from moorland and afforested streams in Wales. (Source: Ormerod *et al.*, 1987; copyright Institute of Terrestrial Ecology)

TABLE 23.4. Potential acid indicator species and their distributions in relation to mean pH

Mean pH	Group	Species absent
<7.0	Crustacea	_Gammarus pulex_
<6.0	Snails	_Lymnaea peregra_ _Ancylus fluviatilis_
	Mayflies	_Baetis muticus_ _Caenis rivulorum_
	Stoneflies	_Perla bipunctata_ _Dinocras cephalotes_
	Beetles	_Esolus parallelepipedus_
	Caddis flies	_Glossosoma_ spp. _Philopotamus montanus_ _Hydropsyche instabilis_ _Sericostoma personatum_
<5.5	Mayflies	_Baetis rhodani_ _Rhithrogena_ sp. _Ecdyonurus_ spp. _Heptagenia lateralis_
	Stoneflies	_Perlodes microcephala_ _Chloroperla tripunctata_
	Caddis flies	_Hydropsyche pellucidula_

all 11 of the districts where the catchments were over 20% afforested were in this category. The loss of fish was not entirely attributed to acidity as there are other factors that can reduce fish populations in forested catchments, such as altered flow regimes, forest debris in streams and loss of light.

Investigations into the causes of decline of fish numbers in acid waters have shown that there is a strong correlation between fish mortality and mean dissolved aluminium concentrations. Typical concentrations of aluminium in acid waters are 100–800 μg L^{-1}, compared with 20 μg L^{-1} in unacidified streams. Work on Welsh streams by Edwards _et al._ (1990) has shown that trout populations are poor or absent when mean dissolved aluminium concentrations exceed 100 μg L^{-1} and when pH <5.4. Studies on streams in England and Wales have shown that the growth of Brown Trout (_Salmo trutta_) can be adversely affected by 20 μg L^{-1} of labile aluminium (Sadler and Lynam, 1987).

Earlier, Howells _et al._ (1983) concluded that the factors that affect fish survival are low pH (<4.5), low calcium (<1 mg L^{-1}) and aluminium concentrations in excess of 250 μg L^{-1}. It appears that the most sensitive stage in the fish's life cycle to the acidity and aluminium is the transition from egg to fry (Haya and Waiwood, 1981; Peterson _et al._, 1982). This leads to a lack of recruitment, and acid waters are typified by a reduced number of larger, older fish which eventually disappear.

In addition to changes in the invertebrate and fish populations, evidence is accumulating that there has been a decline in the Dipper (*Cinclus cinclus*) in acid waters (Ormerod and Tyler, 1991).

AMELIORATIVE MEASURES

It has now been generally accepted that coniferous plantations can have a marked effect on stream water quality and aquatic biota. The most serious problem is that of enhanced acidification, particularly in those areas which receive high atmospheric deposition of SO_4^{2-} and NO_3^-, high rainfall, and where there is low acid-neutralizing capacity in the soil (Department of the Environment and Forestry Commission, 1990). The acidifying effect is most pronounced after canopy closure when the coniferous forest is most efficient at scavenging airborne pollutants.

The Forestry Commission is now well aware of the potential problems associated with coniferous plantations and has produced guidelines for foresters to reduce the impact of their activities on stream water quality. The *Forests and Water Guidelines* (Forestry Commission, 1991c) tackle each of the issues raised in this chapter and suggest ameliorative measures that can be taken. Advice is given about reducing erosion and collecting silt before it enters the main watercourses at both the ground preparation and harvesting stages.

Fertilizer application should take place only after a soil nutrient assessment has been made and should be spread by hand in sensitive areas. The importance of buffer strips along watercourses is emphasized. These riparian areas are valuable for a number of reasons. They can absorb sediment and excess fertilizer from drainage channels and may reduce some of the acidity in areas of high acid deposition. Research on the design and effectiveness of buffer strips is currently being carried out by the Water Research Centre. Buffer strips also act as a corridor for bird life and the dappled shading of the natural vegetation and the litter from it encourages fish and invertebrates. Buffer strips should be at least 5 m wide but up to 10 times the stream width for larger rivers.

There has been considerable discussion on how best to reduce the impact of coniferous plantations on the acidity of receiving streams in sensitive areas. The most obvious remedy is to reduce the pollution in the atmosphere and progress on this has already been made. The annual emissions of SO_2 have been fairly constant since 1984 at a level of 1.8×10^6 t (as S) after a peak value of about 3×10^6 t in the late 1960s. Emissions of NO_x have remained constant at about 0.75×10^6 t (as N) (Department of the Environment and Forestry Commission, 1990), though there is evidence of a slight increase up to 0.82×10^6 t for 1991. As mentioned earlier, the UK is obliged under a EC Directive to reduce SO_2 emissions by up to 60% over the next 10 years.

However, these reductions may take a long time to work through to increases in pH values in surface waters. Work done recently by Jenkins *et al.* (1990) using mathematical modelling has shown that, even with the proposed reductions in pollutant loadings, some streams will continue to be affected by acidity arising from forest drainage because the soil/water system is very sensitive to the inputs. They conclude that, in certain areas, replanting of a felled forest without the addition of lime should not be undertaken even if significant reductions in acid deposition are realized.

The Forestry Commission, with the cooperation of other concerned organizations, has examined the problem of how to allow forestry to develop without adverse effects on stream water quality. The favoured approach has been to examine those areas in the UK where the critical load of pollutants into soils and waters is exceeded. The critical load is defined as the maximum load of a pollutant above which level the ecosystem will be adversely affected. The critical load can be assessed by examining either the acidity in the soil or in the water. In Scotland, the favoured approach is to define the critical load for standing waters so as to ensure the survival of fish and other aquatic biota. In England and Wales, the critical loads were initially evaluated in terms of the sensitivity of the soils but sensitivity maps for fresh water have now been produced.

Freshwater maps have been prepared from chemical data that have been obtained from one standing water in each 10 × 10 km square. If any planned forestry activities are within those squares shown as sensitive, an assessment of the risk to the aquatic environment will have to be carried out before any Woodland Grant Scheme application is approved. A mathematical model has been developed which takes into account likely future reductions in pollutant loads, the scavenging of the trees with increasing maturity and the water chemistry of streams at low and high flows. Figure 23.8 shows the most sensitive 10 × 10 km squares that were identified in the most recent *Forests and Water Guidelines* (Forestry Commission, 1993).

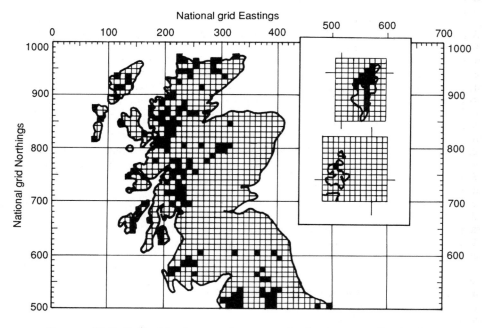

FIGURE 23.8. Critical loads exceedance map for fresh waters, Scotland

REFERENCES

Abrahamson, G. (1980). "Acid precipitation, plant nutrients and forest growth", in *Ecological Impact of Acid Precipitation* (Eds D. Drablos and A. Tollan), pp. 58–63, Oslo (SNSF) Project.

Agren, C. and Elvingson, P. (1992). "EMEP Report 1992", *Acid News*, **5**, 10–12.

Alabaster, J. S. and Lloyd, R. (Eds) (1982). *Water Quality Criteria for Freshwater Fish*, 2nd edition, Butterworths, London.

Austin, R. and Brown, D. (1982). "Solids contamination resulting from drainage works in an upland catchment and its removal by floatation", *Journal of the Institution of Water Engineers and Scientists*, **36**, 281–288.

Bache, B. W. (1984). "Soil – water interactions", *Royal Society of London Philosophical Transactions*, **305**, 393–407.

Barrett, C. F., Atkins, D. A. F., Cape, J. N., Fowler, D., Irwin, J. G., Kallend, A. S., Martin, A., Pitman, J. J., Scriven, R. A. and Tuck, A. F. (1983). *Acid Deposition in the United Kingdom*, Warren Spring Laboratory, Department of the Environment.

Calder, I. R. and Newson, M. D. (1980). "Land use and upland water resources in Britain – a strategic look", *Water Research Series*, B, **15**, 1628–1639.

Clyde River Purification Board (1985). *Annual Report*, East Kilbride.

Crossley, A. and Wilson, D. B. (1990). "Pollution in the upland environment", *International Conference on Acidic Deposition, its Nature and Impacts, Glasgow, 16–21 September*, Royal Society of Edinburgh.

Department of the Environment and Forestry Commission (1990). "Forests and Surface Water Acidification", Blackwell Grange Moat House, Darlington, 25–27 June 1990.

Doughty, C. R. (1990). "Acidity in Scottish rivers", A report by the Scottish River Purification Boards, Department of the Environment, London.

Edwards, R. W., Gee, A. S. and Stoner, J. H. (1990). Acid Waters in Wales, Kluwer Academic Publisher, Dordrecht.

Egglishaw, H., Gardiner, R. and Foster, J. (1986). "Salmon catch decline and forestry in Scotland", *Scottish Geographical Magazine*, **102**, 57–61.

Ferguson, R., Stott, T. and Johnson, R. (1987). "Forestry and sediment yields in upland Scotland", Poster presentation, International Symposium on Erosion and Deposition in Forested Steeplands, Oregan State University, Oregon.

Forestry Commission (1991a). *71st Annual Report 1990–91*, Edinburgh.

Forestry Commission (1991b). *Forests and Water Guidelines*, Edinburgh.

Forestry Commission (1992). *Forestry Facts and Figures*, Edinburgh.

Forestry Commission (1993) *Forests and Water Guidelines*, London.

Fowler, D. and Cape, J. N. (1984). "On the episodic nature of west deposited sulphate and acidity", *Atmospheric Environment*, **18**, 1859–1866.

Fowler, D. and Irwin, J. G. (1988). "The pollution climate of Scotland", *Symposium proceedings, Acidification in Scotland, November 8*, 1988, Scottish Development Department.

Fowler, D., Cape, J. N. and Unsworth, M. H. (1989). "Pollutant deposition on forests", *Philosophical Transactions of the Royal Society of London*, **324**, 247–265.

Fowler, D., Duyzer, J. H. and Baldocchi, D. D. (1991). "Inputs of trace gases, particles and cloud droplets to terrestrial surfaces", *Proceedings of the Royal Society of Edinburgh*, **97B**, 35–39.

Francis, I. S. (1987). "Blanket peat erosion in Mid–Wales: two catchment studies", PhD thesis, University College of Wales.

Gee, J. H. R. and Smith, B. D. (1987). "A survey of macroinvertebrates on the headwaters of the River Wye and Severn", unpublished report, University of Aberystwyth, Aberystwyth.

Gibson, G. E. (1976). "An investigation into the effect of forestry plantations on water quality of upland reservoirs in Northern Ireland", *Water Research*, **10**, 995–998.

Good, J. E. G. (Ed.) (1987). *Environmental Aspects of Plantation Forestry in Wales*, ITE Symposium No. 22 Proceedings, Institute of Terrestrial Ecology, Grange-over-Sands.

Harriman, R. (1978). "Nutrient leaching from fertilised forest watersheds in Scotland", *Journal of Applied Ecology*, **15**, 933–942.

Harriman, R. and Morrison, B. R. S. (1982). "Ecology of streams draining forested and non-forested catchments in an area of central Scotland subject to acid precipitation", *Hydrobiologia*, **88**, 251–263.

Harriman, R. and Wells, D. E. (1985). "Causes and effects of surface water acidification in Scotland", *Journal of the Institute of Water Pollution Control*, **84**, 8–10.

Harriman, R., Morrison, B. R. S., Caines, L. A., Collen, P. and Watt, A. W. (1987). "Long term changes in fish populations of acid streams and lochs in Galloway, South West Scotland", *Water, Air and Soil Pollution*, **32**, 89–112.

Haya, K. and Waiwood, B. (1981). "Acid pH and chlorionase activity of Atlantic salmon (*Salmo salar*) eggs", *Bulletin of Environmental Toxicology*, **27**, 7–12.

Hornung, M. and Newson, M. D. (1986). "Upland afforestation influences on stream hydrology and chemistry", *Soil Use and Management*, **2**, 61–65.

Horning, M., Adamson, J. K., Reynolds, B. and Stevens, P. A. (1986). "Influences of mineral weathering and catchment hydrology on drainage water chemistry in three upland sites in England and Wales", *Journal of Geological Society, London*, **143**, 627–634.

Hornung, M., Stevens, P. A. and Reynolds, B. (1987). "The effects of forestry on soils, soil water and surface water chemistry", in *Environmental Aspects of Plantation Forestry in Wales* (Ed. J. E. G. Good) pp. 25–36, ITE Symposium No. 22, Institute of Terrestrial Ecology, Grange-over-Sands.

Howells, G. D., Brown, D. J. A. and Sadler, K. (1983). "Effects of acidity, calcium and aluminium on fish survival – a review", *Journal of the Science of Food and Agriculture*, **34**, 559–570.

Jenkins, A., Cosby, B. J., Ferrier, R. C., Walker, T. A. B. and Miller, J. D. (1990). "Modelling stream acidification in afforested catchments – An assessment of the relative effects of acid deposition and afforestation", *Journal of Hydrology*, **120**, 163–181.

Leeks, G. J. L. and Roberts, G. (1987). "The effects of forestry on upland streams – with special reference to water quality and sediment transport", in *Environmental Aspects of Plantation Forestry in Wales* (Ed. J. E. Good), pp. 9–24, ITE Symposium No. 22, Institute of Terrestrial Ecology, Grange-over-Sands.

Maitland, P. S., Newson, M. D. and Best, G. A. (1990). "The impact of afforestation and forestry practice in freshwater habitats", *Focus on Nature Conservation No. 23*, Nature Conservancy Council, Peterborough.

Malcolm, D. C. (1991). "Afforestation in Britain – A commentary", *Scottish Forestry*, **45**, 259–274.

Malcolm, D. C. and Cuttle, S. P. (1983). "The application of fertilisers to drained peat. 1. Nutrient losses in drainage", *Forestry*, **56**, 155–174.

Miller, H. G., Millar, J. D. and Cooper, J. M. (1987). "Transformation in rainwater chemistry on passing through forested ecosystems", in *Pollutants Transport and Fate in Ecosystems* (Eds P. J. Coughtry, M. H. Martin and M. H. Unsworth), pp. 171–180, British Ecological Society, Special Publication No. 6, Blackwell Scientific Publications, Oxford.

Nature Conservancy Council (1986). *Nature Conservation and Afforestation in Britain*, Peterborough.

Neal, C., Reynolds, B., Smith, C. J., Hill, S., Neal, M., Conway, T., Ryland, G. P., Jeffrey, H., Robson, A. J. and Fisher, R. (1992). "The impact of conifer harvesting on stream water pH, alkalinity and aluminium concentrations for British uplands: An example for an acidic and acid sensitive catchment in Wales", *The Science of the Total Environment*, **126**, 75–87.

Newson, M. D. (1985). "Forestry and water in the uplands of Britain – the background of hydrological research and options for harmonious land-use", *Quarterly Journal of Forestry*, **29**, 113–120.

Nisbet, T. (1986). "Changes in rain and soil water chemistry on passage through a forested and unafforested site at Loch Fleet, Galloway", in *The Loch Fleet Project – A Report on the*

Pre-Intervention Stage 1984–86, Central Electricity Generating Board, Leatherhead.

Nisbet, T. (1990). *Forests and Surface Water Acidification*, Forestry Commission, Bulletin No 86, Wrecclesham, Farnham, Surrey.

Organisation for Economic Cooperation and Development (1970). *Scientific Fundamentals of the Eutrophication of Lakes and Flowing Waters, with Particular References to Nitrogen and Phosphorus as Factors in Eutrophication*, Paris.

Ormerod, S. J. and Tyler, S. J. (1991). "Exploitations of prey by a river bird, the Dipper (*Cinclus cinclus*) along acidic and circumneutral streams in upland Wales", *Freshwater Biology*, **25**, 105–116.

Ormerod, S. J., Mawle, G. W. and Edwards, R. W. (1987). "The influence of forest on aquatic fauna", in *Environmental Aspects of Plantation Forestry in Wales* (Ed. J. E. G. Good), pp. 37–49, ITE Symposium No. 22, Institute of Terrestrial Ecology, Grange-over-Sands.

Overrein, L. N., Seip, H. M. and Tollan, A. (1980). *Acid Precipitation – Effects on Forests and Fish*, Final report of the SNSF Project 1972–1980, Research Report No. 19/80, Oslo.

Parr, W. (1984). "Consultation or confrontation? A review of forestry activities and developments on water catchment areas in South West Scotland", presented to Scientific Section, Institution of Water Engineers and Scientists, October 1984.

Peterson, R. H., Daye, P. G., Lacroix, G. L. and Garside, E. T. (1982). "Reproduction in fish experiencing acid and metal stress", in *Acid Rain/Fisheries* (Ed. R. E. Johnson), pp. 177 –196, Cornell University, New York.

Pyatt, D. G. (1984). "The effect of afforestation on the quantity of water runoff", Forestry Commission, Research Information Note No. 83, Wrecclesham, Farnham, Surrey.

Reynolds, B., Neal, C., Horning, M. and Stevens, P. A. (1986). "Baseflow buffering of streamwater acidity in five Mid-Wales catchments", *Journal of Hydrology*, **87**, 167–185.

Richards, W. N. (1984). "Problems of water management and water quality arising from forestry activities", in Proceedings of A Symposium, Institute of Biology, 1984, Edinburgh pp. 67–85.

Robinson, M. (1980). *The Effect of Pre-Afforestation Drainage Operations in the Streamflow and Water Quality of a Small Upland Catchment*, Institute of Hydrology, Report No. 73, Wallingford.

Sadler, K. and Lynam, S. (1987). "Some effects on the growth of brown trout from exposure to aluminium at different pH levels", *Journal of Fish Biology*, **31**, 209–219.

Smith, W. H. (1987). "Forest nutrient cycling: Influences of acid precipitation", in *Air Pollution and Forest*, Springer-Verlag, New York.

Solbé, J. F. (1987). "Forestry and the water industry", A Report of a Forestry Commission/ Water Research Centre Workshop Report PRV 1413–M/1, Water Research Centre, Medmenham.

Stevens, P. A. and Hornung, M. (1989). "Nitrate leaching from a felled Sitka Spruce plantation in Beddgelert Forest, North Wales", *Soil Use and Management*, **4**, 3–9.

Stoner, J. H. and Gee, A. S. (1985). "Effects of forestry on water quality and fish in Welsh rivers and lakes", *Journal of the Institution of Water Engineers and Scientists*, **39**, 27–45.

Stretton, C. (1984). "Water supply and forestry – A conflict of interests: Cray Reservoir, a case study", *Journal of the Institution of Water Engineers and Scientists*, **38**, 323–330.

Swift, D. W. (1986). "Phosphorus run-off from Glenorchy Forest", Water Research Centre Report PRV 1699–M, Water Research Centre, Medmenham.

Taylor, C. M. A. (1986). "Forest fertilisation in Great Britain", *Proceedings No. 251*, The Fertiliser Society, London.

Waters, D., Jenkins, A., Staples, T. and Donald, A. (1990). "Impacts of afforestation on water quality trends in upland catchments", *Conference Abstracts, International Conference on Acidic Deposition, Its Nature and Impacts, Glasgow 16–21 September 1990*, Royal Society of Edinburgh.

24

Acidification

B. R. S. MORRISON

Freshwater Fisheries Laboratory, Faskally, Pitlochry, PH16 5LB

INTRODUCTION

Since the start of the industrial revolution in the early 19th century there has been an awareness of the damage caused to human health by atmospheric pollution in the form of acidic waste gases and soot from industrial processes (Smith, 1872). In an attempt to alleviate the situation in Britain, the Clean Air Acts were introduced in 1956 and the use of smokeless fuels became compulsory in many large towns. Taller chimneys for power plants and factories were built to ensure that waste gases and fine particulate matter were carried by air currents well away from densely populated areas. The success of these policies became evident even before the decline of industrial manufacturing during the last decade.

In the 1960s, evidence began to emerge which suggested that sulphur dioxide, one of the primary pollutant gases from the combustion of coal and oil, could be transported great distances in the atmosphere. In 1968, it was demonstrated that precipitation over the Scandinavian countries was gradually becoming more acidic, and that large quantities of the acidifying substances (mainly sulphur compounds) came from the industrial areas of central Europe and Britain (Odén, 1968).

In 1972 Sweden presented a report on pollutant transfer at a meeting of the UN Conference on the Human Environment in Stockholm. This may be regarded as the starting point for most of the current research on acidification. In Scotland, early studies on the effects of acid waters on freshwater biota included work in 1975 by the Freshwater Fisheries Laboratory, Pitlochry, on the survival of trout eggs in streams near Aberfoyle. Investigations in Galloway and the Cairngorms followed. Major investigations in Scotland by several research organizations in the 1980s included:

- a survey of acid lochs by the Institute of Terrestrial Ecology (Maitland *et al.*, 1981);
- the rehabilitation of a fish population in Loch Fleet by the Scottish Electricity Boards, the Central Electricity Generating Board and National Coal (Howells *et al.*, 1992);
- the setting up of the Loch Dee Project by the Solway River Purification Board,

The Fresh Waters of Scotland: A National Resource of International Significance
Edited by P. S. Maitland, P. J. Boon and D. S. McLusky. © 1994 John Wiley & Sons Ltd

the Forestry Commission, and the Freshwater Fisheries Laboratory, Pitlochry, to study long-term changes in stream and loch acidity (Burns *et al.*, 1984);

- palaeolimnological studies of loch sediments by University College London (Flower *et al.*, 1981) to determine historic pH values (see Chapter 7);
- the inclusion of several Scottish waters in monitoring programmes initiated by the Department of the Environment.

This chapter summarizes the range of work on freshwater acidification in Scotland and sets it in a European context. Limitations of space prevent comment on the extensive research undertaken in North America.

SOURCES OF ACID DEPOSITION

Volcanic eruptions, the release of gases from the soil, the breakdown of organic material, and the evaporation of seawater droplets in the atmosphere are all natural sources of the precursors of (sulphur) acidic deposition. Since 90% of sea spray remains in oceanic regions and does not mix with continental air masses, it may be considered to play a secondary role in overland sulphur cycling (Eriksson, 1960). In a Scottish context, however, this can be a major role since sea-salt events are an important feature of stream and loch acidity in many areas (Table 24.1). The major natural sources of nitrogenous precursors are probably biological in origin. In contrast to sulphur, naturally produced nitrogen oxides are thought to comprise a very limited proportion of total atmospheric nitrogen (Söderlund and Svensson, 1976) and even in tropical waters rich in nitrite the NO contribution is estimated to be insignificant in global terms (Zafiriou and McFarland, 1981).

In 1980, when international concern about acid deposition was increasing, it was estimated that 90% of sulphur emissions in northern Europe were man-made in origin, although globally the natural and man-made contributions were of the same order (Swedish Ministry of Agriculture, 1982). At that time, oxides of sulphur from industry and power generation probably contributed about 70% of the polluting gases over Britain with oxides of nitrogen slightly less than 30%. A high proportion of the oxides of nitrogen comes from vehicle exhausts. Figure 24.1 illustrates the main mechanisms by which the various forms of acid deposition are produced.

TABLE 24.1. Effect of sea-salt incursions on the chemical composition of a stream (Allt Eigheach) in central Scotland (after Harriman and Wells, 1985). Concentrations as μeq L^{-1} except pH

Date	Estimated flow	pH	Alkalinity (as $CaCO_3$)	Na$^+$	Ca^{2+}	Mg^{2+}	Cl$^-$	SO$_4{}^{2-}$
22 June 1977	0.1N	6.70	120	160	117	72	128	104
22 Feb 1984	2N	5.07	2	191	49	49	208	107
5 Jan 1984^s	2N	4.70	0	518	123	160	720	123

N = average flow
S – sea-salt event

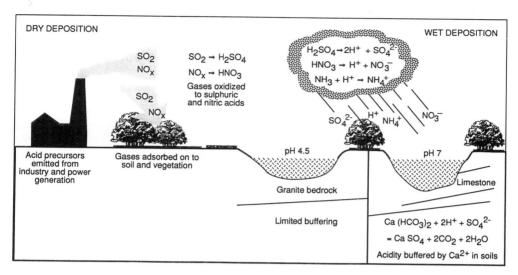

FIGURE 24.1. Sources of dry and wet deposition and the influence of acidity (H⁺) on fresh waters of different buffering capacity

Dry deposition occurs when SO_2 and NO_2 are adsorbed directly by soil, vegetation and water. Contact with water molecules quickly oxidizes the gases to sulphuric and nitric acids. Wet deposition in rain and other forms of precipitation follows oxidation of the pollutant gases by oxidizing agents such as ozone (O_3) and hydrogen peroxide (H_2O_2) in the atmosphere leading to the production of the negative ions SO_4 and NO_3. On reaching the ground these combine with positive ions in the soil or water in order to maintain electrical neutrality. In well-buffered catchments calcium and magnesium ions (Ca^{2+}, Mg^{2+}) are likely to fulfil this role, but in acid conditions hydrogen (H^+) and aluminium (Al^{3+}) will be more important. Transport of hydrogen by sulphate or nitrate ions passing through the soil increases the acidity of the receiving streams, although much of the nitrate is likely to be taken up by the roots of plants.

FACTORS AFFECTING ACIDIFICATION

Fresh waters in the present context may be divided into three types. Permanently acid waters are typical of landscapes with peat greater than 1 to 2 m deep. Their acidity (pH < 5.5) is derived from decomposing organic matter, and the humic acids present form complexes with aluminium, which is very soluble (labile) at these pH values. Free, labile aluminium is toxic to fish in concentrations as low as < 0.1 mg L^{-1} (Muniz, 1984). Calcium levels in these lochs are always low, often close to zero.

At the opposite end of the scale are the permanently alkaline waters in a calcium-rich environment, where the mean pH is above 7, and aluminium values are low because of the limited solubility of the ion complexes of aluminium at pH > 6.

Between these extremes are the fresh waters most affected by acidification processes. These are waters where the buffering capacity is low, that is the quantity of

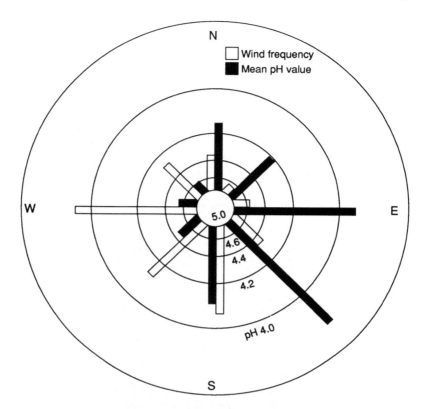

FIGURE 24.2. Frequency of wind direction and mean pH values for rainfall at Loch Dee from April to September 1981. (From Burns *et al.* 1984. Reproduced by permission of Blackwell Scientific Publications)

calcium (as the soluble compound calcium bicarbonate) is limited. Such waters are unable to buffer the larger inputs of acidic materials, although they can reduce the acidity of smaller inputs. Water bodies in areas of shallow, well-leached soils overlying slow-weathering bedrock such as granite come into this category. Calcium levels are generally < 5 mg L^{-1} and labile aluminium values can be high (> 0.1 mg L^{-1}). Large fluctuations in pH, which can vary from around 7 to below 5 within a few hours, result in acid "episodes" which are particularly harmful to juvenile salmonids and their eggs (Harriman *et al.*, 1990).

    Wind direction influences the acidity of fresh waters. The main sources of acidity in Scotland, in addition to those from within the country itself, are from the south and east. Figure 24.2 illustrates the relationship between the pH of precipitation and wind direction for Loch Dee in south-west Scotland. The wind direction factor also helps to explain why there is a decline in sulphate and nitrate concentrations in precipitation towards the north-west of Scotland. In 1986, sulphate levels in the Borders and in Wester Ross were 60 μeq L^{-1} and 10 μeq L^{-1} respectively. The corresponding figures for nitrogen were 34 μeq L^{-1} and 4 μeq L^{-1} (Warren Spring

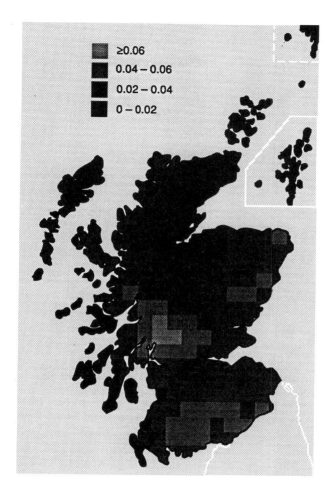

FIGURE 24.3. Wet deposited acidity (H^+) in Scotland in g H^+ m^{-2} (after Fowler and Irwin, 1989)

Laboratory, 1987). However, associated with the effect of wind direction is the fact that the rainfall in the west of the country is greater than in the east. The result is that deposition of pollutants is greater in the west even though the concentration in the atmosphere is less (Figure 24.3).

In coastal areas, enhanced levels of sodium and chloride in precipitation result from the presence of sea-salts. These produce sudden drops in pH by replacing soil hydrogen with sodium thus releasing the H^+ ion (acidity) into the soil water which is then transported into streams and lochs. During these episodes calcium values for stream water are normally high, in contrast to acid episodes with a low input of sea-salts (See Chapter 6).

For the past decade it has been recognized that coniferous forests are able to increase the acidity of streams in planted catchments by scavenging (collecting)

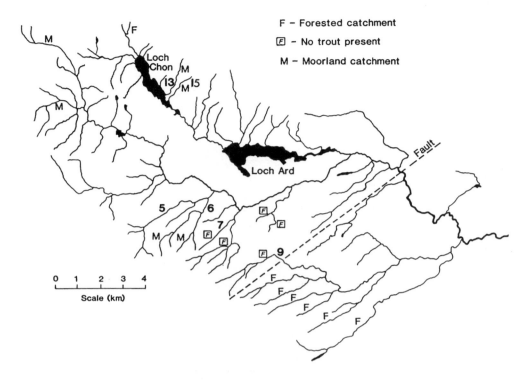

FIGURE 24.4. Loch Ard Forest, central Scotland, showing the distribution of trout in streams surveyed between 1976 and 1982. The numbers refer to those streams listed in Table 24.2. F and M = trout present. $\boxed{F}$ = trout absent from these forested catchments

atmospheric pollutants (Forestry Commission, 1991; Chapter 23). The conditions which bring this about were described by Harriman and Morrison (1982) for Loch Ard Forest near Aberfoyle. The Highland Boundary Fault divides the forest into a north-west section located on peaty soils overlying bedrock which is mainly mica-schist and slate, and a south-east section where the more calcareous soils have a predominantly sandstone base (Figure 24.4). Trout are absent from streams in the northern part of the forest, which are more acid than adjacent moorland streams, but present in forest streams south of the fault. Later work, based on a study of streams with similar buffering capacity in other parts of Scotland, led to the conclusion that changes in acidity are most obvious from the time of canopy closure; that is, when the trees are 15 to 20 years old. This is illustrated in Figure 24.5. For a given value of (Ca + Mg) – a measure of the buffering capacity – the pH of the stream in a mature forest is much lower than that in a young forest or moorland habitat.

Harriman (1989) found that even in north-west Scotland where sulphate ion deposition was very low (12 kg ha^{-1} yr^{-1}) streams in forested catchments were significantly more acidic than moorland streams in the same area. A regional survey by Welsh Water (1986) also revealed a strong correlation between the proportion of catchment covered by forest and the level of labile aluminium in run-off.

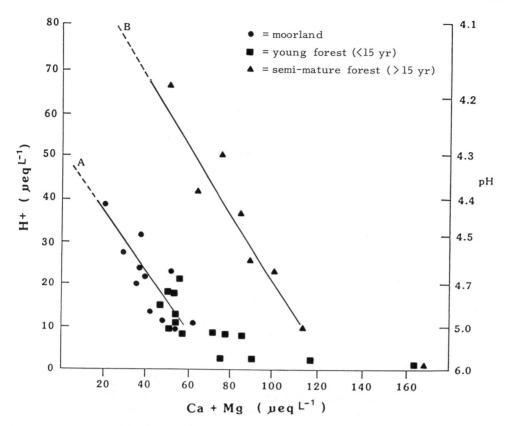

FIGURE 24.5. Relationship between H^+ and excess ($Ca^{2+} + Mg^{2+}$) for surface waters draining moorland, ●; young forest (<15 yr), ■; and semi-mature forest (>15 yr), ▲; (units as μeq L^{-1}. Least-square regression line A, $Y = -0.58x + 49.5$, $R^2 = 0.62$; line B, $Y = -0.82x + 102.2$, $R^2 = 0.91$ where A = young forest and moorland catchments combined, with pH < 5.0. B = semi-mature forest catchments of > 50% forest cover and pH < 5.0. (From Harriman *et al.*, 1987. Reprinted by permission of Kluwer Academic Publishers)

PROBLEM AREAS IN SCOTLAND

The areas of Scotland known to contain waters of pH < 5.6, and regions classed as susceptible to acid deposition on the basis of their geology, are shown in Figure 24.6. This map includes waters which are naturally acid because of their location in areas of deep peat. In broad terms, the central lowlands between the two geological faults, low-lying areas in the extreme south-east, and the land around the Moray Firth are less susceptible to acid deposition than elsewhere. This is because these areas have more calcareous soils and, despite the fact that they are closer to the sources of acid pollution in the midlands of England and central Europe, the buffering capacity of the soils is such that the leaching of acidity into streams and lochs is very much reduced. This is clearly of benefit to Salmon stocks and sport fishing in major rivers in the eastern half of the country, but because of the more acid soils and the influence

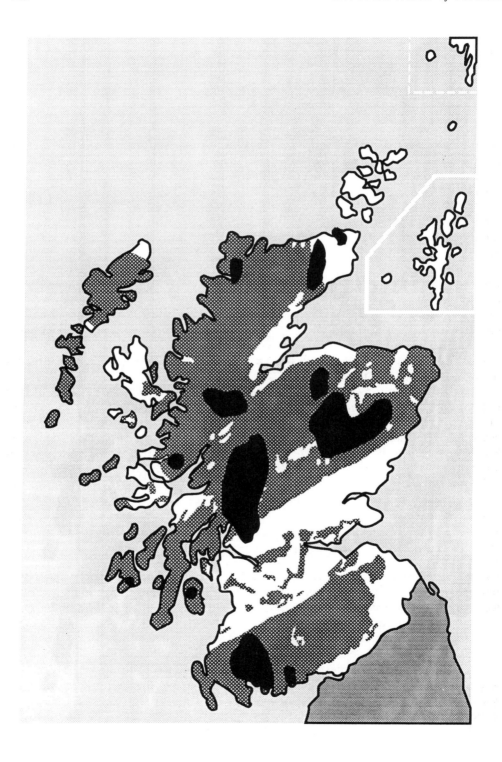

of sea spray in the west and south-west of the country, some fish farmers in Argyll and Galloway have had to resort to treating their farm inflows with some form of lime. A decrease in salmon catches on the River Cree has been attributed to acidification of the headwaters in recent decades (Stephen, 1990).

FRESHWATER ACIDITY IN A EUROPEAN CONTEXT

In central and eastern Europe, in addition to concern about the effects of atmospheric pollution on human health, the relationship between air pollution and forest damage has probably attracted more research than effects on the aquatic environment (Bresser and Salomons, 1990). Much of the damage is the result of the extensive use of brown coal (average sulphur content 2.3%) and mineral oil (average sulphur content 2.1%) in Hungary and other eastern European countries. This, combined with inefficient industrial processes, has produced not only serious local pollution but long-range effects which can be traced as far as southern Norway and the UK (OECD, 1977).

In the countries of north-west Europe, an increase in the acidity of lakes and rivers, coupled with extensive fish mortalities in Norway and Sweden, encouraged the development in the 1970s and 1980s of government-backed programmes of research. Strong pressure from Norway and Sweden for a substantial reduction in global emissions of waste gases led ultimately to an agreement signed by many European nations pledging a reduction in sulphur emissions by 30% of 1980 values by 1993. The British Government funded much of the research done in the UK in the 1980s but did not sign the agreement.

The acidification of lakes in Scandinavia is of particular concern because of their importance to local communities not only as domestic water supplies, but as sources of fish for food and sport. The latter is often of considerable value to the local economy. The acidification of ground waters is also significant since, for example, in Sweden 25% of domestic supplies come from this source. Enhanced amounts of aluminium and other heavy metals present in acidified water are regarded as potentially hazardous both in relation to fish survival and human health (Swedish Ministry of Agriculture, 1982).

Acid conditions are also found in mountainous areas in central and southern Europe. Research in the mid-1980s indicated that the majority of lakes in the Austrian Alps did not appear to be acidified but several were determined to be at high risk. Evidence from 71 small lakes, surveyed between 1983 and 1986, showed that 20% had pH < 6.0 and in 10% the carbonate buffering capacity was exhausted. Precipitation frequently shows a pH of 4.3 to 4.9. On lower ground the soils and water are well-buffered (Orthofer and Kienzl, 1990).

FIGURE 24.6. Distribution of acid waters in Scotland. Location of known acid waters (pH < 5.6) are shown in black. Regions classified as susceptible to acid deposition on the basis of solid geology are stippled. Regions classified as non-susceptible to acid deposition on the basis of solid geology are white (after Harriman 1989)

OBSERVED EFFECTS ON AQUATIC LIFE

It is often difficult to separate effects due directly to low pH from those due to associated phenomena, particularly low calcium levels and increased labile aluminium. The precipitation of phosphorus in acid, oligotrophic waters by aluminium and other heavy metals also restricts the abundance and range of plant species.

Aquatic plants

Probably the most detailed phytoplankton studies in Scotland have been on the use of diatoms for determining historical pH values. The work is discussed elsewhere (see Chapter 7), and is referred to in a later section in this chapter. Numbers of phytoplankton species decline from 30–80 in circumneutral oligotrophic lakes to 10–20 in acidic lakes (Muniz, 1991). In acidic conditions the flora is often dominated by one or more species of Dinophyceae. Studies of these organisms from Galloway lochs showed that some species have an acid- and aluminium-tolerant phosphate metabolism (Smith, 1990).

Hörnström *et al.* (1984) found that the absence of several species of phytoplankton was due not to low pH as such but to a raised aluminium supply from the surrounding environment. This produced oligotrophic conditions by precipitating phosphorus, thus reducing the nutrient supply to the open water. Aluminium itself was also found to be toxic, particularly between pH 5.1 and 5.8. In the laboratory, the growth of 13 out of 19 species tested was inhibited in solutions containing 0.2 mg Al L^{-1}.

Macrophytes in Scottish waters have been studied in a number of areas, and investigations in acid waters in Galloway have been made recently by Murphy *et al.* (1986) at Loch Dee, and Raven (1986) who did a survey of 31 lochs. Both authors noted the wide distribution of *Juncus bulbosus* which tends to restrict the spread of *Lobelia dortmanna* and *Littorella uniflora*, two species common in the littoral zone of less acid waters. Raven also recorded the occurrence of *Sphagnum* spp. in five of the lochs where the pH was < 5.1. In Sweden and the Netherlands increasing acidity is associated with the formation of *Sphagnum* mats (Grahn, 1986) which interfere with sediment/water interchange (Dillon *et al.*, 1984). Raven noted the apparent loss of the calcicole species *Potamogeton lucens* and *P. pusillus* from eight lochs in the area.

Invertebrate fauna

A study of the stream fauna of Loch Ard Forest near Aberfoyle in the late 1970s and early 1980s revealed a limited range of taxa in acid waters (Harriman and Morrison, 1982). The freshwater shrimp, *Gammarus pulex*, molluscs, and mayfly nymphs of the families Baetidae and Heptageniidae, were absent from the more acid streams, but several of these acid-sensitive mayflies were found in neighbouring streams with slightly higher pH (Table 24.2). Research in the Loch Fleet catchment in Galloway in 1984 (Morrison, 1989) produced similar results. A more extensive study covering 145 sites throughout Scotland was made by the River Purification Boards between 1986 and 1988 (Doughty, 1990). This supported the findings of the earlier work and confirmed the scarcity or absence of certain taxa in acid environments. In Loch Dee,

TABLE 24.2. Invertebrate fauna (% abundance in samples) from Loch Ard Streams, March 1983

Stream no.	9	7	5	6	15	13
Mean pH	4.3	4.6	5.2	5.8	6.2	6.7
Oligochaetes	2					1
Mayflies						
Baetis rhodani						22
B. muticus						2
Rhithrogena sp.			4	5	1	5
Heptagenia lateralis					1	4
Stoneflies						
Brachyptera risi		3	57	61	59	16
Amphinemura sulcicollis	69	60	23	10	3	9
Leuctra spp.	12	8	14	12	16	27
Chloroperla torrentium	3	6	2	1	1	5
C. tripunctata				1	2	2
Others	10	5	1	6	2	5
Caddis						
Limnephilidae	1	5	1	1	1	1
Plectrocnemia conspersa	2	10				
Dipterans	2	3		2	14	2
Beetles				1	<1	

in south-west Scotland, where the mean pH was around 5.3 and the calcium level 1 mg L^{-1}, the author found locally distributed snails (*Limnaea peregra*) with soft shells only 6 mm long. In calcareous waters this species may reach 15 mm in length. Low calcium concentration in acid waters is likely to be an important factor controlling the distribution of molluscs, and crustaceans such as *Gammarus*, which require calcium carbonate for shells and exoskeletons. A survey of the littoral benthos of 19 lochs in the Cairngorms between 1983 and 1985 produced a limited range of taxa in the more acid lochs (Morrison and Harriman, 1992).

In addition to the chemical factors which affect the distribution of benthic animals it is important to take into account the physical characteristics of a given water body. Acid lochs, because they are most often located in areas of slow-weathering bedrock, frequently have littoral zones consisting of large boulders and/or large areas of coarse granite grit. Neither substrate is optimal for a wide range of fauna.

The results of the Scottish studies are comparable to those from Wales (Stoner *et al.*, 1984), the English Lake District (Sutcliffe and Carrick, 1973), western Norway (Raddum and Fjellheim, 1984), and Sweden (Engblom and Lingdell, 1984). Benthic invertebrates have been used for several years now as indicators of acid conditions by River Purification Boards because they provide an integrated assessment of the very variable chemistry of running waters. A guide for use by forestry managers has also been prepared (Patterson and Morrison, 1993).

Acid-tolerant and acid-sensitive species are also found among the crustacean zooplankton in lochs. A survey in the Grampian Highlands (Morrison and Harriman, 1992) and in Galloway (Morrison, unpublished) showed that in summer in the open water of lochs with a pH < 5.5 the fauna was limited to one or two dominant species, usually the copepod *Diaptomus gracilis* and the cladoceran *Bosmina coregoni*. Several other species were present in small numbers only. Acid-sensitive species, such as the cladoceran *Daphnia hyalina*, one of the most abundant animals in circumneutral waters, were absent.

Low pH produces stress responses in many invertebrates, including a net loss of sodium ions, thus upsetting the animal's osmoregulation. This has been shown for *Daphnia* spp. (Potts and Fryer, 1979), stoneflies (Twitchen, 1990), and mayflies (Frick and Herrmann, 1990). The last three authors showed that an increase in aluminium may also produce a decrease in sodium ions in body fluids. Aluminium may ameliorate the adverse impact of acidity at around pH 4.0 perhaps by replacing the scarce calcium ions as a barrier to the movement of H^+ ions. Witters *et al.* (1984) demonstrated that *Corixa punctata* is able to control the efficiency of sodium uptake in high aluminium concentrations by transferring Al^{3+} ions from the haemolymph to the tissues.

Invertebrates are affected by ecological as well as chemical changes. The disappearance of fish from acidified waters results in a change in top predators with an increase in the number of carnivorous invertebrates such as dragonfly nymphs (Odonata) and water boatmen (Corixidae) (Nilssen *et al.*, 1984; Lyle and East, 1989).

Fish

Ecological effects of acidification on fish populations in Scotland have been much less severe than in Scandinavia where fish have been eliminated from thousands of lakes (Muniz, 1984). Surveys in what were believed to be the areas most sensitive to acid deposition in Scotland suggest that damage is restricted but that a high proportion of waters have become acidified to some extent (Harriman *et al.*, 1987; Maitland *et al.*, 1987; Morrison and Harriman, 1992).

The most obvious effect of acidification on fish populations in Scotland is the apparent disappearance of Trout (*Salmo trutta*), from five lochs in Galloway which were known to have had Trout populations earlier this century (Harriman *et al.*, 1987), and the disappearance of Arctic Charr, *Salvelinus alpinus*, which had been recorded from Loch Dungeon and Loch Grannoch (Hardie, 1940).

During the surveys mentioned above, Trout populations were found in several lochs with pH values < 5.0 and calcium levels < 2 mg L^{-1}. That this is not necessarily a recent phenomenon can be seen from a paper by Traquair (1882) who dissected three Trout from Loch Enoch. These fish had the deformed fins and tail characteristic of many Trout caught in acid water (Maitland *et al.*, 1987). Traquair noted, however, that the fin rays, although deformed, were complete, and concluded that the effect was due to a scarcity of lime in the water. The scarcity or absence of Trout, however, may also be related to the physical constraints imposed by the environment on these populations. Many of the lochs have very small or no inflow streams. The outflow may be small, sometimes precipitous, sometimes underground for part of its length, and it may dry up during summer. Spawning and nursery facilities in these situations are confined to the loch itself. At higher altitudes, prolonged ice cover will shorten the growing season. Alterations in weather patterns can therefore affect trout survival in these waters.

The greater variability of stream chemistry, as compared with the stability of loch chemistry, puts the eggs and juveniles of salmonid fish at risk. Osmoregulation within the developing egg is adversely affected by the high concentration of H^+ ions in acid water (Potts and Fryer, 1979), but the high rate of mortality at the time of hatching is also due to the failure of the enzyme chorionase to dissolve the inner wall of the egg. This enzyme, produced from the snout of the embryo, has an optimal working pH of about 7.0 and its action is blocked when the pH falls too low (Haya and Waiwood, 1981). Physiological studies on adult fish (Potts *et al.*, 1990) point to failure of the osmoregulatory mechanism as the primary cause of death in acid waters, but the situation is alleviated by enhanced calcium levels (Brown, 1983). The extent to which high calcium values can alleviate the effects of lowered pH during sea-salt episodes is not yet known.

Birds and mammals

Waterfowl and mammals which depend on freshwater organisms for food may be adversely affected by loss of prey. Tyler and Ormerod (1992) found that the breeding density of Dippers, *Cinclus cinclus* is markedly reduced at low pH in both Wales and Scotland. They found that on acidic streams egg-laying was delayed, clutch and brood sizes were significantly reduced, and the time spent foraging was much longer than in circumneutral streams.

CASE HISTORIES

The Arctic Charr of Loch Doon

The disappearance of Arctic Charr from Lochs Dungeon and Grannoch, probably during the first half of this century, leaves Loch Doon (Figure 24.7) as the only water in southern Scotland with an indigenous Charr population as far as is known. Most of the Loch Doon basin is located on the northern tip of the granite mass which forms the Merrick range of hills in south-west Scotland. Several of the lochs which are believed to have lost their Trout populations this century are in the same range of hills. The Trout populations in other lochs in the area are at risk because of the poor buffering capacity of the water (Harriman *et al.*, 1987). A forest plantation covers 25% of the catchment. It was planted in 1973 and canopy closure is taking place; that is; the forest is reaching the stage where it is becoming a more efficient scavenger of atmospheric pollutants. Recorded pH values have so far changed little during the past 15 years (an annual mean of around 5.8), and observations on water chemistry are continuing.

The first mention of Loch Doon Charr in the literature appears to have been by Crawford (1792) who referred to them as "cuddings or char". More recent references are those of Hardie (1940) and Friend (1958). Friend's work has been extended by Maitland *et al.* (1991) who found that populations of both Charr and Trout in the loch are showing signs of decline, with an increase in the size of surviving individuals.

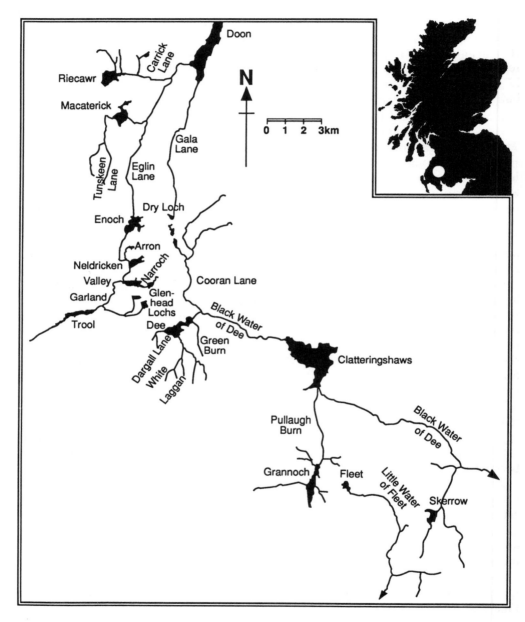

FIGURE 24.7. Location of lochs in area of granite bedrock in Galloway (after Harriman *et al.*, 1987)

There were, however, substantial mortalities during hot, dry summers (Maitland, 1992).

Attempts are now being made to conserve the Loch Doon Charr by transferring young fish and some adults to the Megget and Talla reservoirs near the Scottish border. The young fish came from eggs collected in the years 1986 to 1990 and there is evidence that adult Charr have bred successfully in Talla for two seasons. These reservoirs have a pH of around 7.0 and calcium readings have been quoted as 11 mg L^{-1} (Megget) and 16 mg L^{-1} (Talla) (Maitland, 1992), indicating a relatively good buffering capacity.

Trout angling in Galloway's acid lochs

Most of the lochs in the Merrick range of hills and nearby (Figure 24.7) were fished at some time during the late 19th century (Lyell, 1873). Water chemistry data for those mentioned here are given in Table 24.3. Lochs Enoch, Neldricken and Narroch may have lost their Trout early in the present century but Trout were caught in Loch Valley around 1974 (Maitland, personal communication) In addition to acidification, poor spawning facilities and a short growing season are likely to have been factors contributing to the decline or disappearance of these fish.

Lochs Grannoch and Fleet were fished until the early 1970s. It is clear from the figures for the best baskets that a large number of Trout could be caught during a single visit by one angler (Table 24.4). It also seems probable from these data that the total number of anglers in one year for each of the lochs could have been less than 20. A comparison of the catches from Loch Grannoch in the 1940s and 1970s shows that, latterly, a much greater effort was required to catch a similar number of fish. At the present time, the stock of Trout in Loch Grannoch is probably being maintained largely from a stream entering the southern shore of the loch which is less acid than the loch itself. Despite regular electrofishing, no juveniles have been found in the outflow stream, strongly suggesting that the loch water is not suitable for Trout eggs and young fish. Gill-netting of Loch Fleet on several occasions between 1978 and 1984 failed to produce any Trout, and it was assumed that the fish population had become extinct.

Lochs Riecawr and Macaterick have been fished regularly for over 100 years. Conifers planted in 1973 grow on 70% of the Riecawr catchment and 20% of the catchment around Loch Macaterick. Several hundred Trout are caught each year and until about eight years ago, so far as is known, the stock was entirely natural, with no introduced fish. From the 1950s to the early 1980s there was a general increase in the mean weight of Trout caught (Figure 24.8). Figures for catch per unit effort for Loch Macaterick in the 1950s are not available, but data for effort (angling visits) for Loch Riecawr in the 1950s and 1970s and the corresponding catch data are shown in Figure 24.9. The decline in catch in numbers per unit effort and the increase in the weights of individual fish are evidence of declining recruitment and a total population increasingly dominated by older fish.

The only attempt so far to restore a fish population to an acid loch in the area has been at Loch Fleet. This is referred to in the section on Amelioration.

TABLE 24.3. Physical characteristics and mean ion concentrations of Galloway lochs (after Harriman *et al.*, 1987). Ion concentrations as μeq L^{-1} except for Al (μg L^{-1})

Name	Altitude of sampling site (m)	Forest cover (%)	Forest age (1984)	n	pH	Alk.	Ca^{2+}	Al	SO$_4^{2-}$
Enoch	500	0	0	6	4.42	0	15	114	92
Neldricken	350	0	0	6	4.60	0	30	159	117
Valley	335	0	0	6	4.60	0	25	129	114
Narroch	340	0	0	5	4.55	0	20	222	129
Grannoch	210	30	17	6	4.55	0	50	265	152
Fleet	340	20	16	6	4.33	0	45	213	153
Riecawr	290	70	12	6	5.70	9	50	87	121
Macaterick	300	20	12	5	5.10	0	35	58	120
Doon	230	25	12	5	5.80	27	80	142	141

TABLE 24.4. Fish catches and fishing effort for two lochs in south-west Scotland (Reproduced by permission of Kluwer Academic Publishers from Harriman *et al.*, 1987)

(a) Early records of Trout catches from Loch Fleet

Year	Total catch	Best basket	No. rods
1940	149	13	1
1942	96	17	2
1943	65	14	2
1948	112	11	2

(b) Early records of Trout catches from Loch Grannoch

Year	Total catch	Best basket	No. rods
1940	980	95	3
1942	367	36	2 (caught in 2½hr)
1943	363	59	2
1947	683	56	3
1948	510	46	2

(c) Catches of Trout at Loch Grannoch 1970–1974

Year	Total catch	No. rods
1970	557	228
1971	252	233
1972	151	133
1973	87	61
1974	7	13

PALAEOECOLOGY AND HISTORIC pH DATA

There are few records of lake acidification which involve direct observations of chemical and biological change. In Scotland, the examples available are from seven lochs in Galloway where there is evidence of a rapid decline in pH over a period of 25 years (Figure 24.10, Table 24.5). An indirect method has been to use sediment cores in a way similar to that used by archaeologists and botanists to construct a model of the environment in past ages based on evidence from pollen grains and other artefacts in sediment strata of known age. The strata can be aged from the known rate of decay of radioactive isotopes.

Investigations undertaken by Flower *et. al.* (1987), began with a study of the pH tolerance of present-day diatoms, found in the open water of lochs and on the bed of lochs and streams. The constant rain of dead organisms in a loch builds up slowly (< 1 cm yr^{-1}) on the loch bottom and the silica skeleton of diatoms can be recovered centuries later from mud in sediment cores. The diatoms are then identified and, since their pH tolerance range is known, an estimate can be made of the pH of the loch

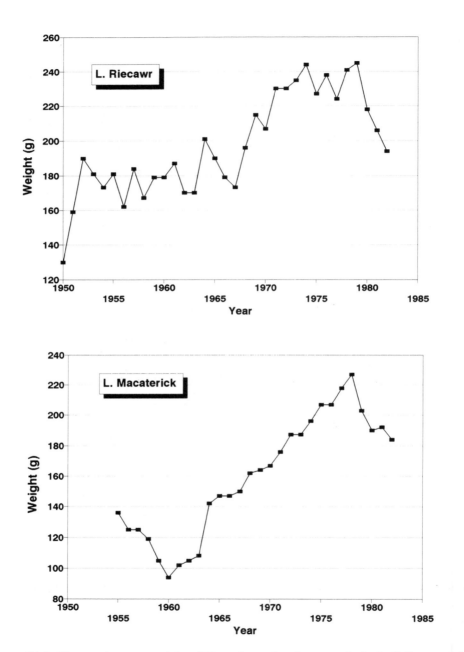

FIGURE 24.8. Changes in mean weight of Trout in catches from two lochs in Galloway, (after Harriman *et al.*, 1987).

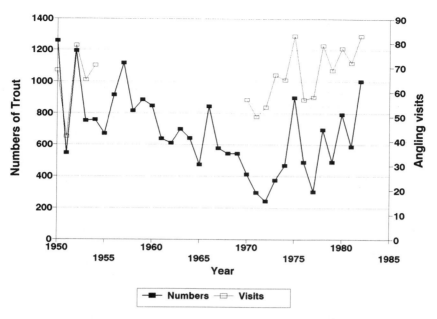

FIGURE 24.9. Fishing effort and catch returns from Loch Riecawr

TABLE 24.5. Comparison of historical pH data (single samples only) with data from 1978 to 1984 for seven lochs in south-west Scotland (Reproduced by permission of Kluwer Academic Publishers from Harriman *et al.*, 1987)

Loch	Historical data		Recent pH maxima
	Year	pH	
Harrow	1953	6.3	5.40
Minnoch	1953	6.1	5.35
Dungeon	1953	6.4	5.20
Neldricken	1958	6.8	4.92
Grannoch	1961	6.6	4.95
Fleet	1961	6.6	4.50
Skerrow	1961	6.8	5.70

water at the time when the diatoms died. The resulting analyses have provided further evidence of acidification.

A more detailed account of this subject is given in Chapter 7.

AMELIORATION

Background

Research into the causes of acidification of fresh waters has been accompanied by work on methods of ameliorating the adverse effects of acidity on the environment.

FIGURE 24.10. An aerial photograph of part of Galloway showing some of the acidified lochs mentioned in the text (cf. Figure 24.7). Photograph: Scottish Office Environment Department

Research on short-term amelioration has concentrated primarily on the use of alkaline materials to counteract acid inputs. The four main groups of chemicals which have been tested are carbonates, oxides, hydroxides and silicates. Of these, calcium carbonate (limestone) has emerged as the preferred material for practical field applications. It is readily available, safe to handle, the cost is relatively low because of its use in agriculture, it is a natural component of the buffering system of fresh waters, and it dissolves slowly, which leads to a gradual rise in pH. Limestone which contains more than 10% magnesium carbonate ($MgCO_3$), for example dolomitic limestone with 35% $MgCO_3$, dissolves too slowly to be of practical use in the neutralization of most acid waters (Sverdrup, 1985). Sodium (as sodium carbonate or soda ash) is a more effective exchanger in cation exchange reactions with lake sediments than calcium, and has been reported to be particularly effective for lake sediment injection methods of increasing the pH of lake water (Lindmark, 1985).

TABLE 24.6. Limestone particle size ranges for various neutralization techniques (from Olem, 1991. Reprinted with permission from *Liming Acidic Surface Waters* by Harvey Olem. Copyright Lewis Publishers, a subsidiary of CRC Press, Boca Raton, Florida)

	Surface area weighted diameter[a]	
Application technique	Acceptable range	Optimal range
Lakes		
Aerial application (dry powder)	0.7–18	3.5–7.5
Aerial application (slurry)	0.7–12	3.5–7.5
Boat (dry powder)	0.7–30	7.5–14
Boat (slurry)	0.7–30	7.5–14
Streams		
Doser (dry powder)	5–13	7.5–12
Doser (slurry)	0.7–5	3.5–5
Diversion well	3–12 mm	6–8 mm
Rotary drum	20–50 mm	38 mm
Limestone carrier	20–50 mm	38 mm

[a]Mean diameter measured in micrometres (μm), unless otherwise indicated. Weighted according to an individual particle's surface area to account for highly irregular shapes of particles

Criteria have been established for the particle size of limestone most suitable for the liming of lakes, streams and catchment areas. Examples of particle size ranges for different methods of application directly to lakes and streams are shown in Table 24.6.

Mathematical models have been developed for determining the quantity of material to be applied. Most are based on titration curves estimating the dosage required to neutralize acidity. The simple model used by the Swedish Environmental Protection Board relates pH and alkalinity of the lake, and the lake's retention time, to the recommended dose. Sverdrup's Dissolution Model is based on the settling rate of different particle sizes in a lake and their relative roles in neutralization as they sink (Sverdrup, 1985). The DePinto model (Scheffe *et al.*, 1986) takes this a stage further and includes aluminium speciation. Similar methods have been developed for streams. A model for the liming of catchments has been produced by Warfvinge and Sverdrup (1988) and takes into account many soil processes including weathering, base cation uptake, nitrification, and evapo-transpiration. This model has been used in British liming programmes.

Lime applications in Scotland

The most detailed work has been in connection with the rehabilitation of a Trout population in Loch Fleet, in south-west Scotland. This is a 17 ha loch at an altitude of 340 m. Before treatment, the pH varied between 4.1 and 5.0; the calcium level was around 1 mg L^{-1} and aluminium values were in the range 120–290 μg L^{-1}. The loch catchment was divided into nine sub-catchments and the most satisfactory dosages for limestone were made using rates varying from 5 to 30 t ha^{-1}. Predictions of water quality, using data from 3.5 years since liming (1986 and 1987), suggest that applications of limestone to this catchment, either as slurry or dry powder, at rates > 20 t ha^{-1}, will maintain acceptable water quality conditions for more than 15 years (Howells *et al.*, 1992).

However, there is considerable concern from conservationists regarding the long-term ecological effects of this type of blanket spreading of lime (Woodin and Skiba, 1990). Damage to terrestrial vegetation, especially *Sphagnum* spp., is very obvious in some areas.

Loch Dee, a 100 ha loch in south-west Scotland, has been managed for almost 20 years as a Trout fishery by the Forestry Commission, and although the pH level of the water was above 5.0 at the start of the management project in 1980, calcium values were often < 1 mg L^{-1}, indicating poor buffering capacity (Lees *et al.*, 1989). Initial applications of limestone chips in winter 1981/82 into the White Laggan Burn (Figure 24.7) and powder to the catchment close to the stream had no obvious effect. In spring 1983, 75 t limestone were applied to the lower reaches of the White Laggan. The calcium concentration in the loch rose to about 1.5 mg L^{-1} but by the end of 1984 it had returned to its former level. It was estimated that by mid-1984 about 50% of the limestone had been lost through the outflow, and 26% had been taken up by the sediment. A similar pattern was found after a further treatment in 1985 when 110 t was applied. The reduction to a pre-treatment level was more rapid than before due to the very wet summer that year. The rapid flow-through of water in Loch Dee (mean value 42 days) and these results indicate that some other improvement strategy is required for long-term effects (Tervet and Harriman, 1988).

Experimental liming of source areas of streams has also been attempted (Scottish Office Agriculture and Fisheries Department, 1992), but the resulting increase in calcium level was not high enough to maintain Salmon eggs or fry in the experimental stream.

Long-term control of acid emissions

Methods for controlling acid emissions at source vary with the nature of the source itself. Reduction of the output of oxides of nitrogen and other gases from vehicle exhausts is being attempted by using lean burn engines, exhaust gas recirculation and catalytic converters. In industry and power generation, oxides of sulphur are the dominant waste gases and particular efforts have been made to control the emission of sulphur dioxide (SO_2). These include: the use of low sulphur fuels or the removal of sulphur from fuel by cleaning; during combustion, by addition of a sorbent to the fuel itself, the combustion vessel, or the ductwork; after combustion, by treatment of the flue gas in a special vessel, a process commonly called Flue Gas Desulphurization (FGD) (Vernon, 1989). The latter is the most widely used approach to SO_2 control. In the non-regenerative process, SO_2 is bound in chemical compounds which must be disposed of. In the regenerative process, the sorbent may be used again, after removal of the SO_2 which is given further treatment. FGD is very expensive. The electricity generating company PowerGen is paying £300 million for the installation at its new coal-burning station at Ratcliffe-on-Soar (Lewis, 1992).

Alternatively, new combustion techniques with low sulphur emission may be used, such as fluidized bed combustion which has been developed since the 1960s and gives sulphur capture efficiencies of over 90% (Vernon, 1989).

The removal of waste products from some of these processes also presents problems. An estimated $500\,000$ t yr^{-1} of gypsum (calcium sulphate) may be produced by a 2000 MW coal-fired power station. An FGD regenerative process such as the Wellman Lord (Vernon, 1989) may produce 50 000 to 80 000 t yr^{-1} sulphur from such a power station. The source of limestone for use in the power stations raises environmental issues. It was suggested that the $320\,000$ t yr^{-1} of high quality limestone required by the Drax B station in Yorkshire might be obtained from the margins of two national parks in that part of the country (Gibbs and Longhurst, 1989)!

PAST TRENDS – FUTURE PROSPECTS

Palaeolimnological studies have demonstrated long-term trends in surface water acidification over past decades. Continuing studies have indicated a change in direction of the trend, with increasing pH estimates for several Scottish waters (see Chapter 7). Direct monitoring of water chemistry during the past 15 years has shown an increase in the pH of the fishless Loch Enoch from 4.3 (1978) to around 4.8 (1989) (Scottish Office Agriculture and Fisheries Department, 1992). Trout held in cages in the loch outflow in 1991 survived for several months. Similarly, an increase in the mean pH of Burn 5 in Loch Ard Forest near Aberfoyle to over 5.5 in 1989 was accompanied by a significant increase in the Trout population (Scottish Office Agriculture and Fisheries Department, 1992) and in 1992, for the first time, Trout fry (0+ age class) were found during electrofishing. Previously only 1+ and older fish, probably immigrants, had been seen.

These promising trends are associated with a decrease in the sulphate content of the rain (Harriman *et al.*, 1990) which may be attributed to the decline in heavy industry as well as to the efforts to remove sulphur from fossil fuels. Whether the trend will continue if industry expands is open to speculation but the importance of controlling sulphur emissions is not in doubt. However, the current controversy about whether or not under the Environmental Protection Act 1990 there is a legal requirement to install FGD plants in power stations burning orimulsion (70% heavy Orinoco crude oil + 30% water and an emulsifier) has re-opened the debate on the very high cost of undertaking these protection measures. It is hoped that the acidifying effects of coniferous forests in acid-sensitive areas will also be limited by the adoption of the different management practices being proposed in the new edition of the *Forests and Water Guidelines* (Forestry Commission, 1993). The emphasis throughout the new edition is on consultation with water and conservation authorities at each stage of a forestry management programme from ground preparation to harvesting. Environmental assessments, such as that at present under way in Strath Halladale (Caithness) are likely to be required in many areas of the country where there is concern about possible long-term effects of plantation. Those currently revising the guidelines recognize that earlier editions have been used by some planning authorities in connection with, for example, Indicative Forestry Strategies, and the new edition has been revised to take account of this use of the guidelines.

Control of damage caused by the long-distance transport of pollutants is the objective of the so-called Critical Loads Programme (Department of the Environment, 1991). Its aim is to identify the areas most sensitive to acid deposition and, by controlling output of waste gases from the appropriate sources of pollution, limit deposition in these sensitive areas. The critical load is the amount of pollutant which may be deposited in a given area without causing ecological damage. In fresh waters, the indicators used to assess damage, and hence indicate the critical load value, are salmonid fish and certain acid-sensitive invertebrates. Initially, the programme was concerned only with sulphur emissions but is now being extended to nitrogen gases.

Research on the long-term effects of acidification and on methods of amelioration and control, is likely to form an important topic of environmental science for many years. Long-term monitoring is now providing evidence of changes in the trends of the 1960s and 1970s but it is the application of advances in fuel technology, in particular the removal of pollutants before, during or after combustion, which should ensure continuing improvement of the aquatic (and terrestrial) environment.

REFERENCES

Bresser, A. H. M. and Salomons, W. (1990). *Acidic Precipitation, vol. 5, International overview and assessment*, Springer Verlag, New York.

Brown, D. J. A. (1983). "The effect of calcium and aluminium concentrations on the survival of brown trout (*Salmo trutta*) at low pH", *Bulletin of Environmental Contamination and Toxicology*, **30**, 582–587.

Burns, J. C., Coy, J. S., Tervet, D. J., Harriman, R., Morrison, B. R. S. and Quine, C. P. (1984). "The Loch Dee Project: a study of the ecological effects of acid precipitation and forest management on an upland catchment in south-west Scotland. 1. Preliminary investigations," *Fisheries Management*, **15**, 145–167.

Crawford, W. (1792). "Parish of Straiton – Ayre", *Statistical Account of Scotland*, **3**, 589–590.

Department of the Environment (1991). *Acid Rain – Critical and Target Loads Maps for the United Kingdom*, HMSO, London.

Dillon, P. J., Yan, N. D. and Harvey, H. H. (1984). "Acidic deposition: Effects on aquatic ecosystems", *CRC Critical Reviews in Environmental Control*, **13**, 167–194.

Doughty, C. R. (1990). *Acidity in Scottish Rivers: a chemical and biological baseline survey*, Scottish River Purification Boards, East Kilbride, Glasgow.

Engblom, E. and Lingdell, P. (1984). "The mapping of short-term acidification with the help of biological pH indicators", *Report, Institute of Freshwater Research, Drottningholm*, **61**, 60–68.

Eriksson, E. (1960). "The yearly circulation of chloride and sulphur in nature: meteorological, geochemical, and pedological implications. Part II", *Tellus*, **12**, 63–109.

Flower, R. J., Battarbee, R. W. and Appleby, P. G. (1987). "The recent palaeolimnology of acid lakes in Galloway, south-west Scotland: diatom analysis, pH trends, and the role of afforestation", *Journal of Ecology*, **75**, 797–824.

Forestry Commission (1991). *Forests and Water Guidelines*, Edinburgh.

Frick, K. G. and Herrmann, J. (1990). "Aluminium and pH effects on sodium-ion-regulation in mayflies", in *The Surface Waters Acidification Programme* (Ed. B. J. Mason), pp. 409–412, Cambridge University Press, Cambridge.

Friend, G. F. (1958). "Loch Doon Charr", *Annual Magazine, Ayrshire Angling Association*, **2**, 8–10.

Gibbs, D. C. and Longhurst, J. W. S. (1989). "Acid deposition abatement: assessing the environmental and economic impact of the UK flue gas desulphurisation programme", in *Acid Deposition: Sources, Effects and Controls* (Ed. J. W. Longhurst), pp. 309–321, British Library Technical Communications, London.

Grahn, O. (1986), "Vegetation structure and primary production in acidified lakes in south-western Sweden", *Experientia*, **42**, 465–470.

Hardie, R. P. (1940). *Ferox and Char in the Lochs of Scotland*, Oliver and Boyd, Edinburgh.

Harriman, R. (1989). "Patterns of surface water acidification in Scotland", in *Acidification in Scotland*, pp. 72–79, Scottish Development Department, Edinburgh.

Harriman, R. and Morrison, B. R. S. (1982), "Ecology of streams draining forested and non-forested catchments in an area of central Scotland subject to acid precipitation", *Hydrobiologia*, **88**, 251–263.

Harriman, R. and Wells, D. E. (1985). "Causes and effects of surface water acidification in Scotland", *Water Pollution Control*, **84**, 215–224.

Harriman, R., Morrison, B. R. S., Caines, L. A., Collen, P. and Watt, A. W. (1987). "Long-term changes in fish populations of acid streams and lochs in Galloway, southwest Scotland", *Water, Air and Soil Pollution*, **32**, 89–112.

Harriman, R., Gillespie, E. and Morrison, B. R. S. (1990). "Factors affecting fish survival in Scottish catchments", in *The Surface Water Acidification Programme* (Ed. B. J. Mason), pp. 343–355, Cambridge University Press, Cambridge.

Haya, K. and Waiwood, B. (1981). "Acid pH and chorionase activity of Atlantic salmon (*Salmo salar*) eggs", *Bulletin of Environmental Toxicology*, **27**, 7–12

Hörnström, E., Ekström, C. and Osama Duraini, M. (1984). "Effects of pH and different levels of aluminium on lake plankton in the Swedish west coast area", *Report, Institute of Freshwater Research, Drottningholm*, **61**, 115–127.

Howells, G., Dalziel, T. R. K. and Turnpenny, A. W. H. (1992). "Loch Fleet: liming to restore a brown trout fishery", *Environmental Pollution*, **78**, 131–139.

Lees, F. M., Tervet, D. J. and Burns, J. C. (1989). "A study of catchment acidification: interim report, 1980 to 1986", *Scottish Development Department*, ARD Report Series, Edinburgh.

Lewis, D. (1992). "Orimulsion's tarnished promise", *Geographical Magazine*, July 1992, 16–19.

Lindmark, G. K. (1985). "Sodium carbonate injected into sediment of acidified lakes: A case study of Lake Lilla Galtsjön treated in 1980", *Lake and Reservoir Management*, **1**, 89–93.

Lyell, J. W. L. (1873). *The Sportsman's Tourist and General Timetables and Guide to the Rivers, Lochs, Moors and Deerforests of Scotland, and to its Places of Natural, Historical and Antiquarian Interest*, Union Bank Buildings, Holborn Circus, London.

Lyle, A. A. and East, K. (1989). "Echo location of corixids in deep water in an acid loch", *Archiv für Hydrobiologie*, **115**, 161–170.

Maitland, P. S. (1992). "The status of Arctic charr, *Salvelinus alpinus* (L.), in southern Scotland: a cause for concern", *Freshwater Forum*, **2**, 212–228.

Maitland, P. S., Lyle, A. A. and Campbell, R. N. B. (1987). *Acidification and Fish in Scottish Lochs*, Institute of Terrestrial Ecology, Grange-over-Sands.

Maitland, P. S., May, L., Jones, D. H. and Doughty, C. R. (1991). "Ecology and conservation of arctic charr, *Salvelinus alpinus* (L.), in Loch Doon, an acidifying loch in south west Scotland", *Biological Conservation*, **55**, 167–197.

Morrison, B. (1989). "Freshwater life in acid streams and lochs", in *Acidification in Scotland*, pp. 82–91, Scottish Development Department, Edinburgh.

Morrison, B. R. S. and Harriman, R. (1992). "Fish populations and invertebrates in some headwaters of the Rivers Dee and Spey, 1983–85", *Scottish Fisheries Research Report* No. 53, HMSO, Edinburgh.

Muniz, J. P. (1984). "The effects of acidification on Scandinavian freshwater fish fauna", *Philosophical Transactions of the Royal Society of London*, **305**B, 517–528.

Muniz, J. P. (1991). "Freshwater acidification: its effects on species and communities of freshwater microbes, plants and animals", in *Acidic Deposition: Its Nature and Impacts* (Eds F. T. Last and R. Watling), pp. 227–254, Proceedings of the Royal Society of Edinburgh, 97B, Edinburgh.

Murphy, K. J., Miller, S. and Anderson, K. (1986). *Aquatic Vegetation of Loch Dee, Galloway 1986*, Department of Botany, University of Glasgow, Glasgow.

Nilssen, J. P., Ostdahl, T. and Potts, W. T. W. (1984). "Species replacements in acidified lakes: physiology, predation or competition?", *Report, Institute of Freshwater Research, Drottningholm*, **61**, 148–153.

Odén, S. (1968). "The acidification of air and precipitation and its consequences on the natural environment", *Swedish Natural Science Research Council, Ecology Committee, Bulletin* No. 1:68 (in Swedish).

OECD (1977). *The OECD (Organisation for Economic Cooperation and Development) Programme on Long Range Transport of Our Pollutants*, Paris.

Olem, H. (1991). *Liming Acidic Surface Waters*, Lewis Publishers, Chelsea, Michigan.

Orthofer, R. and Kienzl K. (1990). "Acidic precipitation and forest damage research in Austria", in *Acidic Precipitation* vol. 5 (Eds A. H. M. Bresser and W. Salomons), pp. 107–138, Springer Verlag, New York.

Patterson, G. and Morrison, B. R. S. (1993). *Invertebrate Animals as Indicators of Acidity in Upland Streams*, Field Book No. 13, Forestry Commission, Edinburgh.

Potts, W. T. W. and Fryer, G. (1979). "The effects of pH and salt content on sodium balance in *Daphnia magna* and *Acantholeberis curvirostris* (Crustacea: Cladocera)", *Journal of Comparative Physiology*, **129**, 289–294.

Potts, W. T. W., Talbot, C., Eddy, F. B. and Williams, M. (1990). "Sodium balance in adult salmon (*Salmo salar* L.) during migration from seawater to freshwater and to acid freshwater", in *The Surface Water Acidification Programme* (Ed. B. J. Mason), pp. 369–382, Cambridge University Press, Cambridge.

Raddum, G. G. and Fjellheim, A. (1984). "Acidification and early warning organisms in western Norway", *Verhandlungen der Internationalen Vereinigung für theoretische und angewandte Limnologie*, **22**, 1973–1980.

Raven, P. J. (1986). *Occurrence of Sphagnum moss in the sublittoral of several Galloway lochs, with particular reference to Loch Fleet*, Palaeoecology Research Unit, University College London, Working Paper No. 13.

Scheffe, R. D., De Pinto, J. V. and Bily, K. R. (1986). "Laboratory and field testing of dose calculation methods for neutralisation of Adirondack lakes", *Water, Air and Soil Pollution*, **31**, 799–807.

Scottish Office Agriculture and Fisheries Department (1992). *Annual Review*, Freshwater Fisheries Laboratory, Pitlochry.

Smith, A. M. (1990). "The ecophysiology of epilithic diatom communities of acid lakes in Galloway, southwest Scotland", *Philosophical Transactions of the Royal Society of London*, **327B**, 25–30.

Smith, R. (1872). *Air and Rain: The Beginnings of Chemical Climatology*, Longmans, Green & Co, London.

Söderlund, R. and Svensson, B. H. (1976). "The global nitrogen cycle", in *Nitrogen, Phosphorus and Sulfur – Global Cycles*, SCOPE Report 7, pp. 22–73, Ecological Bulletins No. 22, Swedish Natural Science Research Council, Stockholm.

Stephen, A. B. (1990). *Annual Report of the West Galloway Fisheries Trust 1989–90*, Newton Stewart.

Stones, J. H., Gee, A. S. and Wade, K. R. (1984). "The effects of acidification on the ecology of streams in the upper Tywi catchment in West Wales", *Environmental Pollution*, A, **35**, 125–157.

Sutcliffe, D. W. and Carrick, T. R. (1973). "Studies of mountain streams in the English Lake District. I. pH, calcium and the distribution of invertebrates in the River Duddon", *Freshwater Biology*, **3**, 437–462.

Sverdrup, H. U. (1985). "Calcite dissolution kinetics and lake neutralisation", PhD thesis, Lund Institute of Technology, Lund.

Swedish Ministry of Agriculture (1982). *Acidification Today and Tomorrow*, a Swedish study prepared for the 1982 Stockholm conference on the acidification of the environment, Stockholm.

Tervet, D. J. and Harriman, R. (1988). "Changes in pH and calcium after selective liming in the catchment of Loch Dee, a sensitive and rapid turnover loch in south-west Scotland", *Journal of Aquaculture and Fisheries Management*, **19**, 191–203.

Traquair, R. H. (1882). "On specimens of 'tailless' trout from Loch Enoch, in Kirkcudbrightshire", *Proceedings of the Royal Philosophical Society of Edinburgh*, **7**, 221–223.

Twitchen, J. D. (1990), "The physiological bases of resistance to low pH among aquatic insect larvae", in *The Surface Waters Acidification Programme* (Ed. B. J. Mason), pp. 413–419, Cambridge University Press, Cambridge.

Tyler, S. J. and Ormerod, S. J. (1992). "A review of the likely causal pathways relating the reduced density of breeding dippers *Cinclus cinclus* to the acidification of upland streams", *Environmental Pollution*, **78**, 49–55.

Vernon, J. (1989). "Technologies for control of sulphur dioxide emissions", in *Acid Deposition:*

Sources, Effects and Controls (Ed. J. W. S. Longhurst), pp. 287–299, British Library, Technical Communications, London.

Warfvinge, P. G., and Sverdrup, H. U. (1988). "Soil liming as a measure to mitigate acid runoff", *Water Resources Research*, **24**, 701–712.

Warren Spring Laboratory (1987). *United Kingdom Acid Rain Monitoring*, Stevenage, Herts.

Welsh Water (1986). *Acid Waters in Wales*, Welsh Water Authority, Brecon.

Witters, H. E., Vangenechten, J. H. D., Van Puymbroeck, S. and Vanderborght, O. L. J. (1984). "The effect of pH and aluminium on the Na-balance in an aquatic insect *Corixa punctata* (Illig)", in *Acid Deposition and the Sulphur Cycle* (Ed. O. L. J. Vanderborght), pp. 287–297, Royal Belgian Academy of Sciences, Letters and Fine Arts, Brussels.

Woodin, S. and Skiba, U, (1990). "Liming fails the acid test", *New Scientist*, 10 March, 50–54.

Zafiriou, O. C. and McFarland, M. (1981). "Nitric oxide from nitrate photolysis in the central equatorial Pacific", *Journal of Geophysical Research*, **86**, 3173–3182.

25

River Flow Regulation

D. J. GILVEAR

Department of Environmental Science, University of Stirling, Stirling, FK9 4LA, UK

INTRODUCTION

Although most of Scotland is characterized by high precipitation, a large number of river systems (an estimated 6628: Smith and Lyle, 1979) and many natural water bodies (an estimated 3798: Smith and Lyle, 1979), rising demands for water and power has led to the development of numerous river flow management schemes. The need for regulation and control is compounded by the spatial disparity between the wettest regions of Scotland and the areas of greatest demand for water (Smith, 1977). Scottish rivers also generally have small catchments and flashy regimes and rapidly show the effects of any rainfall deficiencies. On a typical Scottish highland river, summer flows may be less than 15% of the mean flow and floods over 300 times the magnitude of the dry weather flow; regimes are naturally more subdued, however, where large lochs lie on the stream network or peat blankets much of the catchment.

This review aims to assess the extent of flow regulation and control in Scotland and give an indication of the effects of river management schemes on river flows. It does not provide comprehensive coverage but attempts to give an insight into the history of river flow regulation in Scotland, where, why and how flows are manipulated, and the possible environmental consequences of such regulation.

EARLY FLOW REGULATION SCHEMES

Manipulation of the natural flow of rivers in Scotland goes back many centuries; for example, there are reports of vertical water mills on Scottish rivers in the 12th century (Shaw, 1984). Under the simplest arrangement water was diverted to these mills without the aid of a dam. Sometimes, however, dams diverted other streams in the catchment or dams were built across the main stream using boulders and peat blocks. Thus, by the late 16th century there were a number of relatively complex, if rather small, flow regulation schemes. For example, at Culross on the Firth of Forth, coal mining was only made possible by the provision of water for power, this being supplied by a late 16th century impoundment (Inzivier Dam) on the Torry Burn. By the early 17th century, two more dams had been constructed to supplement the water stored behind Inzivier Dam and an inter-basin transfer scheme implemented which

The Fresh Waters of Scotland: A National Resource of International Significance
Edited by P. S. Maitland, P. J. Boon and D. S. McLusky. © 1994 John Wiley & Sons Ltd

connected Loch Carnock to the Torry Burn. There were also a number of other flow regulation schemes prompted by rather more unusual activities. Loch Morlich, (on the Water of Luineag (Strathspey), was raised in the 17th century to facilitate the floating of timber down the river. Meanwhile, Lord Kames diverted water from the River Teith via a man-made channel on to the Stirling Carse to "float" peat blocks down the River Forth as part of a lowland reclamation project. Incidentally, this was one of the first incidents of river pollution recorded on the River Forth, the breakdown of the peat inducing oxygen depletion downstream within the river and estuary.

It was the arrival of the industrial revolution in Scotland that really prompted the need for river flow regulation. By 1813, for example, there were 29 mills on the White Cart in Strathclyde. Initially, simple weirs were constructed to provide a head of water for mills. In Central Scotland, numerous old weirs alongside mills can still be found on the lowland sections of the rivers Teith, Almond, Ericht, Tay and Allan. Large industrial mills, however, could not afford stoppages due to water shortages and so there was also the need for large headwater reservoirs or inter-basin transfer. Thus, water was diverted from the River Almond to Perth via a 6 km lade to provide water for the textile printing industry (Turner, 1958), while in Greenock a scheme involving an 8 km artificial channel, a major impounding reservoir and six ancillary dams was opened in 1827 to supply mills with water. Meanwhile, on the White Cart 900 acres (364 ha) of storage reservoirs had been created by 1810 in order to supply the large number of mills downstream. River flow regulation did not always involve increasing the surface area of lochs or creation of reservoirs. For example, Loch Leven was lowered 1.5 m in 1833 by means of a new cut and channelization in order to provide more land for agriculture and to improve flows within the River Leven.

The early development of river regulation schemes for water supply began in the late 18th and early 19th centuries in Scotland. For example, up until 1830 Aberdeen relied on wells, springs and a loch for its water supply. Between 1792 and 1851 the population rose from 25 000 to 72 000. As a result, in the 1830s water was pumped from the floodplain gravels of the River Dee. In 1850, abstraction from the River Dee itself was undertaken and by 1885 36.3×10^6 L d^{-1} (1×10^6 L d^{-1} = 11.57 L s^{-1}) was being abstracted. Similarly, Dundee relied upon two small reservoirs, known as South Pond and Clearwater Basin, but in 1869 an impounding reservoir was constructed at Crombie. Edinburgh's first impounding reservoir, designed by Thomas Telford, was completed in 1821 at Glencorse. A fine historical account of the supply of water to Edinburgh and its effect on river flows is provided by Sheil (1985).

The first example in Scotland of a public electricity supply powered by water is believed to have been developed by the monks at the Benedictine Abbey, Fort Augustus, in 1890. The first major commercial hydro-power development was constructed in 1896 by the British Aluminium Corporation to power a smelter on Loch Ness at Foyers. This was followed in the 1920s and 1930s by a 80 MW scheme on the River Tummel and the 100 MW Galloway scheme on the Kirkcudbright River Dee (see Chapter 17).

THE EXTENT, LOCATION AND TYPES OF FLOW REGULATION SCHEMES FOUND IN SCOTLAND

In a recent review paper of regulated rivers in the UK, Petts (1988a) identified 13 major regulated rivers and ranked the degree of regulation according to a number of

indices. The table was headed by three Scottish rivers – the Tay, Conon and Beauly
– and also included the River Tweed. The degree of flow regulation in Scotland is
also reflected in the fact that eight of the 10 largest reservoirs in the UK, ranked
according to capacity, are within Scotland. Table 25.1 lists the major regulated rivers
of Scotland (see also Figure 25.1a).

Within Scotland, river flow regulation has been accomplished according to a variety
of water resource and river management schemes. The primary function of flow
regulation has usually been for the needs of power generation, water supply (domes-

TABLE 25.1. Principal rivers of Scotland with flow
regulation and/or significant abstractions, 300 km
minimum drainage area: H–hydropower,
S–reservoir storage, A–abstraction, R–regulation
involving upstream storage. Areas based on River
Purification Board boundaries

Area/River	Type	Drainage area (km^2)
Highland		
Beauly	H	850
Conon	H	962
Spey	H A	2861
Helmsdale	R	551
Lochy	H	413
Glass	A	375
Shin	H	494
Moriston	H	394
Garry	H	361
Spean	H	312
Tay		
Tay	H	4587
Tummel	S	1717
Earn	H	782
North East		
Deveron	A	441
Dee	A	1844
Ugie	A	325
Tweed		
Tweed	S	4390
Whiteadder	S	503
Forth		
Leven	R	424
Teith	S	518
Solway		
Esk	S	495
Nith	S	799
Clyde		
Doon	H	323

466

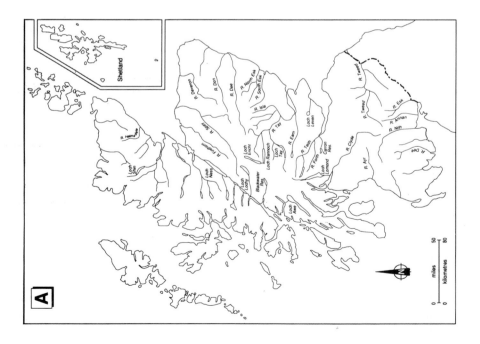

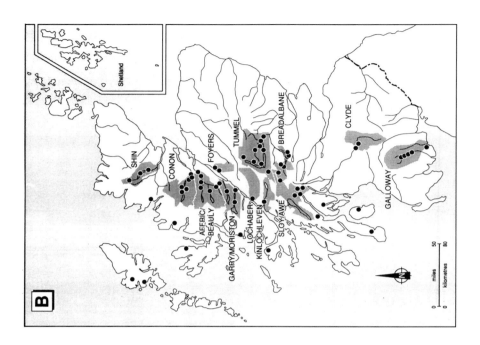

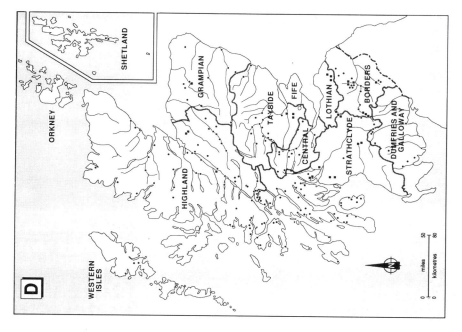

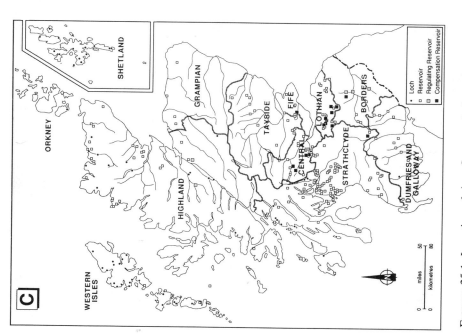

FIGURE 25.1. Location of river flow regulation schemes in Scotland. (a) principal rivers of Scotland, (b) catchments regulated for hydro-power and location of hydro-power stations, (c) location of water-supply reservoirs, (d) location of river (●) and spring (■) water supply abstractions

tic, industrial and agricultural) and flood management. Regulation by impoundment has had the most widespread and significant effect on natural river flows. In Tayside alone there are 77 large raised reservoirs with a volume exceeding 25 000 m^3 (Tayside Regional Council, 1991). In some cases the water levels of pre-existing natural lochs have been raised (Loch Benachally for water supply; Loch Tummel for hydro-power generation) and elsewhere new impoundments have been created (Loch Faskally and Loch Lyon for hydro-power generation; Carron Valley and Meggett Reservoir for water supply). In other circumstances, weirs have been constructed to restrict natural surface water level variations (Loch Earn). Flow regulation is also undertaken by inter-basin transfer (River Garry, Tayside, for hydro-power generation; River Black-water for water supply), direct abstractions from springs and rivers (River Deveron for water supply; West Peffer Burn for spray irrigation) and groundwater (Wrack extraction, Banff for water supply; Forfar for Strathmore Spring Waters). Examples of flood control strategies include flood embankment construction (River Tay), channelization (River Clyde), and floodplain storage (River Conon).

Hydro-power generation schemes

High run-off and relief in the north and west of Scotland has led to hydro-power schemes being implemented on most of the major rivers draining this region (Figure 25.1(b)). There are 11 major catchments with a total generating capacity of over 1000 MW (Johnson, 1988) and a small number of other schemes, primarily on the Western Isles. In total, the schemes comprise 65 major dams, over 200 diversion dams (resulting in inter-basin transfers of water) and approximately 600 km of tunnels, pipes and aqueducts to convey water between catchments and to power stations (see Chapter 17).

A typical hydro-power development – for example, the Tummel Valley scheme – (Figure 25.2a), involves an impounding reservoir, the diversion of run-off from other catchments to the impounding reservoir and, in this case, a high-level tunnel conveying water high above a power station where it descends before discharging to a river or loch at some distance downstream from the impounding reservoir. The high-level tunnel/pipeline may also intercept waters from streams that cross its path (Figure 25.2b). A pumped-storage form of hydro-power scheme is slightly different. Hydro-electricity is generated in the normal way during times of peak demand by allowing water from a high-level reservoir to pass through a power station via a pipeline to a lower-level water body. At times of low electricity demand, water is pumped back to the upper reservoir. Two schemes exist in Scotland: the Cruachan scheme on Loch Awe and the Foyers scheme on Loch Ness; both schemes discharge into lochs and not rivers.

Water supply schemes

Figures 25.1c and 25.1d show the locations of water supply reservoirs and river abstractions in Scotland, the two principal methods by which flow regulation is undertaken for water supply. River flows are also affected by abstractions from springs and lochs, and abstractions for spray irrigation and inter-basin transfer.

The principal method by which water supplies are obtained depends upon geographical location and this obviously has implications for river flows (Figure 25.3). For example, Grampian Region's water supply is primarily maintained by abstractions from rivers and springs while Lothian Region's water supply is mainly provided by three large impounding reservoirs (Figure 25.4). A typical water supply scheme using

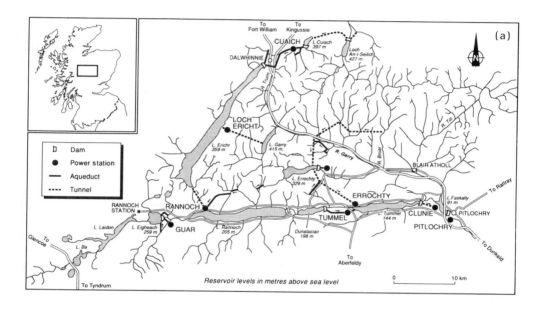

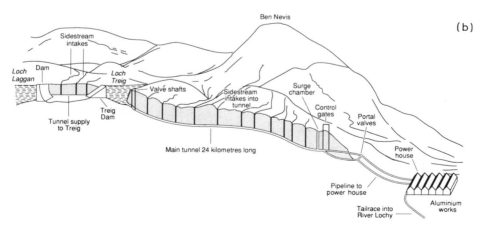

FIGURE 25.2. (a) The River Tummel hydro-electric scheme showing impoundments, power stations and inter-basin transfers. (b) Schematic diagram of the Kinlochleven hydro-electric scheme showing the extent to which flows from headwater tributaries are regulated by diversion dams.

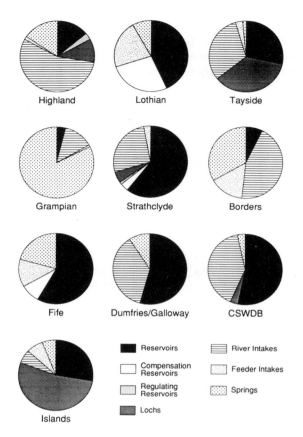

FIGURE 25.3. Spatial variability in water supply sources between Regional Council regions in Scotland (CSWDB: Central Scotland Water Development Board). Statistics are based on number of sources and not water yield (Scottish Office data)

impoundments is the one supplying water to Edinburgh. Talla Reservoir was constructed in 1906 and water supplied directly to Edinburgh by aqueduct; subsequently Fruid Reservoir was built impounding Fruid Burn in 1952. Water collected behind Fruid Dam is diverted to Talla Reservoir via a pipeline which also has an intake on the Menzion Burn (Figure 25.4). The latest stage was the completion of Megget Reservoir in 1983. In addition, water can now be pumped from St Mary's Loch back into Meggett Reservoir. Glasgow's water supply is dominated by abstractions from Loch Katrine, Loch Arklet and Glen Finglas Reservoir on the River Teith, the water being conveyed to Glasgow by two large aqueducts. Both Loch Katrine and Loch Arklet have been raised to increase storage (Crabb and Douglas, 1970).

Flood alleviation schemes

Flood alleviation in Scotland is accomplished primarily by flood warning schemes, together with channelization and flood embankments. Many embankments were initially constructed in the late 18th/early 19th centuries and included channel straight-ening and river diversions. For example, Young (1980) describes 18th century protection works on the River Findhorn and further improvements following a catastrophic flood in 1829. The effect of these works was to reduce the level of Loch Moy by 1.5 m, increase the gradient of the river and constrain a number of braided river channel reaches to a single channel. Reservoirs for hydro-power generation and water supply may also reduce flood magnitudes and frequencies but they are not operated specifically for flood alleviation. All the major rivers in Scotland have flood

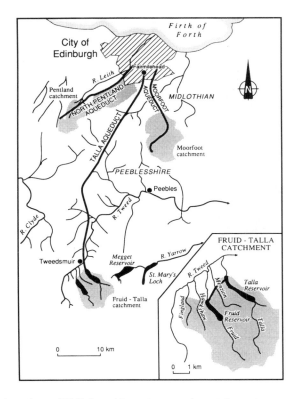

FIGURE 25.4. The location of Edinburgh's water supply catchments, reservoirs and regulated rivers

warning schemes and many of them are either channelized or are bounded by flood embankments, the aim of which is to prevent floodplain inundation during periods of high discharge. However, most of the flood embankments and channelization schemes have been unplanned and have not considered downstream hydrological effects. On the River Conon, due to repeated flood embankment breaches, floodplain storage is also utilized for flood control via a low-level overspill facility, installed in the flood embankment.

EFFECT OF RIVER REGULATION SCHEMES ON RIVER FLOWS AND RESERVOIR LEVELS

Hydro-power

Flood flows

Detailed knowledge of the exact effects of the various hydro-power schemes in Scotland on flood magnitude and frequency is limited because of a lack of data on pre-scheme flood discharges. Reservoirs, however, by virtue of storage capacity and impounded water surface area, attenuate floods and hence reduce their magnitude. Elsewhere in the United Kingdom, dams have been shown, on average, to reduce median flows by 50%, and mean annual floods by 30% (Petts and Higgs, 1988). The precise effect on flood flows will depend on the storage capacity of the reservoir in comparison to run-off from the upstream catchment.

Recently, a number of large floods on the major regulated rivers of Scotland have allowed estimates to be made of the flood alleviation effect of the various hydro-power schemes. Dunn (1989) reports that during the February 1989 floods on the River Conon the peak discharge was reduced by 13%, on the River Garry by 26% and on the River Moriston by 11%. Immediately below the Vaich Dam on the River Conon, Johnson (1990) estimated the peak flow reduction during the February 1989 flood to be 157%. On the Beauly River, upstream flows were stored without dam overspill in Loch Mullardoch and Loch Monar during the same storm in 1989 resulting in no flood flows immediately below the dam. Similarly, Gilvear (unpublished) estimated the flow during a flood on the 10th September 1992 above Loch Beinn a'Mheadhoin in Glen Affric to be 86 m^3 s^{-1}, and yet immediately below the dam the flow was effectively zero! For the River Spey it has been calculated that the Spey Dam would reduce a 1 in 5 year return-interval (RI) flood of 48 hours duration by 60% if empty but by 28% if full. (Cuthbertson and Partners, 1990). At Kincraig, 30 km downstream, only 18% of the catchment is regulated by impoundments and Cuthbertson and Partners calculated that only a 3% reduction in the flood peak of a 1 in 50 year RI flood would occur.

Figure 25.5 shows the effect of the Tummel valley hydro-power schemes on a small flood. Concomitant with three small flood peaks on the unregulated River Tilt, the only fluctuations apparent on the River Tummel below Pitlochry Dam are the daily changes due to hydro-power releases, the flood discharges being absorbed within the reservoir. During large flood events, however, the effects of hydro-power dams are less pronounced, although during the exceptional flood in January 1993 in the Tay catchment the peak run-off per unit area on the River Tummel was only 60% of the essentially unregulated River Garry.

Low flows

A survey of compensation flows below hydro-power dams in Scotland (Gustard, 1991) showed them to vary between 3.4% and 38.7% of mean daily flow with an average value of 13.7%. Gustard (1991) calculated that the average 95 percentile value on the flow duration curve was 18.5% of the mean annual flow for rivers influenced by hydro-

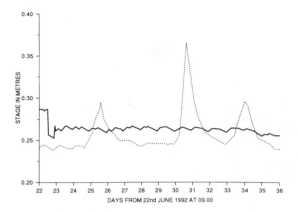

FIGURE 25.5. Comparison of stage changes on the unregulated River Tilt (dotted line) and downstream below Loch Faskally on the river Tummel (solid line) during July 1992 (see Figure 25.2a)

power, 10.7% for natural catchments with no storage and 14.95% for natural catchments with storage. However, values for rivers influenced by hydro-power varied between 6.3% and 30.65%. The primary effect of hydro-power reservoirs is therefore to enhance dry weather flows. On the River Tay, at its junction with the River Almond, it has been estimated that the lowest drought flow has been increased from 10.5 m³ s⁻¹ to 31.6 m³ s⁻¹ (Central Scotland Water Development Board, 1991).

The pattern of compensation flow throughout the year varies between reservoirs; 9.4% of compensation flows have constant discharge, 9.4% are constant discharge with freshets or block grants (see below), 6.2% have seasonally varying compensation flows, and 18.9% are seasonally varying with freshets and block grants. The other 56.1% maintain a constant or seasonally varying discharge at some point downstream and nearly all include freshets.

Compensation flows are not maintained below hydro-electric diversion dams on headwater tributaries (see Figures 25.2a and 25.2b). Except during very high flows and dam overspill there is no flow below the dam (Figure 25.6). In many cases, the flow from every headwater stream is diverted resulting in a substantial reduction in river flows throughout the stream network.

Hydro-power releases

Below hydro-power stations, large and rapid changes in river levels occur, often on a daily basis. Figure 25.7 shows the effects of hydro-power releases on the River Tummel below Rannoch Power Station. Generally in Scotland these hydro-power releases either enter lochs where the effect on water level fluctuations is small, or only affect limited river channel reaches. However, in some instances releases may result in significant changes in water level many kilometres downstream. Thus, on the River Tay the effects of hydro-power releases causing stage changes of 20 cm below Pitlochry Dam can still be detected at Caputh 29 km downstream and at the tidal limit of the river 60 km downstream (Figure 25.8).

FIGURE 25.6. The River Garry below the Trinafour HEP diversion dam. Photograph: D. J. Gilvear

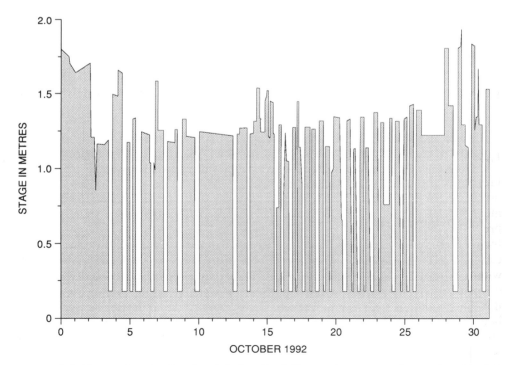

FIGURE 25.7. Fluctuations in river levels below Loch Rannoch power station during October 1992 (see Figure 25.2a)

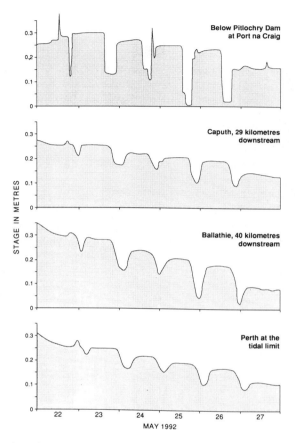

FIGURE 25.8. Fluctuations in river levels on the River Tay resulting from hydro-power releases from Loch Faskally (see Figure 25.2a)

Freshets

Freshets are a common characteristic of many regulated Scottish rivers, and are primarily released at the request of Fisheries Boards and Trusts. The normal agreement is that a "block grant" is allocated for freshets with a maximum release discharge prescribed, the releases being granted at the will of the fishing fraternity. Alternatively, a given number of freshets are allocated with an agreement on whether they can be released at any time throughout the year or only during a prescribed period within the year. The magnitude of freshets from hydro-power dams varies between 0.33% and 82.95% of mean daily flow and between 1.99 and 24.3 times compensation flow (average 7.78). A freshet on the River Garry maintained a stage increase of between 35 cm and 60 cm. Rates of water level change within the regulated river may also be rapid. Close to the dam during the River Garry freshet the period of increase was 13 minutes but 2.1 km downstream this was reduced to 8 minutes (Gilvear, 1987a). This wave-front steepening of freshets in boulder-bed reaches with high roughness has been seen to be a common phenomenon (Gilvear, 1989).

Water supply

Impounded rivers

Most of the reservoirs operated for water supply are of the direct-supply type. Downstream flows are maintained via a compensation flow, tributary inflows and occasionally dam overspill. Many of the earliest dams had by-pass channels to convey excess water around the reservoir thus reducing their effectiveness in attenuating flood flows; for example, Lambielthan Reservoir, Fife (constructed 1900). However, in general the effects of water supply reservoirs on reducing flood flows can only be beneficial, particularly with regard to reducing the magnitude and frequency of small and medium-sized floods.

An analysis of compensation flows from water supply reservoirs showed them to vary between 0.048 and 1.206 of the mean annual flow with a mean value of 0.293. Based on the work of Gustard *et al.* (1987) it is estimated that 75% of all water supply reservoirs have a constant compensation flow. Others have seasonally varying compensation flows with or without freshets, while a few have to maintain a seasonally varying prescribed flow downstream. Freshet releases are generally made available by a block grant allocation to be released over a specified number of months or at any time throughout the year. Freshet discharges vary between 33% and 136% of mean daily flow (3.3 to 40.1 times compensation flow). Perhaps the most enlightened compensation flow is that operated below Loch Lee, Tayside. It is usually set at 0.118 m^3 s^{-1} but this can be varied according to the natural flows inferred from the neighbouring Water of Mark tributary provided it is always in excess of 0.078 m^3 s^{-1}.

The Glenfarg Reservoir Scheme, Tayside, also illustrates the extent to which flows are controlled and diverted for water supply. The natural catchment area is 5.82 km^2 but this was increased to 11.60 km^2 at the time of the dam construction in 1926 by diverting water from the adjacent Slateford Burn, and subsequently by a further 12 km^2 through diversion of run-off from the Water of May. Of the run-off on Slateford Burn and the Water of May 28% is allocated for release as a compensation flow. The compensation flow below Glenfarg Reservoir is 3.0 ML d^{-1} compared to the 84 ML d^{-1} that enters Fife's water supply. Water can also be added to Glenfarg Reservoir at a rate of 15 ML d^{-1} via pumping and a 11.5 km pipeline from the River Earn.

River and spring abstractions

Abstractions are generally small in relation to the mean annual flow and will only have a significant effect on total flow during periods of low flow. The largest river abstractions are 90 ML d^{-1} on the River Glass (Highland Region), 70 ML d^{-1} (Cairnton) and 75 ML d^{-1} (Inchgarth) on the River Dee, 30 ML d^{-1} on the River Deveron (both Grampian Region) and 27 ML d^{-1} on the River Tay. The rising demand for water has necessitated increasing abstractions from rivers. This is well exemplified in the case of the River Dee (Brown, 1985). Figure 25.9 shows the rise in actual and allowable abstraction on the River Dee between 1829 and 1980. The maximum rate of 145 ML d^{-1} (1.678 m^3 s^{-1} equates with 16.78% of the Q90 flow at Woodend. 1992 was also the "green light" year for abstraction to go ahead from a

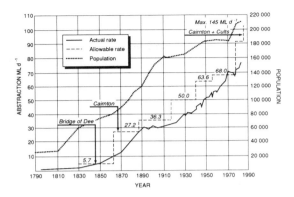

FIGURE 25.9. Increase in water supply abstraction from the River Dee due to increasing demand (1800–1990)

wellfield in the alluvial gravels adjacent to the River Spey just south of Fochabers, at a cost of £26 million. It has been deemed that the abstraction scheme will have little impact on dry weather flows (Mackie-Dawson *et al.*, 1988) but a regional lowering of the floodplain water tables could induce leakage of river water to the floodplain and a downstream reduction in discharge. It is difficult to quantify the effects of the many small abstractions on headwater streams or springs due to the lack of gauging on headwater streams, but although an individual abstraction may be considered insignificant, the cumulative effect of abstractions on downstream flows and river ecology is more difficult to assess. Generally, abstractions for water supply maintain reasonable residual flows downstream.

Flood alleviation schemes

In the context of this chapter, this section examines the extent to which channelization and flood embankment construction has altered flow characteristics and the frequency of floodplain inundation. Certainly the construction of floodbanks on most of the lowland sections of the major rivers of Scotland has reduced the frequency of floodplain inundation, and elsewhere this has occurred through channel bed steepening or channel enlargement. Thus, on the River Nith, after a severe flood in 1982, 2500 m³ of gravel was removed from the channel to increase its bankfull capacity. On the Rivers Nairn, Spey and Tay and elsewhere in Scotland, flood alleviation has involved the removal of meanders and channel steepening, resulting in an increase in the velocity of flood flows. Flood embankment construction has also reduced the time of travel of flood peaks and increased flood peaks downstream owing to the removal of floodplain storage. On the River Tay during the flood of 6 February 1990, a flood embankment breach and inundation of 13 km² of floodplain at Caputh reduced the velocity of the flood peak from above 5 km hr⁻¹ upstream to 1.5 km hr⁻¹ downstream, with a concomitant attenuation of the flood hydrograph (Gilvear, unpublished). During a similar flood in January 1974, when breaching did not occur, the velocity of the flood peak upstream was the same as in 1990, but the downstream flood wave velocity was 8.8 km hr⁻¹. It is estimated that the floodplain inundation at Caputh in

February 1990 reduced the peak discharge at Ballathie by at least 250 m^3 s^{-1} (Babtie, *et al.*, 1990); at Caputh the peak discharge was 1747 m^3 s^{-1} and yet 11 km downstream at Ballathie where the catchment area is 30% greater the peak discharge only increased to 1750 m^3 s^{-1}. Given the ability of floodplain storage to regulate flows full consideration should be given to containing flood waters by channel enlargement and floodplain storage rather than flood embankment construction which can exacerbate flooding downstream.

Occasionally, urban encroachment has reduced channel capacity. In Dumfries on the River Nith, the width of the old bridge decreased from nine to six arches between 1819 and 1850, and approximately 2.7 ha of land has been reclaimed from the margins of the Nith since the early 19th century (Werritty and Acreman, 1985). This will have resulted in higher flood levels and flow velocities for a given discharge through this section of river, increasing the flood risk.

ENVIRONMENTAL EFFECTS OF FLOW REGULATION IN SCOTLAND

Given the extent of flow regulation in Scotland it is surprising that there has been a dearth of Scottish studies examining its environmental effects. This is in striking contrast to England and Wales where a large number of such studies have been carried out in the last 15 years. Useful reviews of the environmental effects of flow regulation in the UK can be found in the journal *Regulated Rivers*, Volume 2, and Langford (1983). This section examines the few Scottish studies and uses findings from other UK work to provide an insight into the possible environmental implications of flow regulation.

Geomorphology

Reservoir sedimentation

Reservoir and diversion dams not only regulate flows but also trap sediments and interrupt the natural movement of sediment downstream. A number of studies have examined sedimentation within Scottish reservoirs (Table 25.2) and these can be used to assess its significance. Rarely has sedimentation led to important losses of storage capacity. For example, Glenfarg and Glenquey Reservoirs in the Ochil Hills have lost only 2.5% and 1.1% of their original storage in 56 and 73 years respectively (Duck and McManus, 1988). However, Dunoon Number 3 Reservoir, Argyll, with a capacity of 9100 m^3, impounded in 1920, underwent slow sedimentation for 40–45 years but subsequently was infilled within 15 years as a result of catchment afforestation (see Chapter 23), the dam being removed in 1982 (Duck and McManus, 1988). Many diversion dams are also periodically infilled and have to be excavated. Richards and McCaig (1985) calculated that 86 m^3 yr^{-1} (25.5 t km^{-2} yr^{-1} – by no means an excessive erosion rate for upland catchments) of sediment was trapped behind check dams above intake No. 11, part of the British Aluminium Company hydro-power scheme at Fort William, on the Allt a 'Mhuillin. The intake itself is annually purged of sediment by sluicing.

TABLE 25.2. Catchment sediment yield derived from reservoir sedimentation studies in Scotland

Catchment yield ($t\ km^{-2}\ yr^{-1}$)	Reservoir	Study
26	North Esk Reservoir, Midlothian	Lovell *et al.*, 1973
41	Kelly Reservoir, Strathclyde	Ledger *et al.*, 1980
9	Glenquey Reservoir, Tayside	McManus and Duck, 1985
60	Glenfarg Reservoir, Tayside	McManus and Duck, 1985

Channel changes

Petts (1980) showed that, in a response to a reduction in flood magnitude and frequency on five impounded rivers in the Southern Uplands, channel capacities were reduced to between 0.16 and 0.54 of their pre-impoundment size over distances of up to 5.5 km below the dam. Immediately downstream from Camps Reservoir (Camps Water) and Leadhills Dam (Elvan Water), clearwater erosion has been observed, but further downstream the river channel width is narrower than before impoundment. The impounded River Tummel has also changed from a braided planform to a meandering planform over the last 200 years but this relates more to flood embankment construction (Gilvear and Winterbottom, 1992).

Reduction in channel capacity occurs principally by the deposition of sediment injected from unregulated tributaries as a result of the reduced competence of the regulated river to transport sediment. Thus, on the River Cannich below Mullardoch Reservoir, tributary junctions are characterized by lobate sediment accumulations within the regulated river. Similarly, below the junction of the unregulated Portail Water and the regulated Daer Water, former pools have been completely infilled due to impoundment upstream (Petts, 1988b). Further downstream on Daer Water, siltation of the substrate was observed with an increase in the percentage of fines (< 2 mm) in the substrate from a natural value of 14% to 25%, and an allied change in the benthic invertebrate community was also observed (Petts, 1988b). This siltation may also adversely affect redds and fish spawning. On the Allt Cuaich, and the Rivers Garry and Truim in Tayside there has been an increase in the percentage of sand blanketing the substrate below hydro-power intakes (Armitage and Petts, 1992). These examples of channel change support the findings of numerous other studies in England and Wales with regard to the geomorphological response of rivers to impoundment (Carling, 1988).

Water quality

Few studies have specifically examined the effects of inter-basin transfers of water and/or impoundment on downstream water quality in Scotland. Certainly, the transfer of water from catchments of markedly different geology, and storage within reservoirs with a long residence time, must affect water quality. Compensation flows above those of the natural dry weather flow will have a beneficial effect on polluted waters, as a result of dilution, but reservoir storage effects or waters collected from other catchments may result in the water being different from the natural low-flow water chemistry. In unpolluted waters, excessive abstraction may lead to deoxygenation by creating shallow, relatively still-water environments (Tay River Purification Board, 1989).

Water quality changes may also occur as a result of reservoir releases and freshets (Petts *et al.*, 1985). Foulger and Petts (1984) showed that the primary effect was to reduce solute concentrations downstream although a short-lived pulse of higher solute concentrations may exist at the time of arrival of the reservoir release at any point downstream. Thus, releases have been made from Castlehill Reservoir on the River Devon to provide dilution during pollution incidents. Similarly, Gilvear (1987b) showed that high turbidity and suspended solids concentrations are typical in reservoir releases for up to two or three hours after the beginning of a release in United Kingdom rivers, particularly where the time since the last release has been lengthy. McDonald *et al.* (1982) have warned of high bacteria concentrations in early release waters from their study of the River Washburn in Yorkshire. Precise water quality and temperature effects are obviously related to whether the waters are derived from the hypolimnion or epilimnion.

Few studies have been undertaken in the UK on the effects of impoundment and river flow regulation on river water temperatures (Lavis and Smith, 1972). This situation contrasts with that of certain other countries, where studies have shown that dam construction may have ecologically significant effects, particularly for projects with a large storage capacity in relation to seasonal discharge. The principal effect of flow regulation by impoundment in the UK is to suppress the natural range of variability of stream water temperatures, both over seasonal and daily timescales (Lavis and Smith, 1972), although artificial flow fluctuations can induce sudden alterations to river water temperature (Petts *et al.*, 1985; Cowx *et al.*, 1987; Webb and Walling, 1988). Artificially induced low flows may also result in unnaturally warm river temperatures in the summer months.

Ecology

Invertebrates

A study of the effects of flow regulation on invertebrate communities in the UK examined five Scottish rivers regulated by hydro-power and affected by spray irrigation abstractions (Armitage and Petts, 1992). No noticeable differences between the invertebrate communities sampled and those expected if the river had been unregulated were found below the hydro-power schemes. On the West Peffer Burn, affected by spray irrigation, changes in invertebrate communities were apparent but the precise effects of the abstractions could not be ascertained because of the problem of disentangling the effects of poor river water quality on the invertebrate populations (Petts, 1991). Studies elsewhere in the UK, however, have shown flow regulation by impoundment and inter-basin transfer to have a significant effect on invertebrate communities (Boon, 1988). Alterations in community structure usually reflect changes in flow, substrate, temperature and water quality. In particular, adverse effects on invertebrates within impounded rivers have been attributed to a reduction in spatial heterogeneity in channel and flow characteristics together with siltation.

Fisheries

Fisheries are affected in at least five important ways by flow regulation schemes: dams obstruct the ascent of fish to their spawning gravels; reservoirs may inundate spawning gravels; river water quality may be affected by inter-basin transfers of water and/or by thermal and chemical stratification in reservoirs; natural flows downstream will be altered; and dams prevent young migratory fish (i.e. smolts) descending to the sea. In addition, indirect affects such as disruption of the food-webs downstream, drying out of redds, stranding of fish during rapid flow fluctuations and siltation of spawning gravels due to the absence of high flows can have adverse affects.

Examples of all these problems can be found in Scottish rivers but in many cases steps have been taken to ameliorate the worst effects. For example, fish ladders and Borland fish lifts have been installed on most Scottish Hydro-Electric storage reservoirs and elsewhere where impoundments have prevented upstream migration of fish. In addition, modification of waterfalls on other tributaries has been carried out to allow upstream migration (e.g. Rivers Lochay and Braan). Struthers (1991) refers to low mortalities of smolt-sized Trout migrating downstream through turbines installed in a low head hydro-power dam (10 m) at Lairg, and Salmon smolt losses through the Pitlochry Dam turbines (15 m). However, on higher head Cashlie Power Station in Glen Lyon around 55% mortality was recorded (Munro, 1965).

Mills (1991) also reports that fish seeking to return to "home waters" may stray because of inter-basin transfers and cites the River Conon as an example, where some water from the River Meig is released via a power station. Unnatural water temperatures may also be important with regard to hatching and as a trigger for fish migration.

Many aspects of river flow regulation and its impact on salmonid fisheries are important, in Scotland, and are covered in Langford (1983) and Mills (1991). Attempts to quantify the varied flow requirements for fish in Scottish rivers have been rare. In some cases compensation flows may be set too high, whereas on other rivers it is obvious that there is too little flow. Baxter (1961) proposed variable compensation flows below dams, based on a study of the seasonal needs of fish in 15 UK rivers (Table 25.3). These recommendations have been adopted below several Lothian reservoirs (e.g. Fruid Reservoir) but further work is needed to assess the precise requirements of Scottish fish stocks.

Aquatic vegetation

Many of the regulated rivers in Scotland have a subdued flow regime in the lower reaches with reduced frequency of floods and elevated low flows. Within these rivers, the standing crop may be increased and higher plants such as Alternate Water-milfoil, *Myriophyllum alterniflorum*, and Bulbous Rush, *Juncus bulbosus*, often thrive. However, in reaches experiencing rapid daily fluctuations in flow, wetting and drying

TABLE 25.3. Schedule of flows proposed by Baxter (1961) for
Atlantic Salmon in Scottish streams

Month	For the smaller rivers and streams (% mean daily flow)	For larger rivers (% mean daily flow)
October	15–12.5	15–12.5
November	25	15
December	25–12.5	15–10
January	12.5	10
February	12.5	10
March	20	15
April	25	20
May	25	20
June	25–20	20–15
July	20–15	15–12.5
August	15	15–12.5
September	15–12.5	15–12.5

Where two values are given the flows should alternate on a weekly
basis. The guidelines may need to be varied according to spawning
times, etc. See Baxter (1961) for full details

cycles, and the scouring effect of releases, the standing crop may be reduced. This is
obviously a gross simplification, however, and no studies have yet examined the effect
of river regulation in Scotland on aquatic macrophytes.

FLOW REGULATION IN A CHANGING ENVIRONMENT

Climate change

Many of the flow regulation operational procedures were designed before 1965 and
were based on limited flow data; since the 1960s the length of flow records and number
of gauging sites has increased. In addition, a number of recent studies have demonstrated that flow regimes in Scottish rivers are not remaining constant. For example,
Smith and Bennett (in press) have shown increases in annual run-off since 1970 on
the Rivers Findhorn, Dee, Tay, Clyde, Nith and Teviot. On the River Dee at
Woodend (Aberdeen), mean flow has increased from 30 to 42 m^3 s^{-1} between 1970
and 1989 – an increase of 40%. This is correlated with a rise in the mean annual
rainfall for Scotland from 1270 mm in the 1970s to 1445 mm in the 1980s; this
constitutes the largest increase between decades in rainfall over Scotland in the last
60 years. Determining changes in flood magnitude–frequency relationships is more
problematic, but on the River Forth at least one flood in each of the years 1989, 1990,
1991 and 1992 exceeded the magnitude of the largest flood in the preceding 16 years
of gauging. Similarly, on the River Tay floods that occurred in February 1990 and
January 1993 ranked in the top six or seven since 1800.

   These changes are reflected in the outflows from a number of regulation schemes.
Gleick (1990) has shown that the sensitivity of water resource systems to climatic

fluctuations depends upon the ratio of storage volume to the quantity of run-off. Thus, on the highly regulated Loch Katrine storage system which supplies water to Glasgow, the reservoirs were full or spilling for an average of 4.2 weeks per year during the 1970s, but this increased to an average of 8 weeks during the 1980s (Smith and Bennett, in press). Also, on the relatively small Loch Faskally, the total volume of water spilled to the River Tummel increased by almost 238% between the 1970s and the 1980s and yet on the larger Loch Eigheach the increase was only 40% (Smith and Bennett, in press) (Figure 25.10).

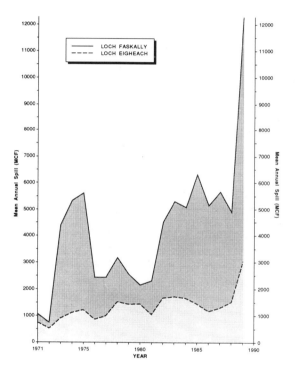

FIGURE 25.10. Reservoir overspill volumes (MCF = Million Cubic Feet) from Lochs Faskally and Eigheach (after Smith and Bennett, in press)

These changes in river flows and the duration of reservoirs at spillweir level have important consequences for water resources and flood management. The increase in uncontrolled spillage of waters represents a loss in potential revenue to the power companies and a loss of water potentially available for supply. Conversely, the increase in the duration of reservoirs at spillweir level represents reduced flood storage and an increase in the magnitude of flood events downstream. Given that the climatic scenarios for Scotland are wetter winters (Arnell *et al.*, 1991; UK Climatic Change Impacts Review Group, 1991), there is a need for an evaluation of current operational flow procedures (see Chapter 19).

Environmental awareness

Flow regulation in Scotland has been undertaken so far without full consideration of the possible environmental effects; serious attention has only been given to the needs for fish migration. Fortunately, rather by luck than judgement, many of the schemes appear not to have resulted in severe downstream degradation. However, because of the paucity of Scottish environmental impact studies and because there is so little pre-flow regulation environmental information, the precise effects of schemes are not known.

There is now an increasing body of scientific information that should be used in the design of new schemes to mitigate most of the environmental impacts of flow regulation (Gore and Petts, 1989). Such information could also be used to revise present flow regulation schemes and operational procedures to restore rivers that have been degraded. There has been considerable research into instream flow requirements for the protection of aquatic organisms (Bullock *et al.*, 1991) and methods have been designed for managing river abstractions and protecting the environment (Drake and Sheriff, 1988). For example, the author believes that the rates of stage rise and fall of reservoir releases and freshets should "mimic" those of the natural river, and that "flushing flows" should periodically be released in regulated rivers that do not (at least occasionally) receive high flows, to prevent excessive stream bed siltation.

More generally, a comprehensive and integrated approach to river management (see Chapter 31), together with the necessary legislation (Brown and Howell, 1992), and a review of instream flow requirements and water resource operational procedures, would bring benefits in terms of the "wise" use of water resources, hazard protection and river conservation. There are some encouraging signs, for example Scottish Hydro-Electric's formulation of environmental guidelines (see Chapter 17), but much more needs to be done. With the establishment of Scottish Natural Heritage, the imminent arrival of the Scottish Environment Protection Agency and the possibility of water privatization, not to mention the recent and possibly long-term alteration in river flow regimes, now is scarcely the time to evaluate the success of Scotland's river regulation schemes.

ACKNOWLEDGEMENTS

I acknowledge the support of numerous staff in the Scottish Office, Regional Councils and River Purification Boards who took time to provide me with information. I also wish to acknowledge the work of Alan Gustard and colleagues at the Institute of Hydrology on compensation flows in Scotland; without access to their work analysis of the effects of flow regulation on river flows would have been a much more onerous task. The excellent diagrams are due to the efforts of Bill Jamieson within the Department of Environmental Science, University of Stirling.

REFERENCES

Armitage, P. D. and Petts, G. E. (1992). "Biotic score and prediction to assess the effects of water abstractions on river macroinvertebrates for conservation purposes", *Aquatic Conservation: Marine and Freshwater Ecosystems*, **2**, 1–17.

Arnell, N. W., Brown, R. P. C. and Reynard, N. S. (1991). *Impact of Climatic Variability and Change of River Flow Regimes in the UK*, Institute of Hydrology, Wallingford.

Babtie, Shaw and Morton (1990). *Flooding in the River Tay Catchment, Volume 1*, Report to Tayside Regional Council, Glasgow.

Baxter, G. (1961). "River utilisation and the preservation of migratory fish life", *Proceedings of the Institution of Civil Engineers*, **18**, 225–244.

Boon, P. J. (1988). "The impact of river regulation on invertebrate communities in the UK", in *Regulated Rivers: Research and Management*, **2**, 389–409.

Brown, A. E. and Howell D. L. (1992). "Conservation of rivers in Scotland: Legislative and organizational limitations", in *River Conservation and Management* (Eds P. J. Boon, P. Calow and G. E. Petts), pp. 407–424, John Wiley, Chichester.

Brown, I. D. (1985). "Water abstraction from the River Dee", in *The Biology and Management of the River Dee* (Ed. D. Jenkins), pp. 407–424, Institute of Terrestrial Ecology, Abbots Ripton.

Bullock, A., Gustard, A. and Grainger, E. S. (1991). *Instream Flow Requirements of Aquatic Ecology in Two British Rivers*, Report No. 115, Institute of Hydrology, Wallingford.

Carling, P. A. (1988), "Channel change and sediment transport in regulated U.K. rivers", in River regulation in the United Kingdom (Eds G. E. Petts and R. Woods), *Regulated Rivers: Research and Management*, **2**, 389–409.

Central Scotland Water Development Board (1991). *Note on proposed scheme for an interregional water supply scheme based on the River Tay*, Glasgow.

Crabb, P. and Douglas, I. (1970). "Water resources management in South West Perthshire", *Scottish Geographical Magazine*, **87**, 203–207.

Cowx, I. G., Young, W. O. and Booth, J. B. (1987). "Thermal characteristics of two regulated rivers in Mid Wales", *Regulated Rivers, Research and Management*, **1**, 85–92.

Cuthbertson, R. H. and Partners (1990). *Flooding in Badenoch and Strathspey*, Report to Highland Regional Council, Volume 1, Edinburgh.

Drake, P. J. and Sheriff, J. D. F. (1988). "A method for managing river abstractions and protecting the environment", *Journal of Water and Environmental Management*, **24**, 27–38.

Duck, R. and McManus, J. (1988). "Sediment yields in lowland Scotland derived from reservoir surveys", *Transactions of the Royal Society of Edinburgh; Earth Sciences*, **78**, 369–377.

Dunn, J. B. (1989). "Philosophy and application of flood control in the Northern Hydro Group", in *East Highlands Floods Symposium, Dingwall, Scotland, SHG, ICE, 27th October 1989*, pp. 1–15, Glasgow.

Foulger, T. R. F. and Petts, G. E. (1984). "Water quality implications of artificial flow fluctuations in regulated rivers", *The Science of The Total Environment*, **37**, 177–185.

Gilvear, D. J. (1987a), "Sediment transport in regulated rivers", Unpublished PhD thesis, University of Loughborough.

Gilvear, D. J. (1987b). "Suspended solids transport within regulated rivers experiencing periodic reservoir releases", in *Regulated Streams, Advances in Ecology* (Eds J. F. Craig and J. B. Kemper), pp. 245–256, Plenum, New York.

Gilvear, D. J. (1989), "Experimental analysis of reservoir release wave routing in upland boulder bed rivers", *Hydrological Processes*, **3**, 261–276.

Gilvear, D. J. and Winterbottom, S. J. (1992). "Channel changes and flood events since 1783 on the regulated river Tay, Scotland: Implications for flood hazard management", *Regulated Rivers: Research and Management*, **7**, 247–260.

Gleick, P. H. (1990). "Vulnerability of water systems", in *Climate Change and US Water Resources* (Ed. P. E. Waggoner), pp. 223–240, John Wiley, Chichester.

Gore, J. and Petts, G. E. (1989). *Alternatives in Regulated River Management*, Butterworths, Boston.

Gustard, A. (1991). "The impact of hydropower development on river flow regimes", Paper presented at *Hydrology and Water Power Development Meeting, British Hydrological Group/ Scottish Hydrological Group, June 14th 1991*.

Gustard, A., Cole, G., Marshall, D. and Bayliss, A. (1987). *A Study of Compensation Flows in the U.K.*, Report No. 99, Institute of Hydrology, Wallingford.

Johnson, F. G. (1988), "Hydropower in Scotland", in River regulation in the United Kingdom, (Eds G. E. Petts and R. Woods), *Regulated Rivers: Research and Management*, **2**, 277–92.

Johnson, F. G. (1990). *Water and Flood Management on Hydro Schemes*, The Peter McCrae Lecture, Scottish Hydraulics Study Group.

Langford, T. E. (1983). *Electricity Generation and the Ecology of Natural Waters*, Liverpool University Press, Liverpool.

Lavis, M. E. and Smith, K. (1972). "Reservoir storage and the thermal regime of rivers, with special reference to the River Lune, Yorkshire", *The Science of the Total Environment*, **1**, 81–90.

Ledger, D. C., Lovell, J. P. B. and Cuttle, S. P. (1980). "Rate of sedimentation in Kelly Reservoir, Strathclyde", *Scottish Journal of Geology*, **16**, 281–285.

Lovell, J. P. B., Ledger, D. C., Davies, I. M. and Tipper, J. C. (1973). "Rate of sedimentation in the North Esk Reservoir, Midlothian", *Scottish Journal of Geology*, **9**, 57–61.

McDonald, A., Kay, D. and Jenkins, A. (1982). "Generation of fecal and total coliform surges by stream flow manipulation in the absence of normal hydrometeorological stimuli", *Applied and Environmental Microbiology*, **44**, 292–300.

Mackie-Dawson, L. A., Walker, A. D., Atkinson, D. and Bibby, J. A. (1988). "Water abstraction from the River Spey area for domestic and agricultural purposes and its effects on agriculture", *Scottish Geographical Magazine*, **104**, 91–96.

McManus, J. and Duck, R. W. (1985). "Sediment yield estimated from reservoir siltation in the Ochil Hills, Scotland", *Earth Surface Processes and Landforms*, **10**, 193–200.

Mills, D. (1991). *Ecology and Management of Atlantic Salmon*, Chapman and Hall, London.

Munro, W. R. (1965). *Fish Migration in Scotland, Freshwater Fisheries Laboratory Working Paper*, Pitlochry.

Petts, G. E. (1980). "Implications of the fluvial process–channel morphology interaction below British reservoirs for stream habitats", *The Science of the Total Environment*, **16**, 149–163.

Petts, G. E. (1988a). "Regulated rivers in the United Kingdom", *Regulated Rivers: Research and Management*, **2**, 201–220.

Petts, G. E. (1988b). "Accumulation of fine sediment within substrate along two regulated rivers, U.K.", *Regulated Rivers: Research and Management*, **2**, 141–153.

Petts, G. E. (1991). "Environmental effects of abstractions: catchwater systems for hydro power in Scotland", Paper presented at *Hydrology and Water Power Development Meeting, British Hydrological Group/Scottish Hydrological Group, June 14th 1991*.

Petts, G. E. and Higgs, G. (1988). "Hydrological changes and river regulation in the UK", *Regulated Rivers: Research and Management*, **2**, 349–368.

Petts, G. E., Foulger, T. T., Gilvear, D. J., Pratts, J. D. and Thoms, M. C. (1985). "Wave-movement and water-quality variations during a controlled release from Kielder Reservoir, North Tyne River, U.K.", *Journal of Hydrology*, **80**, 371–389.

Richards, K. and McCaig, M. (1985). "A medium-term estimate of bedload yield in Allt a'Mhuillin, Ben Nevis, Scotland", *Earth Surface Processes and Landforms*, **10**, 407–411.

Shaw, J. (1984). *Water Power in Scotland*, John Donald Publishers, Edinburgh.

Sheil, J. (1985). "Edinburgh, the Upper Tweed, and the question of compensation water", *Scottish Geographical Magazine*, **101**, 66–76.

Smith, I.R. and Lyle, A.A. (1979). *Distribution of Freshwaters in Great Britain*, Institute of Terrestrial Ecology, Cambridge.

Smith, K. (1977). "Water resource management in Scotland", *Scottish Geographical Magazine*, **93**, 66–79.

Smith, K. and Bennett, A. (in press). "Recently increased wetness in Scotland: Effects of flow hydrology and some implications for water management", *Applied Geography*.

Struthers, G. (1991). "Fish and fishery requirements associated with hydro-electric stations, including facilities for upstream and downstream migration", Paper presented at *Hydrology and Water Power Development Meeting, British Hydrological Group/Scottish Hydrological Group, June 14th 1991*.

Tayside Regional Council (1991). *Water Services Annual Report*, Dundee.

Tay River Purification Board (1989). *Annual Report*, Perth.

Turner, W.H.K. (1958). "The significance of water power in industrial location: some Perthshire examples", *Scottish Geographical Magazine*, **74**, 98–115.

UK Climatic Change Impacts Review Group (1991). *The Potential Effects of Climate Change in the United Kingdom*, HMSO, London.

Webb, B.W. and Walling, D.E. (1988). "Modification of temperature behaviour through regulation of a British river system", *Regulated Rivers: Research and Management*, **2**, 103–116.

Werritty, A. and Acreman, M.C. (1985). "The flood hazard in Scotland", in *Climatic Hazards in Scotland*, (Ed. S.J. Harrison), pp. 25–40, Royal Scottish Geographical Society, University of St Andrews.

Young, J.A.T. (1980). "19th century flood protection schemes around Loch Moy, Inverness-shire", *Scottish Geographical Magazine*, **96**, 166–172.

26

Management of Fish Populations

R. N. CAMPBELL

Tigh-Ur, Bonskeid, Pitlochry, PH16 5NP, UK

P. S. MAITLAND

Fish Conservation Centre, Easter Cringate, Stirling, FK7 9QX, UK

and

R. N. B. CAMPBELL

The Tweed Foundation, Drygrange, Melrose, TD6 9DJ, UK

INTRODUCTION

The management of fish populations in Scotland has had a turbulent history and the present situation is far from satisfactory. Piecemeal legislation, unscientific management by riparian owners, the high value of Salmon fishing overshadowing the value of other species, pressures from poaching and the total absence of a national structured system for fish population management and for angling have led to the present unsatisfactory situation. This chapter deals with the history of fishery management in Scotland from the earliest times to the present; modern management practices and possible future scenarios are reviewed. Common names only are used here; scientific names of all species mentioned are given elsewhere (see Chapter 11, Table 11.1).

Much of the present-day distribution of freshwater fishes in Scotland is the result of re-distribution by humans, for many reasons, intentional and otherwise. However, some natural re-distribution must have taken place also as a result of post-glacial changes in land levels, melting of ice dams and by river capture – though the latter would probably only have affected those stenohaline species living in fast-flowing head waters, such as Minnows, Stone Loach and Bullhead. Presumably at times, some great natural catastrophes must have taken place, such as flooding on a massive scale, resulting in the formation of temporary lakes which might have allowed the colonization of hitherto isolated river systems across low watersheds.

The Fresh Waters of Scotland: A National Resource of International Significance
Edited by P. S. Maitland, P. J. Boon and D. S. McLusky. © 1994 John Wiley & Sons Ltd

The freshwater fish fauna of Scotland is substantially impoverished compared with the communities found further south in Europe. Nevertheless, 42 out of the 55 species recorded from the British Isles as a whole are found here and the number is very gradually increasing as more species appear from the south.

THE PAST

Early settlers

Just over 6000 years ago the first humans appeared in the wilderness of post-glacial Scotland. It was about this time also that the land bridge (which had lasted for about 3000 years) linking south-east England to mainland Europe began to sink and disappear. The first Mesolithic hunter-gatherers are believed to have come across this bridge, though others no doubt appeared by boat (Fleure, 1951). The story of humans in Scotland begins with these hunters and fishers harvesting animal protein. Fish was an important element of their diet, both coastal fish and anadromous salmonids on their annual upstream migration (Ritchie, 1920). These include Atlantic Salmon and Sea Trout and possibly even anadromous Arctic Charr in some places.

These migratory fish seeking out their spawning grounds annually, often far upstream, were readily available to even the crudest means of fishing – often, no doubt, bare hands. The regular appearance of these highly nutritious fish must have contributed substantially to the survival of many inland settlements before the advent of agriculture and animal husbandry – and afterwards as well. Early agriculturalists and stock farmers began to appear some time after 3500 BC – the Neolithic culture that superseded the earlier Mesolithic hunter-gatherer economy.

Because of their regularity of return and high value to primitive communities, it is not surprising that Salmon (and Sea Trout) are commonly part of ancient culture and have a strong symbolism for northern peoples around the globe. In Scotland, there are many Pictish symbol stones from the post-Roman era on which are carved the most accurate outlines of Salmon (Anonymous, 1978). To the Celts, the Salmon was the most ancient of all animals and the source of wisdom itself. This symbolism continues in the form of the coats of arms of several families and Royal Burghs (e.g. Glasgow).

Medieval period

Possibly this traditional respect for Salmon aided the law-makers in medieval times to introduce their stern laws drawn up to prevent over-exploitation of the resource and ensure that the species could complete its life cycle. Such legislation must have been based on a fairly thorough knowledge of the life cycle of Salmon, although it was not until 1527 that Hector Boece (of King's College, Aberdeen) produced a definitive account.

Originally in Scotland the right to catch Salmon was a common right, but because of its increasing value in commerce this right became vested in the Crown and by grants and charters to private individuals. The right to fish for Salmon could be independent of riparian ownership, except in the Northern Isles where the original Norse Udal law linked riparian ownership with fishing rights for Salmon.

Precedents for legislation to conserve Salmon had existed in Scandinavia and other parts of western Europe from early times: both Norse parliaments and Charlemagne drew up protective legislation, but the later Scottish legislation was much more sophisticated in terms of the numbers of laws made to conserve Salmon and regulate the fishery for them. Such legislation dates from David the First and William the Lyon in the 12th century. It aimed to ensure the protection of adult Salmon at spawning time and the safeguarding of smolts on their way to the sea. In order to allow upstream and downstream migration of Salmon, dams and dykes in rivers were required to have a gap wide enough for "a well fed pig" to be able to turn round in.

Fixed engines in rivers were prohibited and in 1424 James I decreed that "all cruives and yaires set in fresche watteris, quhair the sea filles and ebbis the quhilk destroyis the frie of all fisches be destroyed and put awaie for ever mair". However, fixed engines were permitted in the sea. It is likely that such legislation could be enforced only in the more accessible parts of the country and that all forms of trapping continued unabated in remote areas.

18th and 19th centuries

Methods of catching Salmon became more and more restricted. Fixed engines, stake nets and bag nets, with the exception of certain cruives were prohibited in rivers and estuaries with the objective of allowing sufficient escapement of adult fish to reach their spawning grounds (Barbour, 1992). The taking of "baggit fish" (baggots: defined apparently as Salmon about to spawn) was prohibited, weekly close times for netting instituted (i.e. the weekly "slap" period) and an overall close season established.

However, certain cruive rights were granted and some survived well into the present century as part of the commercial fishing effort for Salmon. Towards the end of the 17th century, legislators saw the need to limit the efficiency of Salmon fishing methods to protect stock and certain types of nets were outlawed. "Burning the water" (i.e. the use of spears at night in conjunction with flaming torches) was made illegal, but little attempt was made to enforce this law as it was too much tied up with tradition. More Acts were passed in the early 19th century and the Salmon Fisheries (Scotland) Acts of 1862 and 1868 set up District Fishery Boards, an advance of the first importance, to regulate local matters. These were composed of local Salmon fishing proprietors, allowing them to carry out work on the river which was considered necessary for the protection and improvement of their fishings. The District Fishery Boards are overseen by the Secretary of State for Scotland, but not all areas have such Boards. Fishery statistics for Salmon and Sea Trout, collected and published annually by the Scottish Office, are based on 101 Salmon Fishery Districts which cover the whole country (Williamson, 1991).

Also during the 19th Century the first scientifically designed "salmon ladders" or fish passes were installed from about 1840 onwards to allow adult Salmon to negotiate impassable waterfalls or bypass man-made obstructions. The 380-m-long ladder at Torboll on the River Carnach system (Sutherland) was built in 1865, while the ladder made necessary by the Caledonian Canal cutting off the access of River Lochy Salmon to Loch Lochy and Loch Arkaig was constructed, belatedly, some years later.

Fish translocations

A variety of alien species of fish have been introduced to Scottish waters since medieval times and, certainly in recent years, humans have been the main agents of re-distribution. They imported several fish as food from the Continent, such as Carp, and translocated several native species, presumably for the same reason – for example, Pike and Perch. By tradition, the clergy in particular have been held responsible for much of the re-distribution of Pike and Perch. These two species were ideal for small ponds, moats and lakes, where they could easily be gathered, assuring a dependable supply of fish for Fridays.

There is another factor, too, concerning these two species: both travel very well, especially in cool weather, just wrapped in damp sacking or wet moss, Like this they will stay alive for long periods and their transport would have been a relatively simple matter even by pack animal or slow boat. Carp and Tench also travel well out of water, but their scarcity in the north suggests that either they were not used as much as the former two species or the northern climate did not suit them.

Certainly in Scotland, the distribution of Pike and Perch fits in well with what is known about the locations of early medieval ecclesiastical settlements. References to their presence in Scotland suggest that Pike were well established locally by the mid-17th century and that they were certainly present at the end of the previous century. Perch were known to be present at that time too.

However, results from archaeological excavations carried out at several Scottish burghs so far have not revealed bones of Pike or Perch, although bones of other species were present. At Perth, for instance, bones of these two species were not found during excavations covering the period 1200–1400 AD, a time when they were commonly used as food in English towns. Pike were certainly used as food during the reign of Charles I, as the palace accounts in 1649 reveal. These fish probably came from the Lake of Menteith.

Humans have also introduced and re-distributed fish for sport, particularly those fish which provide both sport and food, such as Brown and Rainbow Trout, Brook, Charr, Grayling, Pike, Carp and Tench. In Scotland during the last century and the early years of the present one, hundreds of waters were stocked with Brown Trout, often from private estate hatcheries which proliferated during that period. Estate staff were sent out with buckets of young Trout to the most isolated lochs – some at altitudes of 600–900 m – which fish were unlikely ever to reach by natural means.

As an indirect result of developing sport fisheries, several other species have become widely re-distributed too. These comprise the bait species such as Gudgeon, Minnow, Roach, Dace and Stone Loach. The Gudgeon and Stone Loach were once popular natural spinning baits for Salmon in northern rivers, as were Minnow and Loach for Trout. Dace and Roach were more often used as live or dead bait for Pike. The end result in many cases was that unused livebait was (and still is) released at the end of a fishing expedition – for convenience and to "improve" the food available to the local predatory fish. Also, anglers were keen to build up a stock of their favourite bait fish locally so that they could collect them on the spot in future. As the railway system moved northwards last century so southern anglers extended the range of their activities.

The process continues to this day; Ruffe, hitherto unknown in Scotland, were first caught in Loch Lomond in 1982, probably released by anglers from the south (Maitland and East, 1989). It is now one of the commonest species in the loch. Recently, Gudgeon, Chub and Dace have also appeared in the same system.

As a result of such activities, Roach, Gudgeon, Stone Loach and Minnow appeared many years ago in several of the great east coast Scottish Salmon rivers as far north as the River Don, while the River Tweed contains Dace as well. Also in Scotland, the practice of using live Minnows for Trout bait has been responsible, particularly in the years since World War II, for their steady advance northwards and they now occur in river systems draining to the Pentland Firth.

As well as Minnows, Three-spined Sticklebacks were sometimes introduced into Trout angling waters to improve the food of Trout there and conversely Pike were introduced to upland lakes to thin out dense populations of stunted Trout – in the hope that a sparser population of larger Trout would result. Evidence of this practice is fairly common in Scotland, where lochs completely isolated from any source of Pike contain populations of that species only. The Trout have usually been long since completely eliminated while the Pike survive, by eating their own young.

Angling

The great angling potential of Scotland was first publicized in the 17th century by Richard Franck (1658) a soldier, who, after coming north with Cromwell's army wrote favourably about angling in Scotland. In the late 18th and early 19th centuries, sportsmen, tourists and naturalists such as Pennant (1769), St John in the 1840s (St John, 1901), Scrope (1843), Stoddart (1847) and others did the same, with the consequence that as the importance of Brown Trout as a human food resource decreased, at the same time its sporting value increased. During the second half of the 19th century angling on many Trout waters in the Highlands was available to patrons of hotels which at that time catered largely for sportsmen. This interest in angling led to the keeping of angling records by hotels and estates and the emergence of experienced advisers; for example, Armistead (1895), Malloch (1910) and Calderwood (1930), who advised estates and landowners how to manage their fisheries.

The steadily increasing number of sporting hotels made efforts to improve their angling – this usually entailed the introduction of "new blood" from hatcheries (Maitland, 1892). Many small private hatcheries were set up at this time to provide young Trout for stocking, while exotic salmonids were introduced widely. Commercial stocking then was often a package deal: the hatchery supplying Loch Leven fingerlings, freshwater shrimps, snails and pondweed (*Elodea canadensis*) – the latter becoming widely distributed in this way.

Some of the earliest developments in fishery management took place in the Scottish Borders where Stewart (1857) recognized the important inverse relationship between the extent of spawning facilities (and the recruitment of young Trout) and the growth and size of fish in the stock. Little notice was taken of this important observation and fishery managers continued (as many do to this day) to overstock waters with young Trout.

THE PRESENT

The earliest formal organizations concerned with Scottish fresh waters and their biota were the Commissioners of the Scotch Salmon Fisheries (established 1862) and their successor, the Fishery Board of Scotland (established 1882), whose Inspectors of Salmon Fisheries published reports from 1883 onwards and were principally concerned with regulating fishing for Salmon (Figure 26.1) and Sea Trout. Also, valuable statistics on Brown Trout catches were recorded by hotels and estates.

After 1945, supervision of basic Salmon research was transferred to the Director of Fisheries Research (at first under the Scottish Home Department, then in 1960 under the Department of Agriculture and Fisheries for Scotland (DAFS) which became the Scottish Office Agriculture and Fisheries Department (SOAFD) in 1991) and was continued at the Freshwater Fisheries Laboratory at Faskally. The origin of the Faskally laboratory is relatively recent. In 1948 the Brown Trout Research Scheme started at Pitlochry and was a joint venture by the Scottish Home Department and the North of Scotland Hydro-Electric Board. The geographic focus of the scheme was the Tummel–Garry catchment, whose hydrology had been substantially altered by the power dams of the Tummel Valley hydro-electric complex.

The Brown Trout scientists were supervised by a committee, their terms of reference being to conduct research into the "factors affecting the number, size and growth of Brown Trout in Scottish waters of varying types and into measures for improving stock" (Figure 26.2). This generous brief gave the scientists the freedom to investigate practically any aspect of the Brown Trout in Scotland and the early work of the laboratory included studies on the growth and reproduction of Brown

FIGURE 26.1. A female Atlantic Salmon from the River Tummel. Most of the legislation and the management of fish populations in Scotland relates to this one species. Photograph: R. Niall Campbell

Trout, availability of food organisms and experiments to improve Trout production in lochs (Campbell, 1971; 1972a; 1972b). During this period much experience was gained and much advice was given to the public on all aspects of fishery management (Pyefinch, 1960).

In 1957, the laboratory was renamed the Freshwater Fisheries Laboratory. The following year a more fundamental change took place when the Supervisory Committee advised the Secretary of State for Scotland that the laboratory had become established as an important freshwater laboratory and should continue as the direct responsibility of the Scottish Home Department's Director of Fisheries Research. This important decision ensured the continuation of the laboratory; it also further recognized the need for the laboratory to take greater account of the more economically important Salmon.

Some earlier work on Salmon had been carried out by the Salmon Inspectorate and in 1945 the supervision of such work was transferred to the Director of Fisheries Research. Some work was done on the River Forss in Caithness in the late 1940s and on tributaries of the Rivers Conon and Lui in the mid-1950s. At Faskally, work centred on problems caused by hydro-electric schemes, and the exploitation of Salmon and Sea Trout by nets and rod. In 1960, responsibility for the laboratory passed to the Department of Agriculture and Fisheries for Scotland, which changed in 1991 to the Scottish Office Agriculture and Fisheries Department.

FIGURE 26.2. Boats and anglers at Loch Leven, once Scotland's most famous Brown Trout fishery, from which stock have been sent to many parts of the world. Photograph: R. Niall Campbell

The District Salmon Fishery Boards were established in 1862 with a remit to regulate local matters. Over the years they have assessed stocks of fish, carried out hatchery work and co-operated in tagging programmes and other research projects.

The present management of fish populations is carried out on a relatively unstructured basis and, within the legal constraints which have been outlined above, relies largely on the actions of Salmon proprietors, riparian owners and of angling clubs. Attempts to structure fishery management, such as the Hunter Committee Reports (1963; 1965), have so far failed and there are few indications of other initiatives from the government. However, many of the Hunter Reports' recommendations have influenced thinking over the years and may have been responsible for the setting up of Protection Orders.

Protection Orders established a valuable machinery for the fishing for Brown Trout (and for coarse fish too) because they take into account the difficult situation involving riparian ownership and associated legal complications. Salmon and Sea Trout are not involved. The owners of a river system or large loch can apply to the Secretary of State for Scotland for a Protection Order for that water. Most of the owners must be in agreement. The principal criterion on which a Protection Order is granted is whether more angling will be made available to the public (provided they abide by the stated regulations for the fishery). The first Protection Order was granted to the Tweed riparian owners in 1987. Protection Orders seem to have had a beneficial effect, because over-exploitation by mass angling has been controlled, and because it is now realistic for owners and lessees (perhaps angling clubs) to try to use various management measures.

Not all applications for a Protection Order have been successful. If the examining body (appointed by the Secretary of State) does not consider that additional angling will result, the application is referred back (e.g. as in the case of the lower Spey). Protection Orders do seem to be a management step on a national scale and are likely to be increasingly important in the future.

Game fishing

Game fishing is the traditional form of angling in Scotland and is still the predominant method used (Mills, 1971; 1980). Exact definitions vary, but game fishing is usually understood to mean angling for salmonid fish, especially (in Scotland) Atlantic Salmon and Trout (both Sea Trout and Brown Trout) and Rainbow Trout. By extension, angling for other Salmonidae which occur in Scotland (Arctic Charr and Brook Charr) is also included in the term, but there is usually some argument as to whether Grayling (Thymallidae) are game fish or not. There is a close season for Salmon and for Trout, but none for Rainbow Trout, Grayling or Arctic Charr.

Thus, most angling and fishery management in Scotland is concerned with game fishing for Salmonidae. Even though coarse fishing is increasing in popularity, game fishing seems likely always to be the dominant sport, certainly outside the central lowlands, because of the highland character of the landscape and consequent unsuitability of most waters for coarse fish species.

Coarse fishing

As with game fishing, there are various interpretations of what exactly the term "coarse fishing" means. Commonly it would certainly include fishing for the larger Cyprinidae – in Scotland: Common Carp, Crucian Carp, Tench, Bream, Rudd, Roach, Chub and Dace. As well as cyprinids, most other large non-salmonid species are also generally regarded as "coarse" fish – for example, Pike, Eels and Perch.

Coarse fishing, formerly not a common pastime in Scotland, has increased in popularity in recent years and there are now several clubs and a large number of anglers devoted to this form of angling. As a result, several coarse fish species have recently been introduced to waters new to them in many parts of the country, especially southern areas, and at least one species, the Ruffe (Maitland and East, 1989), new to Scotland, is now well established.

CURRENT MANAGEMENT PRACTICES

A summary of fishery management practices in Scotland is given in Table 26.1 and they include many activities which are actually harmful to the aquatic environment and some indeed to the fisheries themselves (Maitland and Turner, 1987). Very few data are available on the extent of the various practices described below but subjective estimates are given in Table 26.1.

Removal of unwanted species

As just indicated, and in contrast to many parts of England, the majority of angling in Scotland is for salmonid fish and thus for many anglers all other species are undesirable. For this reason, there has been a regular removal of unwanted species from lochs and rivers in different parts of the country. Various methods have been adopted to remove fish, including poisoning, netting, trapping, electro-fishing and drainage.

A number of lochs (Morrison and Struthers, 1975) and some streams (Morrison, 1977; 1979) in Scotland have been poisoned, in most cases to eliminate unwanted populations of Pike and Perch, or both, usually with the objective of introducing Brown or Rainbow Trout. In a few cases poisoning has been used as a recruitment control measure (Walker, 1975). Occasionally, other species (e.g. Roach or Eels) have been the targets of poisoning. The main poison used has been rotenone (a derivative of derris), for the use of which a licence is required from SOAFD. Usually, relatively small waters have been involved (e.g. Fincastle Loch burn) but occasionally larger water bodies have been poisoned; perhaps notable among these was Loch Choin (Munro, 1957) which was poisoned to eliminate the population of Pike.

Netting to remove unwanted fish has involved the use of both seine nets and gill nets. Seine nets are rarely used directly for this purpose because of the substantial manpower required, but when seine netting is carried out for other reasons, "unwanted" species of fish are often removed. For example, at Loch Lomond over a period of many years during regular seine netting (net and coble) for Atlantic Salmon and Sea Trout, it was common practice to destroy all the Perch and Powan

TABLE 26.1. Summary of fishery/management practices in Scotland. Little quantitative information is available but an assessment of their usage in Scotland is given (++++ = very common, +++ = common, ++ = uncommon, + = rare). Sites and references are listed merely as examples

Practice	Usage	Example	Reference
Removal of fish			
angling	++++	Loch Leven	Bailey-Watts and Maitland (1984)
poisoning	++	Loch Choin	Munro (1957)
netting	++	Loch Leven	Thorpe (1974)
trapping	++	Carbeth Loch	Maitland (unpublished)
electro-fishing	+	River Thurso	Thurso (1984)
drainage	+	Loch Crannoch	Scottish Home Department (1959)
Fish stocking			
eggs	++	River Endrick	Lamond (1931)
juveniles	++++	River Tay	Gardiner (1991)
adults	++++	Loch Fitty	Mackenzie (personal communication)
Fish introductions			
intentional	++	Culcreuch Loch	Burkel (1971)
casual	+++	Loch Lomond	Maitland and East (1989)
accidental	++	River Polly	Maitland (1989)
Groundbaiting	+	Douglas Water	Campbell (unpublished)
Predator control			
fish	+++	River Thurso	Thurso (1984)
birds	++	River North Esk	Carss and Marquiss (1991)
mammals	+	River Endrick	Maitland (unpublished)
humans (poaching)	++++	Loch Lomond	Lamond (1931)

Habitat management

groynes and fishing jetties	+++	River Shiel	Campbell (unpublished)
fishing pools	++	River Thurso	Thurso (1984)
salmonid spawning areas	++	River Polly	Campbell (unpublished)
raising of the water level	+	Swans Water	Maitland (unpublished)
blocking access to inflows	+	Loch Crannoch	Campbell (unpublished)
blocking of outflows	++	Loch Fitty	Mackenzie (personal communication)
removal of barriers	++	River Endrick	Stuart (1962)
provision of fish ladders	++	River Tay	Maitland (unpublished)
addition of fertilizers	++	Loch Kinardochy	Brook and Holden (1957)
liming	++	Loch Dee	Burns et al. (1984)
use of herbicides	+	Loch Rigarry	Campbell (unpublished)
cutting weeds	+	Loch Fitty	Mackenzie (personal communication)
use of Grass Carp	+	Sandyknowes Loch	Campbell (unpublished)
cutting bankside vegetation	+++	River Dee	Oswald (1985)
introduction of "food" species	+	Long Loch	Maitland (unpublished)

Access to fishings

trampling	+++	Various lochs	Tivy (1980)
disturbance	+++	Loch Ruthven	Campbell (unpublished)
lighting of fires	+++	Loch Tummel	Campbell (1972b)
digging turf	+++	River Devon	Maitland (unpublished)
deposition of litter	++++	River Clyde	Clyde River Purification Board (1992)
use of boats	++++	Various lochs	Tivy (1980)

taken – sometimes hundreds of fish in a day. Gill netting is the more usual method of removing unwanted species (especially Pike) and has been carried out at many lochs either as a "one off" management policy or else on a regular, usually annual, basis (e.g. at Loch Leven). Normally the nets used have a large mesh size in order to avoid taking too many, usually smaller, game fish. Gill netting for Pike has been practised regularly on Lochs Lomond, Leven, Menteith and many other Scottish lochs.

Trapping is carried out less frequently for predator control. Sometimes Eel fyke nets are allowed to operate on the basis that a predator and competitor with game fish is being removed and some income is generated from the catch. In a few waters, Perch traps (Le Cren *et al.*, 1967) have been used to remove large numbers of Perch (e.g. at Carbeth Loch). In the past, live Perch trapped in Loch Leven were sold to English coarse fisheries.

Electro-fishing has been used on a number of salmonid nursery streams mainly to remove Brown Trout, assumed to be a competitor and predator of young Atlantic Salmon, thus leaving the habitat free for young Salmon. The Brown Trout removed may be used to stock hill lochs or other angling waters. This practice has operated on the River Thurso for many years (Thurso, 1984).

Drainage is a relatively rare procedure. Partial drainage is recommended before poisoning because it leaves less chance of the target fish species finding poison-free pockets of water in bays or inlets or among littoral vegetation. Occasionally, small reservoirs or lochs (e.g. Kinnaird Loch) have been completely drained to destroy unwanted fish species, allowed to dry out and then refilled and stocked with game fish.

The removal of unwanted species can create various ecological problems, depending on what method is used. Clearly, drainage of the whole system is enormously destructive, especially if the basin is left empty for a long period. Poisoning, too, can cause substantial damage, not only to indigenous fish, but also to various other aquatic species, including Amphibia (Morrison, 1987). The impact of gill netting varies; with coarse mesh only, the target species (usually Pike) may be the only fish directly affected, but with indiscriminate mesh sizes many fish (and some birds) may be killed. The use of seine nets may damage macrophytes and affect the substrates where used regularly, but few fish are killed (i.e. most could be released if wanted), and the same is true of trapping methods and electro-fishing.

Finally it should be remembered that most angling (other than catch-and-release) also removes fish from a water and these numbers must be included in any management plan.

Stocking practices

Stocking practices have varied widely in Scotland in the past and have rarely had any scientific basis. Commonly, stocking is carried out after the removal of unwanted species, but it is also practised at other times – even when there is no indication of lack of stock in the water concerned. Sometimes the objective has been the introduction of "new blood". For over 100 years the principal species involved in Scotland have been salmonids, but in recent years, especially in the central lowlands, many waters have been stocked with cyprinid species. Fish are stocked at all stages of their life cycle – as eggs, juveniles or adults – depending on the objectives and the finance available. The price per fish increases greatly because of rearing costs from egg to adult.

Stocking with adult fish (usually Rainbow Trout) is generally regarded as creating a "put and take" fishery. Often such fish may be caught within hours, usually days, of release. The fisheries involved are frequently intensive ones and the number of fish stocked and caught per year may be very high relative to the size of the water and its natural production of fish.

There is considerable concern, but relatively little information, about the effect of various stocking practices. Obviously, the introduction of diseases or parasites is an important issue, discussed below. If the species being stocked is a new one to the system concerned ("introduced", see below) or is being released in very high numbers, then changes may be expected in the ecosystem concerned via the foodweb or in some other, probably indirect, way. Vulnerable fish or invertebrate species could be eliminated through predation. Often the stocking practice is intended to "enhance" the native (wild) stock in a water but concern is that it may do exactly the opposite. In particular, if the numbers stocked are large compared with the wild population, the latter may be reduced in number or eliminated through competition for food, spawning grounds and other resources. The loss of the genetic integrity of the local native stock which is assumed to have adapted to local conditions over thousands of years is a major issue, discussed more fully elsewhere (Maitland, 1989).

Introductions

All stockings are effectively "introductions" but the latter term is usually reserved for fish which are introduced, (a) intentionally, to create a new population, for example of a desired species (Maitland, 1964) or to develop safeguard stocks of rare species (Maitland and Lyle, 1992); (b) casually, by the release of excess livebait species at the end of a day's fishing or the dumping of unwanted aquarium or pond fish (Maitland, 1971); or (c) through accidental escapes from fish farms or garden ponds. Some species (e.g. the Grayling) owe their entire Scottish distribution to introductions for angling (Gardiner, 1991). Certainly the status of fish stocks in Scotland today owes much to introductions in the past (Wheeler and Maitland, 1973; Maitland, 1977).

The concerns over introductions are similar to those for stocking. However, by definition, new species are involved so, as well as the threat of new diseases and parasites, there is a very real danger of a major impact on the ecosystem concerned (Raat, 1990). The recent introduction of Ruffe (and other species) to the Loch Lomond system (Maitland and East, 1989) is a relevant example here and species new to the loch continue to appear from time to time (Adams and Maitland, 1991).

In Scandinavia, there has been a tradition of introductions of various new species (both invertebrates and fish) to lakes with the objective of "improving" the fisheries there. With hindsight, several of these experiments have clearly been unwise.

In an experiment to improve the feeding available to Brown Trout in Scottish lochs, field trials were carried out some years ago with the crustacean *Lepidurus arcticus* (Department of Agriculture and Fisheries for Scotland, 1978). In August 1977, 1800 adults were flown from Norway and released into three hill lochs in the Invermoriston catchment draining to Loch Ness. Some adults taken back to the laboratory died and no larvae or adults appear to have been seen subsequently in the lochs concerned. While this experiment did have specific and potentially worthwhile objectives it can be criticized on the basis of the sites chosen for the experiment, which drain eventually into Loch Ness – one of Scotland's largest and most important lochs. More isolated waters with no outfall or with outfalls direct to the sea would surely have been a safer choice.

Introductions of invertebrates (and disease) may also result from the use of equipment (including angling tackle) in different waters (Reynoldson *et al.*, 1981).

The majority of planned introductions taking place at the moment are of sport fish and the usual objective is either to diversify and enhance the existing natural population or to provide catchable size fish which can be caught immediately – the "put and take" fishery. Enhancement is very rarely justified and should never be carried out unless the following questions have been asked: "Will it do any harm to the existing fish population and fishery?", "Is it necessary?" and "Is it likely to fulfil its objectives?". If these questions were answered honestly, fewer enhancement introductions would be carried out and less damage would be done to indigenous fish populations.

The popularity of "put and take" fisheries is undoubtedly increasing, though many find it difficult to understand the satisfaction in catching tame, fat fish which come easily to a lure and may only have been released from the fish farm the day before. There they will have been fed on an expensive pellet diet (much of it consisting of meal made from other fish species). Such fish are normally far less attractive than their wild counterparts – often having foreshortened snouts and stunted and worn fins through being kept in close confinement with hundreds of others. In addition to the artificiality of the situation, the introduction of such fish can materially damage the native stock through competition for food and space, the introduction of diseases and the reduction of genetic integrity and fitness.

An additional problem related to "put and take" fisheries is that clearly the fish being introduced have been reared somewhere with all the attendant problems created by fish farms. These include water abstraction, pollution from waste food and faeces, increased demand for industrial fish meal (i.e. more fish will be killed somewhere), introduction of diseases, problems with predators (Herons, Cormorants, Otters, Mink, etc.) attracted to the farm, and impact on native fish from escapees through competition and reduction of genetic integrity. All these factors must be borne in mind when the pros and cons of "put and take" fisheries are discussed.

Perhaps the answer to these various introductions is to accept that they are going to continue to take place in some waters, but to try to identify waters which are important for various reasons and make sure that no introductions take place there. This would seem to be a reasonable compromise which would ensure that the native stocks will continue in some waters and that these truly wild fish will be available to those anglers who wish to use their skill to pursue them.

Diseases and parasites

There is no doubt that various diseases and parasites have been moved around from continent to continent (Maitland and Price, 1969), from country to country and from watershed to watershed. The means of transfer and the outcome have varied greatly from one situation to another (Secombes, 1991).

Maitland and Price (1969) found that a population of the North American Large-mouth Bass, *Micropterus salmoides*, naturalized in a pond in Dorset in England was host to the monogenetic trematode parasite *Urocleidus principalis*. This parasite, which is specific to the genus *Micropterus*, had never before been recorded in Europe but was known as a common parasite of Largemouth Bass in North America. It was assumed that the parasite came to Great Britain with its host and became established here with it.

The outstanding example of parasite transfer in Europe in recent years has been the outbreak of the parasitic fluke *Gyrodactylus salaris* in Norway which has been spread by introductions from farmed salmonids to wild populations, and several native stocks of Salmon have been virtually wiped out (Dolmen, 1987). Over the last decade it has proved necessary to use poison to eradicate entire fish stocks and communities in some rivers as the only means of eliminating the parasite. The original infection appears to have arisen from the import of parasitized stock from fish farms in Sweden, and the parasite is now known from 28 rivers and 11 hatcheries in Norway.

One of the surprising features of the incidence of this parasite in Norway is its virulence in the wild populations, whereas it does not seem to be a problem to Salmon in its native Swedish rivers. It has been suggested that this may be due to the fact that Norwegian wild stocks were unadapted to it and therefore had no resistance, but it is also suggested that the resistance of the wild stocks in Norway had been lowered in genetic terms by the introduction of alien stocks from fish farms over the years.

There are several other examples of problems created by the introduction of diseases and parasites. For example, Norway also created enormous problems for its salmonid fish when it imported furunculosis-infected stock from Denmark in 1966. This caused substantial losses of farmed fish but the effect on the wild fish was not monitored. Thus, there will always be potential dangers from the annual introduction of non-native stocks of fish into lochs via cage systems, however stringent the checks are for disease on these fish.

Groundbaiting

Until recently, the practice of groundbaiting (using cereals, maggots and various other baits) has been of little importance in Scotland because of the lack of interest in coarse fishing. However, it has been used in Grayling fishing and, with interest in coarse fishing expanding rapidly, there is now justification for paying attention to possible problems created by groundbaiting.

Several potential problems are created by groundbaiting where it is carried out over a long period. Although banned on many water supply reservoirs in England, on the grounds of protecting water quality, its contribution to nutrient budgets seems low, except under very high application rates and angler densities (Edwards, 1990). In five out of six reservoirs studied, Edwards and Fouracre (1983) estimated that groundbait contributed less than 0.3% of the phosphorus load. However the contribution in the sixth reservoir was about 6%. In experimental work on a shallow coarse fishing reservoir, Cryer and Edwards (1987) found substantial reductions in the benthic fauna where groundbait was distributed, with the exception of tubificid worms which increased. In addition, the oxygen consumption in these areas increased one-hundred-fold and caused local deoxygenation under warm calm conditions.

Predator control

The loss, or imagined loss, of fish to predators has long been of concern to anglers (Mills, 1987) and in the past many predatory fish, birds and mammals have been persecuted as a result (Draulans, 1987; Carss and Marquiss, 1991). Scientific information on this topic is often fragmentary and sometimes equivocal, leading to heated debate between anglers and conservationists. Usually anglers would like to see some or all of the predators removed but occasionally the reverse is true, for example where Pike (or other predatory fish species) are introduced to populations of stunted fish with the objective of reducing the number and increasing the average size.

The basic argument of anglers is that any fish (of a valued species) eaten by a predator is a loss to them. Arguments countering this attitude point out that (a) often only young fish, with a high natural mortality, are eaten; (b) it is frequently diseased or damaged fish which are vulnerable to predators; (c) it is often stocked fish (from farmed sources) which are most vulnerable because of their reduced capacity to cope in the wild; (d) predators may actually benefit a fishery by reducing dense populations of small fish; (e) the operation of the "sump effect", where individual predators destroyed are simply replaced by others from neighbouring areas, and (f) most predators (e.g. Herons, Kingfishers, Cormorants, sawbill ducks, Otters, Seals) have a high intrinsic value to the public and merit protection.

Obviously, the main conservation problem caused by predator control is the effect on the populations of the predator species concerned and the indirect effects on the ecosystem resulting from its disappearance. The results are often unpredictable. Poaching can also be considered as a form of predation, and in many fisheries considerable effort is given to controlling poachers.

Habitat management

Habitat management is widely practised by fishery managers (Swales and O'Hara, 1983; Murphy and Pearce 1987) and can take many forms, some of them extremely damaging to the integrity of a site, others less so. Management may include any of the following practices: construction of groynes and fishing jetties, creation of fishing pools and loose gravelled salmonid spawning areas, raising of the water level using small dams, cutting off access to spawning streams to control recruitment (Figure 26.3) (Campbell, 1967a,b), blocking of outflows (usually with a grid of some kind) to prevent stocked fish escaping, removal of natural barriers to fish migration (e.g. waterfalls), provision of fish ladders, addition of fertilizers, liming, clearance of aquatic weeds by herbicides (Brooker and Edwards, 1975), cutting or the use of Grass Carp, cutting of bankside vegetation (including trees), and introduction of fish "food" species (usually invertebrates but sometimes small fish species). Several of the other practices described elsewhere (removal of unwanted species, introductions and predator control) are also part of habitat management.

Because this topic involves such a wide range of practices which can be carried out in varying degrees, it is difficult to review all impacts briefly. Presumably a basic start to any consideration is to assume that if the habitat concerned is a pristine one (a condition normally assumed to be desirable by most conservation criteria), then any management could be detrimental. Thus, the opening up of a new spawning tributary to a loch or river (by removing, say, a barrier such as a waterfall) may be regarded as highly desirable by local fishery managers but may be detrimental to conservation interests if the fish (or invertebrates) in the loch, river or tributary are of scientific importance.

FIGURE 26.3. A barrier set across a Brown Trout spawning stream to reduce the extent of spawning grounds from 400 m to 20 m. Photograph: R. Niall Campbell

One of the few biological methods of habitat management developed in recent years has been the use of Grass Carp. The Chinese Grass Carp (*Ctenopharyngodon idella*) has been introduced to a substantial number of waters in Great Britain as a method of biological control of water weeds and to provide sport fishing. The initial introductions were carried out on an experimental basis (Buckley and Stott, 1977; Stott, 1977) and, although its numbers were difficult to estimate once introduced (Stott and Russell, 1979), the research showed that this fish was efficient at controlling weed, was popular with anglers and was never likely to breed naturally here. On this basis its transfer to a number of waters has been encouraged by the Ministry of Agriculture, Fisheries and Food for England and Wales.

Access to fishings

Physical access to fishings and other types of recreation (Sukopp, 1971; Liddle and Scorgie, 1980) can involve a number of issues which relate to the environment. Trampling of sensitive littoral or riparian vegetation is a common problem as is disturbance to nesting birds and other wildlife. Lighting of fires, digging turf to find worms for bait, and deposition of litter (including nylon line and old hooks) can all create environmental problems.

Outside the national and local close seasons for salmonids, there is no legal restriction of access to fishings, provided: (a) permission has been obtained from the owner or lessee of the fishery, (b) permission has been obtained from the riparian owner (not necessarily the same as the owner of the fishery), and (c) the proposed method of fishing is legal.

Legal complications over access rarely cause conservation problems unless ownership is unknown or in dispute, when uncontrolled access could create difficulties. However, physical access may create significant problems for local conservation interests, especially through damage to vegetation and disturbance to wildlife (Cooke, 1987; Cryer *et al.*, 1987a; Jeffries, 1987). Both of these may be difficult to avoid if angling pressure is heavy. However, damage from fires, boating, litter (Bell *et al.*, 1985; Cryer *et al.*, 1987b; Edwards and Cryer, 1987) and bait digging should be perfectly avoidable with proper angler management and good local codes of practice (Mackay, 1987).

THE FUTURE

It can be seen from the above that the best way to describe the present structures for the integrated management of the valuable and internationally famous freshwater fish resources of Scotland is to say they are fragmentary (Chapter 30). This is in contrast to the situation in England and Wales where these resources are the responsibility of a government-funded statutory body, the National Rivers Authority, which also controls most other water-related affairs. The integrated catchment management therefore made possible in England and Wales is in stark contrast to the situation in Scotland where River Purification Boards are concerned with water quality, District Salmon Fishery Boards (DSFBs) with migratory salmonids, landowners with non-migratory Trout and other fish, the Scottish Office with drainage, and local authorities with water supply. It is not clear which of these bodies, if any, is concerned with the quantity of water remaining in watercourses.

The responsibilities of the DSFBs (which are not even present in all parts of Scotland) are also fragmented. They have clear powers to deal with fishing regulations, obstacles to the movement of migratory adults and smolts, and predation, and less clear powers to concern themselves with spawning gravels. The parr stage of the life cycle appears not to come within their remit, except to control predators and prevent parr being killed by anglers. Overall, the general business of the District Boards is more to do with policing than with management.

Owners of fisheries who wished to improve management have been able to consult the SOAFD Freshwater Fisheries Laboratory for several decades. This advice was previously given free (until recently when charges were instituted as a matter of government policy) and survey and other work would be carried out by skilled and experienced staff with all the proper equipment. The other option for a fishery owner or club was to hire a private consultant, but this could have disadvantages and advice was rarely placed in a national context. Continuity of management is a problem as fisheries change hands, estate staff retire or move away, and in clubs as memberships change.

There are several independent organizations concerned with angling and the management of fish populations. The Institute of Fisheries Management is concerned mainly with education and the dissemination of information. The Salmon and Trout Association, the Atlantic Salmon Trust, the Scottish Anglers National Association and other bodies campaign on behalf of anglers and are effective forces against pollution and other factors affecting angling.

In recent years a new factor has appeared on the scene in Scotland – biologists employed by DSFBs or by Trusts set up by these Boards. As yet there are only four such biologists in Scotland – for the Tweed (The Tweed Foundation), the Cree, Bladnoch and Fleet (West Galloway Fisheries Trust), the Spey (Spey Salmon Research Trust) and the Aberdeen Dee (Dee DFSB). There is already an integrated fishery management plan for the Tweed and such plans are envisaged for West Galloway and the Spey. For the first time in Scotland, therefore, some rivers have their own biologists, based locally with equipment to undertake survey and management work, accumulating data for management decisions and able to undertake or advise on management action for the river.

The Tweed experience

As an example of just what is possible, the recent developments on the River Tweed are worth describing in some detail. The management plan for the Tweed has now been in execution since 1990. It is an extensive plan and much of it has not yet been implemented. The parts that have are:

(1) A Trout catch logbooks scheme, in which a few members in most of the angling clubs in the catchment record data on catch and effort.
(2) A Trout marking system by which Trout stocked into the river can be marked specifically for each angling club so that they can assess the return from their stocking.
(3) Scale reading of all Salmon killed at a number of commercial sport fisheries along the river to provide information on the seasonal and geographical variation in the types of Salmon present. This has already identified one tributary as being a particular source of spring Salmon. Around 1500 scale samples are read each year.
(4) Collection and analysis of rod and net catch records to analyze changes in the fisheries over the past century or so. The most notable changes here are in the timing of the return of Salmon. Many of the record books have fallen into disuse and it is proposed to produce a new set of fishing ledgers whose record formats will include information useful for scientific analysis as well as for the angler. A

continuous record of effort data with catches at a sample number of rod fisheries should be possible in this way.

(5) A scientific licence to allow samples of Goosanders to be taken for diet analysis outside the normal culling period. This has shown that coarse fish are the major part of the diet except during smolt migration (which is mainly outside the traditional culling period) when salmonids are significant.

(6) The setting up of electro-fishing sites throughout the river system which will be visited on a periodic basis so that trends in juvenile fish populations can be monitored, as well as the use of both main channel and tributaries by all fish species.

(7) Habitat survey work, both detailed (on the ground) and broad (from aerial photographs) so that nursery stream habitat can be assessed and remedial action identified. The latter has included the fencing of banks to prevent grazing damage, the removal of overhanging trees and the easing of obstacles to fish movement.

As part of the habitat work and the removal of such obstacles, information (which has been lacking in the past) is being provided to local contractors and others on how to construct bridge aprons, elevated fords, culverts, etc. This should limit the number of new problems created as old ones are solved.

The gathering of data both on fish populations and conditions in the streams and their catchments has led to the need for a Geographic Information System. This has already been set up for West Galloway and is being considered for the Tweed.

In these first three years of the Tweed management plan roles additional to the execution of the plan have developed. These have included the assessment of the likely impact of coniferous afforestation on streams, and educational activities for groups such as anglers and local planners. The new Tweed Fish Conservation and Management Centre, which opened in the summer of 1993, does not therefore consist only of laboratories and offices; there is also a visitor centre/meeting room which will have a permanent display of the work of the Tweed Foundation.

Future options

There are several examples of fishery management from other countries which could be followed in Scotland (Campbell, 1973). For example, in the management of sport fisheries in the Maritime Provinces of Canada, the provincial government makes the rules and fishery owners have to comply – even over such details as method (e.g. fly only) and bag limit (e.g. four Salmon per day). Interestingly, this does not depress the market value of private Salmon fishing (e.g. a beat on the Miramichi River costs just as much as a prime beat on a Scottish river).

A study of fishery management in several Commonwealth countries (Campbell, 1973) showed that scientific management based on both pure and applied (sometimes empirical) research is essential. The scale of this scientific support is such that it is quite beyond the means – financial, organizational or technical – of the private sector. As such, a sport fishery conservation service cannot be adequately financed by licence revenue alone. The State has to be prepared to invest funds several times in excess of the revenue – just as happens now through the National Rivers Authority in England and Wales.

One possible way forward in Scotland would be to follow the general guidelines developed in the Hunter Report, based on some form of national fishery structure made up of a number of local management units with professional staff. These units would implement fisheries legislation and be responsible for the sensible scientific management and conservation of all fish species (not just salmonids) within their jurisdiction. The units would look to a central government fisheries laboratory for advice, training and help with research activities. This advice should be free to all, based on the social and economic benefits which surround popular angling. It should be remembered also that there may well be changes necessary because of relationships with the rest of the European Community (Bongers, 1990) and that many other water users have rights (Parry, 1987).

In practice, such a scenario need not be too far away given the proper support from government. A national strategy and structure is needed, but the units are already there (or almost so) in the form of the DSFBs. These would be given a new remit (to cover all fish species) and some support in relation to management, including powers to conclude management agreements for riparian areas with landowners. The existing Freshwater Fisheries Laboratory has already shown itself to be well capable of providing the central scientific support required, given adequate funding and a responsibility for all fish species.

Until recently, the future which appeared to be developing for fisheries management in Scotland was therefore of a central research unit (the SOAFD Freshwater Fisheries Laboratory, Pitlochry) with independent, locally employed biologists resident on large rivers (or groups of smaller rivers). These biologists would liaise informally with the Pitlochry laboratory and each other, working on their rivers with appropriate equipment and accumulating the data necessary for good management, which was then being carried out.

This was made possible by the abolition of local government property rates on Salmon fishings. This freeing of resources allowed them to be diverted, in the four areas mentioned, towards fishery management. Local government in Scotland has many possible sources of funding; fishery management (given the absence of rod licences) has very few. It is to be hoped that in the search for new sources of local government funding the resources needed to manage the valuable fisheries resource are never again diverted for other uses.

Thus it may be that, within the DSFBs, the River Purification Boards (RPBs), the new fisheries biologists and the Protection Order legislation lies the nucleus of a new form of catchment-based management of fish populations in Scotland. In many ways, fisheries management comes down to land-use management and, if the former can be put on a more scientific basis through modernized district boards or management trusts, the possibility exists of fisheries interests joining with RPBs, farming, forestry and water supply and sewerage bodies to form integrated catchment committees for rivers or groups of rivers. Part of this possibility has seemingly been lost already, with the RPBs being taken out of local control and amalgamated into a centralized pollution control authority that will not be concerned with rivers alone. From the catchment management point of view it would have been better to have left the RPBs as local units and expanded them into catchment boards with responsibilities for flood control and river works and with powers to examine land-use practices that affect water quality and quantity. Such catchment boards would be the "providers" of the catchment with other bodies (fisheries, farming, forestry, etc.) being the "users".

It can only be hoped now that the new Scottish Environment Protection Agency will allow its constituent parts enough independence for them to be able to function fully in any local integrated catchment organizations. To be really effective, some sort of statutory underpinning would be required for these, but such a system of locally controlled and based catchment management "federations" could be a valid alternative to the sort of centralized system represented by the National Rivers Authority in England and Wales. It would, in fact, represent subsidiarity for the waters and fisheries of Scotland.

ACKNOWLEDGEMENTS

We are grateful to Dr Philip Boon for useful comments on a draft of this chapter.

REFERENCES

Adams, C. E. and Maitland, P. S. (1991). "Evidence of further invasions of Loch Lomond by non-native fish species with the discovery of a Roach × Bream, *Rutilus rutilus* (L.) × *Abramis brama* (L.), hybrid", *Journal of Fish Biology*, **38**, 961–963.

Anonymous (1978). *Sculptured Monuments in Scotland AD 400–1050*, HMSO, Edinburgh.

Armistead, J. J. (1895). *An Angler's Paradise*, Nelson, London.

Bailey-Watts, A. E. and Maitland, P. S. (1984). "Eutrophication and fisheries in Loch Leven, Kinross, Scotland", *Proceedings of the Institute of Fisheries Management Annual Study Course*, **15**, 170–190.

Barbour, A. (1992). *Atlantic Salmon: An Illustrated History*, Canongate, Edinburgh.

Bell, D. V., Odin, N. and Torres, E. (1985). "Accumulation of angling litter at game and coarse fisheries in South Wales, U. K.", *Biological Conservation*, **34**, 369–379.

Bongers, J. J. A. 1990. "A unified market for European angling", *Proceedings of the Institute of Fisheries Management 21st Anniversary Conference*, 1990, 105–108.

Brook, A. J. and Holden, A. E. (1957). "Fertilisation experiments in Scottish freshwater lochs", *Freshwater and Salmon Fisheries Research*, **17**, 1–30.

Brooker, M. P. and Edwards, R. W. (1975). "Review paper: aquatic herbicides and the control of water weeds", *Water Research*, **9**, 1–15.

Buckley, B. R. and Stott, B. (1977). "Grass Carp in a sport fishery", *Fisheries Management*, **15**, 9–14.

Burkel, D. L. (1971). "Introduction of fish to new water", *Glasgow Naturalist*, **18**, 574–575.

Burns, J. C., Coy, J. S., Tervet, D. J., Harriman, R., Morrison, B. R. S. and Quine, C. P. (1984). "The Loch Dee Project: a study of the ecological effects of acid precipitation and forest management on an upland catchment in south-west Scotland", *Fisheries Management*, **15**, 145–167.

Calderwood, W. L. (1930). *Salmon and Sea Trout*, Arnold, London.

Campbell, R. N. (1967a). "A method of regulating Brown Trout (*Salmo trutta* L.) populations in small lakes", *Salmon & Trout Magazine*, May 1967, 135–142.

Campbell, R. N. (1967b). "Improving highland Trout lochs", *The Flyfishers' Journal*, **56**, 61–69.

Campbell, R. N. (1971). "The growth of Brown Trout *Salmo trutta* L. in northern Scottish lochs with special reference to the improvement of fisheries", *Journal of Fish Biology*, **3**, 1–28.

Campbell R. N. (1972a). "A questionnaire for assessing the angling potential of Brown Trout waters", *Journal of the Institute of Fisheries Management*, **3**, 1–8.

Campbell, R. N. (1972b). "Trout angling in Scotland, past and present", *Proceedings of the Annual Conference of the Salmon and Trout Association, London*, pp. 1–18.

Campbell, R. N. (1973). "A study of the organisation of freshwater sport fisheries in New Zealand, Australia and Canada", Nuffield Travelling Fellowship Report.

Carss, D. N. and Marquiss, M. (1991). "Avian predation at farmed and natural fisheries", *Proceedings of the Institute of Fisheries Management Annual Study Course*, 22, 179–196.

Clyde River Purification Board (1992). *Annual Report*, East Kilbride.

Cooke, A. S. (1987). "Disturbance by anglers of birds at Grafham Water", *Institute of Terrestrial Ecology Symposium*, 19, 15–22.

Cryer, M. and Edwards, R. W. (1987). "The impact of angler ground bait on benthic invertebrates and sediment respiration in a shallow eutrophic reservoir", *Environmental Pollution*, 46, 137–150.

Cryer, M., Linley, N. W., Ward, R. M., Stratford, J. O. and Anderson, P. F. (1987a). "Disturbance of overwintering wildfowl by anglers at two reservoir sites in South Wales", *Bird Study*, 34, 191–199.

Cryer, M., Corbett, J. J. and Winterbotham, M. D. (1987b). "The deposition of hazardous litter by anglers at coastal and inland fisheries in South Wales", *Journal of Environmental Management*, 25, 125–135.

Department of Agriculture and Fisheries for Scotland (1978). "Field trials with the shrimp *Lepidurus arcticus*", *DAFS Triennial Review of Research*, 1976–78, 13, Edinburgh.

Dolmen, D. (1987). "*Gyrodactylus salaris* (Monogenea) in Norway; infestations and management", in *Parasites and Diseases in Natural Waters and Aquaculture in Nordic Countries* (Eds A. Stenmark and O. Malmberg), pp. 63–69, University of Stockholm, Stockholm.

Draulans, D. (1987). "The effectiveness of the attempts to reduce predation by fish-eating birds: a review", *Biological Conservation*, 41, 219–232.

Edwards, R. W. (1990). "The impact of angling on conservation and water quality", *Proceedings of the Institute of Fisheries Management 21st Anniversary Conference*, 1990, 41–50.

Edwards, R. W. and Cryer, M. (1987). "Angler litter", *Institute of Terrestrial Ecology Symposium*, 19, 7–14.

Edwards, R. W. and Fouracre, V. A. (1983). "Is the banning of ground baiting in reservoirs justified?", *Proceedings of the British Freshwater Fisheries Conference*, 3, 89–94.

Fleure, H. J. (1951). *A Natural History of Man in Britain*, Collins, London.

Franck, R. (1658). *Northern Memoirs, Calculated for the Meridian of Scotland*, London.

Gardiner, R. W. (1991). "Scottish Grayling: history and biology of the populations", *Proceedings of the Institute of Fisheries Management Annual Study Course*, 22, 171–178.

Hunter Committee (1963). *Scottish Salmon and Trout Fisheries*, Cmnd 2096, HMSO, London.

Hunter Committee (1965). *Scottish Salmon and Trout Fisheries*, Cmnd, 2691, HMSO, London.

Jeffries, D. J. (1987). "The effects of angling interests on otters, with particular reference to disturbance", *Institute of Terrestrial Ecology Symposium*, 19, 23–30.

Lamond, H. (1931). *Loch Lomond*, Jackson, Glasgow.

Le Cren, E. D., Kipling, C. and McCormack, J. (1967). "A study of the numbers, biomass and year class strengths of Perch (*Perca fluviatilis* L.) in Windermere from 1941–1966", *Journal of Animal Ecology*, 46, 281–307.

Liddle, M. J. and Scorgie, H. R. A. (1980). "The effects of recreation on freshwater plants and animals: a review", *Biological Conservation*, 17, 183–206.

Mackay, D. W. (1987). "Angling and wildlife conservation", *Institute of Terrestrial Ecology Symposium*, 19, 72–75.

Maitland, J. R. G. (1892). *On Stocking Rivers, Streams, Lakes, Ponds and Reservoirs with Salmonidae*, Howietoun Fishery, Stirling.

Maitland, P. S. (1964). "A population of Common Carp (*Cyprinus carpio*) in the Loch Lomond district", *Glasgow Naturalist*, 18, 349–350.

Maitland, P. S. (1971). "A population of coloured Goldfish, *Carassius auratus*, in the Forth and Clyde Canal", *Glasgow Naturalist*, 18, 565–568.

Maitland, P. S. (1977). "Freshwater fish in Scotland in the 18th, 19th and 20th centuries", *Biological Conservation*, 12, 265–278.

Maitland, P. S. (1989). *The Genetic Impact of Farmed Atlantic Salmon on Wild Populations*, Nature Conservancy Council, Edinburgh.

Maitland, P. S. and East, K. (1989). "An increase in numbers of Ruffe, *Gymnocephalus cernua* (L.), in a Scottish loch from 1982 to 1987", *Aquaculture & Fisheries Management*, **20**, 227–228.

Maitland, P. S. and Lyle, A. A. (1992). "Conservation of freshwater fish in the British Isles: proposals for management", *Aquatic Conservation: Marine and Freshwater Ecosystems*, **2**, 165–183.

Maitland P. S. and Price, C. E. (1969). "*Urocleidus principalis* (Mizelle, 1936), a North American monogenetic trematode new to the British Isles, probably introduced with the Largemouth Bass *Micropterus salmoides* (Lacepede, 1802)", *Journal of Fish Biology*, **1**, 17–18.

Maitland, P. S. and Turner, A. K. (1987). "Angling and wildlife conservation – are they incompatible?", *Institute of Terrestrial Ecology Symposium*, **19**, 76–81.

Malloch, P. D. (1920). *Life History of the Salmon, Sea Trout, Trout and other Freshwater Fish*, Black, London.

Mills, D. H. (1971). *Salmon and Trout: A Resource, Its Ecology, Conservation And Management*, Oliver & Boyd, Edinburgh.

Mills, D. H. (1980). *Scotland's King of Fish*, Blackwood, Edinburgh.

Mills, D. H. (1987). "Predator control", *Institute of Terrestrial Ecology Symposium*, **19**, 53–56.

Morrison, B. R. S. (1977). "The effects of rotenone on the invertebrate fauna of three hill streams in Scotland", Fisheries Management, **18**, 128–138.

Morrison, B. R. S. (1979). "An investigation into the effects of the piscicide antimycin A on the fish and invertebrates of a Scottish stream", *Fisheries Management*, **10**, 111–122.

Morrison, B. R. S. (1987). "Use and effects of piscicides", *Institute of Terrestrial Ecology Symposium*, **19**, 47–52.

Morrison, B. R. S. and Struthers, G. (1975). "The effects of rotenone on the invertebrate fauna of three Scottish freshwater lochs", *Fisheries Management*, **6**, 81–91.

Munro, W. R. (1957). "The Pike of Loch Choin", *Freshwater Salmon Fisheries Research, Scotland*, **6**, 1–16.

Murphy, K. J. and Pearce, H. G. (1987). "Habitat modification associated with freshwater angling", *Institute of Terrestrial Ecology Symposium*, **19**, 31–46.

Oswald, J. (1985). "Fishery management on the River Dee", *Institute of Terrestrial Ecology Symposium*, **14**, 117–120.

Parry, M. L. (1987). "Multi-purpose use of waters", *Institute of Terrestrial Ecology Symposium*, **19**, 66–71.

Pennant, T. (1769). *British Zoology*, London.

Pyefinch, K. A. (1960). *Trout in Scotland*, HMSO, Edinburgh.

Raat, A. J. P. (1990). "The impact of fish on aquatic ecosystems: fish stocking in the Netherlands 1950–1990", *Proceedings of the Institute of Fisheries Management 21st Anniversary Conference*, 1990, 299–315.

Reynoldson, T. B., Smith, B. D. and Maitland, P. S. (1981). "A species of North American triclad (Paludicola; Turbellaria) new to Britain found in Loch Ness, Scotland", *Journal of Zoology, London*, **193**, 531–539.

Ritchie, J. (1920). *The Influence of Man on Animal Life in Scotland*, Cambridge University Press, Cambridge.

Scottish Home Department (1959). "Tenth Annual Report of the Supervisory Committee for Brown Trout Research", *Freshwater and Salmon Fisheries Research*, **23**, 1–15.

Scrope, W. (1843). *Days and Nights of Salmon Fishing in the Tweed*, Murray, Edinburgh.

Secombes, C. J. (1991). "Current and future developments in salmonid disease control", *Proceedings of the Institute of Fisheries Management Annual Study Course*, **22**, 81–88.

St John, H. C. (1901). *Charles St John's Note Books, 1846–1853*, Douglas, Edinburgh.

Stewart, W. C. (1857). *The Practical Angler*, Black, London.

Stoddart, T. T. (1847). *The Angler's Companion to the Rivers and Lochs of Scotland*, Edinburgh Printing Co., Edinburgh.

Stott, B. (1977). "On the question of the introduction of the Grass Carp (*Ctenopharyngodon idella* Val.) into the United Kingdom", *Fisheries Management*, **3**, 63–71.

Stott, B. and Russell, I. C. (1979). "An estimate of a fish population which proved to be wrong", *Fisheries Management*, **10**, 169–170.

Stuart, T. A. (1962). "The leaping behaviour of Salmon and Trout at falls and obstructions", *Freshwater and Salmon Fisheries Research*, **28**, 1–46.

Sukopp, H. (1971). "Effects of man, especially recreational activities, on littoral macrophytes", *Hydrobiologia*, **12**, 331–340.

Swales, S. and O'Hara, K. (1983). "A short term study of the effects of a habitat improvement programme on the distribution and abundance of fish stocks in a small lowland river in Shropshire", *Fisheries Management*, **14**, 135–140.

Thorpe, J. E. (1974). "Trout and Perch populations at Loch Leven, Kinross", *Proceedings of the Royal Society of Edinburgh*, **74B**, 295–313.

Thurso, L. (1984). "Management of the River Thurso Salmon resource", *Proceedings of the Institute of Fisheries Management Annual Study Course*, **15**, 15–22.

Tivy, J. (1980). *The Effect of Recreation on Freshwater Lochs and Reservoirs in Scotland*, Countryside Commision for Scotland, Perth.

Walker, A. (1975). "The use of rotenone to control recruitment of juvenile Brown trout (*Salmo trutta* L.) into an 'overpopulated' loch", *Fisheries Management*, **6**, 64–72.

Wheeler, A. and Maitland, P. S. (1973). "The scarcer freshwater fishes of the British Isles. 1. Introduced species", *Journal of Fish Biology*, **5**, 49–68.

Williamson, R. B. (1991). *Salmon Fisheries in Scotland*, Atlantic Salmon Trust, Pitlochry.

SECTION IV

INTEGRATING CONSERVATION AND DEVELOPMENT

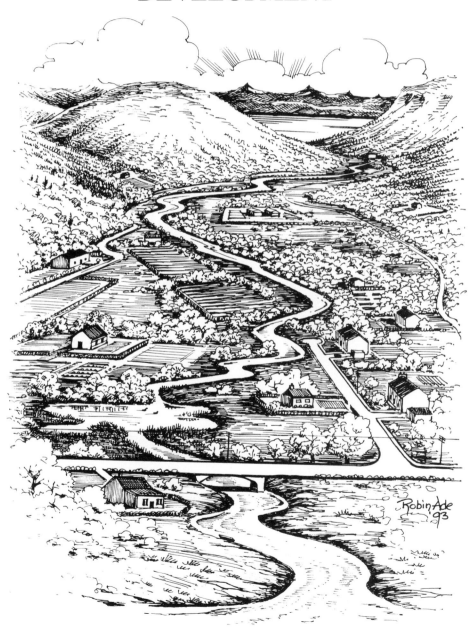

27

Pollution Control

D. W. MACKAY

North East River Purification Board, Greyhope Road, Aberdeen, AB1 3RD, UK

INTRODUCTION

The control of water pollution in Scotland (see Chapter 20) is currently in a state of rapid transition. The steady, if unspectacular, progress achieved by the 10 river purification authorities (RPAs), comprising seven River Purification Boards (RPBs) and three Islands Councils, during the last 30 years (see Chapter 20), is currently being influenced by the introduction of new legislation, in particular the implementation of European Community (EC) Directives. Integrated Pollution Control (IPC) introduced by part 1 of the Environmental Protection Act 1990, provides for the control of emissions to air, land and water from industrial processes by an authorization issued and enforced by a single authority. In practice, this means that many major discharges to water previously controlled by the RPAs will become the responsibility of Her Majesty's Industrial Pollution Inspectorate (HMIPI) with the Authority in a consultative rather than executive role. Recently, the Government announced its intention to form a Scottish Environment Protection Agency (SEPA), bringing together control of water pollution, air pollution and pollution of land under a single management structure.

The seven RPBs, as presently constituted, have numbers of members related to the size of the Board's area, ranging from 12 members for the smallest Board (Tweed) to 24 for the largest (Clyde). Within each Board, one quarter of the members are appointed by Regional Councils and one quarter by District Councils from within their elected memberships; the remaining half of the membership is appointed by the Secretary of State for Scotland to represent industry, conservation, forestry, angling and similar interests. The Boards are defined as Non Departmental Public Bodies (NDPBs) sponsored by the Scottish Office Environment Department (SOEnD), and are increasingly subject to guidance and direction from the sponsors as aquatic environmental protection becomes more influenced by UK and international legislation, rather than the Scottish Acts.

The EC Directives are binding on the UK as a whole and the Government has the duty to interpret and implement them. It does this by the issue of Regulations and

The Fresh Waters of Scotland: A National Resource of International Significance
Edited by P. S. Maitland, P. J. Boon and D. S. McLusky. © 1994 John Wiley & Sons Ltd

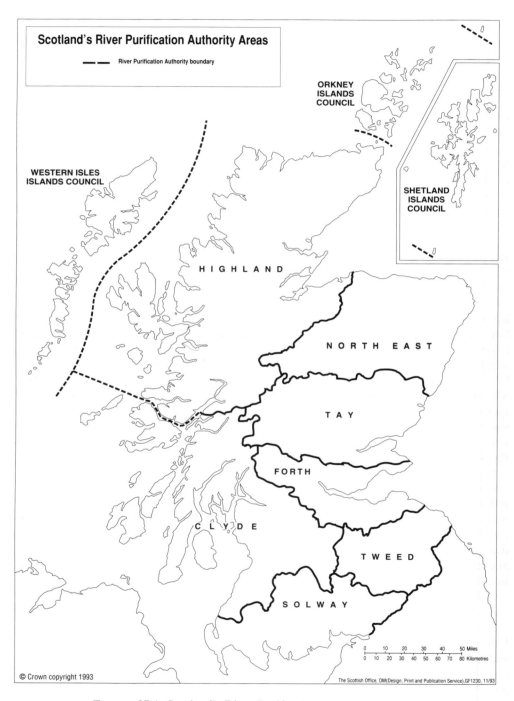

FIGURE 27.1. Scotland's River Purification Authority areas

instructions to identified "competent authorities". The RPAs serve in this role for several of the Directives associated with protection of the aquatic environment.

The seven Boards – Clyde, Forth, Highland, North East, Solway, Tay and Tweed (Figure 27.1) – depend mainly on the Control of Pollution Act 1974 (COPA), as amended by Schedule 23 of the Water Act 1989, to provide the powers to enable them to fulfil their duties. Similarly the three Islands Councils – Orkney, Shetland and the Western Isles – are empowered by COPA to act as RPAs for discharges not of their own making. As single-tier multi-purpose authorities the Islands Councils own and operate sewage treatment works which are controlled by the Secretary of State, through the Scottish Office Environment Department. Since none of the islands has substantial river systems and levels of marine pollution have been identified as low, the approach to controlling and reporting on pollution has been less vigorous in the past than that of the RPBs. This position is now changing with the Islands Councils actively pursuing their responsibilities as RPAs.

The duties of the RPAs are to promote the cleanliness of inland waters (flowing and standing), groundwaters, estuaries and coastal waters. To a large extent, each Board may set its own water quality objectives, but additionally they have to ensure that national water quality standards and objectives, as may be specified by Government or introduced by EC Directives, are achieved.

The Department of the Environment and the Welsh Office (1992) recently published proposals to establish Statutory Water Quality Objectives (SWQOs) in England and Wales. Such an approach, which specifies acceptable levels of water quality taking into account the present situation and economically realistic targets for future improvement, is treated with some suspicion in Scotland where the long-term aim has been traditionally to maintain or restore rivers to their natural condition. While SWQOs may be very useful to measure performance in upgrading rivers of inferior quality, they might equally be used to justify degradation of near pristine rivers to standards which still meet all specified commercial uses. The experience gained in England and Wales may be studied for some time before Scotland chooses to pursue the same path.

Until recently, the Boards' and Islands Councils' main methods of pollution control involved the limitation of discharges of potentially polluting material from point sources by a system of licensing, and the detection and punishment of those who caused pollution by illegal discharges; for example, dumping of polluting materials into controlled waters. Other methods of preventing pollution, by Regulations designed to forestall incidents, by Designations of areas requiring special protection, and by Codes of Good Practice, are now being implemented and are described in the main body of the paper.

CONTROL OF POINT SOURCE POLLUTION

Under Section 34 of the Control of Pollution Act, anyone discharging to controlled waters must apply for, and hold, a consent from the appropriate RPA. The applicant must provide full details of the proposed discharge and the RPA, which cannot unreasonably withhold consent, will take into account the likely effect on the receiving water and set conditions so that water quality objectives are not impaired. Generally the consent will be issued subject to conditions which may refer to the location, design and construction of the discharge outlet, the volume of the discharge, the concentration and loads of particular components in the discharge, and arrangements for taking samples of the discharge.

At the present time, the North East River Purification Board, which is of medium size, has 11 153 active consents to discharge on its Register of Consents, which is open to public inspection. Each year the Board processes approximately 1000 new applications for consent, and since January 1992 makes a charge, currently of £350, for processing the application. For very small discharges arising from up to four dwelling houses or equivalent, the charge is reduced to £50. Other Boards and the Islands Councils operate similar charging schemes, although not introduced at the same time, and charges are also levied for the cost of monitoring consented discharges and the receiving environment.

The consented discharges, including the vast majority of point source discharges in a Board's area, are monitored at regular intervals to measure compliance with the consent conditions. The Boards have recently produced an agreed joint policy document on Consent Compliance Monitoring, which sets out the frequency and type of monitoring appropriate to various types of discharge. The monitoring schedule for a particular discharge may include taking samples of the effluent and the receiving waters for chemical analyses, inspections of the premises and plant, and biological sampling upstream and at intervals downstream of the point of entry to the receiving water of the effluent. Records of all monitoring activities are maintained on the Public Register, and failure to comply with consent conditions is a criminal offence under Section 32 of the Control of Pollution Act and subject to a fine of up to £20 000 per day. For reasons explained below, a breach of consent is not automatically followed by prosecution in Court.

The RPAs have a policy of trying to prevent pollution by promoting rapid remedial action and the provision of better treatment facilities, rather than resorting to reporting every incident to the Procurator Fiscal for consideration as to whether prosecution is appropriate. This policy, a balance between working with dischargers and outright confrontation, has worked well for the environment, but has often been misinterpreted as lack of determination by interested observers and occasionally by dischargers. The Boards have again co-operated in producing a document on Enforcement Policy which may increase understanding on all sides. In comparing Scottish practice with that in England and Wales, it is pertinent that in Scotland the tradition has been to set strict consents with a substantial safety margin, whereas south of the border any breach of the liberal licence conditions is likely to cause pollution in the receiving waters.

Those events described as the "irregular, casual or spontaneous entry of poisonous noxious or polluting matter to controlled waters", which are not controlled by the consent procedure, are offences under Section 31 of the Control of Pollution Act and subject to the same penalties as for Section 32. An example of such an offence would be leakage of silage effluent, oil discharging from a tank, or similar isolated incidents.

The Control of Pollution Act 1974, Section 31a, makes provision for prevention of pollution by anticipating hazards and taking steps to eliminate them before damage occurs. An excellent example of such measures is the Control of Pollution (Silage Slurry and Agricultural Fuel Oil) (Scotland) Regulations 1991. These give RPAs effective powers to survey storage facilities, and if risk of pollution is perceived to order that remedial measures be undertaken within a certain time. Failure to comply with the regulations or a notice issued under the regulations constitutes an offence. The regulations operate in such a way that the operator has strong financial incentives to effect the necessary repairs or precautionary works very promptly since failure to do so may result in the whole storage structure having to be replaced to much higher construction standards than previously obtained. Similar regulations to control the storage of industrial chemicals and oil are likely to be introduced in the near future. Because of the vast range of substances, and the number of industries involved, the production of these regulations is proving more complex but they are now in draft form.

Several other offences are covered by the legislation; for example, Section 49 of COPA covers removal of deposits on the stream bed behind any dam, weir or sluice by causing them to be carried away by the river, or allowing any substantial amount of vegetation cut or uprooted in any inland waters (or so near that it falls into the water) to remain there.

The legislation of which an RPB has to take account is drawn from many Acts, and is complex and difficult to enforce. That which applies to the North East River Purification Board (there are minor differences between Boards) is listed as Appendix 1. There is now an urgent need to draw the relevant legislation together in a small number of documents to facilitate administration.

During 1992, the Courts in Scotland appeared to take a much more serious view of pollution offences than previously, and levels of fines increased very markedly from hundreds of pounds to several thousand pounds.

In summary, pollution from point sources is largely under control. Where it is not, the remedies are generally obvious and only lack of resources may serve as an excuse for the situation not being totally under control.

DIFFUSE SOURCES OF POLLUTION

Pollution from diffuse sources, probably the major problem currently – and for the future – is difficult to control, although EC Directives are proving very helpful since they tackle the important issue of land-use management as a method of limiting pollution. The RPAs, as the competent authorities for Directives on water quality in Scotland, are involved at present with 17 Directives (Appendix 2), the most recent of which – the Urban Waste Water Treatment Directive and the Nitrates Directive – will have considerable influence on water quality management.

The Secretary of State is in the process of issuing to RPAs, guidance on the implementation of European Community Directive 76/464/EEC. This Directive requires that Member States take steps to eliminate pollution of the aquatic environment by List 1 substances. "Pollution" as defined by the Directive is "the discharge by man, directly or indirectly of substances or energy into the aquatic environment, the results of which are such as to cause hazards to human health, harm to living resources and to aquatic ecosystems, damage to amenities or interference with other legitimate users of water". List 1 substances are recognized as being particularly dangerous, but are only specified as such when the Council of Ministers has agreed the terms of a daughter directive specifying limit values.

TABLE 27.1 List I substances and their abbreviations when these are frequently substituted for the full name

Mercury from the chlor-alkali industry	Isodrin
Cadmium	Hexachlorobenzene (HCB)
Mercury from sectors other than the chlor-alkali industry	Hexachlorobutadiene (HCBD)
Hexachlorocyclohexane (HCH)	Chloroform
Carbon Tetrachloride (CTC)	1, 2-Dichloroethane (EDC)
DDT	Trichloroethylene (TRI)
Pentachlorophenol (PCP)	Perchloroethylene (PER)
Aldrin	Trichlorobenzene (TCP)
Dieldrin	Endrin

Table 27.1 lists those substances that have been subjected to the adoption of specific measures and thereby formally confirmed as List I. Other substances included in List I of Directive 76/464/EEC but for which limit values and quality standards have not yet been agreed, are treated as List II substances (Table 27.2). Discharges of List I substances are controlled in the traditional Scottish manner by the RPAs setting emission standards for industrial discharges, so that environmental quality objectives – in this case, those specified by the Community in terms of concentrations of substance which may not be exceeded – are not breached.

The EC standards are to be considered as minima by the control authorities and increasing importance is being placed on reducing discharges to as low a level as technology permits. This policy is welcomed by RPAs as in the relatively pure waters of Scotland considerable loadings of these very dangerous materials could be permitted without breach of the Community water quality objectives. Discharges to sewers are controlled in a similar manner. The system operates in such a way that List I substances should be controlled mainly at the point where they first arise.

For all new plant producing List I substances, discharges may be authorized only if the plant employs the "Best Technical Means Available" (BTMA) which corresponds to the UK description "Best Available Technique" (BAT). Specific programmes to avoid or eliminate discharge to the environment of List I substances from diffuse sources and small point or "multiple" sources will be the responsibility of the Scottish Office Environment Department in consultation with relevant authorities. Appropriate monitoring programmes for discharges and the environment will be the responsibility of the RPAs. List II substances are subject to statutory national quality standards established by the Scottish Office Environment Department.

Altogether the EC has listed 129 substances thought to be the best candidates for priority action. From these and existing List I substances, the UK has selected 23

TABLE 27.2. List II Substances

Lead	Arsenic	Organotins
Chromium	Iron	Mothproofing agents
Zinc	pH	
Copper	Boron	
Nickel	Vanadium	

"Red List" substances which are now subject to control under Sections 6 and 2 of the Environmental Protection Act 1990 as prescribed substances. The Red List includes a large proportion of substances which are likely to enter the aquatic environment through a variety of indirect routes.

IMPLEMENTATION OF NEW EC DIRECTIVES

The recent introduction of two EC Directives – the Urban Waste Water Treatment (UWWT) Directive (91/271/EEC) and the Nitrates Directive (91/676/EEC) – has enforced closer attention to long-standing water quality issues and, under certain conditions, will demand very practical (albeit expensive) pollution control measures.

The UWWT Directive applies to sewage and other specified industrial wastes (either of which qualify depending on "population equivalent") and defines minimum standards for the provision of sewerage systems and sewage treatment. The requirements vary according to the size of the discharge and the nature and sensitivity of the area receiving the discharge. The Directive specifies secondary (biological) treatment as the norm but qualifying discharges to "sensitive" areas may require higher standards of treatment (e.g. nutrient removal). In areas which are "less sensitive", qualifying discharges will normally have at least primary treatment (physical and/or chemical settlement of suspended solids). The key to the application of the Directive is the identification of the "sensitive" and "less sensitive" areas.

The Nitrates Directive concerns the protection of waters against pollution caused by nitrates from agricultural sources. It requires Member States to identify waters affected by pollution by nitrates, or waters which could become affected by nitrate pollution (by 2010) if protective action is not taken. Member States must then designate the areas of land draining into these "polluted waters" as "vulnerable zones" and draw up and implement action programmes to reduce nitrate pollution and prevent any further such pollution. The measures to be included in the action programmes – e.g. limitations on fertilizer or organic manure applications – are specified in the Directive. Outside the "vulnerable zones", Member States must establish and promote codes of good agricultural practice. The key to the application of this Directive, is the identification of "polluted waters". Whilst the UWWT Directive is concerned with the treatment of qualifying point source discharges, and the Nitrates Directive with diffuse sources of agricultural pollution, they nevertheless interrelate by virtue of their respective definitions of "sensitive areas" and "polluted waters" which are very similar. Therefore, waters which meet the common criteria may be both sensitive and polluted. The definitions are:

(a) *(For UWWT "Sensitive Areas" and Nitrate "Vulnerable Zones")*
Surface fresh waters intended for the abstraction of drinking water which contain or may contain more than the concentration of nitrates laid down by the relevant provisions of Council Directive 75/440/EEC (50 mg L^{-1} – Abstraction for Drinking Water Directive) if protective action is not taken.

(b) *(For UWWT "Sensitive Areas" and Nitrate "Vulnerable Zones")*
Fresh waters, estuaries, coastal and marine waters which are eutrophic or which in the near future may become eutrophic if protective action is not taken.

(c) *(For UWWT "Sensitive Areas")*

Areas where treatment more stringent than secondary treatment is required in order to fulfil other Council Directives.

(d) *(For Nitrate "Vulnerable Zones")*
Groundwaters which contain more than 50 mg L^{-1} nitrates or which could contain more than 50 mg L^{-1} if protective action is not taken.

Eutrophication is defined by UWWT as "the enrichment of water by nutrients, especially compounds of nitrogen and/or phosphorus, causing an accumulative quantity of algae and higher forms of plant life to produce an undesirable disturbance to the balance of the organisms present in the water and to the quality of the water concerned" (see Chapter 22). The Nitrates Directive defines eutrophication in a similar way, but with one important difference: the definition is restricted to eutrophication caused by compounds of nitrogen.

The River Purification Authorities are currently monitoring and reviewing data to identify "sensitive areas" and polluted waters, under the terms of the Directives. The phased provision of sewerage systems and sewage treatment under UWWT (mostly required in estuary and marine locations since inland populations are generally well served by appropriate facilities) should be in place from 2001 onwards, and the agricultural measures required by the Nitrates Directive are to be in place by the end of 1997.

The North East River Purification Board has identified one estuary which is likely to qualify as polluted in terms of the Nitrates Directive. If the Government endorses this assessment, then the whole catchment of the river will have to be designated as a Vulnerable Zone. Within that zone, measures will have to be introduced to limit the amounts of nitrogen being applied. These measures may relate to:

(a) Periods when the land application of certain types of fertilizer is prohibited.
(b) Provision of storage vessels for livestock manure so that there is sufficient capacity to cover the longest period during which application is forbidden.
(c) Limitation of the land application of fertilizers, taking various factors into account.

It will be readily obvious that the designation of a Vulnerable Zone will have considerable implications for the freedom of the agricultural community to conduct their farming operations as they see fit. Restrictions may have to be imposed on wide areas for many years before significant changes in the condition of the receiving waters become apparent. The approach to pollution control embodied in legislation such as the Nitrates Directive will, if fully implemented, revolutionize the management of agricultural land in Europe, and there is no obvious reason why the same approach should not be adopted to control pollution by erosion or enrichment arising from afforestation or over-grazing in the uplands. The EC Directives are becoming progressively more specific in their wording and requirements for standards. Combined with much more stringent demands in terms of accurate and timely reporting of environmental data, there seems little doubt that EC Directives will play a major role in determining the quality of the environment and the investment in waste treatment facilities during the next decades.

THE WAY AHEAD

Against the above background, the accomplishments of the seven mainland River Purification Boards and three Islands Councils deserve to be treated with some respect. The 1990 Water Quality Survey of Scotland (Scottish Office, 1992) reported a continuing improvement in the quality of Scotland's surface waters. Of the 51 000 km of rivers, lochs and canals included in the survey, 97% were in Class 1 (unpolluted or recovered from pollution) and only 0.1% in Class 4 (grossly polluted). The report concludes that while a high proportion of Scotland's surface waters are of high quality, there is no room for complacency, and outlines proposals for the establishment of a single independent Scottish Environment Protection Agency (SEPA) to incorporate responsibility for the water environment, along with the pollution control responsibilities of the District and Islands Councils, Her Majesty's Industrial Pollution Inspectorate (HMIPI) and the Hazardous Waste Inspectorate.

While the shape and form of SEPA remain to be established by Government, the RPAs already have some experience of working with HMIPI in implementing Part 1 of the Environmental Protection Act 1990, which deals with those classes of industrial activity prescribed for Integrated Pollution Control. The objectives of the new legislation are laudable, sweeping away the fragmented and outdated legislation and replacing it with a clearly demarcated coherent approach designed to limit pollution at source. For those industries most likely to cause major pollution (the prescribed processes) an Authorization must be applied for and granted by the Enforcing Authority. In Scotland, the Enforcing Authority may be HMIPI or the RPAs, but in practice it appears likely that for the majority of discharges HMIPI will take the lead role. The objective will be to achieve the best practicable environmental option for discharges to air, water and land from an industrial unit by the application of "Best Available Techniques Not Entailing Excessive Cost" (BATNEEC). This, of course, involves an intimate knowledge of each stage of the production process, including the materials employed, the quality of staff, the provision of fail-safe procedures and so on, and will be subject to regular revision and updating. That knowledge will be applied through conditions in the Authorization, and monitoring of performance and standards. If compliance with conditions is not achieved by the industry, then the enforcement authority may issue a Variation Notice which varies the conditions of the Authorization, or an Enforcement Notice which demands compliance with a condition not being adhered to, or a Prohibition Notice which empowers the enforcing authority to call a halt to any activity causing or likely to cause harm to the environment. Finally, the Enforcing Authority may issue a Revocation Notice which cancels the Authorization and effectively closes down the process.

On the face of it, the new system should present a considerable advance on the present approach of the RPAs which, to put it simply, makes a decision on what impact the environment can accept and then leaves it to the discharger to get his emissions down to the consented level by whatever means he sees fit. In defence of the approach it may be argued that since we are talking of large industrial processes (ICI, British Gas, Esso, etc.) it is unlikely that anyone from outside the particular industry will be better qualified to extract the best performance from the system than the plant designers and operators.

The reality of the situation is that, for most discharges to water which are the result of prescribed processes, responsibility for water pollution control will pass from the RPAs with their staff of around 300 to HMIPI with a staff of around 20. A major point of friction which has arisen is that the RPAs may no longer be able to report polluters directly to the Procurator Fiscal; nor will they be able to intercede directly with operators since the enforcement authority will be the channel of all communications. Finally, the RPAs and HMIPI have entirely different philosophies in regard to the extent of self-monitoring by industry which is acceptable, and the overall levels of monitoring which are required. No doubt these problem areas will be resolved, but a period of uncertainty which may be to the detriment of progress in cleaning up the environment is almost inevitable.

REFERENCES

Department of the Environment and the Welsh Office (1992). *River Quality: The Government's Proposals*, London.
Scottish Office (1992). *Water Quality Survey of Scotland 1990*, HMSO, Edinburgh.

APPENDIX 1. LEGISLATION RELEVANT TO RIVER PURIFICATION BOARDS – NORTH EAST RIVER PURIFICATION BOARD

General Acts and Orders

1. Rivers (Prevention of Pollution) (Scotland) Act 1951
2. Spray Irrigation (Scotland) Act 1964
3. Rivers (Prevention of Pollution) (Scotland) Act 1965
4. Local Government (Scotland) Act 1973
5. Control of Pollution Act 1974
6. North East River Purification Board Establishment Order 1975 (SI 236 of 1975)
7. River Purification Board Areas (Scotland) Order 1975 (SI 231 of 1975)
8. Local Government (Scotland) Act 1975
9. Water (Scotland) Act 1980
10. Water Act 1989
11. River Purification Boards (Establishment) Variation (Scotland) Order 1989 (SI 59 of 1989)
12. Environmental Protection Act 1990
13. Natural Heritage (Scotland) Act 1991

Orders and Regulations

A. Made to implement COPA II (and EC legislation where applicable)

1. Control of Pollution Act 1974 (Commencement No. 16) Order 1983 (SI 1175)
2. Control of Pollution Act 1974 (Exemption of Certain Discharges from Control) Order 1983 (SI 1182)
3. Control of Pollution Act 1974 (Commencement No. 17) Order 1984 (SI 853)
4. Control of Pollution (Consents for Discharges) (Notices) Regulations 1984 (SI 864)

5. Control of Pollution (Consents for Discharges) (Secretary of State Functions) Regulations 1984 (SI 865)
6. Control of Pollution (Territorial Sea) (Scotland) Regulations 1984 (SI 867)
7. Control of Pollution (Discharges by Authorities) Regulations 1984 (SI 1200)
8. Control of Pollution (Consents: Transitional Provisions) Regulations 1985 (SI 5)
9. Control of Pollution Act 1974 (Commencement No. 18) Order 1985 (SI 70)
10. Control of Pollution (Territorial Sea) (Scotland) Revocation Regulations 1985 (SI 178)
11. Control of Pollution (Registers) Regulations 1985 (SI 813)
12. Control of Pollution (Exemption of Certain Discharges from Control) (Variation) Order 1986 (SI 1623)
13. Control of Pollution (Landed Ships' Waste) Regulations 1987 (SI 402)
14. Control of Pollution (Anti-fouling Paints and Treatments) Regulations 1987 (SI 783)
15. Control of Pollution (Exemption of Certain Discharges from Control) (Variation) Order 1987 (SI 1782)
16. Control of Pollution (Landed Ships' Waste) (Amendment) Regulations 1989 (SI 65)
17. Controlled Water (Lochs and Ponds) (Scotland) Order 1990 (SI 120)
18. Surface Waters (Classification) (Scotland) Regulations 1990 (SI 121)
19. Surface Waters (Dangerous Substances) (Classification) (Scotland) Regulations 1990 (SI 126)
20. Control of Pollution (Silage, Slurry and Agricultural Fuel Oil) (Scotland) Regulations 1991 (SI 346)
21. Disposal of Controlled Waste (Exceptions) Regulations 1991 (SI 508)
22. Control of Pollution (Continuation of Byelaws) (Scotland) Order 1991 (SI 1156)
23. Control of Pollution Act 1974 (Commencement No. 20) (Scotland) Order 1991 (SI 1173)
24. Bathing Waters (Classification) (Scotland) Regulations 1991 (SI 1609)
25. Control of Pollution (Radioactive Waste) (Scotland) Regulations 1991 (SI 2539)
26. Water (Prevention of Pollution) (Code of Practice) (Scotland) Order 1992 (SI 395)
27. Surface Waters (Dangerous Substances) (Classification) (Scotland) Regulations 1992 (SI 574)
28. Control of Pollution (Licensing of Waste Disposal) (Scotland) Amendments Regulations 1992 (SI 1368)

B. Made to implement Environmental Protection Act 1990

1. Environmental Protection (Prescribed Processes and Substances) Regulations 1991 (SI 472)
2. Environmental Protection (Applications, Appeals and Registers) Regulations 1991 (SI 507)
3. Environmental Protection (Authorisation of Processes) (Determination Periods) Order 1991 (SI 513)
4. Environmental Protection (Amendment of Regulations) Regulations 1991 (SI 836)

5. Litter (Statutory Undertakers) (Designation and Relevant Land) Order 1991 (SI 1043)
6. Environmental Protection Act 1990 (Commencement No 8) Order 1991 (SI 1319)
7. Environmental Protection Act 1990 (Commencement No 10) Order 1991 (SI 2829)
8. Environmental Protection (Duty of Care) Regulations 1991 (SI 2839)
9. Environmental Protection Act 1990 (Commencement No 11) Order 1992 (SI 266)
10. Controlled Waste Regulations 1992 (SI 588)
11. Environmental Protection (Determination of Enforcing Authority, etc.) (Scotland) Regulations 1992 (SI 530)
12. Environmental Protection (Prescribed Processes and Substances) (Amendment) Regulations 1992 (SI 614)

C. Made to implement Water (Scotland) Act 1980 and Water Act 1989

1. Water Act 1989 (Commencement No 3) (Scotland) Order 1989 (SI 1561)
2. Water Act 1989 (Commencement No 5) (Scotland) Order 1991 (SI 1172)
3. Grampian Regional Council (Spey Abstractions Scheme) Water Order 1992 (SI 393)
4. Private Water Supplies (Scotland) Regulations 1992 (SI 575)

D. Made to implement EC legislation

1. Environmental Assessment (Afforestation) Regulations 1988 (SI 1207)
2. Control of Pollution (Special Waste) (Amendment) Regulations 1988 (SI 1790)
3. Sludge (Use in Agriculture) Regulations 1989 (SI 1263)
4. Sludge (Use in Agriculture) (Amendment) Regulations 1990 (SI 880)

E. Miscellaneous

1. Code of Practice for Safe Use of Pesticides on Farms and Holdings 1990 (Food and Environment Protection Act 1985, Part III)
2. Anthrax Order 1991
3. Non-Domestic Rates and Community Charges (Timetable) (Scotland) Regulations 1987 (SI 2167)
4. Surface Waters (Dangerous Substances) (Classification) (Scotland) Direction 1990
5. Surface Waters (Dangerous Substances) (Classification) (Scotland) Direction 1992
6. River Purification Authorities (Bathing Waters) Directions 1992
7. Code of Good Practice; Prevention of Environmental Pollution from Agricultural Activity (March 1992)
8. River Purification Boards (Allowances to Members) Regulations 1975 (SI 332 of 1975)

APPENDIX 2. EC DIRECTIVES AND DECISIONS RELEVANT TO BOARD OPERATIONS

1. Directive 75/440/EEC concerning the quality required of surface water intended for the abstraction of drinking water in the Member States

2. Directive 76/160/EEC concerning the quality of bathing water
3. Directive 76/464/EEC on pollution caused by certain dangerous substances discharged into the aquatic environment of the Community
4. Decision 77/795/EEC establishing the common procedure for the exchange of information on the quality of surface fresh water in the Community
5. Directive 78/659/EEC on the quality of fresh waters needing protection or improvement in order to support fish life
6. Directive 79/869/EEC concerning the methods of measurement and frequency of sampling and analysis of surface water intended for abstraction for drinking in the Member States
7. Directive 80/68/EEC on the protection of ground water against pollution caused by certain dangerous substances
8. Directive 80/778/EEC on the quality of water for human consumption
9. Directive 83/513/EEC on limit values and quality objectives for cadmium discharges
10. Directive 84/156/EEC on limit values and quality objectives for mercury discharges by sectors other than the chlor-alkali electrolysis industry
11. Directive 84/491/EEC on limit values and quality objectives for discharges of hexachlorocyclohexane
12. Directive 86/278/EEC on the protection of the environment, and in particular of the soil, when sewage sludge is used in agriculture
13. Directive 86/280/EEC on limit values and quality objectives for discharges of certain dangerous substances included in List 1 of the Annex to Directive 76/464/EEC (carbon tetrachloride, DDT, pentachlorophenol)
14. Directive 86/574/EEC amending Decision 77/795/EEC establishing a common procedure for the exchange of information of the quality of surface fresh water in the Community
15. Directive 88/347/EEC amending Annex 2 to Directive 86/280/EEC on limit values and quality objectives for discharges of certain dangerous substances included in List I of the Annex to Directive 76/464/EEC (aldrin, dieldrin, endrin and isodrin, hexachlorobenzene, hexachlorobutadiene, and chloroform)
16. Directive 91/271/EEC concerning municipal waste water treatment
17. Directive 91/676/EEC concerning protection of waters against pollution caused by nitrates from agricultural sources

28

Planning

A. D. JAMIESON and J. C. SHELDON

Department of Planning, Lothian Regional Council, Edinburgh, EH1 1PT, UK

INTRODUCTION

> Freshwater is not only a renewable natural resource for which no substitute exists, it also forms an important part of ecosystems and landscapes. (David, 1986)

David's statement emphasizes the dual nature of Scotland's freshwater resources which has particular relevance for planning purposes. On the one hand the supply of fresh water can be a determining factor in certain development strategies for economic growth, while on the other, fresh waters are intrinsic elements of the Scottish environment, as landscape and heritage features, as wildlife habitats and as resources for recreation and amenity.

Scotland is well endowed with freshwater resources but they frequently have to serve the community for a number of different, and sometimes competing, purposes, such as drinking water supply, effluent disposal, agricultural drainage or irrigation, commercial and sport fisheries, water-based recreation and tourism. Consequently, there is great potential for conflict between development and the freshwater environment and for conflict between different users of the resource. While reports of water management disasters are more frequently expected from Bangladesh, the Philippines and other less developed countries, Scotland can produce its own examples of poor planning and management of its water resources, such as flood damage in Strathtay and Strathspey, nutrient enrichment of Loch Leven, acidification of lochs, and conflicts caused by the multiple use of Loch Lomond.

Such conflicts between different land uses within a river catchment have been recorded for nearly 200 years. In 1837 Lord Home (Home, 1837) wrote to the Earl of Montague and complained about the adverse impact of earlier upstream land drainage upon his Salmon fishings on the River Tweed:

> This change has been brought about by the draining of the sheep farms in the hills, the effect produced being that a little summer flood which took a fortnight to three weeks to run off previous to 1795 is now completely run out in eight hours. The rain which formerly filled the bogs or sides of the hills, and yielded a constant and regular supply to the river, is now carried off at once by the drains to the different feeders, causing

The Fresh Waters of Scotland: A National Resource of International Significance
Edited by P. S. Maitland, P. J. Boon and D. S. McLusky. © 1994 John Wiley & Sons Ltd

sudden but violent floods, as short as they are sudden, so that the flood is all run off before the river has time to clear itself, becoming too low for a salmon to rise, yet not clear enough for a fish to see a hook, even were a salmon there to take one.

Ideally, these various conflicts should be capable of resolution within one single planning system but the absence of an integrated system of planning for water in Scotland and the different departmental responsibilities within the Scottish Office do not assist this process. David (1986) recognizes the importance of integrated planning such that:

> Solving the environment versus socioeconomic conflicts generated in river basins by water projects and water related activities (e.g. open cast mining projects, road construction and forest management) will require a comprehensive new approach which will reconcile the different interests and integrate them into a recipe for sustainable development.

THE INTERNATIONAL CONTEXT

The concept of the integrated planning and development of river basins is an old-established one with the Tennessee Valley Authority, for example, founded in the 1950s. The theme was re-emphasized by the United Nations in the 1970s but there are still many international examples of environmental disasters related to the poor planning and management of water resources. Massive flooding, soil erosion, siltation, pollution and loss of economically important fisheries are all commonly reported crises, mainly, but not always, in less developed countries, arising from the lack of an integrated approach to water resource planning.

International progress towards better water planning can be traced through the United Nations Conference on Water in Mar De Plata in 1977 and the resulting "International Drinking Water Supply and Sanitation Decade". The United Nations Environment Programme (UNEP) has seen its projects implemented in many parts of the world, contributing to integrated environmental assessment and impact studies in the planning and decision-making processes for water projects, especially drinking water supply, sanitation and irrigation. In 1985, UNEP launched a new comprehensive water programme for the Environmentally Sound Management of Inland Waters (EMINWA). This programme is designed to assist governments to integrate environmental considerations into the management and development of inland waters, with a view to reconciling conflicting interests and ensuring the regional development of water resources in harmony with the environment.

The integrated planning and management of water resources as a global priority also featured at the UN Conference on Environment and Development (The Earth Summit) held in Rio in 1992. "Agenda 21", which formed one of the key agreements negotiated during the summit, is an action plan to develop strategies for programme measures halting and reversing the effects of environmental degradation. It also promotes environmentally sound and sustainable development in all countries of the world. Chapter 18 on "Water Resources" states that by the year 2000, all states should have action programmes for water management based on catchment basins or sub-basins and efficient programmes of water use. It suggests that these could include the integration of water resource planning with land-use planning and other development and conservation activities such as demand management, re-use and recycling of water. The agreement also seeks protection of water for sustainable urban and rural development and food production. As a signatory to "Agenda 21", the British Government is committed to the establishment of a "Sustainable Development Programme" as a national plan to give effect to the decisions made at the Earth Summit. It must be anticipated that the integrated management of water resources will feature in that plan.

The concept of a comprehensive strategy for water management is already widely adopted throughout the world. Coordinated water management through all-embracing national water agencies is in place in India, Jordan, Israel, Hungary, Egypt, Sudan, Zambia and Zimbabwe. In Canada, France, and to some extent in the UK, water managers have close links with environmental managers through joint ministries while in Israel, Hungary, France and India they maintain links with economic and social policy through planning commissions or coordinating bodies.

THE SCOTTISH CONTEXT

The adoption of a comprehensive viewpoint is a key requirement in relation to the Scottish planning system. Firstly, there is the interrelationship of water development to the development of other resources. Water schemes often have effects upon land resources, as in erosion or the flooding of agricultural land. Similarly, land-use practices can influence both run-off and water quality. It is important, therefore, to identify these interrelationships and consider them in water planning. Secondly, the comprehensive approach requires the integration of water planning with overall economic and social planning. This may be particularly relevant in less developed countries but it has become increasingly so in a number of industrially advanced ones as well, including the UK. Finally, the adoption of a comprehensive viewpoint implies a recognition that water resource management requires input from a wide range of disciplines – from engineering to economics, law, geography, biology and planning.

Under the Local Government (Scotland) Act 1975, impacts resulting from, or likely to result in, pollution are dealt with by the River Purification Boards, under the Control of Pollution Act 1974. However, much of the influence of these Boards in preventing or ameliorating pollution is exercised through the statutory planning process either by their contribution to structure plans and local plans or through their role as statutory consultees on proposals for development requiring planning permission (see Chapters 20 and 27).

Impacts on fresh waters can come from diffuse land-use practices within the catchment as well as from site-specific developments, such as hydro-electricity schemes or industrial sites. Some of these changes (those that come within the legal definition of "development" for planning purposes) can be controlled through the statutory planning process of development control and planning permissions. Activities such as agriculture and forestry, which do not come within planning control, require additional strategies, consultation procedures or non-statutory mechanisms to integrate them with the process of planning for fresh waters. Within the last 10 years this has become an increasingly important feature of freshwater resource management and conservation involving all land-use sectors, including the local authorities through the water and drainage services, which, since 1975, have been the responsibility of Regional Councils.

The statutory planning system – with a strategic planning mechanism at the regional level, through which local plans interrelate – has provided an important opportunity for more effective and positive management and development of freshwater resources. The development of policy in Scotland and the related innovations and initiatives for safeguarding the resource reflects the greater importance now given to freshwater conservation by planners, scientists and engineers.

In Scotland, both the water industry and the statutory planning functions are now within the Scottish Office Environment Department but are operated by different divisions. The Engineering, Water and Waste Directorate is responsible for water supplies, water quality, water pollution control, the River Purification Boards, flood prevention and advice on arterial drainage. The Planning Division is responsible for development planning and policy, and Scottish Natural Heritage for the environmental aspects of agriculture, forestry and fish farming. The Forestry Commission reports directly to the Secretary of State, while agricultural interests, together with freshwater fisheries and aquaculture, are looked after by the Scottish Office Agriculture and Fisheries Department. These divisions of responsibility at national level do not always assist in the achievement of common objectives in planning for fresh waters (Chapter 30).

Effective water planning and management requires the close integration of activities identified by Sewell and Biswas (1986) including monitoring, assessment and surveying of waters, water quality management, conservation of flora and fauna, combined forest and watershed management and river basin planning. It also needs a legal and institutional system, adequate research and training, and public information. In Scotland only certain of these activities come within the remit of the statutory planning system. The first two are dealt with by the River Purification Boards and the water and drainage authorities, which are, at present, the water and drainage departments of the Regional or Islands Councils. Conservation is shared between Scottish Natural Heritage and the statutory planning system of structure and local plans. The statutory planning process makes a large, but not exclusive, contribution to the legal and institutional system and to public information through its consultative procedures. At present, the only procedure for forest and watershed planning and management lies in the limited provisions of the various indicative forestry strategies of the regional structure plans while as yet there is no river basin planning, defined by Sewell and Biswas (1986) as "Multi-criteria planning procedures and systems planning methodology . . . including cost effectiveness analysis".

THE STATUTORY PLANNING SYSTEM

The modern statutory system of town and country planning is described in Young and Rowan-Robinson (1985) and dates from the Town and Country Planning (Scotland) Act 1947. This repealed most of the earlier planning legislation and laid the foundation for what Sir Desmond Heap called "a brand new beginning in the matter of control over land and development". The 1947 Act introduced the concept of development control by planning authorities, within the framework of a development plan. These concepts are still central to the present system of town and country planning in Scotland but planning legislation has been under more or less continuous change since the 1947 Act was introduced. Most of these changes were eventually consolidated in the Town and Country Planning (Scotland) Act 1972 which confirmed a "new style" system of development planning comprising a two-tier system of strategic structure plans and detailed local plans.

The 1972 Act was amended in a number of important respects in the Local Government (Scotland) Act 1973 and was finally brought into force in 1975. This same Local Government Act brought into being the two-tier system of Regional and District Councils which became the planning authorities broadly charged with the preparation of the structure plans and local plans respectively.

The 1973 Act established nine Regional Councils – Highland, Grampian, Tayside, Strathclyde, Fife, Central, Lothian, Borders and Dumfries and Galloway – together with 53 District Councils at a smaller scale. In addition, three general planning authorities were set up in the Islands Councils of the Western Isles, the Orkney Islands and the Shetland Islands with responsibility for both structure and local planning within their areas while three of the Regional Councils – Highland, Borders, and Dumfries and Galloway – are also general planning authorities responsible for both structure and local plans.

The two different tiers of local government have different planning powers and functions. The regional planning functions included the preparation of the original "regional reports", which are no longer required, together with regularly updated analytical "reports of survey" and "structure plans", which provide a corporate approach to strategic land-use planning. The Regional Councils have reserve powers regarding local plans and have powers to "call in" planning applications from the District Councils under certain circumstances, particularly where proposals have major strategic implications. District Councils are charged with the preparation of local plans, the determination of planning applications and the enforcement of planning control. They also have responsibility for the protection of buildings of special architectural or historic interest, powers relating to conservation areas and relating to nature conservation and landscape. Since 1973 there have been further amendments to the planning legislation, most notably in the Local Government (Scotland) Act 1982, which redefined some of the service roles within the established two-tier system and the Planning and Compensation Act 1991 which accorded greater status to development plans in determining applications.

With the publication of the Scottish Office (1992) consultation paper, "The Structure of Local Government in Scotland – Shaping the New Councils", and the recent Local Government (Scotland) Bill, the whole pattern of local government (and ultimately the planning system in Scotland) is under review. The importance of the strategic planning process, however, is recognized by the Government, although the mechanism by which such integrated planning is delivered, is part of the overall review process.

NATIONAL PLANNING GUIDANCE

The system of regional structure plans and local plans does not operate in a vacuum of national policy. Although there is no formal "national planning" system, all structure plans have to be approved by the Secretary of State for Scotland through the Scottish Office Environment Department (SOEnD), formerly called the Scottish Development Department (SDD). Local plans do not need to be so approved, but they do need to conform to the relevant structure plan for the area within which they lie.

In addition to this overview provided by the Secretary of State, planning policy and guidance at national level is exercised through a number of processes and mechanisms such as National Planning Guidelines, Circulars and Planning Advice Notes and can be developed incrementally through the decisions of the Secretary of State on structure plans and planning appeals. It can also be changed through primary legislation in Parliament or through delegated legislation in the forms of Statutory Instruments, Special Development Orders, General Development Orders and Directions.

Where national policy issues need to be resolved, such as the location of major oil platform construction yards or the location of downhill skiing developments, then National Planning Guidelines (NPGs) may be prepared. There have been no NPGs for freshwater resources. Since 1991 NPGs have been replaced by National Planning Policy Guidelines (NPPGs) which are designed to combine policy with locational guidance and are to be regarded as statements of Ministerial policy. These guidelines are therefore an important source of national planning policy for those concerned with the development of land.

SDD Circulars (and now SOEnD Circulars) are widely used by the Secretary of State for drawing attention to changes in legislation, providing guidance in interpretation, and for giving advice on policy to planning authorities. There are Circulars currently in existence for a range of activities including agriculture and for forestry (Scottish Office, 1988c,d), but none for fresh waters.

Planning Advice Notes (PANs) were introduced to assist planning authorities in the preparation of the first round of regional reports but over the years they have expanded in scope to offer national advice on a whole range of planning and resource planning matters. The current list includes PANs on such resources as Agriculture, Forestry, Countryside, Sport, Outdoor Recreation and Tourism, Electricity, Nature Conservation, Fishing Industry, and Geology, but again there is not one on fresh waters.

Further guidance is given to planning authorities from the Scottish Office through a series of Land Use Summary Sheets which provide information and advice on a range of natural resource issues at the national scale. Three of these Land Use Summary Sheets do deal directly with fresh waters – No. 9, *Water Supply*; No.10, *River Conditions* and No.15, *Groundwater* (Scottish Development Department, 1978a,b; 1981a).

Land Use Summary Sheet No. 9, *Water Supply*, summarizes Scotland's freshwater resources from the point of view of water supply for drinking and for development. The SDD had published its first review of available water resources, *A Measure of Plenty*, in 1973, which was subsequently updated in 1985. The Land Use Summary Sheet recognizes that water is one of Scotland's primary natural resources and that few countries are so well endowed with plentiful supplies of high quality water (potentially $200\,000$ ML d^{-1}) and with such a high ratio of total potential supply to total present consumption. However, the Land Use Summary Sheet also notes that the distribution of this water in relation to its customers is less satisfactory; with 85% of the population concentrated in the Central Belt where the rainfall is relatively low, the number of potential sources is limited and the levels of pollution are greatest. It is in this and other lowland areas that it is most difficult to reconcile the various alternative demands on water where the tapping of a loch or river for public consumption (Figure 28.1) places limitations on its use for recreation, agriculture, fishing and effluent disposal. It is considered that integrated planning has been strengthened in Scotland by bringing both the water supply function and the strategic planning function under the same Regional Councils, but other major changes in land use, such as agricultural drainage and large-scale afforestation, both of which are outside planning control, can cause changes in the pattern of rainfall run-off and water quality. Land Use Summary Sheet No.10 deals with *River Conditions* in Scotland in 1978. It similarly emphasizes the multiple uses to which rivers are put for water supply, disposal of sewage and trade effluents, irrigation and land drainage, navigation, commercial fisheries and recreational activities. River water is again identified as an important natural resource which must be carefully protected against damaging levels of pollution. Strict control measures are clearly necessary even though only about 10% of public water supplies in Scotland are drawn from the lower reaches of the rivers where pollution risks are greater.

FIGURE 28.1. Talla Reservoir in Borders Region – a major water supply for Lothian Region and the City of Edinburgh. Photograph: Lothian Regional Council

Land Use Summary Sheet No.15 is concerned with Scotland's *Groundwater* resources and their relevance to planning. It notes that the effect of groundwater can be positive, where the availability of a water resource could aid some types of development, or it could be restrictive because of the need to protect the groundwater from pollution. Planning authorities are warned that planning decisions can directly or indirectly cause pollution of existing groundwater supplies or potentially valuable aquifers. Although many aquifers can reduce the impact of contamination by dispersion and diffusion it is very difficult to reclaim a contaminated aquifer. The locations of aquifers and their recharge areas are therefore a significant factor in land-use planning.

It is clear that national guidance in planning for fresh waters has concentrated upon their value for present and future economic and social development. Rivers offered potential areas for economic activity as fisheries, effluent disposal channels or sources of irrigation for agriculture while surface or groundwater supplies were seen as resources for the development of industry and the expansion of settlements. There appeared to be no consideration, at this time, of the environmental benefits of clean and undeveloped freshwater resources for amenity and as valuable habitats for wildlife, and there was only passing reference to the value of rivers for recreation and for non-commercial fisheries.

STRUCTURE PLANS

National planning guidance is aimed at assisting regional planning authorities in the preparation of their structure plans, which form the main strategic framework for statutory planning in Scotland. The whole of Scotland has now been covered by structure plans which have been prepared by the Regional Councils under the provisions of the 1972 Act on the advice contained in Planning Advice Note 27 – *"Structure Planning"* (Scottish Development Department, 1981b). New guidance under Planning Advice Note 37 (Scottish Development Department, 1992) will have significance for structure plans under review at present and in the future.

The purpose of a structure plan is to provide "a strategic policy framework at regional or sub-regional level for the development and control of the physical environment in the interest of the community" and it has to be prepared against the findings of a Report of Survey which is required to cover a wide range of topics including the principal physical and economic characteristics of the area, the size, composition and distribution of the population and the communications, transport system and traffic of the area and, so far as relevant, of any neighbouring areas.

Each planning authority prepares a Report of Survey for its region on which to base its Structure Plan. The first Report of Survey, published by Lothian Regional Council (1977), was based upon its Regional Report of 1976, which took stock of policies and programmes inherited from predecessor authorities and assisted in the move towards regional policies and priorities. The Report of Survey deals with freshwater resources under the headings of "Infrastructure" and "Environmental Pollution". It refers to the water supply benefits of the proposed Megget Reservoir, to meet projected demands for water well into the next century, and the need to upgrade sewage treatment plants to reduce river and estuary pollution. The Report of Survey summarizes, in map form, the extent of such pollution and describes the substantial improvements achieved in the Water of Leith, the Lothian Esks and the River Tyne, such that the Water of Leith and the lower River Esk could support healthy Trout populations. The survey also highlighted the remaining sewage pollution and identified work in progress to eliminate or reduce it.

Public consultation

There are a number of important statutory stages through which the strategic planning authority must go between announcing its decision to commence the preparation of a structure plan and obtaining the Secretary of State for Scotland's approval of the final document.

Firstly, the authority must give public notice of the intention to prepare or to amend a plan. There must then be consultation and active steps have to be taken to give publicity to the matters to be included in the plan. Adjoining local authorities, statutory and non-statutory bodies, and the general public must be given the opportunity to give their views. These views must be taken into consideration in the preparation of the plan. Consultation on the proposed policies is an important formal stage before the final plan is presented to the Secretary of State for approval and in this there is an opportunity to influence policy and to identify where gaps exist. The Secretary of State may adjust the plan to reflect national policy if he feels that this is necessary and, finally, if there are controversial issues, the Secretary of State may request a public examination of the plan before it eventually receives approval.

Form and content of structure plans

A structure plan must consist of a Written Statement supplemented by diagrams. In general, the written statement has to formulate the authority's policy and general proposals for the development and other use of land in its area, and relate those proposals to the proposals for development and land use in neighbouring areas. The structure plan may also contain such other matter as the planning authority considers relevant, and this gives a degree of discretion on what is included in the plan. The potentially wide range of matters which could be included in a structure plan is, however, constrained by a number of requirements.

Firstly, any item included in the structure plan must serve a planning purpose, and it must be directly related to the development and use of land. Secondly, it must represent a "strategic issue". Not only must the topic be of strategic or regional significance, as opposed to merely a local matter, but it must also be an "issue" – that is, a problem which requires a planning solution. It is up to the local authorities themselves to determine what their strategic issues are but they must take account of any relevant national planning guidelines for incorporation into structure plan policies. Thirdly, the structure plan must be concerned principally with land use. PAN27 suggests that only if there is "an imbalance or conflict among land uses and activities" should it be addressed in the structure plan.

The nature of the issues traditionally tackled in structure plans have been those problems of locating settlement, industry, transport and communications. Planning Advice Note No. 27, however, suggests that countryside conservation, recreation and tourism might be appropriate topics where there are strategic planning interests.

Increasingly, environmental issues have been developed, as a consequence of legislation, government policy and local public concerns. The concept of sustainability now influences land-use planning and, in terms of resource management and development, this becomes a greater determining factor as structure plans are being revised.

The first of the regional structure plans was adopted in the late 1970s and concentrated on such issues as settlement patterns, location of industry and employment, and transportation. Some early structure plans had reference to the countryside, recreation and tourism, under which the amenity aspects of the water resource could be considered.

Lothian Region Structure Plan 1978 (Lothian Regional Council, 1978), for example, contained a commitment to cooperate with the River Purification Board in maintaining and improving water quality, while another policy encouraged the recreational use of river valleys, reservoirs and canals. Other structure plans considered the protection of water catchment areas and the tourism potential of important lochs and river valleys.

By the time the first generation of structure plans was nearing review there was an increasing awareness of the value of water for wildlife conservation. Lothian Region Structure Plan 1985 (Lothian Regional Council, 1985) contained policies promoting the preparation of a conservation and recreation strategy for its reservoirs (Figure 28.2) and requiring wildlife conservation to be considered in the development of recreation and tourism on the Union Canal and other areas of water-based recreation.

FIGURE 28.2. Roseberry Reservoir, south of Edinburgh, one of the many small reservoirs built to provide compensation water of supply water to the city. Photograph: Lothian Regional Council

By 1991, the Borders Region Structure Plan 1991 (Borders Regional Council, 1991a,b) recognized the importance of the River Tweed system for nature conservation, fisheries, the maintenance of the rural economy, recreation and tourism. Policy R19 states:

> The Regional Council recognises the unique value of the River Tweed system as a regional resource and will continue to develop policies reflecting this significance through the medium of such bodies as the recently established Tweed Forum.

This structure plan is therefore taking a holistic view of planning for the whole river system and involving the community through a broad-based forum.

Planning Advice Note No. 37

By 1992 the whole of Scotland was covered by the network of structure plans drawn up, reviewed and updated under the guidance of PAN 27 (Scottish Development Department, 1981b). As a result of the experience gained in this process together with a changing social and economic climate (in particular, the increasing role of the private sector and concerns about the environment) a new Planning Advice Note – No. 37 – was published by the Scottish Development Department (1992). Structure plans will continue to reflect national policies at the regional level. Planning advice and guidance is being reviewed and consolidated and a new series of documents – National Planning Policy Guidance (NPPGs) – is being introduced to provide statements of government policy and, where appropriate, a locational framework on nationally important land-use issues. These issues should not be treated as separate and unrelated. It is vital that structure plans provide a clear locational framework for the promotion and control of development, the coordination of infrastructure investment and the protection of heritage and other resources, including fresh waters.

INDICATIVE FORESTRY STRATEGIES

Forestry is one of the major land uses and influences on fresh waters (see Chapter 23), which does not come under statutory planning control. Mather (1989) summarizes the history of afforestation and planning in Scotland. Although this land use is not subject to statutory planning control, planning authorities are, nevertheless, now required to be consulted by the Forestry Authority under statutory consultation procedures.

The form of these consultations was first laid down in SDD Circular 71/1974 (Scottish Development Department, 1974) and required the Forestry Commission to consult with local authorities and other public authorities, as appropriate, on proposals contained in all applications for grant-aid and felling licences or for approval of draft plans of operations. The objective was to ensure that the implications for agriculture, amenity, recreation, nature conservation and other land-use considerations were taken fully into account. The consultation subsequently requested by Regional Councils was usually promulgated in regional structure plans, and recognized the impact of forestry, particularly on landscape and recreation. For example, the first Lothian Region Structure Plan 1978 called for consultation on any afforestation proposals for the upper moors of the Moorfoot, Lammermuir and Pentland Hills for their strategic landscape value and, more generally, for access agreements to be made where there was public pressure.

The requirements for statutory consultation were amended as a result of SDD Circular 7/1984 (Scottish Development Department, 1984) to speed up and simplify the procedure. In agreement with the Convention of Scottish Local Authorities (COSLA), consultation was restricted to one tier of local authority, that exercising the local planning function. It became the responsibility of that authority to consult with the Regional Council in areas where a two-tier planning system existed. Locally, agreement was reached on the level of consultation, with an emphasis on restricting it to sensitive areas although, in the main, the planning authorities still sought consultation on all applications. At regional level, however, strategic and sensitive areas were generally agreed with both the District Councils and the Commission. At the strategic planning level consultation thus became more specific. For example, the Lothian Region Structure Plan 1985 recommended that:

> In accord with procedures agreed with the Forestry Commission and the District Councils, the Regional Council should be consulted on any afforestation proposals for the proposed Pentland Hills Regional Park and areas of more than 20 ha that fall across or above the 230 m contour, and all proposals within the catchment areas of its reservoirs.

The 20 ha figure, at that time, was the one used by the then Department of Agriculture and Fisheries for Scotland as the cut-off point, below which it did not seek consultation. In such a policy was the recognition of the sensitivity of high amenity areas, important landscape zones and the protection of water catchments.

However, the impacts on other interests, including fresh waters, of the rapid expansion of commercial forestry, encouraged by government policy and aided by tax incentives during the 1980s, led to considerable public concern about insensitive planting schemes destroying nationally important landscapes and nature conservation sites. From this concern arose the need for greater strategic guidance on where afforestation should or should not take place and on the other interests which could be adversely affected by such land-use change. No mechanism existed for such planning involvement, particularly since forestry remained outside the statutory system of planning control.

After 1983 a number of developments affected Scottish forestry. The changing financial and administrative context of forestry over the previous five years had produced uncertainty in the industry, while environmental concerns were becoming major issues. Changes in government financial policy on forestry had made it much more sensitive to economic considerations, while changes in agricultural policy had vastly extended the areas available for planting grant. The introduction of the European Commission Directive in July 1988, requiring environmental assessments of planting proposals in sensitive areas, also required more detailed pre-planning of proposals. Strathclyde Region, along with other regions with extensive areas of afforestable land, had become an increasing focus for forestry investors. To provide more positive planning guidance for the industry, a more explicitly positive approach to forestry policy was considered appropriate by the Regional Council in 1988.

The objective of the Council was to reduce the effort, delay and conflicts of interest by explicit guidance on the relative sensitivity of areas and communities to land afforestation. This led to the preparation of an "Indicative Forestry Strategy", incorporated into the 1988 update to the Strathclyde Region Structure Plan 1981. This innovation was welcomed by the Government, not only in relation to the guidance such strategies would provide, but also because they would be prepared in the context of structure plans.

This first strategy analyzed areas and interests which would be sensitive to land-use changes brought about by afforestation, including areas important for nature conservation, designated scenic areas, archaeological sites, tourist development and water catchments. From this sieving process, three categories could be identified.

- *Preferred Areas*, defined as areas "without major strategic constraints", could accommodate and promote forestry development away from sensitive areas. Nevertheless, promotion of forestry in these areas could only be accepted so long as it was accompanied by the acceptable levels of "good practice" laid down by the Forestry Commission and the private sector representative body, Timber Growers (UK). It was also recognized that further work was needed to provide comprehensive guidelines for those investing in forestry with reference to acidification, archaeology and other issues.
- *Potential Areas* were considered to be able to absorb some further afforestation but their sensitivity precluded their promotion for unrestrained planting. These areas might be considered sensitive for a number of reasons – for example, landscape, nature conservation, agriculture or water supply. In upland water supply catchments, water treatment facilities historically have been kept to the minimum consistent with the long-established balance between land use and water quality or quantity. Intensive conifer planting in such areas is often incompatible with maintaining a long-term supply of wholesome water to the standard of EC Directive 80/778/EEC without extra costs for the water authority. Reduced run-off, siltation during ploughing, nutrient enrichment and acidification were the primary concerns raised by afforestation. In some instances it might be possible to design and manage forestry developments where there is an excess of water yield and suitable treatment capacity but it entails a balance in land-use planning. At the time the anticipated *Forests and Water Guidelines* (Forestry Commission, 1988) were expected only to minimize any detrimental effects on water quality and this is still the point of view of water engineers.
- *Sensitive Areas* were identified as being those where the number, complexity and interaction of the above factors made them extremely sensitive to land-use change, and where tree planting would lead to irrevocable damage, such as Sites of Special Scientific Interest and Scheduled Ancient Monuments.

The issue of forestry had, by 1988, become a major concern of the Convention of Scottish Local Authorities (COSLA, 1988) which published a report *Forestry in Scotland: Planning the Way Ahead* and submitted it to the Secretary of State for Scotland. In welcoming the report, one outcome was national guidance on the preparation of indicative forestry strategies, which came with the publication of the Scottish Development Department (1990) Circular 13/1990. This outlined the Government's policy as seeking to encourage the expansion of forestry in an environmentally acceptable way. It also considered the relationship of indicative forestry strategies to structure plans, yet placed no obligation on all local authorities to prepare such strategies, given the wide variation in the importance of forestry from one area to another. It was also considered not appropriate that forestry issues should generally receive detailed treatment in local plans.

Indicative forestry strategies were intended to represent a broad assessment of the opportunities for new planting, taking account of environmental and other factors and adopted the definitions of preferred, potential and sensitive areas. The Circular concluded that, since new planting could have significant land-use and socioeconomic implications, it was important that an indicative forestry strategy, if prepared, should be incorporated into the structure plan.

In its detailed advice to planning authorities on the preparation of strategies, the Circular recommends the "sieve mapping" of a number of major land-use interests such as forestry potential, prime and important agricultural land, landscape, nature conservation, archaeology, key water supply catchments, and the important sites, areas and routes for recreation and tourism. It also notes that, in some regions, other interests may also need to be taken into account and the distribution of deer populations is cited as an example of a subject for more detailed local study.

Strategies need to be flexible and capable of being updated to take account of new circumstances and some areas may need to be re-allocated between categories as more information becomes available or land-use policies change. Such plans can thus have a short period of relevance, as has been subsequently demonstrated. For example, changing agricultural support mechanisms, as a result of the shift in the EC Common Agricultural Policy away from intensive food production, have potentially brought more agricultural land into the "preferred" planting category. There is also the objective of bringing forestry on to the better agricultural soils which, until recently, were to be protected through national policies from such land-use changes. Nature conservation, too, through wider survey work, can necessitate an upgrading of marginal farmland to the "sensitive" category which might previously have been zoned as "potential", or even "preferred". Indicative forestry strategies are only as good as the information that is fed into them and therefore require regular reviewing.

In the early development of the concept of indicative forestry strategies the freshwater interest tended to be considered in terms of the protection of water supply catchment areas. There was no real consideration of fresh waters as wildlife habitats requiring conservation, or providing avenues for recreation or sustaining economic development and employment through recreational or commercial fisheries in estuarine and coastal areas. However, in March 1991, a Scottish Office Environment Department letter invited planning authorities to give careful consideration to the effects of forestry on salmon and other freshwater fisheries and suggested that, as a matter of course, the Association of Scottish District Salmon Fishery Boards and the Atlantic Salmon Trust should be consulted in the preparation of indicative forestry strategies in most parts of Scotland.

The indicative forestry strategy of Borders Regional Council (1991b) extended the coverage of water issues to identify a number of rivers whose quality would be sensitive to any reduction of flow caused by afforestation. Despite extensive consultation with the River Tweed Commissioners the special sensitivity of salmonid fish populations was not accepted as a separate constraint in the overall strategy but the Forestry Authority agreed to consult with the River Tweed Commissioners on all forestry proposals.

To emphasize the importance of such liaison, the Scottish Office in October 1992 confirmed that it was essential to give careful consideration to the effects of forestry on salmon and freshwater fisheries because of their substantial contribution to the Scottish economy.

Tayside Region Indicative Forestry Strategy, 1992, deals with water both as a resource for exploitation and as a habitat. It considers the importance of fisheries in the Tay and its tributaries and in the North and South Esk, together with the possible effects of land-use change. Despite earlier consultation with the Tay District Salmon Fisheries Board and the River Tay District Advisory Committee the strategy was modified by the Secretary of State who placed a requirement on Tayside Regional Council to collect information relating to the effects of afforestation on fisheries with a view to revising the strategy where appropriate at the earliest opportunity in the light of that information.

The draft indicative forestry strategy for Highland Region was published for public consultation in August 1992 and contains a comprehensive chapter on water resources and freshwater fisheries. This includes a map of water resources which shows not only catchment areas for public water supply and distilleries but also catchments at risk from low flows, eutrophication and acidification. Those rivers and lochs where Salmon are present are shown, in addition to sites known to contain Arctic Charr. This species has been affected by acidification in other parts of Scotland. The chapter also deals with the potentially beneficial effects of broad-leaved planting in improving the chemistry and the food chain of impoverished waters.

The composite strategy map includes "water", in a generic sense, as one of the constraints but does not identify which aspect is significant in specific areas. One of the features of the map of "Key Themes and Priorities" is the large extent of land allocated to the regeneration of native woodland and includes parts of the catchments of the Rivers Spey, Findhorn, Nairn, Ness and Conon and Loch Maree.

The Report of Consultation was published in May 1993 and the final strategy is awaited.

The "Indicative Forestry Strategy" mechanism has been a significant advance in guiding a non-statutory land-use issue. Yet its true value might be argued as having still to be tested because of the slump in afforestation investment during the past 10 years. Where it has been applied, evidence suggests that it has had a mixed success. For example, the "sensitive" category does not actually eliminate forestry but places particular demands on design and integration. However, some interpret it as a "no go" zonation and proposals are refused because of it. On the other hand, there is also evidence provided by forestry agents that proposals for afforestation in "preferred" areas can receive a negative response from the local planning authorities because of the weight of local opinion against the proposal. In such circumstances the relevance of the strategy is of little consequence.

LOCAL PLANS

Local plans are prepared and implemented by District Councils and, by definition, are not required to consider the strategic aspects of freshwater resources. District Councils are, however, the development control authorities, granting or refusing planning permission for most development. They also have specific responsibility for protecting and developing landscape, amenities, recreational and wildlife resources at local level.

Areas of Great Landscape Value are promoted in local plans and frequently feature the freshwater resources of river valleys or lochs. Country Parks are designated and managed primarily by District Councils and feature in local plans. Many of these, such as Monikie Country Park near Dundee, Gartmorn Dam near Alloa, and Beecraigs, near Linlithgow, are based on reservoir water resources, while others at Castle Semple, Strathclyde Country Park and Lochore Meadows in Fife are based on natural or artificial lochs. Local Nature Reserves are also now designated by District Councils and promoted in local plans. Many of these have a freshwater conservation element, as at Gladhouse Reservoir, Midlothian, and at Gartmorn Dam.

A subject local plan is a special type of local plan which is restricted to one or more aspects of planning or specifically deals with a discrete area, often with a linear or clearly defined shape. In Scotland, two subject local plans have dealt specifically with the planning of conservation and recreation on the major water resources of Loch Lomond (1982) and of the Forth and Clyde Canal (1984), while the Subject Local Plan for Conservation and Recreation in the Pentland Hills Regional Park (Lothian Regional Council, 1989), contains policies and proposals for the seven reservoirs which lie within its boundaries.

FISH FARMING

Alongside afforestation, fish farming (see Chapter 21) has been one of the major freshwater issues addressed by the planning system. The planning status of both marine and freshwater fish farming has been a cause of controversy as this industry has expanded over recent years. The marine environment is not under consideration but it should be noted that the statutory jurisdiction of the local planning authorities only extends to the low water mark. Beyond that, the Crown Estate Commission is defined as the competent authority.

Lloyd (1990, 1991) describes the planning position of freshwater fish farms as one of uncertainty in applying planning controls and inconsistency between different areas of Scotland. Some planning authorities have considered that fish farming was an agricultural activity and therefore qualified as "permitted development" while others took an opposite view. There has thus been a growth of Rainbow Trout farming alongside rivers and in such lochs as Tay, Awe and Earn, and smolt rearing in other lochs with variable degrees of public consultation and local authority control.

A consultation paper was issued by the Scottish Development Department in 1989 to try to clarify the position and to eliminate the anomalies. The outcome of the consultation was that the Secretary of State considered that fish farming now comes within the statutory definition of agriculture and therefore a change of use from agriculture to fish farming does not require planning permission. However, the consultation recognized the concerns expressed about the accumulative environmental effects of fish farming in fresh waters and the Secretary of State proposed to make it clear that the permitted development rights associated with agriculture were to be removed from fish farms so that the environmental aspects could be adequately considered by planning authorities. These aspects include not only discharge and effluent levels, but also questions of siting and design where the farm is situated in an area of scenic beauty. Since March 1990 all new freshwater fish farms and new extensions to existing farms have required planning permission. The debate on the environmental effects of freshwater aquaculture was taken forward by the report from the Nature Conservancy Council (1990), prepared by the Institute of Aquaculture, the Institute of Freshwater Ecology and the Institute of Terrestrial Ecology. This report stressed the need for a more integrated approach to the management of fresh waters in Scotland in terms of the existing legislation, the agencies involved and the approach to environmental protection. In particular, it suggested that EC environmental assessmental procedures be used to deal with environmental issues in sensitive locations.

SOEnD Circular 31/1992 (Scottish Office Environment Department, 1992) drew attention to the fact that the placing of cages and other structures in inland waters for fish farming purposes constituted an engineering operation and therefore required planning permission. The circular also advised that a statement of government policy on fish farming development would shortly be issued for consultation in the form of a National Planning Policy Guideline.

ENVIRONMENTAL IMPACT ASSESSMENT

The European Community's interest in environmental impact assessment dates back to 1969 but the first proposal for legislation did not come forward until 1980 and Directive 85/337 "Directive on the assessment of the effects of certain public and private projects on the environment" was formally notified on 3 July 1985 with a compliance date for member states of 3 July 1988. This compliance was implemented by the Scottish Development Department (1988) through SDD Circular 13/1988 against the background of a lukewarm government policy that the Directive should not add significantly to existing procedures.

The main features of the Directive, as summarized by Clark (1988), are that developers of public and private projects which are likely to have significant effects on the environment must submit information on the projects and their environmental effects to a competent authority (normally in the UK a local authority). They, in turn, must make this information available to other public authorities with environmental responsibilities and to the affected public. Any information and opinions received must be taken into consideration by the competent authority when making its decision. In the EC Directive, projects are divided into Annex I and Annex II projects. Annex I projects, such as oil refineries, power stations and motorways, are always expected to have significant effects and will therefore be subject to the articles of this directive. Annex II projects have to be assessed where member states consider "that their characteristics so require". Annex II covers a wide range of projects, some of them not, at present, subject to UK planning control, such as afforestation and marine Salmon farming.

In the Scottish Office Circular 13/1988 the two Annexes are replaced by Schedule 1 and Schedule 2. Schedule 2 projects are identified, rather vaguely, as major projects which are of more than local importance, a few smaller projects proposed for particularly sensitive locations and, in exceptional circumstances, projects with unusually complex and potentially adverse environmental effects where expert and detailed analyses of these effects would be desirable and would not be carried out under normal planning procedures.

The Circular does not offer criteria or thresholds to assist a decision on whether an environmental assessment is required or not but does include indicative criteria. The initial judgement rests with the local planning authority but regulations give the Secretary of State power to direct that an environmental assessment is, or is not, required in any particular case.

For projects normally outside planning control, "Regulations" (1988) were introduced. Those which might have an impact on freshwater systems include trunk roads and motorways, power stations (including those less than 300 MW, if the Secretary of State considers that there will be significant environmental effects), afforestation and land drainage.

Ferguson and Ward (1990) reported that, by the end of 1989, the Nature Conservancy Council, as the government's then official advisers on nature conservation, had been consulted on 60 environmental impact assessments of which none was related to agriculture/water management. Sixteen dealt with afforestation and one with Salmon farming. Extractive industry had been responsible for 10 environmental assessments and waste disposal for seven. At that stage it was already clear that the number of projects which would require assessments had been underestimated and it was also clear that local authorities were taking seriously the definition of "significant" environmental effects in their decisions to call for such assessments.

NON-STATUTORY PLANNING

Despite the limitations of their legal scope and their traditional emphasis on economic and social development issues, statutory structure plans have provided the only strategic framework within which freshwater issues of water supply, drainage, conservation and recreation could be addressed by the planning authorities. Their limitations are that major catchment land uses such as agriculture and forestry do not come within the statutory planning system, although the structure plans have been flexible enough to address forestry issues through statutory consultation procedures and indicative forestry strategies.

Structure plans have been able to develop a corporate approach to the coordination of water and drainage infrastructure of reservoirs and waste water treatment because the water authorities and the strategic planning authorities are integral parts of the same Regional Councils. At the same time, statutory consultation through the strategic planning function has enabled the concerns of the River Purification Boards to be considered at an early stage in the planning process, thus coordinating pollution control with development plans to the extent, in some cases, of placing embargoes on further development in certain river catchments.

Some of the proposals contained in the government's consultation document *Investing for our Future* (Scottish Office, 1992b) and the subsequent Local Government (Scotland) Bill on the proposed re-organization of the Scottish water industry, would separate the water authorities from local government and thereby prejudice this present corporate approach to water planning.

It is clear, however, that structure plans by themselves and the present statutory process in general are unable to address river catchment planning in a fully integrated manner and that other non-statutory mechanisms have to be sought to coordinate catchment land and water use.

In Scotland some progress has been made by developing strategies arising from structure plan policies. Thus, arising from Policy EP 15 of the Lothian Region Structure Plan (1985), the water department and the planning department of the Regional Council prepared a *Strategy for Conservation and Recreation on the Reservoirs owned by Lothian Regional Council* in 1990. This provided a strategic plan for the integrated management of water quality, wildlife conservation and recreation on 26 council-owned reservoirs over a large part of south-east Scotland.

The importance of river valleys for landscape, conservation and recreation has been increasingly recognized in recent years. The "Clean Forth" initiative of the Forth River Purification Board gathered together a range of statutory and voluntary bodies to improve the environment and increase awareness of the waters in the Forth catchment. In support of this initiative, Keep Scotland Beautiful has promoted the establishment of River Trusts in the Allan, Tyne, Devon and Bluther catchments to encourage local interests to look after the amenity of the river valleys. The Water of Leith Conservation Trust was established in 1987 to perform a similar role for the Edinburgh river and in 1992 the Scottish Wildlife Trust appointed a River Valleys Officer to develop, in association with the Conservation Trust and the local authorities, an Integrated Environmental Action Plan for the river valley. Now completed, it is the intention to extend this treatment to the other Lothian rivers.

Similar initiatives in the non-statutory planning and management of river valleys are seen in Strathclyde, where the River Valleys Strategy promotes the protection and enhancement of the Clyde tributaries and there is already a voluntary group, The Friends of the River Kelvin, established for that river. In Borders Region, the charitable trust, the Tweed Foundation, prepared an Integrated Fisheries Management Plan, which dealt solely with the fish populations and their habitat. However, objectives and policies adopted by the 12 statutory and non-statutory bodies involved in implementing the plan were constructive in influencing the policies of the Borders Region Structure Plan 1991 and Indicative Forestry Strategy and encouraging the development of the Tweed Forum as a multi-agency group promoting the conservation and enjoyment of the Tweed river system. These initiatives indicate that there is at least an awareness of the need for an integrated approach to catchment management. The fact that agriculture and forestry are outside planning control limits the scope of structure plans, by themselves, in achieving this.

Water authorities have been particularly concerned about controlling activities in the catchment areas of their reservoirs. Some water authorities have applied byelaws, under the Water Act 1980, which is feasible when the catchments are owned by the water authority. It is not practicable when the catchment area is privately owned and compensation would be expected. Since 1988, forestry practices have been guided by the *Forests and Water Guidelines*, agreed consultation procedures with the Forestry Authority and indicative forestry strategies. It was only in 1992, that the *Prevention of Pollution from Agricultural Activity – Code of Good Practice* was issued by SOAFD (1992) under the Control of Pollution Act 1974 which gave guidance to farmers on how to avoid point-source pollution from silage and slurry and diffuse pollution from fertilizers and pesticides.

These measures assist in the day-to-day management of catchment areas but still do not promote a mechanism for their long-term planning and the integration of agriculture, forestry, water supply, drainage, flood protection, industry, settlement and pollution control.

In England and Wales, the National Rivers Authority (NRA) is seeking to address some of these issues through the mechanism of catchment management plans. Newson (1991) considers that while catchment planning is a policy aim of the NRA it is still at an embryonic stage. He makes a distinction between catchment control and catchment planning and emphasizes the need for a new system of statutory links between the water interests and statutory planning. Newson notes the difference in interpretation within the NRA as to the function of a catchment plan as merely an internal action document to coordinate investment in improving water quality, or as a document to serve a wider and multi-sector purpose. Catchment planning has been used in relation to flood control, pollution control in urban and rural environments, nature conservation and forestry, and Newson concludes that, with the recent publication of statutory water quality objectives, this offers "a perfect recipe for a planning approach in the water quality sector, . . .".

In Scotland the River Purification Boards do not have all the functions of the National Rivers Authority in England and Wales but the Forth River Purification Board is preparing a draft catchment management plan for the River Forth catchment. This will enable it to be more proactive and predictive in assessing the impacts of land-use change on water quality and relating the potential for development to the carrying capacity of fresh waters.

CONCLUSIONS

At a time when all the indications suggest the need for a closer integration between catchment land use, water interests and the planning authorities, Scotland is facing a period of greater separation of these interests and functions.

The Government's current proposals for the re-organization of local government and the creation of unitary planning authorities could weaken the strategic planning function by reducing the size of the planning authorities and requiring the establishment of joint planning boards, with the possible loss of direction and accountability that this could bring.

The Government's current proposals for the re-organization of the water industry may reduce the current corporate approach between the water authorities and the planning authorities and weaken the essential liaison between these two functions. Associated with this issue, the Government's paper (SOEnD, 1993) on a *Code of Practice on Conservation, Access and Recreation for Water, Sewerage and River Purification Authorities* . . . makes little reference to the need for liaison with strategic planning authorities.

In 1995, the River Purification Boards are due to be incorporated into the Scottish Environment Protection Agency (SEPA), and liaison with the statutory planning authorities will be essential to ensure that catchments are managed not just for limited, though important, water quality objectives, but rather for the complete spectrum of economic, social and environmental issues and activities.

Newson (1991) identifies one of the key areas for institutional development in the UK to be the extension of public participation in environmental decision-making. Local involvement becomes more difficult without transferring local government administrative boundaries to catchment boundaries. This has been done with Ontario's Conservation Authorities Act (1985) and allows for the establishment of catchment authorities specifically to plan public projects affecting rivers. The New Zealand catchment boards have a similar but more focused role in halting land abuse in river catchments.

The existing correlation between river catchments and local authority boundaries in Scotland is quite close and, at least at Regional Council level, not too much adjustment would be required to make them the same. At District Council level there is less correlation and this should have been one of the issues addressed in the establishment of boundaries for the new unitary local authorities. However, this does not appear to have been considered.

A similar argument prevails for the boundaries of the new water authorities. To facilitate catchment planning these should also be co-terminous with the boundaries of the River Purification Boards and the strategic planning authorities. This would at least provide common boundaries for catchment planning. Information on the boundaries of the proposed water authorities is not yet available.

However, without a radical redefinition and redesign of the statutory planning system to bring agriculture, forestry and water planning within its scope, achieving the integrated planning of fresh waters in Scotland will have to rely upon closer and more effective liaison and consultation procedures.

REFERENCES

Borders Regional Council (1991a). *Structure Plan – Report of Survey*, Newtown St Boswells.

Borders Regional Council (1991b). *Structure Plan – Written Statement*, Newtown St Boswells.

Clark, B. D. (1988). "EC Directive of the assessment of the effects of certain public and private projects on the environment", *Scottish Planning Law and Practice*, 24, 4–5, The Planning Exchange, Glasgow.

Convention of Scottish Local Authorities (1988). *Forestry in Scotland: Planning the Way Ahead*, Edinburgh.

David, L. (1986). "Environmentally sound management of freshwater resources", *Resources Policy*, 12, 307–316.

EC Directive 85/337/(OJL175 5.7.85). *Directive on the assessment of the effects of certain public and private projects on the environment*, European Commission, Brussels.

Ferguson, M. P. and Ward, S. D. (1990). "Environmental assessments to date – The NCC experience in Scotland", *Scottish Planning Law and Practice*, 29, 9–10, The Planning Exchange, Glasgow.

Fife Regional Council (1991). *Indicative Forestry Strategy*, Glenrothes.

Forestry Commission (1988). *Forests and Water Guidelines*, Forestry Commission, London.

Forth and Clyde Canal Steering Committee (1984). *Forth and Clyde Canal – Subject Local Plan*, Glasgow.

Grampian Regional Council (1984). *Structure Plan – Written Statement*, Aberdeen.

Grampian Regional Council (1991). *Indicative Forestry Strategy*, Aberdeen.

Home, Lord (1837) in *Tweed Foundation Newsletter*, Number 7, November 1992, The Tweed Foundation, Berwick upon Tweed.

Lloyd, M. G. (1990). "Planning for freshwater fish farms", *Scottish Planning Law and Practice*, 29, 3–4, The Planning Exchange, Glasgow.

Lloyd, M. G. (1991). "Freshwater aquaculture and the Scottish environment", *Scottish Planning Law and Practice*, 32, 3, The Planning Exchange, Glasgow.

Loch Lomond Planning Group (1982). *Loch Lomond – Subject Local Plan*, Glasgow.

Lothian Regional Council (1977). *Structure Plan – Report of Survey*, Edinburgh.

Lothian Regional Council (1978). *Structure Plan – Written Statement*, Edinburgh.

Lothian Regional Council (1985). *Structure Plan – Written Statement*, Edinburgh.

Lothian Regional Council (1989). *Pentland Hills Regional Park – Subject Local Plan 1989–1994*, Edinburgh.

Lothian Regional Council (1990). *Strategy for Conservation and Recreation on the Reservoirs owned by Lothian Regional Council*, Edinburgh.

Mather, S. (1989). "Afforestation and planning", *Scottish Planning Law and Practice*, **26**, 4–8, The Planning Exchange, Glasgow.

Nature Conservancy Council (1990). *Fish Farming and the Scottish Freshwater Environment*, Edinburgh.

Newson, M. (1991). "Catchment control and planning – emerging patterns of definition, policy and legislation in UK water management", *Land Use Policy*, **8**, 9–15.

Newson, M. (1992). "Land and water – convergence, divergence and progress in UK policy", *Land Use Policy*, **9**, 111–121.

Scottish Development Department (1971). SDD Circular 84/1971, Scottish Office, Edinburgh.

Scottish Development Department (1974). SDD Circular 71/1974, Scottish Office, Edinburgh.

Scottish Development Department (1978a). National Planning Series, Land Use Summary Sheet No. 9, *Water Supply*, Scottish Office, Edinburgh.

Scottish Development Department (1978b). National Planning Series, Land Use Summary Sheet No. 10, *River Condition*, Scottish Office, Edinburgh.

Scottish Development Department (1981a). National Planning Series, Land Use Summary Sheet No. 15, *Groundwater*, Scottish Office, Edinburgh.

Scottish Development Department (1981b). Planning Advice Note 27, *Structure Planning*, Scottish Office, Edinburgh.

Scottish Development Department (1984). SDD Circular 7/1984, *Forestry: Consultations with Local Authorities etc.*, Scottish Office, Edinburgh.

Scottish Development Department (1985). *A Measure of Plenty*, Scottish Office, Edinburgh.

Scottish Development Department (1988). SDD Circular 13/1988, *Environmental Assessments: Implementation of EC Directive. The Environmental Assessment (Scotland) Regulations 1988*, Scottish Office, Edinburgh.

Scottish Development Department (1989). *Planning Position of Freshwater Fish Farms*, Consultation Paper, Scottish Office, Edinburgh.

Scottish Development Department (1990). SDD Circular 13/1990, *Indicative Forestry Strategies*, Scottish Office, Edinburgh.

Scottish Development Department (1992). Planning Advice Note 37, *Structure Planning*, Scottish Office, Edinburgh.

Scottish Office (1988a). *Environmental Assessment (Scotland) Regulations 1988 (SI No. 1221*, Edinburgh.

Scottish Office (1988b). *Environmental Assessment (Salmon Farming in Marine Waters) Regulations 1988 (SI No. 1218)*, Edinburgh.

Scottish Office (1988c). *Environmental Assessment (Afforestation) Regulations 1988 (SI No. 1207)*, Edinburgh.

Scottish Office (1988d). *Land Drainage Improvement Works (Assessment of Environmental Effects) Regulations 1988 (SI No. 1217)*. Edinburgh.

Scottish Office (1992a). *The Structure of Local Government in Scotland – Shaping the New Councils*, Edinburgh.

Scottish Office (1992b). *Investing for our Future*, Edinburgh.

Scottish Office Agriculture and Fisheries Department (1992). *Prevention of Environmental Pollution from Agricultural Activity – Code of Good Practice*, Edinburgh.

Scottish Office Environment Department (1992). SOEnD Circular 31/1992, *Planning and Compensation Act 1991: Control over Advertisements and Fish Farming*, Scottish Office, Edinburgh.

Scottish Office Environment Department (1993). *Code of Practice on Conservation, Access and Recreation for Water and Sewerage Authorities and River Purification Boards*, Edinburgh.

Sewell, W. R. D. and Biswas, A. K. (1986). "Implementing environmentally sound management of inland waters, *Resources Policy*, **12**, 295–306.

Strathclyde Regional Council (1981). *Structure Plan – Written Statement*, Glasgow.
Tayside Regional Council (1988). *Structure Plan – Written Statement*, Dundee.
Young, E. and Rowan-Robinson, J. (1985). *Scottish Planning Law and Procedure*, William Hodge and Company, Glasgow.

29

Nature Conservation

P. J. BOON

Scottish Natural Heritage, 2 Anderson Place, Edinburgh, EH6 5NP, UK

INTRODUCTION

The term "nature conservation" may be understood at different levels. At its broadest it has been defined as "the regulation of human use of the global ecosystem to sustain its diversity of content indefinitely" (Nature Conservancy Council, 1984). A narrower, more focused definition summarizes the main *raison d'être* of the former Nature Conservancy Council (NCC): ensuring that "the national heritage of wild flora and fauna and geological and physiographic features remains as large and diverse as possible, so that society may use and appreciate its value to the fullest extent" (Nature Conservancy Council, 1984). It is the latter definition (as far as it relates to freshwater habitats and species) that is the main concern of this chapter. No attempt has been made to describe the valuable work undertaken by the voluntary conservation organizations; interested readers should refer to publications such as those by the Scottish Wildlife Trust (1988), Scottish Conservation Projects Trust (1990), and Pritchard *et al.* (1992).

It was shortly after the Second World War that nature conservation in Great Britain developed into an activity promoted by statute. This followed work by the Society for the Promotion of Nature Reserves, and two seminal reports by the Wild Life Conservation Special Committee (England and Wales) (1947) and by the Scottish National Parks Committee and the Scottish Wild Life Conservation Committee (1947) leading ultimately to the establishment of the Nature Conservancy in 1949. This remained intact until 1973 when the Nature Conservancy Council Act divided it into the NCC and a research arm – the Institute of Terrestrial Ecology. In 1991, the NCC was itself re-organized and three new bodies created: the Nature Conservancy Council for England (EN: English Nature), the Nature Conservancy Council for Scotland (NCCS) and the Countryside Council for Wales (CCW). A year later, in April 1992, Scottish Natural Heritage (SNH) was set up (under the Natural Heritage (Scotland) Act 1991) through the merger of NCCS and the Countryside Commission for Scotland, with general aims parallel to those of CCW, namely:

The Fresh Waters of Scotland: A National Resource of International Significance
Edited by P. S. Maitland, P. J. Boon and D. S. McLusky. © 1994 John Wiley & Sons Ltd

(a) to secure the conservation and enhancement of and
(b) to foster understanding and facilitate the enjoyment of the natural heritage of Scotland; and SNH shall have regard to the desirability of securing that anything done, whether by SNH or any other person, in relation to the natural heritage of Scotland is undertaken in a manner which is sustainable.

"The natural heritage of Scotland" includes the flora and fauna of Scotland, its geological and physiographical features, its natural beauty and amenity . . . (Part 1, Section 1).

In some ways it seems inappropriate to include a separate chapter on "nature conservation", yet it illustrates the point that it has become a clearly circumscribed *activity* formalized within government organizations, rather than an *attitude* that permeates the way society and environment interact. This is particularly true for freshwater nature conservation, where it is often seen as merely another competing "use" alongside water supply, fisheries or recreation. Figure 29.1 depicts a simple

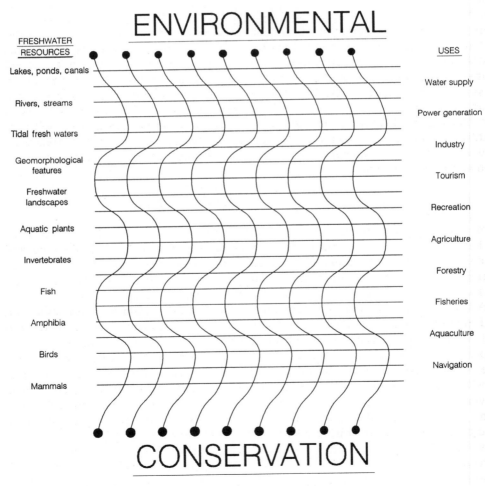

FIGURE 29.1. Freshwater resources and the uses which impinge on them

analogy in which freshwater resources, together with their uses and the pressures impinging on them, are seen as parallel threads in a piece of fabric. The whole area of environmental conservation, incorporating what is usually considered to be "nature conservation", now becomes the weft of the fabric: a system of checks and balances, a way of regulating use and preventing abuse. This analogy demonstrates four advantages of thinking of conservation in this way: (i) it shows how stability can be added to the system; (ii) it emphasizes linkage, not just between organisms and their environment but between man and the rest of nature; (iii) it underlines the need for integration of competing uses; and (iv) it reinstates a sense of orderliness inherent within biological systems, yet so often degraded. In short, this is a view of "sustainable development", of "holism" (in the true sense of the word) in which the whole is more than the sum of the parts.

Strategies for conserving fresh waters will vary according to the condition and perceived value of the system. Cummins (1992), in a discussion of river catchment characteristics, referred to "the arrogance and myth of management", arguing that the best management usually involves minimizing human influence. A practical implication of this is the need to place individual rivers and lakes along a spectrum of "quality" from "natural" to "degraded". The appropriate management option then shifts from one of *preservation* to *limitation* of catchment development, *mitigation* of damaging impacts, *restoration* of damaged systems (by manipulating water quality or physical habitat), and finally to *dereliction* of seriously degraded waters that in the short- or medium-term are irretrievably damaged (Boon, 1992). The tools available for applying this concept to Scotland's fresh waters include both statutory and non-statutory measures. The aim of this chapter is to examine how they have been used, how effective they have been, and how the broader aims of environmental conservation can best be advanced.

ASSESSING THE TASK

Previous chapters have summarized and synthesized information on the wide range of habitats, species and environmental impacts encountered in both standing and running waters. Unlike research workers, or River Purification Boards with a fairly narrow focus, the conservation bodies must try to maintain at least a token interest in most of these areas.

A rough indication of both the scale of the task and the balance of work is shown in Table 29.1, which classifies 470 items of advisory "casework" referred by regional staff to HQ specialists in NCC, NCCS and SNH between 1987 and 1992. It is an imprecise estimate, as (a) it does not permit the classification of items in more than one category, (b) freshwater matters may not be referred from all Regions with equal consistency, and (c) it is not possible to differentiate large items from smaller ones. Nevertheless, three general conclusions can be drawn. First, some topics – acidification, afforestation, and agriculture – seem to have generated surprisingly little casework, perhaps as they have been tackled more as subjects for broader programmes of research and policy development, than for single, short-term pieces of advice. Second, three topics – fisheries management, fish farming and pollution – all feature prominently both in Britain as a whole and in Scotland. Third, Table 29.1 indicates that concern is growing over the incidence of nutrient enrichment on sites of

TABLE 29.1. Synopsis of 470 items of casework in freshwater conservation dealt with by NCC (Chief Scientist Directorate and Scotland HQ) (May 1987 – March 1991), NCCS (HQ) (April 1991 – March 1992), and SNH (Aquatic Environments Branch) (April 1992 – December 1992). Numbers of items expressed as percentages of the totals (A, n = 417; B, n = 107; C, n = 53), and placed into four frequency classes[a]

Subject area	A: GB (1987–91)	B: Items in A referring to Scotland (1987–91)	C: Scotland (1991–92)
Acidification	I	I	–
Afforestation	I	I	I
Agriculture	I	–	I
Land drainage/river engineering	I	II	III
Recreation	I	I	I
Abstraction	II	I	–
Nutrient enrichment	II	I	III
Water regulation	II	II	–
Habitat conservation/site designation	III	II	II
Aquatic weed control	III	IV	III
Civil engineering schemes	III	II	III
Species conservation	III	III	II
Fisheries management	IV	III	IV
Fish farming	IV	IV	IV
Pollution	IV	IV	IV

[a] I = 1–4%; II = >4–8%; III = >8–12%, IV = >12%

conservation importance, with the publicity surrounding cases such as Loch Leven having raised the general awareness of Regional staff.

NATURE CONSERVATION IN PRACTICE

The role of research and survey

Research and survey activities have underpinned the work of the NC, NCC and its successor agencies. During the lifetime of NCC (1973 to 1991) the overall research budget stayed fairly constant at just under £1 million during the 1970s, declined gradually (in "real terms") until the mid-1980s, then rose again to a new peak of £3.7 million in the late 1980s. However, the need to spread this over the entire field of nature conservation meant inevitably that individual subject areas (such as fresh water) received comparatively modest funding.

Figure 29.2 is a four-way analysis of 52 freshwater projects relevant to Scotland, commissioned or carried out by NCC/NCCS/SNH, classifying the division of project funding according to (a) habitat type, (b) species group, (c) project category, and (d) aquatic impacts. The results clearly show a bias towards standing waters (Figure 29.2a), aquatic plants (Figure 29.2b), survey (Figure 29.2c), and water quality issues (Figure 29.2d).

A comparison of these results with advisory output (Table 29.1) suggests that there may be subject areas where new research is required. These might include impacts of water regulation, aquatic weed control, fisheries management, river engineering and others. However, while there may well be a case for re-examining priorities, it would be inappropriate and impractical for SNH to attempt to cover all areas equally. Moreover, there are many other organizations in Scotland (e.g. Freshwater Fisheries Laboratory, Institute of Freshwater Ecology, Institute of Hydrology, Macaulay Land Use Research Institute, Institute of Aquaculture, universities) undertaking freshwater research, some of which is directly relevant to conservation.

This all points to the urgent need for a co-ordinating mechanism – a forum not just for exchanging information about what we are *doing*, but sharing ideas on *what needs to be done*. Ideally, this would extend to programmes of freshwater research elsewhere in the UK to encompass other projects with relevance to Scotland.

The role of legislation

Habitat protection

Freshwater SSSIs While survey and research are basic to an understanding of freshwater systems, an important tool in their conservation is the statutory protection of habitats and species.

In Britain, statutorily protected areas for conservation were first introduced in the same legislation (National Parks and Access to the Countryside Act 1949) that established the Nature Conservancy (NC). This allowed the NC to identify areas of land or water containing plants, animals, geological features or landforms of special interest, and notify planning authorities so that consideration could be given to their conservation in the planning process (Nature Conservancy Council, 1988). In both

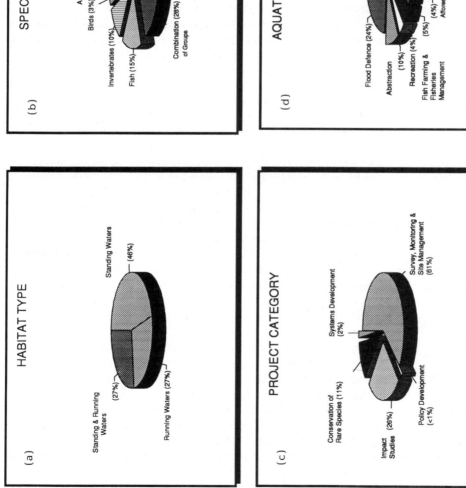

FIGURE 29.2. An analysis of 52 freshwater projects relevant to Scotland, commissioned or carried out by NCC, NCCS, SNH: (a) habitat type, (b) species group, (c) project category, (d) aquatic impacts

the 1949 Act and the Wildlife and Countryside Act 1981, which introduced further provisions for protection, the term "Areas of Special Scientific Interest" is used. By the time the NC had produced its first report in 1952, the word "Area" had been replaced by "Site", and the abbreviation "SSSI" entered the vocabulary from then on.

Under the 1981 Act, an SSSI is formally notified to the owners and occupiers of the land, the appropriate Secretary of State, the local planning authority, and (in England and Wales) to the water or drainage authority. Owners and occupiers receive a list of Potentially Damaging Operations (PDOs) considered likely to damage the interest of the site. The statutory conservation bodies (SNH, EN and CCW) must be given four months' notice in writing of any intention to carry out a PDO. During this period, discussions between the conservation body and the owner may resolve the matter, sometimes entailing financial compensation payable in the form of a "management agreement" to safeguard the nature conservation interest of the site (Nature Conservancy Council, 1988).

An obvious prerequisite of site protection is that sites of high conservation importance can be readily identified using standard criteria. The publication of the *Nature Conservation Review* (NCR) (Ratcliffe, 1977) provided the first systematic appraisal in Britain of the major criteria for selecting areas important for conservation. Ten criteria are discussed: size, diversity, naturalness, rarity, fragility, typicalness (sometimes referred to as "representativeness"), recorded history, position in an ecological/geographical unit, potential value, and intrinsic appeal. A second volume of the NCR gave descriptions of more than 800 nationally (GB) important sites around Britain. Of these, 99 were classified as "Open Waters", of which 40 were in Scotland. This list has not remained static; sites have been deleted for various reasons, some merged with others, and new ones have been added. The present tally of NCR Open Water sites for Scotland includes 37 of the original 40, together with nine sites considered to be of NCR quality since the original list was published. Of the present 46, only five are running waters although another four contain both running and standing waters (Table 29.2).

All biological SSSIs (whether considered NCR quality or not) are selected with reference to guidelines published by the Nature Conservancy Council (1989). These build on the *Nature Conservation Review* and provide a reasoned basis for site selection, both as a means of assisting Regional staff, and as a statement for public information. They also bring a degree of standardization to bear on what might otherwise be a somewhat arbitrary procedure. Both for standing and running waters site selection is based largely on aquatic vegetation, although there is clearly a need, recognized in the guidelines, for taking into account other available information on invertebrates, fish, birds and mammals.

Part of the reason for this emphasis on aquatic plants centres on their usefulness in classifying both rivers and lakes, an essential step in selecting sites representative of different types and different geographical regions. The SSSI guidelines include two classifications: one for standing waters (Palmer, 1989; Palmer *et al.*, 1992), and one for running waters (Holmes, 1983; 1989), each recognizing 10 main Community Types (Chapter 9). Twelve criteria are given for selecting standing water SSSIs, including species richness, presence of a range of *Potamogeton* species, diversity of physical features, and naturalness of the catchment. For rivers, two categories of SSSI

TABLE 29.2. *Nature Conservation Review* (NCR) sites in each of the four Regions of Scottish Natural Heritage. Sites are grouped according to type (i.e. standing waters, running waters, combination of standing and running waters). "OW" is an abbreviation for "Open Waters", and is used with a code number in the *Nature Conservation Review* (Ratcliffe, 1977). Numbers higher than OW 99 refer to sites deemed to be of NCR quality after the *Nature Conservation Review* was published

South-East
OW   63: Gladhouse Reservoir
OW   67: Loch Leven
OW   69: Dupplin Lochs
OW   70: Carsebreck Lochs
OW   71: Loch Laidon (part in NW Region)
OW   72: Tay–Isla Valley
          (a) Monk Myre
          (b) Stormont Loch
          (c) Meikleour
          (d) Loch of Clunie
OW   79: Kilconquhar Loch
OW   80: Drummond Pond
OW   82: Loch Kinnordy
OW   83: Loch Lintrathen
OW 114: Branxholme Wester Loch
OW 117: Lake of Menteith
OW 128: Black Loch

OW   62: River Tweed
OW 126: River Teith

South-West
OW   60: Loch Lomond
OW   61: Mill Loch
OW   64: White Loch
OW   94: Lismore Limestone Lochs

OW   66: River Endrick

North-East
OW   68: Cairngorm Lochs
          (a) Loch Etchachan
          (b) Loch Coire an Lochain
          (c) Lochan Uaine
          (d) Loch Einich
          (e) Loch Avon
OW   74: Loch Insh
OW   76: Loch Kinnord
OW   77: Loch of Strathbeg
OW   78: Lochs Harray and Stenness
OW   84: Loch of Spynie
OW   85: Loch of Spiggie and Loch Brow

OW   73: River Spey
OW   75: River Dee

TABLE 29.2 (*continued*)

North-West
OW 71: Loch Laidon (part in SE Region)
OW 86: Loch Morar
OW 87: Loch an Duin
OW 88: Grogarry Lochs
      (a) Loch Druidibeg
      (b) Loch A'Mhachair and Loch Stilligarry
      (c) The Howmore Estuary, Loch Roag, Loch Fada
OW 89: Durness Lochs and Streams
OW 91: Loch Eye
OW 92: Loch Sionascaig
OW 93: Loch Watten
OW 95: Loch Shiel
OW 121: Loch Ussie
OW 123: Loch Obisary
OW 130: Loch Dola

OW 90: River Strontian
OW 98: Burn of Latheronwheel
OW 129: Forss Water

OW 96: Loch Mhaolach-coire and River Traligill
OW 97: Loch Stack and River Laxford
OW 131: Lochs Brora, Rivers Brora and Blackwater

are recognized: "Whole river SSSIs", to ensure representation of the main River Community Types, or encompassing rivers which show classic and representative transitions along their lengths, and "Sectional SSSIs" – shorter stretches which expand the geographical coverage of river SSSIs and ensure that the best examples of each River Community Type are included in the SSSI series (Nature Conservancy Council, 1989). The definition of appropriate boundaries is essential for all freshwater SSSIs. For example, guidance is given on the inclusion of adjacent semi-natural areas of wet habitat (such as fens, or wet woodland) within the boundary of a river SSSI. There is also a growing recognition of the importance of riparian vegetation, both as habitat and as a modifier of instream physical, chemical and biological conditions, so this is normally included within the site boundary where possible.

It is remarkably difficult to provide an accurate estimate of the number of freshwater SSSIs in Scotland. It is straightforward enough for an individual loch or a stretch of river notified *exclusively* for its aquatic interest, but for many SSSIs the presence of water may be merely a part, perhaps a minor part, of the perceived value of the site.

A compilation has recently been completed of all SSSIs in Scotland containing running waters, defined as those > 5 m wide, shown by a double line on a 1:10 000 OS map (Holmes *et al.*, 1990). The results are given in Table 29.3, where four categories of SSSIs are recognized, from Category 1 in which SSSIs have been designated mainly or wholly on the basis of their riverine interest, to Category 4 in

TABLE 29.3. The numbers of SSSIs in Scotland (in the four Regions of SNH) containing running water interest[a] (Holmes *et al.*, 1990), and the importance of that interest to SSSI status[b]. Numbers of National Nature Reserves (NNRs) containing SSSIs with running waters are also given. Numbers in parentheses represent total numbers of SSSIs (biological and geological) in each Region

SSSI category	SE Region (423)		SW Region (350)		NE Region (230)		NW Region (351)		Total for four regions (1354)	
	SSSIs	NNRs	SSSIs	NNRs	SSSIs	NNRs	SSSIs	NNRs	SSSIs	NNRs
1	5	0	3	0	4	0	5	0	17	0
2	24	1	16	1	2	0	18	2	60	4
3	8	0	11	1	1	1	11	2	31	4
4	35	4	23	4	21	3	48	9	127	20
Regional totals	72	5	53	6	28	4	82	13	235	28

[a] SSSIs containing running waters at least 5 m wide and with at least 500 m present within the site
[b] Category 1: River SSSI – where running water is the main (or one of the main) reasons for notification given in the citation
Category 2: River valley SSSI – sites including the watercourse and the majority of its valley
Category 3: River adds interest – where the SSSI citation clearly states that the river contributes to the biological interest of the site, substantiated with records of plants, animals or habitats of interest
Category 4: River of incidental interest – running water not mentioned in the citation – little information available

which running waters are incidental to the interest of the site, or there is no biological information with which they can be evaluated.

Table 29.3 shows that only 17% of all SSSIs in Scotland contain running waters, and in only 8% do these comprise or contribute to the interest of the site (i.e. Categories 1–3). A mere 1% (17 SSSIs) contain rivers in Category 1. Twenty-eight of the 69 NNRs in Scotland have SSSIs with running waters, but only eight have rivers with features contributing to the interest, and none contains a river or stretch of river classified in Category 1. It should be added that only three Scottish rivers listed in the NCR (Tweed, Strontian, Burn of Latheronwheel) have had significant lengths notified as SSSIs, although it was NCC's intention that this should happen for all NCR sites (Nature Conservancy Council, 1984).

A compilation of SSSI data for standing waters (Table 29.4) shows a slightly different picture. In this case 35% of all SSSIs in Scotland include standing waters, and 24% contain water bodies in Categories 1–3, illustrating the greater effort that has been put into both survey and notification of standing waters than running waters. Similarly, 7% of SSSIs are classified in Category 1, compared with 1% for running waters. Forty NNRs contain standing water, but of these only one – Loch Leven – appears in Category 1. (It should be noted that Lyle and Maitland (1992) have also provided estimates of the numbers of running and standing waters on NNRs as part of their work on British freshwater fish. These figures are not equivalent to those given in Tables 29.3 and 29.4, owing to the different techniques used to collect the data.)

TABLE 29.4. The numbers of SSSIs in Scotland (in the four Regions of SNH) containing standing water interest, and the importance of that interest to SSSI status[a]. Numbers of National Nature Reserves (NNRs) containing SSSIs with standing waters are also given. Numbers in parentheses represent total numbers of SSSIs (biological and geological) in each Region

SSSI category	SE Region (423)		SW Region (350)		NE Region (230)		NW Region (351)		Total for four regions (1354)	
	SSSIs	NNRs	SSSIs	NNRs	SSSIs	NNRs	SSSIs	NNRs	SSSIs	NNRs
1	34	1	17	0	22	0	20	0	93	1
2	60	3	38	4	40	3	82	12	220	22
3	12	0	2	0	1	0	2	0	17	0
4	36	4	30	2	39	6	42	5	147	17
Regional totals	142	8	87	6	102	9	146	17	477	40

[a]Category 1: Standing water SSSI – where standing water is the main (or one of the main) reasons for notification given in the SSSI citation

Category 2: Standing water adds interest – where the SSSI citation clearly states that the standing water contributes to the biological interest of the site, substantiated with records of plants, animals or habitats of interest

Category 3: Standing water with conservation interest at the loch fringes, e.g. delta/marshes at inflow of river to loch, reed beds in bays

Category 4: Standing water of incidental interest and not mentioned in the citation; little information available

The problem of what to do about the large gaps in SSSI coverage of freshwater habitats (especially rivers) is one that SNH will need to address as it continues its general review of site designations. The appropriateness (or otherwise) of using SSSIs in freshwater conservation will inevitably enter the discussion again. The advantages and disadvantages of notifying riverine SSSIs have been considered elsewhere (Boon, 1991), and most of these points are also applicable to lochs to a greater or lesser extent. There are certainly practical difficulties in notifying the frequently large numbers of owners and occupiers, and finding the resources to cope with the volume of casework arising from notification. Furthermore, SSSI boundaries can rarely include more than a small part of the catchment, thus providing little statutory control over damaging activities that may be occurring outside of the SSSI. On the other hand, SSSI notification does place a duty on planning authorities to consult SNH over developments likely to affect the site, and may permit the regulation of activities undertaken by landowners at the water margins (e.g. vegetation removal), zones now recognized as vitally important in the functioning of freshwater systems (Naiman and Décamps, 1990). Equally important is the "spotlight effect" of notification, helping to focus attention on the special interest of the site.

Ramsar sites The Convention on Wetlands of International Importance especially as Waterfowl Habitat was adopted at Ramsar, Iran, in 1971 and ratified by the UK Parliament in 1976. Among other things it requires each contracting party to designate

FIGURE 29.3. Loch Druidibeg (South Uist) – designated as a National Nature Reserve and as a Ramsar site. Photograph: P. Wakely

suitable sites for inclusion in a list of wetlands of international importance, to formulate planning to promote the conservation of wetlands, and generally to promote conservation of wetlands and waterfowl (Pritchard *et al.*, 1992). The term "wetland" is given an inclusive definition by the convention: "... areas of marsh, fen, peatland or water, whether natural or artificial, permanent or temporary, with water that is static or flowing, fresh, brackish or salt ...". Although "in the first instance wetlands of international importance to waterfowl at any season should be included" there is also an option of selecting sites "on account of their international significance in terms of ecology, botany, zoology, limnology or hydrology."

Despite this, very few Ramsar sites in the UK have been designated for interests other than birds. Of the 22 sites so far designated in Scotland (at 1 December 1992), only three fall into this category (Cairngorm Lochs, Grampian and Highland; Loch an Duin, Western Isles; Loch Druidibeg (Figure 29.3), Loch a'Machair and Loch Stilligarry, Western Isles). There are no running water Ramsar sites *per se* on the UK list, and as rivers and wetlands ("traditionally" defined) are very different ecologically, and face distinctive threats, there may be a case for a Ramsar equivalent specifically for running waters (Luther and Rzoska, 1971).

Special Areas of Conservation New conservation designations are on the way. Referred to as "Special Areas of Conservation" (SACs), these will be established under the EC Directive on the Conservation of Natural Habitats and of Wild Fauna and Flora, to form a European network of sites known as "Natura 2000". The UK was notified of this Directive on 5 June 1992, and this is the starting point from which certain procedures must be completed within a timescale specified in the Directive. Thus, by June 1995 a list of proposed sites must be sent to the European Commission, by June 1998 the Commission will agree with each Member State a draft list of Sites of Community Importance, and within a maximum of six years (June 2004) these must be designated as SACs. In the light of earlier comments on SSSIs, it is worth noting that freshwater SACs will probably be implemented through existing SSSI legislation, reinforcing the need to examine current policy and practice in this area.

A number of Annexes to the Directive set out criteria for site selection, and list habitat types (Annex I) and species (Annex II) whose conservation requires the designation of SACs. Table 29.5 reproduces the eight categories of standing waters and the seven categories of rivers as they are described in Annex I. At first glance few of these seem to be readily applicable to Scottish fresh waters. This may be due in part to inconsistencies, ambiguities and unclear definitions, and at the time of writing clarification is being sought from the EC.

Annex II does include freshwater species found in Scotland; these are listed in Table 29.6. Some have already been identified as threatened species (e.g. Allis Shad,

TABLE 29.5. Freshwater habitats listed in Annex I of the EC Directive on the Conservation of Natural Habitats and of Wild Fauna and Flora. Habitats listed in this Annex require the designation of Special Areas of Conservation

Standing Water Habitats
Oligotrophic waters containing very few minerals of Atlantic plains with amphibious vegetation: *Lobelia, Littorella* and *Isoetes*
Oligotrophic waters containing very few minerals of West Mediterranean sandy plains with *Isoetes*
Oligotrophic waters in medio-European and perialpine areas with amphibious vegetation: *Littorella* or *Isoetes* or annual vegetation on exposed banks (*Nanocyperetalia*)
Hard oligo-mesotrophic waters with benthic vegetation of *Chara* formations
Natural eutrophic lakes with *Magnopotamion* or *Hydrocharition*-type vegetation
Dystrophic lakes
Mediterranean temporary ponds
Turloughs (Ireland)

Running water habitats
Alpine rivers and the herbaceous vegetation along their banks
Alpine rivers and their ligneous vegetation with *Myricaria germanica*
Alpine rivers and their ligneous vegetation with *Salix elaegnos*
Constantly flowing Mediterranean rivers with *Glaucium flavum*
Floating vegetation of *Ranunculus* of plain, submountainous rivers
Chenopodietum rubri of submountainous rivers: *Paspalo-Agrostidion* and hanging curtains of *Salix* and *Populus alba*
Intermittently flowing Mediterranean rivers

TABLE 29.6. Species found in Scottish fresh waters and listed in Annex II of the EC Directive on the Conservation of Natural Habitats and of Wild Fauna and Flora[a]

Common name	Scientific name
Otter	*Lutra lutra*
Great Crested Newt	*Triturus cristatus*
Sea Lamprey	*Petromyzon marinus*
River Lamprey	*Lampetra fluviatilis*
Brook Lamprey	*Lampetra planeri*
Atlantic Salmon (fresh water only)	*Salmo salar*
Allis Shad	*Alosa alosa*
Twaite Shad	*Alosa fallax*
Freshwater Pearl Mussel	*Margaritifera margaritifera*
Slender Naiad	*Najas flexilis*

[a]This table does not include introduced species (Atlantic Stream Crayfish, *Austropotamobius pallipes*; Floating-leaved Water-plantain, *Luronium natans*), or vagrants (Sturgeon, *Acipenser sturio*)

Twaite Shad, Freshwater Pearl Mussel), but others (e.g. River Lamprey, Atlantic Salmon) are not at risk. It must be recognized, however, that there is no presumption that SACs will be designated in all countries where listed species are present. Article 4(1) states that "for aquatic species which range over wide areas, such sites will be proposed only where there is a clearly identifiable area representing the physical and biological factors essential to their life and reproduction". It would seem likely for species such as Atlantic Salmon that unless those areas are critical to the health and survival of the species they would be unlikely to be designated as SACs. However, much discussion and clarification will be needed as the process of selection proceeds.

Species protection

Wildlife and Countryside Act 1981   In addition to the indirect benefits that species receive through various habitat designations, some are protected directly through legislation. The Wildlife and Countryside Act 1981 makes certain actions illegal (e.g. intentional killing and injuring, taking, sale), for animals on Schedule 5 and plants on Schedule 8. Table 29.7 lists the 13 animal and six plant species present in Scottish fresh waters which receive full or partial protection in this way.

A more detailed review of statutory protection of freshwater organisms in Britain is given in Boon *et al.* (1992), including some consideration of the effectiveness of protecting species by law. There is certainly little point in scheduling a species subject to insidious threats from pollution or habitat loss. Even those well qualified for inclusion because they are collectable or exploitable in some other way (e.g. Freshwater Pearl Mussel), may still suffer because of the difficulties of enforcing the legislation. Nevertheless, in June 1992 two people were arrested in connection with offences relating to Freshwater Pearl Mussel in the River Spey, although for various reasons the case was not heard.

TABLE 29.7. A list of organisms found in Scottish fresh waters (excluding brackish-water and estuarine species) protected (*) under Schedules 5 (animals) and 8 (plants) of the Wildlife and Countyside Act 1981, with a note of their status under the Bern Convention (Appendices I–III) and the EC Habitats and Species Directive (Annex IV or V). Offences covered under Schedules 5 and 8 are killing and injuring (K/I), taking (T), possessing (P), disturbance at and damage to place of shelter (D/D), picking, uprooting and destroying (P/U/D), sale (S)

Common name	Scientific name	K/I	T	P	D/D	S	EC	Bern
Medicinal Leech	*Hirudo medicinalis*	*	*	*	*	*	V	III
Atlantic Stream Crayfish[a]	*Austropotamobius pallipes*		*			*	V	III
Freshwater Pearl Mussel	*Margaritifera margaritifera*	*					V	III
Common Frog	*Rana temporaria*						V	III
Common Toad	*Bufo bufo*					*		III
Natterjack Toad	*Bufo calamita*	*	*	*	*	*	IV	II
Great Crested Newt	*Triturus cristatus*	*	*	*	*	*	IV	II
Palmate Newt	*Triturus helveticus*					*		III
Smooth Newt	*Triturus vulgaris*					*		III
Allis Shad	*Alosa alosa*	*	*				V	III
Whitefish (Powan)	*Coregonus lavaretus*	*	*			*	V	III
Sturgeon	*Acipenser sturio*	*	*	*	*	*	IV	III
Otter	*Lutra lutra*		*	*	*		IV	II
River Lamprey	*Lampetra fluviatilis*						V	III
Brook Lamprey	*Lampetra planeri*							III
Sea Lamprey	*Petromyzon marinus*							III
Twaite Shad	*Alosa fallax*						V	III
Grayling	*Thymallus thymallus*						V	III
Salmon	*Salmo salar*						V	III
Pigmyweed	*Crassula aquatica*	* (P/U/D)				*		
Bearded Stonewort	*Chara canescens*	*				*		
River Jelly-lichen	*Collema dichotomum*	*				*		
Slender Naiad	*Najas flexilis*	*					IV	I
Floating-leaved Water-plantain[a]	*Luronium natans*	*				*	IV	I
Bog Moss	*Sphagnum* – all species	*				*	V	

[a]Introduced species

Statutory protection of species, as with habitats, clearly does play a valuable role in conservation. It is another tool in the tool-kit; it is not a universal panacea for ensuring the survival of threatened species.

Bern Convention   The aims of the Bern Convention, which came into force in 1982, are (i) to conserve wild flora and fauna and natural habitats, (ii) to promote co-operation between States, and (iii) to give particular attention to endangered and vulnerable species. As with most international conventions, it can only be applied in Britain through domestic legislation. Appendices I and II list plants and animals respectively for which there should be complete protection, while Appendix III lists animals where some exploitation of their populations is permitted. Two freshwater plant species in Scotland (one an introduction) are included in Appendix I, three animal species are listed in Appendix II, and a further 16 are found in Appendix III (Table 29.7).

EC Habitats and Species Directive: Annexes IV and V   Apart from the Annexes that refer to the designation of SACs, the Habitats and Species Directive has two Annexes directly pertaining to species protection. Annex IV lists species "in need of strict protection", and Annex V covers those "whose taking in the wild and exploitation may be subject to management measures". Table 29.7 shows that two species of plant and four species of animal listed on Annex IV are found in Scottish fresh waters. The corresponding figures for Annex V are one and 10.

Ultimate objectives   This brief discussion of species legislation raises other more fundamental points concerning ultimate conservation objectives.

In principle, there must surely be a strong case for broadening conservation effort to encompass other, presently untargeted, species groups. The point made by Maitland (1990) for fish – namely that their conservation suffers because they do not really have a popular following – could be applied with even greater force to most of the aquatic invertebrates or the lower plants. Yet present concerns worldwide for the maintenance of biodiversity also need to address sub-specific levels and ensure that the full range of genetic variation is retained. In Scotland, for example, there are a number of genetically distinctive fish populations worthy of conservation (e.g. races of Arctic Charr (*Salvelinus alpinus*) and Brown Trout (*Salmo trutta*), and spine-deficient Three-spined Stickleback (*Gasterosteus aculeatus*)), a point made explicitly in the SSSI guidelines (Nature Conservancy Council, 1989).

Equally important is the need for a heightened awareness generally of the value of freshwater *habitats* and not merely of a few selected species of conservation interest. This requires attention to preserving habitat integrity and the natural functioning of ecological processes such as nutrient cycling, energy flow, growth and development.

Finally, it is manifest that designating areas for conservation or scheduling certain species can only ever be applied to a small fraction of the freshwater resources of Scotland. Efforts must continue at finding ways of better conserving what is sometimes described as the "wider countryside". In the long term, this must mean devising some workable system for managing whole catchments. Inevitably this will involve some degree of coercion; full, voluntary integration of all activities in a catchment is only possible in an ideal world. In the short-term, it points to the need for achieving greater consensus between conflicting viewpoints.

The role of advocacy and partnership

Both the statutory and the voluntary sectors have many opportunities to achieve positive gains for conservation by using their powers of persuasion at a series of levels throughout society.

As central government's statutory body for advising on nature conservation in Scotland, SNH is consulted on a wide range of matters, some of which are of major importance for freshwater conservation. Such consultations may provide an opportunity for commenting on structural reorganization, such as the present proposal to set up a Scottish Environment Protection Agency. Others may involve more direct participation, as in the recent Scottish Office Working Party preparing a Code of Practice on Conservation, Access and Recreation for the Scottish water and sewerage authorities and River Purification Authorities.

An input at local planning level is also vital. For instance, in recent years NCC (and its successor bodies in Scotland) have contributed data on conservation for the "indicative forestry strategies" drawn up by Regional Councils (see Chapter 28). Where possible, the information supplied has included an assessment of freshwater environments.

Much of the work of advocacy and persuasion is carried out at the level of individual SSSIs or catchments, perhaps over a development plan or an Environmental Impact Assessment. For example, British Nuclear Fuels has put forward proposals for constructing a new nuclear reactor at Chapelcross (SW Scotland). Several options for water supply are under investigation, including water transfer from north-east England, and the construction of a reservoir on a tributary of the River Annan. Part of the EIA involves a detailed study of likely impacts on aquatic plants, invertebrates, fish, water quality and flow regimes, and in these areas SNH is well placed to comment on the possible implications for nature conservation, and suggest ameliorative action if necessary.

It may be many years before anything approaching fully integrated catchment management becomes a reality in Scotland, or in the rest of the UK, but meanwhile there is an urgent need to see what can be achieved by voluntary measures and by partnership approaches. A useful model is provided by the informal liaison group, "Tweed Forum", set up in 1991 with the overall objective of maintaining the well-being of the entire Tweed catchment.

The group comprises a wide range of both statutory and voluntary organizations, including government departments, the Forestry Authority, Tweed River Purification Board, National Rivers Authority (Northumbrian Region), Scottish Natural Heritage, English Nature, Scottish Tourist Board and others (Tweed Forum, 1992). One eventual aim is to produce an informal catchment management plan; until then, useful progress is being made by a number of working groups (such as one on recreation and access), and by a technical group which produces guidance notes entitled *Biologist's Briefing*. These cover topics such as the use of herbicides, or the control of invasive weeds, their purpose being to impart scientific information in a readily understood form and to a wide audience. For example, in just two pages Campbell (1991) explains the importance of bankside vegetation for young salmonids, referring to allochthonous food supply, the relative value of different types of leaves to invertebrates, and the concept of "buffer strips", drawing information from scientific studies in the UK, North America and New Zealand.

THE NEED FOR A CONSERVATION STRATEGY FOR SCOTLAND'S FRESH WATERS

Research and survey, statutory measures for habitat and species protection, advocacy and partnership, as well as many other areas of freshwater conservation, require a framework within which to operate. Without this, policies lack clear direction and the assignment of priorities to research programmes is impossible. In other words, there is an urgent need to design a conservation strategy for Scotland's fresh waters. Some of the themes that should be incorporated in this are listed in Table 29.8, together with some examples of areas that each theme might cover.

Among other things, any strategy should set out the conservation aims for each main habitat type and species group, identify gaps in research, target new areas for policy evolution, determine areas in which legislative changes should be sought, and establish the roles that different organizations might play. An ultimate aim should be the maintenance or restoration of habitat integrity, ecological functioning and genetic diversity of Scotland's freshwater resources.

There seem to be few examples of comprehensive conservation strategies for fresh waters in other countries. In Norway, the need for a national river protection scheme was recognized in the late 1960s. However, this was exclusively to safeguard scenic and scientifically valuable catchments from hydro-power exploitation (Oesthagen, 1988), which is perhaps not surprising in a country where 99.8% of the electricity is produced in this way (Eie and Brittain, 1992). Approximately 200 rivers are now included in a Master Plan for Water Resources (Ministry of Environment, 1986) which lists those projects that should be considered first for a licence when development is deemed necessary, and specifies which rivers should preferably be reserved for uses other than hydro-power development. Regrettably, other significant impacts, such as channel engineering, are not covered in this way (Oesthagen, 1988), but a recent government report has suggested that this situation may soon change (Brittain, personal communication).

In some countries, conservation strategies are oriented towards restoring rather than preserving fresh waters. In Denmark, shallow water bodies have been drained and the area covered by lakes reduced by more than 50% over the last two centuries. Most streams have been dredged or straightened to improve drainage from agricultural land, and 90% of the smallest watercourses have been culverted since the turn of the century. The Nature Management Act 1989 therefore places great emphasis on re-establishing drained lakes and re-aligning streams (Jensen, 1992).

OBSTACLES TO SUCCESS

There is sometimes a tendency to create the impression that the mere utterance of words like "integration", "sustainability", "holistic management" will somehow bring

TABLE 29.8. Some basic themes required in the development of a conservation strategy for Scotland's fresh waters

Theme	Examples
1. Describing the resource	Extending geographical coverage of freshwater habitat surveys; improving knowledge of lesser known groups, e.g. invertebrates in standing waters, algae, etc., and sub-species
2. Classification and evaluation	New techniques for conservation assessment (e.g. SERCON, Boon et al., in press); developing habitat and community approaches to evaluation
3. Developing protective mechanisms	Reviewing/using opportunities offered by existing legislation/designations (e.g. SSSIs, NNRs, SACs, NHAs), species licensing; improving site management techniques
4. Monitoring freshwater habitats and species	Defining objectives; monitoring capabilities/roles of environmental bodies; developing methodologies; species distributions and population dynamics; impacts
5. Restoration and creative conservation	Identifying areas and sites (urban/rural) for restoration; developing techniques for restoring habitat features and water quality; species re-introductions and translocations
6. Research and policy development	Defining areas for policy development; integrating science and policy; research liaison; increase in functional research (e.g. ecological needs of particular species)
7. Working with others	Liaison with government departments/agencies (e.g. SOEnD, SOAFD, RPAs, etc.), NGOs, recreational bodies, landowners, etc.; working towards integrated catchment planning
8. Education and training	Encouraging teaching of freshwater conservation courses in schools/universities/relevant agencies; increase public awareness – media, field centres, etc.; seminars/conferences
9. Systems development	Extension/updating of existing databases e.g. aquatic plants in Scottish lochs and rivers, river invertebrates, fish communities, improving systems for data storage/retrieval
10. UK and international collaboration	Collaborating in research projects with relevant bodies (e.g. EN, CCW, JNCC, DOE (NI)); maintaining awareness of international work and liaising over projects of mutual interest

to an end all problems in resource conservation. Clearly that is far from being the case. Fresh waters, particularly rivers, are subjected to a wider range of human use than almost any other type of natural ecosystem, and conflicts inevitably arise between competing uses.

Some of the issues that need to be addressed are well illustrated by recent events surrounding the conservation of the Rivers Spey and Feshie and the Insh Marshes in north-east Scotland. The Spey is one of the largest rivers in Britain, and for many years this area has been considered nationally important for nature conservation due to its largely unpolluted and relatively natural features, its rich plant and invertebrate communities (Fojt et al., 1987), and its internationally important bird populations (Stroud et al., 1990). Added to this is the geomorphological importance of the River Feshie, a tributary of the Spey, offering a fine example of a forested alluvial fan with active braided channels (Johnson et al., 1991). The conservation importance of the whole area has been recognized by the designation of two SSSIs, its inclusion within the *Nature Conservation Review* as a site of international importance (Ratcliffe, 1977), and through being proposed as a Ramsar site (Stroud et al., 1990).

Several large floods in recent years (especially the winters of 1988/89 and 1989/90) have led to demands from local landowners for mitigating measures to be taken, and for water levels in the Insh Marshes to be lowered. Two engineering options have been proposed – the regrading of a section of the Spey at the confluence with the Feshie, and the re-aligning of the Feshie itself. These schemes have been assessed recently, both for their effectiveness in alleviating floods and in terms of their environmental impact, through a series of individual studies on the various elements of ecological and geomorphological importance (Johnson et al., 1991).

Leaving aside the detailed results of this work, it serves to illustrate three major obstacles to effective conservation. The first is the *problem of perception*: the sometimes difficult task of making the general public more aware of the importance of areas such as the Spey and the Insh Marshes and more sympathetic to the need for their protection. This is partly a consequence of the lack of appreciation for organisms that are not large and furry, or in some other way immediately attractive. It is also because scientists and conservationists have often failed to underline the importance of ecosystems, preferring instead to build their arguments on one or two rare or threatened species. This may provide the headline writers with eye-catching opportunities ("rare beetle stands in the way of new bypass"), but so often fails to ignite the spark of public sympathy for the conservation case.

The second obstacle – an ecological one – could be described as *the problem of prescription*. Defining, or prescribing, the ecological requirements of particular species or communities of conservation importance is rarely straightforward, yet is inherent in the predictive nature of environmental impact assessments. The ecological studies of the Spey/Insh Marshes generated several predictions of the likely impact of the engineering schemes, but forecasting the general consequences that lowered water levels may have on organisms is not the same as determining the specific impacts of varying water depths or different periods of inundation. This problem may recur in many other guises, emphasizing not only the need for continued research, but also the improvidence of dealing with complex biological systems as if they were as predictable as simple pieces of machinery.

The third obstacle is far-reaching, for it touches the value that society places on nature. The *problem of proscription* refers to the difficult task of balancing the many legitimate uses of fresh waters against the need to *proscribe* those that are clearly detrimental to the functioning of healthy ecosystems. In practice, statutory protection, even of nationally and internationally important conservation areas such as the Spey/Insh Marshes, can really only be effective through agreement and incentive. After the statutory negotiating periods have expired, there are few alternatives available for absolute proscription without recourse to lengthy legal procedures.

Scotland is indeed fortunate in possessing an array of fresh waters, many of which are still in a natural or semi-natural state. Overcoming obstacles to their conservation will be part of the challenge of retaining this rich diversity.

ACKNOWLEDGEMENTS

I would like to thank David Howell, Willie Duncan and Karen Sweetman (Scottish Natural Heritage) for their assistance with data collation. John Brittain (Norwegian Water Resources and Energy Administration) and Torben Moth Iversen (National Environmental Research Institute) kindly supplied information from Norway and Denmark respectively. Jackie Graham and Moira Munro (Scottish Natural Heritage) provided valuable help with the diagrams.

REFERENCES

Boon, P. J. (1991). "The role of Sites of Special Scientific Interest (SSSIs) in the conservation of British rivers", *Freshwater Forum*, **1**, 95–108.

Boon, P. J. (1992). "Essential elements in the case for river conservation", in *River Conservation and Management* (Eds P. J. Boon, P. Calow and G. E. Petts), pp. 11–33, John Wiley, Chichester.

Boon, P. J., Morgan, D. H. W. and Palmer, M. A. (1992). "Statutory protection of freshwater flora and fauna in Britain", *Freshwater Forum*, **2**, 91–101.

Boon, P. J., Holmes, N. T. H., Maitland, P. S. and Rowell, T. A. (in press). "A system for evaluating rivers for conservation ('SERCON'): An outline of the underlying principles", *Verhandlungen der Internationalen Vereinigung für theoretische und angewandte Limnologie*.

Campbell, R. N. B. (1991). "Bankside vegetation and young salmonids", *Biologist's Briefing No. 4*, The Tweed Foundation, Berwick-upon-Tweed.

Cummins, K. W. (1992). "Catchment characteristics and river ecosystems", in *River Conservation and Management* (Eds P. J. Boon, P. Calow and G. E. Petts), pp. 125–135, John Wiley, Chichester.

Eie, J. A. and Brittain, J. E. (1992). "Environmental considerations and remedial measures in Norwegian hydropower schemes", in *Hydropower '92* (Eds E. Broch and D. K. Lysne), pp. 289–292, A. A. Balkema, Rotterdam.

Fojt, W., Kirby, K., McLean, I., Palmer, M. and Pienkowski, M. (1987). *The National Importance of the Insh Marshes*, Unpublished report, Nature Conservancy Council, Peterborough.

Holmes, N. T. H. (1983). "Typing British rivers according to their flora", *Focus on Nature Conservation No. 4*, Nature Conservancy Council, Peterborough.

Holmes, N. T. H. (1989). "British rivers – a working classification", *British Wildlife*, **1**, 20–36.

Holmes, N. T. H., Boon, P. J., Brown, A. E., Edwards, C., Howell, D. and White D. A. (1990). *Rivers Within SSSIs: A Classification and Review of Sites in Great Britain*, Unpublished report, Nature Conservancy Council, Peterborough.

Jensen, J. (Ed.) (1992). *Nature Management in Denmark*, The Ministry of the Environment/ The National Forest and Nature Agency, Copenhagen.

Johnson, R. C., Piper, B. S., Acreman, M. C. and Gilman, K. (1991). *Flood Alleviation in Upper Strathspey: Modelling and Environment Study*, Institute of Hydrology, Wallingford.

Luther, H. and Rzoska, J. (1971). *Project Aqua: A Source Book of Inland Waters Proposed for Conservation*, Blackwell, Oxford.

Lyle, A. A. and Maitland P. S. (1992). "Conservation of freshwater fish in the British Isles: the status of fish in National Nature Reserves", *Aquatic Conservation: Marine and Freshwater Ecosystems*, **2**, 19–34.

Maitland, P. S. (1990). *The Conservation of Rare British Freshwater Fish*, Nature Conservancy Council, Peterborough.

Ministry of Environment (1986). *The Master Plan for Water Resources*, Oslo.

Naiman, R. J. and Décamps, H. (Eds) (1990). *The Ecology and Management of Aquatic–Terrestrial Ecotones*, MAB Series, Volume 4, Unesco, Paris and Parthenon Publishing Group, New Jersey.

Nature Conservancy Council (1984). *Nature Conservation in Great Britain*, Peterborough.

Nature Conservancy Council (1988). *Sites of Special Scientific Interest*, Peterborough.

Nature Conservancy Council (1989). *Guidelines for Selection of Biological SSSIs*, Peterborough.

Oesthagen, H. (1988). "Power plants: environmental issues", *Modern Power Systems Supplement*, June 1988, 40–42.

Palmer, M. A. (1989). *A Botanical Classification of Standing Waters in Britain: and a Method for the Use of Macrophyte Flora in Assessing Changes in Water Quality*, Research and Survey in Nature Conservation No. 19, Nature Conservancy Council, Peterborough.

Palmer, M. A., Bell, S. L. and Butterfield, I. (1992). "A botanical classification of standing waters in Britain: applications for conservation and monitoring", *Aquatic Conservation: Marine and Freshwater Ecosystems*, **2**, 125–143.

Pritchard, D. E., Housden, S. D., Mudge, G. P., Galbraith, C. A. and Pienkowski, M. W. (Eds) (1992). *Important Bird Areas in the United Kingdom including the Channel Islands and the Isle of Man*, Royal Society for Protection of Birds, Sandy.

Ratcliffe, D. A. (Ed.) (1977). *A Nature Conservation Review*, Cambridge University Press, Cambridge.

Scottish Conservation Projects Trust (1990). *Operation Brightwater: Information Pack*, Stirling.

Scottish National Parks Committee and the Scottish Wild Life Conservation Committee (1947). *National Parks and the Conservation of Nature in Scotland*, Command Paper Cond 7235, HMSO, Edinburgh.

Scottish Wildlife Trust (1988). *Reserves Handbook*, Edinburgh.

Stroud, D. A., Mudge, G. P. and Pienkowski, M. W. (1990). *Protecting Internationally Important Bird Sites*, Nature Conservancy Council, Peterborough.

Tweed Forum (1992). *Tweed Contacts*, Department of Planning and Development, Borders Regional Council, Melrose.

Wild Life Conservation Special Committee (England and Wales) (1947). *Conservation of Nature in England and Wales*, Command Paper Cond 7122, HMSO, London.

30

Role of Environmental Agencies

D. L. HOWELL

Scottish Natural Heritage, 2 Anderson Place, Edinburgh, EH6 5NP, UK

INTRODUCTION

Resolving the competing and intensifying demands on water resources in industrialized nations poses a great challenge for water managers. Recent years have seen an increasingly widespread acceptance of the need for an integrated approach, based on ecological and geomorphological principles, which recognizes the drainage basin as the appropriate management unit (see for example, Gardiner, 1991; Newson, 1992; and numerous papers in Boon *et al.*, 1992a). The importance of this philosophy is acknowledged at the global level; in updating the 1980 World Conservation Strategy, IUCN *et al.* (1991) identified a number of priorities for action required to achieve their aims of sustainable living and the integration of conservation and development. One of their priorities for fresh waters is that, by 1995:

> All high income countries will have established cross-sectoral mechanisms for integrated water management based on drainage basins and the application of an ecological approach.

In Scotland, the institutional framework does not meet this requirement. The responsibilities for water resource management and protection are split between numerous organizations with different functions and varying scales of geographical jurisdiction (Figure 30.1). In 1992, at the United Nations Conference on Environment and Development in Rio de Janeiro, "Agenda 21" (the conference declaration to which the UK agreed) emphasized the importance of integrated water management, and identified the fragmentation of responsibility amongst sectoral agencies as a major impediment to achieving such integration. Boon (1992a) suggested that the complexity of the water management framework is often a barrier to the effective transfer of technical information to those framing policies, making decisions, or undertaking management. The shortcomings of the Scottish system were noted by the UK Salmon Advisory Committee (1991):

> The Committee believes that integrated management offers the most effective way forward in improving the protection and enhancement of juvenile salmon production.

The Fresh Waters of Scotland: A National Resource of International Significance
Edited by P. S. Maitland, P. J. Boon and D. S. McLusky. © 1994 John Wiley & Sons Ltd

578

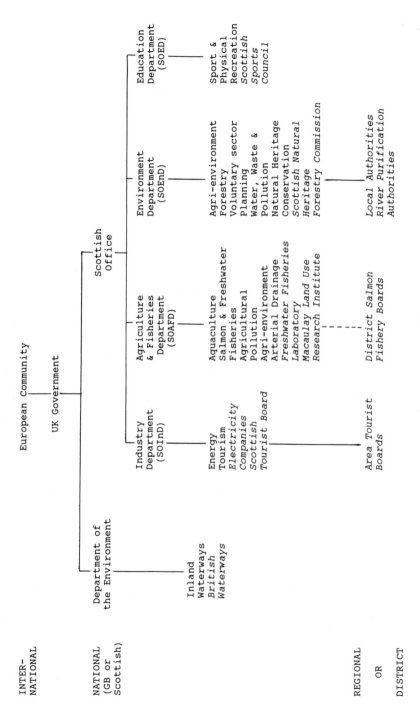

FIGURE 30.1. Scottish fresh waters: the roles of the principal government and statutory bodies (after Brown and Howell, 1992); in practice, links are often more complex than the figure suggests. The names in italics are those agencies responsible for the research and policy areas shown in the figure

There is . . . a need for a stronger and more comprehensive framework in Scotland and
we therefore recommend that the present regulatory structure there should be urgently
reviewed in this context and be amended if appropriate.

The fragmented nature of the water management framework in Scotland, and the
absence of positive statutory conservation duties to underpin and unify the various
water-related functions, have been of concern to conservation bodies for some years.
This chapter will examine the current legislative basis for water management in
Scotland and attempt a critical assessment of the roles of government departments,
statutory agencies and private interests in the light of these concerns. The substantial
upheavals inherent in the Government's proposals to re-organize local government,
re-structure the provision of water and sewerage services and establish a Scottish
Environment Protection Agency, whilst disruptive, provide opportunities to move
towards a more integrated approach to water management. These opportunities will
be discussed, together with some of the associated constraints.

ROLES, POWERS AND DUTIES

As Table 30.1 shows, there are numerous items of legislation, increasingly originating
from the European Commission in recent years, which affect the use and management
of Scottish fresh waters. The statutory regime is implemented and enforced largely
by the Secretary of State for Scotland through Scottish Office Departments and
associated statutory agencies. Roles, powers and duties are widely dispersed, with
formal integration only really possible at the level of the Secretary of State. Comprehensive and detailed overviews of the legislation can be found elsewhere (e.g. Lyall,
1982; Anonymous, 1989a; Robinson, 1990; Haigh, 1992); the following sections will
examine – largely from a nature conservation viewpoint – the implementation of the
main areas of legislation and what this can mean in practice for the quality of the
freshwater resource.

The Secretary of State and the Scottish Office

In the absence of an independent water agency with a comprehensive regulatory
remit, the role of the Secretary of State for Scotland is crucial in overseeing the
implementation of water legislation and associated government policy through the
Scottish Office Departments and the various statutory agencies they sponsor. This
function comes under formal scrutiny through the investigations of advisory and
monitoring committees (see House of Commons Agriculture Committee, 1989;
House of Lords Select Committee on the European Communities, 1991; Salmon
Advisory Committee, 1991; and Royal Commission on Environmental Pollution,
1992, for recent relevant examples) which frequently recommend legislative changes,
although these changes can take many years to appear.

As well as sponsoring many statutory agencies, the Scottish Office also funds a
considerable amount of freshwater research, either in-house (e.g. via the Freshwater
Fisheries Laboratory at Pitlochry), by grant support (e.g. to the Macaulay Land Use
Research Institute or the Scottish Agricultural College) or by external contract.

The legislation imposes numerous duties, powers and functions (Table 30.2) upon
the Secretary of State in virtually every sphere of water management described in the

TABLE 30.1. Scottish fresh waters: examples of relevant domestic and EC legislation

UK and Scottish Acts of Parliament
Salmon Fisheries (Scotland) Acts 1862, 1866
Land Drainage (Scotland) Acts 1930, 1935, 1941
Diseases of Fish Acts 1937, 1983
National Parks and Access to the Countryside Act 1949
Rivers (Prevention of Pollution) (Scotland) Acts 1951, 1965
Salmon and Freshwater Fisheries (Protection) (Scotland) Act 1951
Land Drainage (Scotland) Act 1958
Flood Prevention (Scotland) Act 1961
Spray Irrigation (Scotland) Act 1964
Countryside (Scotland) Act 1967
Sewerage (Scotland) Act 1968
Town and Country Planning (Scotland) Act 1972
Nature Conservancy Council Act 1973
Control of Pollution Act 1974
Freshwater and Salmon Fisheries (Scotland) Act 1976
Import of Live Fish (Scotland) Act 1978
Water (Scotland) Act 1980
Wildlife and Countryside Act 1981
Agriculture Act 1986
Salmon Act 1986
Electricity Act 1989
Water Act 1989
Environmental Protection Act 1990
Natural Heritage (Scotland) Act 1991

European Community Directives
75/440/EEC on the quality of surface water for drinking
76/464/EEC on pollution caused by certain dangerous substances discharged into the aquatic environment of the Community
78/659/EEC on the quality of fresh waters needing protection or improvement in order to support fish life
79/409/EEC on the conservation of wild birds
85/337/EEC on the assessment of the effects of certain public and private projects on the environment
88/609/EEC on large combustion plants
91/271/EEC concerning urban waste water treatment
91/676/EEC concerning the protection of waters against pollution caused by nitrates from agricultural sources
92/43/EEC on the conservation of natural habitats and of wild flora and fauna

sections below. Considerable power and responsibility therefore rests with the Scottish Office, which was felt by Brown and Howell (1992) to be an advantage. However, whilst it appears desirable that the overall adjudication and supervisory role should be retained, the involvement of the Scottish Office in more routine regulatory and operational matters merits careful review, particularly in the light of the Government's support for locally-based decision-making in other areas of public policy (Scottish Development Department 1990a, b; Scottish Office 1991; 1992a, b). Some of the functions carried out by the Scottish Office (e.g. Table 30.2) appear to rest more appropriately with the various statutory agencies, whose roles are discussed in the following sections.

TABLE 30.2. Scottish fresh waters: examples of powers, duties and functions exercised by the Secretary of State

General duties and powers:
- to promote the conservation of the water resources of Scotland; Water (Scotland) Act 1980
- to promote the cleanliness of the rivers and inland and tidal waters of Scotland; Rivers (Prevention of Pollution) (Scotland) Act 1951
- to conduct inquiries and investigations and collect statistics; Salmon and Freshwater Fisheries (Protection) (Scotland) Act 1951

Make regulations:
- to control the storage of agricultural silage, slurry and fuel oil; Control of Pollution Act 1974

Call-in:
- applications for discharge consent; Control of Pollution Act 1974

Hear and determine appeals:
- against refusal of planning permission; Town and Country Planning (Scotland) Act 1972

Issue authorization:
- for land drainage schemes; Land Drainage (Scotland) Act 1958
- for water abstraction or diversion for generation of hydro-electricity; Electricity Act 1989
- to carry out a scheduled industrial process causing release of certain substances; Environmental Protection Act 1990

Make an order:
- increasing the availability of freshwater fishings; Freshwater and Salmon Fisheries (Scotland) Act 1976
- controlling the movement of diseased fish out of a designated area; Diseases of Fish Acts 1937 and 1983

Allow by licence or consent:
- importing fish not native to Scotland; Import of Live Fish (Scotland) Act 1978
- shooting of birds causing serious damage to fisheries; Wildlife and Countryside Act 1981
- discharge of effluent by an Islands Council; Control of Pollution Act 1974

Confirm:
- a byelaw sought by a water authority to prevent pollution of a water supply; Water (Scotland) Act 1980
- a Flood Prevention Scheme proposed by a local authority; Flood Prevention (Scotland) Act 1961

Carry out maintenance:
- of land drainage schemes; Land Drainage (Scotland) Acts 1930–41

Issue grants:
- towards the costs of land drainage works; Land Drainage (Scotland) Act 1958
- towards expenditure incurred by a local authority in carrying out flood prevention operations; Flood Prevention (Scotland) Act 1961

Water supply and sewerage

The provision of these services by the water and sewerage authorities (WSAs) is governed largely by the Sewerage (Scotland) Act 1968 and the Water (Scotland) Act 1980 (see Scottish Office, 1992c, for a useful summary of relevant legislation). The WSA role is fulfilled by Regional and Islands Councils, although the Central Scotland Water Development Board also distributes water to several WSAs from Loch Lomond and Loch Turret.

Under the Water (Scotland) Act 1980, the Secretary of State is required to promote the conservation of Scotland's water resources and ensure the provision of adequate supplies of water through water authorities and development boards. The same Act imposes a duty upon water authorities to provide a piped supply of wholesome water for domestic use throughout their supply area (where this can be done at reasonable cost), and to make water available upon request for non-domestic uses, subject to charging arrangements and other conditions.

The legislation provides numerous supporting powers which allow these duties to be performed, including the acquisition of water rights and land, the impoundment of streams and the making of byelaws (subject to the Secretary of State's confirmation) restricting activities which are wasteful of water or which threaten to pollute supplies. Where water is impounded or abstracted, this requires the Secretary of State's formal approval by Order which may stipulate, amongst other things, an appropriate compensation flow and the circumstances under which abstraction may take place (see following section for more detailed discussion).

In some parts of Scotland (e.g. Lothian Region), water supply reservoirs constitute a major proportion of the total surface water resource, and as such these waters and their catchment areas may be of considerable scenic, conservation or recreational value. This is reflected by the presence of reservoirs in some areas with statutory conservation, landscape and recreation designations (see below).

The Sewerage (Scotland) Act 1968 requires WSAs to provide public sewers for the collection of domestic sewage, surface water and trade effluent, to provide facilities for such materials' treatment and disposal, and to maintain these systems through such actions as inspection, repair and renewal. The authorities are required to accept into the sewers any domestic sewage and surface water drainage, but the discharge of effluent to the sewerage network from trade premises requires the prior agreement or consent of the WSA. The discharge of treated sewage effluent to fresh waters is controlled by the River Purification Authorities (RPAs) under discharge consents procedures which are similar to those used to control trade effluent discharges to sewers (see Chapter 27).

Investment backlogs and European Community Directives on drinking water and sewage treatment require significant additional expenditure on the water and sewerage infrastructure in order to meet the standards and deadlines imposed by the Directives. These pressures on WSA budgets, and the intention to introduce a single-tier approach to local authorities, prompted the Government to explore the options for the future provision of water and sewerage services (Scottish Office, 1992c); the implications of this consultation paper are discussed later.

Control of abstractions, impoundments and water transfers

The present state of the law relating to abstraction and flow regulation is complex, involving a combination of common law and statutory provisions. In summary, the present position is as follows:

- A few private rights are enshrined in statute (e.g. an Act regulating the River Leven's flow by the sluices at the outflow of Loch Leven).
- Private abstraction operations which do not involve a subsequent water discharge exist as common law rights.
- Numerous abstractions are indirectly controlled by discharge consents (e.g. those applying to distilleries, breweries, paper mills, fish farms, food and textile manufacturers). These users may take water from the public supply, or from a natural water (surface or borehole). Where water is an ingredient, as in distilling and brewing, then it is not all returned, but other uses such as cooling or washing may discharge water directly back to the watercourse, indirectly via the sewer and sewage treatment works, or bypass the system altogether if sewage effluent is discharged to the sea. In these circumstances, abstraction rates can be controlled indirectly by setting flow limits in discharge or trade effluent consents, but the volumes of water abstracted and effluent discharged are not necessarily the same.
- Abstractions for public water supply, for hydro-electric generation and for agricultural irrigation are subject to statutory controls under the Water (Scotland) Act 1980, Electricity Act 1989 and Natural Heritage (Scotland) Act 1991 respectively. Of these, only the provisions relating to irrigation confer control powers on the RPAs. The authorization powers for public water supply and hydro-electric impoundments or abstractions rest with the Secretary of State, with the RPAs' role confined to that of consultee in hydro-electric schemes. Each of these uses may involve abstracted water leaving the system altogether; for example, irrigation water lost through evapo-transpiration, reservoir water diverted to other catchments, or domestic and industrial waste water not returning to the hydrological cycle until it is discharged via a marine sewage outfall.

The legislation relating to hydro-electric generation in Scotland (see Chapter 17) has numerous special provisions for protecting Salmon fishery interests (see Mills, 1989, and Robinson, 1990, for fuller accounts), but there have been several bitter disputes over the effects of particular schemes on the quality of the fisheries (Payne, 1988). The modern trend, prompted by financial incentives following the privatization of the electricity industry in 1989, is towards smaller-scale "run-of-river" schemes; Salford Civil Engineering Ltd (1989) identified 823 potential sites for this type of development in Scotland. In the light of these developments, the Salmon Advisory Committee (1993) described the existing regulations regarding fish passes and intake screens as "outdated" and recommended that new regulations should be issued to protect migrating smolts and returning adults.

There have been numerous studies on the effects of impoundment, flow regulation and abstraction on river ecology (e.g. Ward and Stanford, 1979; Petts, 1984; and many papers in the journal *Regulated Rivers: Research & Management*). However, as Armitage (1979) and several authors in Petts and Wood (1988) noted, very few such studies have been carried out in the United Kingdom, let alone Scotland. Thus, although Scotland has numerous schemes to impound, abstract or divert water for hydro-electricity generation and for domestic or industrial supply, there is little evidence of any damaging environmental effects.

Perhaps unsurprisingly, the work that has been done is dominated by investigations of the effects on migratory salmonids, but an examination of the studies reviewed by Mills (1989) shows that this has concentrated on the physical barriers to migration which dams present, with less research devoted to indirect effects on fish such as modified discharge and temperature regimes, altered substrates and changes in the quality, quantity and availability of food organisms. One exception to this is the work of Armitage and Petts (1992), which found that the "RIVPACS" methodology was not able to demonstrate major changes in the benthic community of the River Garry in Tayside, where hydro-electric abstractions can lead to severe flow depletion. Gustard *et al.* (1987) examined the compensation flows of 146 Scottish impoundments, and concluded that compensation regimes had been set according to industrial and political constraints which no longer apply, and were based on inadequate hydrological information, with very little knowledge of the effects of impoundment on downstream flora and fauna.

Ward and Stanford (1993) stressed the need for a combined approach to water quality and quantity with regard to research, management and legislation, and considered it likely that future instream flow regimes would increasingly have to be determined to ensure that diversions and abstractions do not compromise water quality. The case for comprehensive abstraction controls in Scotland has been argued by the RPAs for some years (e.g. Scottish River Purification Boards' Association, 1987), and subsequently supported (Royal Commission on Environmental Pollution, 1992). The Government response has been to issue a consultation paper (Scottish Office, 1993a) setting out proposals for a revised abstraction control regime to be operated by the new Scottish Environment Protection Agency (SEPA, see below).

Pollution control and water quality

As Table 30.2 indicates, the Secretary of State has a number of direct and indirect roles in pollution control and the maintenance of water quality. These include acting as RPA to allow independent control of discharges by the multi-purpose Islands Councils. Also, through Her Majesty's Industrial Pollution Inspectorate (HMIPI) and consultation with the RPAs, the Secretary of State operates the Integrated Pollution Control system of the Environmental Protection Act 1990 to authorize processes which release certain pollutants to more than one environmental medium.

The vast majority of pollution control work is carried out by the 10 RPAs, whose functions originate from the 1951 and 1965 Rivers (Prevention of Pollution) (Scotland) Acts, as amended and repealed by the Control of Pollution Act 1974 and the Water Act 1989. The discharge consent procedures introduced in the 1951 Act, then extended and refined by later legislation, have proved to be the key element of pollution control policy (Hallett *et al.*, 1991). As noted elsewhere in this volume (Chapters 20 and 21), the activities of the RPAs have secured steady improvements in water quality, illustrated in the last two decades by the quinquennial Scottish Office Water Quality Surveys (e.g. Scottish Office, 1992d). However, the relatively crude nature of the classification means that significant deteriorations in water quality can occur before a water body drops from Class 1 (Brown and Howell, 1992), and the most recent review (Scottish Office, 1992d) acknowledges this deficiency in relation to the Class 1 categorization of acidified waters in south-west Scotland. Regrettably, the classification continues to exclude the waters of Shetland, Orkney and the Western Isles, despite some evidence of pollution problems there (e.g. Sinclair *et al.*, 1992; Hennessy, 1993).

Under the Control of Pollution Act 1974 (as amended) the Secretary of State has powers to introduce a statutory water quality classification and to set statutory water quality objectives. These powers (which could be used to improve the current classification) have so far not been used in Scotland, although there are proposals to do so in England and Wales (National Rivers Authority, 1991a; Department of the Environment and Welsh Office, 1992a). Work sponsored by the RPAs is under way to develop a biologically based classification which should provide a more realistic picture of water quality. This development is welcome and to some extent anticipates the proposed EC Directive on the Ecological Quality of Surface Waters. However, the future of this Directive is uncertain, partly because of the current EC debate on "subsidiarity" (Haigh, 1993).

Unfortunately, the success in reducing point-source pollution has not been matched by similar progress on pollution from diffuse sources, largely because the RPAs have insufficient statutory powers in this respect. Four sources of diffuse pollution pose particular threats to Scotland's fresh waters:

(1) atmospheric acid deposition;
(2) careless storage, use or accidental spillages of pollutants leading to unconsented discharges;
(3) land-use activities (e.g. application of fertilizers to agricultural land or forestry plantations); and
(4) the legacy of pollution which remains from Scotland's industrial past (e.g. nutrient releases from enriched loch sediments, toxic leachates from contaminated land, ferruginous acid discharges from abandoned mines).

At present, the options for statutory control of pollution from such sources are limited. Acid deposition is perhaps the most intractable of these, although some acidified waters may recover in the next decade if atmospheric emissions are reduced in line with the EC Large Combustion Plants Directive and other international agreements (see Chapter 24). The reduction of such emissions from Scottish sources is presently the responsibility of HMIPI and local authorities (but see below). In the meantime, the contributory role of coniferous afforestation in acid-sensitive catchments must be minimized by rigorous assessments of planting proposals (Royal Commission on Environmental Pollution, 1992) and water quality issues must be given stronger weight than they have in the past. The role of Indicative Forestry Strategies (see below) is crucial here in identifying acid-sensitive catchments, and the RPAs' monitoring work will continue to be a vital part of this process (see Chapter 23).

The Forestry Commission's role is also important in this context (as competent authority for formal Environmental Assessments of forestry schemes), and its *Forests and Water Guidelines* (Forestry Commission, 1993) provide guidance to forest managers on harmonizing forestry developments with freshwater habitats. The guidelines (which are voluntary) place great importance on the multiple benefits of ensuring that riparian areas are vegetated with native species, with the intention of reducing sediment and nutrient loading, and improving freshwater habitats through the input of leaf litter, bank stabilization and provision of dappled shade.

Riparian habitat restoration also offers an attractive solution to the problem of enrichment from agricultural runoff, which occurs in a number of Scottish fresh waters (see Stewart *et al.*, 1976; Harper and Stewart, 1987; Cuttle, 1989; Bailey-Watts, 1990; Edwards *et al.*, 1990). This approach to reducing nitrogen loading is discussed in some detail by Burt and Haycock (1992) and if, as seems likely, the EC Nitrates Directive requires action to reduce agricultural fertilizer use in some parts of Scotland, the "set-aside" proposals being developed by the Scottish Office Agriculture and Fisheries Department (SOAFD) could form a useful accompaniment which should further reduce fertilizer run-off. The Code of Good Agricultural Practice (Scottish Office, 1992e) also offers a considerable range of advice to farmers on minimizing water pollution risks (See Chapter 21).

Pollution from unconsented discharges continues to be of concern to the RPAs (Scottish River Purification Boards' Association, 1992). The recently introduced Regulations controlling stored agricultural substances are welcome, and their steady implementation by the RPAs should secure significant water quality improvements in rural areas. There is a pressing need for similar measures to control the storage of industrial oils and chemicals, as these substances are a significant source of pollution, particularly in watercourses near industrial estates.

The concerns expressed by Hammerton (1986) over the difficulties of treating acidic ferruginous discharges from abandoned mines are still valid, despite some recent reductions in pollution from these sources (Scottish Office, 1992d). Similar problems exist with releases to water from contaminated land and enriched loch sediments. A solution from Government does not as yet appear to be forthcoming, despite the recommendations of the Royal Commission on Environmental Pollution (1992) for more resources and statutory powers to be directed at these problems.

The seven River Purification Boards (RPBs) underwent a Scottish Office policy review in the late 1980s, but the findings of the review team (Scottish Development Department, 1990a) largely endorsed the status quo. Since then, the RPBs have continued to strengthen their role, and concerns about inconsistencies in the RPAs' approach (Brown and Howell, 1992) have been met recently with welcome statements of common intent (Association of Directors and River Inspectors of Scotland, 1992a, b). The Royal Commission on Environmental Pollution's recent report (1992) made 108 recommendations concerning measures to improve freshwater quality in the UK, and the Scottish Office and the RPAs are already beginning to act on a number of those which apply to Scotland.

Land drainage and flood prevention

The Flood Prevention (Scotland) Act 1961 provides Regional and Islands Councils with discretionary powers to undertake works to prevent flooding of non-agricultural land. Flood prevention on agricultural land is the responsibility of landowners, and grant aid for necessary works is available from SOAFD under the Farm Conservation Grant Scheme or the Land Drainage (Scotland) Act 1958. Civil engineering advice on land drainage and flood defence schemes is provided by the Scottish Office Environment Department (SOEnD), which also issues approval and grant aid for schemes proposed by local authorities under the 1961 Act. The Secretary of State also retains archaic maintenance responsibilities for schemes initiated under the Land Drainage (Scotland) Acts of 1930, 1935 and 1941, which were made to bring or keep land under cultivation during the Depression and the Second World War.

There are 13 schemes still in force under the 1930–41 Acts, 47 under the 1958 Act and 59 under the 1961 Act (Scottish Office, unpublished data). Until recently, these relatively low numbers would appear to support the view of Baldock (1984) that flooding is ". . . a comparatively small problem . . ." on Scottish rivers. However, widespread flooding occurred in Scotland in 1990 and 1993, with the Tay and its tributaries attracting particular attention (e.g. Gilvear and Harrison, 1991; Gilvear and Winterbottom, 1992). Although the catchment flood warning systems established by the RPAs operated efficiently, the magnitude of the flood events meant that damage to housing, commercial and industrial property, agricultural land and roads and railways was severe. Deep concern has been expressed at the piecemeal, site-based approach to land drainage and flood prevention which results from the artificial separation of responsibility for "urban" and "rural" flood defence (see Chapter 25).

In England and Wales, a recent government circular (Department of the Environment *et al.*, 1992) emphasizes that assessment of flood risk by the National Rivers Authority (NRA) should form a key part of the strategic planning process. Planning authorities are instructed to guide development away from flood-prone areas and restrict developments that would increase flood risk. They are expected to heed the advice of the NRA on the appropriateness of floodplain developments – or have good reasons for ignoring or rejecting it. There is obviously a pressing need for similar guidance in Scotland, but it is not clear how it would operate under the present statutory regime.

Fishery management and aquaculture

Fishery management

The management of freshwater fisheries in Scotland (see Chapters 18 and 26) is dominated by the emphasis on Atlantic Salmon and Sea Trout. This is a reflection of their economic importance and the long history of associated legislation reinforcing private rights (see Robinson, 1990, for a full description of Scottish freshwater fishery law). Fisheries for Salmon and Sea Trout are administered principally by District Salmon Fishery Boards under the Salmon Act 1986, which largely replaced the original legislation of the Salmon Fisheries (Scotland) Acts of 1862 and 1868. A Board can only be formed at the instigation of the Salmon fishing proprietors, and the coverage of Scotland by Boards is by no means complete. For example, no Board exists to oversee the return of the Salmon to the Clyde catchment or manage the important fish community of Loch Lomond, and Williamson (1986) suggested that the return of large numbers of Salmon to the Clyde might lead to some conflict in the exercise of Salmon and Trout fishing rights. Separate administrative arrangements apply in the rivers which form a boundary with England, that is, in the rivers flowing into the Solway Firth, and in the Tweed catchment, where the Tweed Commissioners are the fishery authority and have responsibility for managing all freshwater fish species.

Detailed provisions relate to the policing of the fishery to prevent poaching, times when fishing is prohibited, and illegal methods of fish capture. The basic powers to manage fresh waters are much more general, and indeed quite sweeping considering the Boards are essentially private, self-elected bodies. The Salmon Act 1986 allows Boards to:

> do such acts, execute such works and incur such expenses as may appear to them expedient for: the protection and improvement of salmon within the district; the increase of salmon; or the stocking of waters of the district with salmon.

The exercise of these powers to stock headwaters, carry out channel and bank works (Shearer, 1993) or eliminate predatory and competitive species, needs careful thought and planning to ensure such activities are consistent with broader conservation aims. The permission of a Board is required before Salmon or Sea Trout are released into waters within its district, but Boards have no powers to control releases of other species. The release of fish not native to Scotland can be controlled by the Secretary of State using discretionary powers under the Import of Live Fish (Scotland) Act 1978; an order restricting the import of Zander *Stizostedion lucioperca* was made recently because of concerns about the potentially damaging impact of its introduction on native Scottish fish populations.

The River Tweed apart, fishing for other species is largely governed by common law. The main exception to this exists in the Freshwater and Salmon Fisheries (Scotland) Act 1976, which allows owners of fishing rights to seek a Protection Order from the Secretary of State which creates a criminal offence of fishing for freshwater fish without permission. Protection Orders must guarantee improved access to freshwater fishings, and are usually sought to enable statutory controls over unauthorized fishing for Brown Trout. They have been criticized by the Scottish Anglers' National Association, the body governing the sport of game angling in Scotland, because some proprietors have used them to withdraw access and increase rentals for tenant angling clubs (Scottish Anglers' National Association, 1992). A recent wide-ranging review of access for water-based recreation (Brodies, 1992) recommended periodic reviews of each Protection Order to ensure they are being fairly administered.

The management of fisheries for species other than Salmon and Sea Trout has been somewhat neglected. A recent initiative is now under way to try to increase interest in angling for native Brown Trout (Scottish Tourist Board, 1992), but this has not yet gained widespread support. The SOAFD Freshwater Fisheries Laboratory fulfils an important research and advisory role and, although the vast majority of its effort is devoted to Salmon and Trout, recent years have seen an encouraging increase in studies on other species such as Grayling, Eels and Arctic Charr. The appointment of permanent, locally based fishery biologists to advise on the management of fisheries in the Tweed and West Galloway is a positive development, as it combines much-needed technical expertise with the local knowledge and experience of the Boards. However, given increased interest in coarse angling, the possibility of commercial fisheries for the exploitation of Eels and Arctic Charr, and a number of urgent priorities for the conservation of rare and endangered fish populations, a broader approach to freshwater fishery management is still required (Brown and Howell, 1992) and the whole range of legislation should be subject to thorough review (see Chapter 26).

Aquaculture

The growth of the fish farming industry in Scotland in the 1980s (see Chapter 18) rapidly overtook the ability of existing legislation to provide an effective regulatory framework. In introducing his text on the law relating to fish farming in Britain, Howarth (1990) stated: "Aquaculture is a rapidly developing industry striving to fall into ill-fitting legal categories formulated, in many instances, long before modern fish farming practices came into being".

This statement is well illustrated by controversies concerning predator control techniques, the need for discharge consents at fish cages, the potential genetic impact of escaped farmed Salmon on wild populations and the uncertain status of inland fish farms in planning law (see Institute of Aquaculture *et al.*, 1990, for a comprehensive review). Some of these have been resolved: much improved guidance is now available to fish farmers on non-destructive predator control (Howell and Munford, 1992); fish farms were confirmed as trade premises in 1989 and hence cages were subject to discharge consent procedures; freshwater fish farms were brought formally within the scope of the planning legislation in 1990. However, Scottish Office advice on the planning aspects of freshwater fish farming is still awaited, and the growth of the industry has slowed considerably in recent years with many developments (some more appropriate than others) already in place. Concerns remain about the possible genetic impact of escaped farmed Salmon on native stocks, reinforced by recent observations of escapees returning to fresh water to spawn (Webb *et al.*, 1991).

Outbreaks of disease at freshwater fish farms are controlled by SOAFD through the provisions of the Diseases of Fish Acts 1937 and 1983. These allow restrictions to be placed on the import of salmonid fish from overseas, and on the movement of diseased fish within Scotland. However, the onset of the Single European Market (with the associated requirement to remove barriers to trade) prompted the introduction of Regulations on the movement of aquaculture animals and products within the European Community. The implication of this approach is that national disease controls must not present a barrier to trade within the Community, so the relationship with the UK Diseases of Fish Acts needs to be determined.

The controversies surrounding the expansion of freshwater fish farming in the 1980s appear to have subsided somewhat in recent years. If the mistakes of the last decade are not to be repeated, it is vital that the possible diversification of the industry into farming of Arctic Charr, Brown Trout and Eels is more effectively planned and controlled. Highlands and Islands Enterprise (1993) has taken the initiative in producing a forward strategy for aquaculture, and the RPAs are working towards a formal policy on controlling fish farm pollution. The role of the industry's representatives (e.g. Scottish Salmon Growers' Association, National Farmers' Union, British Trout Association) will continue to be crucial, as will effective guidance and controls from all regulatory authorities (see Chapter 21).

Conservation, recreation and access

The Countryside Commission for Scotland (CCS)

The Countryside (Scotland) Act 1967 established CCS with a variety of duties and powers regarding the encouragement of access to and enjoyment of the natural beauty and amenity of the Scottish countryside. These included consultative, educational and advisory roles, powers to give grants and commission or conduct research, and established strong links between CCS and planning authorities. Throughout its history, a substantial proportion of the Commission's budget was devoted to grant-aiding projects and posts in the public and private sector (e.g. habitat and landscape management near fresh waters); provision of visitor facilities (car parks, toilets, interpretative material), particularly along loch sides; support of local authority ranger services in Country and Regional Parks featuring reservoirs as a significant component; assistance to water recreational groups with infrastructure projects (e.g. boathouse and clubhouse facilities).

The Commission embarked on a number of major projects in the 1970s: these included the identification of nationally important landscape areas, culminating in a report (Countryside Commission for Scotland, 1978) which listed 40 National Scenic Areas, many of which contain fresh waters as strong components of the landscape. Other projects examined the effects of water-based recreation on Scottish standing waters (Tivy, 1980) and identified a number of measures suitable for tackling the problem of loch shore erosion (Countryside Commission for Scotland, 1986).

At the request of the Scottish Office, CCS undertook a review of recreation and natural resource management in the mountain areas of Scotland, and the report (Countryside Commission for Scotland, 1990) noted the scenic and wildlife import-ance of upland waters and their sensitivity to pressures such as fish farm development and hydro-electric schemes. The report called for a greater integration between the Secretary of State, government agencies and private interests in mountain areas and made a number of detailed recommendations concerning the management of land-scape, wildlife and recreation, and the need for greater development controls. There was also a recommendation that National Parks should be established to cover the Cairngorms, Loch Lomond and the Trossachs, and Ben Nevis/Glen Coe/Black Mount.

In its latter years CCS embarked on a major review of access to the countryside, and several subsidiary reviews were commissioned to support this exercise. One of these (Brodies, 1992) is a substantial study of the legal basis of access for water-based recreation, which will be an important reference document in the development of these issues by Scottish Natural Heritage (below).

The Nature Conservancy (NC), Nature Conservancy Council (NCC) and Nature Conservancy Council for Scotland (NCCS) (see also Chapter 29)

The history of the NCC is well described elsewhere (e.g. Nature Conservancy Council, 1984a; Moore, 1987; Adams, 1993). Its predecessor, the Nature Conser-vancy, was established by Royal Charter in 1949 with powers in the National Parks and Access to the Countryside Act 1949 to set up nature reserves and a duty to notify planning authorities of any other area considered to be "of special interest by reason of its flora, fauna or geological or physiographical features". These latter areas, which came to be known as Sites of Special Scientific Interest (SSSIs), could include fresh waters, although according to Fisher (1993), in its early years the Conservancy concerned itself almost entirely with truly terrestrial habitats; the study of freshwater habitats was apparently regarded as the preserve of the Freshwater Biological Association.

Legislation in the 1950s and 1960s gave the NC a variety of licensing powers to protect particular species, and the Conservancy became part of the Natural Environment Research Council (NERC) in 1965. The establishment in that year of the Edinburgh-based Wetlands Research Group of the Conservancy marked the beginning of a brief period of intense freshwater research and survey activity which culminated in the commencement of the *Nature Conservation Review* (subsequently published under the editorship of Ratcliffe, 1977) and a major staff involvement in the International Biological Programme study of Loch Leven which ran from 1966 to 1971 (see Anonymous, 1974 for the published findings). The *Nature Conservation Review* identified 40 open water sites in Scotland of national (GB) conservation importance, and work commenced on notifying them as SSSIs where this had not already occurred.

The creation of the Nature Conservancy Council (NCC) by the Nature Conservancy Council Act 1973 transferred the majority of the freshwater specialists (and their associated research expertise) to NERC's Institute of Terrestrial Ecology. The NCC's statutory functions included the selection, establishment and management of National Nature Reserves; the identification and notification of SSSIs; the provision of advice and dissemination of knowledge about nature conservation; and the support and conduct of research relevant to these functions. The Act also provided a power to give grant assistance to suitable projects and initiatives.

Notification of SSSIs continued during the 1970s. The passage of the Wildlife and Countryside Act 1981 was a significant development, as it strengthened the legislation on SSSIs and species protection (see Boon, 1991, and Boon *et al.*, 1992b, for reviews of the application of these provisions to rivers and freshwater species respectively). The Act also reinforced the conservation duties which applied to the water authorities in England and Wales, but not those of their Scottish counterparts (see below). The burdens of renotifying existing SSSIs (and new sites) under the 1981 Act led to a considerable rise in staff numbers during the 1980s, with an associated increase in funding of freshwater research and survey work. Extensive surveys of aquatic macrophyte communities were established, firstly on rivers (Holmes, 1983; 1989) and then lochs (Palmer *et al.*, 1992), followed by a greater involvement in impact-related studies, (Institute of Aquaculture *et al.*, 1990; Rimes *et al.*, 1994) and, more recently, work on invertebrates (Armitage and Petts, 1992; Rundle *et al.*, 1992; Wright *et al.*, 1992) and conservation of rare fish (Maitland and Lyle, 1991; 1992; Lyle and Maitland, 1992). Despite all of this research and survey work, rivers are seriously under-represented in the Scottish SSSI and NNR complement; Brown and Howell (1992) suggested that the lack of river SSSIs in Scotland was due to the considerable resource implications of river notification and concerns about the effectiveness of SSSIs as a means of protecting rivers (see discussion below and Chapter 29).

Work on freshwater policy and liaison with the Scottish Office and its statutory agencies received little attention from NCC, possibly because more effort was devoted to the debates raging in England and Wales over land drainage and flood defence (see Purseglove, 1988). New staff appointments in the 1980s led to greater involvement with other water agencies, particularly the RPBs, although discussions with the latter on the absence of a conservation duty (see below) proved a source of friction for some time. Consultations over applications for discharge consent, forestry grants and planning permission became increasingly routine aspects of daily work at the local level, with complex freshwater conservation issues often arising. In addition, responses to relevant Government consultation papers increasingly called for radical changes to Scottish water policy.

Government proposals for an agency formed by the merger of CCS and the NCC in Scotland were announced in 1989, and developed in some detail by the Scottish Development Department (1990b). This was to follow the abolition of the NCC, a decision which proved very controversial (Scott, 1992; Marren, 1993), but which went ahead under the Environment Protection Act 1990. The Act created a new nature conservation agency in 1991 – the Nature Conservancy Council for Scotland (NCCS) – which derived its funding, supervision and Board appointees from the Secretary of State for Scotland. NCCS existed for one year before it was merged with the Countryside Commission for Scotland to create an entirely new agency, Scottish Natural Heritage.

Scottish Natural Heritage (SNH)

Scottish Natural Heritage was established in April 1992 by the Natural Heritage (Scotland) Act 1991, which combined the statutory functions of its predecessors and added some new ones. Two new functions are of particular interest. The first is SNH's power to recommend areas of outstanding natural heritage value to the Secretary of State for designation as "Natural Heritage Areas", a designation seen by some as an attempt to forestall recommendations for national parks (Taylor, 1991) made by the Countryside Commission for Scotland (1990). The second is the requirement that SNH should "have regard to the desirability of securing that anything done, whether by SNH or any other person, in relation to the natural heritage of Scotland is done in a manner which is sustainable". This latter duty constitutes the first appearance of the concept of "sustainability" in UK legislation and promises to exercise much of SNH's thinking during its early years. Scott (1993) lists a number of difficulties encountered in New Zealand in attempting to reconcile "conventional" economic growth with the statutory requirement to promote sustainable management under the Resource Management Act 1991.

It is perhaps a little early to assess how SNH's approach to Scottish freshwater issues might compare with its predecessors. Work has commenced on a new conservation evaluation system for rivers (Boon *et al.*, in press), the freshwater loch survey (see Chapter 9) has been restarted and fish conservation work has moved on from Charr and Powan to examine the Shad and Smelt populations in the Cree Estuary in Galloway. Pressing for a revision of the *Forests and Water Guidelines* (Forestry Commission, 1991) was a major item of work, prompted principally by the controversial planting proposals in Strath Halladale in the Flow Country. Other highly publicized cases involved pollution and fishery management in Loch Leven and the continued debate about river engineering and flooding at the Spey-Feshie confluence.

Priorities for the future are likely to include assessment of the effects of river engineering and land use on rivers; promotion with fishery interests of the multiple benefits of re-establishing native riparian vegetation; monitoring the development of small-scale hydro-electricity schemes; recommendations on access for water-based recreation following the responses to the Access Review (Scottish Natural Heritage, 1992) and development of strategies which harmonize water recreation with other ways of using and appreciating the resource; monitoring implementation of the forthcoming voluntary Code of Practice for the WSAs and RPAs on Conservation, Access and Recreation and the revised *Forests and Water Guidelines*; development, with the RPAs, of strategies and targets for the restoration of polluted SSSI fresh waters; monitoring progress towards the establishment of SEPA and new water and sewerage undertakings, and compiling lists of waters which support species and habitats of European Community importance for possible designation under the EC Habitats and Species Directive. With such a diverse agenda, numerous collaborative approaches to policy, research and management will be required, and work has now begun on a Scottish freshwater conservation strategy to guide SNH's efforts in all of these areas.

The voluntary sector

Voluntary environmental organizations have widely differing roles and approaches to freshwater conservation. In Scotland, some (FWAG, RSPB, VWT, AST – see Table 30.3 for abbreviations) operate as part of a larger GB or UK organization, or at the international scale (Greenpeace, WWF), whereas others have a distinct Scottish identity (SCP, SWT, NTS, FoE) but with very similar counterparts elsewhere in the UK. Although many of their activities (Table 30.3 and Environment Council, 1993) are those given by statute to SNH (see above), freedom from the protocols of public service has allowed them on occasions to pursue a radical, provocative and confrontational approach. However, the widespread incorporation of their traditional concerns into mainstream thought has led Grove-White (1992) to speculate whether the voluntary bodies could eventually become part of the new "environmentally-aware" political fabric.

Micklewright (1993) suggested that overlaps in the activities of British voluntary conservation bodies could lead to rivalry, competition and dilution of effort, but the existence of Scottish Wildlife and Countryside Link (SWCL) is an attempt to avoid this. SWCL acts as an umbrella body and discussion forum for the Scottish voluntary conservation bodies, and forms *ad hoc* groups to consider particular issues. In the past these have examined forestry and marine fish farming, but following a seminar in 1992 SWCL established a Freshwater Working Group, which could prove particularly timely given the current upheavals in Scottish water policy. A similar group (the Joint Water Group, which includes representation from SNH's equivalent agencies) has existed in England and Wales for some time, where it proved very effective in ensuring that the conservation voice was heard in Parliament and Whitehall during

TABLE 30.3. Scottish fresh waters: summary of activities of selected voluntary environmental bodies. For more details, see Environment Council (1993) and the Annual Reports of individual organizations

	RSPB	SWT	SCP	NTS	AST	WWF	FWAG	VWT	FoE	GP
Site ownership[a]	*	*		*						
Volunteer conservation	*	*	*	*						
Training/advice	*	*	*	*	*		*	*		
Publications/education	*	*	*	*	*	*	*	*	*	*
Campaigning/lobbying	*	*	*		*	*		*	*	*
Grant aid provision						*				
Research and survey	*	*	*	*	*	*	*	*	*	*

[a] e.g. nature reserve, visitor centre; involves management for conservation, interpretation, observation facilities, guided walks, etc

Abbreviations: RSPB – Royal Society for the Protection of Birds
SWT – Scottish Wildlife Trust
SCP – Scottish Conservation Projects
NTS – National Trust for Scotland
AST – Atlantic Salmon Trust
WWF – World Wide Fund for Nature
VWT – Vincent Wildlife Trust
FWAG – Farming and Wildlife Advisory Groups
FoE – Friends of the Earth (Scotland)
GP – Greenpeace

the progress of the Water Bill which privatized the water industry and established the National Rivers Authority.

An important but far less-publicized aspect of the voluntary movement is the attempt by Keep Scotland Beautiful to encourage the establishment of River Trusts. These are generally small community groups which attempt to improve the quality and awareness of their local watercourses through involving people in footpath construction, anti-pollution activities, litter clean-ups, repairing bank erosion, provision of facilities for interpretation, and access improvements. The practical conservation activities of Scottish Conservation Projects' "Operation Brightwater" campaign were very similar (Scottish Conservation Projects, 1990), and both strands of activity have done much to increase local involvement and interest in the management of inland waters, especially in urban areas where water bodies are under severe pressure and often heavily degraded. Expansion of the River Trust network in the future could do much to improve the quality of urban fresh waters in particular as habitats, landscape features and recreational resources.

CONSERVATION DUTIES IN SCOTTISH WATER MANAGEMENT: A CHEQUERED HISTORY

The Countryside (Scotland) Act 1967 stipulates that "in the exercise of their functions every Minister, government department and public body shall have regard to the desirability of conserving the natural beauty and amenity of the countryside". There was little evidence of this having any influence on Scottish water policy and the Countryside Commission for Scotland (1990) regarded the wording as "too cautious and too little heeded". In England and Wales, the Water Act 1973 imposed a similar duty on the newly created water authorities, reinforced by a requirement for NCC to notify the water authorities of any SSSIs in their area. Improvements in conservation awareness began to emerge, but the Wildlife and Countryside Act 1981 marked a real turning point, as it required the water authorities to *further* conservation and consult NCC about any proposals it had to carry out work on SSSIs. This led to the appointment of conservation officers in the authorities and ultimately to changed attitudes within the water industry, particularly with respect to land drainage and flood defence activities which had devastated hundreds of kilometres of waterway (see Purseglove, 1988).

As the 1981 Act amended the 1973 Water Act (which applied to England and Wales), no new conservation duties applied to the water management agencies in Scotland. Concerns expressed by NCC prompted the Scottish Office in 1982 to write to the WSAs and RPAs indicating that whilst no statutory duty applied, they were expected to "act in accordance with the spirit" of the 1981 Act; however, the letter also stated that this new requirement should not involve any departure from existing practice or impose any additional demands on expenditure. Attempts by NCC and the RPBs to reach agreement on the practical implications of this request were hampered by the limited remit of the Boards (Mackay, 1988), and by the above caveat to the letter's principal request.

The Agriculture Act 1986 requires the Secretary of State to achieve a reasonable balance between agricultural developments, nature conservation and the enjoyment of the countryside. It appears that this duty has had little influence on the Scottish

Office in its supervision and maintenance of agricultural land drainage and flood defence schemes. A traditional civil engineering approach still predominates, possibly because that is what is required by many of the outdated Statutory Orders under which most work is carried out.

The Water Act 1989 provided the NRA, Secretary of State for the Environment, the new water companies and Internal Drainage Boards with a duty to *further* conservation in carrying out their statutory functions, with the NRA having an additional free-standing duty (i.e. not linked to its other functions) to *promote* conservation. When the Act was passing through Parliament as a Bill, an RSPB-sponsored amendment was introduced which would have extended a duty to further conservation to the RPBs. In the House of Lords' consideration of the amendment (Anonymous, 1989b), the Scottish Office Minister's reply seemed to indicate that nature conservation was regarded as largely a matter for NCC, and should thus only form a restricted part of the remit of other statutory water interests.

During the passage of the Natural Heritage (Scotland) Bill through Parliament, an amendment was again proposed which sought to extend a formal conservation duty to the RPAs. The amendment failed, but the Scottish Office decided to produce a voluntary Code of Practice on Conservation, Access and Recreation for the RPAs and WSAs. Whilst, ideally, the Code (Scottish Office, 1993b) should have a statutory basis and apply to all the water management functions, it will prove useful in paving the way for the formal statutory duties which are expected for SEPA and the new water and sewerage undertakings.

Recent changes in the approach to river engineering in England and Wales provide a good illustration of the value of supporting traditional water management functions, such as land drainage and flood defence, with positive statutory conservation duties. Damage to the landscape and nature conservation value of fresh waters has been a feature of flood prevention, land drainage and other river engineering schemes in most industrialized societies, and Scotland is no exception. An increasingly sensitive and enlightened engineering approach has in some countries enabled many damaged rivers to be restored, and provided opportunities on new schemes for mitigating damage, or undertaking enhancement work (see Iversen *et al.*, 1993; also numerous examples in Lewis and Williams, 1984; Purseglove, 1988; and Boon *et al.*, 1992a). The production of government guidance documents (Ministry of Agriculture, Fisheries and Food *et al.*, 1991; 1992) has formalized this approach in England and Wales. The conservation duties are taken seriously for the most part and are rapidly becoming incorporated into routine channel maintenance work. The use of pre- and post-project appraisal techniques such as river corridor survey (Nature Conservancy Council, 1984b; National Rivers Authority, 1992a; Heaton, 1993) to minimize damage to species, habitats and landscapes, and the appointment of conservation staff, have both been significant factors in the revolution in thinking and were driven primarily by the conservation duties.

River engineering of this nature often involves an acceptance that floodplains can be allowed to fulfil their hydrological, geomorphological and ecological functions (e.g. to receive and dissipate flood waters). As Ward and Stanford (1993) observed, rivers which are interactive with their floodplains constitute the best flood control systems. It is also important to acknowledge, as does Boon (1992b), that factors such as flooding, channel erosion and sediment deposition – so damaging to the human activities taking place in the floodplains of modern Scotland – may be crucial factors in maintaining features of international nature conservation importance. This is the case in Strathspey, where the floodplain fens of the Insh Marshes on the River Spey and the forested, actively braided alluvial fan at the downstream confluence with the River Feshie are both notified as SSSIs. Pressure to reduce flood risk there through a variety of river engineering and drainage schemes emphasizes the need for a stronger ecological, geomorphological and conservation-based approach to these issues in Scotland (Chapter 29). The evidence from England and Wales suggests that providing a positive statutory conservation duty can accomplish a great deal of environmental benefit without detracting from other more utilitarian water management functions such as land drainage and flood defence.

Even if SEPA's water remit is not extended (see below), the difficulty with simply applying conservation duties to, for example, the fishery management, land drainage and flood defence functions, is that they would sit uneasily beside the existing (largely outdated) statutes. Comprehensive reviews of the legislation are required in these fields to remove, for example, the conflicts between the dredging of river gravel in land drainage schemes and the importance of that gravel as a salmonid spawning ground, or between the Scottish Office's duty to maintain environmentally unsympathetic land drainage schemes made under the 1930–41 Acts, and the same body's proposals for habitat re-creation in river corridors under the planned long-term set-aside scheme.

FUTURE WATER POLICY: INTEGRATION OR SEGREGATION?

Background

The present institutional and statutory framework for Scottish water management has strong roots in the past. Much of the relevant legislation stems from the period 1930–70, when a sectoral approach to agricultural production and protection of agricultural land, water supply, hydro-electricity generation, conservation and management of migratory salmonid fish species and reduction of pollution from traditional point sources, was seen as a strength rather than a weakness.

For example, Hammerton (1987; 1989; 1990) and Mackay (Chapter 27) both argue that the narrow focus of the River Purification Boards is largely responsible for the water quality improvements achieved in Scotland over the last few decades. They contrast this with the multi-functional approach of the National Rivers Authority (NRA) in England and Wales (and its predecessors in the Water Authorities), comparing the two most recent water quality surveys (National Rivers Authority, 1991b; Scottish Office, 1992d) and citing the better performance in Scotland as evidence of a more determined approach to pollution control. Whether the breadth of the NRA's water-related functions inevitably detracts from its role in pollution control is a matter for debate. However, there is ample evidence of a far more conservation-minded approach to water management in England and Wales (e.g. Gardiner, 1991; Heaton, 1993), due largely (in the author's view) to the NRA's status as an independent regulatory authority with a wide-ranging, integrated water remit underpinned by clear statutory conservation duties.

Land use and catchment planning

Much of this chapter has examined the case for integrating water management; the integration of land-use planning and water resource planning is equally important given the powerful influences which catchments exercise over the waters which drain them. A variety of mechanisms exist in Scotland to achieve this end, but not all of them are used to their full potential.

Most development for commercial, industrial or residential purposes (and associated infrastructure) is controlled by the planning authorities through the Town and Country Planning (Scotland) Act 1972, which requires the preparation of Local Plans and regional Structure Plans to provide a strategic basis for the day-to-day operation of the planning procedures (see Chapter 28). Key areas of concern here relate to the role of planning authorities in allowing developments to proceed in areas with inadequate flood defences, or in areas where the water and sewerage systems are overstretched. There is clearly a need for a much stronger water-based input into these aspects of strategic planning (see Gardiner and Cole, 1992, for an example of the application of this approach).

Not all developments affecting fresh waters are within the control of the planning authority; as noted above, the planning status of freshwater fish farming was uncertain for some time, and most activities related to forestry river engineering and agriculture enjoy permitted development rights. The preparation of Indicative Forestry Strategies by Regional Councils has brought a welcome local planning approach to forestry developments, although approval for individual schemes still rests with the Forestry Commission. The strategies produced so far in Scotland have been somewhat tentative in their analysis of the interactions between forestry and fresh waters, in contrast to the often unequivocal statements which are made about the effects of forestry developments on the amenity and conservation value of terrestrial features.

Scottish agricultural and estate management policies illustrate how an insufficient appreciation of land-water interactions can cause significant damage to freshwater habitats. In areas where overgrazing is severe (due to high densities of sheep, deer or cattle), the suppression of woody plant growth has been associated with bank erosion and subsequent siltation of watercourses (Shearer, 1993), leading to loss of instream habitat and reduced species diversity. In arable areas similar problems are associated with land drainage, flood defence and field cultivation, with the added factor of enhanced nutrient loadings arising from fertilizer inputs.

A number of statutory and policy instruments could be used to alleviate these problems. For waters of nature conservation importance the SSSI legislation has limited force unless adjacent land is included within the SSSI boundary (Boon, 1991; Brown and Howell, 1992). Provisions exist in the Control of Pollution Act for the Secretary of State to issue regulations which prohibit or restrict the carrying out of activities which lead to pollution, but these provisions have yet to be used, despite several requests from the RPAs, for reasons which may include a burdensome requirement for evidence and the absence of compensation procedures for those whose activities may be restricted (Brown and Howell, 1992). The Agriculture Act 1986 enables the Secretary of State to designate "Environmentally Sensitive Areas" in which incentives exist to adopt a less intensive approach to agriculture. Ten such areas exist in Scotland, covering some 1.49×10^6 ha, but there does not appear to have been any attempt to focus measures within these areas on freshwater restoration projects – or indeed to assess the extent to which incidental freshwater benefits may be arising through changes in land management.

Surplus agricultural production has prompted the European Community to seek measures to reduce these surpluses, and SOAFD's proposals to take land out of agricultural production ("set-aside") have identified the re-establishment of upland scrub, marshland, damp lowland grassland and waterside habitats as particular long-term priorities. If sufficient funds are available to support these options and they are carefully targeted to particular areas, they could do much to resolve some of the land-use problems discussed above. For example, Harper (1991) has suggested that set-aside land could be used to re-establish floodplain vegetation and act as a flood control measure; Peterken and Hughes (1994) have called for the re-establishment of flood-plain forests.

The Royal Commission on Environmental Pollution (1992) has advocated the use of economic instruments such as a "fertilizer tax" to reduce excessive fertilizer use and subsequent nutrient enrichment problems. The EC Nitrates Directive requires member states to secure reductions in fertilizer use in the catchments of waters experiencing eutrophication from excessive applications of agricultural nitrogen, and it is likely that some areas of Scotland will be affected; however, it is not yet clear whether the necessary reductions in nitrate levels will be achieved by economic or other means.

Difficulties in integrating water-related functions, and relating these to land-use activities, have led to water agencies developing approaches which attempt to do just that through the preparation of Integrated Catchment Management Plans. The value – even necessity – of this approach is widely acknowledged (IUCN *et al.*, 1991; Gardiner and Cole, 1992; Newson, 1992; Royal Commission on Environmental Pollution, 1992) and it is being actively pursued by the National Rivers Authority (1991c), although concerns that the NRA's methodology does not accord sufficient weight to rural land-use issues have prompted others (e.g. Land Use Consultants, 1992) to propose a more comprehensive approach.

In Scotland, the absence of a single co-ordinating water agency makes the application of this approach more difficult, although the advent of "Tweed Forum", which acts as a means of disseminating information amongst the principal bodies with statutory interest in that river, appears to be a small step in the right direction. A similar group was established in 1992 following a toxic algal bloom at Loch Leven, and its regular meetings (and those of technical sub-groups) have done much to engender a spirit of co-operation which perhaps was previously lacking in tackling the loch's well-documented eutrophication problem. Agreement appears to have been reached on the priorities for reducing phosphorus levels in sewage effluents, and attention is now turning to agricultural and other land-use practices in the catchment which could be modified to reduce the loch's external nutrient loading still further. A review of activities in the catchment of Lough Neagh, Northern Ireland (another water with a long history of eutrophication), noted a proliferation of agencies and interest groups with the potential to affect the environment of the lough, and advocated establishing a non-statutory Lough Neagh Development and Advisory Authority, whose key task would be "to manage and wisely develop the resources of the Lough" (Building Design Partnership and Mackay Consultants, 1991). These examples suggest that the voluntary approach to integration of policies for land and water use has some attractions, although there are still strong arguments in favour of bringing responsibility for all regulatory aspects of water management within the remit of one statutory agency.

Reorganization of local government

The plans to create single-tier local authorities (Scottish Office, 1991; 1992a) and the investment needs arising from EC Directives on drinking water quality and sewage treatment raised the question of how water and sewerage services would be funded and provided in Scotland. This was explored in a government consultation paper (Scottish Office, 1992c) which canvassed views on eight options, ranging from outright privatization, through franchising, to public ownership in the new single-tier authorities, joint boards, or new public water authorities.

The issue has excited much public and political debate, and strong public opposition to privatization has been mobilized by local authorities and Opposition parties. Much of the comment has centred around the economic activities of the privatized water companies in England and Wales, such as increased water charges and the disconnections of domestic water users for non-payment. Relatively little attention has been focused on their environmental record, although the recent national water quality survey (National Rivers Authority, 1991b) attributed much of the recorded decline in water quality to continued poor performance by sewage treatment works. Bowers *et al.* (1988) described in some detail the reservoirs, gathering grounds and other landholdings which the water companies would be expected to manage in accordance with their conservation duties, and a recent report (Department of the Environment *et al.*, 1993) suggests that these duties are being carried out in a positive spirit. Numerous conservation staff have been appointed, and all of the water authorities' privatized successors have produced statements of policy on conservation, access and recreation; some reports (e.g. Welsh Water, 1992) claim substantial achievements in these fields.

As noted above, the reservoirs owned or operated by WSAs may often constitute a significant open water resource in terms of nature conservation, recreational potential and scenic value. This is illustrated by the frequency with which reservoirs occur in Regional and Country Parks (e.g. Pentlands Regional Park, Lothian; Lomond Hills Regional Park, Fife; Clatto and Monikie Country Parks, Dundee). Morgan (1972) stressed the difficulties of integrating recreational pursuits on water bodies with nature conservation objectives, and the reservoir management strategy produced by the Planning Department of Lothian Regional Council (1990) appears to be the most comprehensive attempt yet to meet this challenge. A well-publicized example of these difficulties exists around Loch Lomond, parts or all of which have numerous countryside designations (e.g. National Scenic Area, Environmentally Sensitive Area, Regional Park, Site of Special Scientific Interest, National Nature Reserve). The loch also forms a major water supply scheme for the Central Scotland Water Development Board, and experiences intense recreational pressure. The Secretary of State established a working party to examine and report on these and other issues, and its findings (Loch Lomond and the Trossachs Working Party, 1993) have recently been published for consultation.

The Scottish Office (1993c) has announced its proposals for the future of local government in Scotland. These include new arrangements for the provision of water and sewerage services, which involve three new public authorities and a role for the private sector in providing and financing capital investment programmes. The implications of this proposal for the management of, for example, reservoirs and associated land remain unclear but, in the meantime, the Code of Practice (see above) will provide a framework within which the existing WSAs can be expected to operate.

The other area of uncertainty relates to the future responsibility for construction, operation and maintenance of flood defences, which in urban areas often rests with the Water and Sewerage Department of the local authority. At the time of writing, the Government has yet to finalize proposals for the future of flood defences in Scotland.

Scottish Environment Protection Agency

The Government's proposals

In 1991 the Government announced proposals to establish a Scottish Environment Protection Agency (SEPA) by combining the existing pollution-control functions of the RPAs, HMIPI and local authorities (Scottish Office, 1992b). The paper proposed that SEPA should be a national body with a regional structure, perhaps based on the areas of the existing RPAs, with the work of each regional division overseen by an advisory committee. It would have a statutory conservation duty, but its freshwater work would not extend beyond that already carried out by the RPAs. The case for including other water-related functions within SEPA's remit was rejected, using reasoning which was inconsistent with the three key principles underpinning the case for SEPA's cross-media pollution control function. These were:

- to remove overlap and conflict between different regulatory agencies and create a single body with responsibility for controlling discharges of waste to air, water and land;
- to separate operational from regulatory responsibilities (whether conflicts between these roles have existed in the past or not), and
- to ensure that pollution control is carried out with full access to a modern and comprehensive range of specialist expertise and equipment.

The Government considered that these arguments clearly applied to integrated pollution control, but, for reasons not expressed in the paper, not to integrated water management.

A parallel proposal is under consideration in England and Wales where, after some controversy, it appears that all the functions of the NRA will be merged with those of Her Majesty's Inspectorate of Pollution (the equivalent of the Scottish HMIPI) and the functions of local authorities relating to control of waste disposal. Consideration of this proposal by the House of Commons Environment Committee (1992) recommended that an Environment Agency with a Britain-wide remit should be kept as a serious option for the future, and encouraged the Government, in setting up the English/Welsh and Scottish agencies, to ensure that future integration would be possible should it be chosen eventually as an option. The Committee also recommended that an even more wide-ranging remit should be given to the Environment Agency it advocated for Northern Ireland (House of Commons Environment Committee, 1991).

On 25 February 1993 the Secretary of State for Scotland announced to Parliament the outcome of the Scottish consultation exercise. The plans for SEPA would proceed largely as proposed, but further consultation would take place on extensions to the abstraction control system (see below). As the responses to the consultation paper indicated considerable concern about the potential loss of local responsiveness, expertise and accountability associated with passing what are currently locally managed duties to a national agency, a further consultation would also consider these issues.

The case for a broader water remit

Examination of all 168 publicly available responses to the SEPA consultation paper revealed considerable support for the new agency to be given a statutory conservation duty and a broader water management remit amongst consultees commenting on these aspects of the paper (Table 30.4). Such comments were not confined to SNH and the voluntary conservation bodies: they were supported to varying degrees by interests as diverse as local government, owners of salmon fishings, landowners, and pollution control authorities. Whilst only 12 consultees commented on the proposed statutory conservation duty, their support for the proposal was unanimous.

Control of abstractions, impoundments and water transfers

Of the 45 responses to the SEPA consultation exercise which advocated a broader water remit for the new agency, 23 called for broader abstraction control powers. The Government responded to this by issuing a further consultation paper (Scottish Office, 1993a) which set out some limited extensions to the abstraction control regime

TABLE 30.4. Degree of support for providing a Scottish Environment Protection Agency with a statutory conservation duty and an integrated water management remit, as shown by analysis of all 168 publicly available responses to the government consultation paper (Scottish Office, 1992b). Figures represent number of responses commenting on these aspects of the paper; see text for details

	Conservation duty	Integrated water remit
Support	12	18
Part support[a]	0	27
Rejection	0	3
Total	12	48

[a]support that was either partial (only some additional water-related functions should be undertaken by SEPA) or qualified by other statements

which SEPA would administer. The approach set out in the paper is disappointing, as it implies that statutory controls will only be contemplated where localized difficulties pose a threat to water resources. This contrasts strongly with the discharge consents procedures of the pollution-control regime, which provide the RPAs with geographically comprehensive control powers (i.e. there is no need to seek the Scottish Office's approval for catchment-based control areas).

The comparison with pollution control is instructive: Scotland's fresh waters (particularly those in the industrialized areas) experienced many decades of gross pollution before the requirement for consents on virtually all discharges enabled the RPAs to secure water quality improvements (see Chapter 20). Given possible alterations to rainfall patterns, and increased pressures on water resources in expanding areas like the Aberdeen hinterland, it appears prudent to establish a comprehensive statutory regime which anticipates problems in the future, even if the effects are not expected to be as severe or widespread as those experienced in southern Britain in recent years (e.g. Department of the Environment and Welsh Office, 1992b; National Rivers Authority, 1992b).

As Scottish Natural Heritage (1993) stated, SEPA should be given comprehensive (Scotland-wide) powers to control abstractions, impoundments and water transfers, including a power to amend existing compensation water and abstraction regimes, with the Secretary of State retaining oversight and appeal functions. Similar provisions exist for England and Wales through the Water Resources Acts 1963 and 1991. This would entail transferring regulatory responsibility from the Scottish Office (e.g. for setting compensation flows downstream of public water supply and hydroelectric schemes) to SEPA, which will inherit the relevant hydrological and biological expertise from the RPAs.

Although, as noted above, there is little published evidence of over-exploitation of water resources in Scotland, this may simply be a reflection of the greater attention devoted to pollution problems in the past. Absence of evidence does not necessarily mean absence of effect, and any detrimental effects of over-abstraction may be masked by water pollution and other forms of habitat degradation. The consultation paper emphasizes the need to maintain minimum acceptable flows in watercourses for diluting and dispersing pollutants, protecting flora, fauna and natural amenity, but does not discuss the desirability of maintaining variable flow patterns. As illustrated above, many compensation flows have been set on the basis of little hydrological or ecological knowledge. However, modelling techniques developed in North America such as PHABSIM and IFIM (see Milhous *et al.*, 1989, and Bovee, 1982, respectively, both cited in Gore *et al.*, 1992) offer a practical means to integrate ecological requirements with other water resource demands. These techniques are currently being refined for use in England and Wales; the more rigorous approach they embody should be adopted by SEPA with a view to amending controlled flow regimes in Scotland where appropriate.

Flood defence and land drainage

In the SEPA consultation responses, SOEnD was encouraged to provide SEPA with a statutory role in land drainage and flood prevention. This view was put forward by SNH and the voluntary environmental sector, and also, notably, by the bodies representing those currently struggling to maintain flood defences (landowners and local authorities), and those frustrated by their flood warning systems not being matched by similarly effective flood defences (River Purification Authorities). Given current Treasury concerns about the level of public expenditure, the considerable financial implications for SEPA of giving it an operational role in these areas appear likely to dissuade the Government from doing so.

Nonetheless, there is still an urgent need for a more strategic, catchment-based and environmentally-sympathetic approach to all types of channel maintenance in Scotland. If landowners and local authorities were to retain their existing roles, SEPA could usefully be given the following functions:

- conducting catchment-based assessments of flood risk to existing property, and advising local authorities on the types of land use appropriate in areas subject to varying degrees of flood risk;
- operating flood warning systems; and
- offering advice and providing approval for flood defence works, ensuring that nature conservation and landscape requirements are met.

These proposals would still leave maintenance duties with the Secretary of State for the outdated schemes under the 1930–41 Land Drainage (Scotland) Acts. Options for these schemes could include repealing the maintenance duty, passing it to local authorities/landowners, or passing it to SEPA.

Fishery management

Buisson (1991) discussed the land drainage role of the Internal Drainage Boards in England and Wales, and noted that the decision-making process placed power in the hands of those most likely to benefit, but suggested that the system lacked clear policies, an overall strategy and central guidance. The parallels with the District Salmon Fishery Board system in Scotland are quite striking and, as suggested earlier, the present Scottish statutory framework is inadequate for the range of fish conservation issues that need to be addressed. The absence of an independent fishery authority to comment on – and if necessary object to – planning applications, discharge consent proposals, forestry schemes and river engineering projects is a particularly serious omission. The Hunter Committee (1965) advocated the establishment of 13 fishery boards, with responsibilities for all freshwater fish, to cover the whole of Scotland. After some delay, this proposal was largely accepted by Government (Department of Agriculture and Fisheries for Scotland, 1971) but the promised legislation has never materialized.

As noted above, a strong case exists for a thorough review of Scottish freshwater fishery legislation and administration, and the opportunity should be taken to provide SEPA with fishery-related functions. However, the Government's support for separating operation from regulation appears to be uncertain in the field of fishery management, which is understandable not least because of the labyrinthine provisions of Scottish statutory and common law. In addition, examination of the SEPA consultation responses reveals considerable disquiet among Salmon fishing interests at the prospect of SEPA having comprehensive fishery management responsibilities.

Even so, a number of "non-operational" roles should still be considered, including:

- a duty to conserve all native freshwater fish populations, and secure an appropriate balance between fisheries for Salmon, Trout and other species;
- issuing approvals for releases of fish; and
- providing advice on fishery management (e.g. monitoring the status of fish populations, advising on fish habitat improvements).

While some of these options would involve transferring responsibility from the Secretary of State to SEPA, this would then permit a statutory fishery authority to take a strong role in the assessment of development proposals. That possibility does not exist under the present framework.

The experience of previous UK water re-organizations (e.g. the establishment of Water Authorities in England and Wales by the 1973 Water Act and their subsequent abolition under the 1989 Water Act) does not augur well for the prospect of securing a truly integrated water management role for SEPA. The principal objective in creating the new agency appears to be to establish a "one-stop shop" for pollution control (Scottish Office, 1992b), which was confirmed by the Secretary of State's announcement in February 1993. Jordan *et al.* (1977), Bowers (1991) and Buisson (1991), in commenting on the re-organizations in England and Wales, have noted the failure of previous governments to take the opportunities these changes provided to reform other aspects of water law. In both cases the potential existed to revise and update the land drainage legislation, but fear of the agricultural lobby sabotaging the Bill and thus thwarting the Government's main legislative purpose (i.e. to establish public Water Authorities and subsequently to create the NRA and private companies from them), was cited as the reason for the Government's reluctance.

Too often under the current statutory regime, the relevant authorities and Scottish Office Departments seem to have been "forced" together in response to specific incidents (e.g. the flooding in recent winters in Tayside and Strathspey, the toxic blue-green algal bloom at Loch Leven in summer 1992). Effective co-ordination of effort and commonality of purpose between the various Divisions of Scottish Office Departments *and* between the Departments themselves is as important as such integration at all levels outside the Scottish Office.

Whether the legislation to establish SEPA bestows it with a comprehensive regulatory water remit remains to be seen. Whatever the outcome, it is likely that attempts by conservation bodies to influence the Parliamentary Bill will have a better chance of success if they are supported by Scotland's strong agriculture, forestry and salmon fishing lobbies. The views of the Treasury will also be crucial in determining the extent of any operational role for SEPA. With these prospects in mind, Grove-White's observation (1992) that British civil servants are skilled at displacing tensions, rather than addressing the substance of them, has a particular resonance.

ACKNOWLEDGEMENTS

Professor Frank Lyall was a valuable source of information and advice in the early stages of preparing the conference paper, particularly in relation to the range of roles fulfilled by the Secretary of State; I am only sorry that other pressures prevented him from sharing authorship of the final chapter. I am also grateful to colleagues in SNH for their very helpful comments on an earlier version of the chapter.

REFERENCES

Adams, W. M. (1993). "Places for nature: protected areas in British nature conservation", in *Conservation in Progress* (Eds F. B. Goldsmith and A. Warren), pp. 185–208, John Wiley, Chichester.

Anonymous (1974). "The Loch Leven IBP Project", *Proceedings of the Royal Society of Edinburgh*, **74B**, 45–416.

Anonymous (1989a). *Stair Memorial Encyclopedia of the Laws of Scotland*, Law Society of Scotland, Edinburgh.

Anonymous (1989b). *House of Lords Parliamentary Debates (Hansard)*, **508**, cols 1374–1378, HMSO, London.

Armitage, P. D. (1979). "Stream regulation in Great Britain", in *The Ecology of Regulated Streams* (Eds J. V. Ward and J. A. Stanford), pp. 165–181, Plenum, New York.

Armitage, P. D. and Petts, G. E. (1992). "Biotic score and prediction to assess the effects of water abstractions on river macroinvertebrates for conservation purposes", *Aquatic Conservation: Marine and Freshwater Ecosystems*, **2**, 1–17.

Association of Directors and River Inspectors of Scotland (1992a). "A monitoring strategy for water pollution control in Scotland", Unpublished ADRIS report.

Association of Directors and River Inspectors of Scotland (1992b). "Enforcement policy for offences under Sections 31 and 32 of COPA", Unpublished ADRIS report.

Bailey-Watts, A. E. (1990). "Eutrophication: assessment, research and management with special reference to Scotland's freshwaters", *Journal of the Institution of Water and Environmental Management*, **4**, 285–294.

Baldock, D. (1984). *Wetland Drainage in Europe: The Effects of Agricultural Policy in Four EEC Countries*, International Institute for Environment and Development, London.

Boon, P. J. (1991). "The role of Sites of Special Scientific Interest (SSSIs) in the conservation of British rivers", *Freshwater Forum*, **1**, 95–108.

Boon, P. J. (1992a). "Channelling scientific information for the conservation and management of rivers", *Aquatic Conservation: Marine and Freshwater Ecosystems*, **2**, 115–123.

Boon, P. J. (1992b). "Essential elements in the case for conservation", in *River Conservation and Management* (Eds P. J. Boon, P. Calow and G. E. Petts), pp. 11–33, John Wiley, Chichester.

Boon, P. J., Calow, P. and Petts, G. E. (Eds) (1992a). *River Conservation and Management*, John Wiley, Chichester.

Boon, P. J., Morgan, D. H. W. and Palmer, M. A. (1992b). "Statutory protection of freshwater flora and fauna in Britain", *Freshwater Forum*, **2**, 91–101.

Boon, P. J., Holmes, N. T. H., Maitland, P. S. and Rowell, T. A. (in press). "A system for evaluating rivers for conservation ('SERCON'): an outline of the underlying principles", *Verhandlungen der Internationalen Vereinigung für theoretische und angewandte Limnologie*.

Bowers, J. (1991). "Blues for muddy waters", *Ecos*, **12**, 1–2.

Bowers, J., O'Donnell, K. and Whatmore, S. (1988). *Liquid Assets: The Likely Effects of Privatisation of the Water Authorities on Wildlife Habitats and Landscape*, Report to the Council for Protection of Rural England, Royal Society for the Protection of Birds and World Wide Fund for Nature, CPRE, London.

Brodies (1992). *The Law of Access for Water Based Recreation*, Report to the Countryside Commission for Scotland, Brodies Solicitors, Edinburgh.

Brown, A. E. and Howell, D. L. (1992). "Conservation of rivers in Scotland: legislative and organizational limitations", in *River Conservation and Management* (Eds P. J. Boon, P. Calow and G. E. Petts), pp. 407–424, John Wiley, Chichester.

Building Design Partnership and Mackay Consultants (1991). *Lough Neagh Development Study*, Final report to The Consortium of Lough Neagh District Councils and The Northern Ireland Tourist Board, Antrim.

Buisson, R. (1991). "Land drainage revisited", *Ecos*, **12**, 9–12.

Burt, T. P. and Haycock, N. E. (1992). "Catchment planning and the nitrate issue: a UK perspective", *Progress in Physical Geography*, **16**, 379–404.

Countryside Commission for Scotland (1978). *Scotland's Scenic Heritage*, Battleby.

Countryside Commission for Scotland (1986). *Lochshore Management*, Battleby.

Countryside Commission for Scotland (1990). *The Mountain Areas of Scotland: Conservation and Management*, Battleby.

Cuttle, S. P. (1989). "Land use changes and inputs of nitrogen to Loch Leven, Scotland: a desk study", *Agricultural Water Management*, **16**, 119–135.

Department of Agriculture and Fisheries for Scotland (1971). *Salmon and Freshwater Fisheries in Scotland*, HMSO, Edinburgh.

Department of the Environment and Welsh Office (1992a). *River Quality: The Government's Proposals*, DoE, London.

Department of the Environment and Welsh Office (1992b). *Using Water Wisely: A Consultation Paper*, DoE, London.

Department of the Environment, Welsh Office and Ministry of Agriculture Fisheries and Food (1992). *Development and Flood Risk*, Planning Circular 30/92, HMSO, London.

Department of the Environment, Welsh Office and Ministry of Agriculture, Fisheries and Food (1993). *First Report by the Government's Standing Advisory Committee on the Code of Practice on Conservation, Access and Recreation*, London.

Edwards, A. C., Pugh, K., Wright, G., Sinclair, A. H. and Reaves, G. A. (1990). Nitrate status of two major rivers in NE Scotland with respect to land use and fertiliser additions," *Chemistry and Ecology*, **4**, 97–107.

Environment Council (1993). *Who's who in the Environment – Scotland*, Scottish Natural Heritage, Battleby.

Fisher, R. (1993). "Biological aspects of the conservation of wetlands", in *Conservation in Progress* (Eds F. B. Goldsmith and A. Warren), pp. 97–113, John Wiley, Chichester.

Forestry Commission (1993). *Forests and Water Guidelines*, HMSO, Edinburgh.

Gardiner, J. L. (Ed.) (1991). *River Projects and Conservation: A Manual for Holistic Appraisal*, John Wiley, Chichester.

Gardiner, J. L. and Cole, L. (1992). "Catchment planning: the way forward for river protection in the UK", in *River Conservation and Management* (Eds P. J. Boon, P. Calow and G. E. Petts), pp. 397–406, John Wiley, Chichester.

Gilvear, D. J. and Harrison, D. J. (1991). "Channel change and the significance of floodplain stratigraphy: 1990 flood event, Lower River Tay, Scotland", *Earth Surface Processes and Landforms*, **16**, 753–761.

Gilvear, D. J. and Winterbottom, S. J. (1992). "Channel change and flood events since 1783 on the regulated River Tay, Scotland: implications for flood hazard management", *Regulated Rivers: Research & Management*, **7**, 247–260.

Gore, J. A., Layzer, J. B. and Russell, I. A. (1992). "Non-traditional applications of instream flow techniques for conserving habitat of biota in the Sabie River of southern Africa", in *River Conservation and Management* (Eds P. J. Boon, P. Calow and G. E. Petts), pp. 161–177, John Wiley, Chichester.

Grove-White R. (1992). "Environmental debate and society – the role of NGOs", *Ecos*, **13**, 10–14.

Gustard, A., Cole, G., Marshall, D. and Bayliss, A. (1987). *A Study of Compensation Flows in the UK*, Report No. 99, Institute of Hydrology, Wallingford.

Haigh, N. (1992). *Manual of Environmental Policy: The EC and Britain*, Longman, Harlow.

Haigh, N. (1993). "The European perspective", Unpublished paper presented at Institution of Water and Environmental Management seminar "Managing the Environment by Statutory Water Quality Objectives", Churchill College, Cambridge, 17 March 1993.

Hallett, S., Hanley, N., Moffatt, I. and Taylor-Duncan, K. (1991). "UK water pollution control: a review of legislation and practice", *European Environment*, **1**, 7–13.

Hammerton, D. (1986). "Mineral extraction and water quality in Scotland", in *Effects of Land Use on Fresh Waters: Agriculture, Forestry, Mineral Exploitation, Urbanisation* (Ed. J. F. de L. G. Solbé), pp. 127–146, Ellis Horwood, Chichester.

Hammerton, D. (1987). "The impact of environmental legislation", *Water Pollution Control*, **86**, 333–344.

Hammerton, D. (1989). "River basin management in Scotland", *Water Science and Technology*, **21**, 1501–1508.

Hammerton, D. (1990). "Water pollution control in Scotland", *Water Law*, **1**, 70–73.

Harper D. M. (1991). "The National Rivers Authority: a conservation agenda", *Ecos*, **12**, 13–20.

Harper, D. M. and Stewart, W. D. P. (1987). "The effects of land use upon water chemistry, particularly nutrient enrichment, in shallow lowland lakes: comparative studies of three lochs in Scotland", *Hydrobiologia*, **148**, 211–229.

Heaton, A. (1993). "Conservation and the National Rivers Authority", in *Conservation in Progress* (Eds F. B. Goldsmith and A. Warren), pp. 301–320, John Wiley, Chichester.

Hennessy, M. M. (1993). "Water quality and primary production problems in the standing fresh waters of Shetland", Unpublished paper presented at seminar on blue-green algae organized by Grampian Health Board, 28 April 1993, Stonehaven.

Highlands and Islands Enterprise (1993). *Cultivating a Balance – An Aquaculture Strategy for the Highlands and Islands of Scotland*, Inverness.

Holmes, N. T. H. (1983). *Typing British Rivers According to their Flora*, Focus on Nature Conservation No. 4, Nature Conservancy Council, Peterborough.

Holmes, N. T. H. (1989). "British rivers – a working classification", *British Wildlife*, **1**, 20–36.

House of Commons Agriculture Committee (1989). *Fish Farming in the UK*, HMSO, London.

House of Commons Environment Committee (1991). *Environmental Issues in Northern Ireland*, HMSO, London.

House of Commons Environment Committee (1992). *The Government's Proposals for an Environment Agency*, HMSO, London.

House of Lords Select Committee on the European Communities (1991). *Municipal Waste Water Treatment*, HMSO, London.

Howarth, W. (1990). *The Law of Aquaculture*, Fishing News Books, Oxford.

Howell, D. L. and Munford, J. G. (1992). "Predator control on finfish farms", in *Aquaculture and the Environment* (Eds N. de Pauw and J. Joyce), pp. 339–364, European Aquaculture Society Special Publication No. 16, Gent.

Hunter Committee (1965). *Scottish Salmon and Trout Fisheries*, Second report by the Committee appointed by the Secretary of State for Scotland, HMSO, Edinburgh.

Institute of Aquaculture, Institute of Freshwater Ecology and Institute of Terrestrial Ecology (1990). *Fish Farming and the Scottish Freshwater Environment*, Nature Conservancy Council, Edinburgh.

IUCN, UNEP and WWF (1991). *Caring for the Earth: A Strategy for Sustainable Living*, Gland.

Iversen, T. M., Kronvang, B., Madsen, B. L., Markmann, P. and Nielsen, M. B. (1993). "Reestablishment of Danish streams: restoration and maintenance measures", *Aquatic Conservation: Marine and Freshwater Ecosystems*, **3**, 73–92.

Jordan, A. G., Richardson, J. and Kimber, R. H. (1977). "The origins of the Water Act of 1973", *Public Administration*, **55**, 317–334.

Land Use Consultants (1992). "A recommended methodology for integrated catchment management planning", Unpublished report to English Nature, Peterborough.

Lewis, G. and Williams, G. (1984). *Rivers and Wildlife Handbook: A Guide to Practices which Further the Conservation of Wildlife on Rivers*, Royal Society for the Protection of Birds, Sandy, and Royal Society for Nature Conservation, Lincoln.

Loch Lomond and the Trossachs Working Party (1993). *The Management of Loch Lomond and the Trossachs*, Report to the Secretary of State for Scotland, Scottish Office, Edinburgh.

Lothian Regional Council (1990). *Conservation, Access and Recreation: A Strategy for Reservoirs Owned or Operated by Lothian Regional Council*, Edinburgh.

Lyall, F. (1982). *Air, Noise, Water and Waste: A Summary of the Law in Scotland*, The Planning Exchange, Glasgow.

Lyle, A.A. and Maitland, P.S. (1992). "Conservation of freshwater fish in the British Isles: the status of fish in National Nature Reserves", *Aquatic Conservation: Marine and Freshwater Ecosystems*, **2**, 19–33.

Mackay, D. (1988). *Nature Conservation and the Work of the River Purification Boards*, Report to the Nature Conservancy Council, Edinburgh.

Maitland, P.S. and Lyle, A.A. (1991). "Conservation of freshwater fish in the British Isles: the current status and biology of threatened species", *Aquatic Conservation: Marine and Freshwater Ecosystems*, **1**, 25–54.

Maitland, P.S. and Lyle, A.A. (1992). "Conservation of freshwater fish in the British Isles: proposals for management", *Aquatic Conservation: Marine and Freshwater Ecosystems*, **2**, 165–183.

Marren, P. (1993). "The siege of the NCC: nature conservation in the Eighties", in *Conservation in Progress* (Eds F.B. Goldsmith and A. Warren), pp. 283–299, John Wiley, Chichester.

Micklewright, S. (1993). "The voluntary movement", in *Conservation in Progress* (Eds F.B. Goldsmith and A. Warren), pp. 321–334, John Wiley, Chichester.

Mills, D.H. (1989). *Ecology and Management of Atlantic Salmon*, Chapman and Hall, London.

Ministry of Agriculture, Fisheries and Food, Department of the Environment and Welsh, Office (1993). *Conservation Guidelines for Drainage Authorities*, MAFF Publications, London.

Ministry of Agriculture, Fisheries and Food, English Nature and National Rivers Authority (1992). *Environmental Procedures for Inland Flood Defence Works*, MAFF Publications, London.

Moore, N.W. (1987). *The Bird of Time*, Cambridge University Press, Cambridge.

Morgan, N.C. (1972). "Problems of the conservation of freshwater ecosystems", *Symposia of the Zoological Society of London*, **29**, 135–154.

National Rivers Authority (1991a). *Proposals for Statutory Water Quality Objectives*, Bristol.

National Rivers Authority (1991b). *The Quality of Rivers, Canals and Estuaries in England and Wales, Report of the 1990 survey*, Bristol.

National Rivers Authority (1991c). *Catchment Management Planning*, Bristol.

National Rivers Authority (1992a). *River Corridor Surveys*, Bristol.

National Rivers Authority (1992b). *Water Resources Development Strategy: A Discussion Document*, Bristol.

Nature Conservancy Council (1984a). *Nature Conservation in Great Britain*, Peterborough.

Nature Conservancy Council (1984b). *Surveys of Wildlife in River Corridors: Draft Methodology*, Peterborough.

Newson, M. (1992). *Land, Water and Development: River Basins and their Sustainable Management*, Routledge, London.

Palmer, M. A., Bell, S. L. and Butterfield, I. (1992). "A botanical classification of standing waters in Britain: application for conservation and monitoring", *Aquatic Conservation: Marine and Freshwater Ecosystems*, **2**, 125–143.

Payne, P.L. (1988). *The Hydro: A Study of the Development of the Major Hydro-Electric Schemes Undertaken by the North of Scotland Hydro-Electric Board*, Aberdeen University Press, Aberdeen.

Peterken, G. F. and Hughes, F. M. R. (1994). *Restoration of Floodplain Forests*. Unpublished paper presented at the Institute of Chartered Foresters meeting, Edinburgh.

Petts, G. E. (1984). *Impounded Rivers: Perspectives for Ecological Management*, John Wiley, Chichester.

Petts, G. E. and Wood, R. (Eds) (1988). "River regulation in the United Kingdom", *Regulated Rivers: Research & Management*, **2**, 199–477.

Purseglove, J. (1988). *Taming the Flood: A History and Natural History of Rivers and Wetlands*, Oxford University Press, Oxford.

Ratcliffe, D. A. (Ed.) (1977). *A Nature Conservation Review*, Cambridge University Press, Cambridge.

Rimes, C. A., Farmer, A. M. and Howell, D. L. (1994). "A survey of the threat of surface water acidification to the nature conservation interest of fresh waters on Sites of Special Scientific Interest in Britain", *Aquatic Conservation: Marine and Freshwater Ecosystems*, **4**, 30–43.

Robinson, S. S. (1990). *The Law of Game, Salmon and Freshwater Fishing in Scotland*, Butterworths, Edinburgh.

Royal Commission on Environmental Pollution (1992). *Freshwater Quality*, HMSO, London.
Rundle, S. D., Lloyd, E. C. and Ormerod, S. J. (1992). "The effects of riparian management and physicochemistry on macroinvertebrate feeding guilds and community structure in British upland streams", *Aquatic Conservation: Marine and Freshwater Ecosystems*, **2**, 293–307.
Salford Civil Engineering Ltd (1989). *Small-scale Hydroelectric Generation Potential in the UK*, Report to the Energy Technology Support Unit, Department of Energy, London.
Salmon Advisory Committee (1991). *Factors Affecting Natural Smolt Production*, MAFF Publications, London.
Salmon Advisory Committee (1993). *Factors Affecting Emigrating Smolts and Returning Adults*, MAFF Publications, London.
Scott, D. (1993). "New Zealand's Resource Management Act and fresh water", *Aquatic Conservation*, **3**, 53–65.
Scott, M. (1992). "NCC and after – the changing faces of British nature conservation", *British Wildlife*, **3**, 214–221.
Scottish Anglers' National Association (1992). "Policy on Protection Orders and the Freshwater and Salmon Fisheries (Scotland) Act 1976", Unpublished policy paper.
Scottish Conservation Projects (1990). "Operation Brightwater. SCP launches its first national campaign", *Curam*, **6**, 20–23.
Scottish Development Department (1990a). "First policy review of the River Purification Boards", Unpublished report.
Scottish Development Department (1990b). *Scotland's Natural Heritage: The Way Ahead*, HMSO, Edinburgh.
Scottish Natural Heritage (1992). *Enjoying the Outdoors: A Consultation Paper on Access to the Countryside for Enjoyment and Understanding*, Edinburgh.
Scottish Natural Heritage (1993). Unpublished response to Scottish Office consultation paper *Abstraction Controls: A System for Scotland*, Edinburgh.
Scottish Office (1991). *The Structure of Local Government in Scotland: The Case for Change*, HMSO, Edinburgh.
Scottish Office (1992a). *The Structure of Local Government in Scotland: Shaping the New Councils*, HMSO, Edinburgh.
Scottish Office (1992b). *Improving Scotland's Environment: The Way Forward*, HMSO, Edinburgh.
Scottish Office (1992c). *Water and Sewerage in Scotland: Investing for Our Future*, HMSO, Edinburgh.
Scottish Office (1992d). *Water Quality Survey of Scotland 1990*, HMSO, Edinburgh.
Scottish Office (1992e). *Prevention of Environmental Pollution from Agricultural Activity: Code of Good Practice*, HMSO, Edinburgh.
Scottish Office (1993a). *Abstraction Controls: A System for Scotland*, Scottish Office, Edinburgh.
Scottish Office (1993b). *Conservation, Access and Recreation – Code of Practice for Water and Sewerage Authorities and River Purification Authorities*, Edinburgh.
Scottish Office (1993c). *The Structure of Local Government. Shaping the Future – The New Councils*, Scottish Office, Edinburgh.
Scottish River Purification Boards' Association (1987). *Freshwater Quality in Scotland*, Evidence submitted to the Royal Commission on Environmental Pollution, *SRPBA*, Glasgow.
Scottish River Purification Boards' Association (1992). *Annual Report for 1991/92*, Perth.
Scottish Tourist Board (1992). *Going Wild in Scotland: Developing Scottish Brown Trout Fishing*, Edinburgh.
Shearer, W. M. (1993). "Are your fish out of water?", *Landowning in Scotland*, **231**, 24–26.
Sinclair, A. H., Armstrong, G., Young, M., Ford, M. A. and Raffaelli, D. (1992). "The impact of agriculture on water quality in Loch of Harray and feeder burns", Unpublished report to Orkney Islands Council, Scottish Agricultural College, Aberdeen.
Stewart, W. D. P., May, E. and Tuckwell, S. B. (1976). "Nitrogen and phosphorus from agricultural land and urbanization and their fate in shallow freshwater lochs", *MAFF Technical Bulletin*, **32**, 276–305.

Taylor, K. (1991). "Land, wildlife and conservation in the Cairngorms", *British Wildlife*, **2**, 152–161.

Tivy, J. (1980). *The Effect of Recreation on Freshwater Lochs and Reservoirs in Scotland*, Countryside Commission for Scotland, Battleby.

Ward, J. V. and Stanford, J. A. (Eds) (1979). *The Ecology of Regulated Streams*, Plenum, New York.

Ward, J. V. and Stanford, J. A. (1993). "Research needs in regulated river ecology", *Regulated Rivers: Research & Management*, **8**, 205–209.

Webb, J. H., Hay, D. W., Cunningham, P. D. and Youngson, A. F. (1991). "The spawning behaviour of escaped farmed salmon and wild adult salmon (*Salmo salar* L.) in a northern Scottish river", *Aquaculture*, **98**, 97–110.

Welsh Water (1992). *Conservation, Access and Recreation: An Overview*, Brecon.

Williamson, R. B. (1986). "Return of salmon to the Clyde: some legal implications", in *The Return of Salmon to the Clyde* (Eds A. Holden and G. Struthers), pp. 9–12, Institute of Fisheries Management, Pitlochry.

Wright, J. F., Blackburn, J. H., Westlake, D. F., Furse, M. T. and Armitage, P. D. (1992). "Anticipating the consequences of river management for the conservation of macroinvertebrates", in *River Conservation and Management* (Eds P. J. Boon, P. Calow and G. E. Petts), pp. 138–149, John Wiley, Chichester.

31

Integrating Development and Conservation

P. S. MAITLAND

Fish Conservation Centre, Easter Cringate, Stirling, FK7 9QX, UK

D. S. MCLUSKY

Department of Biological and Molecular Sciences, University of Stirling, Stirling, FK9 4LA, UK

and

P. J. BOON

Scottish Natural Heritage, 2 Anderson Place, Edinburgh, EH6 5NP, UK

INTRODUCTION

It is clear from earlier chapters in this volume that the fresh waters of Scotland are a major national resource, covering over 2% of the land surface and comprising over 30 000 lochs and lochans and over 10 000 rivers and burns. These include some of the most spectacular waters in Great Britain as well as the largest – Loch Lomond (greatest area: 71 km^2), Loch Awe (longest: 41 km), Loch Morar (deepest: 310 m) and Loch Ness (greatest volume: 7452 × 10^6 m^3). The River Tay is the largest river by flow (194 m^3 s^{-1}). In all, 91% of the volume of standing fresh water of Great Britain is within Scotland (Chapter 3).

Fresh water has been used by humans from earliest times, at first only for drinking (many of the early settlements in Scotland are related to spring lines and other sources of pure water), but later for fishing and navigation. With improving sanitation, water was used for washing domestic utensils and many other purposes and thus there have developed enormous, sometimes conflicting, demands on this resource. In addition, many activities, especially industry, urbanization and land use, affect water even before it gets into lochs and rivers. Fertilizers, herbicides and pesticides used in agriculture and forestry may end up in nearby watercourses, aided by land drainage which can make water run off faster.

Each person in Scotland uses about 148 litres per day (Water Services in Scotland, 1987) and for security and quality of supply many upland reservoirs have been built.

The Fresh Waters of Scotland: A National Resource of International Significance
Edited by P. S. Maitland, P. J. Boon and D. S. McLusky © 1994 John Wiley & Sons Ltd

Industry too has huge requirements. Wastes from domestic sewage and industry are passed to rivers to be carried to the sea. Fish farming has recently created new demands. Hydro-electric schemes have harnessed many larger mountainous rivers. Finally, water is of major importance for recreation: humans picnic beside it, birdwatch over it, paddle and bathe in it, boat on it and fish in it.

ECONOMIC ASPECTS

As far as the value of its fresh waters is concerned, Scotland is extremely fortunate in its climate and physiography. The most suitable areas for utilizing existing lochs or establishing reservoirs for water supply are in mountainous regions where natural systems are oligotrophic and there is less pollution than in lowlands. The rainfall is also higher in upland than lowland areas. Oligotrophic waters contain low levels of suspended matter (especially algae) and thus require little filtration. Though the geographic regions most suitable for water supply bodies may be far from areas where water is most needed, the altitude of such systems means that water will readily pass by gravity, obviating the need for expensive pumping. As well as the chemical nature of the catchment its physical geology is important, especially where man-made reservoirs are concerned. Local geology affects the amount of direct run-off, the potential underground losses and the mechanics and cost of dam construction. Scotland is favoured in all these respects.

FIGURE 31.1. Loch Morar, Scotland's deepest loch and one of the deepest waters in Europe, has been harnessed at its outflow to provide hydro-power. Photograph: Scottish Tourist Board

There is increasing international pressure on society to move towards greater utilization of clean renewable sources of power, such as hydro-generation. Hydro-electric stations can be constructed only where the topography and water supply are suitable, but in mountainous areas with an adequate rainfall they make a significant contribution to power production (Figure 31.1). In 1991, for instance, 25% of the electricity generated in Scotland was produced by hydro-power (Chapter 17), compared with England and Wales where more than 99% was generated by thermal power.

Factors favourable for hydro-electric production are a high rainfall, preferably with more in winter (when the demand for power is greatest) than in summer, sufficient altitude to give a head for generating purposes, and the absence of prolonged freezing during winter. Scotland is favoured by all these factors and some scope for further hydro-electric generation remains (Chapter 17), notably in run-of-river and pumped-storage schemes. However, the fisheries and conservation aspects of such schemes must be investigated thoroughly before any decision is taken regarding development.

INTERNATIONAL ASPECTS

Not surprisingly in a country which has a surface area less than that of Lake Superior, none of the fresh waters of Scotland is of outstanding importance in terms of its size or other physical features. The nearest approach to this is Loch Ness (Figure 31.2) which is 11th in the world in terms of mean depth (Chapter 3). However, there are aspects of Scotland's freshwater resources which are important internationally — especially in relation to Europe.

The image of the extremely high purity of the freshwater lochs and rivers of Scotland is a major factor in the economy of many sports and industries in Scotland; for example, game fishing (Standing Conference on Countryside Sports, 1992) and the production of whisky, Salmon and more recently bottled water itself. High water quality is linked with the international concept of Scotland as a land with numerous attractive lochs and burns which add so much to the landscape. Thus, fresh waters have a further important aesthetic value in relation to Scotland's large tourist industry.

The high quality of water and the many natural lochs and rivers is reflected in terms of wildlife in Scotland in a number of ways, as described in several earlier chapters. For example, there are several Ramsar sites which are of major importance for their wildfowl. At a species level, Scotland is one of the strongholds of several species which have declined or even disappeared in many other countries; for example, Freshwater Pearl Mussel *Margaritifera margaritifera*, Arctic Charr *Salvelinus alpinus*, Atlantic Salmon *Salmo salar* and Otter *Lutra lutra*. In this connection, it has been pointed out (Chapter 12) that there is a need for nature conservation criteria which recognize the importance of large areas of the country where the status of such species is high. For example, although the Otter still is common over most of Scotland (Chapter 14) this is one of its few remaining strongholds in Europe and should be recognized as such in conservation terms. It is hoped that the international solution to this type of situation may be found in the implementation of the EC Habitats and Species Directive (Chapter 29).

FIGURE 31.2. Loch Ness, famous internationally and a favourite place with tourists, holds more water than all the lakes and reservoirs in England together. Photograph: Scottish Tourist Board

DEVELOPMENT AND CONSERVATION

Clean fresh water is essential to successful modern societies, and indeed in some resource surveys per capita consumption of water is used as a way of comparing the living standards of different nations. Countries with a recognized high standard of living show a high requirement for potable fresh water (*ca.* 100–500 litres per head per day) compared with poorer countries. The improving standards of living in many countries and the increasing human populations combine to make heavy demands on freshwater resources, and result in a range of competing uses for available water.

As has been outlined in several previous chapters, in spite of the extensive resource in Scotland, there are many problems and conflicts, both for humans and for wildlife. Many waters have been so misused that they are unfit for either. Over-enrichment from agricultural fertilizers causes algal blooms on lowland lochs; when these blooms reach a maximum and die, fish kills result. In some cases toxic algae in these blooms have caused sickness in humans and death to pets. Domestic and industrial pollution can eliminate all aquatic plants and animals. These stretches of extreme pollution also act as a barrier to migrating fish which cannot therefore reach clean stretches upstream. Weirs and dams have the same effect. Aerial pollution has acidified a number of hill lochs and some burns, eliminating fish. Other problems are created by the introduction of new plant or fish species or by trampling of vegetation and disturbance to wildlife.

On the positive side, there is no doubt that water quality in rivers subject to pollution has improved markedly in Scotland (as witnessed by the return of Atlantic

Salmon to the Clyde and Sparling *Osmerus eperlanus* to the Forth) and that even the effects of widespread pollutants (e.g. the sulphur dioxide and nitrous gases in the atmosphere causing acid rain) are apparently diminishing. There is, nevertheless, a need for a stronger and more integrated approach to the management of Scotland's fresh waters which will allow maximum sustainable use by the nation on the one hand but full protection for water quality and wildlife on the other. There are three inter-related approaches as to how such a scenario may be developed.

Resource use

The regular increase in the quantity of water required for domestic and industrial (including agricultural) purposes shows no sign of lessening, making it necessary to consider the whole question of water resource and supply on a more extended basis. The demands continue, but national integration of resource use is poor. Water conservation means the preservation, control and development of water resources to ensure that adequate and reliable supplies are available in the most suitable and economic way, while safeguarding all legitimate interests, including the natural environment. Historically, only extremely pure waters were considered as potential water supply sources (Figure 31.3), and this emphasis on quality led to priority

FIGURE 31.3. The River Dee (Grampian Region) at Bridge of Dee. This river is a major source of high quality water for the City of Aberdeen. Photograph: P. Wakely

exploitation of easily available supplies with many impoundments in upland areas. The shortage of water, and the improving means for treatment of contaminated water, have meant that, increasingly, quantity and not quality is now often more important; sources which would not have been considered in the past are now accepted and treated for public supply.

With so many waters in Scotland there should be enough to serve most needs, but present national planning is inadequate and there are many problems and conflicts to

FIGURE 31.4. Loch Lomond, the largest surface area of fresh water in Great Britain, looking south towards the National Nature Reserve at the mouth of the River Endrick. Photograph: P. Wakely

be resolved (Dargie and Briggs, 1991). One solution is the creation of a national framework and policy for the lochs and rivers of Scotland (Maitland, in preparation). This would look at their distribution, quality and value in relation to demands on them. Some are clearly essential to a major need (e.g. hydro-electricity or water supply) and this must be the overriding factor – though other uses may fit in with this. Other waters may be of such high wildlife importance that their conservation needs are paramount. Several of the largest waters are so important nationally that each requires an individual management plan in order to reconcile the needs of potential users with the overwhelming importance of maintaining the quality and value of that water (cf. Lake District National Park, 1993). Loch Lomond (Figure 31.4) is a topical example, where the pressures have become so great that the government has appointed a working party to produce a management strategy (Loch Lomond and the Trossachs Working Party, 1993). In all such cases, users must be prepared to accept compromises and even give up claims somewhere – if not on one water then on another.

The Loch Lomond and the Trossachs Working Party (1993) based its final report on the premise that "The principle of sustaining and enhancing the heritage should be adopted as a fundamental objective, underpinning all planning, management and investment decisions". It concluded that the Secretary of State for Scotland should create a Joint Committee which would implement the Working Party's recommendations, of which there were 82 – covering heritage conservation (13), tourism (12), recreation (10), the water resource (10), land use (10), access into the countryside (5), planning and economic development (10) and administration and finance (12).

Clearly, therefore, some form of national strategy for Scotland's fresh waters must be developed to integrate the present and future needs of society in some form of constructive management system. Such a strategy can only be developed if there is an appropriate interactive database which can hold all the information necessary for making objective management decisions with regard to the wisest use or uses for each water at both local and national levels. Such a database cannot be created overnight. Substantial amounts of information need to be collected and collated in such a way that they are easily available for analysis. Moreover, the various uses must be assessed objectively so that their impacts both on the water body itself and on each other are understood. For example, while it is obvious that noisy power boating (Elson *et al.*, 1989) and contemplative angling (Scottish Anglers' National Association, 1991) are inimical to each other, this is not necessarily true of uses such as water supply and bird watching.

Catchment management

Although the importance of whole catchment management has been realized for many years, scant attention has been paid in most countries to its practice. The combined effect of population growth, increased standards of living and greater leisure time is to place larger and larger demands on available water resources. In many countries these are already insufficient to meet present requirements. It is clear that increased cooperation is required for integrating water use at regional, national and international levels. Water can be conserved only by interrupting the hydrological cycle to make more water available, or to make it available for longer periods, or to use less.

In a few countries, the concept of integrated water usage on the basis of large catchment areas has become accepted as the most rational approach to water conservation. In the United States, the Commission on Water Resources Policy recommended that new proposals for water resource development should be submitted only in the form of programmes which deal with entire river basins and which take into account all relevant features of water and land development (National Research Council, 1992). One of the first areas to develop its water resources under such a concept was the Tennessee Valley Authority, evolved as a single coordinated project for that region. Within this programme there are now more than 30 reservoirs, over half of them designed to include power, navigation and flood control systems. Similar successful examples of multi-purpose river basin development include the Snowy Mountain Authority in Australia, the Helman Valley Authority in Afghanistan, and projects in South America and elsewhere (Allee *et al.*, 1981).

In England and Wales, the National Rivers Authority has already embarked on plans for some aspects of integrated catchment planning and useful background reviews of some rivers e.g, reviews of the River Itchen (National Rivers Authority, 1992a) and the River Test (National Rivers Authority, 1992b) are available as precursors to catchment plans.

In Scotland, there is considerable disappointment that the other water-related functions listed in the Scottish Environment Protection Agency (SEPA) Consultation Paper have been dismissed. It is now widely felt that the Government seems to be pursuing the pollution control role for SEPA without considering the opportunity for change within a wider horizon which SEPA could afford. However, although there are no moves at national level, there are some local initiatives for several catchments, for example those of the Rivers Carron (A. B. Stephen, personal communication), Forth (Forth River Purification Board, 1993) and Tweed (The Tweed Foundation, 1993). It is to be hoped that these may eventually fit into a much broader scheme for Scotland as a whole.

All these schemes and many smaller ones developing in some parts of the world are based largely on economic reasoning. If planned and implemented intelligently, they may lead to improved amenities both from recreational and aesthetic viewpoints – especially in the long term. The end result is a rational use of freshwater resources leading to improved standards of living, clean lakes and rivers, appropriate recreational facilities and increased habitat protection for wildlife.

Sustainability

In developing national strategies for water use and catchment management the question of sustainability must remain paramount. There is little point in promoting wild fisheries in certain rivers and lochs if the fishing effort allowed is so great that stocks decline and disappear; or agreeing to water transfer in the upper reaches of a river if this means that the reaches below virtually dry up in summer. The present condition of the upper River Garry is a glaring example of just such a decision.

Fortunately, fresh water is a renewable resource and substantial amounts of it fall regularly on most parts of Scotland. Thus, within the vagaries of weather and climate change the basic input can be regarded as sustainable – at least in terms of quantity. This is not true, however, of many other components of Scottish freshwater eco-systems and already some facets have been irretrievably lost.

A good example is the Vendace *Coregonus albula* which, in Britain, has been known from only four lakes; two of these are in Scotland near the village of Lochmaben and two are in the English Lake District. Both the Scottish lochs have been subject to eutrophication, fish introductions for angling and other pressures and the Vendace is now extinct in both of them (Maitland and Lyle, 1991). The species is now so rare in Britain that at present it has no commercial or sporting value. In times past, however, it was an important fish at Lochmaben, where an annual festival was arranged each summer by two local "Vendace Clubs", during which Vendace were caught in fine gill nets and then cooked and eaten outdoors while athletic contests took place (Maitland, 1966). Thus there has been a loss, not only to biodiversity, but also to local culture and tradition in Scotland.

Even before the rain falls it has become acidified from atmospheric pollutants (see Chapter 24) and many individual populations of fish (including Brown Trout *Salmo trutta* and Arctic Charr *Salvelinus alpinus*), which have probably been isolated from each other since the last Ice Age, have become extinct in Scotland. Thus if eutrophica-tion and acidification are allowed to continue it will be impossible to sustain stocks of these more sensitive fish and biodiversity will decrease. It is unfortunate that many industries, ironically some of the largest of them owned by the state, only respond to issues after extreme pressure from scientists and conservationists. Although guide-lines are now available (Forestry Commission, 1993), the delay in producing adequate measures to combat the widespread impact of afforestation on fresh waters is a good example.

THE FUTURE

Looking to the future, the concepts of sustainable integrated resource and catchment management which have been discussed above are likely to become increasingly important, as many of the authors of preceding chapters have emphasized. However, there are likely to be difficulties in moving towards this position, not least of which is the lack of any strong indication on the part of the present Government that it intends to move in this direction (Hatton, 1992; HMSO, 1992).

An important element of future management policies is a better understanding of the structure and functioning of Scotland's freshwater systems and the plants and animals within them. In spite of being the scene of some of the earliest limnological studies (Murray and Pullar, 1910), several authors in the present volume have pointed out that further research is needed (e.g. on algae and invertebrates) if we are to understand how lochs and river ecosystems function. In addition, such topics as archaeology have indicated an extensive underwater heritage which has yet to be studied (Chapter 15). Failure to understand the full extent of Scotland's aquatic resources means that there is less chance of understanding and possibly counteracting the effects of new phenomena, such as climate change (United Kingdom Climate Change Impacts Review Group, 1991). As noted above, part of such research must involve the development of a national database as an essential prerequisite to integrated water management in Scotland.

How this management is carried out at national and local levels is the fundamental issue which the State has so far failed to address (HMSO, 1992; Royal Commission on Environmental Pollution, 1992). Given the development of a national strategy in Scotland for integrated water use, and agreement on integrated catchment land use and planning then clearly there must be appropriate agencies and procedures for implementation. The basis for some of these is already there (perhaps in a stronger Scottish Environment Protection Agency than that proposed at present), but in places (e.g. the management of fish populations) there is at present a complete vacuum, other than for some aspects of Atlantic Salmon and Sea Trout *Salmo trutta* (Chapter 26). Given agencies with an appropriate remit there will still be the need for broader groupings (e.g. river or catchment management consortia) to resolve local management issues.

Additional topics related to management include the need to develop less interventionist engineering approaches to river and loch management (this can often be not only cheaper but also less damaging to the landscape and to wildlife) and to improve legislation so that greater controls are available (e.g. to prevent the introduction of alien species of plants and animals).

In Scotland and many other parts of the world the increasing human population, and the leisure time available to it, is placing an enormous demand on what is left of the natural countryside. This is especially true of fresh waters which, as well as being used for domestic and industrial purposes, are often the focus for recreation (e.g. sailing, power-boating, water-skiing, fishing, wildfowling, bathing and picnicking). It is unfortunate that the most important waters for recreation are often not those in urban areas, but those further away. This is because of the natural preference by the public for clean rivers and clear (usually oligotrophic) lochs as opposed to turbid, polluted and eutrophic waters. Unfortunately, it is often these more isolated waters which are the ones most important for wildlife.

Many wetland areas are being actively managed for the benefit of people in different parts of the world. Some are set aside and managed solely on the basis of their scientific interest, with other uses banned or actively discouraged. In other areas, various recreational activities are compatible with the value of the water body. In the USA, natural wetlands are accepted as having a wide variety of uses including nature study, photography, hunting, fishing, swimming, boating, camping and picnicking, as well as economic pursuits such as forestry, haymaking, grazing, mining, petroleum extraction and fur harvesting (Allee *et al.*, 1981). While the primary interest in these areas may be wildlife or recreation, economic operations can yield substantial financial returns, and, with proper safeguards, may even increase the value of the area for the wildlife or recreational activity concerned.

In conclusion, it is hoped that this volume, commemorating the first 25 years of the Scottish Freshwater Group, has presented an objective account of the fresh waters of Scotland – their extent, flora and fauna, value, pressures and problems, and how some of these may be resolved. The editors of this volume are optimistic that, given sound strategies for the future which are sustainable and based on careful research, this valuable national and international resource can continue to be a major part of Scotland's heritage in the future.

ACKNOWLEDGEMENTS

We are grateful to Mr J. C. Currie for helpful comments on an early draft of this chapter.

REFERENCES

Allee, D., Dworsky, L. and North, R. (1981). *Unified River Basin Management*, American Water Resources Association, Minneapolis.

Dargie, T. G. D. and Briggs, D. J. (1991). *State of the Scottish Environment 1991*, Scottish Wildlife and Countryside Link, Perth.

Elson, M. J., Lloyd, J. and Thorpe, J. (1989). *Providing for Motorised Water Sports*, Sports Council, London.

Forestry Commission (1993). *Forests and Water Guidelines*, HMSO, London.

Forth River Purification Board (1993). *Corporate Plan 1994/99*, Edinburgh.

Hatton, C. (1992). *The Habitats Directive: Time for Action*, World Wide Fund for Nature, Godalming.

HMSO (1992). *This Common Inheritance: Britain's Environmental Strategy*, London.

Lake District National Park (1993). *Bassenthwaite Lake Management Plan*, Lake District Special Planning Board, Kendal.

Loch Lomond and the Trossachs Working Party (1993). *The Management of Loch Lomond and the Trossachs*, Scottish Office, Edinburgh.

Maitland, P. S. (1966). "The fish fauna of the Castle and Mill Lochs, Lochmaben, with special reference to the Lochmaben Vendace, *Coregonus vandesius* Richardson", *Transactions of the Dumfriesshire and Galloway Natural History and Antiquarian Society*, **43**, 31–48.

Maitland, P. S. and Lyle, A. A. (1991). "Conservation of freshwater fish in the British Isles: the current status and biology of threatened species", *Aquatic Conservation: Marine and Freshwater Ecosystems*, **1**, 25–54.

Murray, J. and Pullar, L. (1910). *Bathymetrical Survey of the Fresh Water Lochs of Scotland*, Challenger Office, Edinburgh.

National Research Council (1992). *Restoration of Aquatic Ecosystems: Science, Technology and Public Policy*, National Academy Press, Washington.

National Rivers Authority (1992a). *The River Itchen*, Worthing.

National Rivers Authority (1992b). *The River Test*, Worthing.

Royal Commission on Environmental Pollution (1992). *Sixteenth Report: Freshwater Quality*, HMSO, London.

Scottish Anglers' National Association (1991). *Environmental Policy Study: A Study of Members' Environmental Concerns*, Irvine.

Standing Conference on Countryside Sports (1992). *Countryside Sports: Their Economic and Conservation Significance*, Reading.

The Tweed Foundation (1993). *1992 Review and Progress Report*, Berwick-upon-Tweed.

United Kingdom Climate Change Impacts Review Group (1991). *The Potential Effects of Climate Change in the United Kingdom*, Department of the Environment, London.

Water Services in Scotland (1987). *Scotland's Water Services*, Dundee.

Index

Note: Page References in *italics* refer to Figures; those in **bold** refer to Tables

Index compiled by Annette J. Musker